Sociology
of Aging

Sociology of Aging

SECOND EDITION

Diana K. Harris
University of Tennessee

HARPER & ROW, PUBLISHERS, New York
Grand Rapids, Philadelphia, St. Louis, San Francisco,
London, Singapore, Sydney, Tokyo

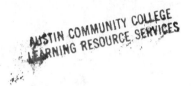

Sponsoring Editor: Alan McClare
Project Editor: Steven Pisano
Art Direction: Heather A. Ziegler
Cover Coordinator: Mary Archondes
Cover Design: Wanda Lubelska Design, Inc.
Production: Beth Maglione

Library of Congress Cataloging-in-Publication Data

Harris, Diana K.
    Sociology of aging / Diana K. Harris.—2nd ed.
      p. cm.
    Includes bibliographical references.
    1. Gerontology—United States.   2. Aged—United States.
I. Title.
HQ1064.U5H27 1990
305.26′0973—dc20   89-26946
ISBN 0-06-042655-1   CIP

90 91 92 9 8 7 6 5 4 3 2 1

Contents

Preface

This volume investigates the subject of aging from a sociological perspective and, as a result, includes much material that is not traditionally found in aging texts. Full chapters are devoted to such areas as socialization, groups, social stratification, and deviance, as well as each of the five basic social institutions: family, economy, political system, religion, and education. Culture is given extensive treatment in three chapters—"Age Norms and Age Status," "Cultural Values," and "Cultural Diversity." I have added a new chapter to this edition dealing with sexuality and aging, a subject that has been almost completely neglected in most aging texts. The title of the chapter on crime has been changed to "Deviance" to reflect a broader coverage in this area. The closing chapter on future trends has been expanded to include technology, a topic of crucial importance to the well-being of the elderly.

Much of the rest of the material in the book has been rewritten, reorganized, and revised with the addition of new material. Throughout the text, wherever relevant, I have included cross-cultural materials. I feel that this not only captures the students' interest, but—and more importantly—it gives them an increased awareness and objectivity toward aging in their own culture, as well as making them more tolerant of cultural differences. An underlying theme throughout the book has been to examine recent research and to show how its results disprove many widely held assumptions and "myth-conceptions" regarding aging and the aged.

Some of the many topics new to this edition include elder abuse, shopping-bag women, the older criminal, intergenerational equity, diagnostic related groups (DRGs), the medicalization of aging, drugs and the elderly, Alzheimer's disease, progeria, the aging homosexual, cryonics, divorce and grandparenthood, emergency response systems, continuing care retirement communities, sexuality in nursing homes, the caregiving burden, and technology and the elderly.

ORGANIZATION

The book is organized into six parts. Part I presents a general overview of the field of aging, some of the research methods that are employed, and the demographic aspects of aging. Part II focuses on culture and socialization, emphasizing the importance of culture and how it shapes human behavior. Socialization is discussed followed by a chapter on the biological and psychological aspects of aging and a chapter on sexuality and the elderly. Part III covers social groups and inequality. The first chapter in this part deals with social groups and organizations. The next two chapters discuss some bases for inequality: class inequality and ethnic and racial inequality. Part IV focuses on the elderly in relation to the five major social institutions. Our concern in Part V is with some of the major problems confronting older people: income, health, housing and transportation, deviance, and death and dying. Finally, in Part VI one chapter discusses some solutions to the problems posed in Part V, while the final chapter deals with future trends and technology.

FEATURES

1. Readings   A new feature for this edition are abridged readings. Many of these readings have been written by outstanding scholars in the field of aging. They have been added at the end of chapters whenever appropriate. Selected mainly from books and journal articles, the words of the authors have been left unchanged.

2. Boxed Inserts   Several types of boxes have been used in this edition. One type of box introduces new material on specific topics, while another type elaborates on what is discussed in the chapter. Other boxes contain interesting and informative material from such sources as journals, books, and newspapers.

3. Readability   I have tried to produce a book that is clearly written, free of jargon, and lively and interesting to read.

4. Chapter Summaries   At the end of each chapter is a numbered summary that reviews the most important concepts and ideas contained in the chapter.

5. Key Terms   Terms are defined when introduced. They are listed again at the end of each chapter and defined again at the end of the book.

6. Glossary   The end of the book contains definitions of all italicized terms used throughout the text as well as some terms that are not italicized or that are not in the text.

7. For Further Study   Some of the newest books as well as classics in the field are listed and annotated at the end of each chapter. The student can turn to these for additional information.

8. Illustrations   The majority of photographs were taken especially for this edition in order to better illuminate and tie-in with many of the major ideas contained in the text.

9. Tables, Charts, and Graphs   These have been designed to be easy to read and to understand. For those with statistics, every attempt has been made to use the latest data available.

10. Instructor's Manual   This manual has been prepared by the author to accompany the text. It includes a chapter outline, major concepts, topics for discussion, multiple-choice and essay questions, and suggestions for films and tapes on aging.

I would like to thank the following reviewers for their help: Linda Belgrove, Case Western Reserve University; Vern L. Bengtson, University of Southern California; Georgia Walker, University of Missouri, Columbia; Robert Kastenbaum, Arizona State University; and Elizabeth Hoobler, University of New Mexico.

D.K.H.

Introduction

Chapter
1

The Field and Its Methods

*T*he aged are frequently seen as infirm, forgetful, isolated, sexually inactive, dependent, irritable, and unhappy. If you think that the preceding sentence presents a distorted view of older people, you are right. Yet thousands of people believe such stereotypes even though much evidence proves that these have little or no basis in fact. Granted, there may be some elderly to whom the foregoing adjectives might apply, but they make up only a small fraction of the elderly population.

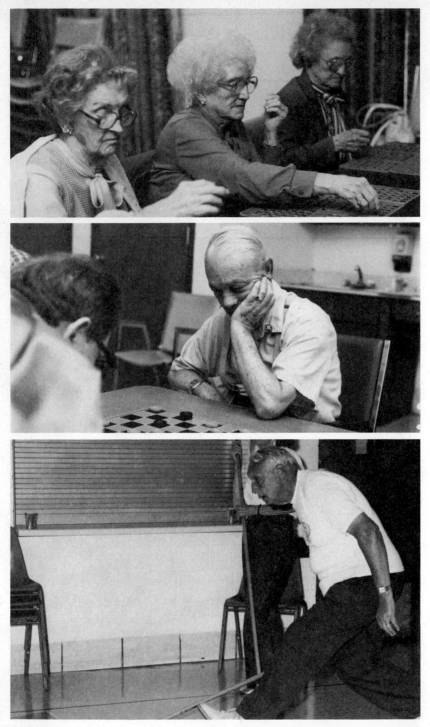

We tend to stereotype the activities of the elderly. Besides sitting in a rocking chair, we often think of older people as playing bingo, checkers, watching television, and playing shuffleboard. (Nick Myers)

STEREOTYPES AND MYTH-CONCEPTIONS

Stereotypes are oversimplified, exaggerated beliefs about a group or category of people. Stereotypes may be positive or negative, but they are always distortions of fact. For example, we generalize when we say that the English are snobbish and reserved, the Irish are witty and pugnacious, intelligent children have high foreheads, and redheads are quick-tempered. These generalizations are erroneous because they do not take into account the many variations within a group and because they indiscriminately attribute the same characteristics to all the members. Many stereotypes or "myth-conceptions" surround older people and the aging process. The following list includes some of the more common myths, along with the chapters in which these ideas are discussed in this text.

1. All older people are alike (Chapter 2).
2. Most older people live in institutions (Chapter 18).
3. The majority of older people are lonely and are isolated from their families (Chapter 12).
4. Older people have more acute illnesses than do younger people (Chapter 18).
5. Retirement is less difficult for women than it is for men (Chapter 13).
6. The majority of people entering a nursing home remain there for the rest of their lives (Chapter 18).
7. Older people cannot learn (Chapter 7).
8. Most older people have no interest in or capacity for sexual activity (Chapter 8).
9. Older people are more fearful of death than are younger people (Chapters 1 and 21).
10. The majority of older people are grouchy and cantankerous (Chapter 7).
11. Alzheimer's disease is to be expected with old age (Chapter 7).
12. Retirement brings poor health and an early death (Chapter 13).
13. Older workers have high accident and absentee rates (Chapters 7 and 13).
14. Most older people prefer to live with their children (Chapter 12).
15. Old age begins at 65 (Chapter 2).
16. The majority of older people are set in their ways, unable to change (Chapters 7 and 13).
17. Older workers are less productive than younger workers (Chapters 7 and 13).
18. Older people vote less frequently than younger people (Chapter 14).
19. Being sick is a necessary part of being old (Chapter 18).
20. People become increasingly religious as they reach old age (Chapters 1 and 15).
21. Older people have higher rates of criminal victimization than younger people (Chapter 20).
22. The majority of older people view themselves as being in poor health (Chapter 18).
23. As people age they become more politically conservative (Chapter 14).

24. At retirement, most people move to Florida or other Sunbelt states (Chapter 2).

25. The majority of older people have incomes below the poverty level (Chapter 17).

How did these myths get started? No one really knows for sure. Many studies of aging in the 1940s and 1950s were based on samples of elderly people who were ill and institutionalized. Those elderly in good health and not in institutions were largely neglected in these studies, with the result that although these studies have some value, they cannot be used as a basis for generalizations about all older people. Also, some research during this period contained methodological weaknesses that made the results invalid. Yet many people continue to accept the conclusions drawn from it. For example, in a compendium of findings of the behavioral sciences prior to 1964, the following statement appears: "In terms of absolute, not relative test performance, mental ability grows rapidly from birth through puberty, somewhat more slowly from then until the early twenties, at which point slow but steady decline sets in, with rather rapid deterioration beginning about age 65" (Berelson & Steiner, 1964). More recent studies, however, reveal that such a pronounced decline in intelligence is a myth and that there is little, if any, intellectual decline for healthy, mentally active individuals up to the age of 80 and beyond (Schaie, 1983).

Myths and stereotypes are perpetuated by the mass media. Probably the most influential medium today is television. A third of all television viewing occurs between the hours of 8:00 to 11:00 each evening, in a period called "prime time." Persons age 65 and over are markedly underrepresented on prime-time television drama and when older people do appear they tend to be cast in minor parts. Their characters are held in less esteem than other characters and are more likely to be treated with disrespect than those in other age groups. In addition, a greater proportion of older characters are portrayed as foolish or eccentric as compared with their younger counterparts. As a result of these unflattering portrayals, negative stereotypes toward older persons are reinforced, especially among heavy viewers. As one researcher concludes, the more television young people watch, the more they tend to perceive the elderly in a negative and unfavorable way (Gerbner, Gross, Signorielli, & Morgan, 1980; Davis & Davis, 1985).

Stereotypes of the elderly are also transmitted and reinforced through humor. Research findings reveal that most of the humor concerning aging and the aged is either negative or ambivalent. From the content analysis of jokes, cartoons, and greeting cards about aging, five recurring themes emerge: physical abilities, mental ability, sexual ability, longevity, and age concealment (Palmore, 1971, 1986).

1. *Physical ability.* Examples of physical decline include such jokes as the elderly couple who got married and spent their honeymoon just trying to get out of the car. Or the old man on bended knee who proposed to a young woman—when she rejects his proposal, he remarks: "Well, if you don't want to marry me, the least you can do is help me up."

2. *Mental ability.* There are many jokes about mental decline. For example, an old man remarks to his friend: "I'd like to live in the past, but I just can't remember any of it."

3. *Sexual ability.* Negative attitudes toward sexuality in old age are conveyed by such jokes as an elderly man staring at a pretty girl as she passes by; his wife witnesses the incident and remarks to a neighbor, "George has a wonderful memory for his age." And a definition of old age: "Where there's a will but no way."

4. *Longevity.* An often-told joke about longevity concerns an old man telling his doctor that if he had known that he was going to live so long, he would have taken better care of himself. Another is a doctor telling an old man that he's in good shape and should live to be 100; the old man replies, "But doc, I *am* 100."

5. *Age concealment.* Nearly all the jokes about age concealment concern women. For example, an elderly man remarks that his wife is a very thrifty lady as she had only 29 candles on her 40th-birthday cake or her cake was beautiful but her arithmetic was terrible.

Some ideas about older people stem from so-called common sense observations. These are often expressed in the form of vague, glib generalizations that many people, both young and old, unquestionably accept as obvious truths about human behavior. Although some common sense maxims may be in accord with scientific knowledge, others—such as "There's no fool like an old fool" and "Old age is a second childhood"—are completely false and quite negative. Sometimes these expressions contradict one another as well as the facts. Common sense maxims tell us, for example, that "Old dogs can't learn new tricks," but "You're never too old to learn." Scientific evidence reveals that the primary ability to learn changes little as one ages. Thus, one aim of research is to separate fact from fallacy and reality from myth.

Box 1.1 **Extraordinary or Ordinary?**

Mary Baker Eddy directed the Christian Science Church at 89.

Albert Schweitzer was in charge of an African hospital at 89.

George Bernard Shaw was writing at 91.

Claude Pepper served as a congressman at 88.

Maggie Kuhn heads the Gray Panthers at 85.

Golda Meir became prime minister of Israel at 71.

Lists such as the foregoing serve only to perpetuate myths about aging. The underlying message is that these people are exceptions to the rule and that ordinarily old people are unproductive, lack vitality and creativity, and are usually sick and senseless. Today we are finding that these exceptions are not that exceptional.

THE DEVELOPMENT OF GERONTOLOGY

Gerontology, the scientific study of aging, is a combination of the Greek words *geront*, meaning "old man," and *logy*, meaning "study of." In 1903 Elie Metchnikoff, a Russian-born biologist, proposed and named this new field of study. However, it did not emerge as a scientific field until about 1940. The rapidly increasing number of older people in the population helped give impetus to gerontological research. Research in gerontology began first with the biological and then with the psychological processes of aging. In the 1950s a subfield of gerontology called *social gerontology* was created; it focused mainly on the social aspects of aging while deemphasizing the biological and psychological aspects. Social gerontology includes specialties in such disciplines as sociology, social psychology, cultural anthropology, political science, and economics.

Early Gerontologists

Lambert A. J. Quetelet, a Belgian scientist and statistician, is considered one of the first gerontologists. His principal work, published in 1835, contains a summary of his statistical research on the average man—both intellectual and physical statistics. In that volume he compares the productivity and age of British and French playwrights.

Another early researcher in this field was Sir Francis Galton, who in 1884 measured 9,337 males and females on such characteristics as their visual acuity and reaction time. From these measurements, Galton was able to show that certain abilities vary with age.

Early in this century, three noted biologists began research in the field of aging. Charles S. Minot compiled his investigations in cytology in *The Problems of Age, Growth, and Death*, published in 1908. That same year Elie Metchnikoff published *The Prolongation of Life*, and in 1922 Raymond Pearl published *The Biology of Death*. In 1926 Pearl researched the lives of more than 5,000 people and showed that alcohol used in moderation did not shorten a person's life. In a later study he analyzed and compared the ancestry of two groups of people in regard to length of life, and he concluded that heredity was an important factor in longevity (Pearl, 1926, 1934). Gerontologists today support the conclusion that genetic factors are important in longevity, but they also recognize that no single factor determines longevity and that it results from the interplay of many factors.

Metchnikoff's interest centered on senescence, death, and specifically the relationship between intestinal flora and aging. According to his hypothesis, toxins that arise from intestinal putrefaction are one of the principal causes of aging. To destroy these toxins and to reduce the onset of aging, Metchnikoff advocated drinking sour milk. He reasoned that sour milk contained acid-producing bacteria that when introduced into the intestine would prevent the breeding of "noxious microbes," which need an alkaline medium. He pointed to such populations as that of the Bulgarians who drank large amounts of fermented milk and who were thought to live a long time (Metchnikoff, 1921).

Metchnikoff failed to consider many organisms that age and die without possess-

"To . . . hell . . . with . . . yogurt." (Drawing by Chas. Addams; © 1979 The New Yorker Magazine, Inc.)

ing large intestines in which putrefaction can take place. His theory, despite its naïveté, has been revived many times. Since the mid-1970s much has been written about the people of the Caucasus Mountains of the Soviet Union who drink large amounts of yogurt-like milk and claim to live to extraordinary ages. However, their claims for unusual longevity are unsubstantiated (see Chapter 2, "The Older Population and Longevity," for further discussion of this topic).

Later Developments

Great strides in the field of gerontology were made in the late 1930s as biologists began studying the changes that take place in cells and tissues as they age and the mechanisms that cause these changes. Cowdry's summarizing volume, *Problems of Aging,* which appeared in 1939, gave further impetus to research in this area. Finally, the formation of the Gerontological Society in 1945 added to the interest in research.

Scientific investigation into the psychological aspects of aging was officially launched around 1930 by the Stanford Later Maturity Research Project, conducted by Walter Miles and his associates. Before this time, little work had been done in the area of aging by psychologists, except for G. Stanley Hall, who in 1922 wrote a book on senescence, which he named; the publication was intended to be a companion volume to his earlier work on adolescence, also named by him. Hall studied religious beliefs and attitudes toward death among older people. His research revealed that as people grow older, they do not necessarily become more religious, nor do they become fearful of death. His findings are still valid today. Many older people worry more about finances than they do about death. Actually, it has been found that younger people fear death more than do the elderly. Since 1946, when the American Psychological Association set up a Division of Later Maturity and Old Age, research into the psychological aspects of aging has grown rapidly.

A pioneering effort in the social sciences was Judson T. Landis's study *Attitudes and Adjustments of Aged Rural People in Iowa,* which appeared in 1940; and in 1945 Leo W. Simmons published his classic work *The Role of the Aged in Primitive Society.* Besides these, there were at this time only a few scattered studies on the social aspects of aging. But in 1943 Ernest W. Burgess, while serving as chairperson of the Social Science Research Council's Committee on Social Adjustment, helped to form the Committee on Social Adjustment in Old Age. The task of this group was to develop an orientation for the study of adjustment problems in old age and to provide suggestions for social research. The report of this committee's work was published in 1948 and laid the foundation for and gave direction to the study of the sociological aspects of aging (Pollack, 1948).

PERSPECTIVES ON AGING

Aging may be defined as all the regular changes that occur in biologically mature individuals as they advance in chronological age (Birren & Renner, 1977). Aging involves a pattern of changes not only in the structure and functioning of the body but also in the adjustment and behavior of the individual. In addition, aging can be viewed as a sequence of changes that takes place in one's statuses and roles over the life course. From these definitions you can see that the study of aging encompasses a wide range of subjects and can be viewed from many perspectives. For our purposes, we will attempt to single out three approaches to the study of aging: the biological, the psychological, and the sociological.

Biological Approach

Research on the biological aspects of aging focuses on the processes that limit the length of life of species and individuals. Or, put another way, such research investigates why species and individuals within a species have fixed life spans. Although opinions differ as to which factors limit the length of life of various species, there is a consensus that these factors are genetically programmed. The goal of biological research is twofold: first, to increase longevity, and second, and more important, to make the added years vigorous and productive ones (Birren, 1968).

Psychological Approach

The psychologist is interested in studying age-related changes and differences in behavior. The subject matter of the psychological aspects of aging includes the effects of aging upon learning, memory, intelligence, skills, personality, motivations, and emotions.

Sociological Approach

A third approach, the one that we will use throughout this book, focuses on the sociological aspects of aging or the sociology of aging. The sociology of aging is an area of specialization within the broader field of sociology; it focuses mainly on one segment of the population—older people. *Sociology* may be defined as the scientific study of human interaction; likewise, we might define the *sociology of aging* as the scientific study of the interaction of older people in society. The key word in both

Interaction refers to the way people act toward one another, interpret one another's behavior, and then respond. (Nick Myers)

definitions is *interaction*. *Interaction* involves acting toward someone who interprets the act and responds to it. For example, suppose an elderly man is walking down one side of the street and an attractive elderly woman is walking down the other. The man sees the woman and whistles at her. By whistling, he is acting toward her. She must then interpret this act before she can respond to it. For instance, she might think that the man is whistling because he has lost his dog, or that he is whistling because he wants to become better acquainted with her. If she interprets his whistling as a search for a dog, she might offer to help him look for it. On the other hand, if she interprets his whistling as an overture, she might smile at him or even cross to his side of the street (Harris & Cole, 1977).

Interaction is simply social behavior between people. People interact in various ways—by means of language, both written and spoken, and by gestures and symbols. The field of aging from the perspective of sociology focuses not on the older individual as a single unit but on his or her interaction with other people. The sociology of aging emphasizes how roles and statuses change with age in relation to the major social institutions and examines the adjustments that individuals make to these changes and the consequences of these actions. It is interested in the impact that the rapidly increasing number of older people have on society, as well as the effect of society on older people.

BASIC RESEARCH METHODS

When we defined the sociology of aging, we referred to it as a *scientific* study. This qualification rests on the assumption that the body of knowledge pertaining to the sociology of aging has been developed through scientific methods of investigation. What are these methods, and how is research done in the field of aging? In the broadest sense there are three basic methods used in sociological research: the sample survey, the experiment, and the case study.

The Sample Survey

A *sample survey*, as the name implies, consists of two elements: a sample and a survey. The group that the researcher plans to study is called a *population*. This population, for example, may consist of college students, voters, housewives, or retirees. Because researchers cannot study all the members in a population, they select a *sample* from the population. The sample must be *representative* of the population—that is, it must contain basically the same distribution of pertinent characteristics as the population from which it was drawn. In this way, findings from the study can be generalized—said to apply—to the population as a whole. The researchers then collect the data on the characteristics of the population being studied by having informants fill out questionnaires, or by asking them questions from interview schedules.

Two studies of aging present an example of how sample surveys are used. In 1975 and again in 1981, Louis Harris and Associates reported on nationwide surveys for the National Council on the Aging that examined the public's expectations of what it is like to be old and to document the views and experiences of older people themselves.

Both studies showed large discrepancies between the problems the elderly personally are experiencing and the problems attributed to them by the 18- to 64-year-old public. For example, in the 1981 study, 68 percent of the public viewed "not having enough money to live on" as a serious problem for most people over age 65. Yet, only 17 percent of the elderly said that lack of money was a serious problem for them. In addition, nearly 75 percent of the public viewed fear of crime as a serious problem for most older persons, but only 25 percent of the elderly supported this view (see Table 1.1).

The 1981 Harris survey also revealed that life satisfaction among those 65 and over is greatest between the ages of 65 and 69 and gradually declines thereafter. Higher scores on life satisfaction were also associated with a higher income ($20,000 and over) and a higher educational attainment. In response to the question "As I look back on my life, I am fairly well satisfied," 87 percent of the respondents agreed. One third agreed that "these are the best years of my life" (Harris and Associates, 1975, 1981).

A great advantage of the sample survey as a research tool is shown by the Harris studies. Certain important questions can be answered only by asking people. Finding out what Americans believe about older people, as well as how the elderly feel about themselves, can be determined only through the sample survey. No experimental study, no matter how well designed, can do this. This method does have disadvantages: Sometimes people purposely conceal their true feelings or express opinions on

Table 1.1   PROBLEMS THAT PEOPLE 65 AND OVER EXPERIENCE COMPARED WITH PROBLEMS ATTRIBUTED TO THEM BY THE PUBLIC

	Persons 65+ who personally are experiencing these problems (percent)	Persons 18–64 who attribute these problems to most people over age 65 (percent)
High cost of energy (e.g. gas, electricity)	42	81
Fear of crime	25	74
Poor health	21	47
Not having enough money to live on	17	68
Transportation to stores, doctors, etc.	14	58
Loneliness	13	65
Not enough medical care	9	45
Not enough education	6	21
Not enough job opportunities	6	51
Poor housing	5	43

Source: Adapted from NCOA. *Aging in the Eighties: America in Transition.* Washington D.C.: The National Council on the Aging, 1981, p.10.

subjects they know nothing about; also, what people say may not always coincide with how they act.

The Experiment

In the *experiment* the investigator controls or manipulates at least one variable being studied and then makes precise measurements or observations of the results. For example, Botwinick (1973) and his associates were interested in finding out whether people become more cautious as they grow older. They wanted to know if older people needed a high degree of certainty before committing themselves to a response. For the experiment, two groups were selected—one old and one young. Ages in the old group ranged from 65 to 71; the young group ranged from 18 to 35 years old. The subjects were shown sets of vertical bars, and they were to judge in each instance which of the two bars was the shorter. Sometimes the difference between the bars was great, making discrimination easy; at other times the difference between the two bars was quite small, making discrimination difficult. Both groups were asked to respond as quickly as possible. The time limit for each judgment was set at two seconds, but the judgments were all made in less time. The older persons responded much more slowly than the younger persons, especially when the bars were nearly the same length.

The experimenter then told both groups that their time for viewing the two bars would be reduced to 0.15 seconds. Both groups made their judgments in less time than before, but the older subjects greatly increased their speed even in cases where discrimination was difficult.

The results of the study showed that the speed of response of the older persons tended to vary with the amount of time they were given. In the first instance, when they had more time to respond, they took it. Later, when they were told they had less time and were pushed by the experimenter to make faster responses, their speed greatly improved.

The investigators concluded that the extra time taken by the older group reflected the increased level of confidence that was required by older persons before giving a response, and not their inability to make correct discriminations in the length of the bars. One reason for this insecurity may be that our society devalues old age—we expect old people to fail; we brand them as inadequate. Because of these societal expectations, older people require more certainty from a situation in order to minimize the chances for their expected failure and in order to avoid being labeled deficient.

The *independent variables* in an experiment are those variables directly manipulated by the investigator. In this experiment, the investigator manipulated both the amount of viewing time and the length of the vertical bars that the subjects were to view, making these the independent variables.

Dependent variables are measured during the experiment; they are affected by the actual process of the experiment. In this illustration, the dependent variable is the response time of the subjects. We can say, then, that the response time (the dependent variable) is a function of the amount of viewing time allowed and the difficulty of the discriminations to be made (the independent variables).

In sociological research, experiments generally take place with small groups of people in limited settings. To do otherwise is not practical because of the expense and time that would be involved. Another point to be considered is that when people know that they are being watched and studied, this knowledge may influence the way they behave or respond. Because of these two factors—the small size of the sample and the behavioral change that may take place with the subjects—an experimental group cannot be said to be representative of the larger population. As a result, findings from experiments are limited in their degree of generalization. A great advantage of laboratory experiments is that we can learn from them exactly how a certain variable affects behavior under a specific condition; this situation would be difficult to control or duplicate in a real-life situation.

The Case Study

The *case study* method focuses on a single case in considerable depth and detail, usually over a long period of time. A case may be the life history of a person or a detailed account of some social process or event. With this method we can also study a work group, a family, or a retirement community.

Participant observation is a technique commonly used by sociologists in case studies. The investigator takes part in whatever group is being studied. For example, William F. Whyte wanted to study a slum gang in Boston, so he joined the gang and participated in all its activities over a period of several years. John Loftland's interest in radical religious groups led him to become a member of the Divine Precepts cult in order to observe and study this group as an insider.

One problem encountered in using this technique is the possible influence or effect on the people that the presence of the observer might have. Also, participant observers must be on guard against getting too involved in the group being investigated and thus losing their objectivity. The participant observer method is an excellent way to get information about groups about which so little is known that other research methods cannot be effectively utilized. The main advantage of participant observation lies in the rich insights and intimate, first-hand knowledge that the investigator gains—information hardly possible to come by through other research methods.

(Reprinted by permission of UFS, Inc.)

The following account shows how a sociologist, Arlie Hochschild, used the participant observation method in studying 43 residents of Merrill Court, a small public-housing apartment building near the shore of San Francisco Bay. Of the 43 residents, 37 were elderly widowed females. In the summer of 1966 Hochschild secured a job as an assistant recreation director of Merrill Court and worked there for the better part of three years. After the first few months, she told the residents that she was a sociologist doing a study, but this fact did not seem to matter to them. During the course of her job at Merrill Court she took part in many activities with the residents and worked with them on recreational projects:

> Initially, my watching went on in the Recreation Room, where I sat and did handiwork at a table with five or six others. As I drove residents to the doctor, to the housing office, to church, and occasionally to funerals, joined them on visits to relatives, shopped with them, kept bowling scores, visited their apartments and took them to mine, I gradually came to know and to like them. Through sharing their lives I came to see how others treated them and how their own behavior changed as their audience did. (Hochschild, 1973)

Hochschild felt that the most outstanding feature of Merrill Court was that it was a vibrant, thriving community, not just an apartment house full of old people. She was interested in finding out the reasons for this cohesiveness. Her study suggests that the communal feeling manifested by Merrill Court residents can be largely attributed to two factors: the homogeneity of the residents and the social arrangements under which they lived.

First of all, the majority of the residents had similar interests and needs. They shared a "we are in the same boat" feeling. Most were white Anglo-Saxon Protestant widowed females in their late sixties who were rural-born and had working-class backgrounds. Nearly all were living on welfare payments, except for a few who received Social Security benefits. They sometimes jokingly referred to themselves as "us poor pensioners." All but one person had been born in the United States, and the majority of them had come from either the Midwest or Southwest.

The second factor that contributed to making Merrill Court a community was the social patterns of the residents. These patterns revolved around upstairs and downstairs roles. Downstairs roles mainly took place in the recreation room and were more formal, whereas upstairs roles involved an informal network of neighboring among residents. The residents enjoyed a particular type of relationship among themselves—a sibling bond. The term *sibling bond* is used by Hochschild to denote a relationship in which there is a reciprocity and sharing among members. Reciprocity results in an almost equal exchange of favors and mutual aid:

> Most residents of Merrill Court are social siblings. The customs of exchanging cups of coffee, lunches, potted plants, and curtain checking suggest reciprocity. Upstairs, one widow usually visited as much as she was visited. In deciding who visits whom, they often remarked, "Well, I came over last time. You come over this time." They traded, in even measure, slips from house plants, kitchen utensils, and food of all sorts. They watched one another's apartments when someone was away on a visit, and they called and took calls for one another.

Hochschild concludes that the family unit, which has held generations together in the past, is declining in strength, and as a result, she predicts, the sibling bond will grow in importance. This bond, she believes, will allow more flexibility in relationships between generations by forging solidarity within generations. She feels that the time is right for sibling-bond interaction and age-segregated communities like Merrill Court.

Because Hochschild's work involved one specific group of older people, we cannot generalize and say that her findings apply to all similar groups. Her in-depth study of Merrill Court does, however, provide much insight, many descriptive examples, and suggestions for perceptive hypotheses.

CROSS-SECTIONAL AND LONGITUDINAL STUDIES

The earliest and still the most frequently used method for studying aging is the *cross-sectional design,* which compares two or more cohorts at one point in time to find out about age differences. *Cohort* refers to persons born within the same year or time period. The previously cited surveys by Louis Harris and Associates illustrate this method. However, if misused, cross-sectional studies are subject to erroneous interpretations because they do not distinguish between the effects of growing older and the time in which one was born. For example, research on the intellectual capacity of the aged was for many years studied only by the cross-sectional method. Investigators administered intelligence tests to a group of young people and a group of old people and then compared the performance levels of the two cohorts. The older persons scored consistently lower than the younger ones, so the conclusion was drawn that as people age, their intellectual levels decline.

We now know through the use of *longitudinal studies* that examine the same individuals over a period of years that much of the lower intellectual abilities of older persons was not because they were growing older (age effect), but rather because they were born at a time when they received less education than young people do today. In other words, people born in 1900 have had a different socialization experience than those persons or cohorts born in 1965. These experiences are referred to as the *cohort effect.* Because age effects and cohort effects are not separated out in cross-sectional studies, this may lead to misinterpretation and the drawing of faulty conclusions.

Another example of the drawing of faulty conclusions regarding age differences is a tongue-in-cheek story related by Robert Kastenbaum:

> Occasionally I have the opportunity to chat with elderly people who live in the communities near by Cushing Hospital. I cannot help but observe that many of these people speak with an Italian accent. I also chat with young adults who live in these same communities. They do not speak with an Italian accent. As a student of human behavior and development I am interested in this discrepancy. I indulge in some deep thinking and come up with the following conclusion: as people grow older they develop Italian accents. (Quoted in Botwinick, 1978)

In both situations the observed age differences were not the result of age effects but rather cohort effects. Whereas cross-sectional studies observe subjects at one point in time and tell us about age differences, longitudinal studies observe the same subjects at two or more points in time and tell us about age changes. Some examples

Table 1.2   COMPARISON OF LONGITUDINAL AND CROSS-SECTIONAL DESIGNS

Type of study design	Time of setting	Data generated	Variables confounded
Cross-Sectional	Subjects observed at one point in time	Age differences	Age effects and cohort effects
Longitudinal	Subjects observed at two or more points in time	Age changes	Age effects and period effects

of these changes might include a slowing down in reaction time or a decline in visual acuity. Although longitudinal studies are not as prone to misinterpretation as cross-sectional studies, they do not distinguish age effects from historical events such as the Depression of the 1930s or the sexual revolution of the 1960s. These events are referred to as *period effects*. Suppose, for example, that you are interested in conducting a longitudinal study to find if attitudes toward sex change with advancing age. You test a group of older subjects in 1960, again in 1970, and finally in 1980. You might find that your subjects had become increasingly more liberal in their sexual attitudes. Does this mean that people get more sexually liberated with age? What is more likely in this situation is that your subjects are simply reflecting the sexual revolution of their times and changing with it. Observed longitudinal differences in the elderly then may be all or partly the result of period effects rather than aging effects (see Table 1.2).

WHY STUDY AGING?

What does studying the subject of aging do for you? Becoming old is something that happens to us all—if we live long enough. What you learn now about this subject will give you a perspective on the problems of aging earlier in your life cycle, will help you plan for a more successful retirement, and will give you a better understanding of the aging process within yourself. Studying aging will also help you to dispel some false beliefs and myths about growing older and, in doing so, may give you a more positive attitude toward getting older, as well as allay some fears associated with aging.

Lastly, studying the sociology of aging may help you in relating to your parents and grandparents and give you a better understanding of some problems that they, as well as other older Americans, face. Helping our nation and its communities to provide a more satisfactory life for the elderly should improve conditions not only for today's older people but also for those who will be old tomorrow.

SUMMARY

1. Many stereotypes about older people are inaccurate. A *stereotype* is an oversimplified belief that is applied indiscriminately to all members of a group or category.
2. *Gerontology* is defined as the scientific study of aging. A subfield of gerontology that focuses on the social aspects of aging is called *social gerontology*.

3. The earliest work on aging was done by Quetelet and Galton. Scientific research in the biological sciences began with such men as Minot, Pearl, and Metchnikoff. Studies on the psychological aspects of aging can be traced back to the work of Hall and Miles; research on the sociological aspects of aging originated with the works of Landis, Simmons, and Pollack.

4. *Aging* refers to the changes that take place in an individual after maturation. The study of aging can be viewed from three main perspectives: the biological, the psychological, and the sociological. The sociological perspective, or the sociology of aging, may be defined as the scientific study of interaction of older people in society.

5. The three basic methods of doing sociological research are the sample survey, the experiment, and the case study. Each of these methods takes place in either a cross-sectional or longitudinal time setting. In a cross-sectional design, the characteristics of a population are studied at one point in time, and this generates data about age differences. In a longitudinal design, the study takes place at two or more points in time, and this generates data about age changes.

KEY TERMS

stereotypes
gerontology
social gerontology
aging
sociology
sociology of aging
interaction
sample survey
population
sample
representative
experiment

independent variable
dependent variable
case study
participant observation
sibling bond
cross-sectional design
cohort
longitudinal studies
age effects
cohort effects
period effects

FOR FURTHER STUDY

Babbie, Earl R. (1986). *The practice of social research.* Belmont, CA: Wadsworth.
  Provides a thorough coverage of social research methods.

Berghorn, Forrest J., Schafer, Donna E., and Associates (1981). *The dynamics of aging.* Boulder, CO: Westview.
  Contains original essays that provide an interdisciplinary approach to the aging process.

Comfort, Alex (1976). *A good age.* New York: Crown.
  A highly readable account of some of the facts about aging.

Cunningham, Walter R., & Brookbank, John W. (1988). *Gerontology: The psychology, biology, and sociology of aging.* New York: Harper & Row.

    Provides an overview of gerontology from three major perspectives.

Quadagno, Jill S. (1980). *Aging, the individual and society: Readings in social gerontology.* New York: St. Martin's.

    A reader that provides a wide variety of articles that focus on the social aspects of aging.

Reading

Stereotypes and Treatment of the Elderly

Pat Moore

At age 26 Pat Moore, an industrial designer, disguised herself as an 85-year-old woman to find out what it is like to be old. With the help of a professional makeup artist, she put on latex wrinkles and a gray wig, wore splints and bandages under her clothes to stiffen her joints, and put plugs in her ears to dull her hearing and baby oil in her eyes to blur her vision. Her research, a form of participant observation, spanned a three-year period. In the following excerpt she describes the feelings she experienced and the treatment she received as an elderly person.

The young are often badly informed about what older people are like, and stereotypes of the elderly abound. Like stereotypes of any kind, they are often inaccurate or downright abusive. Too many younger Americans think of their older counterparts as uniformly deaf, forgetful, arthritic, cranky, and hard to deal with. Many young salesclerks, bank tellers, and waitresses see someone over seventy as a customer who is likely to be troublesome, creating difficulty of some sort.

As with most stereotypes, there is just enough truth to keep the larger fiction alive. If younger people expect elder citizens to fit this negative pattern, they avoid them if they can, give bad service, find ways to ignore them entirely, or treat them

Pat Moore with Charles P. Conn. *Disguised.* Waco, Texas: Word Books, 1985.

with condescension and dismissal. That attitude inevitably increases the likelihood that the older person will behave impatiently, and the spiral of the self-fulfilling prophecy is complete. It is a fundamental truth that people tend to act the way they are expected to act.

When I did my grocery shopping while in character, I learned quickly that the Old Pat Moore behaved—and was treated—differently from the Young Pat Moore. When I was eighty-five, people were more likely to jockey ahead of me in the checkout line. And even more interesting, I found that when it happened, I didn't say anything to the offender, as I certainly would at age twenty-seven. It seemed some-how, even to me, that it was okay for them to do this to the Old Pat Moore, since they were undoubtedly busier than I was anyway. And further, they apparently thought it was okay, too! After all, little old ladies have plenty of time, don't they?

And then when I did get to the checkout counter, the clerk might start yelling, assuming I was deaf, or become immediately testy, assuming I would take a long time to get my money out, or would ask to have the price repeated, or somehow become confused about the transaction. What it all added up to was that people feared I would be trouble, so they tried to have as little to do with me as possible. And the amazing thing is that I began almost to believe it myself. Even though I wasn't genuinely old, I became so intimidated by the attitudes of others, by the fear that they would become exasperated with me, that I absorbed some of their tacitly negative judgment about people of my age.

It was as if, unconsciously, I was saying, in reaction to being ignored and avoided, "You're right. I'm just a lot of trouble. I'm really not as valuable as all these other people, so I'll just get out of your way as soon as possible so you won't be angry with me." . . . I think perhaps the worst thing about aging may be the overwhelming sense that everything around you is letting you know that you are not terribly important any more.

Was the shabby treatment I so often received as Old Pat Moore a reaction to the fact that I was old, or when in character did I just happen to encounter merchants who treated everyone brusquely, regardless of age? I wondered about that, and on several occasions I went twice to the same establishments and engaged in the same transactions with the same personnel—once as the younger and once as the older character. In virtually all these comparisons, the people I encountered showed a more positive attitude toward the younger me. Sometimes it was subtle, but the difference was almost always there, and it always worked against the woman of eighty-five.

Typical of these comparisons was a man who operated a stationery store in Manhattan. He was one of those individuals who appear to become instantly irritated by the presence of an old man or woman. I entered his store one day to buy a ribbon for my typewriter. I was in character, but I honestly did need the ribbon, and I didn't go there with the intention of returning later in younger garb. I began looking for what I needed, patiently, without asking for any help, and could not find it. He stayed at the cash register for several minutes without greeting me or offering to help. It was a small shop, and I was the only customer there at the time. In resignation, he finally approached me.

"Do you need something?" he barked.

"A ribbon for my typewriter," I replied hopefully.

Stepping behind the counter, he asked, "What kind?"

"A black one," I said with a smile. He was so terse that I wondered if I had done something to upset him.

"No, no, no! What kind of typewriter do you have?" By now he made no attempt to hide his irritation; he was addressing me as if I were a half-witted child in a candy store.

"Oh, pardon me. I understand what you mean now," I apologized as sincerely as possible. "I can never remember the name of it. Could you name what you have and I'll know it?"

He sighed in response: "Smith Corona, IBM Selectric, Olivetti, Adler . . ."

"That's it," I interrupted. "Adler. I can never remember that. I should write it down!"

Without speaking, he left to get the ribbon, returned to the cash register, and began to ring up the sale.

"Three dollars and twenty-four cents, with tax," he stated abruptly.

I began to fumble with the latch on my handbag. It was difficult to open, even without gloves and arthritis. For my older self, it was a struggle.

As I wrestled with the change-purse, he heaved such an exasperated sigh that I felt a need to apologize for the delay.

"Darn thing always gives me trouble!"

No response but the same dull glare.

Having successfully opened the purse, I gave him a five-dollar bill.

Without speaking, he placed the change in my hand and put my purchase into a paper bag.

I waited for a moment to see if he intended to hand me the package or address me further. He did neither. Instead, he left the counter, went to the far side of the store, and began busily readjusting the merchandise on a shelf. I picked up the paper sack from the counter and left.

Exactly what transpired in that dreary exchange between the proprietor and the *old* woman? Did it have anything at all to do with an attitude that the *old* are not as important, or not as enjoyable to interact with? Or perhaps it had nothing to do with age; maybe he was just a jerk. Maybe he was rude to everybody.

To test that proposition, I returned to the stationery shop the very next day, hoping to find the same man behind the counter. He was there, and once again he was alone.

I was my younger self now. Sandy-blonde hair curled and falling on my shoulders, sunglasses and sandals. I looked like many other young women from the neighborhood areas around Greenwich Village. I was even wearing the same dress I had worn the day before, but my back wasn't padded to convey a slight hunch, my legs weren't covered by layers of elastic bandages, and the wrinkles and bags were gone from my face.

He looked up immediately as I entered, and gave me his best smile. "Yes, miss? May I help you?" he chirped.

Somehow, I wasn't surprised.

"A ribbon for my typewriter," I said, being careful to repeat the previous day's request.

"And what kind would you like, miss?"

"A black one," I answered simply.

"Oh, no!" he laughed, "I mean what kind of typewriter do you have? They're all different, you know!"

"Oh, now I understand." I returned his smile. "I never remember. Could you name what you have and I'll know it?"

"Sure thing," he replied eagerly. "Let's see, I can help you with an IBM Selectric, a Smith Corona, a Brother, or there's an Olivetti, an Adler . . ."

"That's it!" I exclaimed, just like before. "I can never remember that. I should write it down."

"Oh, lots of people have that problem," he reassured me. "But as long as you know it when you hear it, you're all right."

He was chuckling pleasantly as he placed the ribbon on the counter and pushed the cash register keys.

"Are you sure you don't need anything else with that, now?"

"No, thank you."

"That'll be three dollars and twenty-four cents with the tax," he said politely.

I placed my handbag on the counter. Fumbling with the latch, I repeated my performance from the day before.

"Darn thing always gives me trouble."

"Well, better for it to be nice and tight and take a little longer to open, than to make it easy for the muggers and the pick-pockets," he bantered.

I handed him a five-dollar bill and waited for the change. He counted it out carefully, "That's four and one makes five! Now we'll get you a bag here and you're all set."

He was so nice. I had to fight the urge to scream. Without a word I turned away from the counter and headed toward the door. He scurried behind me.

"Let me get that door for you," he offered. "It sticks sometimes."

"Yeah, I know," I mumbled, and walked out the door.

Chapter
2

The Older Population and Longevity

John Lamb was a college professor. He was a bachelor and lived alone. His health problems became an increasingly important concern to him as he passed the 40-year-old mark. At around age 45, John developed arthritis. By age 50, his arthritis had worsened, and he had developed hypertension. At 59, he decided to give up teaching and to apply for disability retirement. After a long series of conferences and consultations, he was finally granted retirement on the grounds that he was disabled. Now age 65, Lamb, who has suffered a stroke, lives in a nursing home.

Lucille Rogers is 85 years old. She was 65 when she retired as city librarian. At age 75, she made the initial study that formed the basis for many programs and activities of the council on aging in her home city. Lucille is still much in demand as a speaker by groups and organizations concerned with the elderly. Although chronologically aged, Lucille enjoys good health, is energetic, and has youthful attitudes.

Lucille and John illustrate the diversity of conditions found in the category of people we designate as aged or retired. Some people retire at 55, whereas others work until 70 or later. For some individuals, physical decline occurs early; for others it happens much later. In health, vigor, performance, and mental outlook, older people vary as much as, if not more than, young or middle-aged people.

IDENTIFYING THE ELDERLY

There is no fixed time in a person's life when he or she becomes old. Aging is a gradual and sometimes almost imperceptible process. Because of this lack of a clearly defined time, different societies use various criteria for determining when someone has reached the status of an elderly person. Some societies define old age in functional terms such as physical decline or not being able to perform the full range of adult tasks. Among the Kikuyu of Kenya, for example, a man is considered old when he must stop and rest by the side of the road while others pass him by, and when the odor of food no longer awakens him from sleep. The Kikuyu consider a woman old when she can no longer work in the garden, when she cannot carry a small load on her back, and when she keeps dropping the cooking pot (Cox & Mberia, 1977).

Other societies view the beginning of old age socially in terms of role transitions. For instance, the Maricopa Indians of Arizona consider a person old on the birth of his or her first grandchild. In Western society, particularly in the United States, old age is defined chronologically—by how many years a person has lived. In our society we use the age of 65 as the point at which a person is thought to be old. The basis for this belief may be traced back to the Social Security Act of 1935, which was passed during the administration of President Franklin D. Roosevelt. The Act set 65 as the age of eligibility for Social Security payments. American employers then began using 65 as the age for mandatory retirement in order to coincide retirement with the time that Social Security benefits began. Thus the age of 65 was arbitrary and had no basis in reality as the point at which a person actually becomes old. Primarily as a result of Social Security legislation, most gerontological studies use 65 as the age at which people are considered old. For the sake of convenience and clarity, therefore, throughout this book we will refer to those age 65 and over as older people, the elderly, or old. Because age 65 and over spans such a broad category, we will sometimes use the subdivisions of the *young-old* (65–74), the *old-old* (75–84), and the *oldest-old* (85 and over).

In this chapter we will first discuss *demography,* the scientific study of the size of, composition of, distribution of, and changes in human populations. For our purposes, we will be concerned primarily with the population of those persons age 65 and over, or the demography of aging, a subfield of demography. In a later part of this chapter, we will discuss longevity and some of the ideas and beliefs about extending life and youth.

When is a person considered old? Aging proceeds at different rates for different individuals. Such variations have led gerontologists to distinguish between chronological age, functional age, and social age. (Tennessee Valley Authority)

GROWTH OF THE OLDER POPULATION

For most of this century, the number of elderly people in the United States has not only increased at an unprecedented rate, but their numbers also have grown more rapidly than those of any other segment of the population. Every 24 hours, nearly 6,000 persons reach age 65. In 1900 there were 3 million people age 65 and over in the United States, and today there are over 30 million—an increase of over ten times (see Table 2.1 and Figure 2.1). Not only is America growing older, but the old are growing older. One of the fastest-growing age groups in the country is the 85-and-over population, or the oldest-old. What accounts for this phenomenal

Table 2.1 ACTUAL AND PROJECTED GROWTH OF THE POPULATION 65 AND OVER IN THE UNITED STATES 1900–2050

Year	Number (in thousands)	Percent of total population	Year	Number (in thousands)	Percent of total population
1900	3,084	4.0	1980	25,544	11.3
1910	3,950	4.3	1990	31,559	12.6
1920	4,933	4.7	2000	34,882	13.0
1930	6,634	5.4	2010	39,362	13.9
1940	9,019	6.8	2020	52,067	17.7
1950	12,270	8.1	2030	65,604	21.8
1960	16,560	9.2	2040	68,109	22.6
1970	19,980	9.8	2050	68,532	22.9

Source: U.S. Bureau of the Census, *Current Population Reports*, Series P-25, No. 1018, "Projections of the Population of the United States, by Age, Sex, and Race: 1988 to 2080," January 1989. Projection data for 1990–2050 from middle series.

growth of the older population? Primarily, it is due to the high birth rate prior to 1920 and to the dramatic increase in life expectancy, especially during the first half of this century.

MEASURES OF AGING

One of the most significant changes occurring in our nation is the fact that America is aging. Some refer to this phenomenon as the "graying of America," the "graying of our population," and the "age of aging." There are a number of indicators or measures that reflect the aging of our population. Three of these indicators are (1) an increase

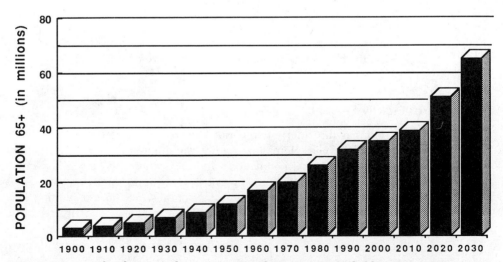

Figure 2.1. Actual and projected increase in population 65 years and older: 1900–2030. In 1900 there were 3 million persons 65 years and over in the population; by 1990 the number had increased to 35.5 million. The older population is expected to reach 65.6 million by 2030.

One of the factors accounting for the dramatic growth of the older population is the high birth rate prior to 1920. Only a part of the children of this Tennessee couple are pictured in this photograph. (Tennessee Valley Authority)

in the proportion of elderly persons, (2) an increase in the proportion of the old in relation to the young, and (3) a rise in the median age.

Proportion of Elderly Persons

Not only has the elderly population grown in numbers, but their proportion in the total population has increased steadily (the number of those 65 and over expressed as a percent of the total population). In 1790, when the first U.S. Census was taken, about 2 percent of the population, or every fiftieth American, was age 65 or over. As Table 2.1 shows, in 1900 the percentage of those age 65 and over in the United States was 4 percent, or 1 person in 25. By 1987 the elderly constituted 12 percent of the population, or 1 in every 8 Americans. This dramatic increase in the proportion of older persons is due mainly to the aging of the pre-1920s group and the decline in the birth rate (creating a "baby bust") after the mid-1960s.

Population aging is not confined to the United States; rather, it is a worldwide phenomenon. As Table 2.2 shows, in 1985 Sweden had the oldest population in the

Table 2.2 POPULATIONS AGE 65 AND OVER IN SELECTED COUNTRIES, 1985

Country	Number (thousands)	Percent of total	Country	Number (thousands)	Percent of total
United States	28,609	12.0	Canada	2,651	10.5
France	6,748	12.4	Japan	12,125	10.0
West Germany	8,812	14.5	China	52,889	5.1
Italy	7,443	13.0	India	32,698	4.3
Sweden	1,415	16.9	Mexico	2,797	3.5
United Kingdom	8,466	15.1			

Source: U.S. Senate Special Committee on Aging, *Aging America: Trends and Projections, 1987–1988.* Washington, D.C.: U.S. Government Printing Office.

world, with 16.9 percent over age 65. Following was the United Kingdom with 15.1 percent and West Germany with 14.5 percent.

One of the best ways to show the change in the proportion of the elderly in the population is to use what sociologists call a *population pyramid,* which graphically depicts the age–sex structure of a population. The population pyramid is based on the number or proportion of males and females in each age group in a population. Five-year intervals are often used. Age groups are represented as horizontal bars in ascending order, with the youngest at the bottom and the oldest at the top. A vertical line in the center of the bars divides the pyramid so that the bars on the left represent males and the bars on the right represent females. The population pyramids for 1900, 1988, and 2030 shown in Figure 2.2 reveal how the age–sex structure of the United States has changed during this century and how it will change again in the early part of the next century. In 1900, when the birth and death rates were high, the bars resembled a pyramid (hence the term "population pyramid"). By 1988, the population pyramid began to take on more of a pear-shaped appearance. Note the huge bulge in the population between the ages of 22 and 40; it represents those persons who were born during America's post–World War II baby boom, from 1946 to 1964. During that period about 76 million children, or about a third of our present population, were born. The baby-boom generation will reach age 65 in the early part of the next century. By 2030 the older population will mushroom to 65.6 million—1 in every 5 Americans will be elderly.

Proportion of the Old in Relation to the Young

As we pointed out previously, in 1900 only 4 percent of the population was age 65 and over. At that time young persons under 18 made up 40 percent of the population. In 1980 the proportion of those persons over age 65 was 11.3 percent, and persons under age 18 made up 28 percent of the population. According to projections by the U.S. Bureau of the Census, the population under 18 will continue to decline while the older population will continue to increase, with the result that the proportion of persons over 65 by 2030 will equal 23 percent and persons under 18 will equal only 18 percent of the population.

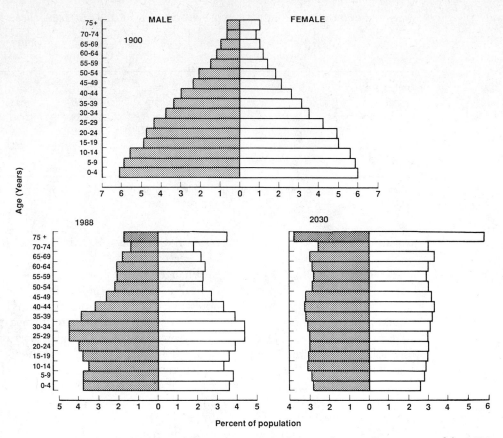

Figure 2.2. U.S. population pyramids: 1900, 1988, and 2030. The population pyramid for 1900 has the shape of a true pyramid. By 1988 the base becomes smaller as the birth rate declines and the top becomes broader indicating an increasing proportion of older people in the population. By 2030 the pyramid takes on a columnar shape except for the top which represents the dramatic increase of older persons in the population.

Median Age

Median age is the age that divides the population into two equal-size segments, one of which is younger than the median and one of which is older. When the median age rises, the population is said to be aging. For example, in 1970 the median age of the U.S. population was about 28 years. It rose to nearly 33 years in 1987. The median age is expected to reach 36 by 2000 and to go as high as 42 by 2030.

WHERE OLDER PEOPLE LIVE

Contrary to popular belief, at retirement most persons do not move to another state but prefer to remain in the same place where they have spent most of their adult lives. In fact, the elderly are less likely to change residence than any other age group. If they do move, they often move within their own community. When older persons move to another state, they tend to migrate to the *Sunbelt* states, those in the South and the Southwest. Florida receives the largest share of older interstate in-migrants, followed by California and Arizona (Flynn et al., 1985).

The traditional notion that Florida also has the largest proportion of older people of any state is true. This high concentration is due to the fact that most of their in-migrants are older people who have relocated there in retirement. Other states such as Pennsylvania, Iowa, Rhode Island, and Arkansas also have high concentrations of older people, but for a different reason—the high rate of out-migration of their younger people (see Table 2.3).

The states with the largest numbers of older people are California, New York, and Florida; each had more then two million persons aged 65 and over in 1987. Pennsylvania, Texas, Illinois, Ohio, and Michigan each had more than a million older residents. About half of all persons 65 and over live in these eight states.

Table 2.3   PERCENT OF PERSONS AGE 65 AND OVER BY STATE: 1988

Rank	State	Percent	Rank	State	Percent
1	Florida	17.8	27	Kentucky	12.4
2	Pennsylvania	14.9	28	Mississippi	12.3
3	Iowa	14.9	29	Indiana	12.2
4	Rhode Island	14.7	30	Illinois	12.2
5	Arkansas	14.6	31	North Carolina	11.9
6	West Virginia	14.3	32	Washington	11.9
7	South Dakota	14.0	33	Vermont	11.8
8	Missouri	13.8	34	Idaho	11.8
9	Nebraska	13.8	35	Delaware	11.7
10	Oregon	13.8	36	Michigan	11.6
11	Massachusetts	13.7	37	New Hampshire	11.3
12	Kansas	13.5	38	South Carolina	10.9
13	North Dakota	13.5	39	Louisiana	10.9
14	Connecticut	13.5	40	Maryland	10.8
15	Maine	13.4	41	Nevada	10.7
16	Wisconsin	13.2	42	Virginia	10.6
17	New Jersey	13.1	43	California	10.6
18	Oklahoma	13.0	44	Hawaii	10.4
19	New York	13.0	45	New Mexico	10.3
20	Arizona	12.8	46	Georgia	10.0
21	Montana	12.8	47	Texas	9.9
22	Ohio	12.6	48	Colorado	9.5
23	Minnesota	12.5	49	Wyoming	9.4
24	Alabama	12.5	50	Utah	8.3
25	Tennessee	12.5	51	Alaska	3.8
26	District of Columbia	12.5		United States total	12.4

Source: U.S. Administration on Aging. Based on data from U.S. Bureau of the Census, Press Release CB89-72, May 4, 1989.

(Reprinted by permission of NEA, Inc.)

LIFE EXPECTANCY

All species have fixed, finite *life spans*. Life span is the average age members of a species can survive under optimum conditions free of disease and accident. For human beings this average age is generally considered to be somewhere between 80 and 90 years, while the *maximum life potential*, the length of life of the longest-lived members of a species, is about 115 years for humans, 150 years for the Galápagos tortoise, and one day for the mayfly (Fries & Crapo, 1981).

Although the human life span has remained constant for at least 100,000 years *life expectancy*—the average number of years remaining at any specified age—has changed dramatically. For example, in 1987, life expectancy at birth in the United States was about 75 years and at age 65 was about 17 years. It is interesting to note that the older one gets, the greater the likelihood of living longer. It is estimated that about 500 B.C. in ancient Greece, life expectancy at birth was around 18 years, and that by A.D. 100 in Rome it had risen to 25 years (see Figure 2.3). Life

---

Box 2.1 # Length of Life in Prehistoric Populations

An archaeologist who has studied the ages of prehistoric skeletons has found that 95 percent of the populations died before they reached 40 and that 75 percent failed to reach 30. The length of life in prehistoric populations has been calculated as follows:

Population	Percentage dead by age:		
	30	40	50
Neanderthal (90,000–40,000 years ago)	8.0	95.0	100.0
Cro-Magnon (35,000–10,000 years ago)	61.7	88.2	90.0
Mesolithic (around 12,000 years ago)	86.3	95.5	97.0

Source: David H. Fischer, *Growing Old in America.* New York: Oxford University Press, 1978, pp. 6–7.

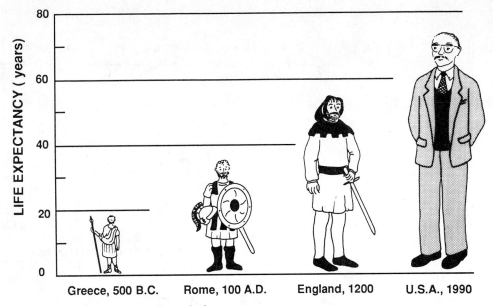

Figure 2.3. Life expectancy through the ages.

expectancy had no significant increase from the late Roman Empire to the eighteenth century.

The earliest data on life expectancy in the United States can be traced back to 1789; in that year individuals in Massachusetts had at birth a life expectancy of approximately 35 years. By 1900 life expectancy for people in the entire nation was 47.3 years, and by 1987 it had increased to 74.7 years. Several reasons account for this 27-year increase in life expectancy during this century: (1) a reduction of infant and child mortality rates, (2) advances in the prevention and cure of most contagious diseases, (3) some decline in death rates during the adult years, and (4) general improvement in the standard of living for the nation.

In 1920 the gap between the sexes in life expectancy was only 1.0 years. The gap began widening up until the 1970s, when life expectancy for females exceeded that of males by about 7.6 years (see Table 2.4). Now the gap in female and male life expectancy appears to have narrowed slightly. As a result of this sex gap, older women outnumber older men three to two—in 1987 there were 18 million women to 12 million men. Because women outlive men and tend to marry men older than they, a large percentage of married women must cope eventually with widowhood.

Why do females outlive males? No one really knows. The population in all the developed countries throughout the world reflects this sex disparity (see Table 2.5).

There is strong evidence that the difference in life expectancy between the sexes is mostly due to biological factors. Several authorities point out that females outlive males not only in the human species but in other species as well, including such varied organisms as spiders, rats, fish, and fruit flies. Some attempts have been made to explain the longer life of the females in genetic terms. One theory is that females have an additional X-chromosome that gives them a biological

Table 2.4   LIFE EXPECTANCY AT BIRTH BY SEX IN THE UNITED STATES, 1900–2000

Year	Male	Female	Difference (female minus male)
1900	46.3	48.3	2.0
1910	48.4	51.8	3.4
1920	53.6	54.6	1.0
1930	58.1	61.6	3.5
1940	60.8	65.2	4.4
1950	65.6	71.1	5.5
1960	66.6	73.1	6.5
1970	67.1	74.7	7.6
1980	70.0	77.4	7.4
1990	72.1	79.0	6.9
2000	73.5	80.4	6.9

Source: U.S. Public Health Service, National Center for Health Statistics, Vital Statistics of the United States, 1986. Life Tables, Vol. II, Section 6, October 1988 (data for 1900–1980). U.S. Bureau of the Census, *Current Population Reports*, Series P-25, No. 1018, "Projections of the Population of the United States, by Age, Sex, and Race: 1988 to 2080," January 1989. Projection data for 1990–2000 from middle series.

advantage over males. Females are also believed to have a better immunization system against disease than males and that whatever the specific disease causing death, females fare better than males at all adult age levels (Rockstein & Sussman, 1979). Another explanation for the difference in life expectancy between the sexes is that women have a superior vitality. With the decrease in contagious diseases, maternal mortality, and degenerative diseases, this superior vitality has become more apparent. Still others point out that the tendency for women to outlive men may be due largely to differences in social roles, attitudes, and lifestyles. For instance, the higher rate of cigarette smoking among males is believed to account for between one-half to one-third of the difference in life expectancy between the

Table 2.5   LIFE EXPECTANCY AT BIRTH BY SEX FOR SELECTED COUNTRIES

Country	Life expectancy in years			Country	Life expectancy in years		
	Year(s)	Male	Female		Year(s)	Male	Female
Australia	1985	72.3	78.7	Italy	1981	71.0	77.7
Austria	1985	70.4	77.3	Japan	1985	74.8	80.4
Belgium	1982	70.0	76.7	Netherlands	1984–1985	72.9	79.6
Canada	1980–1982	71.8	78.9	Norway	1984–1985	72.8	79.5
Denmark	1984–1985	71.6	77.5	Sweden	1985	73.9	79.6
England/Wales	1983–1985	71.8	77.7	Switzerland	1984–1985	73.9	79.6
France	1983–1985	71.0	75.0	United States	1984	71.2	78.2
Greece	1980	72.1	76.3				

Source: United Nations: *Demographic Yearbook*, 1986. New York: United Nations, 1988.

sexes (Palmore & Jeffers, 1971; Retherford, 1975; Waldron, 1976). Whether the disparity in life expectancy between the sexes has a biological or behavioral basis or both, the gap between men and women is expected to remain much the same in the coming decades (for life expectancy self-test, see Box 2.2).

Life expectancy varies not only with sex but also with race. In fact, a sizable disparity in life expectancy occurs between blacks and whites: In 1987, life expectancy at birth for whites was 75.5 years, whereas for blacks it was 69.7 years. For females, the difference was slightly less: Life expectancy at birth was 78.8 for whites and 73.8 for blacks. Some of this discrepancy between the races is due to the lower socioeconomic status of blacks: Because their income as a whole falls below that of whites, the blacks' medical care and living conditions are poorer than the whites', and these factors contribute to the blacks' shorter life expectancy. However, after a certain age, the life expectancies of older blacks and older whites reverse. This is called the *crossover phenomenon*. For example, life expectancy after age 80 is higher for blacks than for whites. Although the existence of this phenomenon has been established for decades, the reasons for it are still unknown (Jackson, 1985). One possible explanation for the crossover is that higher mortality rates in the earlier years of the less robust result in a larger proportion of healthy older survivors (Markides & Machalek, 1984).

THE EXTENSION OF LIFE AND YOUTH

No discussion of life expectancy and longevity would be complete without looking at some of the legends, stories, and methods that reflect the basic desire for a long life and a vigorous old age. Gruman (1966) has classified these accounts into three themes: (1) Methuselah (antediluvian), (2) rejuvenation (fountain), and (3) Shangri-La (hyperborean).

The Methuselah Theme

The Methuselah theme is found in many mythologies and religions. It refers to the belief that people in the past lived much longer than they do today. For example, in Sumerian mythology Larek, the god-king, lived 28,800 years, and the god Dumuzi lived even longer. According to the Old Testament, Methuselah lived 969 years, Noah lived 950 years, and Adam lived 930 years.

The Rejuvenation Theme

From time immemorial people have yearned for long life and at the same time have wished to remain youthful. This theme underlies many legends and stories. It is dramatically illustrated in the Greek legend of Tithonus.

> Eos, the goddess of dawn, fell in love with Tithonus, a handsome Trojan youth. She went to Zeus and asked that Tithonus be given immortality, and Zeus granted her request. But Eos neglected to ask Zeus to allow Tithonus to retain his youthfulness. All went well between the happy pair until Tithonus began to age. In time he became so old and feeble

Box 2.2   # How to Calculate Your Life Expectancy

While there is no sure way to calculate your life expectancy even with computer systems, there are certain guidelines, such as this test, that can give you rough estimates. If you are age 20 to 65 and reasonably healthy, this test provides a life insurance company's statistical view of your life expectancy.

Start with the number 72.

Personal Data:

If you are male, subtract three.

If female, add four.

If you live in an urban area with a population over two million, subtract two.

If you live in a town under 10,000 or on a farm, add two.

If a grandparent lived to 85, add two.

If all four grandparents lived to 80, add six.

If either parent died of a stroke or heart attack before the age of 50, subtract four.

If any parent, brother, or sister under 50 has (or had) cancer or a heart condition, or has had diabetes since childhood, subtract three.

Do you earn over $50,000 a year? Subtract two.

If you finished college, add one. If you have a graduate or professional degree, add two more.

If you are 65 or over and still working, add three.

If you live with a spouse or friend, add five. If not, subtract one for every 10 years alone since age 25.

Health style facts:

If you work behind a desk, subtract three.

If your work requires regular, heavy physical labor, add three.

If you exercise strenuously (tennis, running, swimming, etc.) five times a week for at least a half-hour, add four. Two or three times a week, add two.

Do you sleep more than 10 hours each night? Subtract four.

Are you intense, aggressive, easily angered? Subtract three.

Are you easygoing and relaxed? Add three.

Are you happy? Add one. Unhappy? Subtract two.

Have you had a speeding ticket in the last year? Subtract one.

Do you smoke more than two packs a day? Subtract eight. One to two packs? Subtract six. One-half to one? Subtract three.

Are you overweight by 50 pounds or more? Subtract eight. By 30 to 50 pounds: Subtract four. By 10 to 30 pounds? Subtract two.

If you are a man over 40 and have annual checkups, add two.

If you are a woman and see a gynecologist once a year, add two.

Age adjustment:
If you are between 30 and 40, add two.

If you are between 40 and 50, add three.

If you are between 50 and 70, add four.

If you are over 70, add five.

Add up your score to get your life expectancy at this time. Now compare it to the national average for various ages:

CHECKING YOUR PERSONAL AND CULTURAL HEALTH STATUS

AGE NOW	MALE	FEMALE
0–10	69.8	77.2
11–19	70.3	77.5
20–29	71.2	77.8
30–39	71.3	77.9
40–49	73.5	79.4
50–59	76.1	79.0
60–69	80.2	83.6
70–79	85.9	87.7
80–90	90.0	91.1

If you would like your life expectancy to come out at a later age, look back over the questions relating to health practices and find those in which you subtracted years. Change those to positive health practices and you can add many years to your life expectancy.

Source: Robert F. Allen with Shirley Linde, *Lifegain.* Morristown, NJ: Human Resources Institute, 1981, pp. 19–21.

that he could not move or raise his limbs. Denied death, he was doomed to suffer the infirmities of old age forever.

As this legend illustrates, a long life is not enough—it is the quality of the added years that is important. Throughout history there have been literally hundreds of techniques and substances proposed for bringing about rejuvenation. Some of the earliest attempts were based on the practice of *gerocomy*, the belief that an old man

Box 2.3 **Some Cross-Cultural Prescriptions for a Longer Life**

1. Cultivate body lice. The aged Yukaghirs of Siberia believe that by keeping a few lice on their bodies it prolongs their lives.

2. Tell the truth. The Berbers of Africa believe that persons who are always truthful live longer.

3. Be kind. The Hopi Indians assert that "whosoever is not mean will live long."

4. Wash your face in urine. The Kwakiutl of the Pacific Northwest believe that this practice along with dipping your body in salt water promotes longevity.

5. Get a fetish. The Arunta of Australia make long-life potions from particles scraped off their fetish objects.

6. Be brave. "He who encounters head winds will live a long life," according to the Labrador Eskimos.

7. Pull out all gray hairs. The Xosa of Africa recommend the removal of all gray hairs to delay old age.

8. Avoid your mother-in-law. The Dieri, an Australian aborigine tribe, believe that one can prevent gray hairs by simply staying away from one's mother-in-law.

Source: Adapted from Leo Simmons. *The Role of the Aged in Primitive Society.* New Haven, CT: Yale University Press, 1945, pp. 220–224.

may absorb youth from young women. This custom was widely practiced in many Near Eastern and Far Eastern countries. For example, in the Old Testament, King David's servants secured a young maiden to sleep in his bed to revitalize the aging king with the heat from her body.

The idea of a fountain whose waters bring about rejuvenation can be traced back to the Hindu legend of Cyavana. This legend predates Ponce de Leon's well-known search by more than 2000 years. According to the legend, Cyavana, the aged priest of a Hindu king, gives religious secrets to two demi-gods in exchange for rejuvenation in the Pool of Youth.

A common source of rejuvenation potions and treatments over the centuries has been the sex organs of animals. This use was probably due to the linking of sexual vigor to the prolongation of youth. Many early physicians, including Hippocrates, the father of medicine, administered dried animal organs to their patients, or even advised that they eat the testicles of tigers. Around 1890, the idea of sex organ therapy reappeared. Charles E. Brown-Séquard, a noted French professor of physiology, advocated injections of an extract prepared from animal testicles. Following in Dr. Brown-Séquard's footsteps, Serge Voronoff, a Russian-born French surgeon, achieved fame in the 1920s by grafting pieces of testicles from chimpanzees into aging male patients.

In recent years, two of the more popular techniques used to try to retard the aging process are cell therapy and the drug called Gerovital-H3. Cell therapy, developed in Switzerland by Dr. Paul Niehans, consists of a series of injections. The solution is derived from lamb fetuses taken from specially bred black sheep; certain organs are removed from the fetuses and ground up, and then, the material is suspended in an injectable solution. The theory is that the cells from certain organs of the unborn lamb will revitalize the corresponding organs of the person receiving the injections. The second technique is the drug Gerovital-H3, essentially a form of procaine, which is widely used in dentistry as a local anesthetic. According to Ana Aslan, a Romanian researcher who developed the drug, Gerovital-H3 is an effective treatment for the aging process as well as for a number of degenerative diseases. Although Aslan's claims are highly questionable, Gerovital-H3 may have some use as an antidepressant (Busse & Blazer, 1980).

The Shangri-La Theme

In his famous novel *Lost Horizon*, James Hilton describes a mythical utopia called Shangri-La in which life is extended indefinitely. In this utopia people are "granted the best of both worlds, a long and pleasant youth . . . and an equally long and pleasant old age." Many people today believe that at least three places are comparable to Shangri-La: the village of Vilcabamba in Ecuador, the principality of Hunza in Pakistan, and the Caucasus region of the Soviet Union (especially Abkhasia). Reports indicate that in each of these three areas exist large proportions of centenarians who are amazingly fit and lead vigorous, productive lives. In addition, many of the centenarians claim to be 120, 140, or even older. Before his death in 1973, Shirali Mislimov, an Azerbaijani farmer in the USSR, claimed to be the world's oldest living person at the age of 168. There are no birth records to authenticate the claims of longevity made in these three places. Birth as well as death records were not legally required even in highly industrialized countries until the early part of this century. As Hayflick (1974) points out, "Surely claims of super-longevity should be taken with as much skepticism as any claim unsupported by proof."

After studying longevity in many areas of the USSR, Zhores Medvedev, the distinguished Russian gerontologist, now living in London, concludes that the exceptional longevity claimed by the aged in many areas of the Soviet Union does not exist. Medvedev (1974) suggests several reasons for these claims. First, old people in these areas enjoy high social status; the older a person gets, the more honor, respect, and authority he or she receives from both family and community. Status alone would be motive enough to exaggerate one's age, but another incentive for exaggerated age is the national and international publicity given these centenarians. Pictures and stories about them frequently appear in magazines and newspapers; they are regarded as celebrities and in some cases as national heroes. And for purposes of political propaganda, the government considers these long-lived people a special achievement of the Soviet Union.

Medvedev offers still another explanation for the claim of longevity in the USSR. During World War I and also the Russian Revolution, thousands of men falsified their ages, often using their fathers' documents, to avoid conscription or to mask their desertion from the army. Afterward, many continued the pretense because of the benefits mentioned in the preceding paragraph. An example is a man from Yahutia who was found to be 130 years old in the 1959 census. His picture and an article about him were published in the government newspaper *Isvestia*. Later, a letter arrived from a group of Ukrainian villagers; they recognized him as a fellow villager who had deserted from the army during World War I. It was discovered that this man was only 78 years old and that he had falsified his age in order to avoid further military service.

AMERICA'S CENTENARIANS

For a time the claim of Charlie Smith as being the oldest person in the United States appeared to be authentic. He maintained that he had been born in Liberia in 1842 and after coming to this country was purchased by a Texas cattleman in the New Orleans slave market. In 1955, when Smith was supposedly 113, his age was presumed to have been substantiated when his original bill of sale was located in New Orleans by *Life* magazine. However, recently a researcher associated with *The Guin-*

Mrs. Ellen Miller, an active centenarian, lived 111 years. On her 105th birthday she rode an elephant at the local zoo. She attributed her longevity to working hard all her life, eating the right food, going to bed early, and "not ramblin' around anywhere." (Knoxville News-Sentinel)

Box 2.4　**America's Centenarians**

During the past century, average life expectancy at birth in the United States has increased 30 years. This represents a greater gain than during all of previous human history. Reflecting this increase in average life expectancy, as well as greater numbers of immigrants and births in the late 1800s, the nation is experiencing a steady growth in the number of people aged 100 or more years. In 1980, the number of centenarians was approximately 15,000. By 1985, the number of centenarians had grown to about 25,000. They are projected to number over 100,000 by the year 2000.

Since 1950, the population 65 and over has more than doubled, the number of people 85 and over has increased almost five times, and the number of centenarians has grown more then ten times. While these growth rates are impressive, centenarians are still a very small percentage of the population. In 1986, centenarians constituted only about 1 in 10,000 persons in the total population, and 9 out of every 10,000 elderly (65 and over).

In the past, people rarely reached aged 100, although the chances of living to that age have increased. For those born in 1879, the odds against living 100 years were 400 to 1; the chances for those born in 1874 of reaching age 105 were 2,904 to 1; and for those born in 1869, only one person in 27,823 lived to age 110. Compare these with the odds of people born in 1980 of reaching these ages (based on the mortality rates of the 1979–1981 period): 87 to 1 for age 100, 559 to 1 for age 105, and 4,762 to 1 for age 110.

Sources: U.S. Bureau of the Census, *Current Population Reports,* Series P–23, No. 153. *America's Centenarians,* (data from the 1980 Census). Washington, D.C.: U.S. Government Printing Office, 1987.

---

ness Book of World Records found a Florida marriage license which showed that Smith had added 33 years to his age. He died in 1979 not at the age of 137 but at the age of 104.

The 1980 U.S. Census reported 32,000 Americans as being 100 years of age or over. However, the number was reduced to 15,000 when later analyses revealed processing errors and misstatements by the respondents. Very old people tend to inflate their ages, the opposite of what they do—tend to reduce their ages—during the middle years. The following anecdote illustrates this tendency:

> Take the history of one Bessie Singletree. . . . On her twenty-seventh birthday Miss Singletree became twenty-four years of age and was married. At thirty-five she was thirty. At forty she was thirty-nine until she was close to fifty. At fifty Bessie was forty; at sixty, fifty-five. At sixty-five she was sixty-eight and on her seventieth birthday everyone said Grandmother Singletree was pretty chipper for an octogenarian. At seventy-five she had her picture in the paper as the oldest woman in the country, aged ninety-three. Ten years later she passed away at the ripe old age of one hundred and nine. (Seigel & Passel, 1976)

Until a country's vital registration system or population register has been in existence for at least a century, the exact number of those over the age of 100 cannot be determined. This condition will occur in the United States in about the mid–twenty-first century. At that time, census reports of centenarians can be checked against birth certificates (Seigel & Passel, 1976).

All scientific investigations to date fail to confirm the existence of any substance or technique for rejuvenation or extending the life span. So far there are no human populations with validated super-longevity. Shangri-La continues to be found only in fiction. If and when the extension of the human life span does take place, it probably will not do so until the far distant future. Therefore, our goal for the present should be to employ strategies for postponing the aging process as well as improving the quality of life for the elderly.

SUMMARY

1. Different societies have different ways of determining when a person is old. Our society uses age 65 as the marker for the beginning of old age.
2. America is growing older. Three of the measures that reflect this trend are: the increase in the proportion of the elderly, an increase in the proportion of the old in relation to the young, and a rise in the median age.
3. The state with the largest proportion of older persons is Florida, followed by Pennsylvania and Iowa. California, New York, and Florida have the largest numbers of older persons.
4. Although the human life span has remained unchanged, life expectancy in the United States has increased by 27 years during this century. The maximum life potential for human beings is about 115 years. Life expectancy varies according to sex and race. Expectation of life for females exceeds that of males by about 7 years. Blacks have a shorter life expectancy than whites up to the age of 80; after that point, blacks tend to outlive whites.
5. Early literature on aging can be classified according to three major types of themes: the Methuselah, the belief that in ancient times people lived longer; the rejuvenation, ways to prolong life and youth; and the Shangri-La, the notion that people in some faraway places are living long lives.
6. Three of the areas in the world that claim to have large concentrations of centenarians are the Caucasus region of the USSR, Hunza in Pakistan, and Vilcabamba in Ecuador. There is no scientific proof to validate the ages of these people. The exact number of centenarians in the United States is not known. In the 1980 U.S. Census the number was 15,000.

KEY TERMS

young-old	Sunbelt
old-old	life span
oldest-old	maximum life potential
demography	life expectancy
population pyramid	crossover phenomenon
median age	gerocomy

FOR FURTHER STUDY

Fries, James F., & Crapo, Lawrence M. (1981). *Vitality and aging: Implications of the rectangular curve.* San Francisco: Freeman.

Deals with the changing patterns of human aging and the implications for the future.

Jones, Landon (1981). *Great expectations: America and the baby-boom generation.* New York: Ballantine.

Discusses the past, present, and future effects of the baby-boom generation on American society.

Kammeyer, Kenneth, & Ginn, Dorothy (1986). *An introduction to population.* Chicago: Dorsey.

Presents a good overview of the field of demography.

Rosenfeld, Albert (1985). *Prolongevity II.* New York: Knopf.

A highly readable book that explores the more recent scientific developments on aging and the prospects of prolonging life.

Walford, Roy L. (1983). *Maximum life span.* New York: Norton.

Deals with the science of biological gerontology from the historical, theoretical, practical, and social perspectives.

Reading

The Age of Aging
Robert N. Butler

In this reading, Butler discusses the achievement of increased life expectancy and how many view this as a "collision course" between resources and the needs of an aging society. He points out that instead of perceiving older persons as a burden, we need to encourage and allow them to be productive members of society.

This is the century of old age or, as it has been called, the Age of Aging. It is the first century in which a human being can be expected (at least in those countries where

Robert N. Butler, "Health, Productivity, and Aging: An Overview." In Robert N. Butler and Herbert P. Gleason (Eds.), *Productive Aging: Enhancing Vitality in Later Life.* New York: Springer, 1985, pp. 1–13.

the potential has been realized) more often than otherwise to live out what we presently think of as the life course. It is the first period in history when any child can expect to attain old age. There is an unprecedented increase in the absolute number and relative proportion of older persons. The age structure of society is changing, and this is true not just in the First and Second Worlds, but in the Third World as well. Population aging is a worldwide phenomenon. . . .

One should applaud and celebrate these changes, yet we see and hear much concern. First, there is the concern for dependency—specifically, economic dependency—and the high costs of health care and income maintenance. There is a special subclass of fears of dependency, related to particular forms of debility. One might call it the Struldbrug Effect. The Struldbrugs, whom Gulliver discovered on one of his travels, live forever, but unfortunately also become increasingly decrepit. Especially frightening is senility. Until the various forms of senility, and most particularly senile dementia of the Alzheimer type, have been conquered, the specter of senility is likely to dominate and shape perceptions, attitudes, and fears with regard to old age.

Second, there is a failure to understand the underlying mechanisms of aging, to recognize the distinctions between natural life span and life expectancy. Life span, the genetically determined inherent life span of a species, is not clearly distinguished from the survivorship of the species. Most of us tend to forget yesterday's conquests. In the United States, a polio epidemic was last experienced 22 years ago, yet very few of us are conscious of this reality. Third, and perhaps most important, is a psychological problem that I regard as nearly universal—the difficulty in maintaining a connection between our present self and our future self. Marcel Proust wrote, "Old age perhaps of all the realities is the one we preserve longest in our life as a truly abstract conception." We continue to associate morbidity and mortality with age; therefore, we assume that the increase in life expectancy will increase disproportionately the costs of health care and income maintenance. The last illness has always been the most expensive. It is not that longevity has extended the period of incapacity; rather, it is our inability to adjust our expectations and environments so as to encourage and allow elderly people to exercise their capacities.

There are no data in the United States at least to support the widely held notion, or misperception, that there are growing conflicts between young and old. The data of the Louis Harris polling organization do not show a war between the generations, a phrase used in the American media, including the big news magazines. . . . National magazines such as *Forbes* and *Newsweek* frequently have carried jeremiads regarding the cost and burdens of an aging population. A typical example was the January 24, 1983, issue of *Newsweek* that quite inaccurately showed on its cover one young person holding up nine people older than himself. The title was "The Social Security Crisis: Who Will Pay? The Growing Burden on the Young." It also clearly indicates the failure to perceive the connection between our future selves and our present selves, that the social security burden upon the young is a reflection of the ultimate opportunity for the young person when he gets old to receive appropriate and necessary support. . . .

I believe that significant numbers of people over 60 and 65 can in fact continue to work and contribute to their communities. There are data from a few longitudinal studies in the United States—the National Institutes of Health, the National Institute on Aging, and Duke University—demonstrating that cognitive abilities in older persons, speaking very broadly, decline less and later than had originally been reported in earlier studies. The presence of decrements requires a diagnostic evaluation for possible pathological explanation. There are also data regarding educability and dependability of older workers. Despite stereotypes in the United States, at any one moment only five percent of those 65 and over are in any kind of an institution. There are comparable figures from European and other Western nations. Of all those who survive past 65 in the United States, only about 20 to 25 percent will have any kind of an institutional experience, however brief. Let's put it a little more positively. At any one moment, 95 percent of older persons reside in the community and 80 percent of those who survived past 65 will never have any kind of an institutional experience. There are myriad personal examples of extraordinarily able and contributing older persons.

To mobilize the skills and talents of older persons will benefit both older persons and society. At present, no government or private institution within society has addressed effectively and comprehensively the multiple challenges posed by societal aging. There has been progress, of course, of varying degrees in different countries, including the development of social security programs, social services, research, and education. . . .

It seems there are certain nonsolutions. We certainly don't want to return to the era of high mortality and/or high birth rates. We certainly don't want to blame the victim. We do want to enhance the productive potential of older persons and reduce their dependency.

Culture and Adult Socialization

Chapter 3

Age Norms and Age Statuses

*A*mong the Todas of southern India, thumbing one's nose at another person is a sign of respect. Certain Eskimo tribes offer their wives for the night to a visitor to show hospitality, and in some villages in New Guinea, old persons sleep with pigs for warmth. Why do these people adhere to such practices and customs? The answer is simple: That is the way they were taught. It is their way of life, or more specifically, their culture. *Culture,* in the sociological sense, refers to the social heritage of a society that is transmitted to each generation; it is learned behavior that is shared with others. Culture includes all the beliefs, customs, knowledge, and products of a society. Culture guides the life's activities of a people and may be likened to a blueprint or map for everyday living.

THE MEANING OF CULTURE

Sociologists give *culture* a much broader meaning than is used in everyday speech. Popularly, the term is used to denote good taste and refinement. We think of a cultured person as one who drinks wine with meals, is well read, and enjoys opera and the ballet, rather than one who drinks beer, reads comic books, and shoots craps. To sociologists, however, all human beings and all societies have culture. All people are considered "cultured" in the sense that they are participants in the culture of the society in which they live.

It has been said that the last thing a person who lived under water all of his or her life would discover would be water. We spend our lives so immersed in the culture of the society in which we live that we are often completely unaware of its influence on us. We follow the habits, beliefs, and customs of our culture automatically and unthinkingly. According to Kluckhohn (1944), "Culture regulates our lives at every turn. From the moment we are born until we die there is, whether we are conscious of it or not, constant pressure upon us to follow certain types of behavior." The fact that we prefer steak to fresh worms or caterpillars, that we eat sitting down and not squatting or standing up, or that we believe that a person should have only one spouse at the same time are all patterns of our culture.

To understand the concept of culture more fully, look at the anthropological account of some of the unusual customs and practices that occur in a well-known contemporary society (see Box 3.1). With so many interesting activities to occupy their time, it is hard to understand why old people in this society sometimes complain of being bored and want to resume their official duties.

Box 3.1   # Life in the ASU

When people in this society* reach a certain age, a large feast is prepared in their honor, and they are presented with an apparatus made from a precious metal in which to mark the passage of time. They are then relieved of all their official duties and are expected to remain in their quarters most of the day and to sit on a large piece of wood that is molded to the shape of their body. It is curved at the bottom in order to permit them to move back and forth with the slightest motion.

Sometimes they venture out to a large grassy area where there are long flat pieces of wood to sit on. Here they observe a peculiar type of rite that takes place between two people. Each moves little discs on a small surface covered with squares until all of the discs of one color are gone.

Other times they may attend a ceremony for people of their own age. They all sit together at large rectangular surfaces watching small pieces of paper. One person chants strange sounds while the others place small pellets on the papers from time to time. After a while someone will jump up and yell the name of the ceremony.

* Reverse the letters in ASU.

NORMS

Our culture defines for us what is proper and improper behavior, what is right and wrong, and what we are expected to do and not do. These standards or rules of behavior are called *norms*. Norms help us to predict the behavior of others and, in turn, allow others to know what to expect of us. In our society the expected pattern of behavior, or norm, on being introduced to someone is to extend the right hand. This seems natural to us, but it is not so natural to people in some other societies, who may misinterpret our behavior as being aggressive or even nonsensical. A woman from another culture, after having an American male shake her hand, remarked that she was glad he decided to shake her hand and not her head. The normative behavior for greeting varies from culture to culture. Among some Eskimos, you lick your hands and then draw them first over your own face and then over the face of the stranger whom you are greeting. The Burmese and Mongols greet one another by smelling the other's cheeks. Polynesians embrace and rub each other's back, and in some places people greet by placing one arm around the neck of the other person and tickling him or her under the chin.

Some norms, such as shaking hands, apply to all members of our society, whereas others apply only to certain groups. Such factors as sex and age may determine whether or not a specific norm applies to a group or category of people. For example, in our society norms about bathing attire are determined by sex. A female must cover both the upper and lower parts of the body, whereas a male is required to cover only the lower part. Similarly, males are expected to open doors for females, but females are not expected to do the same for males.

People also have expectations about what is considered proper behavior at different ages. These expectations are called *age norms*. We can understand a 5-year-old kicking and crying for an ice cream cone. But imagine a 21-year-old exhibiting the same type of behavior. We would not expect a college professor to skip into class, suck his or her thumb, and speak in monosyllables. By the same token, we would not expect a 4-year-old to come into a college classroom and deliver a lecture on "The Influence of Age on Chromatin Transcription in Murine Tissues Using a Heterologous and Homologous RNA Polymerase." The familiar phrase "Act your age" reflects our concern for age-appropriate behavior.

How often have you heard someone ask, "Are you still in school?" Once one is out of school, the question changes to "Haven't you found a job yet?" or "Isn't it time you got married?" Later in life the questions asked are "Don't you have any grandchildren yet?" and "Shouldn't you be retired by now?" These phrases are illustrations of age norms that govern the timing of our adult behavior and have been referred to as *social clocks*. These clocks operate to speed up as well as to slow down major life events. Also, people are aware of their own timing and describe themselves as being early, on time, or late regarding certain life events (Neugarten, Moore, & Lowe, 1965).

A high degree of consensus concerning age-appropriate behavior was found in a survey of middle-class, middle-aged people conducted in the late 1950s. Respondents were asked such questions as the best ages to marry, to finish school, to go to work, and to retire. They were also asked with what ages they associated such

All societies have cultural expectations that define the ways in which members of each sex should behave. Although many of our cultural expectations of such behavior are changing, most Americans would typically expect an older woman, and not an older man, to be weaving. (Nick Myers)

phrases as "a young man," "an old man," and "an old woman." Twenty years later, when the same study was repeated with a similar group, the previous consensus had disappeared (see Table 3.1). For instance, in the earlier study nearly 90 percent agreed that the best age for a woman to marry was between 19 and 24; in the later study, only about 40 percent felt this way. In the first study, 84 percent of the respondents believed that 20 to 22 was the best age for people to finish school and go to work; in the second study only 37 percent agreed. When asked if they agreed that the phrase "old woman" referred to a woman between the ages of

Table 3.1 AGE RANGES FOR THE TIMING OF AGE-RELATED TRANSITIONS, LATE 1950S VERSUS LATE 1970S

Age-related transitions and events	Age Range	Late 50s study: Percent who agree		Late 70s study: Percent who agree	
		Men	Women	Men	Women
Best age for a man to marry	20–25	80	90	42	42
Best age for a woman to marry	19–24	85	90	44	36
When most people should become grandparents	45–50	84	79	64	57
Best age for most people to finish school and go to work	20–22	86	82	36	38
When most men should be settled on a career	24–26	74	64	24	26
When most men hold their top jobs	45–50	71	58	38	31
When most people should be ready to retire	60–65	83	86	66	41
When a man has the most responsibilities	35–50	79	75	49	50
When a man accomplishes most	40–50	82	71	46	41
The prime of life for a man	35–50	86	80	59	66
When a woman has the most responsibilities	25–40	93	91	59	53
When a woman accomplishes most	30–45	94	92	57	48
A good-looking woman	20–35	92	82	33	24
A young man	18–22	84	83	29	22
A middle-aged man	40–50	86	75	41	47
An old man	65–75	75	57	52	37
A young woman	18–24	89	88	41	25
A middle-aged woman	40–50	87	87	49	50
An old woman	60–75	83	87	50	44

Source: Patricia M. Passuth, David R. Maines, and Bernice L. Neugarten, "Age Norms and Age Constraints Twenty Years Later." Paper presented at the annual meeting of the Midwest Sociological Society, Chicago, 1984.

60 and 75, in the first study 85 percent agreed, whereas in the second study agreement dropped to 47 percent. These findings illustrate that people today have different perceptions of the type of behavior that is appropriate at various ages. Age norms are changing, becoming more flexible and less constraining. We may be moving toward what Neugarten (1980) has described as an age-irrelevant society in which there is no particular age or age range for taking on certain social roles. She points out that it no longer surprises us to hear of a 50-year-old retiree or a 35-year-old grandmother. No one is shocked at a 70-year-old college student or the 60-year-old man who becomes a father for the first time.

Sociologists distinguish among norms by their degree of importance and by the type of sanctions applied when they are violated. Norms may be grouped into three types: folkways, mores, and laws.

Folkways

Most of the rules that govern the conventions and routines of everyday life and define what is socially correct consist of *folkways*. These range from using the proper fork to keeping your grass cut. Folkways are enforced informally, but effectively, by such means of social control as gossip, raised eyebrows, or ridicule. Because folkways are not considered important to the well-being of the group, only mild disapproval results when they are violated.

Many age norms fall into this category. Appropriate behavior for older people is often specified in the folkways. We expect older people not to be interested in sex or

We ordinarily do not expect to see an older woman playing ball. Age norms in our society specify that the elderly should give up strenuous activities. (Nick Myers)

(Drawing by Shanahan; © 1989 The New Yorker Magazine, Inc.)

in subjects having to do with sex. An older man who makes suggestive remarks or tells jokes about sex may be dubbed a "dirty old man." ("He shouldn't think about sex at his age.") We expect older people to wear conservative styles of clothing. ("She's too old to dress like that.") An elderly woman wearing a bikini on the beach would definitely raise eyebrows and be subjected to uncomplimentary remarks. We expect older people not to do strenuous work. ("He shouldn't be doing that type of work at his age.")

Folkways also define the proper etiquette toward the elderly. The following are expectations regarding behavior toward the elderly, some of which are gradually disappearing today. For example, a Boy Scout is expected to help an elderly woman across the street. A young person is supposed to offer a seat to an older person on a crowded bus or subway. A younger person is expected to allow an elderly person to go first through a doorway and is supposed to pick up an object dropped by an older person. In other situations, a younger individual is supposed to offer to carry a heavy parcel or suitcase for an elderly person.

Certain folkways govern housing, intergenerational obligations, and finances. The preferred residence pattern is for older persons to live in their own homes, but to be near their children and relatives. Older people expect their children and relatives to maintain frequent contact with them. Grandparents are expected to show an interest in their grandchildren; some grandparents even overconform to this expectation. People are expected to save money while they are young in order to support themselves when they stop working. Adults are supposed to give financial aid to their aged parents in need. By the same token, the aged parents are expected to help their children if circumstances permit.

Mores

In contrast to folkways, *mores* relate to the basic needs of a society and are considered extremely important for the welfare of the group. Violations of the mores, unlike those of the folkways, are considered very serious and carry with them strong negative sanctions. When they are violated, people react with disgust, shock, or horror. Mores define what is morally right or wrong.

When mores are expressed in the negative form of "must not" and "thou shalt not," they are called taboos. Many of the Ten Commandments fall into this category. What are some of the mores of our society? We must not murder, steal, or eat human flesh. Americans are expected to be sexually faithful to their spouses, be loyal to their country, and have only one spouse at a time.

Some age norms can be classified as mores. For example, an old woman dating a young man violates our mores. We believe that an elderly woman should not date and certainly should not marry a man who is much younger than she. An elderly couple who divorce after having been married for 40 or 50 years will be much more severely censured than a younger couple. Some older couples violate the mores when they live together without being married, and some adult children violate the mores when they abuse an elderly parent.

The mores of some cultures prescribe that old people should be killed outright or abandoned when they become feeble and infirm. To us, these are shocking practices that offend our sense of decency and morality. One reason the concept of euthanasia is a difficult one for us is that it involves the violation of a deeply ingrained norm.

The dividing line between folkways and mores is not always sharp. They can best be viewed as being on a continuum ranging from those norms that elicit mild disapproval to those that elicit strong disapproval (see Figure 3.1). Both folkways and mores regulate human behavior and are enforced by informal social controls.

Laws

Informal social controls alone are not sufficient to guarantee that a complex society functions in an orderly manner. A more formalized type of control is needed—namely, laws. *Laws* are rules enacted by those who exert political power and are enforced by the police and other officials who have been given the authority to do so. They maintain social order through force or the threat of force.

Some laws, such as those against bigamy and murder, are supported by the mores. The violation of these laws is considered both immoral and illegal. Laws firmly rooted in our mores are the most effective because most people want to conform to

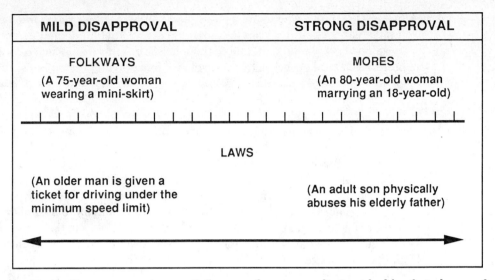

Figure 3.1. Normative continuum. Folkways and mores are distinguished by their degree of disapproval. Laws may carry mild or strong disapproval depending on the law violated.

them and exert informal pressure on others to do likewise. At times, laws may conflict with the folkways and mores; these laws are difficult, if not impossible, to enforce. A classic example was the Prohibition amendment to the U.S. Constitution, which did not express the beliefs of the majority of our population and was repealed after 15 years. Most traffic laws are not backed by folkways or mores and are widely violated. The 55-mile-an-hour speed limit is a case in point.

Just as there are folkways and mores associated with age, there are also laws related to certain ages in a society. At 18 an individual is considered eligible to vote, at 30 generally eligible for public office; and from ages 62 to 65 one may begin receiving Social Security benefits. In 1965 the Older Americans Act, outlining a national policy to improve the situation of older persons, was passed. Some objectives included in this statute are adequate income, housing, and employment for the elderly.

The Age Discrimination in Employment Act (ADEA), passed in 1967, barred employers from denying job opportunities or dismissing employees between the ages of 40 to 65 solely on the basis of age. In 1978 the law was amended to include persons up to age 70, and in 1986 it was amended once more to remove the upper limit of age 70 for nearly all workers. The ADEA now protects virtually all workers age 40 and older (see Chapter 13, "The Economy: Work and Retirement," for a discussion of this topic).

NORMS FOR OLDER PEOPLE

Rosow (1974) argues that not only are there fewer significant norms for older people to follow, but they tend to be more ambiguous and less clear-cut than norms for younger persons. In other words, our culture does not provide the elderly with meaningful norms as it does at all the previous stages of the life course. The activities that older people should pursue, how they should use their time, or in what way they should pattern their lives are for the most part without guidelines and structure. For instance, older persons are told to remain active, but no guidance is given about the preferred nature of such activity. Instead of meaningful prescriptions, the elderly are given meaningless platitudes: "Take care of yourself," "Stay out of drafts," "Don't overdo." With fewer and less specific norms to guide their behavior in old age, older people are left in an ambiguous position, uncertain of what to do or what is expected of them. Furthermore, this uncertainty can be a source of anxiety and alienation for some older people.

While Rosow emphasizes the negative aspects of the decrease in normative expectations with age, Bengtson (1976) argues that this decrease can have positive consequences, such as an increase in personal freedom. The very lack of definite, prescribed norms for older people to follow allows them more flexibility and freedom in their behavior and permits them a wide range of options in their lives. He indicates that the decrease in specific norms "represents a potential opportunity to pick and choose among alternative behaviors—a degree of freedom from societal restraints that is perhaps greater than at any other period of the life cycle . . . to those who choose (and have the capability) to exploit it."

THE DOUBLE STANDARD OF AGING

Since ancient times, people have believed that the onset of old age takes place earlier for women than for men. According to Hippocrates, old age began at about 55 to 60 years for men and at 45 to 55 years for women. Plato set the prime of life for a man at 30 and at 20 for a woman. Today in our society, people still believe that women age sooner than men. Table 3.1 shows that society defines an "old man" as one 65 to 75 years old, whereas old age for a woman is thought to begin 5 years earlier, between 60 and 75 years. What is being reflected here are sex norms associated with aging, or a *double standard of aging*—how aging takes different forms for men and women in our society.

Women can expect to live longer than men, and they also tend to have less-serious health problems than men. Yet, why does our society picture them as aging much more rapidly than their male counterparts? One reason is that women in our society are more dependent on their physical appearance for status and self-concept than men. Femininity is associated with sexual attractiveness, while masculinity is associated with power and position. Men derive their status and self-concept from money, occupation, and leadership—all of which are sexually enhancing and diminish more slowly than physical appearance. In contrast to women, how men look is not as important as what they do. Many men, even unattractive men, can stay sexually eligible well into old age. In fact, it is not unusual for a man to be more successful romantically at 45 or 50 than he was at 25 (Sontag, 1972).

Television reflects society's double standard of aging. Women age faster than men on prime-time television programs. Among characters 65 and over, 72 percent of the men will be cast as "old" in contrast to 90 percent of the women. The chances of women being given roles with romantic possibilities rapidly decrease with age. Aging women are portrayed as becoming increasingly sexless while aging men are portrayed

Growing old is particularly difficult for women in our society. Unlike men, much of their self-concept and status is derived from their physical appearance. (Nick Myers)

as becoming increasingly sexually attractive (Gerbner, Gross, Signorielli, & Morgan, 1980; Davis & Davis, 1985).

Our culture, then, defines women as growing old much sooner than men. This may explain in part why women are more evasive than men in telling their age. Remember all the "old maid" jokes you've heard? Now think for a minute about "old bachelor" jokes. The chances are that you have not heard one. Palmore, (1971), in his study of humor and aging, discusses jokes about old maids but reports that there are no "old bachelor" jokes. According to Palmore, "While the term 'old maid' generally has negative connotations, there is no corresponding negative term for men such as 'old bachelor.' " Obviously, being old and unmarried is acceptable for a man in our society, but not for a woman. Our norms prescribe that a woman should be married by a certain age; otherwise, she is to be pitied. The same norm does not hold true for a man.

Norms governing the age of marital partners also differ. A woman is supposed to marry a man her own age or older, and certainly no more than a few years her junior. A man, however, may marry a woman 25 or 30 years younger than he, and this act is not only acceptable but is sometimes even laudable. Romantic involvements between an older man and a younger woman have been reinforced by novels, plays, television, and movies.

> The mass media glamorize and legitimate the older man–younger woman relationship. Successful actors continue to play romantic leads well into their fifties and sometimes sixties. Frequently, they are cast opposite actresses at least half their age, and the story line rarely even acknowledges the difference. They are simply an average romantic couple. The question of whether the 20-year-old heroine is out of her mind to marry the graying 55-year-old hero is not even raised. (Bell, 1976).

As we mentioned earlier, an older woman's marrying a younger man is met with strong disapproval in our culture. Some may argue how illogical this kind of normative behavior is. After all, since women live on the average about seven to eight years longer than men, would it not be more rational for a woman to marry a younger man instead of an older one and thus avoid a long period of windowhood? But our culture defines what are approved and disapproved standards for our behavior, and we judge behavior not by its being logical or reasonable but by its conformity to the norms.

AGE STATUS SYSTEM

Status is like a calling card: It identifies who we are and defines our position. As we move from one group to another, we occupy a different status. In the classroom we have the status of student, in the dormitory the status of roommate, and at home the status of son or daughter, or wife or husband. Each individual then has many statuses,

---

Box 3.2   **The Dirty Old Man**

In our humor it is sometimes possible to see evidence of social norms. A current bumper sticker proclaims, "I'm not a dirty old man—I'm a sexy senior citizen." But here also is evidence of a cultural double standard for males compared to females. While the dirty old man may be humorous, the sensual old woman is not.

Source: Vern L. Bengtson, Ron C. Manuel, and Linda M. Burton, "Competence and Loss: Perspectives on the Sociology of Aging." In Richard H. Davis (Ed.) *Aging: Prospects and Issues.* Los Angeles: University of Southern California Press, 1981, p. 28.

Box 3.3 **The Negative Characterization of Older Women**

The terms used to characterize old women have a much longer history of negative connotation than those for old men. Words for old women have generally reflected their perceived lower status. There has also been a long tradition of associating old women with evil and with spiritual forces. This was made most visible by the labelling of many old women as witches. This tendency continues in the present use of language in the images of old women as the archetype for witches. Old men were seldom associated with evil and witchcraft in the same sense as old women.

Source: Herbert C. Covey, "Historical Terminology Used to Represent Old People." *The Gerontologist* (28), 1988, p. 297.

---

and with each status go certain rights and obligations. When people put these rights and obligations into effect, they are performing their roles. A *role* is the expected behavior of one who holds a certain status. Just as a person has many statuses, he or she also has many roles. Usually a person's occupation is considered the key or *master status*, and this generally determines his or her general social position in society.

Statuses may be classified into two types: ascribed and achieved. *Ascribed statuses* are those assigned to us by society; we don't have to earn them. *Achieved statuses* are those, as the name implies, achieved by our own efforts. Being a doctor, a wife or husband, or student is an achieved status. Sex is an ascribed status. This status is assigned at birth without regard to individual ability. Basic to all societies is the ascription of statuses with regard to sex. All groups specify different attitudes, behavior, and activities for men and women. We discussed earlier how these differences are reflected in the norms of our society.

Age Status

Another important way of establishing status is by the use of age. Like sex, our age is ascribed. All societies have at least three or four age categories (infant and/or child, adult, and old), and some have delineated many more. Poets and writers have long described the succession of age statuses that individuals pass through in the course of their lives. Ancient writers divided the life course into five to ten stages. For example, Solon, an Athenian poet of the seventh century B.C., suggested ten-stages, each stage lasting seven years. The idea of seven ages of man, originally proposed by Hippocrates, was popularized by Shakespeare in *As You Like It*. Modern scholars, such as Erik Erikson, view the life course in terms of eight categories, and Rosow has suggested a series of nine age statuses that most people may normally expect to occupy.

(Drawing by Chas. Addams; © 1983 The New Yorker Magazine, Inc.)

The term *age status* refers to the differential rights and obligations awarded to individuals on the basis of age. All members of society move from one age category to the next as they progress through the *life course*. Each new category represents a new status and requires the learning of new roles and culturally defined patterns of behavior. All societies are faced with the tasks of preparing members for their new statuses and making the transition as smooth as possible. To accomplish this, they employ what are called *rites-of-passage* ceremonies. These ceremonies mark the transition from one status to the next and publicly announce the new status.

Rites of Passage

Van Gennep (1960) in his classic work *Rites of Passage* distinguished three phases of such a ceremony: separation or removal from a former status, transition, and incorporation of the person into a new status. He noted that the person who moves to a new status may often find the change disturbing and that rites of passage ease the adjustment and help to incorporate the individual into a new status in the group. Van Gennep said:

> The life of an individual in any society is a series of passages from one age to another and from one occupation to another. . . . [These passages all have] similar ends and beginnings: birth, social puberty, marriage, fatherhood, advancement to a higher class, occupational specialization, and death. For every one of these events there are ceremonies whose essential purpose is to enable the individual to pass from one defined position to another which is equally well defined.

According to Linton (1942), one of the most universally observed status changes is the transition to adulthood, which in most societies occurs with the marriage ceremony. In some societies, although the husband is given adult status at marriage, the wife does not receive it until the birth of her first child. Another ceremonial observance involves puberty rites, which mark the transition of the child to the adolescent or adult category, depending on the society. In primitive societies, this observance is usually marked by hazing, physical ordeals, and instruction in the history, skills, and crafts of the tribe. The closest ceremonies to puberty rites in our society are confirmations, bar mitzvahs, and debuts.

Transition to Old Age

The change from adult status to aged status receives little social recognition in most societies. One reason for this lack is because the onset of old age is so gradual and almost imperceptible that we cannot pinpoint when it occurs. In addition, the transition from adult to old-age status is often accompanied by feelings of regret and reluctance, and the individuals concerned are not eager for public acknowledgment of the change.

A few societies have what may be called retirement ceremonies. In these instances a man gives his successor the powers that he formerly possessed, or he may relinquish some prerogatives of his adult male status. Formerly among the Comanche Indians when a man became too old to actively participate in war, he was expected to give up his "medicines," at which time he was then eligible for the position of peace chief. In modern Japan there is a special retirement celebration in which families honor individuals who have reached 61 years of age.

> On the sixty-first birthday the elder dons a bright kimono, such as those worn by children, to symbolize that he or she is no longer bound by the somber duties of middleage. Traditionally, all the children and close relatives gather to celebrate this transition. On this day also, or whenever the woman formally retires as mistress of the house, the woman traditionally presents her daughter-in-law with the family rice ladle as the baton of domestic authority. The elder couple then literally retire to a separate

room; if possible, a separate retirement cottage may be built for them, and they are referred to as "those living in retirement" (*inkyo*). (Palmore, 1975)

The nearest equivalent in our society to a retirement rite is a dinner given by a company or organization for an employee or group of employees who have reached the age of 65 or thereabouts and are retiring. After the meal, some speeches, and a few jokes, the retirees are presented with a gift (often the traditional gold watch) in recognition of their years of service.

Compared with other age passages, the transition to old age is the most difficult to make. Whereas younger members of a society look forward to moving on to the next age status, most people are not eager to achieve the status of an elderly person. In fact, in nearly all societies the individual who enjoys the prospect of getting old is atypical (Linton, 1936). In order to induce people to assume this status, some societies accord the aged much power and prestige. In certain societies, as women age, their freedom and authority increase; they may then be exempt from the social and ceremonial restrictions that were once imposed on them. In our society the entry into old-age status is associated with retirement and the relinquishing of many adult responsibilities. Many individuals, depending on their personalities are glad to be relieved of their obligations, whereas others are reluctant to let go of them and may miss the power they wielded.

SUMMARY

1. The term *culture* has a specific meaning in sociology that differs from the popular meaning of the word. Culture is the social heritage of a society that is transmitted to each generation. It is learned behavior that is shared with others. Often we are completely unaware of the extent to which our lives and behavior are influenced by our culture.

2. Norms are standards or rules of behavior. Norms help us to predict the behavior of others, as well as to permit others to know what to expect of us. Not all norms apply to all members of a society. Such factors as sex and age may determine the application of some norms.

3. Norms may be divided into three broad types: folkways, mores, and laws. Folkways are not considered too important, but mores are considered essential to the group's welfare. Both folkways and mores are informally enforced, whereas laws are backed by the coercive power of the government.

4. Age norms are expectations about what is considered proper behavior at different ages. They also govern the timing of adult behavior. In the last few decades, age norms have become flexible and less constraining. As persons age, there are fewer and less specific norms to guide their behavior. Our society has what is called a "double standard of aging" in that aging takes different forms for the sexes. These double standards are reflected in the fact that our society views women as losing their sexual attractiveness sooner and aging earlier than men.

5. Status identifies who we are and defines our position, whereas a role is the behavior expected of a person who holds a certain status. Statuses may be

classified into two kinds: achieved and ascribed. Age and sex are two types of ascribed statuses.

6. All societies are divided into different age-status levels. An individual moves from one level to the next as he or she progresses from infancy to old age. Ceremonies marking these transitions are called rites of passage. In our society the entry into the status of old age receives the least ritual observance and is the most difficult transition to make.

KEY TERMS

culture	*status*
norms	*role*
age norms	*master status*
social clocks	*ascribed statuses*
folkways	*achieved statuses*
mores	*age status*
laws	*life course*
double standard of aging	*rites of passage*

FOR FURTHER STUDY

Lesnoff-Caravaglia, Gari (Ed.) (1984). *The world of the older woman.* New York: Human Sciences Press.

A collection of articles dealing with issues and problems that confront older women.

Neugarten, Bernice L. (1968). *Middle age and aging.* Chicago: University of Chicago Press.

Part I contains a collection of papers dealing with age status and age norms in our society.

Silverman, Philip (Ed.). (1987). *The elderly as modern pioneers.* Bloomington, IN: University of Indiana Press.

Using the conceptual scheme of the life course perspective, this volume of original essays integrates material from biology, psychology, sociology, and anthropology.

Sumner, William Grant (1906). *Folkways.* Boston: Ginn.

A classic discussion of folkways and mores.

Reading

The Changing Meanings of Age

Bernice L. Neugarten and Dail A. Neugarten

For many individuals, the social clock is no longer as important or compelling as it once was. In today's society, age norms are becoming more flexible, and the distinction between life periods are becoming more blurred.

In our society, as in others, age is a major dimension of social organization. Our school system, to name one example, is carefully arranged around the students' ages, and the behavior of all students is clearly differentiated from the behavior of adult teachers. Similarly, to a greater or lesser extent, families, corporations, even whole communities are organized by age.

Age also plays an important part in how people relate to one another across the whole range of everyday experience. When a young man sits down in an airplane and glances at the person in the next seat, the first thing to cross his mind is likely to be "That's an old man" or "That's a young man like me," and he automatically adjusts his behavior accordingly—his language, manners and conversation.

Age is also a major touchstone by which individuals organize and interpret their own lives. Both children and adults continually ask of themselves, "How well am I doing for my age?" . . .

In all societies, lifetime is divided into socially relevant periods, age distinctions become systematized and rights and responsibilities are distributed according to social age. Even the simplest societies define at least three periods: childhood, adulthood and old age. In more complex societies, a greater number of life periods are differentiated, and transition points are differently timed in different areas of life. . . . The distinctions between life periods are blurring in today's society. . . .

When, then, does old age now begin? The usual view has been that it starts at 65, when most people retire. But in the United States today the majority begin to take their Social Security retirement benefits at 62 or 63; and at ages 55 to 64

Bernice L. Neugarten and Dail A. Neugarten, "The Changing Meanings of Age." *Psychology Today*, May 1987.

fewer than three of every four men are in the labor force. At the same time, with continued good health, some people are staying at work, full-time or part-time, into their 80s. So age 65 and retirement are no longer clear dividers between middle age and old age. . . .

It is not only in the second half of life that the blurring of life periods can be seen. Adults of all ages are experiencing changes in the traditional rhythm and timing of events of the life cycle. More men and women marry, divorce, remarry and divorce again up through their 70s. More stay single. More women have their first child before they are 15, and more do so after 35. The result is that people are becoming grandparents for the first time at ages ranging from 35 to 75. . . .

The blurring of traditional life periods does not mean that age norms are disappearing altogether. We still have our regulations about the ages at which children enter and exit from school, when people can marry without the consent of parents, when they are eligible for Social Security benefits. And less formal norms are still operating. Someone who moves to the Sunbelt to lead a life of leisure is socially approved if he is 70, but not if he is 30. An unmarried mother meets with greater disapproval if she is 15 than if she is 35. A couple in their 40s who decide to have another child are criticized for embarrassing their adolescent children. At the door of a discotheque a young person who cannot give proof of being "old enough" may be refused admission, while inside a gray-haired man who dances like those he calls youngsters meets the raised eyebrows and mocking remarks of the other dancers. As in these examples, expectations regarding age-appropriate behavior still form an elaborate and pervasive system of norms, expectations that are woven into the cultural fabric.

Both legal and cultural age norms are mirrored in the ways people behave and the ways they think about their lives. Today, as in the past, most people by the time they are adolescents develop a set of anticipations of the normal, expectable life cycle: expectations of what the major life events and turning points will be and when they should occur. People internalize a social clock that tells them if they are on time or not. . . .

The life events that occur on time do not usually precipitate life crises, for they have been anticipated and rehearsed. The so-called "empty nest," for instance, is not itself stressful for most middle-aged parents. Instead, it is when children do not leave home at the appropriate time that stress occurs in both the parents and the child. For most older men, if it does not occur earlier than planned, retirement is taken in stride as a normal, expectable event. Widowhood is less often a crisis if it occurs at 65 rather than 40.

It is the events that upset the expected sequence and rhythm of the life cycle that cause problems—as when the death of a parent comes during one's adolescence rather than in middle age; when marriage is delayed too long; when the birth of a child comes too early; when the empty nest, grandparenthood, retirement, major illness or widowhood occurs "out of sync." Traditional timetables still operate.

For the many reasons suggested earlier, the traditional time schedules do not in today's society produce the regularities anticipated by adolescents or young adults. For many men and women, to be out of sync may have lost some of its importance, but for others, the social clocks have not stopped ticking. The incongruities between the traditional norms and the fluid life cycle represent new freedoms for many people; for other people, new uncertainties and strains. . . .

Shall we say that individuals are paying less or more attention to age as a prod or brake upon their behavior? That age consciousness is decreasing or increasing? Whether or not historical change is occurring, it is fair to say that one's own age remains crucial to every individual, all the way from early childhood through advanced old age. A person uses age as a guide in accommodating to others, in giving meaning to the life course, and in contemplating the time that is past and the time that remains.

Cultural Values

*C*an you imagine running in a race in which you are not supposed to run faster than the other participants or you will be disqualified? Such a race makes no sense to us. Yet, among the Zuni Indians of the Southwest, who value cooperation, not competition, a person who continually wins races is not only unpopular, but also is not allowed to race because it spoils the fun for everyone else. By contrast, competition is a dominant value in American society. It is not just reflected in sports; we also compete for many other things including jobs, grades, political office, parental affection, and sexual attention.

DOMINANT AMERICAN VALUE THEMES

Every society has certain dominant or core values that give it a distinctive character and differentiate it from other societies. Values justify and give meaning to behavior. *Values* are socially learned and shared conceptions of what is desirable, good, or right; they serve as criteria for judging ideas, behavior, events, people, and things. For example, most Americans believe that honesty is good, that prejudice is wrong, that Abraham Lincoln was a great man, and that communism is bad. Americans believe in freedom, fair play, equality, democracy, and patriotism. These values are culturally approved sentiments that people support and about which they feel strongly.

One approach to studying aging and the behavior of others toward the elderly is to analyze some of the dominant values in American society. For this purpose we will single out only a few of our core values: (1) youth orientation, (2) the work ethic, (3) independence and self-reliance, (4) education, and (5) progress. After discussing each value, we will examine how it affects the elderly.

Youth Orientation

Americans live in a youth-oriented society. Young people and the virtues of youth are extolled. We believe that youth is a time of energy and enthusiasm. The young are thought to be inventive, resourceful, and resilient—qualities that were highly valued in the development of this country and are still considered characteristic of most Americans.

In seventeenth-century America, young people behaved with deference, respect, and veneration toward the elderly. Youth were told to venerate the elderly, and in turn the elderly were expected to condescend toward the young. This behavior was especially predominant among the Puritans, who made a cult of old age. The pattern of exalting old age was manifested in such customs as reserving the choice seats in New England meeting houses for the oldest men and women. Old men held high offices until they died, fathers waited until their sixties to turn over their land to their sons, and the elderly maintained a position of authority within the family.

According to Fischer (1978) the devaluation of old age and the exaltation of youth began during the French and American revolutions—also a time of social revolution in attitudes toward the elderly. "On the surface it introduced a spirit of age equality. . . . But beneath that surface a new sort of inequality was being born, a new hierarchy of generations in which youth acquired the moral advantage that age had lost."

In the nineteenth century a youth cult began to develop in the United States. This emphasis on youth has grown rapidly since World War II. The young have influenced American society in recent years in the areas of our domestic and foreign policy and in our culture, especially music, fashions, recreation, even language.

The power of the young consumers is keenly felt in the marketplace. In fact, some American marketeers have gone to extremes to try to gain their share of the youth market. One observer remarks that as he watches television commercials these days, he sometimes wonders if anyone besides himself is over 30. There seems to be a conscious denial of middle age—and there certainly is one of old age. He notes that usually the only time an old face shows up is in commercials for laxatives and denture adhesives (Adams, 1971) (see Box 4.1).

A common belief that permeates American life is that the best years of life are those of youth, and that after this period, maturity and old age are largely downhill. We tell our young people to enjoy themselves while they can because later they will be tied down with responsibilities. In a 1975 Harris Poll, 69 percent of the general

---

Box 4.1   **Aging and TV Advertising**

This is an open letter to the nation's manufacturers of consumer products and the creative geniuses who plan their advertising.

On television there are only three commercials aimed directly at us—two of them about keeping regular and the other for a product that is guaranteed to keep our dentures tight while we grind away at the roots and bark husks that are supposed to keep us regular.

To look at most television advertising today one would have to conclude that no one over 65 drives a car, drinks popular soft drinks, takes a bath in fragrant soaps, buys clothes other than support hose, travels—except in an ambulance to the hospital—uses cosmetics or engages in any of the hundreds of other activities that require the products being pushed by all those young, pretty and plastic Ken and Barbie dolls who are supposed to represent Mr. and Mrs. America.

For the most part, in advertising, mature citizens are never where the action is. I mean where the REAL action is.

I'm not sure why those bright, young advertising whizzes haven't found this out yet, but someone should tell them that my crowd does indeed drive cars—even fast ones. We drink soft drinks and often we buy wine—even before its time.

Some of us bathe regularly, like to smell good, dress neatly and occasionally wear Foster Grants.

Not all of us suffer from loose teeth and constipation.

Source: Barnard K. Leiter. School of Journalism, College of Communications, University of Tennessee, Knoxville, Tennessee, 1988 [personal communication].

---

public considered the teens, twenties, and thirties as the best years of a person's life. Only 2 percent of the public felt that way about the sixties. In contrast, both old and young Samoans consider old age the best years of a person's life. For them, it is a time of great personal freedom, fewer demands, and maximum security. If old people so desire, they may relax while their relatives and children support them, or they may continue to work and contribute to the group.

Most Americans feel that adventure, excitement, and opportunity belong to youth. The science fiction writer Isaac Asimov (1974) wryly remarks:

> It is generally accepted that past a certain age, what is worthwhile in life is gone. Creative thought is for the young only; beauty and charm are for the young only; sexual activity is for the young only. Make the mistake of growing old and all the world will tell you that you cannot learn new tricks, that you are either sexually neutral or perverted, that you can do nothing more useful than remain out of the way.

Because of the beliefs cited in the foregoing paragraph, many people experience fear and panic as they age. Advertisers prey on this fear and help reinforce the desire to remain young looking as long as possible; they make us feel that we must rid

"No, I don't want to look young and beautiful. I want to look old and beautiful."

ourselves of the signs of the aging process. We are told to keep our hair its "natural" color, not to let it get gray. We are urged to eliminate bald spots through having hair transplants, or by wearing wigs or toupees. Claims are made for many creams, ranging from turtle oil to Retin-A, that they help defy the skin's aging process. The face lift is being popularized, and plastic surgery is also available for nearly every other part of the body.

Palmore and Maeda (1985) observe major differences between American and Japanese attitudes toward aging:

> One key difference in the attitudes of Japanese and Americans toward aging: most Japanese over sixty-five do not try to hide their age, while most Americans do. In fact, most Japanese men and many women tend to be proud of their elder status. It is considered polite and proper to ask an older Japanese his or her age and to congratulate him/her on it. Most Americans know it is impolite to ask an older American his or her age, and if the truth comes out, the best one can do is to reassure the older person that he/she does not look "that old." The popularity of hair dyes and cosmetics to conceal wrinkles attests to the prevalence of age concealment among older Americans. Some middle-aged Japanese women also dye their graying hair, but most older Japanese do not. It would be an exaggeration to say that most Japanese believe "gray is beautiful," but at least they believe it is natural and should be accepted as it is.

Stearns (1976) points out that leisure-time activities and sports reflect our society's emphasis on the youth culture. For example, if a 40-year-old professional football player kicks the ball or sometimes plays the quarterback position, we consider his performance amazing. We think such a person exceptional, although he is not really old. "But in spending so much time watching the young excel in sports, and yearning with jealous amazement when someone around 40 can even stay in the game," Stearns writes, "we seem to confirm the hold of youth upon us."

Box 4.2   # But You Don't Look It

During the past 7 to 10 years, many people to whom I have told my age have said, "But you don't look 62"—or 60, or whatever I was at the time. That's considered a compliment in this society, which worships youth and denigrates age. For a long time I was vaguely distressed every time I heard this so-called compliment. I found it hard to conceptualize in my own mind—let alone tell the person—why it bothered me. But it did.

Then one day it came to me: If I don't look or act (another "compliment") 62, how exactly is a 62-year-old woman supposed to look and act? Why is looking and acting your age—when that age happens to be over 40 or 50 or 60—such an insult (opposite of compliment, right?)? And why should I feel so damned good about not looking 62 (or 72 or 82) when first, I'm bound to look that way eventually, and second, when I do, I don't want to be excluded from anything? Get it?

Source: Unknown.

It is difficult to grow old in a society that values youth and devalues old age. Older people are made to feel that they are useless, out of date, and incapable of adapting to new and changing conditions. In this environment, no wonder people clutch frantically to youth and try to deny and postpone old age as long as possible.

The Work Ethic

A second major orientation in American culture is the work ethic. Americans place a high value on work and believe that staying busy is important. "Americans are not merely optimistic believers that 'work counts,'" notes Kluckhohn (1944) but adds "Their creed insists that anyone, anywhere in the social structure, can and should 'make the effort.'"

Williams (1970) cites three reasons why work has become an inherent part of the American value system. First, in early America work was necessary for group survival along the frontier. If people did not work, they were told that they could not eat. Secondly, the early settlers were mostly people of the working class from Great Britain and elsewhere in Europe, and hard work was part of their way of life. Lastly, the strong influence of the Protestant ethic emphasized dedication to work as a means of serving God.

The *Protestant ethic* refers to a cluster of values and attitudes embodied in certain religious groups, particularly seventeenth-century Calvinists. The underlying basis for the ethic stems from the Calvinist doctrine of predestination. According to this doctrine, God has foreordained the salvation of individual souls, and nothing done during one's lifetime can achieve salvation if one is not already chosen. Believers in the doctrine became anxious to find out whether they were among the elect, and they sought some outward sign to let them know. To reduce their uncertainty, the Puritans began to interpret success in an individual's occupation or calling as such a sign. They believed that if a person worked hard at an occupation and accumulated wealth in this world, this success would mean that he or she had hopes of salvation.

The Puritans regarded work as one of the highest forms of moral activity. It was considered a defense against temptations, including religious doubts. And no matter how successful Puritans were in their occupations, they could not relax but continued to work even harder because they had no guarantee of divine favor. They also needed to convince themselves of their worth. Their values are clearly expressed in the maxims of Benjamin Franklin: "Early to bed and early to rise, makes a man healthy, wealthy, and wise"; "Plough deep while sluggards sleep"; "God gives all things to industry"; and "Remember that time is money." Almost two centuries later, President Calvin Coolidge said at his inaugural address in 1925: "The business of America is business. The man who builds a factory builds a temple. The man who works there, worships there."

Over the years, there has been a gradual shift away from the Protestant ethic and its religious overtones, but the work ethic endures and is perhaps strongest in older people.

Our elderly, then, have grown up in a work-ethic society that maintains it is good to be busy, and it is bad to be idle. At retirement, a person gives up his or her work role, and in its place is offered leisure. But the long-standing values of the work ethic are not easily put aside. How does a retired person legitimate full-time leisure?

To adapt to this dilemma, Ekerdt (1986) argues that leisure is legitimated by what he terms a *busy ethic*. This ethic refers to the emphasis that people place on keeping busy in retirement, and it is consistent with the ideals of the work ethic. The busy ethic places a high value on leisure that is filled with activity.

Granted, some people are truly active in retirement, but it is not the actual pace of activity that counts. What is important is that people believe that it is desirable to be busy, and because they believe it, they will say they are busy whether they are or not. No one can talk to retirees very long without hearing the rhetoric of busyness: "How did I ever find time to work?" "The only way to rest in retirement is to go back to work." "Since I retired, I've never been busier." The busy ethic functions to legitimate the leisure of retirement, it defends retirees against the judgments of others as being "over the hill" and useless, and helps adapt individuals to retirement as well as adapting retirement to prevailing societal values.

Independence and Self-Reliance

Independence and self-reliance are highly praised values in our society. These characteristics are reflected in such phrases as "People should stand on their own two feet"; "He's a self-made man"; "I've never asked anyone for anything." We point with pride to such cultural heroes as Andrew Carnegie and Abraham Lincoln, who "pulled themselves up by their own bootstraps." Parents stress the importance of being independent and often deride their children for lack of independence. A child's peers reinforce the need for independence by disapproving certain dependent types of behavior.

We are taught that dependency is a sign of weakness, of a lack of character, or even of a sickness. A dependent person is frequently the object of ridicule and hostility and is sometimes called derogatory terms, such as *moocher, good-for-nothing, sponge, leech,* or *bum.*

Margaret Mead (1971) argues that we pay a high price for our emphasis on independence and self-reliance:

> Old people in this country have been influenced by an American ideal of independence and autonomy. The most important thing in the world is to be independent. So old people live alone, perhaps on the verge of starvation, in time without friends—but we are independent. . . . It is a poor ideal and pursuing it does a great deal of harm. . . . We have reached the point where we think the only thing we can do for our children is to stay out of their hair. . . . Old people's homes, even the best, are filled with older people who believe the only thing they can do for their children is to look cheerful when they come to visit. So in the end older people have to devote their energies to "not being a burden."

Many cultures do not have the American ideal of independence and self-reliance; they neither promote it nor take pride in it. Francis Hsu (1972) notes that in traditional China, aged parents would be happy and proud if their children could support them in a lifestyle better than the parents had been accustomed to. They would tell everyone what good children they were. If a similar situation occurred in our society, not only would the parent not brag about it, but the parent might even be ashamed of such support. In fact, the desire for independence is so strong in our culture that a parent would probably resent being supported by his or her children and would seek to become independent at the earliest opportunity.

In their study of mentally well and mentally ill older people in San Francisco, Clark and Anderson (1967) found that the most frequently cited source of self-esteem was independence. They noted that one of the striking findings of their research is the singularity of the subjects in it. "This singularity is interpreted by these subjects in many ways: it is proud independence; it is an autonomy prized as befitting 'a good, upstanding American,' or it is shrinking from others for fear of rejection, . . . or the offering of unwanted 'charity.' " The importance of preserving independence, self-reliance, and autonomy in order to maintain self-esteem was expressed in such statements as:

> I hope to always be able to take care of myself and continue in good health.
> I wouldn't want to get on welfare. I just wouldn't go to see them. I wouldn't want to do that.
> The most important things my parents did for me was that they . . . taught me how to be independent and self-reliant.
> It's very important that I do not become a burden on somebody.

When the respondents were asked to express their sources of depression or dissatisfaction, dependency (either financial or physical) ranked first on the list. Other sources of dissatisfaction, in order of rank, were: physical discomfort, loneliness, and boredom. Although other losses can be tolerated, it appears that the loss of independence is the hardest to bear. Clark and Anderson point out the extremes that some older people will go to to avoid dependence:

> Such people will draw their curtains to avoid critical appraisals for their helplessness; they will not get enough to eat; they will stay away from the doctor and forego even vital drugs; they will shiver with the cold; they will live in filth and squalor—but pride they will relinquish only as a last resort.

Two sets of reasons for wanting to avoid dependence were given by the subjects in this study. One set Clark and Anderson called adaptive, and the other, maladaptive. Taking pride in being independent and not wanting to be an inconvenience or burden to others are adaptive reasons. By not impinging on the freedom of loved ones, the elderly feel that they can maintain their own self-respect, as well as the respect of others. Maladaptive reasons center on fears and mistrust of others. Independence is seen as a defense against the possibility of bad treatment and neglect. By isolating themselves, these persons avoid any potential rejection and manipulation. Clark and Anderson conclude:

> In America, one must simply not admit that, when one grows old, one will need to lean more and more upon others. In America *no adult* has any *right* to do this. At all costs, the major work must be done, the major values must be acted out. Those who cannot do these things are either "children" or fools, useless or obsolete. It is the central values of American culture which lay down such cruel alternatives.

If the self-esteem of older people in our society tends to rest heavily on the cultural values of independence and self-reliance, then what happens when we reach the point where we are no longer able to maintain our autonomy and need the assistance and support of others? Here lies the crux of the problem. We socialize people in our society to believe that independence is good and that dependence is bad. If we live long enough, eventually we all become dependent on others.

Education

A British professor once predicted that, given the way Americans emphasize mass education, soon after an American baby is born, someone will simply hang a bachelor's degree around its neck. Most foreign observers are struck by the faith and high value that most Americans place on education. Many Americans believe that, no matter what the problem—poverty, crime, or discrimination—education is the cure-all for social ills. Williams (1970) notes: "To some Americans education is a magic panacea, the prime agency of progress; and America's faith in universal public education is its greatest asset." We believe that everyone is entitled to some formal education, and great resources are directed toward achieving this goal.

This American value of education has existed for a long time and is based on several perceptions. First, in a democracy people need to be educated in order to be responsible citizens. Second, to have a unified country despite differences in language and culture brought by immigrants, most of American society must acquire the same language and values. Finally, part of the American ideology is that talents are to be rewarded on the basis of ability alone, so all must have equal educational opportunities. For the individual, education affords one the best opportunities to improve his or her economic and social position in society.

The system of public education as we know it today was not achieved until the middle of the nineteenth century. At that time, public elementary schools began appearing in large numbers in most states. In 1852 Massachusetts was the first state to pass a law requiring compulsory attendance at school, and by 1918 all states had enacted similar statutes. By the time of the Civil War, many states began establishing free public high schools, and the movement for higher education expanded rapidly. The expansion of mass education in the United States since the end of the nineteenth century has been unparalleled. In 1900 about 7 percent of American students were graduated from high school. Today, more than 80 percent are. Four percent of the high school graduates attended college in 1900, compared with the current enrollment of about 40 percent.

Despite the great increase in persons with higher education, many older Americans have had little or no formal schooling. In addition, in a technological society like ours, change occurs so rapidly that even those elderly whose education or training was adequate when they were young find that their knowledge is often considered obsolete and outmoded. The educational attainment measured in terms of median years of school completed or the percent of high school graduates is much lower for older persons than for younger persons. In 1986, elderly persons were much less likely to have graduated high school than the entire population 25 years and older. About 49 percent of the elderly were high school graduates, compared with 75 percent of the rest of the population.

The elderly who lack formal schooling in a society that values education find their

Many of today's elderly attended school in a one-room schoolhouse. Although mass secondary education grew rapidly during the early part of the twentieth century, higher education was still the privilege of a small minority. (Tennessee Valley Authority)

prestige further diminished. In contrast, in preliterate societies the elderly derive much authority from possessing superior knowledge through experience. In a society without books, schools, and other specialized educational institutions, the older person's role as the source of knowledge becomes indispensable. Older people in our society have lost their teaching function because many of their skills are considered obsolete and useless, whereas in preliterate societies the old are the chief instructors of the young.

A common activity of the aged in many societies is story telling, which both instructs and entertains. Simmons (1945) observes how the old people among the Hopi, as is the case in many preliterate societies, are the repositories of knowledge, traditions, and skills:

> Often they alone knew the old land boundaries, the sites of distant shrines, and the complicated rituals. . . . Aged women were technicians in pottery and basketry, and old men were skilled instructors in weaving and the tanning of hides. Old men watched the sun, kept the calendar, and supervised dates for crop-planting katchina dances, rain-making ceremonies, and harvest regulations.

Still another factor operates in American society to work against older people: the concept of *human investment* in education. Instead of viewing the cost of education

The traditional role of the elderly as teachers has almost disappeared with the acceleration of social change in our society. Most notable among the skills of the elderly are those in the area of arts and crafts. This elderly man is passing on the technique of making a wooden bucket to his grandson. (Tennessee Valley Authority)

as a necessary expense like that of food or clothing, education is now regarded as a capital investment, in much the same way as buildings, machines, or materials are. People will invest money to train and educate young persons with a view to a future payoff, but they are not willing to do the same for older people. The obvious reason for this reluctance is that an older person's remaining years are limited, and the return would not be enough to justify such an investment. Robert Butler (1975) observes that "we create 'old fogies' if we continue to dispose of non-reusable human beings rather than recycle people through retraining."

Progress

The American emphasis on youth and education relates to our belief in *progress*. We stress the future, rather than the past or present. "Throughout their history Americans have insisted that the best was yet to be. . . . The American knew nothing was impossible in his brave new world. . . . Progress was not, to him, a mere philosophical ideal but a commonplace of experience" (Commager, 1970). Such expressions as *outmoded, out of date, old-fashioned, backward,* and *stagnant* have taken on negative connotations. We assume that the new is better than the old, that it is better to move forward than backward, and that by standing still we stagnate.

Belief in progress is based on the idea that we are moving in a definite, desirable direction. The belief that progress will go on indefinitely, and that things will continue to get better as we progress toward an ever-increasing enlightenment and perfection, has been a driving force throughout our history. The idea of progress and an optimistic view of the future reached its peak during the nineteenth and early part of the twentieth century. Many disillusioning events, beginning with the Depression of the 1930s and World War II, have caused some to seriously question the American faith in progress.

Progress is social change of a desirable nature and implies a value judgment that the change taking place is for the better. In a certain population some people may view various changes as progressive, whereas others may consider them retrogressive. Progress is thus a subjective, not a scientific, concept.

A society's rate of social change greatly affects the status and role of the elderly. In those traditional societies in which change proceeds slowly, the elderly seem to be more highly regarded. Simmons (1959) comments on this tendency:

> There is a pattern of participation for the aged that becomes relatively fixed in stable societies but suffers disruption with rapid social change. . . . The general principle seems to be: In the long and steady strides of the social order, the aging get themselves fixed and favored in positions, power, and performance. They have what we call seniority rights. But when social conditions become unstable and the rate of change reaches a galloping pace, the aged are riding for an early fall and the more youthful associates take their seats in the saddle.

Gordon Streib (1972) notes that in Ireland there is a shift now taking place from a traditional society, oriented to slow change, to one that emphasizes rapid change, youth orientation, and technological development. "If Ireland decides to take her place along with the other nations of Europe," Streib writes, "some of the traditional ways of thinking and behaving will have to be left behind. The veneration of the old may be one of the casualties of progress."

In a future-oriented society like our own in which social change is occurring at a rapid pace, the elderly have been stripped of an important social function. Manney (1975) describes this situation: "Progressive American society also deprives the old person of the one role he has had in most traditional cultures: the role of elder statesman who epitomizes social stability and continuity with the past. A society which treasures the . . . future has little need for someone to embody the past."

Urbanization, residential mobility, and changes in technology and occupational systems have adversely affected the lives of older Americans. For a case in point, let us look briefly at occupational specialization. In the past few decades, occupational specialties have increased enormously. Their growth has resulted in an even greater level of technological progress. As technology becomes more complex, skills become outdated more rapidly. This condition may leave the older worker in a state of occupational obsolescence.

Automation has caused many older workers to lose their jobs to computerized operations and to younger employees. Often older people find it difficult to get other jobs. Many job opportunities lie in specialties for which older persons have no training, and employers are reluctant to train them. Another outgrowth of our expanding technology has been the lowering of the retirement age. This change has occurred partly because technical ability is considered more important than seniority, because some workers prefer early retirement, and because in some cases this lower retirement age has been used to get rid of older workers, who have been dubbed "dead wood." "An emphasis on youth and newness has replaced the older stress on continuity and experience," Manney continues. "Young people are valued partly because of their superior technical education, but also simply because they are young."

The accelerated rate of social and technological change in our society has served to further undermine the position of older people. They have lost some functions that they performed in the past and, because of this, they have also experienced diminished status and prestige. In a country that equates the latest, the newest, and the most modern with the finest and the best, experience and continuity with the past and its traditions have little value. With epithets like *old-fashioned, out of date,* and *over the hill,* old people are made to feel like anachronisms and superannuated members of a progress-oriented society.

This simplified view of five major value orientations in American society is bound to be imprecise, subject to many exceptions, and controversial. Nevertheless, these abstracted patterns are useful because they provide a greater understanding of our culture and insight into the problems and conflicts of America's elderly.

VALUE SIMILARITIES AND DIFFERENCES BETWEEN GENERATIONS

The Youth and the Elderly

Some values that create problems for older people in our society may do the same for younger people. Kalish (1969) argues that some of the same values that discriminate against the elderly also tend to discriminate against the young, specifically college students. These values include productivity, achievement, material gain, independence, and hard work. He maintains that in many ways the old and young are both caught in the same bind and makes the following comparisons between the two generations:

1. *The youth and the elderly belong to somewhat segregated groups.* They are both stereotyped in ways that the middle-aged group seldom faces.
2. *Both generations are continually reminded of their nonproductive roles in society.* Both are taking out of the system rather than putting into it, and because of this circumstance, they are discriminated against by the working-age group.
3. *Both young and old persons have a lot of unstructured time.* Working-age adults structure their time around their jobs. But college youth and older people have less routine and more free time.
4. *Both groups desire to be financially independent.* The young want to be independent of their parents, whereas the elderly want to be independent of their children. Both the elderly and the young receive a large share of their money and maintenance from sources not related to what they are doing.
5. *Both generations are poor.* This condition makes them weak and vulnerable. They are looked upon as living on a kind of charity offered by the working group.

Kalish concludes that the young and old have much in common; in fact, he sees them as "generation-gap allies." Other observers have also noted a closeness between

Many observers note the affinity between youth and the elderly. Dan Smith, of the Retired Senior Volunteer Program (RSVP), regularly entertains children at an elementary school with his stories, riddles, songs, and games. (ACTION)

the first and third generations. Maggie Kuhn (1973), leader of the Gray Panthers, remarks: "Our society is age-ist . . . age-ism goes both ways—hurting both the young and the old—depriving both groups of the right to control their own lives. The same issues oppress us both . . . the first and third generations get along fine. The gaps are between the middle-aged and both groups." Flemming (1971) echoes her sentiments: "There may be a generation gap between youth and the middle-aged, but . . . There's a real affinity between the aged and youth . . . because they face a common enemy— the middle-aged. The middle-aged tell youth, 'You're too young to deal with the problems,' and they tell the old people, 'You're over the hill.'"

The Generation Gap

So much has been written in the last decades about the relations between generations along with the differences between them that the term *generation gap* has become commonplace. Social scientists who have examined this area usually take one of three approaches: the great-gap position, the gap-is-an-illusion position, or the selective-continuity-and-difference position (Bengtson, 1970).

The Great-Gap Position   Social scientists who subscribe to the great-gap perspective argue that profound differences exist between today's young people and adults with respect to values, interaction, communication, power, and authority. Some research-ers maintain that a social revolution between generations is occurring, while others view the problem as a psychological disease that is pulling age groups in our society apart. The great-gap position stresses that certain basic differences between age groups in our society cannot be resolved, and that these differences supply the impetus for a cultural transformation. Old responses and adaptions no longer suit a rapidly changing society.

The Gap-Is-an-Illusion Position   In contrast to the great-gap position, the gap-is-an-illusion perspective stresses continuity, rather than discontinuity, between gen-erations. Proponents of this view argue that the differences between age groups are greatly exaggerated and offer historical documentation to show that conflict between age groups is inevitable and recurrent.

The Selective-Continuity-and-Difference Position   The selective-continuity-and-difference perspective combines the two preceding positions. It maintains that, in most respects, generational conflict is marginal and that there is substantial solidarity and continuity of values between all age groups. Like the first position, this one stresses that the rapid rate of change in our society requires new adaptions and modes of behavior.

Studies Comparing Three Generations

Most work in the area of the generation gap has concentrated on the relation between youth and their parents. Bengtson, Olander, & Haddad (1976) note that, with a few exceptions, little attention has been given to analyzing the generation gap with regard

Box 4.3   # Intergenerational Equity or the New Ageism?

Older people are being made into targets of what I call the "New Ageism." I refer to, among other things, journalistic-hype articles in respectable publications bemoaning the growth of an elderly population as a drag on younger Americans and on our economy.

Indeed, the elderly of America are being made into scapegoats for many of the alleged ills of our society. For some exponents of the "intergenerational equity" move-ment, the elderly are resented because of the presumed burden they impose on others. For another group of exponents, the elderly are envied because of the progress made in lowering the poverty ratio among them, progress often believed to have been achieved unfairly. Yet, some of the most vocal organizations and spokesmen for this New Ageism—despite their complaints of public and private discrimination against the young in favor of the old—have rarely been among the advocates for legislation or funding aimed at improving services and policies for the young. It seems, therefore, that "equity" is to be achieved through lowering the socioeconomic status of the elderly, rather than by working to improve the lot of all age groups.

In the perspective of the New Ageism, an aging society is synonymous with insur-mountable problems and decline, not with challenges and new solutions. Rather than devote their energies and fervor to "solutions" based on pessimism and notions of a permanent downward trend in our economic and technological capacities, the propo-nents of the New Ageism should be persuaded to concentrate on the search for greater progress on remedies and on creating effective policies for prevention. This search is the essence of the history of bio-medicine, technology, and social inventions.

Proponents of the new ageism should also consider whether the facts support their notion that the progress of the older population has been made at the expense of young Americans. Richard Easterlin of the University of Southern California has examined this proposition and found it to be without empirical foundation. Writing in the June, 1987, issue of *Population and Development Review,* he makes clear in his empirical analysis that the divergent trends in the progress of the old and the young "reflect two different and largely independent causes." Even without government programs benefiting the elderly (notably Social Security), the rise in the poverty rate among children, for example, would still have taken place. "This is not to say there is no need for improving govern-ment programs for children."

So far, at least, the New Ageism does not appear to have penetrated very deeply into the public mind. As a matter of fact, public opinion polls seem to show the very opposite. One study, by the Commonwealth Fund, even contradicts the widely accepted image of older Americans as "takers" and not "givers." The proportion of the elderly giving to children and grandchildren turns out to be four times the proportion of young people helping out their elderly parents!

Unfortunately, little has been done to disseminate such findings in the mass media. The question also remains whether the media would give these and similar findings the level of attention they deserve, as a means of presenting to the public a balanced perspective on the aging population. In the meantime, the scapegoating of the elderly in the name of "intergeneration equity" continues, and these notions and values may eventually gain influence if allowed to persist without challenge.

Source: Harold L. Sheppard, "Intergeneration Equity or the New Ageism." *Aging and Vision News* (1), July 1988, p. 6.

to older people. These authors see the generation gap affecting older persons in two ways, the first being at their cohort level, which refers to the differences in standards of behavior between their own age group and those younger. The second, and the position that we will discuss, is at the lineage level, which refers to the differences between generations in the same family.

Lineage studies investigate similarities, as well as differences, in values between, say, a 72-year-old woman, her 48-year-old daughter, and her 21-year-old granddaughter. Kalish and Johnson (1972) made such a study and found that the grandmothers and the mothers appeared to be the furthest apart, whereas the mothers and the daughters were the closest in their values. A similar finding was made by Aldous and Hill (1965) in an earlier study.

The middle-aged group had more fear of aging and less regard for older people than either the daughters or the grandmothers, according to Kalish and Johnson. Older people were found to be less afraid of death and dying than were the other two generations. Although old people may discuss death frequently, they do not, contrary to popular belief, seem to be fearful of it. Perhaps the elderly feel that they have lived their lives and that, unlike those who die young, they have had their share of time and experience. Kalish and Johnson note that "values held by the young women in our sample were substantially related to values held by their mothers and their grandmothers. And, even though substantial differences were found between children and their parents, equally substantial differences were found between parents and grandparents."

In a similar study, Fengler and Wood (1972) focused on value differences among three generations. The sample studied consisted of college students, together with both parents and one grandparent of each student; these subjects were asked how they felt about six issues. Each generation was found to be twice as liberal as the generation preceding it on such issues as drugs, race relations, and religion. In the area of sexual norms, the gap was far wider between the middle-aged group and their elderly parents than it was between students and their parents. Again, this result points out that generational differences are not limited to today's young people and their parents. However, on the issue of "distribution of political and economic power," there was more agreement between the students and their grandparents than between students and their parents. "The relatively powerless state of both students and grandparents," write Fengler and Wood, "suggests a situational alliance on this issue."

Bengtson's (1975) study of three-generational families explored two value dimensions: humanism versus materialism, and collectivism versus individualism. He found two main differences in values between generations. First, the young and the old generations rated humanism and materialism similarly, and the middle-aged were found to be the most materialistic of the three. Secondly, the young generation seemed the most individualistic, and the elderly, the most collectivistic or traditionally oriented. But overall, Bengtson's study suggests no marked differences between generations nor any great gaps in values.

The findings from three-generational studies indicate the following:

1. Generational differences in values occur not only between the second and third generations, but also between the first and second.

2. Differences between generations often depend on which issues or values are involved.

3. Differences tend to be greater between the middle and the oldest generations than between the youngest generation and their parents.

4. There is a similarity in certain values between parents, children, and grandchildren.

5. People often feel that there is a greater generation gap in the larger society than exists in their own family.

SUMMARY

1. Values are socially learned and shared conceptions of what is desirable, good, or right. One approach toward interpreting and understanding the problems of older people is through an examination of some of our society's basic values. Among these values are youth orientation, the work ethic, independence, education, and progress.

2. Americans place a high value on youth and feel that this period is the best time in one's life. Many people fear old age because they see it as a time when a person is devalued and cast aside by society. As a result, many aging persons frantically try to stay young and to deny their old age as long as possible.

3. Another value emphasized is hard work, an attitude that stems in part from the Protestant ethic. Although some of its influence has faded, the work ethic continues to occupy a central place in most Americans' lives. When the work role is lost after retirement, many older people attempt to make legitimate leisure as a full-time pursuit through what has been termed "the busy ethic."

4. Independence and self-reliance are values highly promoted and praised in America. One dilemma confronting its older people is the desire for independence, coupled with the fact that often in old age they unavoidably become dependent and need others.

5. Americans have a strong faith in education and a belief that everyone is entitled to formal schooling. The high percentage of students finishing high school and attending college in recent years reflects this emphasis. In a society in which the young are better educated than their elders, this situation tends to further undermine the power of old people and strips them of roles as instructors.

6. Another dominant value in American society is progress. Americans have always believed in moving ahead and have always looked optimistically toward the future. In doing so, they tend to devalue traditions and continuity with the past. The elderly have lost some of their previous roles because of our rapidly changing society and are made to feel that they have become outmoded.

7. Many observers feel that there is a great affinity between the first and third generations, and Kalish has pointed out some parallels in their situations. In recent years, much has been written about the generation gap, the bulk of

the research centering on the relationships between young people and their parents. But only a few studies have investigated the generation gap by considering three generations, including older people; these studies have explored the similarities and differences in values that exist between generations.

KEY TERMS

values
Protestant ethic
busy ethic
progress

generation gap
New Ageism
"intergenerational equity" movement

FOR FURTHER STUDY

Achenbaum, W. Andrew (1983). *Shades of gray: Old age, American values, and federal policies since 1920.* Boston: Little, Brown.

Examines some of the ways Americans have dealt with the challenge of an aging society during the twentieth century.

Bellah, Robert N., et al. (1985). *Habits of the heart* Berkeley: University of California Press.

A study of American values and national character that focuses on the dilemma of individualism versus the need for community and commitment in our lives.

Cowgill, Donald O. (1986). *Aging around the world.* Belmont, CA: Wadsworth.

Discusses both similarities and differences in the aging experience from various cultures. Chapter 3 contains a perceptive discussion of value systems and aging.

Lasch, Christopher. (1979). *The culture narcissism.* New York: Warner Books.

Argues that a major shift in American cultural values is taking place in what he calls the search for self-fulfillment that gives rise to the narcissistic personality.

Mead, Margaret. (1970). *Culture and commitment: A study of the generation gap.* Garden City, NY: Doubleday.

A good discussion of some significant discontinuities among primitive, historical, and contemporary cultures.

Williams, Robin A. (1970). *American society: A sociological interpretation.* New York: Knopf.

See Chapter 11 for what is considered one of the most comprehensive analyses of American values to date.

Reading

Traditional Cultural Patterns: China and the United States

Gordon F. Streib

This excerpt describes the impact of different cultural patterns upon the older population in two societies.

[A] major determinant of the situation of the elderly consists of the traditional cultural patterns: norms, roles, relationships—those ways of organizing social life that tend to persist from year to year and more important, from generation to generation. Some of these patterns are deeply embedded in centuries of Chinese tradition. In American society, there are also traditional determinants—rules and relationships that have a shorter history but that significantly affect the ways in which old and young interact and the kinds of services and care provided by families and public agencies. The characteristics of Chinese and American society categorized under this rubric are presented separately from economic development determinants so as to highlight the fact that the situation of the elderly must be placed in historical perspective. Here we are emphasizing those ways of defining social life and of behaving that have continuity with earlier periods.

Filial piety [respect and devotion to parents] has been a paramount value in China for centuries and has welded the generations together (Hsu 1948; Parish and Whyte 1978). After the Communist revolution, Marxists at first stressed equality of the generations and tried to reduce the power of parents by abolishing their control over children's marriages. However, filial piety is so deeply embedded in Confucian norms that it remains a strong theme in Chinese life that results in an almost automatic sense of obligation to care for one's frail parents.

The traditional respect for authority is a related Chinese attribute that has significant implications for the elderly. Hsu-Balzer et al. (1974, p. xii) remind us that the Chinese do not have a concept of freedom and volition. They state:

Gordon F. Streib, "Old Age in Sociocultural Context: China and the United States." *Journal of Aging Studies*, 1, 1987, pp. 101–103. [Readers interested in full source citations are referred to the original article.]

Authority means that commands must be given and obeyed, that it is perfectly in accordance with the order of things for the people to be divided into the governors and the governed. The former should be wise and experienced, and able to guide the less wise and less experienced. . . . Consequently, Chinese parents do not have to play the friendship game with their children. Growing up does not imply the change of a vertical relationship with the parents into a horizontal one as American educators, under the influence of the attribute of volition, would theorize. Since Chinese parents maintain their position of superiority, as parents, maturity in the Chinese scheme of things has always meant the acquisition of the wisdom and the experience to know how to act as sons with reference to parents and how to act as parents with reference to sons.

Such an attitude gives the elderly automatic respect. They are not concerned if their needs and wishes interfere with their children's lives or activities.

In the United States, a contrast, the dominant themes have been youthfulness, equality, free choice, and independence. American parents expect their children to leave home and establish separate families. They accept the fact that children may move to other sections of the country because of career mobility, and they usually relinquish parental authority when the child becomes employed. In China, however, the authority patterns of the elderly, the respect and deference of the young to the old, the close patterns of daily living throughout their lifetime interact in such a way that family units have a more cohesive quality than in the United States. Although the Communist revolution modified some family patterns, intergenerational living, with the elderly preserving their dignity and power, causes Chinese society to have a kin-bound integration that is not found in more developed societies.

Another aspect of Chinese tradition that has continuity from earlier periods is the lack of emphasis on sexuality. Hsu has said that Chinese society has been described as asexual, with the main emphasis in man-woman relations being procreational. Davis-Freidmann (1983) agrees with this description and states that in pre-1949 families, parent-child loyalties took precedence over those between husband and wife, and sexual relations were important because they resulted in children. She adds that this perspective on sexuality is involved in the positive attitudes toward the elderly, for the physical attractiveness of youth is not essential for a positive self-image. Widows and widowers are included in the ordinary round of social life inside or outside the family, and continue to participate fully in social activities.

Chinese clothing generally reduces awareness of sexuality, says Davis-Freidmann. Men and women of all ages wear somewhat loose-fitting garments that mask body contours, unlike Western dress. Thus the elderly in China do not stand out in stark contrast to younger people in their dress and appearance.

However, in the United States there is a preoccupation with youthfulness and sexual attractiveness. These emphases are closely integrated with an economy geared toward creating high consumer demand for products that are advertised and sold by the use of overt and covert sexual appeals. The patterning of these behaviors is related obviously to the emphasis on youth and vigor, and the fragility of the marital and family ties is correlated with individual choice and sexual freedom. . . .

Traditional patterns of child rearing in China also have repercussions on the attitudes to the elderly and their roles. The Chinese have long had a cultural ideal that support of the parents comes before all other obligations and that this obligation must be fulfilled even at the expense of the children (Hsu, 1972). This ideal has been emphasized in literature, theater, paintings, and poetry.

Chinese children are socialized to see the world in terms of social relationships; they must submit to parents, and later to the school, the work group, and the state. In contrast, American children are encouraged very early to do things for themselves, to express themselves, to explore, question, master skills, and follow predilections. When American children are socialized in this manner, it is perhaps unreasonable to expect that they will switch priorities 50 years later, and suddenly put the needs of the parents first. Thus, the situation of the elderly may have its roots in child-rearing practices decades earlier. Butterfield states (1982, p. 20):

> Chinese parents don't ask what they can do for their children, as American fathers and mothers do—but what their children can do for them. This is a carry over of the old virtue of filial piety, which lay at the heart of Chinese personal relations.

Differences in child-rearing practices in the two countries are also involved in the role of the elderly. In the United States, child-rearing norms are derived from the emphasis on individual development and the freedom to choose, while in China they involve socializing the child to fit into the group. Visitors to China are surprised at the "well-behaved" children they observe, and contrast this with American children who are often noisy, willful, determined, exploratory, and at times, obnoxious. In contrast, Chinese babies will sit quietly in grandparents' arms—gazing serenely at the passing scene. There are few strollers or carriages, so infants are held a good deal of the time, in many cases even when they are sleeping. Furthermore, Chinese children are taught to conform at an early age—to fit in with the group—to subdue their individual desires. The net result of this is to produce children who can be reared by grandparents without an excessive amount of strain or friction. In contrast, most American elderly people do not want the responsibility of rearing their grandchildren, for they find it too exhausting. They are often willing to care for the children occasionally, but most do not want to be tied down to full-time child care. In summary, the Chinese grandparents have an important role in child rearing that American elderly do not have and usually do not want.

Parish and Whyte (1978) observe that the most feared kind of misbehaviors by Chinese parents are those that lead to conflicts between families. Since Chinese peasants live and work in close contact with their neighbors, parents and grandparents are anxious to maintain harmonious relations. "Indeed, one could argue that the collectivization of agriculture has made harmonious relations more important than before, since family income is now more dependent on cooperation with neighbors" (Paris and Whyte, 1978, p. 226). The techniques of discipline show how the cultural patterns of today have continuity with the past and that older family members are an integral part of the disciplinary process.

Another set of social norms that have significance in many aspects of social life relates to privacy. The two cultures attach vastly different priorities to privacy. "Individual privacy, which Americans value so highly, has never been a point of

Chinese contention," says Hsu-Balzer et al. (1974, p. xii). Butterfield (1982, p. 42) notes that the "Chinese simply do not recognize privacy: indeed, there is no word for privacy in the 50,000 characters of the Chinese language." In contrast, Americans value privacy highly. One of the reasons most American elderly insist on living alone and resist moving in with relatives is that they fear they would lose their privacy.

Chapter

5

Cultural Diversity

CULTURAL UNIVERSALS

Every society has some characteristics that are unique, some that it shares with certain other societies, and some that it has in common with all societies. The general traits or characteristics that all societies have are called *cultural universals*. Some years ago, the anthropologist George Murdock (1945) compiled a list of these features. Among them are athletic sports, bodily adornment, calendar, cleanliness training, courtship, dancing, decorative art, division of labor, education, ethics, etiquette, family, feasting, folklore, funeral rites, games, gift giving, greetings, hospitality, incest taboos, inheritance rules, joking, marriage, mourning, obstetrics, residence rules, status differentiation, toolmaking, and weather control.

Cultural universals represent general categories and not specific content of particular cultures. For example, "the family" is a universal category: No known society exists or can exist without some type of family organization. Family organization, however, may and does take many different forms. In some societies a man can have only one wife *(monogamy)*, in others he can have two or more wives *(polygyny)*, and in a few places he may be one among several husbands of the same woman (poly-andry). All societies, then, address themselves to the same general questions, but each devises its own solutions.

Simmons (1945) lists certain recurrent and persistent interests among the elderly in all societies:

1. To live as long as possible, or at least until life's satisfactions no longer compensate for its privations, or until the advantages of death seem to outweigh the burdens of life.
2. To get more rest, or . . . to get some release from the necessity of wearisome exertion at humdrum tasks and to have protection from too great exposure to physical hazards—opportunities, in short, to safeguard and preserve the waning physical energies. Old people have to hoard their diminished resources.
3. To safeguard or even strengthen any prerogatives acquired in mid-life such as skills, possessions, rights, authority, and prestige. The aged want to hold on to whatever they have. Thus seniority rights are zealously guarded.
4. To remain active participants in the affairs of life, in either operational or supervisory roles. Any sharing in group interests being preferred to idleness and indifference. . . .
5. Finally, to withdraw from life when necessity requires it, as timely, honorably, and comfortably as possible and with maximal prospects for an attractive hereafter.

Simmons maintains that the foregoing five interests of the elderly can be summed up in two words, *influence* and *security*. The goals of aging involve a reciprocal relationship between the individual and his or her group. On the one hand are the attitudes and obligations of the group toward elderly people; on the other hand is their desire to be assured of care, support, and a place in the group.

Cowgill and Holmes (1972) have identified the following demographic principles that they consider to be universal and to affect the social conditions under which aging occurs:

1. The aged always constitute a minority within the total population.
2. In an older population, females outnumber males.
3. Widows comprise a high proportion of an older population.
4. In all societies, some people are classified as old and are treated differently because they are so classified.
5. There is a widespread tendency for people defined as old to shift to more sedentary, advisory, or supervisory roles involving less physical exertion and more concerned with group maintenance than with economical production.
6. In all societies, some old persons continue to act as political, judicial and civic leaders.
7. In all societies, the mores prescribe some mutual responsibility between old people and their adult children.
8. All societies value life and seek to prolong it, even in old age.

CULTURAL VARIATIONS

Although the similarities between societies are impressive, the immense diversity among them is equally great. For instance, in many societies the old are given tedious, monotonous tasks requiring little physical strength. In other places, older people are expected to take things easy while their children and relatives support them. In some societies when the elderly become feeble and can no longer work or be useful, they are neglected or abandoned.

Ethnocentrism

Foods that people eat differ enormously from society to society. Some relish dog meat, some mosquito or ant larvae, and others rodents. Among the Aranda of central Australia, older men and women of the tribe exercise their authority by reserving the choicest delicacies, such as lizards and emu fat, for themselves. These foods sound unpalatable to Americans, but by the same token, many foods that we enjoy are defined as inedible by others. A Hindu may be sickened by beef, or a Muslim by pork. We consider milk not only healthful but pleasant to drink, yet many people in the world—for example, those of southeastern Asia—regard it as disgusting and harmful. They react to the thought of drinking a nice, cold glass of milk as we might react to the thought of drinking a "nice, cold glass" of cow saliva (Harris, 1985). Having grown up in our society, we find it difficult to understand that some people believe that milk and steak are unfit for human consumption, and yet they eat rats. (See Box 5.1.)

Marriage and other practices vary among societies. We think monogamy is more desirable than polyandry or polygyny. The thought of being one of many wives of the same man at the same time is hard for an American female to accept. But in many societies in which this form of marriage prevails, women welcome the additional

---

Box 5.1   # Food and Status in Different Cultures

Some cultures set people apart or define their status by assigning them different types of foods or diets, according to the age they have attained. There are children's, adults,' and old folks' foods in many cultures—foods one is old enough, or too old, to eat according to this cultural classification.

Preindustrial societies that are supportive of their elders include food in their care. . . . Among the Muslims of Sri Lanka, a son-in-law is obliged to give his father- and mother-in-law a rice meal every day. The Chinese venerate old people. Cantonese have special foods for those without teeth, a kind of concentrated essence of proteins (from beef or chicken) to substitute for the soups taken by younger people. In villages in Japan, grandparents cook and eat separately from the rest of the family (although living with them) as a symbol of retirement from active household headship.

There are other cultures in which people too old to function normally are discarded or discard themselves by stopping eating. Among the Numa of western North America, "suicide" by starvation by its old women was held to be meritorious. Death of a well-respected family member may lead all survivors to alter food consumption temporarily to items less well-liked. Widows may be singled out for longer abstention from familiar foods because these would remind them of the departed. The extreme case may be South India, where a widow eats one meal a day. It is thought that eating more in this state would be unhealthy.

Source: Christine S. Wilson. "Nutrition and Aging Considered Cross-Culturally." In Heather Strange and Michele Teitelbaum (Eds.), *Aging and Cultural Diversity*. South Hadley, MA: Bergin and Garvey, 1987.

wives acquired by their husbands because the extra hands lighten the workload. These women would no doubt pity the poor Western woman who has no other wives to help with domestic chores. Again, wife purchase seems like a strange and barbaric custom to us; we cannot understand how a father could sell his daughter to another man. Yet, in societies in which this is the custom, the people find it strange that a woman could give herself away. Finally, the Eskimo practice of leaving their aged parents in igloos to freeze to death seems detestable to us. But our practice of placing old people in nursing homes and leaving them there until they die would probably seem abhorrent to the Eskimo.

These examples show that we believe that the values, norms, and tastes of our culture are preferable to all others, and that at the same time people in other societies feel the same preference for their own. The tendency to regard one's own culture as superior to all others is called *ethnocentrism*, a universal phenomenon found in every known society. Our own culture becomes the standard by which we evaluate all other cultures. Those societies with values and norms very different from our own are judged to be greatly inferior, whereas those societies that most resemble ours are considered to be more progressive and civilized.

Cultural Relativism

Part of being ethnocentric is not understanding what a particular pattern of behavior in another culture means to the people who practice it. Therefore, to understand other cultures, we must examine the actions of their people in terms of their values and beliefs and not in terms of our own. Let us return to Eskimo *geronticide* (killing of the old) and look at it from the Eskimo point of view. Eskimos live in a harsh, demanding environment, which means that all must do their share of the work in order for the group to survive. When an old person becomes so feeble that he or she cannot contribute to the group's welfare or cannot travel great distances in search of food, then the lives of some others or even of the entire community may be placed in jeopardy. In addition, Eskimos believe that generations are linked together in a timeless system; people do not really die but instead live on, cycling from one generation to the next (Guemple, 1983). Thus, to understand other societies, we must take the position of *cultural relativism*, which implies that all patterns of behavior should be analyzed in the cultural context in which they are found and not by the standards of another culture. There are no universal standards of right and wrong, good and bad, moral and immoral. Standards are relative to the culture in which they occur.

Abandonment of the elderly is not unique to the Eskimo society. As a matter of custom the *Obasute*, "discarding granny," has been a recurrent theme in Japanese literature since the sixth century (Plath, 1972). The following modern-day version of the *Obasute* theme clearly demonstrates that an act we consider unthinkably immoral can be moral in another cultural setting:

> [Old] Rin, a woman nearly seventy years old, of outstanding piety and abnegation, and much beloved by her son Tappei, hears the Narayama song in the street; this song says that when three years have passed one is three years older, and its intention is to make the old people understand that the time for the "pilgrimage" is coming near. The day before the Feast of the Dead those who must "go to the mountain" invite the villagers who have already taken their parents up; this is the only great feast of the year—they eat white

rice, the most valued food, and they drink rice-wine. [Old] Rin determines to celebrate the feast this very year. She has made all her preparations, and what is more her son is about to marry again; there will be a woman to look after the house. She is still strong, she can work, and she has all her teeth; this indeed is a source of anxiety for her, for in a village that is so near starvation it is disgraceful still to be able to eat every kind of food at her age. One of her grandsons has made up a song in which he mocks her, calling her the old woman with thirty-two teeth, and all the children hum it. She manages to break two with a stone, but the mockery does not stop. The eldest of her grandsons marries; now that there are two young women in the house she feels useless and she thinks about the pilgrimage more and more. Her son and her daughter-in-law weep when she tells them of her decision. The feast takes place. She hopes that it will snow up there, for snow would mean that she will be welcomed in the next world. At dawn she sets herself upon a plank and Tappei carries it on his shoulders. In the customary way they steal silently out of the village, no longer exchanging so much as a word. They climb the mountain. As they get near the top they see dead bodies and skeletons beneath the rocks. Watchful crows are flying about. The top itself is covered with bones. The son puts the old woman down on the ground; under a rock she spreads a mat that she has brought with her, sets a bowl of rice upon it, and sits down. She does not utter a word, but she makes violent gestures to send her son away. He goes, weeping. While he is making his way down the mountain the snow begins to fall. He comes back to tell his mother. It is snowing on the mountain-top as well; she is quite covered with white flakes and she is chanting a prayer. He calls out, "It is snowing; the omen is good." Once again she waves him away and he goes. He loves his mother dearly, but his filial love has evolved within the frame of reference provided by the society he belongs to, and since necessity has dictated this custom, it is by carrying [Old] Rin to the top of the mountain that he proves himself to be an affectionate, dutiful son. (de Beauvoir, 1972)

As this story illustrates, the mother does not think that being abandoned on the mountain is a sign of cruelty or ingratitude on the part of her son. On the contrary, abandonment in this situation shows love and respect. Both mother and son are merely following the normative behavior prescribed by their culture. This way of life was worked out by the group to adapt to the environment, as was also the case of the Eskimos.

The status of the aged varies from time to time and from place to place. In some societies the aged are powerful, and in others they are powerless. In some societies the aged are highly esteemed, and in others they are merely tolerated. As we will see, the status and the role of the aged in *preindustrial societies* are often quite different from their status and role in modern industrial societies.

PREINDUSTRIAL SOCIETIES

One of the earliest and best-known works on the elderly in preindustrial societies is Leo Simmons's *The Role of the Aged in Primitive Society* (1945). According to Simmons, in most preindustrial societies (societies whose economy is based on hunting and gathering, herding, or agriculture) the elderly are accorded considerable respect. This respect is generally based on some special asset that the elderly possess, or on some functions that they perform. Often they are able to render a useful service by assisting others at various economic and household chores. The elderly are highly regarded for their knowledge, skills, and experience, which they utilize to their advantage in such roles as priests, shamans, and political leaders. In addition, they command much respect and authority through their control of property and the exercising of their family prerogatives.

Work Roles

Agricultural societies afford the elderly the greatest opportunity to continue working. As people age in these societies, they are given less strenuous tasks to perform—usually helping others to garden, to farm, or to do household tasks. In this way the elderly can continue to be useful as long as they live. The Hopi Indians of northeastern Arizona, still mainly a herding and farming people, illustrate this point:

> Old men tend their flocks until feeble and nearly blind. When they can no longer follow the herd, they work on in their fields and orchards, frequently lying down on the ground to rest. They also make shorter and shorter trips to gather herbs, roots, and fuel. When unable to go to the fields any longer, they sit in the house or kiva where they card and spin, knit, weave blankets, carve wood or make sandals. Some continue to spin when they are blind or unable to walk, and it is a common saying that "an old man can spin to the end of his life." Corn shelling is woman's work, but men will do it, especially in their dotage. Old women will cultivate their garden patches until very old and feeble and "carry wood and water as long as they are able to move their legs." They prepare milling stones, weave baskets and plaques out of rabbit weed, make pots and bowls from clay, grind corn, darn old clothes, care for children, and guard the house; and, when there is nothing else to do, they will sit out in the sun and watch the drying fruit. The old frequently express the desire to "keep on working" until they die. (Simmons, 1960)

Shifting the elderly from less physically demanding work to lighter tasks is a common pattern. For example, among the Baganda in Uganda, older persons are given lighter work loads and increased time for leisure. As Eskimo men become old and can no longer hunt on a regular basis, they help in making and repairing tools for the younger hunters (Nahemow, 1983; Guemple, 1983).

Knowledge, Magic, and Religion

Besides performing menial tasks in the field and home, the elderly often find other, more prestigious ways to utilize their talents and abilities. These ways require brains, not brawn, and are well suited to an older person's declining physical strength. For instance, in nonliterate societies in which information must be transmitted orally and retained in the memory, the elderly are the custodians of knowledge, wisdom, and traditions. In this way the elderly perform an invaluable function for the group. Their control of useful information results in their enjoying high prestige in these societies (Maxwell and Silverman, 1970). For example, among the !Kung Bushmen, the elderly perform a valuable function as the repositories of detailed knowledge of plant and animal life and water sources (Biesele and Howell, 1981); most of the elderly Kirghiz men of Afghanistan are well versed in local history and ecology (Shahrani, 1981). Among the Coast Salish Indians, the old men and old women have high status because of the information they possess about old ritual practices, as well as knowledge about canoe making (Amoss, 1981).

The elderly use their knowledge not only in teaching and advising others, but also in enacting their roles as shamans and priests. They monopolize the ritual roles that control the welfare of the individual and the group. "Shamans who have the power to inflict fatal illness and cure it are all old. Mediums who can see ghosts and who officiate after funerals, when food is burned to placate the ghosts, are also old men or women" (Amoss, 1981). In these roles they provide comfort to the distraught, diagnose illnesses, and serve as mediators between the individual and the unknown. During times of crisis, they are the ones to whom people turn for advice and guidance. Because of their advanced age, it is believed that the older persons will soon be spirits, and people attribute a supernatural power to them, an advantage in their roles as shamans or priests.

Among the Polar Eskimos some old shamans are believed to be so powerful that they can perform many miraculous feats:

This wooden Eskimo shaman mask represents a sea-mammal spirit. (Lowie Museum of Anthropology, University of California, Berkeley)

Certain old men among the Polar Eskimo were reputedly able to raise storms, produce calms, call up or drive off birds and seals, steal men's souls out of their bodies, and cripple anyone for life. They could fly up to heaven or dive down to the bottom of the sea, remove their skins like dirty garments and put them on again. Old women often made "soul flights" to the realm of the dead in order to save the lives of very sick persons. All these mighty works were said to be wrought by magic words. (Simmons, 1945)

On one occasion, after a heavy snowstorm a group of Eskimos became terrified when the ice underneath their camp began to split. They gave presents to the shaman and begged him to stop the oncoming catastrophe. He went into a deep trance and communicated with a young caribou spirit, which helped uncover the fact that a young girl had violated a sewing taboo by repairing a hole in her boot. Once she confessed, the ice stopped cracking, and the whole camp was saved.

Religious and ceremonial functions, like magic, give the elderly an opportunity to use their knowledge and wisdom, as well as to hold a prestigious position in the community. Many old people serve as keepers of shrines and temples and are leaders in performing prayers, ceremonies, and sacrifices (Simmons, 1945).

Political Activities

Other effective and important roles for the elderly lie in political, civil, and judicial affairs. The position of chief is found in nearly all primitive societies, and often it is occupied by an old man. Among the Dahomeans of West Africa the chief of each clan is always the oldest living male member regardless of his wealth, reputation, or ability. He cannot be replaced unless he becomes senile, and in that event the next-oldest clan member may govern in his name. The tremendous power and respect enjoyed by the chief is reflected in the way the Dahomeans must approach him: They must bare their heads and torsos and kneel until their foreheads touch the ground. The oldest living women are treated with similar respect (Murdock, 1934).

Some preindustrial societies have a type of government in which a group of old men rules by virtue of the superior knowledge they are supposed to possess because of their age. This is called a *gerontocracy*. Literally, the term means "rule by old men." Places where gerontocracies exist include Ethiopia, Australia, and Africa. The Sidamo of Ethiopia are ruled by an assembly of old men who make the important decisions for the group and settle disputes (Hammer, 1972). In Australia, the Aranda have a council of elders that consists of the oldest and most respected men of the group, who act as advisers to the totem chief. They are called on for such matters as conducting ceremonies, dealing with strangers, and organizing groups to avenge crimes. Among the Samburu of Northern Kenya, the older men possess both political and ritual powers. The distribution of scarce resources is in their favor (Keith, 1982).

Property Rights

Property rights have always been an important source of authority and respect for the elderly. The power that comes from holding property has afforded the elderly with a means to control others, despite declining strength. Aged persons with property are assured better treatment and command more respect than those without property (Simmons, 1945; Silverman and Maxwell, 1983). The authority that old men derive from owning property is vividly illustrated by the Chukchi and Yakut peoples of northeastern Siberia. Adult sons let their old fathers beat them with sticks or whips, and they dare not retaliate or repel their fathers' blows for fear that it would affect their inheritance.

The question of timing is also important in maintaining control and authority through property rights. Aged Laplanders of northern Europe hide their wealth from their heirs by burying it. When an elderly man is about to die, he will tell his heirs where the secret hiding place is. Sometimes a dying man refuses to reveal where his wealth is buried, and it is lost. Perhaps this custom allows an elderly father to use his possessions to reward or to punish his children, depending on the type of treatment he receives from them. This usage seems to be the case among the Banks Islanders of Oceania, where an old man buries a portion of his wealth and reveals its hiding place only if he feels that his son has taken good care of him in his old age. When an aged Hopi Indian has property, he receives better care in life and death because the kin who buried him were entitled to extra shares of his possessions (Simmons, 1945).

Family

Old people can also acquire power and exercise their prerogatives through family relationships. Elderly people in some preindustrial societies often gain advantage through such relationships by marrying younger mates. An old woman will often urge her husband to marry a strong, young woman to help lighten her work. Often the young wife is relegated to the position of maid and does all the household chores for the old couple. Elderly men and women both maintain considerable authority and prestige within the family circle and through kinship ties. In some societies the old men exercise supreme authority over their wives and children.

An old person's prestige in a family often lasts not only into extreme old age but sometimes until death. Among Samoans the old men, especially chiefs, were once honored and esteemed by being buried alive. Furthermore, if this honorific burial was not performed, the chief's family was disgraced. Turner (1884) gives the following account of such a burial:

> When an old man felt sick and infirm, and thought he was dying, he deliberately told his children and friends to get all ready and bury him. They yielded to his wishes, dug a round deep pit, wound a number of fine mats around his body, and lowered down the poor old man into his grave in a sitting posture. Live pigs were then brought, and tied, each with a separate cord, the one end of the cord to the pig, and the other end to the arm of the old man. The cords were cut in the middle, leaving the one half hanging at the arm of the old man, and the pigs were taken to be killed and baked for the burial feast; the old man, however, was supposed still to take the pigs with him to the world of spirits. . . . His grave was filled up, and his dying groans drowned amid the weeping and wailing of the living. (pp. 335–336)

By attending his own funeral the elderly Samoan could appreciate the high regard in which he was held by the community as evidenced by the large number of people attending his funeral, the many gifts of food, and the speeches extolling his virtues.

High status for the aged is a dominant characteristic in many preindustrial societies. The reasons for this, as we have discussed, are the opportunities that they have to make full use of their talents and abilities. They are able to utilize the knowledge gained through years of experience to acquire important roles in religious, magical, and political affairs of the community. The positions of the elderly are further reinforced by their control and exercise of property rights and their authority and power within the family unit. But what happens to the status and role of the elderly when a society is transformed from a preindustrial to an industrial society and the process of modernization takes place?

MODERNIZATION

Modernization is a broad concept that refers to major social changes that occur when a preindustrial society develops economically and the workplace shifts from the home to the factory *(industrialization)*, people move from farms into cities where the jobs are *(urbanization)*, and large-scale formal organizations emerge *(bureaucratization)*. These three components of modernization—industrialization, urbanization, and bureaucratization—lead to changes in the major social institutions—the family, the economy, the political system, religion, and education—and these changes in turn

At the beginning of the twentieth century, economic modernization disrupted the elderly's basic means of support through the loss of their role in agriculture. Modernization changed society from a relatively rural way of life based on animal power to a predominantly urban way of life based on inanimate sources of power. (Tennessee Valley Authority)

affect the elderly. For example, the role of the elderly as transmitters and custodians of knowledge becomes obsolete in a modernized society with advanced technology for recording and retrieving information.

Modernization theory can be traced to the writings of Emile Durkheim (1893) and Max Weber (1922). While neither was concerned with the subject of aging in itself, "Both contrasted the position of the elderly in traditional society, where they played active and often powerful roles, with their situation in modern society, where their power and prestige were at best negligible" (Silverman, 1987).

Simmons (1960) pointed out that the participation pattern for the elderly in stable societies is relatively fixed but becomes disrupted with rapid social change. Under these conditions the elderly suffer a decline in status with the loss of their positions of power and performance.

From a cross-national survey of aging in selected European countries, Ernest W. Burgess (1960) concluded that the consequences of industrialization impinge upon older persons. He pointed out, "The differences in the state of industrial growth appear to be more important for the status of the aging than variations of these countries in cultural heritage or historical background. . . . Other differences significant for the welfare of older people among the countries seem to be largely the result of the degree of industrialization."

MODERNIZATION THEORY AND THE ELDERLY

Cowgill and Holmes have done the most comprehensive and detailed work on modernization and aging to date. Using data from 14 different and diverse societies, they derived their major hypothesis: The status of the elderly declines as the degree of modernization in a society increases. Later, in a revision of their modernization theory, Cowgill (1974) selected four aspects of modernization—health technology, economic technology, urbanization, and education—and related them to the elderly's lowered status:

1. *Health technology*. Medical advances and improvements in sanitation have resulted in an increase in life expectancy, leading to a rise in the number of older people in the population. This in turn, according to Cowgill, results in an intergenerational competition for jobs, with older persons being pushed out of the labor force into retirement. The loss of income in retirement contributes to a decline in the elderly's status.

2. *Economic technology*. Developments in the economic sector create newer, more specialized occupations. Younger workers, with their technological training, are attracted to these jobs. At the same time, many of the elderly's jobs become obsolete. As a result, there is pressure toward early retirement and with it a loss in income and status.

3. *Urbanization*. Young people in modernizing societies move from the rural areas to the cities, where the new jobs and opportunites are. In doing so, they leave the elderly behind. As they come to earn their own living without dependence on their elders' land or animals, it is inevitable that the older people's authority and control over them are weakened. Not only do the young become financially independent, but they generally surpass their elders in wealth and prestige.

4. *Education.* Literacy, mass education, and technical training are prerequisites for modernization. As a consequence, the young are often better educated than the old, and this allows them to hold better-paying and more prestigious jobs, creating an inversion of status. Thus not only are the elderly deprived of their earlier educational function, but they also become intellectually segregated from the young. (See Figure 5.1.)

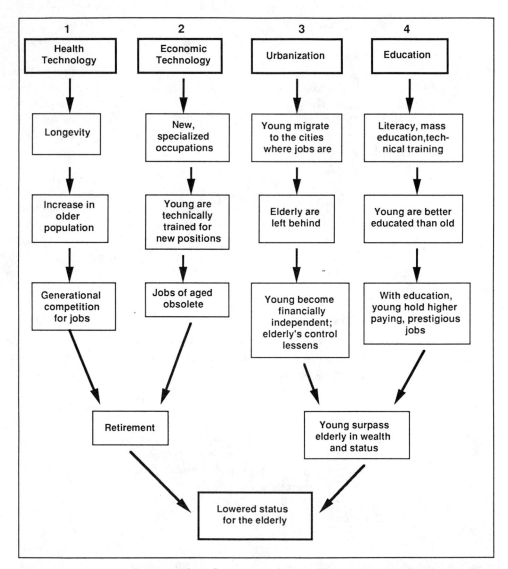

Figure 5.1. Diagram of aging and modernization theory, showing how the four most salient aspects of modernization—modern health technology, modern economic technology, urbanization, and increasing levels of education—all tend to have a depressing effect on the status of the elderly.

Some researchers argue that the relationship between modernization and the status of the elderly is not a simple straight-line relationship but instead is cyclical. They maintain that the overall status of the elderly rises as societies shift from hunting and gathering to agriculture. Then it declines again in the early stages of modernization and rises again in the later stages. For example, a study done by Palmore and Manton (1974) correlated indicators of modernization with indicators of status in 31 countries with varying levels of economic development. Their work reveals that while modernization undermines the status of the elderly in its early stages, the trend may "bottom out," and the status of the elderly may begin to improve in the advanced stages of modernization.

Modernization theory has been challenged by historians for its before-and-after-approach in assuming that before modernization the elderly in Western societies were highly regarded and after modernization they were not (Achenbaum, 1978; Stearns, 1982). Modernization theorists have been accused of romanticizing the past and assuming that the elderly in preindustrial societies enjoyed an ideal existence. In doing so, they fall prey to what Laslett (1983) refers to as the *"world we have lost"* myth. Finally, critics of modernization theory assert that the theory does not take into account the variations within societies in the status of the elderly by such factors as social class, sex, and racial groups. Although modernization theory has its limitations, it does provide a useful framework for describing and explaining historical continuities and changes in the status of the elderly as well as increasing our understanding of the factors that influence their status.

SUMMARY

1. All societies share a number of general traits or characteristics called cultural universals. These universals represent only broad categories found in all cultures and do not include specific patterns or content of a culture.
2. In a survey of preindustrial societies, Simmons found the following interests of older people to be universal: having a longer life, getting more rest, retaining seniority rights, remaining an active participant in the social group, and experiencing an easy and dignified release.
3. Societies vary tremendously. Most people are habituated to the patterns of their culture, and they consider them preferable to those of other societies. The tendency to regard one's own culture as superior to all others is called ethnocentrism.
4. Cultural relativism refers to the fact that if we are to understand the behavioral patterns of other groups, we must analyze these patterns in terms of the cultural setting in which they appear.
5. The aged are highly regarded in most preindustrial societies. This respect is often accorded the elderly because of their knowlege and experience, their property rights, and the important roles that they perform. The aged fill many important positions in primitive societies as shamans, priests, and political leaders.
6. Modernization theorists assert that the status of the elderly declines as the degree of modernization increases. Four aspects of modernization consid-

ered detrimental to the status of the aged are health technology, economic technology, urbanization, and education. Modernization theory has been criticized for asserting that there is a linear relationship between the degree of modernization and the status of the elderly, for romanticizing the past, and for not taking into account the variations that occur within societies in the status of older persons.

KEY TERMS

cultural universals   preindustrial societies
monogamy   gerontocracy
polygyny   modernization
polyandry   industrialization
ethnocentrism   urbanization
geronticide   bureaucratization
cultural relativism   "world we have lost" myth

FOR FURTHER STUDY

Cowgill, Donald O., & Holmes, Lowell D. (Eds.) (1972). *Aging and modernization.* New York: Appleton-Century-Crofts.

A survey of aging in a wide range of cultural groups and national societies in which the authors conclude that as a society modernizes, the status of the elderly declines.

Holmes, Lowell D. (1983). *Other cultures, elder years.* Minneapolis: Burgess.

A summary and theoretical statement of the field of cultural anthropology as it relates to aging. Includes discussions of such topics as retirement, longevity, and cultural change.

Simmons, Leo (1945). *The aged in primitive society.* New Haven: Yale University Press.

A classic study of aging in a variety of societies.

Sokolovsky, Jay (Ed.) (1983). *Growing old in different societies.* Belmont, CA: Wadsworth.

A collection of cross-cultural articles that deals with a variety of gerontological topics.

Reading

The Honorable Elders

Erdman B. Palmore and Daisaku Maeda

This selection describes the traditional respect for the elderly in Japan. It points out some basic differences between Japan and the United States in their attitudes and treatment of older people.

Perhaps the most pervasive form of respect for elders in the family (as well as outside the family) is the honorific language used in speaking to or about elders. English and other languages have polite and impolite forms for some words, but Japanese is unusual in its extreme elaboration of different forms to show the proper degree of respect or deference. Differential respect is reflected not only in the different nouns, verbs, prefixes, suffixes, and other parts of speech, but also in the basic grammar and syntax of the language. There are three basic forms of speech in Japanese: the honorific form, which is used in speaking to or referring to someone who is older or otherwise socially superior to the speaker; the middle form, which is used in speaking to someone on approximately the same social level; and the plain or blunt form, which is usually used in speaking to younger persons and others socially inferior to the speaker. There are many other complications, depending on whether the speaker and listener and person referred to are in the same or different "in-group" or whether the setting is formal or informal, etc. Nevertheless, respect for elders is one of the basic dimensions built into the Japanese language. This is one of the main reasons why it is so difficult for foreigners to learn to speak proper Japanese; not only must they learn the many different forms, but they also must understand the culture enough to know which relationships call for which form.

Another traditional form of respect for elder family members is seating arrangement. The main room of a Japanese house, which usually doubles as a dining-living room during the day and a bedroom at night, contains a *tokonoma*, an alcove in which various scrolls, art objects, or flower arrangements are displayed, depending on the season or occasion. The seat nearest the *tokonoma* is the seat with the highest honor,

Erdman B. Palmore and Daisaku Maeda. *The Honorable Elders Revisited*. Durham, NC: Duke University Press, 1985. [Readers interested in full source citations are referred to the original source.]

and the honor of each seat is ranked by its distance from the *tokonoma*. Traditionally, the seat with the highest honor is occupied by the oldest male in the family. His wife would usually occupy the second highest seat, and all the other household members would be arranged in descending order according to age and sex. In many modern households, if the oldest male has retired from being head of the household, the highest seat will be given to the present head of the household, and the oldest male (retired) will be moved down to the second or third highest seat.

The same order of prestige is followed in serving. The oldest male is usually served first; the youngest female is served last. An exception is made for an infant who is usually not made to wait as long as others who are actually higher in status. Not only are the elders served first, they also get the choicest portions of whatever is served.

A similar order of precedence is usually followed in all household matters. The elders and head of household go through doors before younger persons and walk down the street in front of younger persons. The elders and head of household also get to use the family bath *(ofuro)* first. The advantage of this requires some explanation: The *ofuro* is a deep tub of very hot water in which Japanese soak after washing and rinsing off outside the tub. This same water is used for soaking by every one bathing during one evening. Therefore, each person soaking in the *ofuro* leaves a residue of body oils, perspiration, etc., which gradually reduces the purity of the water. Thus, the first user gets the cleanest water.

In cooking, also, the tastes of the elders are often given precedence. If the elders like the rice cooked soft for easier chewing, it will usually be cooked soft even if the young want it firm. If the elders like the food salty or sour, it will usually be salty or sour regardless of the others' tastes. The elders and head of household usually get the rooms with the best exposure (usually the sunny one or the one with the best view). They also usually get the best silks, decorations, and bedding *(futon)*. When guests bring gifts, the gifts will often be chosen primarily to please the elders.

Adult children who have left the family home show respect and affection for their parents by returning to the family home to celebrate their parents' birthdays and special holidays, such as Respect for the Aged Day, *O-bon* festivals, [and] New Year's Day. . . . Throughout the year dutiful sons and daughters keep in close contact with their parents through frequent visits, letters, and phone calls. Many adult children call their parents every day even when they must use long distance.

There are four special birthday celebrations in old age. Age seventy is called *koki*, which means "rare old age," because in the past it was rare for anyone to live to that age. The seventy-seventh year is called the "pleasure age" *(kiju)* because the character for seventy-seven is similar to the one for "pleasure." The eighty-eighth year is called the "rice age" *(bei ju)* because the character for eighty-eight is similar to that for rice. Since rice is the basic food in Japan (indeed, the word for cooked rice, *gohan,* can also mean food in general), the "rice year" is considered to be a fortunate and important year. The ninety-ninth year is the "purity year" *(haku ju)* because the character for white or purity has one less stroke then the character for one hundred and therefore can represent ninety-nine. The birthdays marking the beginning of these special years become special occasions for family celebrations to honor the elder parent.

In the United States there is usually little ceremony at family occasions. In

Japan it is precisely in the family where respect for elders is learned and meticulously observed. Benedict (1946) observed:

> While the mother still carries the baby strapped to her back she will push his head down with her hand (to bow), and his first lessons as a toddler are to observe respect behavior to his father or older brother (or grandparents). . . . It is no empty gesture. It means that the one who bows acknowledges the right of the other to have his way in things he might well prefer to manage himself, and the one who receives the bow acknowledges in his turn certain responsibilities incumbent upon his station. Hierarchy based on sex and generation and primogeniture are part and parcel of family life. [pp. 48ff.]

This is still generally true today. When a younger person bows to his elder, the younger person bows lower and stays down longer than the elder. The elder may acknowledge the bow with a simple nod of his head.

There are popular sayings that illustrate family respect for the elders. One riddle says, "Why is a son who wants to offer advice to his parents like a Buddhist priest who wants to have hair on the top of his head?" (Buddhist priests, of course, shave their heads.) The answer is, "However much he wants to do it, he can't" (Benedict, 1945). The following dilemma is often posed: If a man's mother and his wife were both drowning at the same time, whom should the man rescue first? In earlier times the answer usually given was his mother because she is elder to his wife. These days the proper answer is not so clear, and there is considerable debate about whether a man's mother or his wife should take precedence. This may be contrasted with the United States where the usual answer would clearly be his wife because a man's primary loyalty is expected to be his wife.

You may notice that we have often used the terms *respect* and *affection* together, and you may question whether these two different attitudes can go together or whether they are mutually incompatible. To contemporary Americans with their strong eglitarian values, it may seem unlikely that you could be truly affectionate toward one before whom you must bow and continually demonstrate subservience. The Japanese do not usually view this as a problem. In fact, they tend to regard a vertical relationship, with authority and responsibility on one side and respect and subservience on the other, to be conducive to affection between the persons involved. They simply do not value independence and equality in personal relations as much as Americans do, but rather they value dependence and deference in most relationships (Nakane, 1972).

It should be understood that the prerogatives of age are usually balanced by responsibilities and concepts of fairness.

> The prerogatives of generation, sex, and age in Japan are great. But those who exercise these privileges act as trustees rather than as arbitrary autocrats. The father or the elder brother is responsible for the household, whether its members are living, dead, or yet unborn. He must make weighty decisions and see that they are carried out. He does not, however, have unconditional authority. He is expected to act responsibly for the honor of the house. . . . The master of the house saddles himself with great difficulties if he acts without regard for group opinion. [Benedict, 1946, p. 54]

Thus, the elder normally "earns" affection and respect from younger family members through his fairness, wisdom, and aid. . . .

The question remains: How widespread is such family respect for elders in contemporary Japan? Our interviews with Japanese of all ages in rural and urban areas found estimates ranging from 90 percent in rural areas to a minority among young urban people. It is safe to say that there is more respect for elders in rural areas, in traditional occupations and households, and among middle-aged or older persons than in urban areas, "modern" households, and younger persons. This can also be inferred from the statistics showing differences by place of residence and age as to living arrangements and support patterns. . . .

Respect for Elders Day (*Keirō No Hi*) is one of the most dramatic expressions of respect and affection for the elders. Ceremonies in honor of the elders have been widespread for more than three hundred years, but in 1963 Respect for Elders Day became a national holiday. The law specifies that "the governments of various levels should hold suitable activities to evoke the people's interest in and understanding of the welfare needs of the aged as well as to encourage old people to improve and enrich their own lives." On each September 15 the Ministry of Health and Welfare presents a silver cup and a letter from the premier congratulating each person who reached the age of one hundred during the past year. In Tokyo the Metropolitan Government presents a silver fan to those who became one hundred during the year; a "respect for elders" medal to those who became seventy-five; and gifts of 5,000 yen (about $20) to each of the more than 200,000 persons over the age of seventy-five in the city. Newspapers run feature articles on the aged and on the celebrations and rallies that are held in most cities. Even small hamlets usually have some kind of ceremony and celebration with gifts of honor for the elders in the community. In large cities there are usually several different celebrations, which include music and entertainment, speeches by important officials, and gifts to honor the very old and those who have worked to help elders during the year.

A more traditional form of respect for elders was the practice of younger persons giving their seats to elders on public vehicles such as buses, subways, and trains. Traditionally, all younger persons were supposed to give their seats to any older person when there were no other seats, simply to show their respect, regardless of whether they appeared infirm or not. In recent years there have been many complaints, especially from older persons, that younger people were no longer giving their seats to elders.

As a result, starting on Respect for Elders Day in 1973, the Tokyo railways and subways reserved six seats on every fourth car for use by the aged and the physically handicapped. The seats are silver-gray in color (instead of the usual blue) and are called "silver seats." Prominent signs on the outside and inside of the cars explain that the aged and physically handicapped have priority in the use of these seats.

The program has been quite successful, so successful that there is now talk of eliminating them because most people now give their seats to elders and handicapped regardless of whether the seats are designated as "silver seats" or not.

Chapter

6

Socialization

*I*n the preceding three chapters we have seen how important culture is in the shaping of human behavior. Now let us turn to the process through which an individual learns his or her culture—*socialization*. Through socialization people acquire the skills, attitudes, values, and roles that make it possible for them to become members of their society. "Without this process of molding which we call 'socialization,' the society could not perpetuate itself beyond a single generation and culture could not exist. Nor could the individual become a person; for without the ever-repeated renewal of culture within him [or her] there could be no human mentality, no human personality" (Davis, 1949).

SOCIALIZATION AS A LIFELONG PROCESS

The most obvious phase of socialization takes place during childhood, but the process does not stop there. Socialization gained in childhood cannot fully prepare us for the multiplicity of *roles* that we perform as adults. Socialization occurs throughout the life course and is a continuing, never-ending process. Each new social possition that one attains—such as entering college, beginning a new job, getting married, becoming a parent or a grandparent—requires the learning of a new social role. Socialization, then, may be defined as a lifelong process through which individuals learn and internalize the culture and social roles of their society.

Inkeles (1969) divides the life course into these stages: infancy and early childhood, late childhood and adolescence, adulthood, and old age. He identifies four elements in socialization that occur at each stage: (1) the *main issue* of socialization that dominates the attention of the one being socialized, as well as that of those doing the socializing; (2) the *agents* of socialization that play the most significant roles in the socialization process; (3) the *objectives* that these agents set as goals for successful socialization; and (4) the *main task* of the one being socialized, such as the skill to be learned or the problem to be solved (Table 6.1).

The main issue of infancy and early childhood is the total helplessness and dependency of the child. The central objective is to help the child move on to the next stage of development. For the child, the main task is mastering control over his or her body, which includes becoming toilet trained and learning how to walk and talk, and to feed and dress himself or herself.

In late childhood and adolescence, the significant issues revolve around the capacity of the individual to adjust to physical and mental changes, and society's adaptation to the impact of these adjustments. The individual begins to acquire roles that precede or fall within the scope of adult roles. The objective of the agents of

Table 6.1   INDIVIDUAL SOCIALIZATION THROUGH THE LIFE COURSE

Elements	Stages			
	Infancy and early childhood	Late childhood and adolescence	Adulthood	Old age
1. Main issue	Helplessness	Adjustment to changes in physical and mental capacity	Acceptance and performance of multiple roles	Acquisition of new skills and changes in habits
2. Agent of socialization	Family and adult kin	School, teachers, peers, etc.	Formal organizational agencies	Peer group
3. Objective of agent	To move child to next stage of development	To help adolescent assume adult roles	To motivate adults to attain highly specific and defined objectives	To help elderly to accept new status
4. Task of the one being socialized	To gain mastery over one's own body	To manage the changes in oneself	To fit into the large set of new statuses	To give up previously held positions

Source: Adapted from discussion in Alex Inkeles, ''Social Structure and Socialization.'' In David A. Goslin (Ed.), *Handbook of Socialization Theory and Research*. Chicago: Rand McNally, 1969, pp. 618–629.

socialization at this period is to help train the adolescent for his or her adult roles as effectively as possible. The family is replaced as socializing agent by a diverse group, including teachers, the school, peer groups, religious specialists, public and local heroes, and so on.

The key issue in adulthood is the degree to which the individual accepts and performs the multiplicity of roles that accompany the statuses of adulthood. The task of the one being socialized is to take over these new roles and statuses and to accept adult responsibilities. In old age, one adjusts to physical changes that necessitate learning new skills and changing patterns of behavior. An important part of the older person's task is to relinquish previously held statuses and roles, along with the prestige, power, and economic rewards accompanying them. Learning new roles and skills may be required, especially those suitable to full-time leisure. In old age, one's peer group again becomes an agent of socialization. Children and others whom the elderly had previously socialized also act as socializing agents during this period and encourage the older person to accept the new status.

The most significant aspect of adult socialization is the acquisition of social roles. As individuals move through adulthood into old age, they must constantly learn to perform new or altered roles and give up old ones. As we mentioned earlier, a role is the expected behavior of one who holds a certain status. A single status may involve a number of associated roles. For example, the status of college professor involves not only the role of teacher in relation to students but also includes a cluster of other roles in relation to colleagues, secretaries, and administrators. All these roles constitute a *role set*, which may be defined as the entire array of related roles associated with a particular status that an individual occupies.

SOCIALIZATION AND OLD AGE

A person's role sets change during the stages of the life cycle. New roles are added to the sets, and old ones are discarded. An individual discards the role of a single person in taking on the new role of husband or wife. When one is graduated from college and gets a full-time job, the role of student is exchanged for that of employee. In each instance, the individual relinquishes one role and is given a new role in return. The single person may look forward to marriage, and the college student to a job. But old age differs from other stages in the life cycle because, while roles continue to be discarded, new roles often do not take their place. Eventually the role sets of the elderly begin to shrink.

Role Loss

The major *role losses* that characterize old age come with retirement, widowhood, and institutionalization. The loss of the work role or marital role differs from role losses in earlier years because one's participation in the occupational structure and the nuclear family, respectively, are ended. As a rule, the majority of retired persons never return to the labor force as full-time workers, and most widows do not remarry

(Blau, 1981). The physical decline that often occurs in the later years results in additional role losses, especially when it leads to institutionalization. Unlike earlier transitions, retirement, widowhood, and institutionalization involve the loss of highly respected roles—those of worker, spouse, and community resident—in exchange for roles that have less social worth (Foner, 1986).

Research by Lowenthal and Haven (1968) found that having a close relationship with someone in whom one can confide serves as a buffer and social support against role losses. Despite role losses, persons with confidants were more likely to be satisfied and less likely to be depressed than persons without confidants (see Table 6.2). This finding held true even with those who suffered role losses such as widowhood and retirement. The study also found that an individual who had been widowed within seven years of marriage but who had a confidant had a higher morale than a person who, though married, had no confidant. Similarly, the morale of retired persons having confidants was the same as the morale of those still working but without confidants.

The type of role losses experienced by the elderly underlies the basis for two theories of successful aging: the disengagement theory and the activity theory.

Box 6.1 **The Looking-Glass Self**

The feelings we have about ourselves, the notion of the kind of persons we think we are—this knowledge is gained through the reactions of others toward us. Although these feelings and notions are formed early in life, they are constantly being modified and reevaluated throughout life. Cooley (1902) called the process of discovering the nature of the self from the responses of others to us the *looking-glass self*. In other words, society provides a looking glass—a mirror—in which people discover their image or self-concept: We see ourselves as others see us. According to Cooley, there are three steps in building the looking-glass self:

1. How we imagine we appear to others.

2. How we imagine they are judging us.

3. Our feelings about their judgments (positive or negative).

For instance, an elderly man may believe that he has lost weight and looks great in his new bathing suit. He then imagines how others are judging his appearance because he knows that people generally consider slim people more attractive. Finally, he experiences a feeling of pride on the basis of what he believes others' judgments to be. Similarly, at the death of her husband a woman imagines how she, as a widow, appears to the couples with which she and her deceased husband associated. Next, she imagines how they are judging her. She is aware, for example, that people typically think of a widow as a "fifth wheel." Finally, she experiences feelings such as anger and resentment about what she believes their judgments to be.

Table 6.2   EFFECT OF CONFIDANT ON MORALE
IN THE CONTEXTS OF WIDOWHOOD
AND RETIREMENT

	Satisfied (percent)	Depressed (percent)
Widowed within 7 years		
Has confidant	55	45
No confidant	(27)[a]	(73)
Married		
Has confidant	65	35
No confidant	(47)	(53)
Retired within 7 years		
Has confidant	50	50
No confidant	(36)	(64)
Not retired		
Has confidant	70	30
No confidant	50	50

[a]Percentages are placed in parentheses when the numbers on which they are based are less than 20.

Source: Marjorie Fiske Lowenthal and Clayton Haven, "Interaction and Adaptation: Intimacy as a Critical Variable." *American Sociological Review* (33), no. 1 (1968), p. 27.

The Disengagement Theory   Developed by Elaine Cumming and William Henry from their work in Kansas City, Missouri, in the 1950s, the *disengagement theory* was the first formal theory to attempt to explain the aging process. It is based on the premise that aging involves a gradual relinquishment of social roles and a decrease in social interaction. Cumming and Henry (1961) contend that both the individual and society prepare for the ultimate disengagement (death) through a gradual, mutually beneficial process during which the individual and society withdraw from each other. Their statement follows:

> In our theory, aging is an inevitable mutual withdrawal or disengagement, resulting in decreased interaction between the aging person and others in the social system he belongs to. The process may be initiated by the individual or by others in the situation. The aging person may withdraw more markedly from some classes of people while remaining relatively close in others. His withdrawal may be accompanied from the outset by an increased preoccupation with himself; certain institutions in society may make this withdrawal easy for him. When the aging process is complete, the equilibrium which existed in middle life between the individual and his society has given way to a new equilibrium characterized by a greater distance and an altered type of relationship.

To Cumming and Henry, disengagement is inevitable because death is inevitable. Old people prepare for their deaths by divesting themselves of social relationships and social functions. Society, in turn, encourages its members to do this so that their deaths will not be disruptive to its equilibrium. In other words, disengagement is a two-way process whereby the individual withdraws from society and society withdraws from the individual. When the process is complete, the individual has shifted from being preoccupied with society to self-preoccupation.

These authors believe that their theory of disengagement is universal and applies to all societies, though they acknowledge that cultural variations occur in the initiation of the process. For instance, in our society old persons may resist the process of disengagement until it is forced upon them, while in traditional societies the elderly may initiate the process.

Since its emergence, disengagement theory has received extensive criticism (Rose, 1965; Maddox, 1964; Hochschild, 1975, 1976). In a critique of the disengagement theory, Rose argues that the process of disengagement is not inevitable. He points out that a significant proportion of older people never disengage and continue to be socially involved all their lives. This counterevidence, according to the authors, does not refute the theory. They regard those persons who do not disengage as making an unsuccessful adjustment to aging, being "off-time," or belonging to a "biological or psychological elite." Hochschild refers to this explanation as an "escape clause" in the theory. Disengagement, according to Comfort (1976), is "often, alas, sludge language for being ejected, excluded, or demeaned, and liking it—an attribute wished on the newly created old to plaster our guilt and provide a piece of jargon to excuse our conduct."

In spite of its many limitations, disengagement theory has encouraged much research and debate as well as the development of other theories over the past 30 years. Recently, some elements of this theory—such as society's role in excluding the elderly from valued roles—have been revived (Passuth & Bengtson, 1988).

The Activity Theory   In contrast to the disengagement theory is the *activity theory*, often referred to as the "common-sense theory" of aging (Cavan, 1949; Havighurst & Albrecht, 1953). Whereas the disengagement theory emphasizes withdrawal from roles, the activity theory stresses a continuation of role performances. In this view, when roles are lost, such as in retirement and widowhood, the individual is expected to find substitutes. Havighurst, Neugarten, & Tobin (1968) sum up the main premise of the activity theory:

> The older person who ages optimally is the person who stays active and who manages to resist the shrinkage of his social world. He maintains the activities of middle age as long as possible and then finds substitutes for those activities he is forced to relinquish: substitutes for work when he is forced to retire; substitutes for friends and loved ones whom he loses by death.

Although withdrawal is considered mutual in the disengagement theory, in the activity theory it is not. The activity theory holds that society withdraws from the aging person, but this is against the person's will or desire. To minimize this withdrawal, the person must try to be active, keep busy, and stay "young." The underlying theme seems to be that "it is better to wear out than rust out," or better still, "to die with one's boots on." Many old and young people subscribe to this philosophy,

Some people have no desire to sustain high levels of activity as they grow older. They are content to disengage from many of their former roles, whereas others continue to be socially involved all their lives. (Nick Myers)

as do most of the practical workers in gerontology. This theory is certainly more in keeping with the American value system than the disengagement theory is.

Despite all the bromides on keeping active, many people have no desire to sustain the high levels of activity and the attitudes of middle age as they grow older; they may not want to replace some of the activities they have lost. Research has shown that life satisfaction among the elderly is dependent not on the amount but on the type of activities in which they are involved. For example, informal activities tend to be positively related to life satisfaction, solitary activities have no effect on life satisfaction, and formal activities have a negative effect (Lemon, Bengtson & Peterson, 1972; Longino & Kart, 1982).

As we have seen from the foregoing discussion, both the activity and the disengagement theory have their limitations and neither offers an adequate explanation of the complexities of the aging process.

Role Ambiguity

Brim and Wheeler (1966) state that the three main purposes of socialization are to help an individual acquire knowledge, ability, and motivation. Before a person can perform a role adequately, that person must know what the normative expectations of the role are, must have the ability to meet the requirements of the role, and must possess the desire or motivation to fulfill the role. These three basic conditions are necessary for successful socialization. Of these conditions, in most cases, the elderly have the ability to perform their roles, but they are seriously hampered by the other two requirements, knowledge and motivation.

For learning to take place efficiently and effectively, the knowledge that one is expected to acquire should be explicit and clearly stated. Students are well aware of this in the classroom. They are often confused and bewildered by instructors who speak in vague generalities and who cannot express their thoughts clearly. A similar situation occurs in learning a role when the content of the role is vague and ambiguous.

Role ambiguity occurs, therefore, when there are no clearly defined guidelines or expectations concerning the requirements of a given role. Role ambiguity is not uncommon. For example, today a lack of consensus exists on what the role of a woman in our society should be. Should she get married, have children, and remain in the home, or should she pursue an independent career? Role ambiguity also exists for parents and their adolescent children because there is no clearly defined time in our

(Drawing by Modell; © 1986 The New Yorker Magazine, Inc.)

According to research, life satisfaction is positively related to informal group activities while solitary activities have no effect on life satisfaction. (Tennessee Commission on Aging)

society when an adolescent becomes an adult. At some point we expect young people to stop being children, and yet we do not view them as adults. In some situations they are treated like children, whereas in others they are given the responsibilities of adults. Thus, many adolescents become confused about their role and its inconsistencies. In certain states—Tennessee, for example—at 16 persons are considered mature enough to drive and can marry with the permission of parents, but they must wait until 21 before being legally able to buy a bottle of beer.

Many primitive societies have rites-of-passage ceremonies that mark the transition into adult status, thus eliminating any confusion. Such ceremonies perform the function of letting a person know where he or she stands and of announcing the new status publicly.

The transition into old age and retirement is often characterized by role ambiguity, as there are few established norms regarding these roles. Not only the elderly themselves, but others are uncertain about the proper role for the aged and retired. For instance, when we think of persons who are doctors, plumbers, teachers, or police officers, we have a fairly good idea of what each role entails. But think for a moment of retired persons. What is their role? Do we expect them to sit and watch TV, play bingo, go fishing? Our expectations are uncertain and vague (see Chapter 3's section on norms). There are few guidelines to give structure and direction to their lives.

Three decades ago, Burgess (1960) in the following classic statement referred to the ambiguous position of older people in our society at retirement as being an essentially "roleless role."

The retired older man and his wife are imprisoned in a roleless role. They have no vital function to perform. . . . Nor are they offered a ceremonial role by society to make up in part for their lost functional role. The roleless role is thrust by society upon the older person at retirement, and to a greater or lesser degree he has accepted it or become resigned to it.

Today most people disagree with Burgess and maintain that there *is* a retirement role, even though it is quite vague. Retired persons, for example, are expected to manage their own affairs, to live within their income, and to avoid being dependent on their families or communities (Atchley, 1976). As Rosow (1973) points out, the retiree is told to find a hobby and to stay active, but it is usually not specified at what he or she is expected to stay active.

Equally ambiguous is the widowhood role in our society. Besides the vague prescriptions of learning to live independently and to interact as a widowed person, there are few clear expectations of what to do; there are mostly expectations of what persons should not do. For example, widowers should not expect to be socially active or to have much of a sex life; widows should not go out with men much younger than they (Bengtson, Manuel, & Burton, 1981).

Without clear-cut norms to measure conformity to or deviation from a role, there can be no positive sanctions or rewards for performing a role successfully. This lack deprives the older person of motivation, which in turn impedes the socialization process. Clearly, two of Brim's necessary conditions for socialization, knowledge and motivation, have not been met in the retirement and widowhood roles.

Role Discontinuity

For many roles in our society, we often prepare ourselves. For example, a college student studying to be an engineer, besides taking the necessary courses, gets a summer job working for an engineering firm, begins reading the engineering journals, and joins an engineering society. Or, a mother returns to school to finish her degree when her children are nearing high school age so that she may become certified as a teacher. In both cases, there is a continuity of socialization for a new role. Role continuity refers to the learning of new skills, norms, and attitudes that prepare one for the next stage. Such socialization facilitates the movement and adjustment to a new role.

Benedict (1938) describes continuity in the socialization process among the Cheyenne Indians:

At birth the little boy was presented with a toy bow, and from the time he could run about serviceable bows suited to his stature were specially made for him by the man of the family. Animals and birds were taught him in a graded series beginning with those most easily taken, and as he brought in his first of each species his family duly made a feast of it, accepting his contribution as gravely as the buffalo his father brought. When he finally killed a buffalo, it was only the final step of his childhood conditioning, not a new adult role with which his childhood experience had been at variance.

This description shows how Cheyenne youths are systematically trained from childhood for their adult role. In most societies, people are trained, formally or informally, for their future roles by learning expected behavior and values. In this way, transition from one role to the next is made easy and smooth.

But a lack of preparation and consistency in training for a role that one will take on at the next consecutive stage results in *role discontinuity*. In our society, some serious discontinuities occur in the socialization process. Transitions from the dating role to the marriage role and from the work role to the retirement role are situations involving role discontinuity. What is learned in socialization at one age level may be useless at the next or may conflict with what has previously been learned, necessitating unlearning.

Linton (1936) provides an example of how socialization into old age can be a difficult one to make. He points out that among some societies, such as those of the Comanche and most of the Plains tribes, the transition was made even harder by the fact that the status of adulthood had a different personality ascribed it from that of old age. The adult male was expected to be a warrior—vigorous, self-reliant, and aggressive; his relationships were characterized in terms of competition. To settle one's differences or ignore slights was a sign of weakness and resulted in a loss of prestige. By contrast, the old man was expected to be wise and gentle, willing to overlook slights, and even to endure abuse. While young men strived for war and honor, old men worked for peace and tranquility. The transition to old age was so difficult for the Comanche warriors that many preferred death in battle to old age. When a warrior became too old to fight and was forced to assume the new role, he did so grudgingly.

In our society, transitions into the old-age role can also be problematic. Ekerdt (1986) raises the question: "At retirement what does a person do with a work ethic when they do not work anymore?" This lack of consistency and integration with the existing values and norms of the person, according to Ekerdt, creates a discontinuity in moving from the role of worker to that of retiree, and he makes the following suggestion:

> In the abstract, retirement ought to entail the unlearning of values and attitudes—in particular, the work ethic—so that these should be no obstacle to adaptation. Upon withdrawal from work, emotional investment in, and commitment to, the work ethic should by rights be extinguished in favor of accepting leisure as a morally desirable lifestyle.

When an individual moves from one role to the next and there are conflicting norms and values between the two roles, this situation imposes a strain on the role transition and results in role discontinuity. Role discontinuity in later life occurs not only at retirement but also in widowhood and institutionalization. For instance, the role of a wife or husband does not prepare one for widowhood, nor does the role of a community resident prepare one for the role of a nursing-home resident.

ANTICIPATORY SOCIALIZATION

Closely related to role discontinuity is the concept of *anticipatory socialization*. This is the process of preparing for a new role before assuming it. Such socialization tends to make the transition and the adjustment to the new role easier. For instance, some informal socialization for retirement takes place as a worker discusses the subject with family, friends, and co-workers as well as observing persons who have already retired. A more formal type of anticipatory socialization for retirement occurs through retirement planning programs. These programs provide the preretiree with some knowledge about retirement: what to expect, what problems to anticipate, and how to prepare for them.

Generally, two approaches are used—individual counseling and group sessions. Individual counseling consists of scheduling interviews with an employee and often his or her spouse to discuss financial planning for retirement. Besides the financial aspect of retirement, other areas dealing with adjustment to retirement may also be included. Interviews are usually conducted by a trained member of the personnel staff and often begin three to five years prior to retirement.

Group sessions are considered by many to be the most effective method of retirement preparation. They give employees the opportunity to exchange ideas and information freely and to discuss retirement problems with one another. Each session, which usually lasts about two hours, focuses on one major topic involved in retirement preparation. These topics generally include finances, health, the sociological and psychological aspects of retirement, living arrangements and locale, legal aspects of retirement, and the use of leisure time. New topics that now are being introduced into these programs include part-time employment during retirement and caring for one's aging parents (Dennis, 1988).

Most group programs schedule weekly meetings, ranging anywhere over a period of from 6 to 12 weeks; employees are given time off during working hours to attend

Most retirement planning programs are offered as an employee benefit by private and public employers. In general the evidence indicates that these programs are helpful in easing the transition from work to retirement.

the sessions. Some firms hold their meetings in the evenings to enable the employees' spouses to attend.

Preretirement programs have been growing in popularity during the past three decades, not only among business and industrial firms but also in labor unions and in federal, state, and local governments. In recent years, preparation for retirement has been adopted by many universities, community colleges, and public schools as part of their instructional offerings. Such groups as senior citizen centers, community centers, churches, and libraries also sponsor pre-retirement programs.

Some companies offer their employees the option of gradual retirement, which involves giving an employee increasing amounts of time away from the job in the form of extended vacations or shorter working hours. Gradual retirement is a type of *role rehearsal* that enables individuals to act out behavior required in their future role. Although the opportunity to rehearse future roles fosters the socialization process, in the case of the ambiguous retirement role a person is limited in what to rehearse. Probably the greatest advantage of gradual retirement is that it allows individuals to experience retirement in small doses. In this way, they gain insight into the adjustments and problems that they will experience later in retirement, and they can use this knowledge to plan accordingly. Also, by gradually getting used to being away from the job, people find that the transition from full-time employment to full-time leisure tends to be less traumatic (see Box 6.2).

Box 6.2   ## Employees Get a Shot at Testing Retirement

BOSTON (AP)—When Allen Metcalfe was ready to retire from Polaroid Corp. he was given three months to decide whether he liked his new lifestyle. If he didn't, the company would take him back, no questions asked.

Polaroid officials said they established the unusual three month "rehearsal retirement" program because many employees find the adjustment traumatic and some would rather continue working.

"From the morale point of view, this is a biggie," said Joseph Perkins, Polaroid's corporate retirement manager. About 50 people, or 10 percent of those eligible to retire, have opted for the tryout retirement since the plan began, Perkins said, adding that the company continues to offer the program as a goodwill gesture.

Metcalfe said Polaroid's retirement office advised him that he needed time to decide what retirement would do for him. "When I was getting ready for retirement, I didn't know whether I was going to like it," he said. "I didn't know if I'd fit in with it or what was going to happen. It was a very, very uncertain thing."

During his three months off, Metcalfe spent more time participating in what had previously been a hobby—polishing stones. "Now I'm into lapidary work, making custom jewelry," said Metcalfe, 73.

Source: *Knoxville News-Sentinel*, January 22, 1988.

Like retirement, widowhood is not a clearly defined role, making anticipatory socialization to it more difficult. Because men die at younger ages than women, the role of widowhood is primarily for older women. Older women may "rehearse for widowhood" by observing the behavior of friends and relatives who are already widowed or by having nursed one's husband through an extended illness prior to his death.

The impact of institutionalization can also be eased by preparation. Anticipatory socialization might include not only the appraisal of one's situation but also knowledge about the institution, visiting it, or even living there on a trial basis.

RESOCIALIZATION

Some role transitions require *resocialization*—the replacement of former norms and values with new ones. For instance, at retirement one replaces a commitment to work with a commitment to leisure, or at widowhood one replaces dependence with independence. The most effective type of resocialization occurs in special settings such as prisons, boarding schools, monasteries, and nursing homes. Goffman (1961) has called these facilities *total institutions*. They are "total" in the sense that people spend almost all their time in them, cut off from the rest of society, for an appreciable period of time. In addition, all aspects and activities of daily life are scheduled and regulated by a hierarchy of custodians who do not consult the participants.

Entering a nursing home requires that an elderly person undergo resocialization to restructure his or her way of life; this includes the acquisition of institutional values and norms to replace former ones. In a nursing home a formal routine prescribes when one gets up or goes to bed, what one eats, when one eats, and what leisure activities one pursues. In many cases one must also adjust to the idiosyncrasies of a roommate. Privacy is at a premium. Because of the limitation of space, most of one's possessions, which provide a sense of the past, must be left behind. Being separated from one's possessions may contribute not only to a loss of sense of the past but also to one even of self. Finally, nursing-home residents are cut off from their former roles. They are no longer able to perform the roles of parent, grandparent, or friend the way they once did. Resocialization for the nursing-home patient, then, includes giving up independence and control over one's life as well as an erosion of social roles. The initial consequences of this resocialization experience has been referred as the "first-month syndrome" (Tobin & Lieberman, 1976).

ROLE MODELS

The late Elvis Presley served as a role model for many aspiring young singers during the 1960s and most of the 1970s. His innovative style of strumming a guitar and gyrating his hips while singing were and still are emulated. A *role model* is an individual whose behavior in a certain role provides a pattern for another individual to follow in performing the same role. By having appropriate role models with which to identify, an individual can learn a new role with greater ease. Parents generally act as role models to socialize their children for age, sex, or occupational roles. Role models may range from a public figure to a legendary hero. Hess (1974) notes:

> In a society in which youthfulness is the valued state of being, in which wrinkles, gray hair, lack of zap, and irregularity must be eradicated along with spotty glassware, grimy sinks, and dirty floors . . . where are role models who can demonstrate successful aging? This question becomes crucial when we remember that today's old people are the first to survive in large numbers into an old age of retirement from work and family roles, in fair health, and with a good deal of confidence in their capacities for coping. Because this is a new stage in life, there are few models to follow and few institutionalized norms to guide them.

Rosow argues that older people do have role models, but these models are often inappropriate because they are youthful. For older persons to judge themselves according to youthful standards seriously hampers their socialization to old age. The elderly who are most admired and who serve as role models tend to be those who act youthful, look well preserved, and maintain middle-age lifestyles. Any deviations from these models are often regarded as undesirable and negative.

Much documented evidence shows that most people in their sixties deny their age and continue to think of themselves as middle-aged, although they are considered old by society's standards. Older people maintain that they are middle-aged as long as possible mainly because old age is devalued in a youth-oriented society. Often an old person recognizes that others are old but somehow exempts himself or herself from that category—like the woman who went to her high school reunion and was amazed at how everyone had aged but she.

As we have seen in this chapter, the elderly are called upon to be the most creative and adaptive group in our society. They are expected to provide for their own socialization into old age with no incentives in our society to embrace their age and few meaningful norms by which to live. They must not only redesign their own status, but they must then socialize themselves to fit it (Cain, 1968; Rosow, 1974). A summary of some of the major points covered in this chapter regarding major role transitions in later life along with their socialization properties are given in Table 6.3.

SUMMARY

1. Socialization, the learning of one's culture, makes it possible for people to become members of their society. The process is not limited to the childhood years but rather continues throughout life.
2. At each stage of the life course, there are four principal elements in the socialization process; the main issue, the agents, the objectives, and the central task.
3. Acquiring social roles is the most important single aspect of adult socialization. Each person performs many roles that constitute his or her role sets. In old age, the individual discards old rules without acquiring new ones, making the role sets fewer in number.

Table 6.3 MAJOR ROLE TRANSITIONS IN THE LATER YEARS

Socialization Properties	Retirement	Widowhood	Institutionalization
Role loss: Giving up of a role	Loss of worker role	Loss of spouse role	Loss of community resident role
Role ambiguity: Vague and ill-defined role	Retiree's role is vague	Widow/widower's role is vague	Nursing-home resident role is not vague but instead is well structured
Role discontinuity: Lack of preparation for new role	Worker role to retiree role results in conflict in values and norms	Spouse role to widow role results in conflict in values and norms	Community resident role to nursing-home resident role results in conflict in values and norms
Anticipatory socialization: Preparation for new role	Retirement planning programs/friends, co-workers, and retirees	Watching those already widowed; nursing sick mate	Visiting nursing home; trial period
Resocialization: Replacing of old values and norms with new ones	Replacing work commitment with leisure commitment	Replacing dependence with independence	Replacing independence with dependence

4. The major role losses that occur in later life are caused by the events of retirement and widowhood. Lowenthal and Haven in their research on role loss found that having a close friend in whom to confide helps to soften the loss of major roles. Those persons with confidants were found to be less depressed and better satisfied than those without confidants.

5. Two major theories in gerontology are the disengagement theory and the activity theory. The disengagement theory maintains that aging results in a loss of roles because of the inevitable and mutual withdrawal of the individual and society from each other. The activity theory stresses a continuation of the individual's role performance through substitutes for the roles relinquished. Neither theory adequately explains the aging process.

6. Role ambiguity occurs when there are no clearly defined expectations governing a role, and there is considerable role ambiguity in the transitions to retirement and old age.

7. Role discontinuity results from a lack of preparation for the new roles acquired at each stage of life. In our society there is a discontinuity in the socialization process for old age.

8. The most effective type of resocialization occurs in total institutions such as nursing homes. On entering a nursing home, the older person needs some resocialization to help him or her adapt to the new social world.

9. A role model is an individual whose behavior in a certain role provides a pattern for others. Rosow argues that older people have role models, but that they are inappropriate.

KEY TERMS

socialization   *role discontinuity*
role   *anticipatory socialization*
role set   *role rehearsal*
role loss   *gradual retirement*
disengagement theory   *resocialization*
activity theory   *total institution*
looking-glass self   *role model*
role ambiguity

FOR FURTHER STUDY

Achenbaum, Andrew (1980). *Old age in the new land.* Baltimore: Johns Hopkins University Press.

Offers a detailed account of the role and status of the elderly in the United States since 1790.

Blau, Zena S. (1981). *Aging in a changing society.* New York: Watts.

Primarily focuses on the status of the elderly and the relationships between identity and role losses.

George, Linda K. (1980). *Role transitions in later life.* Monterey, CA: Brooks/Cole.

Explores the types of transitions commonly encountered as one ages and traces their consequences.

Rosow, Irving (1974). *Socialization to old age.* Berkeley: University of California Press.

An excellent book on adult socialization theory.

Chapter
7

Changes and Adaptations in Later Life

Why do we age? This question has posed a fascinating puzzle for scientists for centuries. Hayflick (1987) suggests that instead of asking why we age, the proper question might be: "Why do we live as long as we do?" Old age is an experience that involves a complex balance of biological, social, and psychological factors; all three are interdependent. For example, a person who is lonely may not eat well and as a result may develop symptoms of malnutrition, which in turn can interfere with mental functioning. A person with a hearing loss may become socially isolated, which can lead to an emotional disorder as well as a decline in mental competence. Or a grieving widower may develop psychosomatic symptoms and be forced to retire (Butler & Lewis, 1977).

Because of the close-knit interrelationship of these three factors, we will now give some attention to the biological and psychological aspects of aging. In this chapter, we will first briefly examine some of the biological theories of aging, and then discuss some of the physiological changes and psychological aspects of aging, followed by some functional and organic disorders related to aging.

BIOLOGICAL THEORIES OF AGING

Many theories have been suggested to try to explain the enigma of aging. It has been estimated that there are more than 20 biological theories of aging. Shock (1977) has classified these theories into three principal groups. The first group, genetic theories, explains aging in terms of defects that occur in the transmission of information to the cells. The second group, nongenetic theories, focuses on changes that take place in the cells that interfere with their performance. The third group, physiological theories, explains aging on the basis of the malfunction of a single organ system or some impairment of the regulatory and control mechanisms of the body. Some examples from each group are given in Box 7.1.

Today the autoimmune theory and the immune system are the focus of much gerontological research because they appear to have great promise in increasing our understanding of the sources of aging and many of the more harmful diseases associated with aging. The immune system protects the body from invasion by unfriendly proteins (antigens). With age the system is no longer able faultlessly to distinguish friend from foe and, as a result, it may produce antibodies to attack and destroy the very cells it is supposed to protect.

Substantial evidence shows that with age the autoimmune antibodies increase in the blood. Also such "immune type" diseases as rheumatoid arthritis, anemia, adult-onset diabetes and cancer tend to be age related. Makinodan and his associates (1977, 1985) experimented with old mice by injecting them with cells from young mice. He found that their resistance to disease increased so dramatically that they survived large doses of disease-producing bacteria that previously would have been deadly. Some scientists speculate that in the future, people could have their white blood cells frozen and stored away during youth, and then could use them in old age to revitalize their immune systems.

Box 7.1   **Biological Theories of Aging**

Genetic Theories

1. *Somatic mutation theory.* Cells become injured from radiation or from other causes and change in their inherited characteristics. These mutations accumulate in the cells and eventually produce functional failure.

2. *Error catastrophe theory.* As cells continue to function, random errors may occur in the process of new protein synthesis. In time these errors accumulate and eventually cause death.

Nongenetic Theories

1. *Wear-and-tear theory.* Assumes that the living organism is like a machine: from extended usage, its parts wear out and the machine breaks down. Similarly, aging is seen as a product of the gradual deterioration of the organs of the body.

2. *Waste-accumulation theory.* Harmful substances and waste products that cannot be eliminated build up within the various cells. In time, these wastes interfere with the normal functioning of the cells.

3. *Cross-linking theory.* Cross-linkages or bonds occur between parts of the same molecule or between the molecules themselves. These bonds, which tend to accumulate over time, change the properties of the molecules and hamper their function.

4. *Free radical theory.* Asserts that aging and cell death occur from the damaging effects of free radicals. These chemical components are produced during metabolism and are a by-product of normal cells. However, if they are allowed to accumulate they can damage the cell as well as cause mutations of chromosomes.

Physiological Theories

1. *Stress theory.* Proposes that aging results from a gradual build-up of stresses in daily life. These stresses leave residuals that persist, accumulate, and eventually exhaust the reserve capacities of the body.

2. *Single-organ theories.* The most popular of the single-organ theories attempts to explain aging in terms of the failure of the cardiovascular system. This failure is caused by arteriosclerosis, a disease that deteriorates the blood vessels.

3. *Autoimmune theory.* Postulates that aging results from the development of antibodies that attack and destroy the normal cells in the body that they are supposed to protect. With age, defects occur in the body's immune system with the result that it cannot distinguish itself from foreign substances.

Source: Adapted from Nathan W. Shock, "Biological Theories of Aging." In James E. Birren and K. Warner Schaie (Eds.), *Handbook of the Psychology of Aging.* New York: Van Nostrand Reinhold, 1977, pp. 103–113.

The fact that each species has a fixed life span has led scientists to conclude that the major factors setting the upper limits of the life span must be genetically programmed. Work done by Hayflick (1965) shows that certain cells of the body are capable of only a limited number of divisions, after which the cells die. Hayflick put human embryo cells in a culture; they doubled approximately 50 times and then stopped. In contrast, cells taken from old animals undergo from 20 to 25 cell divisions only. The finite capacity for cells to divide is now called the *Hayflick limit*. His work suggests that there is a cellular clock within us that runs down at a certain predetermined time.

At present, no single theory explains the complexities of the aging process. Most theories do not view aging in terms of the total organism and fail to take into account the relationships and interdependence between tissues, cells, and organs. Perhaps, instead of a single theory, a combination of theories is needed to explain the various aspects of aging.

PHYSIOLOGICAL CHANGES

Although we are not exactly sure why people age, we do know that, despite popular belief, no one dies of old age. Aging is not a disease. Aging simply increases the chances that a person may die of any one of a host of diseases. We also know that aging is a universal phenomenon. Animals such as mice, horses, dogs, and rabbits all grow old in ways similar to human beings. Furthermore, different organs of the body age at various rates. Because of this fact, it is possible for a 65-year-old person to have, in effect, a 55-year-old heart and 70-year-old lungs.

Not only are there variations within people as far as aging is concerned, but there are variations among people. Individuals age at such varying rates that it is hard to determine what the "average" physical changes in old age are. Not all of the physical changes described in the following discussion will happen to everyone. Also, the degree to which people are affected by these changes will vary.

Skin

The first tell-tale signs of aging are in the skin and hair. The skin may become dry and lose its elasticity; there is a lessening of the fat and supportive tissue. These conditions cause the skin to wrinkle. About middle age or sometimes even sooner, the hair begins to gray and later turns white. Besides inherited baldness, in males, there is a thinning of the hair in both men and women due to the atrophy of hair follicles. The loss of subcutaneous tissue and the decrease in the number of nerve cells of the skin, often referred to as heat and cold receptors, are in part responsible for older people's diminished ability to maintain a constant body temperature. This is why older people often complain of being cold while young people in the room find the temperature quite comfortable.

Skeletal System

Although a slight reduction in height occurs with age, some of this shrinkage is due to a bent posture. An older person may walk slightly stooped, with hips and knees partially bent and the neck flexed. Much of this postural change is due to the thinning

"Fred got his second wind at eighty. (Drawing by Ross; © 1989 The New Yorker Magazine, Inc.)

of the cartilage between the spinal discs, which causes the spine to compress and bend. Bones become lighter, increasingly porous, and brittle as calcium is depleted; elasticity in joints and joint cartilage is lost to a varying degree.

Muscle strength declines at varying ages depending on the complexity of the task. For example, in a task involving a single muscle group such as pulling and pushing stationary objects, muscle strength tends to decline after age 40. But in the task of turning a crank, requiring coordination of opposing muscle groups, the decline in performance begins as early as age 25 (Shock, 1985).

Heart

Studies in the 1950s reported that cardiac output, the volume of blood pumped per minute by the heart, declined at the rate of 1 percent yearly beginning at about age 20. Recent research has found no such decline. It now appears that coronary artery disease, physical conditioning, and other such factors accounted for this decline in the earlier studies and not aging itself (Fleg, 1987).

Lungs

The vital capacity of the lungs, which is the total amount of air one can breathe in and out in a single breath, reduces with age. At age 70, this vital capacity is reduced to less than 50 percent of what it was at age 30. The change is related to the weakening of the muscles in the rib cage and the decreased elasticity of the lungs.

Gastrointestinal Tract

The great preoccupation of older people with food intake and elimination stems from several factors. Difficulties in eating may be related to poorly fitting dentures, loss of teeth, or a decrease in the production of digestive juices. The decline in the muscular contractions that push materials along the digestive tract, along with the weakened muscles, may contribute to constipation, a common ailment of the elderly.

Urinary Tract

Starting around middle age, there is a decline in the function of the kidneys. Although they lose about one-third of their efficiency by age 70, they still are able to maintain waste products in the blood at normal level. The bladder does not change significantly with age but there is a diminished capacity for urine retention, causing older persons to get up during the night to urinate. Also, enlargement of the prostate gland, a common occurrence in males after about age 50, requires frequent urination because of the difficulty in completely emptying the bladder.

Reproductive Organs

Most age-related changes in the reproductive organs occur very gradually except for menopause, which may begin rather abruptly. The "change of life" usually occurs between ages 45 and 55 in females, accompanied by an atrophy of the reproductive organs. Some maintain that a similar, though less dramatic, condition occurs in males. Often a woman's sexual desire may increase following menopause because she has been freed from the fear of pregnancy. Much research shows that probably two-thirds of elderly people maintain sexual interest and activity well into their seventies. Many people are sexually active in their eighties and beyond. If an elderly person is in good health and has a suitable partner, he or she is as capable of having sex as a younger person. (See Chapter 8, "Sexuality, Aging, and Society," for a discussion of this topic.)

Senses

A familiar complaint of people as they age is that their arms have gotten too short for them to hold a newspaper or a book so they can read it. One of the most common visual problems associated with aging is *presbyopia,* or farsightedness, which is the loss of ability to focus on close objects. This condition generally occurs between 40 and 50 years of age. Opacity of the eye lens, known as a *cataract,* is also common among elderly people. The condition necessitates surgery only when it interferes with useful vision. With age, more light is required for maximum vision as the pupil becomes smaller in size. For example, people past 60 need twice as might light as they needed when they were 40.

Changes in hearing begin around middle age. The most common source of auditory decline is a gradual loss of the ability to hear high frequencies. This condition is due to the loss of the eardrum's elasticity. Hearing impairments are among the most common chronic conditions affecting the elderly.

Most research about the senses reveals that in old age there is a decline in taste and smell sensitivity. These losses may result from a combination of factors, including aging, disease conditions, or drugs. With age the preference for stronger, more tart, and less sweet tastes increases. Because the elderly perceive a range of smells as less intense than the young, they are more tolerant of unpleasant odors and less proficient in identifying common odors (Schiffman & Covery, 1984).

PSYCHOLOGICAL CHANGES

Although there is some general agreement on the many physical changes occurring with advanced age—such as the skin wrinkles or the lungs take in less air—the same agreement does not exist regarding the psychological changes associated with aging, such as intellectual functioning. Psychological changes are not as clear cut and are more difficult to measure and assess. The question of whether or not intelligence declines in old age is a controversial one. Some reasons for this controversy relate to the type of research methods used to measure intelligence.

Intelligence

The Army-Apha test, an early intelligence test developed during World War I, was administered to soldiers between the ages of 18 and 60. The findings showed that intelligence peaked at early adulthood and then began to decline. Similar results were obtained in the early 1930s when the test was given to residents of a New England community. Later, David Wechsler (1958), whose intelligence tests have been among the most widely used in the United States, developed the Wechsler Adult Intelligence Scale (WAIS), which was adjusted for different age groups. The results from the 1955 standardized version of this test also showed a drop in intelligence with age. Wechsler found that mental abilities peaked at about age 24, with a decline beginning after age 30 and continuing into old age.

A major methodological issue of these studies was that they were cross-sectional, in that each subject was tested at a given point in time and the results then compared with other age groups (see Chapter 1, "The Field and Its Methods"). But people of different ages differ in generations—the cohorts that they belong to. Therefore, differences in test scores from a cross-sectional study could be due to age, or to cohort differences, or both. Longitudinal studies attempt to overcome this problem by comparing the same individual at several points in time. Though some weaknesses are associated with the longitudinal design (such as differentiating age-related changes-from those changes due to events in the environment, and dealing with the problem

Box 7.2 ## Premature Aging

There is a rare childhood disease that serves as a model for accelerated aging. The disease is *progeria*, which has been referred to as nature's unnatural experiment in premature aging. The victims of this disease resemble very old, small people. At birth progeria victims appear normal but at about 1 to 3 years of age, their growth becomes retarded, their skin begins to wrinkle, and they lose their hair. Although their heads are of normal size, they appear larger because of their small bodies. They weigh no more than about 30 pounds and never get any larger than a 3- to 5-year-old. Progeria victims bear a close resemblance to one another because of their small faces, prominent eyes and beak-shaped noses. They are normal to above normal in intelligence.

By the time the child reaches 10 to 15, he or she is likely to suffer from atherosclerosis, high blood pressure, and congestive heart failure. Most progeric children only live to their teens and usually die of heart disease. The exact causes of progeria are unknown but it is believed to be related to an inherited defect based on a recessive trait.

Sources: Ewald W. Busse and Dan G. Blazer. ''The Theories and Processes of Aging.'' In E. W. Busse and D. G. Blazer (Eds.), *Handbook of Geriatric Psychiatry*. New York: Van Nostrand Reinhold, 1980, pp. 3–45; W. Ted Brown. ''Progeroid Syndromes.'' In George L. Maddox (Ed.), *The Encyclopedia of Aging*. New York: Springer, 1987, pp. 542–543. (Photograph by Joe Vericker.)

of dropouts and death), overall the longitudinal method is far superior to the cross-sectional design in investigating age changes within individuals.

The first longitudinal studies of intelligence began in the 1950s and revealed quite different results from the previous cross-sectional ones. The longitudinal studies helped put an end to the myth that people lose their intellectual abilities after age 25 and steadily decline into incompetence by their sixties. Schaie and associates (1983) gave intelligence tests to people ranging in age from 22 to 70 over a period of 21 years. On the basis of the longitudinal data collected, Schaie concludes that there is little, if any, decline for five mental abilities—verbal meaning, reasoning ability, numerical ability, word fluency, and spatial visualization—until the sixties, and even then the decline is slight. In some areas such as knowledge and information, there is an increase.

According to James Birren (1976):

> There appears to be a continual increase in the amount of information that we have stored within us. All things being equal, if you have good health, you will continue to store information as you age. Your vocabulary is going to be significantly larger at age sixty-five than it was at forty, or even than it was when you graduated from college. Your vocabulary may double, in fact, over these years. As a college graduate you may have known 20,000 words and at sixty-five you may know over 40,000 words. This means that intellectual functioning defined as stored information, is increasing as you age.

In general, much of the evidence today points to very little, if any, intellectual decline up to age 80 and beyond if one stays in reasonably good health and continues to be active intellectually. The one aspect of mental performance that does appear to change in most cases, however, is a slowing down in the speed of response.

Motor Performance

The time an older person takes to cross a street is longer than the time a younger person takes to do the same thing. Older people are slower in sizing up situations regarding oncoming cars and traffic lights. When they step off the curb, they do so

---

Box 7.3   Reversing Intellectual Decline

In a study conducted by K. Warner Schaie and Sherry L. Willis, a group of people whose average age was over 72 were given five one-hour training sessions, then tested and compared with their own levels of cognitive ability of 14 years earlier. The training brought 40 percent back to their previous mark and helped many others to a less dramatic extent.

A substantial proportion of older people, Schaie and Willis conclude, were victims of the "use it or lose it" rule: Their intellectual abilities properly declined because of disuse and were not really lost. They can be regained, at least in part, through relatively simply and inexpensive educational training techniques.

Source: Alfie Kohn. "You Know What They Say. . .," *Psychology Today*, April 1988, p. 41.

more cautiously and often monitor their movements visually to avoid losing their balance and falling. By watching their feet, they slow down, and some of their attention to the environment is reduced. They then walk across the street at a slow pace, often following younger people.

This slowness of behavior, one of the most distinguishing characteristics of older persons, is due to processes within the central nervous system. These processes involve such factors as the loss of nerve cells, limitation of transmission speed, and a decline in neural excitability. As a result, the elderly are limited to the number of behaviors they can emit per unit of time. This slowness of response with age is found in animals as well.

An elderly person adapts to slowness of response by avoiding situations with unusual time pressures. This avoidance is clearly demonstrated in work situations.

(Drawing by Stevenson; © 1989 The New Yorker Magazine, Inc.)

Older workers are seldom found in jobs that require continuous activity under paced conditions. An interesting finding, confirmed by several studies, is that men engaged in moderately heavy work tended to be older than those doing lighter work: The performance of heavy work is usually slower and more self-paced, which in the long run is easier for an older person than light work carried out under pressure (Welford, 1977).

Most studies show that the performance and productivity of older workers are in most cases the same as or better than those of younger workers. What older workers lose in speed, they tend to make up in accuracy, experience, and commitment. Contrary to popular opinion, accident rates are usually higher for younger workers than for older workers, which may be explained in part by the fact that the older workers exert more caution, take fewer chances, and exercise better judgment on the job. Other research indicates that, in general, older workers have fewer absences because of illness than do younger workers. When older workers do become ill, however, the time off required for recovery tends to be longer than that for younger workers.

The worker over 65, it should be remembered, is a highly select sample of the total population. Workers who could not perform well or who were less skilled or in poor health have left their jobs earlier. Those who continue to work beyond 65 exemplify the survival of the fittest. Birren (1964) notes: "If total job behavior is considered, the older worker is sometimes found to be better in comparison with the young worker, particularly if such characteristics as accuracy, absenteeism, and motivation are considered."

Learning and Memory

If a young or middle-aged man when leaving a social gathering does not remember where he left his hat, observed Samuel Johnson, it is nothing—people will overlook his behavior and explain it as carelessness. But if the same thing happens to an old man, people will shrug their shoulders and say, "His memory is going." Memory lapses occur at all ages, but the interpretation depends on one's stage in the life course.

Memory is often divided into primary and secondary memory. *Primary memory* refers to a temporary memory system that stores information from a few seconds to a minute or so and has a limited capacity of about seven or eight items. Information from primary memory is often forgotten, an example being a telephone number that one obtains from directory assistance and then forgets after dialing it. Most research reports little or no decline in primary memory capacity with age. However, what most people think of when they think of memory is *secondary memory*. This memory system stores information for long periods of time or even permanently (except in cases of brain injury or disease) and holds limitless amounts of information.

Unlike primary memory, there is a marked decline in secondary memory with age. A major function of secondary memory involves the acquisition of information or learning. Many research studies reveal that although older persons can and do learn, they just do not learn as fast as younger people. Laboratory tasks often require responses that are too quick for many older persons. But when ample time is given, elderly persons show significant improvements in their performance. Much of what appears to be a learning deficit in old age may actually be more of a response limitation (Botwinick, 1984).

A major problem related to learning is the attitude and expectation of society toward older people. Society expects older people to be incompetent and to fail. Because of this, many older people become anxious in learning situations and avoid any chance of failure by not answering even when they know the correct responses. If they do respond, they proceed cautiously and slowly to minimize error. Many older people accept the negative conception society has of them. This acceptance in turn undermines their self-confidence and their ability to learn. It is much like a self-fulfilling prophesy: One begins with a false definition of the situation that elicits a new behavior that makes the originally false conception come true (see Chapter 1).

Creativity

Lehman (1953) reports that the outstanding achievements of creative persons—the achievements for which people are best known—occurred early in life. He found a sharp rise from the twenties to a peak in the thirties or early forties, and from then on a gradual decline takes place. But his sample included many short-lived persons; their presence caused the average age of greatest notable achievement to be lower and thus exaggerated the declines with aging.

Using a different approach, Dennis (1966) studied only people who lived to the age of 79 or older, and his research focused on the quantity of creative output instead of quality. He classified their fields of work into three major categories: scholarship (history, philosophy, and literature), the sciences, and the arts (music, poetry, and drama). He found that peak productivity for scholars occurred in their later years—up to their seventies. Scientists were the most productive between their forties and sixties, and artists had their highest outputs in their thirties and forties. Furthermore, Dennis asserted that there was a correlation between high productivity and high quality. In order to test this assertion, Simonton (1984) analyzed the productivity of ten of the most highly regarded composers of classical music. He found quality and quantity to be correlated: The times at which the composers created their most notable works were also times of high productivity. His findings also reveal that high-quality creative work can occur throughout the entire life course. There have been many people who have produced notable achievements, if not their most outstanding achievements, in their old age.

ADAPTATION

Does personality change with age? Does personality influence how one adapts to aging? Do different personality types age differently? The following are two classic studies that investigated the relationship between personality type and aging.

Personality Types

Reichard, Livson, and Petersen (1962) studied 87 elderly men aged 55 to 84. From their data based on interviews, the researchers identified three types that adapted well to aging and retirement and two types that adapted poorly. The first group that

This painting of an aged musician reflects young Picasso's own sense of isolation and gloom at the age of 22. Throughout his lifetime, he produced about 14,000 paintings and drawings, 100,000 prints; 34,000 book illustrations and 3000 models and sculptural works. He continued to be productive until his death at age 92. (The Art Institute of Chicago)

adapted well was identified as the "mature": They felt that their lives had been rewarding, and they faced aging without regret. These men continued to participate in many satisfying activities and social relationships and moved easily into aging and made the most of it. A second group, the "rocking-chair men," also adapted success-fully to aging, but in another way: They welcomed the opportunity to be free of responsibilities and were content to take it easy. The third group that adapted well was called the "armored"; they had strong defenses against growing old and fought off the fear of aging by staying active and keeping busy. To them, activity was a compulsion instead of a source of enjoyment.

Among the poorly adapting men were two groups: the "angry men" and the "self-haters." The angry men felt that they had failed in life and blamed others for their failures; they found aging difficult. The self-haters looked back on their lives with much regret, and they blamed themselves, instead of others, for their misfortunes and failures. These men felt depressed, worthless, and inferior.

Reichard and her associates note that the histories of both the armored and rocking-chair types suggest that their personalities showed very little change throughout their lives. Furthermore, the rocking-chair type shows that disengagement can be a satisfactory adaptation for some older people. Also, the researchers found that the poor adaptations made by the angry men and self-haters were a continuation of lifelong personality problems. By the same token, the mature group suggests that the same factors that led to a good adaptation in the earlier years continue to exert their influence in the later years.

In the second study of personality and aging, Bernice Neugarten and her associates (1968) studied 59 men and women aged 70 to 79. They made assessments in three areas: personality type, amount of role activity, and degree of life satisfaction. From these data they derived four major personality types, which they called the "integrated," the "armored-defended," the "passive dependent," and the "unintegrated." These four groups were then further divided into 8 patterns.

The first type, the integrated, was composed of persons who functioned well, whose abilities had not declined, and who had feelings of high regard for themselves. All scored high in life satisfaction, they were in control of their impulses, they were flexible and mature. Three patterns of aging emerged from this type. Those in the pattern called the "reorganizers" engaged in a wide variety of activities and tried to keep active. As one activity was lost, they found another to replace it. Another pattern was the "focused"; this group was selective in its activities and concentrated only on a few activities that were important to them. The third pattern was the "disengaged," made up of persons who had voluntarily moved away from many of their social contacts and role commitments. Their approach to aging was one of calmness, contentment, and withdrawal. They epitomized the rocking-chair type of aging.

The second major type of personality was the armored or the defended. These persons were ambitious, striving, and oriented toward success and achievement, and they maintained strong defenses against aging. This group was divided into two patterns of aging: the "holding-on" and the "constricted." The holding-on pattern consisted of persons who embodied the "I'll die with my boots on" philosophy. To them old age was a threat, and they believed that keeping busy would help ward off anxieties about aging. Their life satisfaction ranged from medium to high. The second pattern, constricted, included people who tried to defend themselves against aging by limiting their social contacts and conserving their energies to fend off "what they seem to regard as imminent collapse." Their life satisfaction was high to medium.

The third type of personality, the passive dependent, yielded two patterns of aging. The "succorance-seeking" included those persons who were very dependent on others for emotional support and managed well as long as they had one or two persons to lean on. The second pattern, the "apathetic," was composed of very passive and submissive individuals who were low in role activity.

The last type, the unintegrated personality, showed a "disorganized" pattern of aging and consisted of persons who suffered deterioration in their thought processes and experienced loss of control over their emotions. They barely managed to maintain themselves in their communities. Table 7.1 gives a summary of the personality types that we have been discussing.

Neugarten and her associates conclude that personality type is the central factor in predicting which individuals will age successfully and which ones will not. These eight patterns are probably predictable and well established by middle age. The key concept appears to be adaptation. Furthermore, they note that there are no dramatic

Table 7.1 PERSONALITY PATTERNS IN AGING

Personality type	Characteristics of the type	Role activity	Life satisfaction
Integrated	Well-adjusted persons with high self-regard, mature; maintain comfortable degree of control over life's impulses		
Reorganizer	Competent people, engaged in many activities, who substitute new activities for lost ones	High	High
Focused	Persons selective in their activities and who concentrate on one or two roles	Medium	High
Disengaged	Those who voluntarily move away from role commitments and social relations; they are calm, contented, and withdrawn	Low	High
Armored-Defended	Striving and ambitious persons with high defenses against anxieties associated with aging		
Holding-on	Those who try to maintain patterns of middle age as long as possible; to them old age is a threat	High or medium	High
Constricted	Persons who defend themselves against aging by limiting their social contacts and trying to conserve their energies	Low or medium	High or medium
Passive-Dependent			
Succorance-seeking	Those people who are dependent on others for emotional support	High or medium	High or medium
Apathetic	Persons who are passive and submissive	Low	Medium or low
Unintegrated			
Disorganized	Persons with defects in psychological functions	Low	Medium or low

Source: Adapted from Bernice L. Neugarten, Robert J. Havighurst, and Sheldon S. Tobin, "Personality and Patterns of Aging." In Bernice L. Neugarten (Ed.), *Middle Age and Aging.* Chicago: The University of Chicago Press, 1968, pp. 173–177.

changes or sharp discontinuities of personality with age, but rather a trend toward increasing consistency. More recently, the findings from a major longitudinal study done by McCrae and Costa (1984) are consistent with the work of Neugarten and her associates in that they reveal that "People stay much the same in their basic dispositions." Personality traits appear to be enduring and stable. In other words, unhappy, complaining middle-aged people are likely to become unhappy, complaining old people. And contrary to what many believe, old people do not get grouchy; grouchy people get old.

Stress and Illness

Some people tend to tolerate change with minimal stress, whereas change can have a devastating effect on others. According to Holmes and Rahe (1967), any type of change that substantially alters one's normal routine is stressful; it makes no difference whether the change is pleasant or unpleasant. To evaluate empirically how stress from major changes in one's daily life may affect susceptibility to an illness or precede the onset of disease, Holmes and Rahe developed the "Social Readjustment Rating Scale" shown in Table 7.2. They ranked 43 commonly occurring life events that cause stress and assigned mean values to them to coincide with the impact of each specific event on one's life. The items range from the death of a spouse, with a mean value of 100, to a minor traffic violation, with a value of 11. Though the death of a spouse carries the highest mean value, other stressful experiences likely in the life of an older person rate fairly high. For example, death of a close family member rates 63; personal injury or illness, 53; retirement, 45; change in financial state, 38; death of a close friend, 37; and change in living conditions, 23. According to the mean values Holmes and Rahe assigned to life events, some of the most stressful changes in life occur in old age.

Research reveals that widowhood has been found to bring negative changes in physical health along with increased mortality rates. Older persons who recently lost a spouse were more likely to report the development of a new illness than those elderly whose marriages remained intact. Numerous other studies have supported the work of Holmes and Rahe and documented the link between stress and illness (Gallagher & Thompson, 1983; Thompson, Breckenridge, Gallagher, and Peterson, 1984).

Most older people, then, must constantly adapt to changes within themselves as well as to changes in their social world. Many changes result from loss in one form or another and place great stress on emotions. They may be physiological or psychological losses, such as losses in sensory acuities, decline in physical health and strength, changes in bodily appearance, or a slowing down in reaction time. Or they may be social or extrinsic losses, such as loss of significant others, a decline in standard of living, and losses of prestige, occupational status, and social roles.

Adaptation to these losses, along with the problems and crises that accompany them, are a main part of the tasks that confront the elderly. But how does one adapt to these losses? Pfeiffer (1977) notes that adaptation involves replacing some social losses with new relationships, acquiring new roles to take the place of those relinquished, and retraining lost capacities, such as receiving speech or physical therapy after a stroke.

Table 7.2   THE SOCIAL READJUSTMENT RATING SCALE

Rank	Life event	Mean value
1	Death of spouse	100
2	Divorce	73
3	Marital separation	65
4	Jail term	63
5	Death of close family member	63
6	Personal injury or illness	53
7	Marriage	50
8	Fired at work	47
9	Marital reconciliation	45
10	Retirement	45
11	Change in health of family member	44
12	Pregnancy	40
13	Sex difficulties	39
14	Gain of new family member	39
15	Business readjustment	39
16	Change in financial state	38
17	Death of a close friend	37
18	Change to different line of work	36
19	Change in number of arguments with spouse	35
20	Mortgage over $10,000	31
21	Foreclosure of mortgage or loan	30
22	Change in responsibilities at work	29
23	Son or daughter leaving home	29
24	Trouble with in-laws	29
25	Outstanding personal achievement	28
26	Wife begin or stop work	26
27	Begin or end school	26
28	Change in living conditions	25
29	Revision of personal habits	24
30	Trouble with boss	23
31	Change in work hours or conditions	20
32	Change in residence	20
33	Change in schools	20
34	Change in recreation	19
35	Change in church activities	19
36	Change in social activities	18
37	Mortgage or loan less than $10,000	17
38	Change in sleeping habits	16
39	Change in number of family get-togethers	15
40	Change in eating habits	15
41	Vacation	13
42	Christmas	12
43	Minor violations of the law	11

Source: Reprinted with permission from *Journal of Psychosomatic Research,* 11 (1967), 216, Thomas H. Holmes and Richard Rahe, ''The Social Readjustment Rating Scale.'' Copyright 1967 Pergamon Press, Ltd.

Defense Mechanisms

All persons at one time or another use various defense mechanisms to respond to inner conflicts and frustrations. With age, they continue to use some of the adaptive techniques of earlier years, or they may add some new ones. The following are some defense mechanisms most often utilized by older people to respond to frustrating situations and the anxieties generated by the losses associated with aging (Butler & Lewis, 1982).

1. *Denial.* Many elderly people refuse to accept the fact that they are old. They continue to think of themselves as middle-aged or younger. Denial of old age and death manifests itself in the "Peter Pan" syndrome, an older person pretending to be young.
2. *Counterphobia.* A defense mechanism, related to denial, in which one over-compensates for feared situations. For example, an elderly man experiencing dizzy spells may climb a ladder to paint his house.
3. *Projection.* Some older persons, in an effort to relieve their anxieties, attribute their own undesirable feelings and attitudes to others. They may accuse merchants of cheating them, neighbors of stealing from them, or their children of neglecting them. Some of their complaints may be legitimate, but many are not. Nevertheless, projection does occur, and at times older people may manifest fears and suspicions to the point of being paranoid.
4. *Displacement.* Older persons may adjust to situations by shifting the blame from the real cause of difficulties to other persons, objects, or situations. An older woman, for example, may blame her husband for her poor health.
5. *Selective memory.* Many older persons try to forget unhappy and painful present situations and events by talking about the past, when they were happier and more content. Selective memory occurs when older people screen out the unpleasant events of the past, often referring to the past as "the good old days." Actually, a more accurate description would probably be "the good and bad old days."

FUNCTIONAL AND ORGANIC DISORDERS

Sometimes when losses occur in rapid succession, the emotional stress becomes too great, and an individual may find that the adaptive mechanisms previously used in coping with situations are no longer adequate. This lack of ability to cope may result in a *functional disorder*—a disorder for which no physical cause has been found and whose origin appears to be emotional. In contrast to a functional disorder, an *organic disorder* has a clearly established physical basis.

Depression

The most frequent functional disorder of old age is depression. It occurs with varying degrees of intensity and duration. Some periods of depression last for only a few minutes, while others may last for several days or longer. Depressive periods are often a pathological response to the loss of a significant person or object. Guilt, unresolved grief, anger and loneliness may be the underlying causes of depressive reactions. Psychological characteristics of depression include discouragement, a sense of uselessness, a loss of self-esteem, apathy, and pessimism about the present and future. Depression can interfere with thought processes and can slow down speech and physical movements. Such symptoms as loss of appetite, insomnia, and fatigue frequently accompany depression. Severe depression is the most common cause of suicide (see Chapter 20 for a discussion of this topic).

Alzheimer's Disease

An example of an organic disorder is *Alzheimer's disease,* the most prevalent brain impairment of old age and one of the principal reasons for institutionalizing the elderly. It is estimated that the disease affects 2.5 to 3 million older Americans. The

Depression is one of the most common complaints of older people. (Nick Myers)

cost to society of care and treatment for Alzheimer's patients is estimated at $48 billion annually (U.S. Senate Special Committee on Aging, 1988). Some estimates run as high as $60 billion to $80 billion per year.

Named for the German neurologist Alois Alzheimer, who first recognized the disease in 1907, Alzheimer's disease is characterized by a progressive deterioration of mental functioning. Its range of symptoms includes loss of memory, especially of recent events; impairment of judgment and abstract thinking; and a deterioration of personality. In the later stages an individual may become totally dependent, requiring 24-hour care. This round-the-clock attention places a strain on the family. In fact, being a caregiver to an Alzheimer's patient is so exhausting that it has been dubbed the "the 36-hour day" (Mace & Rabins, 1981). As a result, many who suffer from this disease end up in nursing homes.

The two most prominent brain changes as a result of Alzheimer's disease are neuritic plaques and neurofibrillary tangles. Neuritic plaques are clusters of degenerating nerve endings that are found outside the nerve cells and surround a core of abnormal protein. Neurofibrillary tangles consist of nerve fibers of the brain cells that become twisted around each other. Although heredity does not play an obvious role, there is an increased chance of developing the disease if one's parents have or had it. The chances for developing the disease increases with age and with being female. There are a number of theories as to the cause of Alzheimer's disease, but at present its cause and cure still remain a mystery. (For an Alzheimer's quiz, see Box 7.4.)

THE POSITIVE SIDE OF AGING

Most research and writing about the elderly appears to concentrate on the negative aspects of aging, stressing mental and physical decline, with little or no attention being given to the positive side of growing old. In fact, having just read this sentence, you are probably asking yourself whether there *are* any positive aspects to aging. We need to change the popular, negative concept of aging and achieve a more balanced view of both its positive and negative aspects.

Among the plus factors of later maturity is, first of all, an increase in general knowledge. The longer a person lives, the more facts and information that person is likely to accumulate. As we pointed out earlier, older people know more words and have a larger vocabulary.

Second, through experience a person develops better judgment and what is frequently referred to as wisdom. With maturity, an individual can meet new situations with greater deliberation and poise, which are the basis of good judgment: Busse and Pfeiffer (1977) note that "wisdom and judgment . . . come to full flower in old age, at least in some [persons]. Certain qualities, such as statesmanship, seem to be found more often in those of advanced years." Also, an older person is likely to have a higher level of occupational skill; this has been gained through long years of experience and practice, which no young person can possess.

Learning becomes more efficient with age. Young people deal with bits and pieces of information because they have not acquired the "filing system" that older

Box 7.4   **Alzheimer's Quiz**

Alzheimer's disease, named for German neurologist Alois Alzheimer, is much in the news these days. But how much do you really know about the disorder? Political scientist Neal B. Cutler of the Andrus Gerontology Center gave the following questions to a 1,500-person cross section of people older than 45 in the United States in November 1985. To compare your answers with theirs and with the correct answers, turn to page 149.

	True	False	Don't know
1. Alzheimer's disease can be contagious.	____	____	____
2. A person will almost certainly get Alzheimer's if they just live long enough.	____	____	____
3. Alzheimer's disease is a form of insanity.	____	____	____
4. Alzheimer's disease is a normal part of getting older, like gray hair or wrinkles.	____	____	____
5. There is no cure for Alzheimer's disease at present.	____	____	____
6. A person who has Alzheimer's disease will experience both mental and physical decline.	____	____	____
7. The primary symptom of Alzheimer's disease is memory loss.	____	____	____
8. Among persons older than age 75, forgetfulness most likely indicates the beginning of Alzheimer's disease.	____	____	____
9. When the husband or wife of an older person dies, the surviving spouse may suffer from a kind of depression that looks like Alzheimer's disease.	____	____	____
10. Stuttering is an inevitable part of Alzheimer's disease.	____	____	____
11. An older man is more likely to develop Alzheimer's disease than an older woman.	____	____	____
12. Alzheimer's disease is usually fatal.	____	____	____
13. The vast majority of persons suffering from Alzheimer's disease live in nursing homes.	____	____	____
14. Aluminum has been identified as a significant cause of Alzheimer's disease.	____	____	____
15. Alzheimer's disease can be diagnosed by a blood test.	____	____	____
16. Nursing-home expenses for Alzheimer's disease patients are covered by Medicare.	____	____	____
17. Medicine taken for high blood pressure can cause symptoms that look like Alzheimer's disease.	____	____	____

people possess because of their ability to assimilate and organize knowledge into conceptual compartments. Birren (1976) explains:

> With maturation comes a greater conceptual grasp so that we can size up the situation and then look to the relevant items in our store. This is what I call the race between the chunks and the bits. While younger people, say those between 18 and 22, can process more bits per second, and even though by age sixty the number may be halved, the older person may process bigger chunks. The race may go to the tortoise because he is chunking, and not to the hare because he is just bitting along.

With age, a person has achieved a real identity and is a "completed" being. The young person is still trying to find out who he or she is and to establish a sense of identity. With age, many potentials of earlier years have been realized: an established place in an occupation, in a family, with friends, and in a community. The individual has become a known entity. Only through the passage of time does one become a "real person"; time also makes one a more interesting person because over the years an individual has seen many things, met many people, and had many experiences. These give a person more to talk about and make the person more interesting to talk to (Tyson, 1975).

Another positive consequence of aging is an increase in personal freedom. After retirement, a person's time is no longer structured around an eight-hour work day. A person becomes his or her own boss. As children have reached adulthood, the parents' responsibilities are considerably diminished. Though income is likely to be less, obligations are fewer. Although the elderly have lost many roles at this point in the life cycle, they have gained greater freedom and an opportunity to do as they please (Bengtson & Manuel, 1981).

Lastly, Butler and Lewis (1982) note that older people experience a personal sense of the life cycle, something that younger people cannot have. "An inner sense of the life cycle . . . produces a profound awareness of change and evolution . . . and therefore a profound but nonmorbid realization of the previous and limited quantity of life. For older people it is not the same as 'feeling old'; it is instead a deep understanding of what it means to be human."

Box 7.5   # Aging Has Its Advantages

I must get into a topic . . . that I think has been overlooked by many, and it is easy to see why. I want to discuss the advantages of growing old. For one thing, it is a great satisfaction to be around fewer and fewer people who can say "You are too young to remember . . ." Or "That was before your time." Or "When I was your age . . ." I myself now know the pleasure of saying such things, effectively putting down the young, including those who are only in their early sixties.

Source: Richard Armour, *Going Like Sixty: A Light-hearted Look at the Later Years,* McGraw-Hill, New York, 1974, p. 49.

SUMMARY

1. There are many theories regarding why people age. These theories fall primarily into three major categories: genetic, nongenetic, and physiological. The two theories that seem to hold the greatest promise are the cross-linking and autoimmune theories.

2. Aging varies not only between persons but also within a person. Different systems of the body age at different rates. Though many physiological changes occur as one ages, not all of these changes happen to everyone or to the same degree.

3. In general there is little, if any, intellectual decline up to age 80 if one stays reasonably healthy and continues to be active mentally. However, there is a slowing down in response speed. The slowness of behavior is one of the most distinguishing characteristics of older persons.

4. Memory may be divided into types: primary and secondary. Primary memory (temporary memory) shows little or no decline with the aging process, whereas secondary memory (acquiring of information or learning) does show a marked decline. Older persons continue to learn, but just not as fast as younger persons.

5. Creativity, according to recent studies, can occur throughout the life course. Many persons have produced their most outstanding achievements in their old age. Personality type is a major factor in predicting whether one will age well or poorly. Personality does not change with age but is enduring and stable. People tend to have the same basic dispositions all their lives.

6. Various studies have documented the link between stress and illness. The loss of a spouse can bring negative changes in health along with increased mortality rates. Functional disorders are those that have no physical cause but are emotional in origin, such as depression; organic disorders, on the other hand, have a clearly established physical basis. Alzheimer's disease is an example of an organic disorder and is the most prevalent brain impairment of the elderly, affecting between 2.5 and 3 million older persons.

KEY TERMS

Hayflick limit
presbyopia
cataract
progeria
primary memory
secondary memory
denial

counterphobia
projection
displacement
selective memory
functional disorder
organic disorder
Alzheimer's disease

FOR FURTHER STUDY

Belsky, Janet (1984). *The psychology of aging: Theory, research and practice.* Monterey, CA: Brooks/Cole.

Examines gerontological psychology from the perspectives of research and practice.

Butler, Robert N., & Lewis, Myrna I. (1982). *Aging and mental health.* St. Louis: C. V. Mosby.

Emphasizes the emotional and mental disorders of old age and the principles that apply in their treatment and prevention.

Schaie, K. Warner, & Willis, Sherry L. (1986). *Adult development and aging.* Boston: Little, Brown.

A clearly written text on current psychological theory and research on the major stages of adult life.

Spence, Alexander P. (1989). *Biology of aging.* Englewood Cliffs, NJ: Prentice-Hall.

A highly readable book that discusses the biological changes that occur with the aging process.

Answers to Alzheimer's Quiz

	True	False	Don't know
1. **False.** There is no evidence that Alzheimer's is contagious, but given the concern and confusion about AIDS, it is encouraging that nearly everyone knows this fact about Alzheimer's.	3%	83%	14%
2. **False.** Alzheimer's is associated with old age, but it is a disease and not the inevitable consequence of aging.	9	80	11
3. **False.** Alzheimer's is a disease of the brain, but it is not a form of insanity. The fact that most people understand the distinction contrasts with the results of public-opinion studies concerning epilepsy that were done 35 years ago. At that time, almost half of the public thought that epilepsy, another disease of the brain, was a form of insanity.	7	78	15
4. **False.** Again, most of the public knows that Alzheimer's is not an inevitable part of aging.	10	77	13
5. **True.** Despite announcements of "breakthroughs," biomedical research is in the early laboratory and experimental stages and there is no known cure for the disease	75	8	17

(continued)

Answers to Alzheimer's Quiz (*Continued*)

	True	False	Don't know
6. **True.** Memory and cognitive decline are characteristic of the earlier stages of Alzheimer's disease, but physical decline follows in the later stages.	74	10	16
7. **True.** Most people know that this is the earliest sign of Alzheimer's disease.	62	19	19
8. **False.** Most people also know that while Alzheimer's produces memory loss, memory loss may have some other cause.	16	61	23
9. **True.** This question, like number 8, measures how well people recognize that other problems can mirror Alzheimer's symptoms. This is crucial because many of these other problems are treatable. In particular, depression can cause disorientation that looks like Alzheimer's.	49	20	30
10. **False.** Stuttering has never been linked to Alzheimer's. The question was designed to measure how willing people were to attribute virtually anything to a devastating disease.	12	46	42
11. **False.** Apart from age, research has not uncovered any reliable demographic or ethnic patterns. While there are more older women than men, both sexes are equally likely to get Alzheimer's.	15	45	40
12. **True.** Alzheimer's produces mental and physical decline that is eventually fatal, although the progression varies greatly among individuals.	40	33	27
13. **False.** The early and middle stages of the disease usually do not require institutional care. Only a small percentage of those with the disease live in nursing homes.	37	40	23
14. **False.** There is no evidence that using aluminum cooking utensils, pots or foil causes Alzheimer's, although aluminum compounds have been found in the brain tissue of many Alzheimer's patients. They may simply be side effects of the disease.	8	25	66
15. **False.** At present there is no definitive blood test that can determine with certainty that a patient has Alzheimer's disease. Accurate diagnosis is possible only upon autopsy. Recent studies suggest that genetic or blood testing may be able to identify Alzheimer's, but more research with humans is needed.	12	24	64

	True	False	Don't know
16. **False.** Medicare generally pays only for short-term nursing-home care subsequent to hospitalization and not for long-term care. Medicaid can pay for long-term nursing-home care, but since it is a state-directed program for the medically indigent, coverage for Alzheimer's patients depends upon state regulations and on the income of the patient and family.	16	23	61
17. **True.** As mentioned earlier, many medical problems have Alzheimer's-like symptoms and most of these other causes are treatable. Considering how much medicine older people take, it is unfortunate that so few people know that medications such as those used to treat high blood pressure can cause these symptoms.	20	19	61

Chapter
8

Sexuality, Aging, and
Society

One of the least-understood aspects of life in the later years is sexuality. As a result, there are numerous "myth-conceptions" concerning the sexual behavior of the elderly. These erroneous beliefs fall mainly into two broad categories: the "no sex" myths and the "if they do, they shouldn't" myths.

MYTHS ABOUT SEX

Old age is often thought of as a period devoid of sexuality in which the elderly are often relegated to a neuter status. Promulgators of this myth assume that older persons are not interested in sex and, even if they were, are incapable of sexual activity. As Alex Comfort (1976) comments: "Older people weren't asked in surveys

The need for sexual expression and the capacity to enjoy it are lifelong. (Nick Myers)

about their sexual activity because everyone knew they had none, and they were assumed to have none because nobody asked." The truth is that the requirement for sexual expression and the capacity to enjoy it are lifelong. We never outgrow our need to be close to another human being, to be touched or caressed.

Another common set of attitudes that persists in our society is that sexuality of any kind in the later years is abnormal, perverted, unhealthy, or disgusting. An older man who makes suggestive remarks or shows interest in sex is quickly censured and referred to as a "dirty old man." "Shame on you, at your age!" people may say. Similarly, a female may be called a "frustrated, indecent, old woman." Children and grandchildren often make older persons feel guilty about having an interest in sex. One reason for this attitude is the myth that sex is only for the young because only they are physically attractive and sexually appealing. All of us are accustomed to associating sex and love exclusively with youth. Sexual activity of any kind on the part of older persons is rarely referred to except in derogatory terms. According to our folklore, what is " 'virility' at twenty-five becomes 'lechery' at sixty-five" (Rubin, 1965). Such misconceptions prompted a husband to write for advice: "My wife and I are over 65 and we still like to have sexual intercourse very much. Please give us advice in this case. What should we do?" (Huyck, 1974).

Many people, including older people themselves, also believe that the elderly should refrain from sexual activity because it is dangerous (they might have a heart attack) and it can be harmful because they are so fragile (their bones might break). According to Butler and Lewis (1982), sex requires no more exertion than taking a brisk walk or climbing a flight of stairs. A conservative estimate is that 1 percent of heart attacks occur during intercourse. Contrary to what many people believe, sex is healthy for older persons. It helps them to stay in good physical condition and reduces both mental and physical stress.

STUDIES OF HUMAN SEXUALITY

It is difficult to imagine today how shocked the American public was when the first Kinsey Report was published in 1948. Up until that time, the scientific study of human sexual behavior had been taboo. Perhaps one of the greatest contributions of Kinsey and his associates was to pave the way for other investigators to study sexual behavior.

The Kinsey Reports

Alfred Kinsey's two volumes, *Sexual Behavior in the Human Male* (1948) and *Sexual Behavior in the Human Female* (1953), represent a monumental compilation of statistics gathered through interviews. Kinsey's work remains today the most extensive research ever undertaken on human sexuality. Despite some methodological difficulties, later studies have supported many of Kinsey's early findings. Although older

---

Box 8.1   # Elderly Sex in China

The newspaper *China Daily* recently advised its readers that an active sex life was no longer the exclusive province of the young. Reporting on a Shanghai conference dealing with the health problems of the aged, it said that sex relations between elderly persons acted as "special medicine" slowing the aging process and promoting longevity. The traditional Chinese belief that sex among the elderly was ridiculous and shameful, the daily declared, was wrong and should be discarded.

Source: *Parade* magazine, October, 18, 1987, p. 17.

persons were underrepresented in both of his samples, he was still able to draw some conclusions about their sexual behavior. First, he found that, in general, there is a decline in sexual activity in the later years. Second, one of Kinsey's most interesting findings regarding aging is that the male reaches his peak for sexual responsiveness in adolescence, and from then into old age it drops at a constant rate with no acceleration in the later years. The female, by comparison, does not reach her peak until her late twenties or her thirties. However, unlike the male, the female's sexual responsiveness continues at the same level, with little or no change, into her sixties.

Duke Longitudinal Studies

Whereas Kinsey's study was cross-sectional, the findings from Duke were based on data from two longitudinal studies. The first Duke Longitudinal Study began in 1955 with 271 persons aged 60 to 90, and the second study in 1968 with 502 persons aged 46 to 70. Both studies ended in 1976. The Duke Studies support Kinsey's work by finding that, overall, sexual activity tends to decline gradually with age. However, substantial proportions of persons of all ages reported stable or increased levels of sexual activity over time. Almost half of the married women in the studies remained sexually active in their sixties, and about the same amount of married men continued to be sexually active in their seventies. The Duke Studies also show that substantial proportions of older married persons continued sexual activity until at least their eighties. The evidence reveals that sexual activity is a contributing factor to better health and for maintaining life satisfaction in the later years (Palmore, 1981).

Masters and Johnson

Using direct observation and physical measurement in a laboratory setting, William Masters and Virginia Johnson (1966) investigated the anatomy and physiology of human sexual response patterns. They were interested in finding out what physical reactions and behavior occur as males and females respond to sexual stimulation. Like Kinsey's, theirs was a landmark study, and, like Kinsey's, their sample underrepresented persons over the age of 60. One of Masters and Johnson's major findings pertinent to aging is that "there is no time limit drawn by advancing years to female sexuality." For the male, there is a slowing down in the reaction pattern, but it does not necessarily diminish satisfactory sexual activity. Masters and Johnson conclude:

> There is every reason to believe that maintained regularity of sexual expression coupled with adequate physical well-being and healthy mental orientation to the aging process will combine to provide a sexually stimulating climate within a marriage. This climate will, in turn, improve sexual tension and provide a capacity for sexual performance that frequently may extend to and beyond the 80-year age level.

The Starr-Weiner Report

How do older persons feel about sex? How do their attitudes toward sex differ from those of younger persons? To find answers to such questions as these, Starr and Weiner (1981) collected questionnaire data from 800 respondents between the ages of 60 and 91. The questionnaire consisted of 50 open-ended questions. The majority of the respondents in the survey, 65 percent, were female, and 35 percent were male.

The respondents had reached adulthood long before the sexual revolution of the 1960s. Although many had been raised with Victorian standards, their responses to the changes in our sexual norms were surprising. When Starr and Weiner asked, for example, "How do you feel about older people who are not married having sexual relations and living together?" the overwhelming majority (91 percent) approved of such practices. Both men (95 percent) and women (89 percent) enthusiastically endorsed this arrangement. It appears that these older people had not only changed with the times but were in tune with them. They believed that they should have the same rights as the younger generation.

The majority of the respondents in the survey did not agree with the double standard of aging in our society (see Chapter 3, "Age Norms and Age Status"). When asked, "How do you feel about older women having younger lovers?" 83 percent of the respondents sanctioned the older woman–younger man combination. In answer to the question "How do you feel about older men having younger lovers?" 86 percent, as might be expected, approved of this combination. Most of the respondents felt that age was irrelevant in both situations. In answer to the question "How do you feel about older men and women without sexual partners going to prostitutes to relieve sexual needs?" 64 percent of the women and 74 percent of the men approved. Finally, the respondents were asked to rate the actual experience of sex: "How does sex feel now compared with when you were younger?" About 75 percent of the respondents, both male and female, said that sex is the same or better now compared with when they were younger. More than a third (36 percent) reported that sex is better in the later years.

Additional findings from this survey indicate that the respondents continue to be interested in sex, and a substantial number are sexually active. They believe that sex is important for physical and mental health. Most are satisfied with their sex lives and see them remaining much the same as they get even older.

PROBLEMS OF OLDER WOMEN

Many older women give up sexual activity not from lack of desire but from lack of a partner. Women are continuing to outlive men their own age by about seven years. Because of this difference in life expectancy and the fact that men usually marry women younger than they, in 1985 more than 68 percent of women age 75 and over were widowed whereas 67 percent of the men in this age group were married. A woman's chances for dating or remarriage are quite limited. There just aren't enough older men to go around, and those who are available usually go around with younger women (Huyck, 1983). The scarcity of male partners for older women has prompted numerous writers to suggest possible options to fulfill their needs for sexual expression.

1. *Polygyny.* This pattern of marriage in which one man has two or more wives at the same time is not likely to be a popular choice for many older women

Box 8.2 ## Popcorn and Sexuality

I should like to propose a . . . view of sexuality as it applies to the elderly. For the lack of a better term, I shall call it the popcorn theory. There are several characteristics of popcorn which seem better to describe sexuality than the essential vitamin model. In the first place, popcorn is probably the one food that has fewest prescriptions about it, either to eat it or not. We seldom hear parents admonish "Eat your popcorn, it's good for you." Nor is a parent likely to shout, "Don't eat that popcorn, it will ruin your teeth." Relieved of prescriptions or proscriptions, we can simply enjoy it for the fun of eating it.

Now, suppose that we came across a society in which the elderly had been strongly discouraged from eating popcorn. There might be instances in which elderly couples who were caught eating popcorn together would be ridiculed, perhaps forcibly separated. An occasional horror story would emerge in which it came to light that married couples were prevented from eating popcorn in the privacy of their room and were in fact made to eat it in separate quarters.

There would certainly be a need for enlightened gerontologists to point out the manifest ageism involved in such behavior. They could prove their point by doing surveys to show that the elderly are as capable of eating popcorn as younger persons. To be sure, they would have to admit that older persons probably have to eat it more slowly, and they may not eat as much or as often. But there would certainly be instances of persons actively enjoying popcorn into the eighth and ninth decades of life.

Source: L. Eugene Thomas, "Sexuality and Aging: Essential Vitamin or Popcorn?" *The Gerontologist,* 1982, 22(3), pp. 240–243.

now or in the future. Besides the problem of overcoming cultural norms, it is questionable whether one older man could adequately satisfy the sexual needs of many women. (See Chapter 12, "The Family," for further discussion of this topic.)

2. *Older woman–younger man combinations.* This combination makes sense in that women reach their peak of sexuality much later than men and there is no cutoff point to their sexual capacity. The Starr-Weiner Report indicated that older women would welcome this solution. However, such relationships still remain uncommon, and those involved in them are often ridiculed.

3. *Male prostitutes.* Both female-oriented counterparts to such magazines as *Playboy* and male strippers emerged in the 1970s. It may be that in the next decade or so, male prostitutes may afford a viable alternative for older females.

4. *Lesbian relationships.* Although it may be practical for a previously heterosexual older woman to turn to a relationship with a person of the same sex because of the shortage of older men, it is difficult to determine if such a dramatic change in one's sexual preference is possible (Turner & Adams,

For many older people, especially women, the greatest limiting factor in sexual activity is the lack of a partner. (Nick Myers)

1983). According to Walz and Blum (1987), some women may discover that they prefer a same-sex relationship in later life as aging may allow a latent lesbian to acknowledge her sexual preference.

SEXUALITY IN NURSING HOMES

The sexuality of nursing-home residents and those in similar facilities is often ignored, denied, or censured. Few nursing homes provide opportunities or places for privacy. In most places, room doors must be kept open, and personal visits to an individual's room are restricted. In addition, the sexes are usually segregated, they are allowed to mix only in public lounge areas and under supervision. Even married residents in some institutions are separated and are subjected to the watchful eye of the staff.

Silverstone and Wynter (1975) report on a geriatric institution that decided to move males and females together on the same floor. They found that this new type of living arrangement resulted in an improved social life and social adjustment for both sexes. In addition, the men appeared better groomed and were more cautious in their use of profanity with the women around.

> To the surprise of the staff, no difficulties were encountered with the exception of one incident when a male resident walked naked in the hall, greatly upsetting one of the female residents. The same lady was openly involved in a sexual affair with another man on the floor, which drew much criticism from the nursing staff.

The policy of many nursing homes is to have a taboo on any expression of sexuality, ranging from a simple exchange of affection to getting into bed together.

After age 65 there are four single women for every single man. As a result, older women must compete not only with those in their age group but with younger women as well in finding suitable men to date and marry. (Nick Myers)

Residents are kept in line by scolding or by medication. This policy is primarily for the convenience of the staff as well as to eliminate complaints from the families of residents. As one writer put it, "Better blah than bliss."

OLDER MALE AND FEMALE HOMOSEXUALS

The term *homosexual* refers to preferential sexual attraction for persons of the same sex. It is derived from the Greek root *homo*, meaning sameness or alike, and should not be confused with *homo*, Latin for man. The term *gay* is commonly used to refer to men and women who engage mainly in homosexual relations as well as to a male homosexual, whereas *lesbian* is used to refer only to a female homosexual. Although sexual attraction often occurs with sexual relations, there is no one-to-one correlation between them. For example, it is possible to be attracted to persons of the same sex without wanting to have sexual relations with them. "Sexual preference" is a term that is being used more frequently as studies reveal that few persons are exclusively heterosexual or homosexual. Most people have had some feelings or experiences of both kinds but have a definite preference for one or the other. It was Kinsey who in 1948 first pointed out that the sexual orientation or preference of individuals can be classified on a continuum. He constructed a seven-point scale to show the varying degrees between the two extremes: completely heterosexual and completely homosexual (see Figure 8.1).

Kimmel (1978) estimates that about 10 percent of the population in the United States can be considered exclusively or predominantly homosexual. On the basis of this estimate, we can conclude that there are about 1 million homosexuals aged 65 and over. Most research on older homosexuality has focused on men because of the difficulty of collecting sufficient data on older lesbians (Berger, 1982). There is no evidence that the number or percentage of gay persons in the population has increased in recent years, only their visibility as they have become organized at both a community and a political level to fight for legislation to ban discrimination toward homosexuals and to lobby for more federal funds for AIDS (acquired immune deficiency syndrome) research.

Facts About Homosexuality and Aging

What are older homosexuals like? Does being a gay male or a lesbian cause problems in old age? Many beliefs about homosexuals are inaccurate and have been dispelled by recent research. The following quiz concerns some of the more widely held beliefs about homosexuality. On the basis of your present knowledge, decide which statements are true and which are false.

_____ 1. Older male and female homosexuals are lonely, isolated, and without friends.

_____ 2. Older male homosexuals are sexually frustrated.

_____ 3. Male and female homosexuals perceive themselves as aging earlier than heterosexuals.

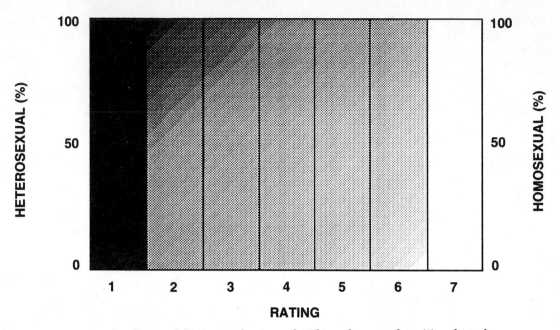

Figure 8.1. Kinsey heterosexual–homosexual rating scale. This scale ranges from (1) exclusively heterosexual acts or feelings to those that are (2) predominantly heterosexual, only incidentally homosexual, (3) predominantly heterosexual but more than incidentally homosexual, (4) equally heterosexual and homosexual, (5) predominantly homosexual, but more than incidentally heterosexual, (6) predominantly homosexual but incidentally heterosexual, and (7) exclusively homosexual. Kinsey was the first to point out that both heterosexual and homosexual elements are found in most individuals.

_____ 4. Older male and female homosexuals have a special preference for younger sex partners.

_____ 5. Older gay males have as many different sex partners as do younger gay males.

If you found all five statements false, then you have a perfect score.

1. In general, older male and female homosexuals tend to have more friends than their heterosexual counterparts. Homosexuals tend to form strong friendship ties with their age peers in the gay community. Because their sexual preference usually results in some degree of alienation from their families, these friendships help to replace the loss of familial support.

2. Research reveals that most older male homosexuals are content with their sex lives (Kelly, 1977). Berger (1982) reports that nearly three-fourths of the men in his study were somewhat or very satisfied with their sex lives.

3. Male homosexuals do not perceive themselves as aging any sooner than male heterosexuals, and lesbians do not experience aging as early as heterosexual women (Minnigerode, 1976; Laner, 1978, 1979).

4. Older gay males and lesbians are no more likely to seek younger sex partners

than their heterosexual counterparts. They prefer partners their own age (Laner, 1978, 1979; Kelly, 1980).

5. With age there is decrease in the number of sex partners among homosexual males. Older gay males tend to limit their sexual activities to fewer partners and often just to one partner. However, with the appearance of AIDS many younger gay males who were previously promiscuous may also be staying with one partner (Berger, 1982).

Homosexuality and Adaptation to Aging

The homosexual experience may in some ways facilitate the adjustment to aging. Kimmel points out that male homosexuals consciously prepare to become more self-reliant in the later years and that they have experience in the skills needed for maintaining themselves and their homes. Also, the friendship networks and social supports that homosexuals have created in the earlier years help to buffer them from some of the stresses and losses associated with old age. Another way in which homosexuality may help one adapt to aging is that early in life homosexuals have faced the crisis of managing their stigmatized identities; therefore, the coping mechanisms needed to manage the stigma of old age and its devaluation are already in place (Johnson & Kelly, 1979; Berger, 1982b). One researcher suggests that as far as aging is concerned, lesbians may have an advantage over heterosexual women: "The field of eligibles for lesbians, even though they are a minority among women in general, may be effectively larger than the experienced field of eligibles for heterosexual women who continue to seek the traditional 'male older/female younger' age distribution in relationships" (Laner, 1979). Growing older may also lessen some of the problems faced by younger homosexuals; with age there tends to be a more stable self-concept and less need for concern about one's sexual orientation being exposed. One man expressed relief at retirement because he no longer had to worry about the possibility of his employer's learning of his homosexuality (Kelly, 1977; Weinberg & Williams, 1974; Berger, 1982).

Problems Faced by Homosexuals

As we have noted, little evidence suggests that homosexuality causes problems in old age, but the societal stigma attached to it does (Kelly, 1977). A number of special problems of discrimination are faced by homosexuals. For example, only the immediate family is permitted to visit the patient in the intensive care unit of most hospitals or make decisions about treatment if the patient is unable to do so; the patient's long-term partner is very often excluded. Older homosexuals living in nursing homes may often experience anxiety over becoming ostracized by other residents or being mistreated by the staff. Nursing homes also prevent homosexuals from sharing rooms or (possibly at the instruction of the family) from having visits from gay friends. When death occurs to one's long-term partner, the bereaved partner often is excluded from funeral planning and attendance and usually must grieve in private. Another problem faced by the surviving partner concerns inheritance and property ownership. For instance, if there is no will when one's partner dies, the deceased's family can claim the entire inheritance. Also, if a partner dies without a will, the ownership of a house or business can very well pass to the deceased's family regardless of the partner's contribution (Kelly, 1977; Kimmel, 1978; Berger, 1982b).

SUMMARY

1. There are a number of myths about sexuality in the later years. Most of them regard old age as a period of asexuality or a period when sexuality of any kind is considered unhealthy, abnormal, and perverted.

2. The work of Kinsey and his associates, the premier study of human sexuality, found that the male reaches his peak of sexual responsiveness in adolescence, whereas the female reaches her peak much later. Other important research includes the Duke Longitudinal Studies, which indicate that sexual activity may continue into the eighties, and that of Masters and Johnson, who noted there is no age limit to female sexuality.

3. The Starr-Weiner Report found that many older persons have responded to the sexual revolution of the 1960s. They have updated many of the sexual norms that they grew up with, and their norms are now more in keeping with those of the younger generation.

4. Older women become sexually inactive because of the lack of opportunity and because of social conventions. Various writers have proposed some ways to overcome these obstacles. These suggestions include polygyny, older woman–younger man combinations, male prostitutes, and lesbian relationships. Few nursing homes provide any opportunities for the residents to express their sexuality.

5. Just as there are myths about aging and sexuality, there are also myths about older male and female homosexuals. In some ways, the homosexual experience may be helpful in adapting to old age. Homosexuals face special problems of discrimination in our society.

KEY TERMS

polygyny
homosexual
gay

lesbian
sexual preference

FOR FURTHER STUDY

Hammond, Doris B. (1987). *My parents never had sex.* Buffalo: Promethus.
    Written to help children and grandchildren to accept the sexuality of their elders and to dispel the many myths of sexual aging.

Solnick, R. R. (Ed.) (1980). *Sexuality and aging.* Los Angeles: University of Southern California Press.
    A collection of articles on the various aspects of sexuality and the older adult.

Starr, Bernard D., & Weiner, Marcella B. (1981). *The Starr-Weiner report on sex and sexuality in the mature years.* New York: McGraw-Hill.

Reports on a study of the sexual activities of more than 800 men and women over the age of 60.

Waltz, Thomas H., & Blum, Nancee S. (1987). *Sexual health in later life.* Lexington, MA: Lexington Books.

Discusses how the aging body as well as attitudes and mental states may affect sexual functioning in later life.

Weg, Ruth B. (Ed.) (1983). *Sexuality in the later years: Roles and behavior.* New York: Academic Press.

Focuses on options and possibilities for the individualization of sex roles and sexual behavior of the elderly.

Reading

Never Too Late

Kris Bulcroft and Margaret O'Conner-Roden

Contrary to the popular notion that passion and romance are only for the young, this article reveals that there are quite a few older single people who are dating and who are sexually active.

What is the age of love? The star-crossed lovers Romeo and Juliet were teenagers; Antony and Cleopatra's torrid affair occurred at the prime of their health and beauty; Lady Diana Spencer was barely 20 when she married her Prince Charming. How old is too old for the sparkle in the eye and the blush in the cheek?

The message our culture often gives us is that love is only for the young and the beautiful—people over 65 are no longer interested in or suited for things such as romance and passion. Few of us imagine older couples taking an interest in the opposite sex other than for companionship—maybe a game of bridge or conversation

Kris Bulcroft and Margaret O'Conner-Roden, "Never Too Late." *Psychology Today*, June 1986, pp. 66–69.

out on the porch. But, in fact, there are quite a few older single people who not only date but are involved sexually with someone.

Statistically there are good reasons for older people to be dating. At the turn of the century only about 4 percent of the total American population was 65 years of age or older. Today that number has soared to approximately 11 percent, with the total expected to increase to about 20 percent by the year 2050. In addition, older people are living longer and staying healthier, and they are less likely than before to have children living at home. And an increasing number of divorces among the elderly is casting many of these older people back into the singles' pool. All of these factors create an expanded life stage, made up of healthy and active people looking for meaningful ways to spend their leisure.

The question of whether older people date, fall in love and behave romantically, just as the young do, occurred to us while we were observing singles' dances for older people at a senior center. We noticed a sense of anticipation, festive dress and flirtatious behavior that was strikingly familiar to us as women recently involved in the dating scene. Although our observations indicated that older people dated, when we looked for empirical research on the topic we found there was none. We concluded this was due partly to the difficulty in finding representative samples of older daters and partly to the underlying stereotype of asexual elders. So we decided to go out and talk to older daters ourselves. Once we began looking, we were surprised at the numbers of dating elders who came forward to talk to us. We compared their responses to those from earlier studies on romance and dating, in which the people were much younger.

Dating, as defined by our sample of older people, meant a committed, long-term, monogamous relationship, similar to going steady at younger ages. The vast majority of elderly daters did not approach dating with the more casual attitude of many younger single people who are "playing the field." All respondents clearly saw dating as quite distinct from friendship, although companionship was an important characteristic of over-60 dating.

One of our major findings was the similarity between how older and younger daters feel when they fall in love—what we've come to call the "sweaty palm syndrome." This includes all the physiological and psychological somersaults, such as a heightened sense of reality, perspiring hands, a feeling of awkwardness, inability to concentrate, anxiety when away from the loved one and heart palpitations. A 65-year-old man told us, "Love is when you look across the room at someone and your heart goes pitty-pat." A widow, aged 72, said, "You know you're in love when the one you love is away and you feel empty." Or as a 68-year-old divorcée said, "When you fall in love at my age there's initially a kind of 'oh, gee!' feeling . . . and it's just a little scary."

We also found a similarity in how both older and younger daters defined romance. Older people were just as likely to want to participate in romantic displays such as candlelight dinners, long walks in the park and giving flowers and candy. Older men, just like younger ones, tended to equate romance with sexuality. As a 71-year-old widower told us, "You can talk about candlelight dinners and sitting in front of the fireplace, but I still think the most romantic thing I've ever done is to go to bed with her."

A major question for us was "What do older people do on dates?" The popular image may suggest a prim, card-playing couple perhaps holding hands at some senior center. We found that not only do older couples' dates include the same activities as those of younger people, but they are often far more varied and creative. In addition to traditional dates such as going to the movies, out for pizza and to dances, older couples said they went camping, enjoyed the opera and flew to Hawaii for the weekend.

Not only was the dating behavior more varied, but the pace of the relationship was greatly accelerated in later life. People told us that there simply was "not much time for playing the field." They favored the direct, no-game-playing approach in building a relationship with a member of the opposite sex. As one elderly dater commented, "Touching people is important, and I know from watching my father and mother that you might just as well say when lunch is ready . . . and I don't mean that literally."

Sexuality was an important part of the dating relationship for most of those we spoke to, and sexual involvement tended to develop rapidly. While sexuality for these couples included intercourse, the stronger emphasis was on the nuances of sexual behavior such as hugging, kissing and touching. This physical closeness helped fulfill the intimacy needs of older people, needs that were especially important to those living alone whose sole source of human touch was often the dating partner. The intimacy provided through sex also contributed to self-esteem by making people feel desired and needed. As one 77-year-old woman said, "Sex isn't as important when you're older, but in a way you need it more."

A major distinction we found between older and younger daters was in their attitudes toward passionate love, or what the Greeks called "the madness from the gods." Psychologists Elaine Hatfield, of the University of Hawaii in Manoa, and G. William Walster, of Los Gatos, California, have similarly defined passionate love as explosive, filled with fervor and short-lived. According to their theory of love, young people tend to equate passionate love with being in love. Once the first, intense love experience has faded, young lovers often seek a new partner.

For older daters, it is different. They have learned from experience that passionate love cannot be sustained with the same early level of intensity. But since most of them have been in marriages that lasted for decades, they also know the value of companionate love, that "steady burning fire" that not only endures but tends to grow deeper over time. As one older man put it, "Yeah, passion is nice . . . it's the frosting on the cake. But it's her personality that's really important. The first time I was in love it was only the excitement that mattered, but now it's the friendship . . . the ways we spend our time together that count."

Nonetheless, the pursuit of intimacy caused special problems for older people. Unlike younger daters, older people are faced with a lack of social cues indicating whether sexual behavior is appropriate in the dating relationship. Choosing to have a sexual relationship outside of marriage often goes against the system of values that they have followed during their entire lives.

Older couples also felt the need to hide the intimate aspects of their dating relationship because of a fear of social disapproval, creating a variety of covert behaviors. As one 63-year-old retiree said, "Yeah, my girlfriend (age 64) lives just down the hall from me . . . when she spends the night she usually brings her cordless phone

. . . just in case her daughter calls." One 61-year-old woman told us that even though her 68-year-old boyfriend has been spending three or four nights a week at her house for the past year, she has not been able to tell her family. "I have a tendency to hide his shoes when my grandchildren are coming over."

Despite the fact that marriage would solve the problem of how to deal with the sexual aspects of the relationship, very few of these couples were interested in marriage. Some had assumed when they began dating that they would eventually marry but discovered as time went on that they weren't willing to give up their independence. For women especially, their divorce or widowhood marked the first time in their lives that they had been on their own. Although it was often difficult in the beginning, many discovered that they enjoyed their independence. Older people also said they didn't have the same reasons for marriage that younger people do: beginning a life together and starting a family. Another reason some elders were reluctant to marry was the possibility of deteriorating health. Many said they would not want to become a caretaker for an ill spouse.

Contrary to the popular belief that family would be protective and jealous of the dating relative, family members tended to be supportive of older couples' dating and often included the dating partner in family gatherings. The attitude that individuals have the right to personal happiness may be partially responsible for families' positive attitudes. But more importantly, many families realize that a significant other for an older person places fewer social demands on family members.

Peers also tended to be supportive, although many women reported sensing jealousy among their female friends, who were possibly unhappy because of their inability to find dating partners themselves and hurt because the dating woman didn't have as much time to spend with them.

Our interviews with older daters revealed that the dating relationship is a critical, central part of elders' lives that provides something that cannot be supplied by family or friends. As one 65-year-old man told us, "I'm very happy with life right now. I'd be lost without my dating partner. I really would."

Our initial question, "What is the age of love?" is best answered in the words of one 64-year-old woman: "I suppose that hope does spring eternal in the human breast as far as love is concerned. People are always looking for the ultimate, perfect relationship. No matter how old they are, they are looking for this thing called love."

PART
THREE

Social Groups and Inequality

Chapter 9

Social Groups and Organizations

*F*or nearly five years, Tommy Seddon, a 61-year-old former machinist in Manchester, England, was shunned by his fellow workers because he refused to join a one-day union walkout. After that, not one of his co-workers would talk to him. Commenting on the wall of silence, Seddon said: "It upset me at first but it doesn't hurt now. I seem to have found a strength to endure the isolation just as long as it is imposed upon me. Initially, it did come hard. These were the men that I drank with, talked to, laughed with." But all that ended after the strike. Seddon felt that it would have been harder if he had not known that he was right. He said that the work stoppage was politically motivated and that he could not be a party to it. Tommy Seddon's ostracism by his work group ended when he and his co-workers' jobs were eliminated in a factory cutback (*Manchester Evening News,* 1973, 1975).

Whether extended isolation is social, as in Tommy's case, or physical, such as solitary confinement in a prison cell, for most people it is intolerable. Human beings are social animals and as such are interdependent on one another. Our interaction with others is necessary for our survival and the satisfaction of our needs.

COLLECTIVITIES

We spend our lives in the company of others and in the context of such groups as the family, peer groups, occupational groups, religious groups, and the community. A *group* is two or more people who interact with one another in a standardized pattern and who share a sense of common identity. An individual who is a member of a group has a sense of belonging to it. By the same token, the individual belongs to a group when others who consider themselves members accept that individual as part of the group.

People who have some characteristic in common, such as the same occupation, hobby, or age, do not constitute a social group; they are best classified as a *social category.* But if members of a social category begin to interact and develop a sense of identification with one another, then the category may be transformed into a group. One task of the sociologist is to study the conditions under which a category becomes a group. Broom and Selznick (1973) note:

> The aged are a significant social category, and there is considerable interest today in the kinds of groups older people are likely to form or accept. Is there an old-age style of life that can be the natural basis for separate housing? Or do older people feel little sense of identity with each other despite their similar age and dependency? There have been some old-age political pressure groups, such as the Townsend movement of the 1930s. Should more and increasingly powerful groups of this sort be expected as the number of older people in the population rises? What effect would this have on the political order? These questions indicate the problems raised when the group potential of a social category is explored.

Rose (1965) argues that older Americans are now in the process of changing from a category to a group. He maintains that this is due to the group consciousness forming among those older people who are beginning to feel a sense of positive identification with other elderly people and who see themselves as members of an aging group. Rose states:

> For the growing minority that has reacted against the negative self-conception characteristic of the aging in our society and has seen the problems of aging in a group context, there are all the signs of group identification. There is a desire to associate with fellow-agers, especially in formal associations, and to exclude younger adults from these associations. There are expressions of group pride. . . . With this group pride has come self-acceptance as a member of an esteemed group. . . . There are manifestations of a feeling of resentment at "the way older people are being mistreated," and indications of

their taking social action to remove the sources of their resentment. There are the signs of group-identification that previous sociological studies have found in ethnic minority groups.

THE AGING SUBCULTURE

Rose not only contends that the elderly are in the process of being transformed from a social category into a group, but he also sees a subculture of the aging also developing. He points out that the elderly tend to interact more with one another as they grow older, and less with younger persons, because of the common interests and concerns that the elderly share and, to some extent, because they are excluded from interacting with other age groups. This segregation results in the development of an *aging subculture*, similar to the adolescent subculture in our society. A subculture, though part of the total culture, usually contains some of its own distinctive lifestyles, values, norms, and language. For example, a subculture based on age, such as the adolescent one in our society, has its own special clothing, style of life, music, behavior, and vocabulary.

Rose claims that certain demographic and social trends, favorable for the emergence of an aging subculture, are occurring. These trends include:

1. the growing number and proportion of older people
2. the trend toward self-segregating retirement communities
3. the institutionalization of retirement, which has resulted in a decreased amount of interaction with younger workers
4. the increasing number of older people with more money, education, and leisure time
5. the emergence of organizations and groups that are exclusively for older people

Today there is growing evidence of the potential for a subculture of aging to develop. The creation of such groups as the American Association of Retired Persons (AARP) and the Gray Panthers lend support to Rose's argument (Passuth & Bengtson, 1988).

REFERENCE GROUPS

People may be influenced not only by the groups to which they belong, but also by groups to which they do not belong. Any group or social category that we use as a standard of comparison and by which we measure our accomplishments and failures is called a *reference group*. Such groups or categories may include friends, immediate family members, occupational group, or social class. A reference group may also provide a person with a set of norms, attitudes, and values. For example, a person who aspires to move ahead socially may begin to pattern behavior after a higher status group and acquire its tastes.

Bultena and Powers (1976) observe that the aged as yet have no reference groups to provide a specific set of age norms; however, they feel that the social category of the aged constitutes an important reference group with which the elderly can compare themselves. The fact that our society has many negative stereotypes regarding the aged as a social category may work to the advantage of the elderly in one respect: When older people make comparisons of their personal situation, they are likely to judge themselves against these negative stereotypes and feel that their personal situation is not different from, or not as bad as, that of other elderly.

In a study of older people in Iowa, Bultena and Powers sought to determine the relationship between reference-group comparisons and the adjustment made to aging. Their data indicate that a large majority of the respondents felt that they were in a comparable or better position than others their age regarding health, income, physical mobility, and social interaction. Also, the respondents who assessed themselves favorably in comparison with others tended to have high levels of life satisfaction and morale.

With advancing age, the elderly lose friends along with reference groups. Bengtson and Manuel (1981) recount the following incident:

> So, what happens when the individual reaches the age of seventy and his friends begin to die? One of the authors once interviewed a man who had just celebrated his 104th birthday. He said as he talked about the problems of growing old, "You know, I haven't had a friend since I was 77. That's when my last friend died." It is difficult to imagine living for 27 years without someone who is regarded as a friend! This represents not only loss of a confidant, of contact with an intimate, but also loss of reference group. To what group can this man who is 104 years old refer so he can judge the appropriateness of his behavior, or reinforce his identity? Many older people judge themselves by the standards of middle age, a criterion by which they invariably are at a disadvantage.

PRIMARY GROUPS

Another approach to analyzing groups is to look at the type of relationship that exists between its members. A group in which the members have an intimate, direct, personal relationship with one another is called a *primary group*. The members of primary groups interact face to face in relationships that involve many aspects of their personalities, and these relationships are valued solely for themselves and not as a means to an end. One of the most important primary groups is the family. Other examples are a clique of workers in an office and a group of friends at a retirement community.

Primary groups are of necessity small in size. It is not possible for large numbers of people to interact on a close, intimate basis. For intimacy to arise and be maintained, face-to-face contact is usually necessary, and so is the persistence of the group relationship over time.

Functions of Primary Groups

Primary groups fulfill a number of functions for their members. The following are some of the ones that relate to the elderly.

1. *Primary groups help to support and sustain the individual.* All human beings need the emotional support and intimate companionship of others. Lowenthal and Haven (1968) found that older people who have a close friend seem to be happier and in better mental health than those who do not. The presence of close relationships is essential to personal adjustment and emotional sustenance. They serve as a buffer against the age-linked losses of retirement and widowhood.

2. *Primary groups function as important instruments of social control.* In her study of the residents of Merrill Court, a small apartment house composed of older people who were mostly widows, Hochschild (1973) observed a pressure toward conformity (see Chapter 1, "The Field and Its Methods"). One resident named Daisy wanted to keep to herself. The group chastised her and made her feel uncomfortable about this desire. The residents felt it was their duty to try to help her to be more sociable and to get involved in their activities. She was the topic of much discussion and gossip.

   The residents were pressured into being active and involved, as well as acting "proper." Another resident, Beatrice, like Daisy, was also considered a deviant, but for a different reason. Beatrice flagrantly disregarded the group's conventions. Everyone disapproved of her behavior and gossiped about her. Many wanted to exclude her from their service club for her actions. The case of Tommy, the English machinist mentioned earlier, is still another illustration of how a group penalizes those who do not conform to its expectations.

3. *Primary groups serve as havens.* In such groups people can be themselves. They do not feel that they have to be on guard or worry about the impression they make. Hochschild points out that when no younger people were around, the elderly widows of Merrill Court sang and danced without fear of what others would think. She also notes that their topics of conversation were different.

   > When the old people were together alone, everyone was a representative of the past, and no one had to instruct or interpret. They felt free mentally to move back a generation and speak of themselves less as grandmothers and mothers and more as sisters and children of their own deceased parents.

4. *Primary groups are major links between the individual and society.* All persons in modern societies must deal with large-scale formal organizations, and most family members, including the elderly, look to their relatives for assistance. The family often acts as a mediator for the elderly in their dealings with such formal organizations as hospitals, the Social Security system, and nursing homes (Shanas & Sussman, 1977).

Types of Primary Groups

Three major kinds of primary groups—family, friends, and neighbors—are particularly relevant in our discussion of the elderly.

Family   Research findings reveal that families provide the major part of social support for the elderly and in times of need are the first source of help to which elderly persons turn. However, when the family is nonexistent or not available, friends and neighbors become important in the provision of social support. A study in a lower-class district in East London found that older persons without families intensified their relationships with friends and neighbors through frequent visits and mutual aid (Young & Willmott, 1962). However, most studies suggest that a substantial proportion of older persons have family living nearby to provide support. Research by Kivett and Atkinson (1984) reveals that 58 percent of the elderly respondents in their sample reported having two or more children living within a 30-minute car ride from their homes.

It is interesting to note that regular contact with one's children makes no difference in the morale of older persons. Arling (1976) found no significant association between morale and the number of children living nearby or the frequency of contact with them. A study by Zena Blau (1981) reported no significant differences in the morale of retired and widowed persons who had regular contact with their children as compared with those who did not.

Friendship   Friends seem to be more important to the morale of older people than contacts with their adult children, their grandchildren, or their siblings. Sharing memories and experiences with friends helps to preserve one's identity following role losses associated with aging. Friendships provide an effective way to forestall demoralization in old age.

Research reveals that older women tend to have a greater capacity and need for friendships than do older men and, as a result, have more intense and long-lasting friendships than their male counterparts. Men are less likely to have close friends. Generally, men name their wives as the only person they would talk with about their personal problems, whereas women often designate friends of their own sex. It appears, then, that a man satisfies his need for a confidant mainly within marriage, whereas a woman fulfills this need outside of marriage with a woman friend (Blau, 1981).

Neighbors   A study by Muriel Cantor (1979) of inner-city elderly revealed that about two-thirds of the residents knew one or more neighbors well. The level of mutual aid between neighbors was substantial. Sixty percent reported that "they and their neighbors help each other out either in emergencies or a lot of the time." Although neighbors provide aid to one another, it differs in amount and type from the aid given by one's family. Neighbors tend to supplement instead of substitute for the family's support (Peters & Kaiser, 1985).

Neighboring among older persons tends to increase in housing arrangements with high concentrations of elderly persons. Rosow (1967) found that elderly persons who live in apartment buildings containing a larger number of persons their own age have more friends and more opportunities for mutual aid than those living in buildings with a lower concentration of elderly residents. Similarly, age-segregated living arrangements such as public-housing or retirement communities tend to promote a higher degree of friendship formation and neighboring than do age-integrated environments (Carp, 1966; Osgood, 1982).

FORMAL ORGANIZATIONS

In contrast to primary groups are *formal organizations*, which are large, impersonal secondary groups that are deliberately designed to achieve specific goals. Their members perform more narrowly defined roles and have fewer emotional ties than do primary group members. Unlike primary groups, which are informally structured, organizations have a formal structure in that they have stated rules, policies, and procedures that define the activities of the members of the organization. The formal structure functions to help the organization meet its goals most efficiently. The mechanisms of this structure include the organization chart, which sets out the formal lines of authority or chains of commands within a formal organization (see Figure 9.1). Examples of formal organizations include corporations, government agencies, hospitals, and multipurpose senior centers.

Primary Groups and Formal Organizations

Much has been written about the decline of primary groups and the rise of formal organizations in modern societies. While the significance of formal organizations is great, it is well documented that primary groups persist and also remain essential to modern life. Although formal organizations and primary groups have contradictory structures and different goals, they work best when they work closely together, especially in the management of the problems of the elderly. To explain this paradox, Litwak (1985) has proposed the theory of shared functions. According to his theory, most tasks have one aspect that can be managed best by people with technical knowledge and training and another that requires everyday experience and continued contact. As a result, to accomplish most tasks both primary groups and formal organizations are needed.

Which tasks are best managed by primary groups? Those involving unpredictable events (giving first aid to an elderly woman who has fallen in her home), those too simple to be divided (assisting an older person in dressing), and situations in which quick and flexible decisions, uninhibited by policies and procedures, are required. Which tasks are best managed by formal organizations? Those that require the impartial, uniform application of technical skill and knowledge to large numbers of people. An example of a formal organization would be a hospital. In a hospital some persons are technically competent to give X-rays, others are competent to make diagnoses, still others are competent to give round-the-clock nursing care, and so on. Suppose that the elderly woman mentioned previously was injured when she fell. The primary group (the woman's daughter and son-in-law) administers first aid and then takes her to the hospital, where members of the formal organization take over. A technician X-rays the patient, finding a broken rib. A physician then bandages the woman's rib and prescribes some medication for pain, after which the daughter and son-in-law take the patient home.

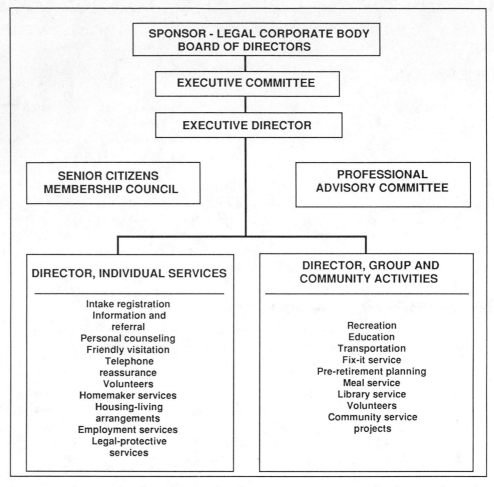

Figure 9.1. Organization chart of a typical multipurpose senior center. This diagram shows the chains of command within a formal organization such as a senior center.

Both the primary group and the formal organization have worked together to help restore the elderly woman's health. In the best interest of older persons, coordination between primary groups and formal organizations is necessary. However, argues Litwak, there must be some midpoint of distance between the two groups. This point should be close enough so that the groups can work together, but not so close as to lead to conflict between them.

Voluntary Associations

A type of formal organization that individuals join by choice, is nonprofit, and has a specific purpose is called a *voluntary association*. Our society is characterized by a vast array of associations, ranging from the American Red Cross and the National Rifle

Association to the American Association of Retired Persons. Some associations have a religious orientation, such as the National Conference of Christians and Jews; some are recreational, such as the National Contest Association; and others are occupational, such as the American Association of University Professors. Still other associations are charitable, political, social, or service groups.

Older people belong to three main categories of voluntary associations: (1) ones in which elderly persons participate, but that are not particularly geared to their specific needs; (2) associations that are organized by and for older people to meet their needs and interests; and (3) those in which others provide services for older people (Rose, 1960).

Voluntary Associations in Which Older People Participate   If a person participated in voluntary associations when young, this pattern tends to persist in later life. A study by Babchuk et al. (1979) reveals that the elderly have a high rate of participation in associations and that no sharp decline in affiliation occurs even for those persons 80 years or older. However, older persons in better health and of higher socioeconomic status belong to more associations and are more involved than those older persons in poorer health and of lower socioeconomic status (Cutler, 1973).

Although there are no significant differences in association memberships and attendance rates between the sexes, there are differences between the races. Older blacks belong to more associations and have higher rates of attendance than do older whites (Clemente, Rexroad, & Hirsch, 1975). As far as types of voluntary associations are concerned, older persons are the most likely to belong to church-affiliated and fraternal groups and the least likely to belong to sports-related groups (Cutler, 1976).

Voluntary Associations Organized for and by Older People   The Townsend Movement was one of the first associations of older people in this country. Originally called the Old Age and Revolving Pensions, Ltd., it was organized in 1934 by Francis E. Townsend, a retired California physician. The goal of the organization was to persuade Congress to pass a law giving all persons over the age of 60 a pension of $200 per month on the condition that they would not work and that they would spend all the money by the last day of every month. Townsend argued that making older persons the "circulators of money" would stimulate the economy, end the Depression, and help eliminate poverty among the elderly.

The movement—with its motto, "Youth for Work, Age for Leisure"—grew rapidly, and by 1936 there were several thousand local clubs attracting about a half a million members. Rose (1960) observed: "Participants in the clubs were given some hope that their economic needs would be amply met and were brought together in sociable groups. Moreover, the clubs created their first insights of themselves as a social group with common problems."

With the implementation of social security legislation, the main thrust of the Townsend Movement was blunted. The organization then shifted its purpose to the promotion of recreational and social activities for older people. By 1953 the membership had dropped to 23,000 and since that time the movement has disappeared.

Today, several voluntary associations link their purposes to the needs, problems, and interests of older people. The largest of these is the American Association of

Retired Persons (AARP), which is open to persons over 50 years of age, retired or not. The association was founded in 1958 by Ethel Percy Andrus, a 72-year-old retired high school principal, as the National Retired Teachers Association (NRTA). Today AARP has more than 3,300 local chapters and a membership exceeding 30 million. It provides many direct membership benefits including a mail-service pharmacy, adult education, a temporary employment service, preretirement programs, and travel services. In addition, AARP serves its members through legislative representation at both the federal and state levels.

Next to AARP in size and power is the National Council of Senior Citizens (NCSC), which was founded in 1961 by two major unions, the United Automobile Workers and the United Steelworkers. Their present membership of 4.5 million comes from organizations of older people like senior citizen clubs and councils, as well as from labor unions. NCSC helps the low-income elderly through a program that assists them to obtain affordable housing and through an employment program (Senior Community Service Employment Program) that provides them with part-time work. NCSC encourages its members to involve themselves in political and social action, legislation, and education. "A better life for *all* Americans" is its stated goal.

In contrast to the AARP and NCSC is an intergenerational advocacy movement of about 60,000 social activists called the Gray Panthers—a name that a television-program director gave them because of their radical tactics on some occasions. The leader of the Gray Panthers is the charismatic, 85-year-old Maggie Kuhn, who started the association in 1970 when she was forced into mandatory retirement after 25 years of service with the Presbyterian Church. Kuhn has been described as "the feisty old lady from Philadelphia." (See Box 9.1.)

Loosely structured and lacking the organization of AARP and NCSC, the Gray Panthers are a coalition of both young and old whose primary objectives are to promote a positive attitude toward aging, to fight against age discrimination, and to

---

Box 9.1 ## Maggie Kuhn on the Detroit Syndrome

I'd like to elaborate just a little on the wastefulness of our society, what I call the "Detroit" syndrome. The Detroit syndrome builds obsolescence into all our thinking and production. Only the new model is desirable, marketable, profitable. The Detroit mentality has taken us over as a society. We are a wasteful society. We've been wasting people who cannot produce at what we consider to be productive peaks. They're surplus, they're scrap. . . . We scrap-pile our old people like wornout car hulks. . . . We warehouse away our so-called senior citizens in senior high-rises and nursing homes—or, as I prefer to call them, "glorified playpens." . . . Old people should not be treated as wrinkled babies.

Sources: Dieter T. Hessel, *Maggie Kuhn on Aging.* Philadelphia: Westminster Press, 1977; George Michaelson, "Maggie Kuhn: Gray Panther on the Prowl." *Parade,* December 18, 1977.

influence social policies. Some of the issues that the Gray Panthers have consistently championed include accessible health care for all age groups, more accurate media portrayals of the elderly, and nursing-home reform. In addition, the Panthers stress the importance of involvement in the political process at the grassroots level. Each of the 120 chapters is given autonomy to pursue those problems and issues that it believes are most important to its own community.

Voluntary Associations That Provide Services for Older People   Probably the most prevalent type of voluntary association providing services for the elderly is the *multipurpose senior center*. The first senior center was started in New York City by its Welfare Department in 1943 for the purpose of reducing isolation and loneliness among older people.

The programs of the early senior centers were largely limited to recreational activities, but they have gradually expanded their programs until today most centers have become multipurpose in scope. A multipurpose senior center is a designated community facility for older people that offers a wide variety of activities and services.

Maggie Kuhn, founder and leader of the Gray Panthers, a national organization of social activists who are dedicated to ending age discrimination. (Julie Jensen/photography)

Multipurpose senior centers offer instruction in a wide variety of activities including art and dancing.

These include health, employment, and housing services; leadership development; consumer education; and volunteer opportunities. Many centers serve as a neighborhood or community social agency. Often representatives from community agencies are on hand to offer counseling to the elderly with personal problems and other assistance in obtaining needed services. Most centers provide some form of transportation for members, as well as low-cost well-balanced meals in a communal dining room. Instruction in language skills and arts and crafts is also common. Field trips and camping are also part of many center programs, as are plays, musicals, dances, and other forms of entertainment and recreation (see Figure 9.1).

The growth of senior centers has been phenomenal. The first directory of the National Council on the Aging (NCOA) in 1966 identified 360 centers. By 1970 its directory listed 1200 centers; by 1974 it listed 2362 centers. Estimates are that there are more than 8000 centers throughout the country serving about 8 million older persons.

A number of factors are related to the use of centers by the elderly. Neighborhood location and accessibility have an important effect on the use of a center, especially for the minority elderly. Users of the centers are more likely to be widowed, have a higher income, and belong to more associations than nonusers. In addition, nonusers tend to have serious health problems or rate their health problems as very serious as compared with those of users. Loss of a spouse is often given as a reason for center attendance, but the most frequently given reason is the wish to meet others (National Council on the Aging, 1972; National Institute of Senior Centers, 1974).

COMMUNITIES

Thus far we have been discussing the various types of groups in which we participate and of which we are members. These groups function within a larger territorial group in which people pursue their daily needs and activities. When we speak of this larger, more inclusive territorial group, we are referring to the community. The community differs from other groups in that membership is based on the sharing of the same general locality. A *community* is a grouping of people who live in a limited territorial area where they have a sense of belonging and fulfill most of their daily needs and activities.

The various types of communities, such as rural, urban, and suburban, can be categorized in many ways. One analysis includes these criteria to classify communities: (1) the size and density of the population; (2) the specialized functions of the community within the whole society; and (3) the kind of organization the community has. To these we will add a fourth criterion—age. Although the concept of having whole communities composed of an aged population is not new, only in recent years have retirement communities emerged in this country.

Retirement Communities

One cannot discuss the subject of *retirement communities* for long without making some distinctions between the different types. One way to differentiate retirement communities is on the basis of whether they are unplanned or planned. *Unplanned retirement communities* are places that were not designed as retirement communities but have become popular places for retirement migration, attracting retirees in large numbers. Examples of such communities are found along the east and west coasts of Florida. On the other hand, *planned retirement communities* are those that have been deliberately designed by developers as retirement communities. They fall into two types: subsidized and nonsubsidized. Public housing provided by the Department of Housing and Urban Development (HUD), such as Merrill Court, the apartment building studied by Hochschild, is an example of a *subsidized retirement community* (Longino, 1981). In a *nonsubsidized retirement community*, persons may buy their homes and the land on which they are built or the developer may retain ownership of the land. An example of a well-known nonsubsidized retirement community is Sun City, Arizona, one of the largest retirement communities in the world with more than 47,000 residents.

Another way to classify retirement communities is according to such variations as size, age, and health of the residents; services; and sponsorship. Using this classification scheme, five types of retirement communities have been identified: new towns, villages, subdivisions, residences, and continuing care centers (Marans, Hunt, & Vakalo, 1984). Table 9.1 summarizes the characteristics of these types.

The wide variation in the classification of retirement communities, as we have just noted, makes defining them difficult. However, for our purposes, we will define a retirement community as a planned, relatively self-sufficient entity, partially separated from the larger community, and whose residents are mainly retired or semiretired. Residents of retirement communities tend to be active and relatively healthy,

An aerial view of Sun City, one of the largest retirement communities in the world, located near Phoenix, Arizona. (Jerry Svendson)

Table 9.1   CHARACTERISTICS OF FIVE TYPES OF RETIREMENT COMMUNITIES

Type of community	Size	Resident characteristics at entry	Services	Sponsorship
Retirement new town	Large	Young, predominantly healthy	Extensive health, outdoor recreational, and other	Profit
Retirement village	Medium	Young, predominantly healthy	Limited/no health; extensive outdoor recreational and other	Profit
Retirement subdivision	Large, medium, or small	Young, predominantly healthy	Limited/no health, outdoor recreational, and other	Profit
Retirement residence	Small	Old, predominantly healthy	Limited/no health, outdoor recreational; extensive other	Nonprofit
Continuing-care retirement center	Small	Old, mixed healthy and frail	Extensive health; limited outdoor recreational; extensive other	Nonprofit

Source: Robert W. Marans, Michael E. Hunt, and Kathleen L. Vakalo. "Retirement Communities." In Irwin Altman, M. Powell Lawton, and Joachim F. Wohlwill (Eds.), *Elderly People and The Environment.* New York: Plenum Press, 1984, pp. 57–93.

with the exception of continuing care centers in which there is a mixture of healthy and frail residents (see Box 9.2).

The rapid growth of retirement communities following World War II has provoked much controversy about whether or not they are desirable alternatives for older people. Some people argue that the retirement community is an unnatural environment and can lead only to stagnation and boredom, while others criticize it for being a pleasure-seeking community dominated by a "fun morality." Another view is that age-segregated communities put undue stress on their residents because of their lack of privacy and the pressure on members to be active and sociable. On the other hand, others claim that retirement communities are beneficial because they afford the elderly a higher degree of social interaction and in this way alleviate the problems of loneliness and isolation. Some feel that adjustment to retirement is made easier in such communities. (See the Reading at the end of this chapter concerning an age-segregated retirement community.)

Much of the sociological research on retirement communities has focused on the effects of age segregation on the residents. A classic study by Bultena and Wood (1969) compared retired persons in age-integrated communities and age-segregated communities. They found that those who had moved to retirement communities rated twice as high in life satisfaction as those who settled in age-integrated communities

Box 9.2   **Continuing Care Retirement Communities**

In contrast to retirement communities that are designed primarily for the healthy, active young-old, continuing care retirement communities (also referred to as life-care communities) are geared more toward serving the older and often frail elderly. A relatively new and unique option for the elderly, they combine housing, personal care, and nursing home care. While the older continuing care communities provided only the two extremes of care—independent living and nursing home care—the newer communities provide a continuum of care ranging from independent living, personal care, some health-related care to skilled nursing care. Typically, residents move from one level to another as their needs change.

Upon entering the community, residents sign a contract which requires them to pay an entrance fee ranging from $40,000 to over $150,000, along with monthly fees ($500 to $2,000), in exchange for the services that they will receive. The contract usually remains in effect for the rest of the resident's life. For these fees, residents are provided with health care and nursing home care services at less than the full cost of such care if and when the need arises. This arrangement may be viewed as a type of long-term care insurance as those residents who require fewer health and nursing home care services pay in part for those who need more of such services. The average age at entering a continuing care community is about 75. For those living in apartment units, the average age is 80; for those in the nursing home units, the average age is 85.

Most continuing care communities are operated by private, nonprofit organizations and some by religious organizations. It is estimated that presently there are 300 communities of this type serving over 90,000 residents. Their number has doubled in the last decade and it is expected to increase rapidly in the future.

Sources: Joel P. Weeden, Robert J. Newcomer, and Thomas O. Byerts, "Housing and Shelter for Frail and Nonfrail Elders: Current Options and Future Directions." In R. J. Newcomer, M. P. Lawton, T. O. Byerts (Eds.), *Housing an Aging Society: Issues, Alternatives, and Policy.* New York: Van Nostrand Reinhold, 1986, pp. 181–188; U.S. Senate Special Committee on Aging. *Developments in Aging: 1987.* Washington, DC: U.S. Government Printing Office, 1988.

(Table 9.2). Bultena and Wood attribute these high levels of life satisfaction of retirement community residents to several factors.

First, the persons in the retirement community had higher incomes, as well as higher educational and occupational levels; in addition, they perceived their health as being better than that of those in the regular communities. Secondly, the features of the retirement community contribute positively to the adaptation of the retirement role. Those persons in the retirement community were found to be similar not only in age but in socioeconomic status and background. Such homogeneity promotes a high degree of social interaction and facilitates the formation of new friendships. Compared with those in regular communities, a smaller proportion of the migrants to retirement communities reported a decline in close friends as a result of the move,

Table 9.2   PERCENTAGE DISTRIBUTION ON
             LIFE SATISFACTION SCORES OF
             AGED MIGRANTS IN RETIREMENT
             AND REGULAR COMMUNITIES IN
             ARIZONA

Life satisfaction	Retirement communities N = 322	Regular communities N = 199
Low morale	3	10
Medium morale	40	63
High morale	57	27

Source: Gordon L. Bultena and Vivian Wood, "The American Retirement Community: Bane or Blessing?" *Journal of Gerontology* (24), no. 2 (1969), p. 211.

and there was less dissatisfaction with the number of friends they had made. Furthermore, the retirement community has a strong orientation to full-time leisure pursuits as opposed to the orientation to productivity and the work ethic in a regular community. Persons oriented toward leisure-time activities find support for this from other residents in the retirement community.

In comparing communities, an important point to consider is the factor of selective migration. Many persons who choose retirement communities come from backgrounds characterized by high levels of social participation, and they are attracted to these communities because of the social and recreational activities provided. Those persons who are not predisposed to such activities and have lifelong patterns of minimal social participation might be unhappy and demoralized in such a setting. Seventy-five percent of the respondents from the regular community in Arizona expressed negative attitudes toward retirement communities. Bultena and Wood point out that "older persons, just as those of other ages, have a diversity of social-interaction styles and that these require differential social structures to maintain morale." It seems evident that retirement communities are not suited to everyone's needs, but for some people they can have a beneficial effect on morale and satisfaction with retirement.

Age-segregated communities are often criticized for being unnatural environments. In his case study of Fun City, a planned retirement community in the West, Jerry Jacobs observed older persons' adjustment to this environment.

> Fun City had no children, young adults, or ethnic minorities. . . . The complete lack of children and/or young adults in Fun City led many new residents to consider their environment unnatural even if they were glad or at least ambivalent about the state of affairs. After all, if one had lived for seventy years in the outside world, one saw or at least knew of all kinds of people. . . . Insofar as one did not encounter, for the first time in his life, all kinds, Fun City was experienced by many residents as unnatural and a place that took some getting used to. In short, new residents in Fun City experienced a form of culture shock.

Originally, retirement communities were found predominantly in the Sunbelt (Southern and Southwestern states), but recently they have been developing at an increasing rate in other sections of the country. A study of Katherine Heintz of 1033 New Jersey residents in five retirement communities found that they attracted mostly residents who had formerly lived in nearby cities in New York, Pennsylvania, and New Jersey. There appears to be a nationwide trend for the elderly to move short distances from their former urban homes and to relocate in the metropolitan fringe areas so that they can be close to their families and friends in nearby cities.

Most of the reasons given by the residents for their move to a New Jersey retirement community involved antipathy toward city life, reflected in such phrases as "sick of city life," "bad neighbors," "neighborhood deteriorating," "pollution," "too many kids," "tired of city's rat race," and "closed-in feeling." Two important factors influencing the decision to move were the economic advantages and the proximity to their former residences. Although the people did not specify availability of planned leisure activities as a primary reason for moving to a retirement community, the appeal of such activities is shown by the fact that almost three-fourths of the residents participated in them.

The residents indicated that they were highly satisfied with their retirement community. Satisfaction was found to be positively correlated with the length of residence; that is, the longer people lived there, the more content they were. This high level of satisfaction was supported by the fact that 90 percent said they would recommend such a community to their friends who were planning to move.

Most studies indicate high levels of social interaction among the residents of age-segregated communities. When work, family, and other roles are lost with age, retirement communities afford the elderly an opportunity to acquire new roles to take their place. On the other hand, retirement communities are definitely not for all older persons. Some cannot afford them, others do not wish to be isolated from younger age groups or to be pressured into participating in social and recreational activities. But for those elderly who are leisure-oriented and who have the money and desire for this type of lifestyle, retirement communities represent a highly satisfactory living arrangement.

SUMMARY

1. A group is two or more people who interact with one another in a standardized pattern and who share a sense of common identity. People who have some particular attribute in common are considered a category, not a group. But if members of a category begin to interact with one another and to share a sense of relatedness, they may become a group. Rose argues that older people in our society are in the process of being transformed from a category into a group. He also asserts that because of certain demographic and social trends that are occurring in our society, a subculture of aging is emerging. The creation of such groups as the AARP and Gray Panthers support Rose's contention.

2. Groups that we use to compare ourselves to and to measure our successes and failures against are called reference groups. Reference groups provide us

with a set of norms, attitudes, and values. At present, there is a lack of age-appropriate reference groups for the elderly, and for this reason, many older people continue to judge themselves by middle-age standards.

3. Groups may be analyzed by the type of relationship that exists among their members. Relationships that are intimate, personal, and sentimental characterize those found in primary groups. Primary groups help to support and sustain the individual, and they function as instruments of social control.

4. Examples of primary groups are family, friends, and neighbors. Formal organizations, unlike primary groups, are large and impersonal groups that are designed to achieve specific goals. Examples of formal organizations are government agencies and hospitals. To accomplish most tasks, both primary groups and formal organizations work together.

5. Voluntary associations are one type of formal organization in which membership is based on choice. The largest voluntary association for older people is the American Association of Retired Persons (AARP), followed by the National Council on Senior Citizens (NCSC). Senior centers have grown rapidly since their beginning in 1943. Today the multipurpose center offers activities ranging from arts and crafts instruction to employment and housing services.

6. Retirement communities may be classified by whether they are planned or unplanned. Planned communities may be subsidized or unsubsidized. Another way of classifying retirement communities is by size, types of residents, services, and sponsorship. Most studies indicate that the residents of retirement communities manifest a high degree of social interaction and activity. Although retirement communities are not a universal solution to the problems of older people, for some they are proving to be a most satisfactory one.

KEY TERMS

group
social category
aging subculture
reference group
primary group
formal organizations
theory of shared functions
voluntary association

multipurpose senior center
community
retirement communities
unplanned retirement communities
planned retirement communities
subsidized retirement community
nonsubsidized retirement community

FOR FURTHER STUDY

Carp, Frances M. (1966). *A future for the aged: Victoria Plaza and its residents.* Austin: University of Texas Press.

A study of a public-housing complex for the elderly that focuses on life satisfaction and adjustment among residents.

Heintz, Katherine M. (1976). *Retirement communities: For adults only*. New Brunswick: The Center for Urban Policy Research/Rutgers, The State University of New Jersey.

Focuses on the characteristics of retirement communities, their occupants, and their impact upon the municipal environment.

Jacobs, Jerry. 1975. Older persons and retirement communities. Springfield, IL: Charles C. Thomas.

Contains case studies of a retirement complex, a retirement community, and an apartment building for retired persons.

Peterson, Warren A., & Jill Quadagno (Eds.) (1985). *Social bonds in later life: Aging and interdependence*. Beverly Hills, CA: Sage.

Unified by the theme of interdependence in social relationships, the papers in this volume cover a wide variety of subjects ranging from marital relationships and support systems to social services.

Reading

Senior Settlers

Nancy Osgood

The issue of age-segregation versus age-integration of the elderly has been debated for several decades. The following selection, taken from a case study of a large planned retirement community in Arizona, helps us to understand how age-segregated communities affect older persons.

Upon first entering this small, rather isolated desert Shangri-la, one is struck first by the breathtaking beauty of the community. The scenic view of the mountains and desert is unparalleled. In many respects, the community itself resembles a typical middle-class suburb of a medium-sized city, yet it differs in a few significant respects. Upon entering the community, one is greeted by a very large sign that reads: "Get that Hidden Valley grin that comes from living good again." The beautiful streets are considerably wider than average, and they are immaculately clean; most of the inhabitants who walk along the sidewalks or who maneuver along the streets in their cars or golf carts are over 60 years of age and are dressed as if they were on their way

Nancy J. Osgood: *Senior Settlers: Social Integration in Retirement Communities*. New York: Praeger, 1982.

to play a few holes of golf, swim in a nearby pool, or engage in other casual outdoor activities—which, in reality, most of them are. Conspicuously absent from the town are fast food places, movie theaters, bowling alleys, and elementary and high schools. The two land development offices located on the main street, the bulldozers and construction crews, and half-constructed homes located throughout the community are the outward symbols of community growth and development. Unlike most typical suburbs, at 2:00 in the afternoon the streets of Hidden Valley are filled with people usually in pairs or small groups. The main street is fairly congested at any time of the day or early evening. . . .

A wide variety of living arrangements are available to residents of Hidden Valley. Living quarters range from small one-bedroom rental apartments in the center of town to large ranchettes on several acres of land outside the town. Several residents live in two- and three-bedroom single-family dwellings, built in the Spanish style and situated in rows on tree-lined streets in or near the town. Mobile home living is also available to residents of Hidden Valley. . . .

Several facilities catch the eye of the newcomer to Hidden Valley. Perhaps most notable is the 10,000-square foot recreation facility, complete with large meeting rooms, facilities for ceramics, photography, general arts and crafts, and card rooms indoors, as well as an Olympic-sized swimming pool, shuffleboard and tennis courts, and the "Par 3" golf course outside. What is most impressive is the fact that the parking lot is so filled with cars nearly every weekday at any time of the day that it is almost impossible to find a parking space in order to go in to see what is going on. Once inside one cannot but be impressed by the complete facilities and meeting rooms, as well as by the large number of residents who are engaged in activities inside the facility and in golfing, swimming, and playing shuffleboard outside.

Another popular and visible part of the community is the private golf course and country club on the outskirts of town. The country club does a booming lunchtime business, and a major complaint of residents is that the golf course is so crowded that not everyone who wants to play always get a chance.

The shopping center in the heart of town is another notable feature. Most Hidden Valley businesses are located in the Hidden Valley Shopping Mall. . . .

The Mall was specifically designed to accommodate the needs of the retired citizens of Hidden Valley with ramps, spacious sitting areas, and well-landscaped open spaces. The Mall not only serves as a shopping facility, but also is Hidden Valley's "downtown" area, supplying financial, legal, investment, and retail services. . . .

ORGANIZED SOCIAL LIFE

The organized social life of Hidden Valley residents revolves around eight churches, some 100 different organizations, organized recreational pursuits, and various involvements in community-wide projects and organizations, as well as involvement in community decision-making and local self-government. . . .

Clubs and Organizations

Nearly everyone interviewed mentioned their involvement in some club or organization as one of the activities which keeps them busy now that they are retired from gainful employment. When asked to judge how many in Hidden Valley are active in clubs and organizations, most of those interviewed stated somewhere in the range of 75 to 80 percent of all residents. The local land development people and the local service providers (priest, doctor, dentist, psychiatrist) agreed that nearly 80 percent of all residents are involved in one or more clubs or organizations. One resident stated: "We know everybody in town. This is a very 'social' community; people are active in clubs and organizations, community projects, and community-wide events—not like any other place I've been in the country." Another resident, discussing the availability of clubs and organizations, told me: "It's like my preacher said, 'If there are two people here with the same interest, they'll find each other.' The wide variety of clubs and organizations makes it possible for everyone to find something to do that they enjoy, and friends there who enjoy doing it, too.". . .

Organized Recreation

From the beginning, there has been a major emphasis on all types of recreation and leisure activities at Hidden Valley. The developers stress the availability of golf courses, swimming pools, shuffleboard courts, numerous arts and crafts classes, and hobby clubs in order to attract new residents. Brochures are filled with pictures of recreational facilities, and various arts and crafts items are displayed in the recreational center. The guided tour for prospective residents hits all the major recreation centers and a few of the arts and crafts classes. Several of the residents made the comment: "When I saw all the facilities and classes, I bought my house the same day." And a younger man whose parents moved to Hidden Valley put it in a similar way when he told me: "Man, they just show them those swimming pools and all those classes in ceramics and the woodworking shop and they are just like little kids in a candy store. Can't wait to get there to have fun." This comment was not offered as a negative one. This young man's father is now one of the most active members of the community and very happy with this new life. . . .

Interviews with residents revealed that golf and bridge are the two favorite activities. Several residents, when asked, indicated that over half of the residents golf at Hidden Valley. Another popular activity is ceramics. The ceramics group became so large that they have now split and offer two classes. . . .

INFORMAL SOCIAL ORGANIZATION

In addition to the formally organized social life, there are several forms of informal social interaction that occur on a daily basis in the community. Friendship groups, neighboring, visiting, and mutual aid in times of sickness or emergency permeate daily life. In fact, residents who were interviewed told me that Hidden Valleyans pride themselves on the fact that they are not judged and do not judge residents on the basis of how much money they have or their social position, but rather on their quality as people and on their "sociability."

Friendships

Most residents interviewed indicated that they have more friends in Hidden Valley than they ever had in other communities in which they lived. Most residents found their friends at church, in organizations and activities, or in the local neighborhood centers. Most of them participated in activities with friends, had coffee or lunch together, went shopping together, golfed or played bridge in one another's homes, or took trips to Tucson or Mexico together. Nearly everyone interviewed stated that all or most of their friends were living in Hidden Valley.

Informal visiting was a favorite pastime and generally occurred on a neighborhood basis. Residents indicated that neighbors would drop in with cookies or pies or just to chat and share a cup of coffee. They saw neighbors riding by on their bikes. They also met outside while they were working in the yard or having a barbecue.

Certain places become the scene for informal socializing. Residents can be seen in the shopping mall and the local post office, chatting with friends or sharing lunch or a cup of coffee. The same group of people generally frequent the post office every day at the same time, and it has become a sort of informal meeting place where friends interact on a regular basis. Usually those who arrived alone can be seen leaving in twos or threes after chatting informally for a while.

The cocktail party in Hidden Valley is one of the primary means of informal socializing. Residents, without fail, have friends and neighbors in for cocktails nearly every day at 5:00 P.M. This practice has resulted in several outsiders noting the "alcohol problem" in Hidden Valley. Residents themselves were less likely to perceive that they had an "alcohol problem." Most of those interviewed cited the parties as their major means of meeting and entertaining friends. . . .

One resident told me she had sworn all her life that she would never come to a community where everyone was older, but after living in Hidden Valley for the past three years she has changed her mind. She said: "I love it here. People here like what I like, and we are friends and can do all kinds of things together. I'd never leave." Another resident commented on how the similarity of the residents contributed to the formation of friendships: "There is a real sense of community here. It is the people. They are all from similar backgrounds and value the same things, share the same interests, so we can all work together and get real close." Another resident said: "There is a neighborliness about the community, an intense desire to make people comfortable. There is a helpfulness and openness, and everybody has the feeling of being wanted in Hidden Valley." The Catholic priest put it this way:

> People here have the time to help each other out, to do things together, to socialize. They all have similar interests and like to do the same things, so it promotes friendships and intimacy.

. . . In addition to friendship and neighboring, several patterns of mutual aid were discovered in Hidden Valley. Residents exchange all kinds of services, from dog sitting and watching out for each other's houses when the neighbors are gone to taking care of an older, sicker member every day. One woman interviewed jokingly re-marked: "My husband is always up on other people's roofs. If I can't find him I just look up." Another related the story of their close friend who had recently lost her husband. "We keep her under our wing. We visit her, walk her dog. We are really concerned about her. We help her fix things around the house, and we talk to her and let her cry to us.". . .

HOW RESIDENTS VIEW THEMSELVES AND THEIR COMMUNITY

Interviews with residents revealed a very strong positive identification with their community and a host of positive images of Hidden Valley life. Most of those inter-viewed stressed their pride in the community and its cleanliness, the high quality of people, of the various community groups, and of the projects, such as the work of the Community Fund. None of the residents interviewed wanted to live anywhere else. Most of the residents took great pride in their own homes and lawns, spending long hours improving the interior of homes, building on extra rooms, making furniture or various arts and crafts items to adorn the inside of their homes. Nearly all those interviewed saw themselves as a cut above other communities, a higher quality people, strong and independent and hard working. One woman summed up the view of many when she said: "We are a higher quality people here. We are all educated and from interesting occupational backgrounds. We all worked hard in our commu-nities before coming here, and we work hard to make this a better community now."

"Modern-Day Pioneers"

Probably the most frequently mentioned image of themselves expressed in interviews and casual conversations was that of modern-day pioneers. Over and over again residents described themselves as pioneers in a new land, carving an existence out of what used to be just a piece of desert. The "pioneering spirit" of life in the community was referred to by several. One of the very first residents to move into Hidden Valley expressed it in these terms:

> The few of us who were here in the early days were all from somewhere else; and we were lonesome for our home and families, just like the early pioneers who came out West. So we had to pull together and build a community together, and we did.

Another long-term resident revealed:

> There is a strong sense of community here that developed long ago when the people had to band together to protect their rights when the developers changed so much. Now they want to stick together.

Another expressed her views this way: "We all had to pull up stakes and leave our family and old friends and come to a new place. We had to cling to one another or we wouldn't make it. The ones of us who came are stronger and more independent spirits than others our age, like the early pioneers. It is not easy to leave your home and your family and friends, but like the early pioneers who came out West, we came seeking an even better life. Some of us came for the adventure and excitement, just like the early settlers.". . .

Many of the residents stressed the trauma of leaving old friends, family, familiar communities, and well-known surroundings as responsible, in part, for the need to cling to each other in Hidden Valley. This trauma helps explain the need to "stick together," to build a community together, and to form friendships to replace former friendships and former involvement in community.

"We're All Equal"

Another equally powerful image residents hold of themselves is the view that they are all equal, free from the distinctions based on social status and income in larger society. They are no longer forced to keep up with the Joneses and to compete for money, status, and social position. Most noted that fellow residents were honored and respected for their neighborliness, sociability, and their efforts to work for and improve the community, as well as their talents and skills in various arts and crafts and organizations which they share with fellow residents. Residents denied emphatically that former career or amount of money were important in Hidden Valley. One resident put it this way: "When we come here, we start all over again. Our fellow residents don't know or care what we did, how many cars we had or what kind of house we lived in. They don't care how much money we made or now have. We have to prove ourselves as people here. The kind of person we are is all that counts, not those outward symbols of success that younger people value. If you are kind and charitable and interested in your fellows, then you make it here.". . .

"It's Fun Living with Others Your Own Age"

Another often uttered phrase in interviews with residents was "It's fun living with others your own age." The reasons were many: (1) they wanted to escape the noise and destructiveness of small children and teenagers; (2) they wanted a ready pool of people who also had the time and desire to golf or swim with them or engage in other activities; (3) they wanted to feel free to be themselves and not live up to younger people's expectations; nor did they want to have to "act their age" for those younger people; (4) they felt they shared more experiences and values with others their own age; and as a result, they could become closer to others and have deeper, more intimate relationships, which are so important at this stage in life when friends and spouses die and when sickness and death are imminent. . . .

Several who preferred age-segregation pointed out that they felt more free to be themselves and have fun in such a setting. One woman said: "Here you don't have to compete with beautiful girls and their pretty figures and all that energy. Here you can feel like you can swim and not feel foolish." Another man put it similarly when he remarked: "You can be free and relaxed when you are with others your own age. You can be yourself. You don't have to 'act your age,' whatever that is, like you are expected to by younger people. If I want to get out and dance the polka and make a fool of myself, I can do it here. Nobody laughs at me. In fact, they usually join in with me."

The most commonly repeated advantage of living among age peers was that it provides a ready source of friends and people who share interests and activities together, which is not possible to find in mixed-age neighborhoods where you are the only one on the block who is retired and you have no one to do anything with. . . .

THOSE WHO DON'T FIT IN: "OUTSIDERS"

It should be clear from the discussion above that Hidden Valley residents are united in sharing a common set of values. Residents highly value their leisure-oriented lifestyle and the leisure ethic. They also stress active involvement in activities, clubs, and organizations, as well as community involvement and service. Neighborliness and sociability are also valued by Hidden Valleyans. Most pride themselves on being vibrant and healthy, as well. Residents take pride in their homes and yards and in the beauty of their community and the surrounding countryside. They are happy to be among their age peers and do not like children and teenagers. Interviews and observations confirm these basic values, which serve to unite the residents in their common life.

Those who do not or cannot participate in the active lifestyle are the outsiders in Hidden Valley. As one resident, who is shunned put it: "If you don't golf here, they treat you like a bum, like you don't even exist." Some residents were never "joiners" in their adult lives, and they do not join organized activities, nor do they participate in the "active lifestyle" that most Hidden Valleyans cherish. These individuals are not befriended by other residents. They are talked about. They are avoided. They are not invited to other people's homes. It is as though they did not exist. One woman who described herself as "an introvert" does not join group activities. She talked at length in the interview of her loneliness and total lack of friends: "I'd like to have friends, but no one has come to ask me to be a friend or to join in their social groups. They probably can see that I'm not the sociable type and, well, you have to be here or you are just lonely, very lonely.". . .

One resident who came to the door unshaven and in his pajamas was very bitter. He confided that he did not have one friend in Hidden Valley because he did not like golf or bridge or any of the activities. Consequently, nobody cared to associate with him. He also loved his family and had grandchildren visit often. This man had a heart attack earlier in the year and he described the pain in his arm and chest and his experience of falling on the floor. He lay there for seventeen hours in a half-awake, half-asleep state until he finally got to the phone and called a doctor. He said: "I could have died there and nobody would have known for days. I don't have one friend here." Another resident related a similar incident about a neighbor who had died recently, an older woman who never negaged in organized activities and, as a result, had no friends in the community. The woman had died, and no one even knew she was dead until three days later when a maintenance man found her. One resident remarked bitterly: "Oh, we have a few friends; but if we were drinkers, we'd have triple the friends. People here are really into their cocktail parties, and they know we don't drink, so they don't invite us over." Another resident interviewed confided: "Loneliness is a problem for some of us who just don't seem to fit here. I think people who are not mixers, those who are kind of shy and don't know how to just strike up a conversation with someone or go out and get involved in community activities, just get excluded from life here. We have to just sit home alone and do the best we can."

Comments such as these indicate that residents of Hidden Valley have created boundaries within their community. It is important to them to view themselves as healthy, active, involved community members. Perhaps they are trying very hard to avoid the negative stereotype of the poor, disengaged older person who sits out life rocking in a rocking chair. Those who do not engage in this active lifestyle are ostracized and shunned by fellow residents. They are effectively "eliminated.". . .

Individuals who do not take pride in their homes and yards are also "deviants" in the community. They are severely controlled by the local homeowner's associations, that enforce the deed restrictions. No one is allowed to have laundry hanging outside, or recreational vehicles parked out front, or any towers or apparatus that obstruct neighbors' views of the mountains. One explanation for the tight social control in this area is that residents no longer have families or full-time jobs to put their time and energy into and to really care about. They therefore shift all their time and work into building a beautiful community and into their homes and yards.

Chapter
10

Social Stratification and Aging

"*A*ll men are created equal, but some are more equal than others" is a common saying. Inequality and social stratification are certainly inherent and pervasive in social life. Archaeological evidence reveals that social stratification was present among the ancient Greeks and Persians as well as among early preliterate societies. Yet people have always dreamed of a classless society in which equality and distinctions of rank do not exist.

For thousands of years, social stratification has been a source of conflict and controversy and a subject of philosophical debate. Stratification not only dates back to antiquity, but it is found in all known societies today. *Stratification* involves the ranking of individuals and families into higher and lower social positions according to their share of social rewards. Or it may simply be referred to as structured social inequality.

DIMENSIONS OF STRATIFICATION

The pioneering work on stratification was done by Karl Marx. He viewed stratification along a single dimension: economic organization. According to Marx, social classes are derived from the system of production. Those who own and control the means of production compose the ruling class or the bourgeoisie, and those who work for them and have nothing to sell but their labor compose the working class or proletariat. The German sociologist Max Weber (1922/1968) recognized the importance of the economic basis of stratification, but he asserted that Marx's view of stratification was too simplified. Weber saw stratification as being encompassed by a three-dimensional scheme that can be translated into: wealth, power, and prestige. We will now discuss each of these as they pertain to the elderly.

Wealth and Income

Huge inequalities continue to exist in this country between the very rich and the very poor. Proportionately, the rich are getting richer and the poor are getting poorer. The gap between the rich and the poor continued to widen between 1977 and 1988. During that period the majority of the population experienced an income stagnation. But the average family income of the top five percent (those earning more than $124,651 a year before taxes) grew by $33,895 and the top one percent (those earning more than $303,900) grew by $129,402. The pattern of the distribution of wealth, which is based on what people own (such as property, stocks or bonds), seems to be fairly stable and even more highly concentrated than income distribution that is based on what people receive. In fact, the distribution of wealth has remained much the same in this country for about the last 200 years (Edsall, 1988; Smelser, 1988).

Wealth   The *wealth* of the elderly is far more varied than that of any other age group. In 1984, 15.4 percent of elderly households had a net worth (assets minus debts) below $5,000, while 8.2 percent had a net worth of $250,000 or more (U.S. Bureau of the Census, 1986). *Forbes* magazine (1986) made a study of the 400 richest people in America and found that the average age of these individuals was 62.3 years and that they had an average net worth of $390 million each. Typically, a millionaire is a self-made entrepreneur who is in his or her early sixties (*U.S. News & World Report*, 1986). Thus, it is interesting to note that although the aged are more likely than other adults to be poor, they are also overrepresented in the very rich segment of the population.

The wealth of most elderly persons is mainly in the form of home equity. Nearly 75 percent of older persons own their homes, and of these, 80 percent are free of any mortgage. However, although many older persons' homes provide them with a sizable asset, in most cases these homes produce no income to help with daily living expenses. This situation has led to some elderly's being referred to as "house rich" but "cash poor" (U.S. Senate Special Committee on Aging, 1987–1988).

After home equity, the assets of the elderly are mostly in checking and savings accounts. Because savings tend to erode in times of inflation, studies on the effect of inflation on the distribution of wealth among households reveal that the largest decline in wealth occurs among families headed by elderly persons (Schulz, 1985).

Income   Although most younger persons get income from wages or salaries, this source accounts for only 17 percent of the elderly's income. The major source of *income* for the elderly is Social Security. About 38 percent of all income received by the elderly comes from this source. Income falls sharply at retirement. In 1987 the median income of families with heads age 65 and older was $20,808, while the median income of families with heads age 25 to 64 was $34,275 (U.S. Senate Special Committee on Aging, 1989). Social Security benefits, pensions, and assets accumulated over a lifetime often do not afford the majority of older people the same standard of living they had before retirement.

In a study of employed as well as of retired blue-collar workers, Rosenberg (1970) noted an inverse relationship between age and income level. He found that about 15 percent were poor among those persons between the ages of 45 and 54. The proportion of poverty rose to 25 percent in the 55-to-64 age group; in the 65-to-79 age category, the proportion of poor reached 55 percent.

Some maintain that the decline in income for older people poses little or no problem for them because they do not need as much money as younger persons. The "old need less" argument asserts that elderly persons voluntarily curtail their consumption patterns and, as a result, spend less. On the other hand, others argue that the old spend less because they have less to spend (Streib, 1985; Dowd, 1980).

Power

Another dimension of stratification closely related to the possession of money is power. Although there is not always a one-to-one correlation between them—not all powerful people are wealthy, and not all wealthy people are powerful—in general, a strong relationship between them does exist. Power may be divided into two main types: individual and societal. *Individual power* is the ability to control one's own life, whereas *societal power* is the ability to influence the lives of others.

Individual Power   In Shakespeare's *King Lear*, Lear divides his kingdom among his daughters. The gratitude of his daughters turns out to be far less than he had expected, and he finds that he has made the mistake of placing himself in a dependent and powerless position (Goody, 1977). Throughout history the owning and retaining of property has given the elderly power over younger family members. For example, Fischer (1978) writes that in seventeenth-century New England fathers held onto their property as a way of preserving power and authority over their sons. In rural Ireland, property is used by the father as a form of blackmail through which he is able to keep his sons in submission to his authority—even into their thirties and forties— by refusing to reveal which son will take over his farm until he is ready to retire

(Streib, 1972). Today in our society even small amounts of wealth and property are sufficient for the elderly to exercise power. Many older persons maintain leverage over their relatives by threatening to change their will or by keeping them guessing about its provisions (Streib, 1985).

Another form of individual power is being able to choose the quality and type of life that one wishes to lead and to have access to the goods and services that one desires with the minimum amount of dependence upon other persons. This often boils down to having adequate financial resources. Many older people, because of their meager circumstances, are deprived of this type of power; they lack the freedom of choice and the power to control their own lives, and thus they feel helpless and dependent.

Power and dependence also play an important role in social exchange relationships. Briefly stated, *exchange theory* is based on the premise that much social interaction can be reduced to rewards and costs. People tend to maximize rewards and reduce costs (Homans, 1961; Blau, 1964). Rewards include money, knowledge, services, and respect; costs have to do with the unpleasantness experienced in obtaining a reward. Persons will continue to interact as long as each perceives the relationship as being rewarding rather than costly. If a person provides more rewards than his or her exchange partner can return, this situation creates an imbalance with the result that the partner with the greatest valued resources gains power over the other. "Power" is used in this sense to refer to the state of relative independence that results from having a greater share of valued resources than one's exchange partner.

Dowd (1975, 1980) has applied the exchange theory to the elderly, maintaining that because of their limited power resources some older people become increasingly unable to enter into a balanced exchange relationship with other individuals and are thus placed in a docile, dependent position. The elderly's costs in yielding to the wishes and demands of others steadily increase until a point is reached at which additional costs become so high that often they choose to withdraw from the relationship. For example, suppose that an impoverished elderly woman has no transportation to church. A young neighbor offers her a ride. The relationship becomes unbalanced as the older woman has no way to repay the neighbor, her exchange partner. Even if she were able to afford to give her money for the ride, such payment would be inappropriate. Because of the limited power resources that she possesses, the only thing the elderly woman has to offer is dependence and compliance. After several months, she decides that the cost of going to church becomes too high a price to pay in terms of her self-respect, and she withdraws from the relationship.

Societal Power   Elderly persons are disproportionately represented in positions of political power. In fact, in most advanced industrialized nations like our own, as a rule there is a relationship between advancing age and the holding of major political office. Because of the long-standing seniority system in the U.S. Congress, for example, which grants special privileges such as committee chairmanships to members who have served for many years, older politicians have substantially greater power over the outcome of legislation than their younger counterparts (Williamson Evans & Powell, 1982).

Though much has been written about "senior power" and "gray power," the elderly do not vote as a bloc. As a result, they do not have the political clout that many people think they do. Also, it is unlikely that they will gain power in the future by forming a political bloc of voters. Whatever political or social gains the elderly have made in the past were due more to their uniting with other, more powerful groups rather than the influence of senior power (Binstock, 1974; Williamson Evans & Powell, 1982). (This topic will be discussed more fully in Chapter 14, "The Political System.")

Prestige

A third dimension of social stratification is prestige. *Prestige* refers to the social recognition and respect that one receives from others. Usually a person's occupation is the major determinant of prestige. Prestige in American society comes to those who are employed in such fields as science, law, and medicine. A study by Friedmann and Havighurst (1954) in which physicians over age 65 were interviewed on what their profession meant to them revealed the importance of prestige.

> Some doctors stated that to be a physician meant that one belonged to an elite class. It meant that one associated with important people and was in a position of leadership in the community. This feeling was expressed by Dr. I., who described his work as . . . "a nice clean profession. It has prestige and you can get into so many inaccessible places just by sending in your card." Dr. I. told of the time that he wanted to visit someone who was in jail. The attendant told him that he could not possibly get in. He just gave the attendant his card and the latter said with reverence, "Oh, come in, doctor."

At retirement, individuals suffer a decline in status mainly because they are no longer productive in a predominantly work-oriented society and because of the negative stereotypes that are associated with being old. Professionals and other persons of high occupational status frequently continue to identify with their occupations after retirement, and in this way they retain their titles and some of their former prestige. This practice is especially characteristic of retired doctors, professors, and judges, who continue to be called by their titles. Also, military officers of high rank are often addressed by their former titles long after retirement.

STATUS INCONSISTENCY

As a rule, older persons (as well as younger persons) who are poor also have little prestige and power. Conversely, some statuses as that of lawyer or physician rank high in all three dimensions: wealth, prestige, and power. But there are some instances in which one status level may be independent of the other two. For example, a university professor may rank high in prestige but low in wealth and power, or a drug dealer may have a high income but little prestige and power. This situation is called *status inconsistency.*

As persons age, they often experience this inconsistency. For instance, some persons at retirement are well off financially but have little prestige and power; there are others at retirement who have a high level of prestige but little power or income.

Occupational prestige has been remarkably consistent throughout the years in this country. Occupations such as physicians and scientists continue to rank among the highest in prestige; street cleaners rank among the lowest. (Nick Myers)

Some studies reveal that status inconsistency may result in some degree of social withdrawal or lead to psychological stress, and in some cases it may manifest itself physically in psychosomatic symptoms. People with inconsistent statuses generally compensate by attempting to claim their highest status as their overall or master status, and they expect others to treat them on the basis of their highest status. A retired president of a large corporation, for example, may continually remind others of his or her former rank and seek the deference that he or she was shown in the previous position (Trela, 1976).

SOCIAL CLASS

We have been discussing the reasons for social stratification in society—the unequal distribution of wealth, power, and prestige. Now let us examine the patterns that social stratification takes or the social class system in our society that results from these inequalities.

Social class may be defined as a category of individuals and families who share relatively equal amounts of social rewards. To determine class divisions, sociologists popularly use three criteria that are closely associated with one another—occupation, education, and income. In most cases, education is related to a good job, and a good job is usually related to a high income. Because of this correlation, it is not always necessary to know all three factors about a person to establish his or her social class membership. By knowing one factor—especially occupation, which is the main indicator of social class—we can make assumptions about the other two.

Class Divisions

Identifying distinct classes in the United States is difficult. The number of social classes is not fixed, and the boundaries between them are often blurred. Although some sociologists identify only three classes—the upper class, the middle class, and the lower class—most sociologists generally prefer to use five or six classes. One of the earliest studies of social class in a modern community was done by Warner and Lunt (1941). They analyzed a small New England town, that they called Yankee City, and identified six classes by dividing each of the major classes into an upper and lower level. Later, when he studied a city in the Midwest, Warner (1949) used only five classes, by not dividing the upper class.

The type of home and neighborhood an older person lives in generally indicates his or her social class as well as reflecting significant differences in lifestyles. (Nick Myers)

Class and Life Chances

Social class has far-reaching consequences that penetrate every aspect of a person's daily life and social interaction. Few aspects of life have more effect on the way we think and behave as does social class. It influences our life-opportunities or *life chances:* the probability that we will obtain the opportunities that affect health, longevity, and happiness. As Birren (1964) notes, "Although each individual is unique, with particular genetic, psychological and social characteristics, the accumulated effects of social class have an impact upon the way in which humans age." Let us now look at some of the factors associated with class membership and how they relate to aging and the aged:

1. *Life expectancy.* How long a person may be expected to live is influenced by social class. The chances of longevity are definitely greater in the higher social classes.

2. *Illness.* Persons in the lower class are not only likely to die earlier than those in the upper class, but they also suffer more from physical and mental illness. A study by Dovenmuehle and his associates (1970)—of 256 persons 60 years of age and older—found that persons of higher social levels had fewer limitations on physical functioning than those of lower levels. In addition, persons in the lower levels have a higher incidence of impairment of vision, arteriosclerosis, cardiovascular disease, hypertension, pulmonary disease, and arthritis.

   One of the most striking differences between the social classes is in the area of mental illness. Contrary to popular belief, for the population as a whole there is a lower incidence of mental illness in the upper classes than in the lower classes; this tends to be the case for older people as well.

   Clark and Anderson (1967) compared the social levels of persons 60 years of age and over who had undergone, or were in the process of undergoing, treatment in a San Francisco hospital for mental disorders with the social levels of mentally healthy persons of similar ages who lived in the community. The researchers found that the majority of hospital patients came from a considerably lower social level than the community residents did. Sixty-three percent of the community sample were from a high social level, compared with only 23 percent of the discharged hospital patients and with 14 percent of the hospital patients.

3. *Friendship patterns.* Various studies reveal that the number of friends a person has in old age appears to be related to social class. Middle-class people have a larger number of friends than those in the working class (manual workers including blue-collar workers; often used interchangeably with lower class). Also, members of the working class are dependent on neighbors as a source of friends, whereas middle-class persons rely on other sources of friendship. As a corollary, Blau (1981) reports that widows in the working class are more isolated and have fewer social opportunities than widows in the middle class.

4. *Age identification.* Feeling old tends to be related to social class. Rosow (1967) found in his Cleveland study that middle-class people aged 65 and over feel young or middle-aged as often as they feel old. Among the working-class sample, three out of every four persons thought of themselves as being older. Although few persons look forward to the prospect of growing old, it seems that working-class people can more readily accept it.

5. *Retirement adaptation.* Retirement patterns vary with status level. In her study of 306 male retirees, Simpson (1973) grouped workers into three general strata: upper white-collar workers, composed of professionals and executives; middle stratum, consisting of clerical workers, salespeople, and skilled craftsmen and foremen; and lower blue-collar workers, composed of semiskilled service workers and laborers. Of these three status levels, she found that though the upper white-collar workers received the greatest satisfaction from their work, they also made the most successful adaptation to retirement. Their adaptation was facilitated by their varied interests, their high level of community participation, and the freedom that their jobs afforded them to structure their own work routines. Although few of these men looked forward to retirement, when it came they adjusted well and were able to find meaningful substitutes for their work.

    The middle level anticipated retirement the most. Their work had little intrinsic meaning, and they looked forward to a life of leisure. In comparison to the upper white-collar workers, they had fewer interests and community roles, so they experienced more difficulty in finding substitutes for work.

    The blue-collar workers were not as enthusiastic about retirement as the middle level. They worried more about finances and felt a sense of helplessness toward life's events. In addition, their social relationships were limited to their family or neighbors, thus giving them the fewest outlets in retirement. The blue-collar workers were the least successful in adapting to retirement.

6. *Family interaction.* Studies of the relationship between social class and visiting patterns have found that working-class persons visit older members of their family more often than middle-class persons do. However, when geographic distance is not a factor, middle-class persons visit their relatives as much as, if not more than, members of the working class. It appears, then, that social class affects visiting patterns because middle-class persons tend to move more and live farther from their relatives than those in the working class (Bengtson, Olander, & Haddad, 1976).

    Family-help patterns also vary by social class. Generally, parents in the middle class help their adult children by giving them financial assistance. Those in the lower classes supply less in the way of finances and rely more on the exchange of services.

    In a study of grandparent roles, Albrecht (1973) found that males in the white-collar groups have more interaction with their grandchildren than those in the working class do. Overall, there was no significant difference in the grandmother role. Other researchers have found that a stronger tie existed between grandparents and their grandchildren when they lived nearby, especially for those in the middle and upper classes (Troll, Miller, & Atchley, 1979).

7. *Social participation*. Older persons in higher social levels participate more in community activities and tend to be more socially integrated into society than those in lower levels. In addition, the higher the level of income and education (often used as an index of social class), the greater the number of memberships in voluntary associations a person is likely to have. For older persons in the lower classes, social participation appears to revolve largely around their families and neighbors.

8. *Residential mobility*. Change of residence takes place twice as often for older people in the lower classes, compared with those in the upper classes. Some research reveals that the poor elderly in urban areas continuously search for different housing. When older persons in the upper classes decide to relocate, they tend to move to age-segregated apartment complexes or to retirement communities.

9. *Life satisfaction*. A strong correlation exists between being satisfied with life and holding high social status. Older persons from the upper classes are more likely to be satisfied with their lives than those in the lower classes. Family income appears to be one of the most important determinants of life satisfaction (Palmore, 1981).

10. *Leisure time*. How people use their leisure time varies with social class. Havighurst (1961) obtained information on leisure-time activities from a sample of 234 men and women in Kansas City between the ages of 40 and 70. He found that the favorite activities of the upper–middle class were flower and landscape gardening and participation in sports and voluntary associations, whereas the lower–middle class and lower-class people preferred television and manual-manipulative activities, such as home repair and woodworking. Members of the lower–middle and upper–lower classes especially favored fishing. Visiting friends and relatives ranked highest among the lower–lower class, as did vegetable gardening. All classes chose reading as a leisure-time activity about equally, with the exception of the lower class, who showed the least interest in it.

SOCIAL MOBILITY

Social mobility refers to the vertical movement of persons from one social class to another. Most people think of vertical social mobility as getting ahead and moving up the social ladder as success. Getting a better job, marrying a person of higher status, or moving to a better neighborhood are all examples of upward social mobility. But vertical mobility can be downward as well. Instances of downward mobility include loss or reduction of income or a job demotion.

Differences in leisure pursuits tend to vary with social class. A favorite activity of the upper-middle class is flower gardening.

Social Mobility and Aging

The process of social mobility is curvilinear in our society. Typically, there is a rise in mobility after young adulthood that then peaks in the middle years before leveling off and then gradually declining in the later years (Foner, 1986). Some older persons, especially single women and widows, have insufficient incomes to sustain an adequate standard of living. The following excerpt (Butler, 1975) is an example of downward mobility in old age as a result of widowhood:

Box 10.1 # Age Stratification Model

Social class is only one of the several bases of social stratification or structured social inequality. Just as all societies are stratified by social class, they are also stratified by age, race and ethnicity, and sex. According to Riley and her associates, who developed the *age stratification model,* the age structure of roles, much like social class, organizes society into a hierarchy. Age, like class, divides the population into strata or categories on the basis of the amount of wealth, power, and prestige (social rewards) they possess. Riley maintains that age functions as a means of control over society's rewards because it is built into the social structure as a criterion for when one takes on or gives up certain roles. In this way, age leads to inequality among the various age strata (e.g., young, middle-aged, and old) because people in some age strata have less access than others to valued roles and social rewards. For example, in our society the middle-aged have the greatest access to social rewards and the youth and the elderly the least.

Nancy Foner (1988) points out that social inequalities based on age do not inevitably produce tension and conflict between those at the bottom of the hierarchy and those above them, but the potential is there. For example, adolescents may resent the dominance of the middle-aged, and older persons who have suffered the loss of valued roles and social rewards may resent the more successful younger persons.

Furthermore, the age stratification model analyzes the movement of successive *cohorts* (individuals born within the same year or specified period) across time. Each cohort is considered unique because each experiences certain historical events (e.g., the Great Depression, World War II) that in turn influence its members' attitudes and behaviors.

The age stratification model has its limitations. It has been criticized for overemphasizing the power of one's age in explaining the distribution of societal rewards. Also the model assumes that there is little variation between individuals of the same birth cohort. Research has revealed that members of the same cohort often experience aging in a number of ways and that situational factors in the lives of the members within a cohort must be taken into account (Passuth and Bengtson, 1988).

Sources: Matilda W. Riley, Marilyn Johnson, and Anne Foner, *Aging and Society, Vol. 3: A Sociology of Age Stratification.* New York: Russell Sage Foundation, 1972; Matilda W. Riley, Anne Foner, and Joan Waring, ''Sociology of Age.'' In Neil J. Smelser (Ed.), *Handbook of Sociology.* Newbury Park, CA: Sage, 1988, pp. 243–290; Nancy Foner, *Ages in Conflict.* New York: Columbia University Press, 1984; Patricia M. Passuth and Vern L. Bengtson, *Sociological Theories of Aging: Current Perspectives and Future Directions.* New York: Springer, 1988.

Mrs. Woods: an old lady with a lightly made, stately body, carried with pride and some pain. Her beautifully wrinkled skin was almost translucent, showing her high cheekbones.

She would be pretty if not for the worried strain in her voice, face and hands, the shifting feet, distant eyes. A successful lawyer's wife, she had always been able to live in comfortable circumstances but was now under increasing financial pressure. She had outlived her savings.

When her lawyer makes a visit she puts on the violet and blue print dress. She does not change her flat brown shoes. She pins her hair in a soft white knot in back. The lawyer was the family attorney for years. He comes to receive her endorsed checks and pay her bills. He makes out a check to the realty company for rent, and two other checks, one for the housekeeper who comes once a week, the other for food. He continues to help her now, when she is on public assistance of $92 per month.

According to Foner and Schwab (1981), for many older persons the retirement role may be viewed as socially imposed downward mobility. By "socially imposed" they mean that the economic resources available to retirees are affected by circumstances that are beyond their control, such as the state of the economy, Social Security, and the soundness of pension programs.

Rosow (1967) investigated downward social mobility among older people in the middle and working classes, using loss of income as an indicator of downward mobility. Members in both social classes were equally matched in the proportion of retirees and widows who said they experienced a loss of income. As Table 10.1 shows, about one-fourth of the working class acknowledged that their class position declined, whereas only 14 percent of the middle class admitted a downward change. Rosow explains that growing old appears to be more threatening and demoralizing to people in higher-class positions because they have more to lose. Thus members of the middle class are more likely than those of the lower class to deny or minimize any loss in status.

Open and Closed Systems

The amount of upward mobility in a society is an important indicator of whether or not it has an open- or closed-class system. Theoretically, an *open-class system* permits its members to move up or down the social hierarchy, depending on their own accomplishments or failings. An example of a relatively open-class system is a modern industrial society like that of the United States. In a *closed-class system*, on the other hand, mobility is severely restricted. A person is assigned a certain status, usually at

Table 10.1   SOCIAL MOBILITY OF THE RETIRED AND WIDOWED BY SOCIAL CLASS

	Mobility		
Social class	Upward (percent)	Stable (percent)	Downward (percent)
Working class	9	65	26
Middle class	8	78	14

Source: Irving Rosow, *Social Integration of the Aged.* New York: Free Press, 1967, p. 282.

birth, that cannot be changed. The Indian caste system before the time of Gandhi is an example of such a system. No class system is completely open or totally closed, but all systems can be placed on an open-to-closed continuum.

Rosenberg (1970) studied the images that older and younger blue-collar workers in Philadelphia had about the class system. When workers were asked whether or not they thought the class system was open or closed in terms of their own experience in getting ahead, a larger proportion of younger than of older workers indicated that it was a closed-class system. Those men currently in the labor force appeared to be more discontented and exhibited more resentment than those who were retired. To explore beliefs about the class system in the future, the men were asked what they thought would be the chance of working people's getting ahead in the next ten years. Those still in the labor force tended to be more pessimistic about the future. A greater proportion of the younger men than of the older men believed that a closed-class system will prevent working-class advancement in the future. Rosenberg also examined the relationship between the economic context of the neighborhood where the workers lived and their image of the class system. He found that those older men who lived in the poorest neighborhoods were most likely to have a conception of a closed-class system.

SUMMARY

1. Social stratification or structured social inequality is found in every known human society. Stratification is the ranking of individuals and families into higher and lower social positions according to their share of social rewards. These rewards are wealth, power, and prestige.

2. Much inequality and variation exist in the distribution of wealth and income in the United States, especially among the older population. Power is also unequally distributed and may be divided into two types: individual and societal. Prestige, the social recognition that one receives from others, is largely determined by occupation. At retirement, a decline in prestige usually results.

3. Social classes are generally defined by occupation, education, and income. Though the number of social classes is not fixed and the divisions between the classes are often indistinct, most sociologists generally identify five or six classes. Class membership relates to one's life chances and opportunities. Factors correlated with social class include life expectancy, illness, friendship patterns, age identification, retirement adaptation, family interaction, social participation, residential mobility, life satisfaction, and leisure time.

4. Social mobility is the vertical movement of persons or groups from one social class to another. Downward mobility is frequently found among those who are retired or widowed. Social mobility is an important indicator of whether or not a society has an open- or closed-class system. According to Rosenberg's study of blue-collar workers, more older workers tend to see the American class system as open as compared with younger workers, who were less optimistic about their opportunities for advancement.

KEY TERMS

stratification
wealth
income
individual power
societal power
exchange theory
prestige
status inconsistency

social class
life chances
social mobility
age stratification model
cohort
open-class system
closed-class system

FOR FURTHER STUDY

Dowd, James J. (1980). *Stratification among the aged.* Monterey, CA: Brooks/Cole.

Emphasizes the relationship of the aging process to social class membership and society's stratification system.

Riley, Matilda W., Johnson, Marilyn & Foner, Anne (1972). *Aging and society: A sociology of age stratification,* Vol. 3. New York: Russell Sage Foundation.

Proposes a theory of age stratification that is in some ways similar to social class stratification.

Streib, Gordon F. (1985). "Social Stratification and Aging." In Robert H. Binstock and Ethel Shanas (Eds.), *Handbook of aging and the social sciences.* New York: Van Nostrand Reinhold, 1985.

Discusses some of the major dimensions of aging and stratification along with age consciousness and stratification in Great Britain and the Soviet Union.

Chapter
11

The Minority Elderly

One of the key characteristics of American society is the ethnic diversity of its population. Although such diversity has greatly enriched our culture, it also has contributed to conflict and social inequality. As we saw in Chapter 10 ("Social Stratification and Aging"), one way of stratifying society—the unequal distribution of social rewards—is by social class. Another way of stratifying society is by ethnicity. An *ethnic group* may be defined as a group of people that differs from the larger society in such characteristics as race, religion, nationality, language, or customs. Within this broad classification are *minority groups*—certain ethnic groups who are subject to prejudice and discrimination.

MINORITY GROUPS

The sociological concept of "minority group" is not used in a numerical sense; but it is used to denote some form of dominance. For instance, in the United States the blacks are a minority group and constitute about 12 percent of the population. But in the Union of South Africa, where blacks make up 75 percent of the population, they are still considered a minority group because they are socially, politically, and economically dominated by the whites.

In the United States the dominant group has been and continues to be native-born, white Anglo-Saxon Protestants (WASPs). Generally speaking, those in the population who do not share the characteristics of the dominant group are singled out for minority status. In essence then, a minority group is a group of people who in some ways differs from the dominant group in society and who, because of these differences, are the object of prejudice and discrimination, resulting in their being disadvantaged.

Prejudice is a state of mind and entails feelings and attitudes. A major feature of prejudice is stereotyping. As we saw in Chapter 1 ("The Field and Its Methods"), with stereotyped thinking we assume that certain traits apply to all members of a group or category. For instance, a person who is prejudiced against a minority group will have a negative attitude toward any member of that group because he or she assumes that each member possesses the undesirable traits ascribed to that group. Whereas prejudice refers to attitudes, *discrimination* involves actions in which members of a minority are treated unfavorably. Although prejudice and discrimination often occur together, they are not one and the same. It is possible to be prejudiced without showing discrimination, and the reverse is true as well.

Minority group members have less access to the rewards of society—wealth, power, and prestige—than members of the dominant group do. Minority status limits opportunities and privileges, and as a result, minorities are often barred from full participation in society. Because of these conditions, some gerontologists argue that the elderly constitute a minority group.

THE ELDERLY AS A MINORITY GROUP

Breen (1960) points out that in many ways the elderly manifest characteristics of a minority group. They have high visibility, they are subject to stereotyping, and they are objects of prejudice and discrimination, especially in employment practices. Blau (1973) also feels that the aged constitute a minority group to the "extent that they are barred from full and equal participation in the occupational structure, which in contemporary society is the principal determinant of status, wealth, and power." A similar point of view is expressed by Busse and Pfeiffer (1977), who believe that the aged hold the status of a deprived minority group. They feel that older people, especially those who are retired, are often denied their share of the opportunities and advantages available to the majority of our society. And more recently, Levin and Levin (1980) maintain that the elderly constitute a minority group whose members are victims of *ageism*. (See Box 11.1.)

In contrast to these views, Streib (1965) claims that the elderly are not a minority group. He lists six criteria associated with minority group status and argues that they do not apply to the condition of the elderly in our society:

1. Does the characteristic identify all who possess it throughout the life cycle?
2. Does the dominant group hold stereotypes and clichés about the aged regarding work performance and appropriate activities?

Box 11.1 ## Ageism and Language

Just as racism and sexism discriminate against persons on the basis of their skin color and sex, to these Butler (1969, 1987) adds a third "ism"—ageism, which is prejudice and discrimination against persons simply because they are old. Ageism is manifested in stereotyping older persons (e.g., believing that all old persons are senseless, sexless, and sick), discriminating against them in housing and employment, and demeaning them through jokes and cartoons. We also demean the elderly through language. Ageism is reflected in the words that we use to refer to older persons (*fossil, geezer,* and *witch*), many of which are preceded by "old." Ageism is also reflected in the characteristics that we attribute exclusively to the elderly (*decrepit, cranky,* and *rambling*). Following is a selected list of ageist terms compiled by Frank Nuessel (1982). Note that some terms refer to both sexes and others to one sex, but all are derogatory.

bag	dotage	little old lady
bat	fart	miser
battle ax	feebleminded	old-fashioned
biddy	fogy	over the hill
cantankerous	fool	rambling
codger	fossil	rickety
constipated	fuddy-duddy	second childhood
coot	gaffer	senility
crank	geezer	spinster
cranky	Geritol generation	superannuated
crone	goat	toothless
decrepit	grump	witch
dirty old man	hag	wizened

Sources: Robert N. Butler, "Age-ism: Another Form of Bigotry." *The Gerontologist* (9), 1969, pp. 243–246; Robert N. Butler. "Ageism." In George L. Maddox (Ed.), *Encyclopedia of Aging.* New York: Springer, 1987, pp. 22–23; Frank Nuessel, "The Language of Ageism." *The Gerontologist* (22), 1982, pp. 243–246.

---

3. Do the aged view themselves as a separate and distinct group?
4. Is there a readiness to organize as an identifiable pressure group?
5. Do they have differential access to power, privileges, and rights?
6. Are the elderly deprived of economic and social security, as well as being subjected to residential and social isolation?

Streib claims that to view the elderly as a minority group only obscures their social role in society instead of clarifying it.

The aged do not share a distinct and separate culture; membership in the group defined as "aged" is not exclusive and permanent, but awaits all members of our society who live long enough. As a result, age is a less distinguishing group characteristic than others such as sex, occupation, social class, and the like. True, many aged persons possess distinctive physical characteristics. But even here there is a broad spectrum, and these "stigmata" do not normally justify differential and discriminatory treatment by others. The aged have little feeling of identification with their age group: they have a low degree of collective consciousness. . . . They are not herded in ghettos, deprived of civil rights, excluded from public facilities, or from jobs they are qualified to perform. . . .

Jacobs (1974) contends that much of Streib's refutation of the aged as a minority group applies to the elderly who are still working and part of the greater community and not to retired persons, especially those living in retirement communities like Fun City. He points out that

Fun City residents exhibit a "sense of consciousness of kind," are subject to "restrictions on political roles and activities," do not have "access to work," are "subject to residential segregation" (by way of subjecting others to it), do experience "social [and geographic] isolation," are as a group looked upon by the greater community as "less deserving of respect and consideration" (indeed, this is their self-perception of how others view them), and experience "less economic and social security" (real or perceived).

As the elderly continue to develop more group identification and group consciousness—both of which are already becoming quite pronounced in many retirement communities—they will become increasingly more like a minority group. But whether or not the elderly constitute a "true" minority group is debatable. Undoubtedly, however, they possess many characteristics associated with minority group status.

Related to the view of the elderly as a minority group is the concept of *double jeopardy*, which characterizes minority group members as bearing a double burden: They are devalued because of old age and they are disadvantaged because of their minority status (Dowd & Bengtson, 1978). The double jeopardy hypothesis predicts

---

Box 11.2 **Age Prejudice**

Age prejudice not only has a bad effect on its victims, but, according to Alex Comfort, it corrupts us all, as he explains in the following excerpt.

Other victims of vulgar prejudice suffer from it lifelong, but we all *become* old. One wonders what Archie Bunker would feel about immigrants if he knew that on his sixty-fifth birthday he would turn into a Puerto Rican. White racists don't turn black, black racists don't become white, male chauvinists don't become women, anti-Semites don't wake up and find themselves Jewish—but we have a lifetime of indoctrination with the idea of the difference and inferiority of the old, and on reaching old age we may be prejudiced against ourselves.

Source: Alex Comfort, *Social Policy*, November/December 1976.

that an older minority group member will have lower status than a younger person of the same group and that an elderly minority group member will have a lower status than an elderly person who is not a member of that minority group (Weeks, 1984). The term "double jeopardy" was first used by Tally and Kaplan (1956) to refer only to being old and black, but now it has been expanded to include all minority groups. Although the double jeopardy hypothesis has failed to obtain empirical support to date, it nevertheless remains an important concept for studying stratification and minority groups (Jackson, 1985).

THE ELDERLY IN MINORITY GROUPS

America is a nation composed of hundreds of minority groups. These minority groups originated from three principal sources: the indigenous Indian population, the blacks brought from Africa as servants and slaves, and the immigrants who settled on our shores.

The five principal minority groups in the United States are the blacks, the Hispanics, the Native Americans, the Chinese-Americans, and the Japanese-Americans. Brief sketches of the history and the experience of each group in this country follow, with a discussion of their present situation and the problems of their elderly.

The Blacks

Americans of African ancestry, the largest minority group in the nation, number more than 28 million. Their history in this country includes more than 100 years of exploitation and degradation.

The first blacks came to the New World as explorers and servants, not slaves. The precedent for slavery in America was established by the Spanish and Portuguese and later adopted by the English. The black population grew very slowly at first, even after slavery was legally established in the English Colonies. With the advent of the industrial revolution, which created a demand for raw materials, especially cotton, the demand for black slaves rapidly increased. By 1860 there were nearly 4 million blacks in slavery. A healthy male between the ages of 16 and 24 was sold for $1,800 on the New Orleans slave market.

To protect the sizable investments of the slave owners, laws known as the slave codes were enacted. These laws did not allow the slaves to leave the premises without written permission of their owners. Slaves were not allowed to own property, to give evidence in court, or to make contracts. In addition, it was forbidden to teach them reading or writing.

In 1865, when the Thirteenth Amendment abolished slavery and involuntary servitude, discrimination and intimidation of the blacks still continued. The Jim Crow statutes of the 1890s served to make the blacks second-class citizens by excluding them from all private and public facilities used by whites. In 1896 the U.S. Supreme Court made "separate but equal" facilities the law of the land. This law stayed in effect until after World War II.

Since World War II, there has been an unprecedented migration of blacks from the South to northern cities. In 1940, 77 percent of the nation's blacks lived in the South, and by 1970 only slightly more than half remained there. This migration can be attributed primarily to the better opportunities for employment in the North. Also, after the war mechanization of Southern farms increased greatly, and many rural blacks could no longer find work as field laborers or sharecroppers.

The Supreme Court declared segregation unconstitutional in 1954, and the Civil Rights Act was passed some ten years later. Since these events, black Americans have made great strides in the areas of employment, income, education, and housing. Yet, despite these gains, there is still a considerable gap between the races; it is even more pronounced among many elderly blacks, who are said to experience the triple jeopardy of being black, old, and poor.

Although the overall status of the elderly has improved in recent years, the black elderly continue to lag behind their white counterparts in social and economic status. (Peter Rustin Harris)

The Black Elderly In 1987 there were 2.4 million blacks aged 65 and over in the United States. In general, they had lower incomes and less education than their white counterparts. The median income for elderly black males in 1987 was $7,167, as compared with $12,398 for elderly white males. The median income of aged black females was $4,494, and for white females it was $7,055. Although the proportion of older persons living below the poverty level has fallen steadily in recent years, the poverty rate among older blacks was 33.9 percent in 1987, more than triple the rate (10.1 percent) among older whites. The level of educational attainment also differs between the races. In 1986, 40 percent of the older blacks age 60–64 had completed high school as compared with 70 percent of the older whites.

Another disparity between the races is in the area of nursing homes. The percentage of blacks in these facilities is much lower than it is for whites; they are found at less than one-third the rate that their population would suggest. Some argue that nonwhites are underrepresented in nursing homes because of discrimination or because they cannot afford the cost. Others maintain that the reason is that blacks and other minority groups prefer to have their elderly remain within the home so that the family can care for them (Kalish, 1975).

Recent research documents the fact that the black family is a highly integrated unit that functions as a strong support system for its elderly members. It provides them with a wide range of services and assistance, and, in turn, the elderly assist the younger family members by helping to maintain and support them (Markides & Mindel, 1987).

The Hispanics

Next to blacks, the second-largest minority group in the United States is Hispanic Americans or Americans of Spanish origin. Because Hispanics are one of the fastest growing minority groups in this country, they are expected to be the largest after the year 2000 (Torres-Gil, 1986). In 1986, there were 18 million Hispanics, or 7.6 percent of the U.S. population. The term *Hispanic* American includes Mexican-Americans (Chicanos), Puerto Ricans, and Cuban-Americans. The majority of Hispanics (60 percent) are Mexican-Americans. They are heavily concentrated in the five Southwestern states of California, Arizona, New Mexico, Colorado, and Texas. For our purposes, we will focus mainly on the Mexican-Americans—not only because they are the largest group in the Hispanic population, but also because much of the research on older Hispanics has been conducted on Mexican-Americans.

Some Mexican-Americans are descendants of the original settlers who occupied the Southwestern part of the United States long before New England was colonized. At the end of the Mexican-American War in 1848, Mexico recognized the annexation of Texas by the United States and ceded to the United States the territory that now makes up the states of California, Nevada, and Utah, and parts of Arizona, New Mexico, Colorado, and Wyoming. The people living on these lands were given the option to move to Mexico or to become American citizens. Many of them remained, and today their descendants number about 1 million.

During the Mexican Revolution of 1911 to 1922, many well-to-do Mexicans began emigrating to the United States as political refugees. Others came because of the

Box 11.3 **The Economic Future of the Black and Hispanic Elderly**

The skills and educational backgrounds of today's ethnic minority populations are somewhat ill-suited to the needs of urban America. Traditional blue-collar jobs have moved to outlying areas or to non-metropolitan areas. This has enabled white farmers to obtain industrial jobs, but has been impractical for those in the inner city. The deconcentration of employment has rendered existing public transportation less than useful for reaching industrial jobs. Some inner-city poor with automobiles can make the daily commute to the suburbs, but many are less fortunate. It has been estimated, for example, that 4 out of 5 inner-city Blacks in Chicago do not own automobiles (Kasarda, 1983). Among the only economic activities in the inner city directly affecting the lower classes are the thriving welfare and underground economies.

The growth of high-tech industries has been particularly evident in the Southwest, including Texas. That in the new urban economy there is little demand for cheap unskilled labor is evident in Austin's much greater ability to attract high-tech companies than nearby San Antonio, with its large Hispanic population. Although San Antonio has also had some success in attracting a few high-tech companies, it is uncertain whether these industries will directly benefit the poorer Hispanics.

This is a time of optimism regarding the economic future of American society. The growth of high-tech industries was never anticipated to reach its current and prospective levels. Although this growth promises a great deal to an increasing number of skilled and educated people, it may have little to offer to the urban poor, most of whom are Blacks and Hispanics. It should not be expected that rapid technological change will enable these populations to experience the necessary upward mobility to become economically assimilated into the larger society, as was the case with European immigrant groups at the end of the 19th and the beginning of the 20th centuries. Most poor Hispanics and Blacks are likely to continue to grow old isolated from the economic mainstream of urban America. Despite minor improvements in the educational attainments of these groups, there is little reason for optimism that the lot of elderly Hispanics and Blacks will improve relative to that of the majority of white elderly. Watson (1986) has recently concluded that the economic future of aged Blacks is bleak because few Blacks today are able to move out of the "peripheral" labor market and into more "core" types of employment. Similarly, Torres-Gil (1986) has concluded that future cohorts of elderly Hispanics will continue to be relatively disadvantaged. Hispanics are less likely than even Blacks to be covered by pensions, a factor that is sure to adversely affect their economic circumstances in later life. In addition, the continued influx of unskilled immigrants from Mexico and Central America is likely to ensure that the economic disadvantage of the overall Hispanic population will remain. As the Black and Hispanic populations continue to age demographically, programs and support services for meeting their needs will become increasingly important. Yet the current economic climate is likely to deprive them of resources they are finally beginning to live long enough to enjoy.

Source: Kyriakos S. Markides and Jeffrey S. Levin. "The Changing Economy and the Future of the Minority Aged." *The Gerontologist* (27), 1987, pp. 273–274.

Mexican-American elderly generally have good relationships with their children and grand-children. They also have higher levels of contact with their families than do whites. (ACTION)

attraction of the agricultural labor market. It is estimated that between 1910 and 1930, about a million Mexicans entered this country. During the Depression of the 1930s, immigration from Mexico was brought to a halt. Also, many Mexican laborers, though U.S. citizens by birth, were sent by the truckload to Mexico in an effort to relieve the unemployment situation in this country. Beginning about World War II, Mexican immigration resumed and has continued to the present time. Most of the recent immigrants have come in search of agricultural work. Thousands have entered this country illegally by wading or swimming across the Rio Grande.

Mexican-Americans have continued to preserve their language, along with many cultural traditions and values. Most live in distinct and relatively closed urban communities known as *barrios*, which serve to reinforce their cultural identity. Though the Mexican-Americans have not been socially excluded to the extent of the blacks, they have shared somewhat similar experiences in residential and school segregation.

Both have suffered discrimination in employment and have been denied access to public accommodations. An 83-year-old Mexican-American woman whose ancestry in this country can be traced back for four centuries remarked, "You bend with the wind. And Anglo people are a strong wind. They want their own way; they can be like a tornado, out to pass over everyone as they go somewhere. . . . But we are outsiders in a land that is ours" (Coles, 1974).

The Hispanic Elderly   The Hispanics have a smaller proportion of elderly than do whites or blacks. In 1987 only 5 percent of the nearly 1 million Hispanics were age 65 and older, as compared with 13 percent for whites and 8 percent for blacks. This difference is largely a result of a higher fertility rate among Hispanics, which results in a disproportionate number of young persons in the population. One of the most striking differences between whites and Hispanics was in their living arrangements. Only 26 percent of older white widows lived with their children or other family members, compared with 53 percent of older Hispanic widows who did.

The median income among Hispanics is low and the poverty rate high. For instance, in 1987, the median income of older Hispanic males was $6,803 and $4,526 for older Hispanic women. The poverty rate in 1987 among Hispanic elderly was 27.4 percent, or more than double the poverty rate (10.1) among white elderly. Of all the

Many Mexican–Americans continue to maintain their cultural values and ethnic heritage. (Alex Harris)

minority elderly, Hispanics are the most educationally disadvantaged. In 1987, 30.9 percent of older Hispanic men and 31.5 percent of older Hispanic women were functionally illiterate—that is, they had fewer than 5 years of schooling. This rate is 6 to 7 times as great for older whites.

Because of their poverty and low educational attainment, and especially because of their language barrier, most older Mexican-Americans are separated from and uninformed about the larger society. Diffusing information to them becomes a difficult problem. Carp (1970) investigated the communication habits of older Mexican-Americans and the ways in which they obtain information. She found that the difficulty in communication arises because the usual techniques for disseminating information are relatively ineffective. Though most listened regularly to the radio and watched television, two-thirds of the group said that they never read a newspaper. ". . . For this generation of old people, there is little hope of improving information dissemination through the printed word because their reading skills are very poor, both in English and in Spanish."

Perception of aging appears to vary among different groups in the population. In a west Texas study of older Mexican-Americans, Crouch (1972) found that nearly two-thirds of the sample considered old age to begin at 60 or below. A similar finding was reported by Bengtson and his associates (1977) in southern California, where they compared Mexican-Americans, blacks, and whites. The respondents were asked whether they thought of themselves as old, middle-aged, or young. More than 30 percent of the Mexican-Americans replied that they were old at age 60 (others felt old at younger ages), blacks replied at age 65, and whites did not feel old until they were about 70. These studies, as well as those cited earlier, indicate that perception of aging is related to socioeconomic status. Those of a lower socioeconomic status perceive the onset of old age as beginning much earlier than do those of a higher socioeconomic status. Because blacks and Mexican-Americans are deprived minorities of essentially the same lower socioeconomic level, it is to be expected that they would perceive old age as starting sooner—and they do.

Bengtson reports that both Mexican-Americans and blacks view old age more negatively than whites do. This negative view may in part reflect whether older people judge their own health to be good or bad. He found that in the 65-to-74 age group, 23 percent of Mexican-Americans considered their health poor, as did 27 percent of the blacks. In contrast, only 4 percent of the whites felt that they were in poor health. See Table 11.1 for a comparison of some selected characteristics of whites, blacks, and Hispanics.

The Native Americans

No other minority group in the United States has suffered more injustice or abuse than the American Indian. Their deprivation and poverty is unequaled by any group in our society. The 1980 census enumerated 1.4 million Native Americans (Indian and Alaskan natives). Native Americans are the only minority group that is less urbanized than the general population; in 1980, 46 percent lived in rural areas. Slightly more than half of the American Indian population lives in the Western part of the United States, with a concentration in three states—Arizona, California, and Oklahoma.

Table 11.1   DEMOGRAPHIC AND SOCIOECONOMIC CHARACTERISTICS BY RACE AND HISPANIC ORIGIN OF POPULATION 65 AND OVER: 1987

	Number (in thousands)	Percent of 65+ population	Median income	Poverty rate	Education (median years of school)	Widows living with family
White	26,865	13%	$8,975	10.1%	12.1	26%
Black	2,448	8	5,081	33.9	8.4	41
Hispanic[1]	947	5	5,282	27.4	7.4	53

Source: U.S. Bureau of the Census, various reports.
[1] Hispanic persons may be of any race.

It is estimated that at the time of Columbus more than a million Indians lived in the territory that now is the United States. They represented several hundred major tribes with countless subdivisions. Each of these tribal groups had its own distinctive culture and language. It has been said that the American Indians spoke more different languages than were used in the entire Old World.

At first the relationship between the early European settlers and their Indian neighbors was a peaceful one. In many cases, the Indians turned over large portions of land to them in return for goods, not understanding the European meaning of property rights. But later, when the white settlers made additional demands for land, bitter disputes arose. If the Indians resisted, they were either driven away or annihilated.

As the invading whites moved westward, the policies of the federal government toward the Indians shifted between assimilation, leaving them alone, and extermination. In the first half of the nineteenth century an estimated 100,000 Indians were moved to the territories in the west. Many Indians died en route because of the harsh conditions under which they were forced to travel. Diseases introduced by Europeans also took a toll of Indian lives.

The first of 267 reservations was established in the middle part of the nineteenth century. One purpose of the reservation was to help assimilate the Indians into the American way of life. In 1871 Congress declared that no Indian tribe could be recognized as an independent power, and the Indians were made wards of the federal government. In the years that followed, the government program to break up the tribal organizations and to force the Indians to "Americanize" met with utter failure. In 1933 the policy of the federal government toward the Indians was reversed. Instead of trying to assimilate the Indians, they were given freedom to preserve their identity and to retain the values and customs of their cultures. A year later the Indian Reorganization Act was passed; it allowed the Indians to form businesses and agricultural enterprises and to set up self-governing units. The first Americans were granted citizenship in 1924.

The Native American Elderly   The proportion of elderly among the Native American population has grown faster than that of other minority groups. In 1980 about 79,000,

By the latter part of the nineteenth century, Congress declared that no Indian tribe could be recognized as an independent power, and the Indians were made wards of the federal government. (The Smithsonian Institution)

or 5 percent, were age 65 and over. Approximately one-quarter of Native American elderly live on American Indian reservations or in Alaskan Native villages.

Although life expectancy at birth for Native Americans increased from 65 years in 1970 to 71.1 years in 1980, it still lagged 3.3 years behind that of the white population. Few of the elderly have ever worked steadily, and because of this and the fact that many who were employed were not covered under Social Security, a large proportion are ineligible for Social Security benefits. In most cases, older Indians cannot look to their children for financial assistance because the children also have inadequate incomes.

Being the poorest of the poor, the elderly Native Americans suffer from malnutrition and have a high incidence of disease, especially tuberculosis. A contributing factor to their poor health is their substandard and overcrowded living conditions. A substantial number are without plumbing and other modern conveniences.

> Many older Native Americans live in crowded homes where there are from one to three families. Physical crowding promotes the spread of infectious diseases. Water, usually from wells, is often contaminated and the lack of refrigeration in many homes leads to contamination of foods. Open fires and stoves which are used for heating and cooking present burn hazards. Leaky roofs and damp houses contribute to colds, pneumonia, and lowered resistance to other diseases. (U.S. Department of Health, Education, and Welfare, 1976)

The lack of nursing homes and extended-care facilities as well as their inaccessibility is still another problem. Some states will not license nursing homes on Indian reservations. Often Indians are forced to go outside their communities to obtain this type of care.

> When a sick elderly Indian must be moved to a nursing home facility, it is usually not within his own community but several hundred miles away or even in another state. The normal trauma of being uprooted from home and familiar surroundings is intensified for the elderly Indian because he is surrounded by strangers who do not understand his language or cultural values and is too far from home for relatives or friends to visit. The attitude of many is typified by a remark one older Apache reportedly made to his relatives as he was being taken to a nursing home in Phoenix, Arizona. "Goodbye," he said. "The next time you see me I will be in a pine box." (U.S. Department of Health, Education, and Welfare, 1976)

The plight of older Indians is further aggravated by their social and physical isolation. Most have little or no education. Many cannot speak English, and for those who do, it is a second language. A large percentage of elderly Indians live on or near reservations, generally in isolated rural areas and miles from a major urban center. Poor roads and lack of transportation make medical services and other facilities in these centers often inaccessible.

The Chinese-Americans

Much of the past prejudice and discrimination against Chinese-Americans has declined. In recent years their number has increased mostly because of immigration. The last census enumerated 806,027 Chinese-Americans, nearly all living in urban areas.

The Chinese and Japanese, though both Asian minorities in the United States, differ greatly in their history in this country. The first large influx of Chinese to the United States began in the 1850s, precipitated by the famine in the Canton region of China and the need for contract laborers ("coolies") to help build U.S. railroads and to work in the California gold mines. Many of those who had originally intended to return to China after improving their economic situation remained permanently. Later the Chinese began to shift to other occupations, including working on the farms and orchards of the West Coast. Because of the shortage of women in the Old West, many Chinese found it profitable to open small restaurants and hand laundries.

With the completion of the Central Pacific Railroad and the rise in unemployment, many whites began to fear competition from cheap Chinese labor. Anti-Chinese feelings intensified, and open hostility ensued: Many Chinese were beaten, harassed, and even lynched. In 1882, Congress passed the Chinese Exclusion Act, making all Chinese immigration illegal. The Act was not repealed until 1943, when China became our military ally in World War II.

The Chinese-American Elderly About 7 percent, or 27,000, of the total Chinese-American population was age 65 and over in 1980. The Chinese population in the United States has been predominantly male since the beginning of this century. Though the differential between the sexes has been gradually decreasing, even by 1970 elderly males still made up 57 percent of their population and females only 43 percent. This unusual sex ratio reflects the earlier immigration patterns in which Chinese men left the women behind when they came to this country.

The elderly Chinese have high poverty rates. More than half the Chinese elderly who are poor live alone, and most are males who never married because of the scarcity of Chinese women.

Traditionally, the Chinese have emphasized education, especially for males. As Table 11.2 shows, 18.5 percent of older males have completed 4 or more years of college, as compared with 10.5 percent for whites. Notice the gap between elderly Chinese males and females in educational attainment.

Elderly Chinese fall into two principal groups: those who came here as early immigrants to work as laborers, and recent immigrants who came as political refugees, when they were old, from the Communist takeover. A major problem facing both groups is the language barrier, which separates them from the mainstream of American society as well as from other Chinese speaking another of the many different Chinese dialects.

Table 11.2 PERCENTAGE OF CHINESE-AMERICANS AND WHITE POPULATION AGE 65 AND OVER COMPLETING FOUR YEARS OR MORE OF COLLEGE BY SEX: 1980

Race	Male (percent)	Female (percent)
Chinese	18.5	6.8
White	10.5	7.6

Source: Elena S. H. Yu, "Health of the Chinese Elderly in America." *Research on Aging* (8), 1986, p. 89.

Born in 1905, Alice Fong Yu remembers the days before Chinese children were admitted in school. In the 1920s she became the first Chinese teacher in San Francisco and she taught until her retirement in 1970. (Pam Valois)

In addition, not speaking English hampers their capacity to obtain many needed services, such as health care. In a study of health-care needs of elderly persons in San Francisco's Chinatown, Karp and Kataoka (1976) found that though serious health problems existed among the older residents, their resources for obtaining medical services on their own were extremely limited. Besides the problem of communicating with the physician, they found that the majority of older Chinese-Americans live below the poverty level and therefore cannot afford medical care. Eighty percent of the Chinese-American elderly who were interviewed in the study lived in a household with a yearly income of less than $4000—nearly a third of them with a family income under $2000. Most of the elderly respondents had no means of transportation and were thus restricted to those medical services that were within walking distance.

Many people believe that because of the Confucian concept of filial piety, respect, and devotion to parents, the aged Chinese have no problems and will be taken care of by their children (see Box 11.4). This practice is not generally followed in this country. As younger Chinese families have become Americanized, children have taken the highest position in the family and are considered more important than parents. Although many Chinese-Americans still give lip service to the concept of filial piety and believe it should be preserved, a discrepancy exists between the ideal and actual practice. In a study of Chinese aged in Los Angeles, Wu (1975) notes that "financial support of parents was an ideal approved by both aged and middle-aged, but in practice, this support was rare."

Box 11.4 <u>**Filial Piety**</u>

The following is an illustration of the concept of *filial piety* that has dominated the teachings of the Chinese for centuries: Kuo Chu was a poor man burdened with a wife, mother, and child. One day he said to his wife, "We are so poor that we cannot even support mother. Moreover, the little one shares mother's food. Why not bury this child? We may have another, but if mother should die, we could not get another one." The wife did not dare to contradict him. He began to dig the grave and suddenly discovered a vase full of gold, "A gift of heaven to the filial son."

Source: Frances Y. T. Wu, "Mandarin-Speaking Aged Chinese in the Los Angeles Area." *The Gerontologist* (15), no. 3 (1975), p. 274.

The Japanese-Americans

Japanese immigrants began arriving in this country about 1880, 30 years after the Chinese. Like the Chinese, most were unskilled laborers who planned to return home after earning some money. Some worked on farms and in mines, while others went to the cities to become small merchants or to work as domestics or gardeners. Soon the prejudice against Chinese workers was also directed toward the Japanese. To decrease their immigration, President Theodore Roosevelt entered into a "Gentleman's Agreement" with the Japanese government in 1908. Under the agreement, Japan was not to permit laborers to emigrate to the United States. The Japanese government was, however, allowed to issue passports to the wives of Japanese men living in this country; many Japanese women were married by proxy so that they could come to the United States as wives.

In 1942, following the attack on Pearl Harbor, 100,000 Japanese citizens and aliens were removed from the West Coast and interned in "security" camps in other parts of the country. The reason given for their evacuation was that all Americans of Japanese ancestry were considered potential traitors and saboteurs. Before leaving the West Coast, they were forced to sell their businesses and property within a few weeks, and because of this, they suffered great financial losses. After the war, many Japanese-Americans, depleted of their resources, found it difficult to start over again and to return to their former occupations.

Despite their financial losses during World War II and the retention by the general society of some prejudice against them, the Japanese have been remarkably successful in the last 30 years in that they have achieved one of the highest socioeconomic levels of any minority group in the United States.

The Japanese-American Elderly   Unlike the Chinese, the Japanese population has shifted from being predominantly male to being largely female. This shift is due not only to female longevity but also to a higher percentage of female immigrants. In 1980 there were 700,747 Japanese-Americans in this country; 47,000 were age 65 and over.

In general, the Japanese-American elderly are the most advantaged of the minority group elderly in terms of income, health, housing, and transportation.

The elderly Japanese-Americans represent two generations—the old-old, who are called the *Issei* (first generation), and the young-old who are referred to as the *Nisei* (second generation). One study found that 56 percent of the Issei and 44 percent of the Nisei agreed that adult children are obligated to take care of their parents. About one-third of the Issei interviewed lived with their children, as compared with only 6 percent of the Nisei. Most Nisei wanted to be cared for by their children but not live with them (Weeks, 1984). In addition, the Nisei have achieved higher educational and occupational attainments than their Issei parents and, as a result, enjoy a higher socioeconomic status. In spite of the upward mobility of the second generation, ties between children and parents have tended to remain strong and supportive (Osako & Liu, 1986).

Minorities differ markedly from one another because each is a product of its distinctive cultural background and its own history in this country. But, because of their minority status and the prejudice and discrimination experienced, these groups share certain characteristics. Their histories reflect a disproportionate amount of unemployment and poverty, low wages, substandard housing, and inadequate medical care.

The minority elderly not only endure the same deprived conditions that they did when younger, but their position has worsened. The elderly in each of the five minorities discussed in this chapter have the highest rate of poverty for their group. Because they trail far behind the younger members in education and language skills, they are often isolated, even within their own group. And to the existing discrimination pervading their lives, a new dimension is added—age discrimination.

SUMMARY

1. Societies are stratified by not only social class but also by ethnicity. An ethnic group is one that differs from the larger society in such characteristics as race, religion, and nationality. A minority group is a group that in some ways differs from the dominant group in society and that because of these differences is subject to prejudice and discrimination. Prejudice and discrimination are not the same. Although they often occur together, there is no one-to-one correlation between them. Prejudice has to do with attitudes, whereas discrimination has to do with actions.

2. Whether or not the elderly constitute a true minority group has been debated for several decades. But there is a consensus that they do possess many characteristics associated with minority group status. The term "double jeopardy" is often used to describe elderly members of a minority group; they are considered to be doubly disadvantaged because they belong to a minority group and because they are old.

3. There are five principal minority groups in the United States: the blacks, the Hispanics, the Native Americans, the Chinese-Americans, and the Japanese-

Americans. The blacks, the largest minority group in the United States, have lower educational and income levels than their white counterparts. Next to the blacks in size are Hispanic Americans, who have the most educationally disadvantaged of all the minority elderly.

4. The Native Americans have suffered more injustice than any other minority group. They are the least urbanized of all the minority groups. Native Americans have a high incidence of disease and malnutrition, especially tuberculosis. The Chinese-American population has been predominantly male since the beginning of this century. Because of the scarcity of Chinese women, a substantial number of older Chinese males have never married. Traditionally, the Chinese have stressed education, especially for males. The elderly Japanese represent two generations—the Issei (the first generation) and the Nisei (the second generation). Ties between the two generations remain strong.

KEY TERMS

ethnic group
minority group
prejudice
discrimination
ageism
double jeopardy

Hispanic
barrios
Issei
Nisei
filial piety

FOR FURTHER STUDY

Jackson, Jacquelyne J. (1980). *Minorities and aging.* Belmont, CA: Wadsworth.

> *Focuses on the issues and problems associated with minority aging and examines how nine minority groups are affected by the aging process.*

Jackson, James S. (Ed.) (1986). *The black American elderly: Research on physical and psychosocial health.* New York: Springer.

> *Deals with the biological, psychological, and social aspects of aging among the black population.*

Levin, Jack, & Levin, William C. (1980). *Ageism: Prejudice and discrimination against the elderly.* Belmont, CA: Wadsworth.

> *Discusses stereotypes of and prejudice and discrimination against the elderly and compares their status and treatment with those of minority group members.*

Markides, Kyriakos S., & Mindel, Charles H. (1987). *Aging and ethnicity.* Newbury Park, CA: Sage.

> *Examines aging in relation to race and ethnicity.*

McNeely, R. L., & Colen, John J. (Eds.) (1983). *Aging in minority groups.* Beverly Hills, CA: Sage.

> *A collection of papers and essays that provides a description of the various aspects of minority aging.*

Reading

Current Perspectives in Ethnicity and Aging

Donald E. Gelfand and Charles M. Barresi

This essay deals with a number of important issues, problems, and future challenges relating to ethnicity and aging.

As the field of aging has grown, the complexity of the aging process and society's reaction to older persons has become more evident. To some degree this complexity results from the changing racial and ethnic composition of the American population. The numbers of native-born White, Black, Asian, Hispanic, and Native American elderly will increase dramatically over the next 50 years. The effects of these demographic changes will be compounded by the effects of current immigration patterns.

The inception of the quota system in 1924 to determine the number of new immigrants symbolized an effort to maintain domination by Northern European groups. Until 1965 immigration was limited. Quotas from southern and eastern Europe were oversubscribed, accompanied by a corresponding paucity of immigrants from northern and western Europe. As this system became riddled with exceptions (such as the acts that allowed American soldiers to bring their Japanese or Korean brides into the United States), calls for immigration reform began to be more commonly heard.

The repeal of the quota system in 1965 opened American borders to large numbers of individuals who entered the country with visas, others who entered the United States as refugees, and the large, basically uncounted numbers of individuals who continue to enter illegally. What is important is not only the numbers of immigrants but the fact that this current immigration represents an influx of Hispanics and Asians whose cultural backgrounds bring a new dimension into the society. This

Donald E. Gelfand and Charles M. Barresi. 1987. "Current Perspectives in Ethnicity and Aging." In D. E. Gelfand and C. M. Barresi (Eds.), *Ethnic Dimensions of Aging*. New York: Springer, pp. 5–17. [Readers interested in full source citations are referred to the original source.]

new immigration since 1965 has had a decided impact on the field of aging. There are now not only older Americans with varied ethnic backgrounds but also substantial numbers of older Americans who are first-generation immigrants. This creates a mix of generations within these ethnic groups, whose needs for services and support are varied. . . .

METHODOLOGICAL ISSUES IN ETHNICITY AND AGING

The first hurdles to be overcome in probing the relationships of ethnicity to aging are methodological. In the 1970s it was necessary to convince investigators of the value of including ethnicity as a variable. This problem has now largely been overcome. The majority of investigators are now careful to include Black, Hispanic, and perhaps Asian elderly in their sampling design when possible. When unable to accomplish this type of sampling, we at least can expect to find disclaimers about the generalizability of the findings beyond White elderly.

Among minority elderly the most notable gap is the sparseness of research about older Native Americans. This situation can be accounted for by general lack of interest in Native Americans among the public and by the difficulties of gaining access to Native American communities, which are generally suspicious of outsiders. Based on the tragic history of these groups, their suspicions extend not only to White investigators but also to cooperative Native Americans, who are viewed pejoratively as "apples" (red on the outside, white on the inside). As infant mortality decreases and the percentage of elderly among Native Americans increases, this lack of basic and programatically relevant knowledge will be especially harmful. . . .

THE IMPACT OF ETHNICITY

Age as a Leveler

Bringing ethnicity into the models used in studying aging has been difficult not only because of our difficulty dealing with ethnicity as a changing phenomenon but also because of the continuing strong, and often unspoken, tendency to view age as a leveler. Current analyses of drinking behavior among older persons provides an example of this tendency. When drinking behavior is discussed, the common approach is to assert that the consumption of alcohol is usually reduced among older people because of lower tolerance for alcohol and the reduction in social situations encountered in which alcohol is being served. Almost no discussion can be found in the literature about differential alcohol consumption among older ethnic group members, with perhaps the exception of alcohol problems among Native Americans. The unspoken assumption is that the reductions in alcohol usage are equivalent among all ethnic groups. This assumption has yet to be proved.

Life expectancy is one major area related to basic physical characteristics of aging where ethnic differences have been acknowledged. Statistics continue to show decreasing differences in life expectancies among White and minority elderly. Complicating the picture, however, is the so-called crossover effect in which Blacks who live into their seventies have longer life expectancies than their White peers. This difference in life expectancy is now also shown to exist among Native Americans and perhaps Asians as well (Manson & Callaway, 1985). Whether related to selective survival among these groups or to susceptibility to specific diseases, these differentials continue to be a topic of discussion among researchers (Manton & Stallard, 1984).

The lack of similar attention to social and behavioral differences among ethnic and minority aged is related to the tendency to regard age as a leveler that counteracts differences existing among the elderly. Clearly, the current tendency in ethnic research is to simplify the world in order to make it more orderly and easier to comprehend. Using the age-as-leveler bias, however, neglects important elements that shape an older person's existence. Ethnicity is for many older individuals one of the more important of these elements.

Positive and Negative Ethnicity

At times it would appear that investigators assume that the existence of an ethnic identity among their subjects is ipso facto a positive factor in their aging process. According to this view, ethnicity serves as an important link to a cultural heritage that specifies how things should be done, including thinking and behaving in old age, relationships with family, and involvement in the larger community. In a supposedly rootless world, ethnic identity provides the individual with roots not easily destroyed by the decrements associated with the aging process in industrial society.

Less attention is paid to the negative impact of ethnicity on the older person. . . . For the older Vietnamese, adherence to traditional culture may include an expectation that children will provide the respect and deference they believe should be afforded elders. Faced with the demands of survival in American society, adult Vietnamese children may not have either the inclination nor the ability to afford the expenditure of time and energy necessary to fulfill these expectations (Cox & Gelfand, in press). . . . [P]roblems arise from the differences in allegiance to the traditional ethnic culture by older parents and their children. Unburdened by the demands of surviving in a foreign and strange culture, the Vietnamese family in Vietnam may not face these problems.

The traditional culture thus may not create the unalloyed positive experience that many authors assume. Indeed, some recent writers have argued that the importance attached to ethnic culture as a means of identity or as a base for social mobility is a myth (Steinberg, 1981). . . . [I]t is important to note that membership in an ethnic culture may be the reason for some problems experienced by older persons as well as providing a foundation for their successful aging. Understanding an ethnic culture and its effect on aging requires knowledge not only of the manner in which an ethnic culture can assist elderly in coping with the demands of late life but also of the problems that might be created by adherence to this culture.

ETHNICITY AS A POLITICAL AGENDA

All of the aforementioned factors make the assessment of the impact of ethnicity on the aging process a difficult task. Complicating the situation even further is the fact that ethnicity is not a topic that is viewed by many with objectivity. Advocates argue for its importance in any assessment and planning activity; others argue that it has ceased to be relevant in American life except among the most recent immigrants. The rhetoric that pours forth from both camps is not merely the result of differing positions on the issue but also because of the real benefits or losses stemming from the ultimate outcome. The potential benefits include funds for programs oriented to specific ethnic groups. . . .

Advocates for minority elderly have argued that programming must be developed to meet their specific needs (Jackson, 1980). Some of these needs stem from the greater extent of poverty, malnutrition, and poor health that minority elderly experience. Lower life expectancy among minority groups in general, when compared with the dominant majority, is a direct result of neglect in meeting these vital needs. Among the elderly, the lowest life expectancy recorded is among Native Americans. Given that life expectancy among minority groups is less than among Whites, then perhaps the definition of eligibility for programs under the Older Americans Act should be reduced from one standardized at age 60 to one more relevant to the life expectancy of each respective minority group.

FUTURE ISSUES IN ETHNICITY AND AGING

Despite the complex relationships between ethnicity and aging there are some important implications that can be drawn from current data on ethnic groups. These implications are not necessarily positive for all groups of ethnic aged. A survey of older individuals in New York City who arrived in the United States before 1950 indicates a strong reliance on a foreign tongue (Lee, 1985). It is reasonable to expect that these individuals have some rather specific service needs. The most recent census figures indicate that "among those persons 65 years and over speaking a language other than English at home, 1 in 5 did not speak English well and 1 in 10 did not speak English at all" (U.S. Bureau of the Census, 1984, p. 24). This limited ability in communication makes it difficult for these elderly to avail themselves of services and also creates problems for service providers. . . .

. . . Because of the effects of earlier patterns of discrimination older minority group members may suffer from both poorer health and lower income. This is reflected in the higher illness and poverty rates among minority elderly. Moreover, among groups such as Native Americans the specific living situation on the reservation may also produce conditions that are less than favorable for healthy longevity (Manson & Callaway, 1985). It is important to note that both of these groups, despite their American nativity and long family history in the United States, still display rather glaring unmet service needs.

Among Native American groups, it is possible that tribal memberships also reflect distinct attitudes toward the aging process. However, even these attitudes may be undergoing change among more recent generations of Native Americans. This assertion raises perhaps the most crucial and certainly most difficult issue for research in ethnicity; the relationship between social class and ethnicity. If upward social mobility reduces the influence of ethnicity, then it may be possible to argue that ethnicity will become less and less relevant as upward social mobility of the majority of these groups in the United States increases.

The relationship between ethnicity and aging is even more complex among Hispanics and Asians. Hispanics represent a variety of cultures and nationalities. Aggregating these groups under the term *Hispanics* also neglects the distinctions between those families who have been settled on American soil for five or six generations and recent immigrants. Even among Chicanos there are distinct differences in attitudes and cultures in various southwestern states, depending on the history of the state. As Lukas (1985) correctly notes in his analysis of the effects of school busing on three Boston families, this is not to imply that there are no differences among Blacks.

The situation among Asians is even more problematic because of both the diversity and the rapid growth of the Asian population in the United States. During the 1970s the Asian-American population increased by more than 141%, in comparison to an increase of 17% among Blacks and 39% among Hispanics. The Asian-American population is also estimated to have increased by 50% since 1980 and may be 4% of the U.S. population by the year 2000. Between 1980 and 1984 the number of legal immigrants from Asia exceeded the number of legal immigrants from Latin America (Gardner, Robey, & Smith, 1985).

Although this growth pattern is very clear, the situation becomes less distinct when we move beyond the basic figures. The first complexity is the number of ethnic groups represented under the term *Asian*. At present there are at least eight large groups and three "others" that are classified as Asian. These groups are diverse in cultural attitudes. Because of their recent immigration, the tendency is to think of Asians as primarily a young population. Even this assumption is an oversimplification. For example, the median age of Whites in 1980 was 31.3 years. The median age of Chinese Americans was 29.6 years and of Japanese Americans 33.5 years. The Chinese-American figure reflects recent immigration of Chinese into the United States, but the median age of Japanese Americans reflects the long tenure of this group in the United States. The relative needs of Chinese, Vietnamese, Filipino, or Japanese elderly will thus be different because of their differential tenure in American society and the proportion of elderly in their respective groups.

The status of the elderly may also vary according to the numbers of children available to assist the older person. On this parameter, Asian-American populations, except for Vietnamese, rank lower than Whites (1,358 children per 1,000 individuals), Blacks (1,806 children per 1,000), or Hispanics (1,817 children per 1,000 individuals). There are also differences among groups in the average size of the household. In 1980 these ranged from 2.7 persons among White families to 4.4 individuals among Vietnamese. . . .

There are some indications in these data about the future status and problems among minority elderly. The proportion of high school graduates among Asian-Americans is currently above that of Whites, Blacks, and Hispanics. A recent study notes that Asian-Americans are already well represented among managerial and professional ranks. "Among Japanese, Filipino and Asian-Indian immigrants the proportion in the highest occupational category in 1980 not only exceeded the White figure but also the proportions for the U.S. born workers in these groups" (Gardner et al., 1985, p. 32). On the basis of this information it can be expected that Asian-Americans who reach old age will have economic and social resources comparable to those of White elderly and far superior to their Black and Hispanic age peers. This is already evident from the fact that a smaller number of Asian-American families (except for Vietnamese) are below the poverty level than either Black or Hispanic families (Gardner et al., 1985).

The meaning of ethnicity for the older person in American society is undergoing change. The meaning of these changes must form the basis for our research agenda over the next 50 years. Along with an aging society, the complex ethnic composition of the United States is being altered by the major numbers of immigrants from areas formerly underrepresented in the population. As the number of older Hispanics and Asians increases, the need to understand the role of ethnicity in aging will also increase.

FOUR

Social Institutions and the Elderly

Chapter

12

The Family

A wit once remarked, "Marriage is a great institution, but who wants to live in an institution?" This statement combines both the popular usage and the sociological meaning of *institution*. Most people think of an institution as a place of complete or partial confinement in which a specific group of individuals lives—for example, prisons, hospitals, orphanages, schools, and nursing homes. In sociology, the term *institution* is used as an abstraction and refers to normative patterns and established procedures, not to a particular place or a concrete entity. In the socio-logical sense, you cannot see, belong to, or live in an institution.

INSTITUTIONS

An institution may be thought of as a regulatory agency that channels human action much in the way that instincts channel animal behavior. Berger (1963) notes that "institutions provide procedures through which human conduct is patterned, com-pelled to go, in grooves deemed desirable to society." An institution, then, may be defined as an organized cluster of norms—folkways, mores, and laws—that surround an important social need or activity of a society. In other words, an institution is a conventional way of pursuing an activity important to society.

Every known society has these five basic social institutions in one form or an-other: the family, the economy, the political system, religion, and education. So necessary are institutions that no society could survive without them. Each institution fulfills at least one major function (see Table 12.1).

In Part Four we will examine these five social institutions, emphasizing the roles of the elderly in them and how roles in each of these institutions change with age. Now let us discuss the first institution to which all human beings are introduced—the family.

PATTERNS OF FAMILY ORGANIZATION

Anthropologists and sociologists have recorded an amazing variety of family patterns that exist or have existed in different societies of the world. Many patterns differ greatly from our own and seem strange to us. By the same token, American family patterns appear strange to people of other cultures, who are equally ethnocentric.

A Cross-Cultural Perspective

Societies vary greatly in their processes for selecting mates. In many places, marriage arrangements are made by the heads of families. Their authority in these matters is often reinforced by the requirement that a bride price be paid to the girl's family by

Table 12.1   THE FIVE BASIC SOCIAL INSTITUTIONS AND THEIR FUNCTIONS

Institution	Function
Family	Procreation and child rearing
Economy	The production and distribution of goods and services
Political system	Maintenance of societal order
Religion	Preservation and reaffirmation of sacred traditions and shared values
Education	The transmission of cultural values, knowledge, and skills

the boy's parents. In ancient Greece and in China until recently, brides and grooms did not see each other until just before the wedding ceremony. In some societies, girls and boys are married when only two or three years of age. Up to about a generation ago, an Arab's choice of a wife was often restricted to marrying his cousin on his father's side. In many societies it is a common custom for young girls to marry elderly men; as a result, the young men experience difficulty obtaining wives and often have to marry old women or widows.

Societies also differ in the degree of interaction between family members. Mother-in-law avoidance is a common custom among many peoples; the Aranda of Australia, for instance, do not allow the men to look at, or even speak to their mothers-in-law. The Semang believe in a certain amount of avoidance between mother and son and between father and daughter, and the Baganda often send their first child to live with the father's brother. In an Israeli kibbutz, children live apart from their parents and visit them only at certain times each day. This last style of living is designed to weaken ties between parents and children and to eliminate family-centeredness. The kibbutz provides us with an example of family life very different from our own.

According to Talmon (1971), the Israeli *kibbutzim* (plural of *kibbutz*) are agricultural settlements organized around the principle of communal living. All able-bodied adults work for the welfare of the collective at whatever task is assigned to them. The task of child rearing is taken over by communal institutions; children are trained and educated by special nurses and teachers. The parents' role is limited to a warm, affectionate, indulgent relationship without involving discipline or other means of socializing the child. This pattern is more like the interaction between grandparents and grandchildren in American society.

The kibbutz has solved many problems associated with aging. A fixed retirement age does not exist; instead, a person gradually withdraws from the occupational sphere beginning at age 55. Older persons work shorter hours and are given lighter, less strenuous tasks. The elderly who can no longer work are secure—all their basic needs, including food, housing, and health care, are provided. According to Talmon, however, the emphasis on work and productivity, characteristic of all kibbutzim, produces feelings of guilt among nonproductive older members.

Older people tend to compensate for the loss of their work role by shifting their focus to the family. The parent–child relationship assumes greater importance for them, and grandchildren become a major preoccupation. Even though communal institutions take over most child care, grandparents assist parents. For example, when children visit their parents at the end of the work day, sometimes grandparents help out by entertaining the children. Or, when the parents go on vacations or leave the kibbutz, grandparents take their place. In most families, emotional ties between grandparents and their grandchildren are strong. Though the bulk of older persons' needs are provided by the kibbutz, children perform important domestic and personal chores for them when they become sick or incapacitated. Talmon observes:

> In the support and care of aged relatives the children only supplement collective institutions. Their limited liabilities and duties do not, in most cases, interfere with their normal life routines. The curtailment and limitation of obligations seem to reinforce rather than weaken family relationships. As a rule, it does not undermine the sense of

responsibility toward old parents; quite the contrary; the children are able to help spontaneously and generously. The relationship is free of the feeling of resentment and of the sense of guilt engendered by too heavy responsibilities.

Older people with no children, or whose children have left the collective, tend to compensate for this lack by increased participation in communal affairs. Friends and neighbors usually take over some functions that children normally perform and serve as foster families. Some older people who are childless attach themselves to the family of a friend or neighbor and act as additional grandparents.

Nuclear and Extended Families

The *nuclear family*, the most basic of all family types, is composed of a husband, a wife, and their children. When several nuclear families are joined together by an extension of parent–child relationships, this is called an *extended*, or three-generation, *family*—typically a married couple, their unmarried children, their married children and spouses, and their grandchildren, all living together.

The general thesis throughout much sociological literature is that the extended family, the norm in early agrarian America, has greatly declined, and that today the nuclear family is the dominant form. Many sociologists argue that this change in family organization is responsible for many problems that confront the elderly.

The major cause of this shift from the extended to the nuclear family is considered to be industrialization. Proponents of this view argue that with industrialization, workers are required to move to where job opportunities are available. This geographical mobility tends to undermine the kinship bonds in the extended family by decreasing the frequency and intimacy of contact between its members. Popenoe (1977) observes that industrialization has made it possible for women to work outside the home, a practice that diminishes the importance of some basic functions of the extended family. At the same time, the nuclear family, with its more limited set of responsibilities, has been strengthened. Finally, and probably the most important reason given for the change in family organization, according to Popenoe, is the loss of the family as a productive unit:

> In an agrarian society, each member of the family does economically productive work. Children, the elderly, and the handicapped do less than able-bodied adults, but they each make a contribution to the economic welfare of the family unit. The extended family thus offers an economic advantage. In an industrial society, however, the young, the elderly, and the physically handicapped are unemployable. They produce little for the family unit, yet they consume at the same rate as a producer. The extended family unit, with aged parents or other dependent relatives, becomes a burden rather than an advantage.

In the transformation of the extended family into the nuclear family, it was believed that not only did older people lose their economic role in the household, along with other functions, but they also became isolated from their children and relatives. Recent studies have contradicted these notions. First, it has been found that extended families were no more prevalent in the past then they are now. So the family did not evolve from an extended into an nuclear family form but has remained much the same. Tibbitts (1968) points out that "it is now clear that the nuclear parent–child family has always been the modal family type in the United States and that three-generation families have always been relatively rare."

Since few people lived to old age in the past, it would have been impossible for the extended family to be the predominant family type. Much of the nostalgia for the farm family of the past, in which older people enjoyed the economic security and emotional satisfaction of being part of a large household of kinfolk, is based on fiction and not fact. Goode (1963) asserts that idealization of the classical American family of the past only obscures much of its real character.

> When we penetrate the confusing mists of recent history, we find few examples of this "classical" family. Grandma's farm was not economically self-sufficient. Few families stayed together as large aggregations of kinfolk. Most houses were small, not large. We now *see* more large old houses than small ones; they survived longer because they were likely to have been better constructed. The one-room cabins rotted away. . . . Indeed, we find, as in so many other pictures of the glowing past, that in each past generation people write of a period *still* more remote, *their* grandparents' generation, when things really were much better.

Another misconception that has been examined is that old people who live alone or apart from their children are isolated from them. This myth of alienation is based on two sources: professional social workers and the elderly themselves. Professional social workers often develop a distorted view because they deal with older clients alienated from their families or with some family problems that more than likely began before they became old. About one-fifth of all elderly people in the United States are childless, and they are the most likely of all to believe that aged parents are abandoned by their children (Blenkner, 1965). (See Box 12.1.)

INTERGENERATIONAL RELATIONSHIPS

Nearly all studies find that older people prefer to live near, but not with, their children. This preference for separate residences is often referred to as *intimacy at a distance* (Rosenmayr & Kocheis, 1963). Most elderly desire to remain in their own homes to retain their independence and to avoid impinging on their children's freedom. However, separate homes are not always possible in situations in which older people are in poor health or lack adequate finances to live alone.

Interaction with Children

The majority of older people who live alone enjoy a high degree of interaction with one or more of their adult children. In their study of the elderly in Denmark, Great Britain, and the United States, Shanas and her associates (1968) found that while most older parents live apart from their children, they maintain regular contact with at least one child. Nearly two-thirds of the older people surveyed said that they had seen at least one child during the 24-hour period preceding the interview. In all three countries the majority of older people had at least one child who lived within a

Much of the nostalgia for the family of the past that lived on Grandma's farm is based on fiction not fact. (Tennessee Valley Authority)

30-minute distance from them. Other studies reveal that even when geographic distances are great, regular contact is maintained between parents and their children by letters, telephone, and extended visits. "Feelings of affection toward kin, especially aging parents, seem to override spatial distances" (Bengtson, Olander, & Haddad, 1976).

The old maxim that "a son's a son till he gets a wife and a daughter's a daughter all her life" appears to have some validity. Married daughters seem to have closer ties and contact with their parents than married sons do (Sussman, 1965). Some investigators have found that females keep in closer touch with relatives on both sides of the family than do males, and that a middle-aged couple tends to be closer to the wife's family than to the husband's family (Kalish, 1975).

Some gerontologists maintain that as parents age, the parent–child relationship reverses itself: The parent assumes the former dependency role of the child, and the child takes on the supportive role of the parent. Blenkner (1965) disagrees, arguing that *role reversal* is not a normal but rather a pathological condition of neurotic or

Box 12.1 # The Myth of Abandonment

From the time we are young, we soak up a pervasive myth and accept it meekly: People used to care for their elders but we, callously, will abandon our parents in old age, just as our children will abandon us. The persistence of this myth is remarkable because of overwhelming evidence that the opposite is true. Not only are more people—many of whom are old themselves—caring for their aged parents, but they are providing care for more difficult problems and for longer periods than ever before.

A recent congressional study reported that family *caregivers* provide between 80 and 90 percent of medically related care, personal care, household maintenance and assistance with transportation and shopping needed by older people. What's more, the duration and extent of care have changed since "the good old days." Whereas people typically used to care for parents during an acute, ultimately fatal illness, people today live long after chronic disease and disability set in. "It is long-term parent care that has become the norm—expectable, though usually unexpected," says Elaine Brody of the Philadelphia Geriatric Center.

Some researchers equate parent care with other developmental stages that occur in the normal course of life. It differs, however, in that parent care is not linked to specific age periods. Need for parent care may arise as adult children rear their own young, as they enter and advance through middle age or as they adjust to the realities of their own old age.

Unfortunately, despite benefits such as companionship, feelings of usefulness and improved senses of self-worth, many people find that stress is a tiresome companion to their caregiving responsibilities. Studies repeatedly identify emotional strain as a widespread and deeply felt consequence. Shifting roles and competing demands for time disrupt comfortable balances in both the caregiver's workplace and at home. Relationships between husbands and wives, among adult siblings and between adult caregiver and younger offspring must be adjusted, often for long and indefinite periods during which the needy relative is likely to grow ever more dependent.

Sociologist Samuel H. Preston, of the University of Pennsylvania, reports that for the first time in American history, the average married couple, by the time they are 40 years old, has more parents than children. While many men, particularly spouses of the care recipient, readily fulfill caregiving roles, the job overwhelmingly falls to women. Authorities believe this reflects acceptance by both men and women of traditional sex roles, rather than the sons' deficient sense of responsibility. Daughters are twice as likely as sons to become *primary caregivers,* and when the son is the official caregiver, the daughter-in-law often assumes the caregiving tasks.

The potential for conflict is especially great for Brody's so-called *"women in the middle"* who are squeezed between dramatic demographic shifts and changes in women's life-styles. Many women in this generation are mothers and are employed in addition to their responsibilities as primary caregivers. Given the sex differences in life expectancy, experts say that many of these women will care for dependent husbands in the future.

(continued)

As family caregivers mete out untold hours of parent care, why don't they feel they are doing enough? Why do they continue to believe that most elderly parents are abandoned and that their children, in turn, will abandon them? Why does the "myth of abandonment" persist?

"The myth does not die because at its heart is a fundamental truth," Brody suggests. "At some level, members of all generations expect that the devotion and care given by the young parent to the infant and child should be repaid in kind when the parent, now old, becomes dependent." But that level of devotion is not possible for most adult caregivers, and consequently they feel guilty. The good old days, she explains, may not be an earlier period in our social history but an earlier period in each individual's and family's history to which no one can return. "Not only does the myth persist because the guilt persists," she says, "but the guilt persists because the myth persists."

Source: "Myth of Abandonment," *Psychology Today*, April 1988, p. 47.

emotionally immature or disturbed older persons. She believes that instead of the adult child assuming the parental role, he or she takes on a more mature filial role. This role is seen as a natural outgrowth of the increasing maturity of the adult child as he or she reaches middle age. The role "involves being depended on and therefore being dependable insofar as the parent is concerned." Blenkner refers to this stage as *filial maturity*. She sees it as a part of the developmental process in which children begin to recognize parents as individuals with their own needs, rights, limitations, and distinctive life histories.

Patterns of Mutual Assistance

Many studies of intergenerational family relationships have concentrated on the mutual-aid patterns that exist between parents and their adult children. Mutual aid flows in two directions: from adult children to their parents, and from the parents to their children.

Stehouwer (1968) has distinguished two forms of help. The first type is composed of nonessential, informal services that people perform for one another when they live nearby; these services require little effort, such as a son carrying packages for his elderly mother. The second type is deliberately organized and constitutes essential help—for example, when an older couple takes over their daughter's household responsibilities in an emergency.

Sussman and Burchinal (1962) have pinpointed a number of help patterns that seem to be more prevalent among middle-class and working-class families: the exchange of gifts, advice, economic assistance, and various services. Certain services that adult children are expected to perform on a regular basis for their aged parents are considered acts of filial responsibility and are done voluntarily. These services include physical care, the providing of shelter, escorting, shopping, performing household tasks, sharing of leisure time, and so on. Other forms of help may be given periodically for such ceremonial occasions as funerals or in time of crisis or illness.

The type of mutual aid tends to vary by the sexes of the parents and the children. Older men typically assist their children in household repairs, while elderly women often help out with baby-sitting and cooking. Sons and daughters do not generally receive the same kind of assistance; adult male children are likely to receive financial aid, and daughters to receive a greater share of services from their parents.

Economic aid between parents and their adult children also varies with social class. As a rule, the lower classes supply less in the way of finances and rely more on the exchange of services and shared living arrangements. The middle classes are more likely to provide financial help. But contrary to what most people believe, regardless of class, the direction of financial assistance most frequently flows from parents to children than in the reverse direction (Sussman, 1985).

In recent years there has been a trend toward a decrease in the financial reliance of older people on their children. The elderly today look to public and private pensions for the bulk of their economic maintenance. In other words, responsibility for the support of parents has shifted from an individual to a collective responsibility.

This trend is reflected in the marked increase in the number of financial-assistance programs administered by large-scale governmental organizations or bureaucracies. In addition to Social Security, older people are guaranteed a minimum income through Supplemental Security Income (SSI) and are given medical coverage through Medicare and Medicaid. Other governmental aids include subsidized housing, meal programs, and income tax exemptions. Older people often rely on their children and other relatives for information about these programs and for assistance in dealing with them. Sussman (1965) notes that many relationships of older people with their children today center on coping with bureaucratic organizations. Children often act as mediators and buffers between the organizations and their aged parents.

GRANDPARENT–GRANDCHILD RELATIONSHIPS

Important shifts in grandparenthood have taken place in recent years as a result of increased life expectancy. More people are becoming grandparents today than ever before. Many grandparents are also becoming great-grandparents and even great-great-grandparents. About three-quarters of persons age 65 and over are grandparents, and nearly half of all grandparents will also become great-grandparents (Shanas, 1980). Not unlike retirement, being a grandparent is often looked upon as an ambiguous role in that there are no clearly defined guidelines or norms attached to grandparenting (see Chapter 6, "Socialization," for a discussion of role ambiguity). Furthermore, as Troll (1982) observes, often grandmothers are not differentiated from grandfathers, and sometimes the line between grandparents and great-grandparents is also blurred.

Perceptions of Grandparents

In a study of 70 middle-class older couples, Neugarten and Weinstein (1968) found that not everyone enjoys being a grandparent. A third of the respondents experienced difficulty in performing the grandparent role satisfactorily and felt that the role was

Even though the role of the grandparent is ambiguous, it does not interfere with the development of rewarding relationships between grandparents and their grandchildren. (Nick Myers)

uncomfortable, unrewarding, and disappointing. The study also revealed that the grandparent role holds different meanings for different people. For some, it gives a feeling of biological renewal and continuity; they derive a sense of immortality through their grandchildren. Others feel that the grandparent role provides them with emotional self-fulfillment and the satisfaction of being a teacher and a resource person. A few saw grandparenthood as a chance for vicarious achievement—that is, they felt that grandchildren might accomplish what they and their children had not. The grandparent role tends to be so varied that Neugarten and Weinstein were able to distinguish five types of grandparents:

1. The *formal* grandparent enjoys giving presents and indulging grandchildren but is careful not to encroach on the parents' responsibility and authority.
2. The *fun seeker* has an informal, playful relationship with grandchildren and often sees them as a source of leisure activity. The grandparents in this group, instead of indulging their grandchildren, tend to emphasize mutual satisfaction.
3. The *surrogate parent* role pertains to grandmothers whose daughters work and who are responsible for the care of grandchildren during the day.
4. The *reservoir of family wisdom* type refers mostly to grandfathers who maintain an authoritarian position in the family and dispense knowledge and special skills.
5. The *distant figure* grandparent has only brief contacts with grandchildren on holidays and special occasions, seeing them infrequently otherwise.

The style of grandparenting also relates to age. The fun seekers and distant figure types are found more frequently among younger grandparents, whereas the formal grandparents are more typical of older grandparents.

Perceptions of Grandchildren

The type of grandparent that one prefers tends to be related to the age of the grandchild. Kahana and Kahana (1970) found that pre–school age children valued indulgent grandparents who gave them food and presents, whereas slightly older ones wanted grandparents to be active and "fun sharing." Robertson (1976) reports that young adults between the ages of 18 and 26 described the ideal grandparent as "one who loves and enjoys grandchildren," "who visits them," "shows interest," and "is helpful when needed."

A survey of 500 junior high and high school students found that most of the respondents had a positive attitude toward their grandparents (Cole & Harris, 1977). When asked what they liked most about their grandparents, the most frequent response was "they are nice," followed by "they are easier to talk to than my parents," and "they listen to me and understand my problems." The most often repeated criticism of grandparents was they were "old-fashioned." Some students felt that grandparents complained too much, while others found them boring and too talk-ative. When the students were asked in what ways they could help their grandpar-ents, they replied, "visiting them or writing them more often," "doing work around their house," and "loving them."

The attitudes of children toward the elderly are often influenced by their own experience within the family. One study found that young people who had grand-parents and great-grandparents had fewer prejudices against older persons than those who did not (Bekker & Taylor, 1966). Gilford and Black (1972) explored how grand-children develop positive sentiments for their grandparents. Their findings suggest that attitudes and feelings toward grandparents are largely transmitted from parent to child and tend to persist into adulthood. There has been some speculation that children observe how their parents relate to their (the children's) grandparents and often treat their parents similarly when they get old. The following version of a common European folk tale illustrates this point:

> A family would not let the grandfather eat at the table with the rest of them. Instead, they placed his food in a little wooden trough some distance from the others, and there, out of sight and hearing, the old man ate his meals. One day the middle-aged father came across his young son hammering some nails into a couple of boards. "What are you doing?" his father asked. Glancing up from his work, the son replied, "It's for you when you get old." Shocked by that glimpse of his own future, the father hastily invited the old man to rejoin the family at the table. (Jones, 1977)

The Foster Grandparent Program, even though outside the family situation, demonstrates the value of the grandchild–grandparent relationship. This program provides an opportunity for older persons to work on a one-to-one basis with special-needs children in a variety of residential and community settings.

> The unusual aspect of the Foster Grandparent Program is that it is of enormous benefit to both the doer and the recipient. For the children, the kindness, patience, and love that they receive improve their lives. In many cases, the children served show improvement in their physical, social, and psychological development. In some cases, the individual attention that each older volunteer gives each child results in early release of the child from the institution or the early termination of costly special treatment. (Baumhover, & Jones, 1977)

In addition, this program gives older persons a chance to make a valuable contribution to their communities and, in so doing, feel useful and needed. Many foster grandparents attest to the fact that the satisfaction and increased sense of self-esteem derived from working with children contribute to their physical and mental well-being.

Divorce and Grandparenthood

Each year about 1 million additional children are affected by divorce, and in turn, a growing number of grandparents face a change or loss in the grandparent role (Robertson, Tice, & Loeb, 1985). A study by Beal (1979) found that adult children may punish grandparents by denying them access to their grandchildren in situations in which the divorce was resolved with bitterness between the parents or if the divorce created friction between the grandparents and the adult child. Another study (Matthews & Sprey, 1984), which explored the impact of divorce on the grandparent–grandchild relationship, found that the contact between grandparents and their grandchildren was affected by whether one's own child or the in-law child was awarded custody of the grandchildren. A larger percentage of cases in which contact was maintained involved situations in which the respondents' own child had been awarded custody. For instance, when the daughters received custody of the grandchildren, all but two of the grandparents on the maternal side in their sample reported no change or even an increased amount of contact with their grandchildren.

Traditionally, grandparents have had no legal standing in cases involving the visitation of their grandchildren in the event of divorce. In recent years some laws have been passed to offer legal support to grandparents in response to the legal frictions created by the high incidence of divorced parents with children and the pressures created by grandparent activist groups (Wilson & DeShane, 1982). One such group is Grandparents Anonymous, formed in 1976 by Luella M. Davison. Its purpose is to help grandparents who are denied legal visitation of their grandchildren and to promote the well-being of grandchildren. In 1981 another group, Grandparents'/Children's Rights, was established for the purpose of promoting and organizing lobbying efforts toward uniform laws safeguarding the rights of children, grandparents, and grandparents' visitation rights.

By the late 1970s, 21 states had passed laws permitting grandparents some visitation rights with regard to their grandchildren. The grandparent movements have steadily gained momentum until today all 50 states have adopted statutory provisions for grandparent visitation.

OLDER HUSBAND-AND-WIFE RELATIONSHIPS

At the beginning of this century, more than half of all marriages were broken by the death of one partner, usually the husband, before the last child left home. Today the average couple can expect to live together an additional 15 years or more after the departure of the last child. The increase in the postparental years is due mainly to longer life expectancies and smaller, more closely spaced families. Researchers have found that couples often enjoy greater satisfaction with their marriages after the children have left home. Some sociologists feel that this upswing continues into the later years, while others find that it is limited to the immediate "post-launching" period.

Thompson and Streib (1961) have divided the postparental period into these stages: (1) the family of late maturity, in which the husband and wife are between the ages of 45 and 54; (2) the family of pre-retirement, in the 55-to-64 age range; (3) the family of early retirement, between ages 65 to 74; and (4) the family of later retirement, for those still together at age 75 and over. Our interest lies in the last two postparental stages and their consequences for the marital relationship.

The high male mortality rate characterizes the family of early retirement. In 1986, about 80 percent of the males in the 65-to-74 age bracket were married and living with their spouses, as compared with only 49 percent of women in this age group. Studies of the effects of retirement on the marital relationship focus mainly on the changes in role differentiation and sharing of household chores. After retirement, husbands usually become more involved with household tasks. Kerchoff (1966) found that in households in which husbands participated in domestic chores, the morale of both the husband and wife was higher than in households in which husbands did not participate. On the other hand, some husbands may consider housework degrading, and some wives may resent their husbands' interference in the domestic domain.

Several studies suggest that some wives do not look forward to their husbands' retirement. Many wives feel that their daily routines will be disrupted by their husbands' being home all day and that they will have to live on a lower income.

On the other hand, a husband's retirement is likely to bring a couple together in a way that they have not experienced since the first years of their marriage. Before retiring, their interests centered on child rearing and earning a living; now their interests are directed toward each other. For some couples the intense interaction of the retirement years may increase their appreciation of each other and bring them closer together. For others the intimacy of the relationship may put a strain on the marriage: "Daily absence from home except over the weekends may have enabled many husbands to adjust to the marital relationship which under conditions of close contact they might have found explosive or intolerable" (Donahue, Orbach, & Pollak, 1960). A study of Vinick and Ekerdt (1989) compared the marital complaints of retired couples with a matched sample of couples in which the husbands were still working. They report that, in general, couples complained about the same issues both before and after retirement. They indicate, as does much of the research evidence, that there is a tendency toward a continuity of marital satisfaction and that marriages that were happy or unhappy before retirement will be the same after retirement.

Clark and Anderson (1967) have observed that, as couples reach the later retirement stage, age 75 and over, successful marriages are based on a mutual interdependency that has a symbiotic quality. This is especially true in situations where the husband or wife or both are ill and need the care and support of the other. In addition, they report that happy older marriages are based on a greater social equality in the relationship. "Rather than the feminine subordination to a husband, . . . husband and wife appear more as social equals, dividing up the labor of the household, blending the masculine and feminine into one tight little social unit."

WIDOWHOOD

One of the greatest fears of happily married husbands and wives is the fear of widowhood. In 1987 nearly half (49 percent) of all women over age 65 were widows; there were 8.1 million widows as compared with 1.6 million widowers. Widowhood is primarily a women's problem because of their longer life expectancies and their tendency to marry men older than they are.

Some sociologists have suggested that the problems of widowhood are more serious for women than men; widows tend to fare worse in terms of remarriage and finances. Because of the greater availability of women over 65, the widower has a wide choice of women from which to choose. In addition, unlike the older woman, the widower is not limited by societal standards to his own age group but can, and often does, select a marital partner much younger than he. The remarriage rate for older men is more than eight times higher than for women. Though social relationships with the opposite sex are limited for older women and their chances for remarriage slight, they find some compensation in the likelihood of having a large group of other widows from which to select friends.

On the other hand, other sociologists argue that the problems a surviving husband faces are more difficult than those of a surviving wife. The widower is often confronted with the management of household affairs for which he may be totally unprepared. For some men, domestic tasks and responsibilities appear overwhelming. Furthermore, the widower experiences more difficulty in finding an adequate substitute for the intimacy of the primary relationship that was once provided by the wife (Bernardo, 1970).

Perhaps because widowhood is more often encountered by older wives than older husbands, studies find that more women than men are likely to report that they had thought about the possibility of losing their mates. Thus, many women go through a *rehearsal for widowhood,* in which they begin to prepare themselves psychologically for some of the problems and adjustments they are likely to encounter when their husbands die (Neugarten, 1968; Kalish, 1975). However, whether or not a widow's rehearsal for the role of widowhood facilitates adjustment to bereavement is debatable (Hill, Thompson, & Gallagher, 1988). (For a cross-cultural perspective on widowhood, see the Reading at the end of this chapter.)

Because women outlive men and tend to marry men older than themselves, a large percentage of married women must cope eventually with the problems of widowhood. (Nick Myers)

ALTERNATIVE FORMS OF FAMILY

After the death of a spouse, many older people are unwilling or unable to live alone. The traditional alternatives previously open to them were either to move in with their children or to live in a nursing home or some other institution for the aged. Today a growing proportion of older people are rejecting these choices and, like some in the younger generation, are experimenting with new, alternative forms of family life.

Senior Communes

Communal living is not new, but the fact that such an arrangement might meet the needs of the elderly is new. According to Streib and Streib (1975), two social trends in our society have led to the idea of communal living for the older population. First, because of the increased number and proportion of people 65 and over, more attention is being given to their needs and problems, including their living environment. Second, the emergence of a communal movement among young people has given rise to the idea that communal arrangements might provide a solution to some problems of older people. Streib and Streib suggest that "since old age and retirement for many are marked by a shift in roles and activities which deemphasize work, individualism, competition, and the accumulation of wealth, it is argued that the elderly might benefit from an environment involving cooperation, sharing of expenses, and the provision of emotional supports."

One noteworthy example of a modified form of communal living is the Share-A-Home Association, which consists of a network of private residences located primarily in Florida. Started in 1960 as a nonprofit organization, these homes allow older persons to live together as a family by sharing expenses and functioning as a single household unit. In this environment the members not only fulfill their basic needs but also provide one another with companionship and emotional support. The power and decision making in the household rest solely in the hands of the residents. Their authority ranges from hiring and firing the staff and voting on new members to decisions regarding menus and entertainment.

A case involving a Share-A-Home group in Winter Park, Florida, gave a new legal definition to what constitutes a family (Sussman, 1976). In 1971 the Orange County Board of Commissioners filed a suit against a Share-A-Home Association, claiming that it was a boarding house and as such was in violation of the single-family zoning ordinance in that neighborhood. The Share-A-Home group in question consisted of 12 older people, aged 61 to 94, who had formed a communal-type family and were living in an old 27-room house. The Orange County code defines a family as "one or more persons occupying a dwelling and living as a single housekeeping unit." Because these persons were living in the same household, sharing the same kitchen, splitting living costs, and giving one another support and understanding, they were found to be a bona fide family. (The main argument for not recognizing them as family was that they were not related.) The presiding judge ruled that the group met the legal definition of a family and that "any group that pools its resources with the intention of sharing the joys and sorrows of family life is a family."

The Share-A-Home Association is set up so that the home is truly a home and not an institution. By pooling their financial resources, persons can enjoy a higher standard of living than they could afford alone. For those elderly who have limited incomes, are lonely, and are no longer totally independent, the Share-A-Home Association appears to offer them a viable solution.

Polygyny

Several gerontologists have suggested that polygynous marriages for older people (when a husband has two or more wives at the same time) would compensate for the excess of women in that age category. A leading exponent of this marriage alternative is Victor Kessel (1970). Instead of facing 15 to 20 years of widowhood, a woman over 60 would have a chance to remarry if men over 60 married two to five wives. This marital arrangement would not only afford older people the opportunity to establish a new family group consisting of wives and their spouse, but, according to Kessel, such an arrangement would include at least seven advantages.

First, he notes that married couples have a more balanced diet than widows or widowers, who often have little or no incentive to cook for themselves and do not enjoy eating alone. By living as a family, members would find the mealtime atmosphere greatly improved. Secondly, by family members' pooling their resources, they could live more adequately and graciously.

A third advantage of *polygyny,* according to Kessel, is that in the event of illness, the husband and wives could share the burden of nursing. Also, many elderly are hospitalized because they live alone and have no one to take care of them; in this situation, infirm persons could remain at home with people to look after them.

Sometimes older people do not have the stamina or strength to do all the work necessary to maintain a household. Thus, a fourth advantage would be that several women working together and dividing the domestic tasks could lighten the load considerably.

Many older widows who grew up in a society that considered sex outside marriage a serious transgression cannot accept such relationships; their sexual activity ceased with the deaths of their husbands. The fifth advantage of a polygynous marriage would be for an older woman to have a legally sanctioned sexual partner.

A sixth benefit of a polygynous family arrangement is that it would help combat depression resulting from feelings of loneliness and uselessness. "It is knowing that one is a member of a distinct group that produces a feeling of belonging, with a consequent reason to live." Last, because of the rivalry that exists in a polygynous family, Kessel believes that it can increase pride in appearance and emphasize good grooming. Although he acknowledges that jealousy and rivalry may often lead to family disruption, he feels that all the other advantages of plural marriage far outweigh this disadvantage.

Rosenberg (1970) raises objections to a polygynous family structure for the elderly. In particular, he feels that monogamous values are so firmly implanted in our society that there is no reason to believe an older woman can or would want to discard these values. Furthermore, he notes that a polygynous remarriage would have economic consequences on kinship ties, especially where inheritance is involved. Polygyny, in his view, would lead to a dispersal of inheritance outside the original family lineage and, in turn, would be disruptive to the present kinship system.

Cohabitation

Another variant family form is *cohabitation*, commonly referred to as "living together." In recent years this lifestyle has been adopted by varied segments of the population from young adults to the elderly. Living together has proved to be a satisfactory solution for some older people. A significant proportion of the elderly do so because they fear being penalized financially. In the past, many older men and women avoided remarriage in order to draw maximum social security benefits, but social security requirements were changed in 1979 and again in 1984 to allow unreduced benefits for widows, widowers, and surviving divorced spouses who remarry after the age of 60. In some cases women do not remarry in order to retain their widow's benefits from private pension plans. Also, the problems that each older person faces with his or her children over inheritance are minimized in this type of living arrangement.

A variety of alternatives to conventional marriage, in addition to the ones discussed here, may offer solutions to the needs of some elderly. Today, the changing demographic structure of our population—the growth in the percentage of older people in the population and the large number of women who survive their husbands—requires that we explore new types of relationships between the sexes. Many older people may choose to have either conventional relationships or none at all. But for those who wish to try alternatives, the option should be open to them.

SUMMARY

1. An institution is a cluster of norms surrounding an important social need of a society. Every known society has five basic social institutions: the family, the economy, the political system, religion, and education. Family patterns vary widely in different societies. Many patterns in other cultures seem strange to Americans, and our ways seem equally strange to them.

2. The most basic of all family types is the nuclear family. When several nuclear families are combined generationally they form an extended family. Contrary to what many believe, the extended family was no more prevalent in the past than it is today. The nuclear family has always represented the modal pattern for the elderly in American society.

3. Though most older people live apart from their children, they are not isolated from them. They maintain contact with at least one child on a regular basis. Although mutual aid flows in two directions, it most frequently flows from parents to children.

4. Today more people are becoming grandparents, great-grandparents, and great-great-grandparents than ever before. Neugarten and Weinstein distinguish five types of grandparents: the formal grandparent, the fun seeker, the surrogate parent, the reservoir of family wisdom, and the distant grandparent. In recent years some laws have been passed to offer legal support to grandparents of children whose parents have been divorced.

5. Most studies of the effects of retirement on the marital relationship focus on the changes in role differentiation and the sharing of household chores. Some studies suggest that a significant proportion of wives do not look forward to

their husbands' retirement. Successful marriages in the family of the late retirement years are based on mutual interdependence.

6. Widowhood is primarily a women's problem because of their longer life expectancies and their tendency to marry men older than they. Although widows tend to fare worse in terms of remarriage and finances than widowers, some argue that widowhood is more difficult for men.

7. Today many older people are experimenting with new, alternative forms of family life. One example is Share-A-Home, in which older people live together as a family unit. Kessel has proposed polygynous marriages for people age 60 and over. Cohabitation is another lifestyle that has been adopted by some elderly persons. These and other alternatives to traditional marriage may prove to be satisfactory solutions for the elderly of the future.

KEY TERMS

institution	the myth of abandonment
kibbutzim	caregiver
nuclear family	primary caregiver
extended family	women in the middle
intimacy at a distance	rehearsal for widowhood
role reversal	polygyny
filial maturity	cohabitation

FOR FURTHER STUDY

Bahr, Stephen J., & Peterson, Evan T. (Eds.) (1989). *Aging and the family*. Lexington, MA: Lexington Books.
A collection of papers that provides an introduction to aging from a family perspective.

Brubaker, Timothy H. (1985). *Later life families*. Beverly Hills, CA: Sage.
Provides a review of studies on later-life family patterns.

Cherlin, Andrew & Furstenberg, Frank F. (1986). *The new American grandparent: A place in the family, a life apart*. New York: Basic Books.
Based on a national study of grandparents, this volume provides an in-depth portrait of grandparenthood.

Lopata, Helena Z. (1973). *Widowhood in an American city*. Cambridge, MA: Schenkman.
Probably the most comprehensive study of widowhood to date.

Pifer, Alan & Bronte, Lydia (1986). *Our aging society: Paradox and promise*. New York: Norton.
The eighteen essays in this volume address the major social institutions along with problems and issues related to an aging population.

Troll, Lillian E., Miller, Sheila J., & Atchley, Robert C. (1979). *Families in later life*. Belmont, CA: Wadsworth.
Offers a concise coverage of the literature of the familial lives of older people.

Reading

Widowhood Among the Maloese

Robert L. Rubinstein

This account examines the resources and integration of widows in Malo, a small island in the South Pacific, and reveals the contrast between the lifestyles of widows in our society and those in another culture. The Malo society is based mainly on the growing of yams and the breeding and raising of pigs; these form the basis of their economy. Most weddings and many land transactions involve the payment or exchange of pigs.

The Maloese say, "Men stand on the land and women leave it," referring both to sons who stay and carry on and to daughters who marry out. . . . Women—as daughters and sisters—are dispossessed from their natal land at the time of their marriage. As one man put it, "My daughter belongs to me and when she marries, she'll belong to another man." At marriage, exchanges of pigs, yams, and other valuables "place" the bride at her husband's land; they socially fix any of her biological offspring as her husband's children. . . .

From the Western point of view, marriage is the union of two individuals that may involve two families. From the Malo point of view, marriage is the union of two individuals, but it always involves families and represents a complex series of arrangements between persons of two lands. Basic to the notion of marriage is the idea that a transaction must accompany it. A payment must go from the groom to the bride's family (specifically to her father; mother; and brothers). . . .

Traditionally, and until recent decades, most marriages were arranged, of older men to young girls (age five or ten) and polygyny was practiced. Nowadays, notions of romantic love have dictated alliances of individuals of more equal age and there are few polygynous relationships. Some of these occur in non-Maloese villages.

It is within this general context of gender and land conceptualizations that widowhood should be viewed. A widow is called a *buotinau* in the Malo language; as far as I am aware, there is no complementary term for widower; who remains a "man"

Robert L. Rubinstein, "Women as Widows on Malo (Natamambo), Vanatu (South Pacific)." In Helena Z. Lopata (Ed.), *Widows, Vol. 1: The Middle East, Asia, and the Pacific.* Durham, NC: Duke University Press, 1987, pp. 24–42. [Readers interested in full source citations are referred to the original source.]

or a "person." There are only a small number of widows on Malo at the present time, perhaps thirty. Most are elderly.

When a woman is widowed there are a number of alternatives for her. She may continue to live on her husband's land, at her husband's place, as a widow; she may marry a husband's brother; or, she may marry the son of her deceased husband's cowife. It is also possible that she may be "claimed" by her husband's sister's son as part of that individual's rights in the deceased's property. A further option is that she may remarry another man who is not related to her former husband. Several factors govern the choosing of these alternatives: land relations and contending legal principles, the age of the widow, and the population of potential mates.

A woman belongs "legally" to the land of the man to whom she was married. This is her place, an attachment that has its legal foundation in *kastom* and in the social strength of transaction (because there has been a payment to transfer her and any of her children to her husband's land), and its emotional foundation in her relations with her husband (in the fact that this is her children's place and in ongoing human struggles and activities). Thus, when her husband dies, a woman continues to "belong" to his land and, in a sense, to the men of that land, her husband's "brothers." . . .

The death of an individual sets off a period of intense activity that, when the deceased is a married man, involves the widow and, always, other close family members and other mourners. Traditionally, if the deceased was an important man in the pig-killing system, special ceremonies marked the tenth and hundredth day after his day. His widows covered their bodies in ash, were expected to "sit" and sleep at his grave site until the one-hundredth day, to restrict the types and amounts of food they consumed, to cry and wail daily, and to not wash nor don normal dress. Currently, the most intense period of mourning lasts to the tenth day, when a ceremony called "Tenth Day" is held. At this occasion wealth—in the form of yams taken from the deceased's gardens, his pigs, and his money—is given out to those who have come to mourn. . . .

During this mourning period society draws together to help patch the social tear: This is true even to the extent that relatives from the other side of the island, or those who are living on other islands, and who have not been to visit in months or years, come to mourn. These persons stay for several days or until the tenth day. Local relatives, friends, and other mourners come daily, bringing food, and helping to cook for the crowd. The close family—widow, children, siblings, nieces, and nephews—mourn daily by wailing a stylized song of mourning with a doleful cadence and with words selected by each individual to tell of his or her relations with the deceased. Often, survivors dream of or experience the spirit of the deceased, which lingers, visiting its corporeal haunts and usual pathways, before it departs.

On the tenth day, after the distribution of the deceased's wealth, most of the mourners depart, leaving the widow and her immediate family. A kind of veil of privacy then falls. This period, the few months following the Tenth Day ceremony, can be the most difficult for a widow. Grief remains as she decides what her options are. One older widow noted, at the time of her last husband's death, that she had buried several husbands, had survived them all, and was obviously no good for men, so that she would not remarry. Besides the question of remarriage, widows must face a variety of other important issues involving possible residential moves, disposition of property, and future activities.

If a widow is elderly and does not remarry, she will, as we have noted, tend to remain at the place of her deceased husband. For the rest of her life her children and grandchildren will be her main supporters and care-givers. As has been so often noted for the West (Shanas, 1981a, 1981b; Brody, 1981), children are the primary providers of care and support for elderly widows and other elderly individuals. The same appears to be true for many non-Western societies (Rubinstein & Johnson, 1984). On Malo, this is certainly the case. But rather than sons and daughters specifically, it is usually sons' wives who carry the care-giving burden for widows, primarily because daughters have married away from the land at which their elderly mother is living and because there are considerable restrictions on the care-giving interaction between a mature man and his mother. . . . Generally, Maloese distinguish two levels of social help. The first is the cooperative help of kinly good fellowship and mutual concern (*tuania*, "help"), as when a man and his wife, along with his elderly widowed mother who resides on another land, make a garden together or may work together to prepare one another's garden land. The second is care (*mataci*, from *mata*, "eye"), the support, watchfulness and personal care over one—such as a child or an elder—who is weak or infirm.

If a widow has no children, she is definitely at a disadvantage. If she has daughters who are married out into other lands, or if she has sons who are not yet married, she is also at a disadvantage. Nydegger (1983) has noted that in Third World societies, the position of elderly persons without children is often quite bad. While this is not precisely true for Malo, there is some degree of truth in such a generalization. Generally, all widows have children (albeit not children who are their own); but, in the case of a childless widow, it is sisters' children and children of land relatives who theoretically should provide help. However, the strategic interests of these individuals may be elsewhere, and they may fail to respond to needs in specific instances.

The widow without enough support may need to adapt by taking over types of activities that were traditionally performed by a husband, such as heavier garden work—male activities including climbing trees and the like. There is some social stigma attached to the taking over of gender-inappropriate tasks, although an allowance is made if the need is clear. In such instances a widow is said to be "taking on the work of two" (certainly an honorable description in a society that values ability to work hard and long) or "taking on men's work" (a less-honorable estate for women).

Support can vary depending on the number of children and grandchildren. It further varies on the marital status of the children. Having married sons is an important resource for an elderly widow. . . .

Besides help from immediate children and children-in-law; widows may receive support from children of land relatives. This form of support is especially significant when older widows have no children of their own or children who are not in a position to give them support. . . .

Older widows (and married women as well) sometimes act as "initiators" of sexual experiences for young men. I have collected data on several instances of such affairs between older women and young men. Such surreptitious alliances may be uncovered by a third party and circulate as public gossip, or they may be hidden but "told out" by the widow as part of a deathbed confession.

Chapter
13

The Economy: Work and Retirement

*U*nlike the solitary wasp, virtually no human being can live by his or her own efforts alone. In human society, cultural adaptation implies an interdependent relationship among its members to produce the necessities for existence (e.g., food, clothing, and shelter), along with a host of other needs. This interdependence entails a division of labor and a specialization that evoke the need for some system of exchange. A society, then, must not only provide for the production of goods and services, but it must also devise some orderly and efficient means of allocation given the inevitable scarcity of these items.

The norms and ideas controlling the production and distribution of scarce goods and services in a society constitute its *economic institutions.* These institutions frame the world of work. This chapter focuses primarily on work and the departure from it—retirement—in relation to the older person.

THE MEANING AND FUNCTION OF WORK

Historically, *work* has carried different meanings at various times and places. Among the ancient Greeks the word for work, *ponos*, was derived from the word for sorrow. Work was regarded as fit only for slaves, because affluent Greeks felt that it degraded the mind and corrupted the soul. The Latin word for labor means both work and toil in the sense of suffering. The Hebrews looked on work as Adam's punishment, the necessity of having to toil for a living: "In the sweat of thy face shalt thou eat bread." The first Christians did work as a penance.

With the advent of the Protestant Reformation, the Christian concept of work took on a totally new meaning. Work began to be characterized as a religious devotion. The Calvinist doctrine of predestination held that only through hard work could individuals get evidence that they had God's favor and were chosen for salvation. Work was equated with prayer and was considered a personal calling or mission.

Though most people in our society today do not look on work as a sign of salvation, they are still guided by a strong work ethic. Friedmann and Havighurst (1954) identify five general functions that work performs in the lives of individuals. The first and most obvious function is that the job gives persons income or some financial return with which to maintain themselves. In exchange, workers are expected to produce something or to make some economic contribution. A second function of work is that of regulating life activity. Work usually requires the individual to be at a certain place during certain days and hours. In this way, the job determines to a great extent where, when, and how people are to spend a large portion of their time. This demand gives order and routine to their lives.

A third function of work is that it gives a person a sense of identity. The job helps them describe themselves. As Hughes (1970) has noted, "A man's job is his price tag and calling card." Most people describe themselves by their occupation or by the company or organization for which they work. When you meet someone for the first time, "How do you do?" is soon followed by "What do you do?" The importance of this job-related identification becomes most pronounced at retirement, when individuals feel a sudden loss of identity. Along with the identity, persons carry the position or status that society has attached to their particular job. Although each person occupies many different statuses, usually the job provides the master status and bears heavily on social standing in the community (see Box 13.1).

A fourth function of work is that a job serves as a base for social relationships. It is a principal source of social contact and of a major reference group. Finally, a fifth function of work is that it affords the worker a cluster of meaningful life experiences. "It is a source of contacts with persons, objects, and ideas. It is a market place where the worker's store of life-experience is enriched through interaction with the world about him and where he receives new ideas, expresses his own ideas, and modifies his conception of the work and of himself in relation to it" (Friedmann & Havighurst, 1954).

Although work fulfills certain functions for all workers, its meaning and the

---

Box 13.1 # Retirement Means Losing the Important Part of One's Name

I have yet to see anyone mention one problem that bothers most men when they retire. This problem is the sudden loss of personal identification except for a name. This is what I mean. Let's take a fellow named John Jones. He has worked for a firm named General Endeavor (or General Motors or General Electric) for 30 or 40 years. He has long been accustomed to thinking of himself in relation to his firm. When introducing himself to a stranger, he has said, "I'm Jones of General Endeavor." He knew he had a fixed place in the business world, and he was identified with his organization. He was accustomed to thinking of himself as part of his firm.

Then John Jones retired, and one day he walked into a room filled with strangers and heard his own voice saying, "I'm John Jones." It shook him to realize that he no longer was John Jones of General Endeavor. He was just John Jones period. He was on his own. The experience left him feeling curiously adrift without the old anchor of identification he had always thrown out when meeting someone. He felt as though he were floating about in space without identity, even though he had a name and was a member of the human race. "I'm John Jones and I belong to the human race" was hardly adequate. . . .

Source: Don Whitehead, *Knoxville News-Sentinel*, October 4, 1977, p. 24.

---

relative importance of certain aspects of work vary. A 1981 Harris poll asked people what they missed about their jobs after they stopped working. As Table 13.1 shows, a substantial majority cited "the money" and "the people." Other aspects of the job missed were "the work itself" and "the importance of being useful."

Table 13.1 JOB ASPECTS MISSED BY RETIRED PEOPLE AGE 65 AND OVER

	Missed (percent)	Not missed (percent)	Not sure (percent)
The money it brings in	71	28	2
The people at work	70	28	2
The work itself	57	41	2
The feeling of being useful	55	43	2
Things happening around me	51	46	3
The respect of others	48	49	3
Having a fixed schedule every day	44	54	3

Source: Louis Harris and Associates, *Aging in the Eighties: America in Transition*. Washington, DC: National Council on the Aging, 1981.

Labor-Force Participation

The economy in this country has changed dramatically since the turn of the century, with a shift from agriculture and smokestack industries to white-collar and service industries. In 1900 farm workers composed 40 percent of the entire work force, and by 1980 they made up only 3 percent. Today about 70 percent of all workers are employed in white-collar and service occupations. These changes are reflected in the employment trends among older workers. For example, in 1987, nearly three-fourths of workers age 65 and older were in white-collar and service jobs.

The rates of older men remaining in the work force after age 65 have significantly declined in the past 35 years. Table 13.2 shows that in 1950, 45.8 percent of all men 65 and over were in the labor force, in 1960 it was down to 33.1 percent, and by 1986–1988 the figure had dropped to around 16 percent. This drop reflects the decline in self-employment and the trend toward retiring before age 65. For instance, in 1988, nearly 90 percent of men ages 50 to 54 were in the labor force, whereas only about 55 percent of those in the 60- to 64-age bracket continued to work. Put another way, nearly half of older men are out of the labor force before age 65 (U.S. Senate Special Committee on Aging, 1989). In contrast, the rates of older women in the labor force have varied only slightly. In 1950 close to 10 percent of older women were working, and by 1988 it was 7.9 percent.

Historically, the extent of labor-force participation for black women 65 years and older has been slightly higher than for their white counterparts. Presently, the rates are 8 percent for older white women and 10 percent for older black women. The rate of labor-force participation for older black men in 1988 was 14 percent, as compared with 17 percent for older white men.

Characteristics of Older Workers

When compared with the younger adult population, older workers have a disadvantaged position in the labor force. This situation is due to erroneous beliefs about older workers. The U.S. Department of Labor has listed some of the more common myths about older workers and the facts concerning them.

Table 13.2   PERCENT OF POPULATION AGE 65 AND OVER IN THE LABOR FORCE: 1950–1988

Sex	1950	1960	1970	1975	1980	1986	1988
Male	45.8	33.1	26.8	21.7	20.1	16.0	16.5
Female	9.7	10.8	9.7	8.3	8.0	7.4	7.9

Source: U.S. Bureau of the Census, *Current Population Reports,* Special Studies Series, P-23, No. 59, Washington, DC: U.S. Government Printing Office, 1976; U.S. Department of Labor, Bureau of Labor Statistics. Employment and Earnings, Vol. 34, No.1 (January 1987) and Vol. 36, No. 1 (January 1989).

1. *Older workers are too slow—they can't meet the production requirements.* Studies show no significant drop in performance and productivity in older workers. Many older workers exceed the average output of younger employees.

2. *Older workers can't meet the physical demands of our jobs.* Job analysis indicates that fewer than 14 percent of jobs today require great strength and heavy lifting. Labor-saving machinery makes it possible for older workers to handle most jobs without difficulty.

3. *You can't depend on older workers—they're absent from work too often.* According to surveys, workers 65 and over have a good record of attendance in comparison with other age groups.

4. *Older workers are not adaptable—they're hard to train because they can't accept change.* Evaluations of older job seekers show that a high proportion are flexible in accepting change in their occupation and earnings. Adaptability depends on the individual: Many young people are set in their ways, and many older workers adjust to change readily.

Other reasons that account for the disadvantaged position of older workers include their lower educational attainment, their obsolescent skills, and management's preference for younger workers in a competitive economy.

Older people are often found in the self-employed category because it affords them the advantages of setting their own hours and work pace. The proportion of men employed in service occupations increases steadily with age. Such jobs as janitor, desk clerk in a hotel or motel, night watchman, or guard are more apt to be filled by older men. Older women are frequently employed to do baby-sitting or light housework (Loether, 1975).

Older workers are less occupationally mobile than their younger counterparts. By the age of 50, few workers are apt to change jobs voluntarily, for several reasons. In middle age, workers are more likely to be settled down in jobs that they consider permanent. Workers, as a rule, do not want to give up their seniority or their fringe benefits. But probably the most significant reason why older workers refrain from leaving their job is the fear of not being able to find another. This fear is not without justification. After age 45, finding a job becomes more difficult and this is reflected in the fact that duration of unemployment tends to increase with age. In 1987 the average period of unemployment for workers between the ages of 55 and 64 was about 22 weeks, whereas for workers age 20 to 24 it was 11 weeks (U.S. Senate Special Committee on Aging, 1989).

Despite the fact that older workers encounter great problems in finding another job once they are unemployed, the unemployment rates for older workers are low. Though at first this seems paradoxical, the situation is explained by what is called *hidden unemployment.* The unemployment rate reflects only those *actively* seeking work and omits those older workers who become discouraged and drop out of the labor force after finding their search for employment futile. These people are then no longer classified as unemployed. Thus the line of least resistance for older workers is to declare themselves retired because being out of the labor force is more respectable than being out of a job.

The proportion of men employed in service occupations such as guard or night watchman increases steadily with age. (Nick Myers)

Age Discrimination in Employment

One of the most publicized age-discrimination cases to date was that of the I. Magnin clothing store chain (*Cancellier* v. *Federated Department Stores*, 1982). It involved the firing of three employees—Philip Cancellier, a vice president, age 51; John Costello, a merchandise manager, age 51; and Zelma Ritter, a buyer, age 52. The three had worked for Magnin 25, 17, and 18 years, respectively. The company felt that Cancellier had reached his full potential at age 50, and he was told to take a demotion or go. He was replaced by a 33-year-old. Costello and Ritter were considered no longer promotable at their ages. These firings were prompted by Magnin's concern about the youth market, the company wanted to attract young customers and believed that younger personnel could reach this market by selling and merchandising in tune with the times. What made matters even worse was that the company had a plan that gave executives with a certain number of years of service extra benefits at retirement; by firing these people before they became eligible to receive these benefits, it appeared as if the company were trying to save money by double-crossing its executives. The trial lasted six weeks. Though the plaintiffs did not get their jobs back, a jury awarded them nearly $2 million in damages (Friedman, 1984).

Since 1967, when the *Age Discrimination in Employment Act (ADEA)* was passed, there have been hundreds of court cases on age discrimination, and the numbers keep growing. The Equal Employment Opportunity Commission (EEOC), which enforces the laws prohibiting discrimination, in 1988 received more than 11,400 age-discrimination complaints (U.S. Senate Special Committee on Aging, 1989). The ADEA bans age discrimination in hiring, promoting, and dismissing employees and makes it unlawful for an employment agency to refuse to refer a client to a prospective employer for a job because of age. Also, it is illegal for prospective employers to state age preferences in help-wanted advertisements, whether directly or indirectly. Furthermore, employers are not allowed to treat older workers differently from younger workers, such as requiring only older workers to pass physical or mental tests or using different promotional standards for them (Levine, 1988). Table 13.3 highlights some of the most important pieces of legislation for older workers.

Originally the ADEA was designed to protect workers between the ages of 40 and 65. In 1978 it was amended to extend protection to persons up to 70 years of age. These changes officially outlawed 65 as the age of mandatory retirement in the United States for most workers and abolished it altogether for federal employees. Although many proponents of flexible retirement policies looked on this legislation as a significant step in the right direction, they felt that the law did not go far enough. They argued that the upper limit of age 70 should be removed. In 1986, amendments were passed eliminating the upper age of 70 and making age-based mandatory retirement

---

Table 13.3 MAJOR LEGISLATION FOR OLDER WORKERS

1956 Social Security Act Amendments: Allowed women to receive Social Security benefits at the age of 62 instead of 65 (however, the amount is permanently reduced by 20 percent).

1961 Social Security Act Amendments: Allowed men to also receive early benefits.

1967 Age Discrimination in Employment Act (ADEA): Prohibited age discrimination in hiring, promoting, and firing employees between the ages of 40 and 65.

1974 Employee Retirement Income Security Act (ERISA): Regulated private pension plans and set minimum pension standards.

1978 Amendments to Age Discrimination in Employment Act (ADEA): Raised upper age limit to 70.

1983 Social Security Act Amendments: Raised the age of eligibility for full retirement benefits from age 65 to age 66 beginning in the year 2009 and to age 67 beginning in the year 2027.

1986 Amendments to Age Discrimination in Employment Act (ADEA): Ended mandatory retirement.

against the law. Twenty states had already enacted similar laws. Thus the debate between flexible versus mandatory retirement policies (forced retirement at a certain age), always a perennial issue in gerontology, was finally ended. Table 13.4 lists some of the major arguments that surrounded this debate.

Despite legal protection against mandatory retirement, age discrimination in employment persists. Discriminatory practices include relocating older employees to undesirable locations in hopes that they will resign, offering older workers early-retirement incentives, and giving older employees smaller pay raises as well as poor evaluations for no valid reason. In addition, older workers often are not given the same opportunity as younger workers for needed training to keep up with technological changes.

THE MEANING OF RETIREMENT

In many places of the world, retirement as we know it is a rarity. Cessation of work in most preindustrial societies occurs only when individuals are too feeble to perform any type of productive activity. A gradual reduction of participation in economic activities is the most common pattern of aging throughout the world. The aged are expected to continue to engage in whatever economic function that they are capable of doing, shifting from tasks that are physically demanding to lighter, less strenuous ones. For instance, among the !Kung Bushmen of the Kalahari Desert, when a man is no longer able to hunt big game, he shifts to trapping and making weapons. Old women continue to gather berries and tubers as long as they are able (Biesele & Howell, 1981).

Retirement is a relatively recent development in modern industrialized societies. The term itself has several meanings. At the individual level, retirement entails an event that marks the end of one's primary occupational life and is then followed by the process of adjusting to being a retired person. At the societal level it refers to "an economically non-productive role for large numbers of people whose labor is not considered essential to or necessary for the functioning of the economic order" (Orbach, 1963). Retirement entails the transition from a clearly

Table 13.4   ARGUMENTS FOR FLEXIBLE VERSUS MANDATORY RETIREMENT

Flexible retirement	Mandatory retirement
Mandatory retirement is discriminatory and contrary to the principle of equal employment opportunities	Mandatory retirement assures everyone equal and fair treatment
Age is not an accurate indicator of the abilities of older people	Older people are not as productive as younger workers
Flexible retirement would more fully utilize the experience, skills, and potential of older people	A fixed retirement age is needed to open up jobs and promotional opportunities for young people

"Gosh, Grandma, what a big office you have!" (Drawing by Ross; © 1987 The New Yorker Magazine, Inc.)

defined role to a vague and ambiguous role. This lack of clear-cut norms in the retirement role is due to the retiree's new and unique social position, for which there is no precedence. People used to work throughout their adult lives out of necessity. Today a new period has been added to the life course in which people live out their last 15 to 20 years without having to work. They constitute a new social category known as retirees.

Gerontological literature in the 1960s often emphasized only the negative aspects of retirement. The literature focused on such problems as economic deprivation and the loss of occupational identity and social status. Burgess (1960) referred to retirement as a "roleless role," whereas others saw it as a social identity crisis and a stressful transition (Rosow, 1962; Miller, 1965).

In the past two decades a number of economic and social factors have helped ease the transition to retirement and to make it a more rewarding experience. As a result, retirement has gained popular acceptance and is now being viewed more positively both before and after the event. For instance, retirement planning programs are becoming increasingly available along with flexible retirement policies such as gradual or phased retirement. Phased retirement permits workers to withdraw gradually from their work-life routines in order to prepare for a life with more discretionary time (see Chapter 6, "Socialization," for further discussion of this topic). Increased pension coverage and benefits have made retirement more attractive as well as attainable at earlier ages. Next, the dramatic increase in the number of retired persons has helped facilitate adjustment to the retirement role and created a favorable social environment for retirement. Also, many products and services are being geared toward this expanding consumer market, including retirement housing, travel services, and senior citizen discounts, which enhance the retirement lifestyle. In addition, there has been a significant expansion in organizational support for the elderly in the form of clubs, centers, and government-sponsored programs (Foner & Schwab, 1983).

Although reactions to retirement have become increasingly positive, it is important to keep in mind that for some people retirement is a dismal, unhappy experience with serious financial, social, and psychological problems. Retirement, like work, does not have the same meaning for all individuals. There are wide individual differences. For some, retirement is the realization of a lifelong goal; it may be a welcome relief from an unpleasant job or work situation or the chance to begin a new life or start a second career. For others, it is a time of bitterness, the beginning of diminished roles and the end of self-worth and power.

Early Retirement

It is paradoxical that at a time when persons are living longer, they are also retiring earlier. *Early retirement* (retiring before the age of 65) has recently become established as a norm in American society as workers continue to opt for early retirement in increasing numbers. As we noted earlier, today nearly half of all older men retire before age 65. Some studies report even higher rates. A survey by Louis Harris and Associates (1979) found that nearly two-thirds of retirees had left work before age 65, with the median age of the sample being 60.6 years. A study of recent Social Security beneficiaries revealed that 76 percent of the men and 84 percent of the women began drawing benefits before they reached age 65 (Sherman, 1985), and another study done by the General Accounting Office in 1985 (U.S. Senate Special Committee on Aging, 1987) found that almost half of the individuals who receive private pensions start receiving them by age 62.

The trend toward increasingly early retirement gained momentum in the early 1960s as more and more industrial workers were given options to retire early along with increased benefits. In recent years labor unions have bargained successfully for earlier retirement provisions. The most notable of these is the United Automobile Workers union, which has adopted the "30 and out plan" allowing automobile workers to collect a pension after 30 years of service, regardless of age. Many workers as young as 48 or 49 are able to qualify for full pension benefits.

Early retirement has caught on not only with blue-collar workers but with managerial and professional workers as well. Today 9 out of 10 private pension plans offer financial inducements for early retirement. Employers encourage early retirement by offering the "open window" or "golden handshake" option, which gives employees a very attractive lump-sum benefit and early pension benefits in exchange for their retirement. Another factor that has given further impetus to this trend is the lowering of the age of eligibility for Social Security benefits. Since 1961, men have been allowed to receive reduced Social Security benefits beginning at age 62—instead of having to wait until age 65—giving them the same option granted to women in 1956. As a result, there has been a major increase in the number of workers choosing early retirement. Some employers offer pension supplements to early retirees to bridge the gap until Social Security benefits become available at age 62. Such incentives make the retirement decision more economically feasible than it would have been otherwise. Early retirement allows some workers to start second careers at younger ages, and for others it provides a way out when they are in poor health or having employment problems. Employers use early retirement as a means of adjusting the size and age structure of the labor force. It also helps to minimize the layoffs of younger workers as well as open up managerial positions for them.

On the other hand, early-retirement programs sometimes are not as voluntary as they appear to be. Many employees are subtly pressured into retiring. Sometimes workers take voluntary retirement rather than risk being laid off or trying to find another job. Another problem is that early-retirement incentive programs can be costly to finance as well as wasteful of human resources. Companies lose some of their best employees through these plans as the most experienced and talented workers are often indiscriminately discarded (Alsop, 1984).

One serious long-term consequence for the economy is that there will be an acute labor shortage in the 1990s if workers continue to retire early. The early-retirement trend also places a burden on both private and public pension plans. As workers retire at younger ages, pension costs increase at dramatic rates. As Schulz (1988) points out

> Pension costs increase by about 50 percent once the normal age of retirement is reduced from age 65 to 60. Some private plans today allow people to retire below the age of 60 with no serious penalty. The cost of earlier retirement is measured not only by costs of the pension benefits paid, but also by the reduced economic output resulting when fewer workers remain in the labor force.

In an effort to reverse the trend, federal legislation was enacted in 1983 that raised the age of eligibility for full Social Security benefits from 65 to 66 beginning in 2009 and to 67 beginning in 2027. Congress also has approved a more generous formula for computing "delayed retirement benefits" for those who work beyond age 65 and up to age 70 that will be phased in between 1990 and 2009. However, it is questionable whether such legislation will have a significant effect on retirement patterns. There is little evidence that the trend toward increasingly early retirement will slow down. It reflects not only a positive response to Social Security and private pension incentives but also a strong desire for more leisure time.

The Retirement Decision

Retirement is one of the most important decisions that an individual has to make. A number of factors influence the decision to retire and the timing of retirement. Economists view retirement as a work–leisure trade-off. Schulz (1988) points out that work produces goods and services and in turn provides the money to purchase the goods and services of others. Leisure provides time to be used in nonpaid, voluntary, unobligated activities. A person can get more leisure, but only at the expense of having less money to spend. Persons will be motivated to retire when they believe that their anticipated retirement income is adequate to meet their financial needs and the rewards of leisure outweigh the rewards of work (Atchley, 1988).

Health and the ability to continue to perform on the job are major considerations in the retirement decision. Workers in poor health are more likely to decide to retire earlier than those in good health. About 25 to 30 percent of all retirees cite poor health as the major reason for early retirement (Sherman, 1985).

Individual factors are not the only criteria for the retirement decision; there are also external factors, societal and institutional, that enter into the decision. For one thing, the attitudes toward retirement have changed drastically. Retirement is looked on much more positively than ever before as the numbers of retired persons continue to rise. The availability and increased size of Social Security benefits and employer-sponsored pension programs, as well as early-retirement incentive programs, are powerful influences on the retirement decision. Other factors affecting the retirement decision in the workplace include opportunities for increased earnings, job security, and prospects for continued employment (Schulz, 1988).

Satisfaction with Retirement

A number of studies over the past few decades consistently find that substantial numbers of older persons are satisfied with retirement. For instance, in a study of retirement among both men and women, Streib and Schneider (1971) report that about one-third (31 percent) of their respondents were satisfied with retirement and felt that retirement turned out better than expected. Nearly two-thirds (65 percent) said that it turned out about the way they expected. Four percent felt that it was worse. In 1981 Louis Harris and Associates asked retired people: "Do you now think that you made the right decision to retire when you did, did you retire too early, or do you now think you retired too late?" An impressive majority of 90 percent reported that they had made the right decision. Finally, a study of retired college and university faculty, administrators, and support staff reveal that 51 percent were very satisfied, and 41 percent reasonably satisfied, with retirement. When they were asked to name the factors contributing most to retirement satisfaction, "comfortable financial situation" ranked first, followed by "health" (Milletti, 1984). Studies on retirement reveal that a more satisfactory retirement is experienced by those individuals who have good health and an adequate income.

Thompson (1958) indicates that besides health and wealth, two other important factors contributing to retirement satisfaction are having an accurate preconception of retirement and a favorable preretirement attitude toward retirement. In line with this view, numerous retirement planning programs have been developed in the last two decades by business, industry, labor unions, educational institutions, and various other organizations. (See Chapter 6, "Socialization," for a further discussion of this topic.) In addition to giving workers some idea of what retirement will be like and what to expect, most programs attempt to encourage participants to plan constructively for retirement and to act on these plans before they retire.

Most studies consistently report that older people experience a high degree of satisfaction in retirement. Are retirees really as satisfied as they claim to be? It is important to keep in mind that there are many people who have spent years working at unrewarding, undesirable jobs, and retirement serves as a welcome escape for them. Their high level of satisfaction may hinge on the fact that retirement is much better than what they had before. Also, it may be that older people tend to lower their expectations. They may be satisfied because they do not have the same high hopes and aspirations they had in earlier years. Furthermore, there is a tendency for people to accept to some degree whatever part of the life course they may be in and to adjust and make the best of it (Sheppard, 1976; Foner & Schwab, 1983).

The Consequences of Retirement

One of the most researched topics in gerontology is the affect of retirement on the individual. Yet in spite of the abundance of research, it is still a topic about which there is much misinformation.

1. *Physical health*. One of the most popular beliefs about retirement is that it has a deleterious effect on health and in some instances can lead to a premature death. It is generally assumed that the abrupt cessation of a pattern of high activity and the shift to a slower pace at retirement contribute to physical decline. Stories are common about people who worked "day and night" and then, several months after retirement, died suddenly.

   Research findings reveal that retirement has no adverse effects on health; in fact, in some cases one's health may actually improve after retirement. Although the retired population does contain a disproportionate number of people in poor health, retirement did not cause their health to decline; they retired because they were in poor health. (See the Reading on retirement and health at the end of this chapter.)

2. *Mental health*. Because of the belief that work has a therapeutic value, it is popularly assumed that without work, mental ailments ensue. Lifelong patterns of mental problems before retirement have often been overlooked as the basic cause of mental illness after retirement. The prevalent notion that retirement triggers mental illness is not substantiated by research.

3. *Income*. At retirement most people experience a reduction in income. On the average they retain about one-half to two-thirds of their preretirement earnings. An adequate retirement income, as we have previously noted, is a key element in retirement satisfaction.

4. *Social relationships*. Another popular belief is that retirement marks a decline in social relationships. Research reveals that in most cases withdrawal from the labor force does not automatically result in a reduction of social contact with family, friends, or neighbors. Retirees are no more likely than workers to change their patterns of seeing their children, visiting with family and friends, and participating in community and associational activities. Simpson and her associates (1966) found that the factor having the most influence on social participation in retirement is the status of the retiree's occupation. Retired professionals have the highest degree of involvement,

followed by middle-status workers, with the semiskilled having the least involvement. The researchers also discovered that if social involvements are not established before retirement, it is highly unlikely that they will be initiated after retirement.

5. *The marital relationship.* When the husband retires, the wife must adjust her daily routines to his presence. Some consensus is usually reached regarding the division of household tasks. Although some wives complain of "half as much income and twice as much husband," they also report that their husband's retirement affords them greater companionship. Generally, if a husband and wife enjoy a good relationship prior to retirement, retirement will increase, rather than decrease, marital satisfaction. But spouses who were able to adjust to each other only because they were apart each day may find that retirement creates a strain on their relationship. A couple's marital history before retirement, thus, is one of the most important factors in understanding the dynamics of the marital relationship after retirement (Brubaker, 1985). (See Chapter 12, "The Family.")

Women and Retirement

People generally believe that retirement is not as significant for women as it is for men. Some writers point out that a female worker has the roles of homemaker and career person; she retains the former, which alleviates the impact of retirement (Butler & Lewis, 1977). Others suggest that retirement is easier for a woman because she has "effectively retired once before from her primary family role as mother and thus by age 65 has already negotiated one more or less successful transition" (Bengtson, Kasschau, & Ragan, 1977).

Other researchers have questioned these assumptions and indicate that retirement may be more difficult for women than it is for men. Streib and Schneider (1971) report that women are more unwilling to retire than men are. Among the female retirees in their sample, 57 percent were reluctant to retire, compared with 49 percent of the men. These researchers point out that women who are still working at 65 are those who have consciously selected the work role in preference to the homemaker role and, consequently, are more committed to it. Also, the widely held belief that retired women become full-time homemakers is largely erroneous. The majority of retired women show no increased interest in household activities after retirement (Szinovacz, 1982).

Several studies report that women frequently have more difficulty in adjusting to retirement and find it more psychologically stressful than their male counterparts (Atchley, 1976; Stone, 1985). A major factor contributing to this stress is that female retirees are among the most economically disadvantaged segment of the population. Many suffer substantial reductions in income at retirement because of their being disproportionately represented in low-paying jobs and in industries with unfavorable pension coverage. Also, many women receive decreased retirement benefits because of interruptions in their work histories due to family needs.

Evidence shows that the marital status of women is related to the timing of their retirement. Married women retire earlier than their unmarried counterparts in order to retire at the same time that their typically older husbands do. This situation has been referred to as *synchronized retirement* (Brubaker, 1985). Women who are single, widowed, divorced, or separated are more likely to retire late because of economic need (Atchley & Miller, 1983; Silverman, 1987).

It is generally assumed that women who have worked have a more restricted social network after retirement because they have not had time to make friends outside of the workplace. To investigate this assumption, Fox (1977) studied the effect of retirement on the social life of middle-class women. She found that women who have worked much of their lives have the same social involvement as, if not more than, lifelong homemakers do. At retirement women tend to accelerate their interaction with friends and neighbors to compensate for the loss of work-related friendships. Keith (1982) found that involvement in formal organizations (both civic and religious) was more important to the well-being of retired women than of homemakers. She suggests that retired women may turn to organizational involvement because it provides a place for the continued use of skills from the workplace. These skills may also be the same ones that make participation in organizations more satisfying and meaningful.

Work After Retirement

About 14 percent of American males and 7 percent of the females continue to work after the traditional retirement age of 65 and are sometimes referred to as the *"working retired."* Fillenbaum (1971) in a study of working-retired men tried to determine which variables are most closely associated with work after retirement. Her findings reveal that the working-retired differ mainly from the non–working-retired in that they have more education, have intended to continue working when retired, and are less likely to report a decline in health. She indicates that the major reasons inducing certain persons to continue working after officially retiring are their greater work commitment and high level of job satisfaction.

Individuals who work beyond the traditional retirement age tend to fall into these categories: (1) those who retire and take a part-time job; (2) those who embark on a second career; and (3) those who continue working at the same job. The largest proportion of workers aged 65 and over who continue to work do so on a part-time basis. This situation is due mainly to their preference for part-time work and to the earnings' limitation ceiling of the Social Security system, which discourages full-time employment.

According to Louis Harris and Associates (1981), 73 percent of all persons age 65 and over prefer some kind of part-time work after retirement. A substantial majority (82 percent) would rather continue with the same kind of work instead of changing to a different type of job.

Another group of people are successful in launching new careers after retirement. Some persons go into a new career because they are bored and disappointed with retirement, others because of financial reasons, and some because they want to fulfill a lifelong dream. Although second careers are not the modal pattern in American society, they are becoming a more frequent phenomenon, especially with the trend

Persons who work after the age of 65 are often self-employed. (Nick Myers)

toward earlier retirement. Second careers have long been a pattern for military personnel because of the 20-year-minimum requirement for retirement, which means that many military personnel can retire in their early forties. General Dwight D. Eisenhower after his retirement from the army began his second career as a college president at the age of 58, and started a third career at 62 as president of the United States. (See Box 13.2.)

The third category, those who continue to work at their occupations, often are self-employed. Barfield and Morgan (1969) found that self-employment is the most important factor in determining a late retirement, that is, retirement at age 70 or older. Other significant factors include an expected low retirement income and a current low income.

In recent years much change has taken place regarding retirement. The negative connotations that the word *retirement* once carried in everyday speech have faded. It does not appear to be the traumatic transition and disruptive experience that social scientists and commentators in the 1960s once thought it to be. As the number of retirees continues to mushroom, the retirement role has become institutionalized,

---

Box 13.2 ## A New Career After Retirement?

George Washington retired three times; each time, he became depressed and intro-spective. The first time at the age of 26 while in command of the Virginia Militia in 1758, he decided to retire because of poor health. In a letter to a friend he wrote, "I have not too much reason to apprehend an approaching decay." With the outbreak of the Rev-olutionary War, he was recalled from retirement and, against his wish, was placed in command of the Continental Army. In 1783, he retired again; his words, "The scene is at length closed. I will move gently down the stream of life until I sleep with my fathers." But again, at 51, he was recalled to serve as the first president of the Constitutional Convention.

Source: Edward L. Bortz, "Beyond Retirement." In Frances M. Carp (Ed.), *Retirement*. New York: Behavioral Publications, 1972, pp. 352–353.

---

which in turn has made the workers' transition and adjustment to it easier. The age of 65, long considered the appropriate retirement age, has been replaced by ages in the early sixties. Early retirement is now the norm. Today, with higher private and public pension benefit levels, retirees are better off financially than ever before. Study after study reports that most older people are satisfied with retirement. Although it appears that satisfaction runs high among a substantial proportion of retir-ees, it is well to keep in mind that most of these studies tend to concentrate on the early phases of retirement. More studies are needed of persons who have been retired for longer periods of time in order to help us more fully understand the retirement process.

SUMMARY

1. Through the ages, work has had a variety of meanings and has fulfilled numerous functions. Today, work performs five general functions for most individuals: (1) it provides income; (2) it regulates life activity; (3) it gives a person a sense of identity; (4) it is the source of social relationships; and (5) it offers a set of meaningful life experiences.

2. The proportion of older males, both white and black, in the labor force has steadily declined during this century. The number of older women in the labor force has changed only slightly in the past decades.

3. There are many misconceptions about older workers' productivity, absen-teeism rates, and adaptability. Older workers are less mobile occupationally than younger workers are; after age 50, few change jobs voluntarily because it is difficult for them to get a new job. Many times when older people cannot find work, they drop out of the labor force and declare themselves retired.

4. The Age Discrimination in Employment Act of 1967 (ADEA) protects workers between the ages of 40 and 65 from discriminatory practices in hiring, promoting, and firing workers. The Act was amended in 1978 to raise the top limit from age 65 to 70, and in 1986 it was amended again to remove the top limit—thus making age discrimination illegal.

5. Retirement has become a new stage in the life course in which people spend the last 15 to 20 years of their life without having to work. Early retirement has become increasingly popular in recent years. Nearly half of all older men retire before age 65 today. If workers continue to retire early, there may be an acute labor shortage in the near future.

6. Two key factors affecting the decision to retire are health and income. Studies show that most people are satisfied with retirement. Contrary to popular belief, retirement has no negative effect on one's physical or mental health. Income is often reduced to nearly half at retirement.

7. Research reveals that women are often more unwilling to retire than men and often find it more stressful. Married women tend to retire earlier than unmarried women.

8. Persons who are deeply involved in their work and are successful are the most likely to continue working past retirement age. Individuals who continue to work after the customary retirement age can be divided into three groups: those who work at part-time jobs, those who pursue a second career, and those who continue working at the same job.

KEY TERMS

economic institutions
hidden unemployment
*Age Discrimination in Employment
  Act (ADEA)*
mandatory retirement

roleless role
early retirement
synchronized retirement
working retired

FOR FURTHER STUDY

Atchley, Robert C. (1976). *The sociology of retirement.* Cambridge, MA: Schenkman.
A concise book covering the various aspects of retirement.

Foner, Anne, & Schwab, Karen (1981). *Aging and retirement.* Monterey, CA: Brooks/Cole.
A good review of the major issues in the area of retirement, including myths concerning early retirement and adjustment to retirement.

Graber, William (1980). *A history of retirement.* New Haven, CT: Yale University Press.
Deals with the historical relationships between pensions and employment practices of management, unions, and the government.

Palmore, Erdman B., et al. (1985). *Retirement: Causes and consequences.* New York: Springer.
Based on data from seven longitudinal data sets, this study examines the reasons that persons retire and the consequences of retirement.

Ricardo-Campbell, Rita, & Lazear, Edward P. (Eds.) (1988). *Issues in contemporary retire-ment.* Stanford, CA: Hoover Institution Press.
> *Explores the issues of early retirement, labor-force trends, retirement patterns, Social Security, and other issues related to retirement.*

Reading

Why the Notion Persists That Retirement Harms Health

David J. Ekerdt

The idea that retirement is likely to harm the physical health of older workers is due in part to the availability of vivid anecdotes, the tendency to interpret big events as major causes of illness, the cultural celebration of work, theoretical perspectives in gerontology fostering expectations that retirement is disruptive, and the misinterpretation of research findings.

In January of 1983, just 37 days after he had retired as head football coach at the University of Alabama, Paul "Bear" Bryant, at that time the most successful coach in college football history, died of a heart attack at the age of 69. To the casual observer who had not followed recent details of Bryant's legendary career, this event may have looked like another instance of retirement contributing to a premature death. This, however, would have been the wrong lesson to take away. Although the *New York Times* obituary and related articles for that day made no mention of Bryant's health in his later years, it was reported in a sports page item on the following day that Bryant had struggled with serious health problems for 3 years before his death and that his personal physician had placed him under a rigorous medical regimen (Rawls, 1983). Whatever the effect of retirement on Bear Bryant's health, it was his failing health, rather, that prompted his retirement.

David J. Ekerdt, "Why the Notion Persists That Retirement Harms Health." *The Gerontologist* (27) 4, 1987, pp. 454–456. [Readers interested in full source citations are referred to the original article.]

It is fairly easy to summarize the research conclusions about retirement's impact on physical health. Studies from the 1950s onward have found, with one exception, that retirement increases neither deterioration in health nor the risk of death (Ekerdt et al., 1983a; Kasl, 1980; Palmore et al., 1985; Portnoi, 1981; Streib & Schneider, 1971). Still there are issues that remain to be investigated (see Kasl, 1980 for a useful discussion of these issues). For example, the experience of women and certain occupational groups warrants more detailed study, as does the extent to which retirement might benefit existing medical conditions (Ekerdt et al., 1983b). Nevertheless, a careful reading of the research literature contains virtually nothing to encourage the notion that retirement is likely to harm an older worker's health. It is, of course, possible that retirement can lead to the deterioration of health, but it has not been established that such cases are more than rare events.

And yet the idea persists in popular, medical, and scientific circles that retirement is a significant threat to health. It is more than just an idea, for it can be the basis for individuals' retirement decisions and for the lifestyle advice offered by professionals and practitioners to people of retirement age. The stubbornness of this myth of aging even in the face of contradictory evidence is an impressive phenomenon that should command attention. Several reasons are provided about why the view that retirement harms health has such considerable staying power.

ANECDOTES FROM POPULAR AND CLINICAL OBSERVATION

On a day-to-day basis, familiar stories about friends, relatives, and co-workers continually nourish the idea that retirement harms health. Anecdotal momentum is maintained by a common bias in everyday judgments about probability; namely, that an event will seem more frequent or plausible to the extent that people can easily imagine it (Tversky & Kahneman, 1982). Observations about ailing retirees and comparatively healthy workers have some basis in fact because some 25% to 30% of retirements occur primarily due to illness or disability (Sherman, 1985). As in the case of Bear Bryant, health deterioration soon after retirement is likely to be a continuation of preretirement illness. Narrators of anecdotes, however, may not be privy to detailed health histories or personal reasons leading up to the retirement decision. Health professionals can also overgeneralize from selective observations, extending the experience of their distressed clients to characterize the wider lot of retirees (Strieb, 1983).

THE NATURE OF RETIREMENT AS A LIFE EVENT

The onset of illness in someone who was healthy when last seen usually evokes reflection on the past. The obvious intervening event of retirement can become a convenient explanation for health and other behavioral changes. Brim and Ryff (1980) have observed that "most people, in thinking about life events and their effects on behavior, tend to attribute causality to a single, large, vivid, and recent event." People fall into this fallacy by seizing on a vivid or prominent event as the particular cause of resulting change, often ignoring earlier events or experience of some duration. According to Brim and Ryff (1980), there is a tendency to overlook various cumulative and interacting events in favor of assuming that big events are big causes. In the present case, the interpretation of health change is simplified by pointing to retirement, an interpretation drawn from the stock of conventional wisdom.

THE CULTURAL CELEBRATION OF WORK

There is another and more basic reason why retirement's adverse effect on health is a credible notion. Negative views of retirement are consistent with the cultural ideology that celebrates work as the source of self-worth, self-esteem, identity, and personal fulfillment. People can say disparaging things about retirement and health to defend their own commitment to work or to offer general instructions to others about the importance of work. Chrysler Chairman Lee Iacocca (Anderson & Witteman, 1985) recently described his zest for work by using a bit of lore about retirement. Said Iacocca, "Some guys in this business slow down, retire and take it easy. A couple of months later, they're dead." Hyperbole perhaps, but it is a common enough device to portray work and retirement as the inverse of each other, extolling the glory of work by stressing the peril of retirement.

There are also certain occupational groups who find their work fulfilling, who are committed more to their profession than their jobs, and who are characteristically unenthusiastic about conventional retirement. Ironically, it is members of these groups who are frequently looked to as authorities on the subject of retirement's effect on well-being, particularly physicians, academics, and high-priced consultants.

Negative statements about retirement and health are useful when it comes to endorsing the tonic qualities of work. It is interesting to note that warnings about the unhealthfulness of retirement surfaced repeatedly during the 1977 Congressional hearings on retirement age policies. In their enthusiasm for relaxing mandatory retirement rules, several participants in these hearings noted that longer working lives would forestall health decline. One congressman, for example, stated: "The case files of physicians and psychiatrists bulge with tragedy—the records of patients whose health deteriorates rapidly once they retire. Lacking the challenge that will get them up and going each morning, [mandatory retirees] literally fall apart and find an early grave" (U.S. Congress, 1977). Other testimony to this effect took as its authority a pamphlet of the American Medical Association (1972) in which it was observed that mandatory retirement on the basis of age impairs the health of many individuals who are emotionally involved in their jobs. Similar opinion was recently offered in Massachusetts as the state legislature considered bills to discourage age discrimination in employment (Reiff, 1984).

A PRIORI REASONING IN GERONTOLOGY

Common sense ways of thinking about retirement have their analogues in scientific conceptions. Some 20 years ago Martin and Doran (1966) noted the "seductive power" of the hypothesis that retirement threatens health and the way it leads gerontologists to engage in a priori reasoning that retirement must have some effect. Two theoretical perspectives in particular have encouraged this expectation, in both of which the tendency is to regard retirement as a disruptive, externally imposed experience with the potential for personal disorganization.

The early, implicit "activity theory" of aging legitimated inclinations to view retirement negatively by equating successful aging with full social integration and participation. Conceptions of retirement's impact on individuals, which developed while the retirement role was still gaining popular acceptance, foresaw withdrawal from work as a crisis for personal identity that needed compensation or substitutes if retirement was to be successful.

Although subsequent research showed that the maladaptive potential of retirement had been overstated, the negative effect hypothesis found new theoretical support in the "stressful life events" paradigm which flowered in the 1970s. The idea that life stress could affect susceptibility to illness was provocative and it revived gerontology's attention to the "big events" of later life as possible "big causes" of illness. Indeed, retirement had been scaled as the 10th most readjustment-requiring life event on the popular Social Readjustment Rating Scale (Eisdorfer & Wilkie, 1977). The purported stressfulness of retirement began to appear as the rationale underpinning research hypotheses that retirement might contribute to a decline in health status (Kremer, 1985; Palmore et al., 1979; Wan, 1982), though these hypotheses, too, routinely failed to find empirical support. This is not to imply that retirement cannot be stressful, only that it has not been shown to be stressful to the point of causing illness. By way of explanation for this theoretical dry hole, Kasl (1980) has discussed the limited relevance of the stressful events framework to the study of retirement and health.

MISCONSTRUAL OF RESEARCH FINDINGS

Whereas investigators have repeatedly concluded that retirement has no adverse impact on physical health, there is nonetheless a style of reviewing the literature that underplays the consistency of these findings in favor of reciting their methodological flaws. Existing studies are regarded with considerable reservation because samples may have been too small or inappropriate, or because data were cross-sectional, or because health was measured by self-report. The collective limitations of previous research have, from one reviewer's perspective, left an "uncertain legacy" as to the health effects of retirement (Minkler, 1981). Another reviewer, in order to hedge bets about the conclusiveness of previous research on retirement and mortality, confounded scientific logic by stating that ". . . although there has been no clear-cut evidence that retirement predicts death, there has been no demonstration that retirement does not affect subsequent mortality rates" (Rowland, 1977).

Ambiguous interpretations of research findings have also appeared in original work. In two studies of retirement and mortality (Adams & Lefebvre, 1981; Haynes et al., 1978), in which it was reported that retirement was not detrimental to survival, the door was, nevertheless, left ajar to the opposite conclusion by reading year-by-year fluctuations in post-retirement mortality rates as possibly indicating periods of stress or disenchantment with retirement. Speculations such as these are available throughout literature reviews.

Research findings can also be overplayed. The sole research report of a negative health effect of retirement came from an epidemiological study of coffee-drinking and coronary mortality in Florida (Casscells et al., 1980). Using a case-control design and relying on wives' retrospective reports about their husbands, the investigators found a significantly greater incidence of coronary mortality in retirees compared with men who had not retired. The authors themselves, it must be emphasized, did not misconstrue their research findings and were careful to conclude, "We believe that these data merely raise the question that this association may exist, rather than provide conclusive evidence in its support."

Not so circumspect, however, was the initial publicity that followed an earlier presentation of these findings at a meeting of the American Heart Association. "Well, retirement may be bad for you," was Walter Cronkite's lead into an item about the study that was broadcast on the CBS Evening News (1979). The study was also reported by news services and by other national media such as the *Wall Street Journal*. Not long after, the *Journal of the American Medical Association* ran a feature piece headlined, "Retiring may predispose to fatal heart attack" (Gonzales, 1980), an article in which previous studies of the subject were characterized as "numerous but equivocal." This entire episode, along with the unnamed editors and news directors who created it, put a stamp of scientific proof on something that everyone already "knows" and undoubtedly contributed further to public perceptions that retirement can harm health.

CONCLUSION

Gerontology has enjoyed some success debunking certain myths of aging that portray later life in a negative light: for example, that older people are socially abandoned, or are sexually inactive and disinterested. But myths are not for nothing. Be they true or false, they are controlling images that people use to make sense of their lives and experience: Myths satisfy the human need for meaning (Cole, 1983).

The idea that retirement harms health is a falsehood that, for a number of reasons, has continued value. The idea can be understood, most simply, in terms of people's penchant for post hoc, propter hoc reasoning when they wish to interpret health decline in someone who has recently retired. Nonretirees may also want to maintain that retirement is a health threat because it affirms the wisdom of their commitment to work. Others may promote it out of an attempt to control the image of retirement, be it in daily interaction or in settings for formal policy-making. Finally, the idea that retirement harms health is useful to illustrate pre-existing theories about the importance of an active lifestyle or about the corrosive effects of life stress. Even as society grows more familiar with retirement, the perpetuation of this negative notion indicates a continuing measure of public wariness about quality of life in the postretirement years.

Chapter
14

The Political System

M an is not only a social animal, but according to Aristotle he is also a political animal. Some form of political system or government is found even in the simplest societies. The *political institution* serves to maintain social order, to protect against outside enemies, and to plan and coordinate for the general welfare. In addition to these functions, the political institution also provides for the distribution of power.

The process by which people acquire and exercise power over others is known as *politics*. Politics has been referred to as the science of "who gets what, when and how" (Laswell,1936). In other words, it determines who shall be given what power in government, and when and how it shall be given. In this chapter we shall examine the attitudes and participation of older people in politics. What is the impact of senior citizen organizations on the political system? What is the government's involvement in programs for the elderly? Finally, what is the future of the aged in politics?

POLITICAL ATTITUDES AND BEHAVIOR

It is popularly assumed that with age people become more politically conservative. Cross-sectional studies, which account for the bulk of the research in this area, show that in comparison with younger adults, older people do tend to be more conservative. But cross-sectional studies do not tell us whether or not there is a change in political attitudes with age.

Attitudes and Issues

To fully understand the political attitudes and behavior of older people, three distinct but interrelated factors must be taken into account: the *cohort* to which older people belong, that is, individuals born during approximately the same time period; the aging process throughout the life course; and the period or historical effects on all age groups in the population (see Chapter 1, "The Field and Its Methods"). First, the cohort effect must be considered, because the time in which people grew up and received their early socialization plays an important part in interpreting their political attitudes and behavior.

> Data on persons who are old at the time of measurement may reveal more about the shared experiences and perceptions of that particular older generation—exposure at approximately the same age and time to common patterns of schooling, family life, economic cycles, wars and political events—than about anything intrinsic to the processes of aging. (Hudson & Binstock, 1976)

Second, political attitudes may be influenced by the aging process or by the maturational changes that occur at different stages in the life course. For instance, the elderly's support of government programs for medical aid may increase; also, physical decline may curtail political participation. Third, period or historical effects must be considered, as social and political events greatly alter the patterns of party identification and change the degree of popularity of the two major American parties.

By a technique called *cohort analysis*, which examines cross-sectional and longitudinal data at the same time, these three factors may be more readily observed and identified. Briefly, cohort analysis when used to study political attitudes does so through a sequence of cross-sectional attitude surveys. Each survey is arranged in such a way that persons of similar ages may be followed over a period of time. For example, suppose we had data from three attitude surveys taken ten years apart, from 1950 to 1970, in which the respondents had been placed into age groups of five-year intervals. Those respondents who had been 30 to 35 years old in 1950 would be 40 to 45 in 1960, and 50 to 55 in 1970. In this way it is possible to trace different cohorts over time through a series of surveys.

Through this method of analysis, Glenn (1974) found two important facts about the relationship between age and social, economic, and political attitudes. First, "People have typically become less, rather than more, conservative as they have grown older, in conformity with general societal trends." Second, persons in their fifties and sixties generally are more liberal than they were in their thirties and forties. Older people's attitudes have changed in the same direction and at about the same rate as the general population. Thus, compared with others in the population, the elderly appear to be more conservative, but compared with their own younger attitudes, they actually have become more liberal.

As to preferences regarding specific issues between age groups, there are some small differences but major differences are uncommon (Hudson & Strate, 1985) (see Box 14.1). While we would expect older persons to support issues affecting their self-interests, it is significant that a 1981 Harris poll revealed that a majority of persons of all ages support raising Social Security taxes if necessary to provide adequate income for older people. The poll also found that most Americans look to the government and the children of the elderly to assume greater responsibility than they do now for older people. These findings of the Harris poll and other public opinion polls and surveys are in direct contradiction to the issues raised by such groups as Americans for Generational Equity (Age), "the intergenerational equity" movement, or what one author has called the "New Ageism." These groups contend that the American people resent the expenditures for the elderly who they believe have too many advantages as it is. The major thrust of their argument is that the elderly's financial gains have been achieved at the expense of the young. It is true that the overall condition of children has deteriorated in recent years (about 20 percent live in poverty), but severe cutbacks in the areas of nutrition, health care, and education following the $750 billion tax cut by the Reagan administration have contributed to this condition, not the elderly people (Butler, 1989). (See Box 4.3, Chapter 4, "Cultural Values.")

Box 14.1 Attitudes For Old and Young Change Evenly

Another bit of conventional wisdom challenged: the belief that social and political attitudes become more conservative and more rigid as people age.

Not so, say University of Vermont sociologists Stephen Cutler and Nicholas Danigelis. They found that as people grow older, their attitudes change in the same general direction—and at about the same pace—as the views of society at large. The changes, Cutler says, "aren't due to some ingredient of the aging process."

The Vermont researchers tracked the views of four age groups based on answers to national polling questions in the past 25 years. The questions covered such issues as residential desegregation, premarital sex, distribution of birth-control information, the death penalty, and willingness to vote for a qualified black or a qualified woman for president.

All four age groups became consistently more liberal on issues involving race, sex and gender during the 25 years—and on almost every issue the oldest group moved in line with the younger ones. On law-enforcement issues, the country became more liberal on legalizing marijuana but more conservative on capital punishment; on this last topic, the oldest group actually is the most liberal.

Source: Allan L. Otten, "People Patterns," *Wall Street Journal*, January 3, 1989.

Party Attachments

As people age, do they tend to affiliate with the Republican party? An early study by Crittenden (1962) based on cross-sectional comparisons found that as persons grew older, they changed from the Democratic to the Republican party. Later studies found that by applying cohort analysis to longitudinal and cross-sectional data, there was no increase in Republicanism as a result of the aging process. Research evidence indicates that the disproportionate number of Republicans among older people is a result of early socialization in an era that was dominated by the Republican party and not as a result of the aging process (Hudson & Strate, 1985).

By the same token, it is well documented that party attachment tends to be stronger among older people than among younger age groups. Again, this attachment is not due to the aging process, but rather to the fact that older persons were socialized in a time when the two major parties were more prominent in American life than they are today (Glenn & Hefner, 1972; Cutler, 1981).

Voting Behavior and Political Interest

Older people have higher voter participation rates than the rest of the population. In the 1988 presidential election, persons 65 and older represented 19 percent of those who reported voting, and in the 1984 presidential election they account for 18 percent of those who reported voting. As Table 14.1 shows, the 55-to-64 and 65-to-74 age groups participate more in elections than any other age groups. It is interesting to note that in the last five elections those 75 and over (the old-old) were more likely to vote than those under 35, even though after age 75 there is a decline in voting. This

Table 14.1   PERCENTAGE OF PERSONS WHO
REPORTED VOTING IN NATIONAL
ELECTIONS, BY AGE GROUP: 1980–1988

Age group	1980	1982	1984	1986	1988
18-plus	59.2	48.5	59.9	46.0	57.4
18–20	35.7	19.8	36.7	18.6	33.2
21–24	43.1	28.4	43.5	24.2	38.3
25–34	54.6	40.4	54.5	35.1	48.0
35–44	64.4	52.2	63.5	49.3	61.3
45–54	67.5	60.1	67.5	54.8	66.6
55–64	71.3	64.4	72.1	62.7	69.3
65–74	69.3	64.8	71.8	65.1	73.1
75-plus	57.6	51.9	61.2	54.0	62.2

Source: U.S. Senate Special Committee on Aging, *Aging America: Trends and Projections,* 1987–1988. Washington, DC: U.S. Government Printing Office and U.S. Bureau of the Census, Current Population Reports, Series P 20, No. 435, "Voting and Registration in the Election of November 1988 (Advance Report)," February 1989.

decline, however, is usually due to factors other than age. One reason is that the older population has a preponderance of females, and women usually vote less frequently than men, so this partly accounts for the drop in voting. Another is that because educational attainment is positively associated with voting participation, and older people, especially the old-old, tend to have lower educational levels than younger persons have, the elderly tend to vote less.

Although older persons constitute a large aggregate of participating voters, they do not vote as a bloc. (But many people, including politicians, believe that they do.) For example, Table 14.2 shows the percentage of voters by age in two recent presidential elections. Notice how the votes of older people are distributed among candidates in about the same proportion as those of the rest of the population.

Older people not only vote more frequently than younger persons do, but they also manifest higher levels of political interest. Glenn and Grimes (1968) found the highest percentage reporting a great deal of interest in politics to be people aged 60 and older. They explain that older people do not have the distractions that they had at earlier stages of the life cycle; when they were young, their immediate problems of families and careers made demands on their time and energy, and this continued in a modified form in their middle years. By retirement age, fewer distractions allow more time for political matters. Glenn and Grimes note also that with age, political

Table 14.2   NATIONWIDE VOTE DISTRIBUTION, BY AGE GROUPS, IN RECENT ELECTIONS FOR U.S. PRESIDENT

	1980			1984	
	Reagan	Carter	Anderson	Reagan	Mondale
Percent of All Voters	51	41	7	59	41
Percent of Men					
18–29 years old	47	39	11	61	37
30–44 years old	59	31	4	62	37
45–59 years old	60	34	5	63	36
60+	56	40	3	62	37
Percent of Women					
18–29 years old	39	49	10	55	45
30–44 years old	50	41	8	54	46
44–59 years old	50	44	5	58	41
60+	52	43	4	64	35
Percent of Adults					
18–29 years old	43	44	11	58	41
30–44 years old	54	36	8	58	42
44–59 years old	55	39	5	60	39
60+	54	41	4	63	36

Source: Robert H. Binstock, "Aging, Politics, and Public Policy." *The World and I,* December 1988, p. 540.

Congressman Claude Pepper was the nation's unrivaled champion and principal spokesman for the older Americans for many decades. According to Horace Deets, Director of AARP, "Claude Pepper, more than anyone else in our lifetimes, helped us as a nation realize the contributions that older Americans can make to our country if given a chance."

Pepper's legislative efforts include being the principal co-sponsor of the Older Americans Act (1965) and a leader in supporting the passage of Medicare and Medicaid (1965). He led the fight against the cutting of Social Security benefits in 1981, and was the driving force behind the legislation to outlaw mandatory retirement (1986). Serving longer than any other person in the United States Congress, as well as being the oldest, Claude Pepper died in 1989 at the age of 88.

activity may become a source of satisfaction and an end itself, rather than a means toward achieving an ideal or pursuing self-interests.

AGE AND LEADERSHIP

Older people also appear to occupy a disproportionate number of leadership positions. Such positions of high rank as Supreme Court justice or president of the United States are often dominated by persons in their middle or later years. Lehman's study *Age and Achievement* (1953), reveals that the largest number of Supreme Court justices began their appointment between the ages of 55 and 59. Although some served in their thirties and others in their nineties, the majority served between the ages of 65 and 69. Lehman notes that 80 percent of Supreme Court service has been rendered by men over 65.

Lehman also found that presidents of the United States were most frequently between the ages of 55 and 59 when first elected. Furthermore, the two parties are most likely to choose presidential candidates, both successful and unsuccessful, in this age range. Before Ronald Reagan's election in 1980 at the age of 69, only one other president in history, William Henry Harrison, was over age 65 at the time he assumed office.

Schlesinger (1966) reports an age timetable for political leaders that corresponds to the hierarchy of offices. For instance, United States representatives usually enter the House between the ages of 35 and 40, governors are elected between 45 and 50, and senators are elected for the first time between 50 and 55. He concludes that the older a politician is, the higher the office he or she is likely to hold.

OLD-AGE INTEREST GROUPS

In recent years, older people have become increasingly mobilized politically through their membership and participation in age-based organizations such as the American Association of Retired Persons (AARP) and the National Council of Senior Citizens (NCSC). Public officials have begun to recognize the credentials of these groups, and more and more they are being included in the national policy processes and in decisions that concern the elderly. Binstock (1974, 1988) points out that these organizations have basically three types of power available to them. First, their ready access to public officials gives them a chance to present their own proposals regarding such matters as Social Security, Medicare, and long-term care, as well as the opportunity to block the proposals of others. Second, this access to public officials permits them to obtain public platforms on subjects affecting the elderly in national conferences, through congressional hearings, and in the media. From these platforms they have the opportunity to frame many issues of policy concerned with aging and to initiate issues for public debate. A third type of power is the "electoral bluff." Although the large membership of many of the aged-based organizations seems formidable, these organizations do not have the ability to swing a decisive bloc of older voters. For example, in the 1980 presidential campaign, a number of age-based organizations endorsed Jimmy Carter instead of Ronald Reagan. However, as Table 14.2 shows, the majority of older persons voted for Reagan, as did younger persons. Yet, politicians do not wish to offend these organizations, even though their potential power is a bluff.

Binstock (1988) concludes that the power of age-based organizations is limited, and they have not performed a major role in shaping aging programs and policies for older persons. Furthermore, he notes that, "The impact of these organizations has been confined largely to the creation and maintenance of relatively minor policies that have distributed benefits primarily to researchers, educators, clinicians, and other practitioners in the field of aging rather than directly to older persons themselves."

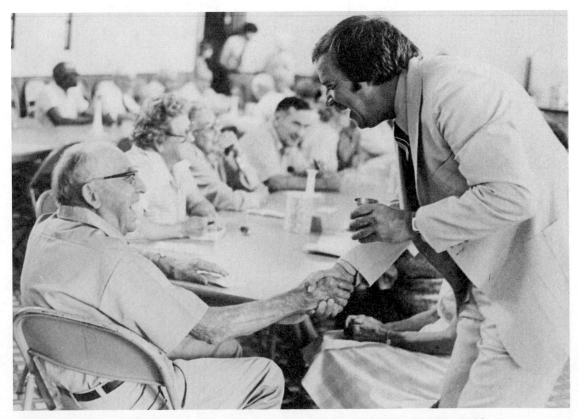

Although aged-based organizations do not have the power to swing a decisive bloc of older voters, many politicians do not wish to offend these organizations. (Tennessee Commission on Aging)

GOVERNMENT INVOLVEMENT

When the Social Security Act was signed into law in 1935, President Franklin D. Roosevelt remarked: "We can never insure one hundred per cent of the population against one hundred per cent of the hazards and vicissitudes of life, but we have tried to frame a law which will give some measure of protection . . . against poverty-ridden old age" (Rosenman, 1938). This act marked the beginning of the government's involvement in the problems of the elderly.

Exactly thirty years elapsed before the enactment of two other important pieces of legislation that have greatly affected the lives of older people. In 1965 Congress passed the Medicare Bill and the Older Americans Act (OAA). The Older Americans Act established the Administration on Aging (AoA), which is the principal agency for carrying out the provisions of the Older Americans Act. Its functions and duties include developing and conducting research in the field of aging, coordinating and assisting federal, state, and local agencies in planning and developing programs for older persons, and disseminating information relating to the problems of the elderly. The Older Americans Act, which was amended ten times between 1965 and 1987, spells out specific government responsibilities and objectives for the elderly.

1. An adequate income in retirement in accordance with the American standard of living.
2. The best possible physical and mental health that science can make available and without regard to economic status.
3. Obtaining and maintaining suitable housing, independently selected, designed and located with reference to special needs and available at costs that older citizens can afford.
4. Full restorative services for those who require institutional care.
5. Opportunity for employment with no discriminatory personnel practices because of age.
6. Retirement in health, honor, dignity—after years of contribution to the economy.
7. Participating and contributing to meaningful activity within the widest range of civic, cultural, and recreational opportunities.
8. Efficient community services, including access to low-cost transportation, that provide social assistance in a coordinated manner and that are readily available when needed.
9. Immediate benefit from proven research knowledge that sustains and improves health and happiness.
10. Freedom, independence, and the free exercise of individual initiative in planning and managing their own lives . . . and protection against abuse, neglect, and exploitation.

The 1960s are often thought of as the turning point in our government's responsiveness to the needs of the elderly. Prior to that time, older Americans not only suffered from the lack of concern for their problems, but with the exception of Social Security, the federal government almost totally failed to recognize that the elderly had any problems at all.

The government's awareness of its responsibilities for older people was evidenced in 1960 when Congress authorized a White House Conference on Aging to be held in 1961. Each state assessed the needs of its older people through a series of studies and inventories and reported its findings to the conference. From these proceedings emerged a comprehensive set of recommendations for action on a nationwide basis to meet the needs of the elderly. It is generally recognized that this conference made a major contribution to the enactment of Medicare. It also laid the groundwork for the Older Americans Act. Since 1961, White House Conferences on Aging have been held every ten years.

Gold (1974) classifies into six categories the government's programs and services designed to improve the circumstances of the elderly. First, cash-transfer programs, such as Social Security and Supplemental Security Income (SSI), help assure older people a more adequate income. SSI, which replaced the Old Age Assistance Program, establishes an income floor for the elderly. The second category includes noncash benefits and services that have a measurable economic value, exemplified by Medicare, Medicaid, housing subsidies, and food stamps. The third area is the protection of the rights of older people through legislation, such as the Age Discrimination in Employment Act and pension-reform legislation. The Employee Retirement Income Security Act expanded previous legislation regulating private pension plans and, for the first time, set certain minimum pension standards. The support of biomedical, social, and behavioral research related to the aging process is a fourth area. The Research on Aging Act of 1974 authorized the establishment of the National Institute on Aging to conduct research and to study the diseases and special problems of the elderly. A fifth role of the government is the delivery of services to the elderly through grants to private and public organizations at the state and local level. Finally, the sixth role is the coordination at state and local levels of the resources, services, and programs made available in the five preceding categories.

The government's concern for the elderly may be limited in the long run by the expansion of their needs. With the increasing numbers of persons who are chronologically aged and of those who are retiring from the labor force at earlier ages, the government may find it more difficult in the future to meet their needs and to fulfill the responsibilities that it has already undertaken.

THE AGED IN FUTURE POLITICS

Though much has been written about senior power, there is no evidence at this time that older people are likely to exercise this power and to vote as a bloc. Binstock (1974) points out that even if the proportion of older voters during the next few decades were to double, it is unlikely that it would result in a cohesive aging vote that could determine the outcome of elections. The generational cohorts who will be 65 years of age between now and 2020 have already demonstrated their political diversity.

> And because each age cohort includes people who differ profoundly in many important conditions of life, it is not likely that any age group will be very homogenous in its attitudes. The evidence which national surveys provide us does in fact demonstrate that

Older persons in the future will be even more involved in political affairs than the elderly of today. (Nick Myers)

attitudinal differences between age groups are far less impressive than those within age groups. . . . Age groups will continue to remain as heterogeneous in economic, social, and geographical characteristics as they are now, and this heterogeneity will frustrate attempts to make common cause among people who resemble each other only in their age. (Campbell, 1971)

Although Cutler and Schmidhauser (1975) agree that the elderly are not likely to vote as a cohesive bloc, they do suggest that age is going to play an increasingly important role in politics in the future. They cite several factors to support this conclusion, including changes in the demographic and educational composition of the population. The size and proportion of the older population is steadily increasing and will continue to do so for some time. It is estimated that by the year 2020, there will be about 52 million persons aged 65 and over, representing more than 17 percent of the population. As the size of the older population increases, more retirees will be economically dependent on a relatively decreasing number of workers. In addition, the fact that the average age of retirement is becoming lower will further increase the economic burden on the working population. Because Social Security and other pension systems ultimately pose a political question, age will be an important issue in politics in the future.

A second factor to consider is whether the aged themselves will substantially be involved in politics in the future. Because of changes in educational opportunities, the electorate has become better educated. In 2020, those persons aged 65 and over will be represented by a cohort that already has high levels of educational attainment. Since education is a major predictor of political participation, it may be assumed that tomorrow's elderly will be even more involved in political affairs than older people today.

SUMMARY

1. To gain a clearer understanding of the political attitudes and behavior of older people, the cohort, the aging, and the period effects must be taken into account. Through the technique of cohort analysis, which examines cross-sectional and longitudinal data at the same time, these effects are more readily observed.

2. Instead of people becoming more conservative with age, Glenn reports that they have actually become more liberal, in conformity with the general trends of society. Though older persons tend to be more conservative than younger persons, in comparison with their younger selves they have become more liberal.

3. The relationship between age and political issues is not clear cut. The way people respond to political issues tends to be governed more by their early socialization and present circumstances than by age. Although there is no increase in Republicanism as a result of aging, aging does tend to be associated with party identification because party identification increases with age. Party ties are strongest among older people, and they are the least susceptible to shifting their allegiance to another party.

4. Persons in the 55-to-64 and 65-to-74 age brackets have the highest voting turnout of any age group. Glenn and Grimes found that the highest percentage of people reporting a great deal of interest in politics was among people age 60 and over.

5. Positions of leadership are occupied by a disproportionate number of older people. The majority of Supreme Court justices have served between the ages of 65 to 69, and presidents of the United States are most often between 55 and 59 years of age when they take office.

6. The elderly have become increasingly mobilized politically through their membership in old-age interest groups. But the power of these groups is limited.

7. The government's involvement with the problems of the elderly began with the passage of the Social Security Act in 1935. Since that time, two of the most significant pieces of legislation for the elderly have been the Medicare Bill and the Older Americans Act. The federal government performs many services for older people. These include cash-transfer programs, noncash

benefits and services, the protection of the rights of older people, the support of research on aging, and the delivery and coordination of services to the elderly.

8. Most authorities agree that there is little evidence at this time that older people vote as a cohesive bloc. However, it is likely that age will play an important part in future politics for two reasons: Social Security and other pension systems are ultimately a political question, and a more highly educated older population will become even more involved in politics in the future.

KEY TERMS

political institution   cohort analysis
politics   senior power
cohort

FOR FURTHER STUDY

Lockett, Betty A. (1983). *Aging, politics, and research*. New York: Springer.

Deals with the background and history of the creation of the federal agency of the National Institute on Health and its most recent component, the National Institute on Aging.

Pratt, Henry J. (1976). *The gray lobby*. Chicago: University of Chicago Press.

An account of the factors that have intervened between the elderly and the official decision makers.

Williamson, John B., Evans, Linda, & Powell, Lawrence A. (1982). *The politics of aging: power and policy*. Springfield, MA: Charles C Thomas.

Provides an analysis of power relations as they concern the elderly, including their voting participation and political attitudes.

Chapter
15

Religion

When King Tutankhamen's tomb was discovered in the 1920s, the world was awed by the magnificent 3,300-year-old treasures that it contained. Among the gilt and gold objects were amulets to protect the king in his travels through the underworld, as well as tools to do any labor that the gods might assign to him. The Neanderthal burial sites dating back over 100,000 years reveal that the departed were also supplied with tools for the afterlife. Though made of stone and certainly not as elaborate as those of King Tut, they attest to the presence of religion even then (Howells, 1948).

Religion is a pervasive and universal phenomenon. Every society from earliest known times has had some system of religious beliefs and practices. The variations are endless. Some people believe in many gods. For instance, the Ifugoas of the Philippines have some 1,500 distinct gods. A few religious groups believe in one god; still others do not believe in any gods. Instead of gods, some religions focus on souls or spirits. In different times and places, a large variety of things have been deified, ranging from oceans, mountains, and trees to ducks, rabbits, cows, lizards, frogs, and worms. In Africa, the Dahomey believe that all people have at least three souls and that adult males have four. Some groups think that after death the soul journeys to a spirit world in the West or to an underworld beneath the sea.

The revered writings of the Torah are an example of the sacred, one of the most distinctive features of religion. (Nick Myers)

Because *religion* exists in such diverse forms, defining it is difficult and a number of definitions have been proposed. One sociologist defines it as "a system of beliefs and practices by which a group of people interprets and responds to what they feel is sacred, and, usually, supernatural as well" (Johnstone, 1988). The *sacred* is found in all religions and is made up of those elements that evoke attitudes of respect and awe and are separated from the everyday world. Some examples of the sacred in our society include such objects as the cross and the star of David, or the writings of the Bible and the Torah.

OLD AGE AND RELIGION

Old age has characteristically been associated with religion in many primitive societies. The elderly are for several reasons peculiarly qualified to perform a dominant role in the religious life of preliterate people. First, because they have lived so long, older persons have had the opportunity to accumulate a vast knowledge of religious affairs and practices. Second, it has been generally accepted that they would soon be spirits themselves; they were the logical intermediaries between this world and the next, and between the living and their ancestors (Goody, 1976). Finally, "survival to a great age was sufficiently uncommon to seem unnatural or even supernatural. One way of making sense of such a world was to believe that age was itself endowed with supernatural properties" (Fischer, 1978).

Thus, it is not surprising that the highest religious offices of the Aztecs, Incas, and Todas were held by old men. In some societies old women also performed religious duties. The aged patriarchs were the family priests among the Samoans and the Ainu of Japan. Simmons (1945) observes that the attributes of old age were assigned to the various gods in primitive societies: "They were almost always described as worldly wise and very powerful—and, although aged, never stupid or senile. . . . It would almost appear that the aged have created gods in their own image."

The tendency to visualize deities or religious figures as old persons occurs throughout history. In seventeenth-century America, Puritan writers often described God as an old man with a white beard, an image that has persisted. But the Puritan concept of an angel was quite different from the one most people hold today. They pictured an angel as a man in his seventies. In early America, according to Fischer, "When a white-haired septuagenarian suddenly appeared in the New England town of Hadley, some of the inhabitants mistook him for a heavenly messenger."

The close tie between old age and religion is also reflected in word usage. For example, *priest* is derived from the Greek word *presbyteros*, meaning elder. The word *venerable* is used as a title for an Anglican archdeacon. In the Roman Catholic Church, *veneration* is used for those who have obtained the first of the three degrees of sanctity. In addition, the popes of the Catholic Church have usually been older men; from 1800 to the present, the average age of a pope at the time of his election has been 65.

Lehman (1953) plotted the ages at which 51 men served as popes of the Roman Catholic Church, the ages at which 101 persons served as presidents of religious organizations, and the ages at which 54 persons founded religious sects and societies. His data reveal that more than 97 percent of the popes were past age 50, and more than 65 percent were 65 years of age and over. Ninety-three percent of the presidents of non-Catholic religious organizations served when they were past 50, and 56 percent when they were past 65. In addition, he found that out of 148 Protestant bishops, most served as bishops between the ages of 70 and 74. His study further suggests that though new religious movements are most likely to be started by individuals in their thirties, their leadership is likely to come from older persons after they become well established. Writing in 1922, G. Stanley Hall observed:

> Thus it came that, while men in their prime conceived the great religions, the old made them prevail. Thus, too, instituted and dogmatic religion owes its existence chiefly to men past the meridian of life. The old did not invent belief in supernatural powers or persons but needed and used it to sustain their position when physical inferiority would have otherwise compelled them to step aside and so they made themselves mediators between gods and men. They directed and presided over rites and ceremonies and took possession of the keys of the next world, enforced orthodoxies for the sake of the order, and established and equipped the young to aid them in their work. They were behind the scenes and held the secrets, realizing the utility to society and also to themselves.

DIMENSIONS OF RELIGIOSITY

A popularly held view in our society is that people become increasingly more religious as they age and that there is an inevitable turning toward religion in later life. Presumably, the religious fervor of the elderly is related to the problem of their approaching demise, as well as to their concern with the hereafter. In addition, since the elderly have so much time for contemplation, it is only natural that they think more about religion.

This common sense view about age and religion has little or no basis in fact. It is contrary to research findings about religious attitudes and activities of the elderly. Yet this folklore is widely accepted not only by the general public but also by some social scientists as well.

Studying and measuring *religiosity*—interest and involvement in religious activities—are difficult to do scientifically. One of the major problems facing the researcher is that religiosity consists of many dimensions and sometimes the various dimensions are not highly related. For example, in the past some researchers used only one dimension—church attendance—as a measure of religiosity (Bahr, 1960; Orbach, 1961). These studies often concluded that religiosity declined in old age. This method gave distorted results because it did not take into account that while some older persons may no longer attend church because of poor health or lack of transportation, they are able to compensate by engaging in religious activities in their own homes.

Glock (1962) has analyzed religiosity in terms of five dimensions. The *ideological dimension* involves the religious beliefs that one holds. The *ritualistic dimension* refers to participation in religious activities. The knowledge that one has about his or her religion is the *intellectual* dimension. The *experiential* dimension refers to one's emotions and feelings toward God. Finally, the *consequential* dimension pertains to the way one's behavior is affected by the other four dimensions and is more directly linked to one's relationship with God (Moberg, 1984). In the following section, our discussion will focus mainly on the ideological dimension and the ritualistic dimension.

The Ideological Dimension

Studies show that belief in God is stronger among the elderly than in other age groups. A Gallup survey (1966) found that the largest percentage (86 percent) of those that were "absolutely certain" there was a God were age 65 and over. The percentages successively declined in younger age categories. Another Gallup survey (1976) reported that 96 percent of the older respondents said they believed in God.

Most of the available evidence indicates that religion appears to be more important to older people than to younger people. According to a 1975 Harris poll, the highest percentage of people reporting that religion is important in their lives were in their eighties and over, followed by persons in their seventies and sixties (see Table 15.1). A 1982 Gallup survey reported that 82 percent of the elderly felt that religious faith was the most important influence in their lives, and 23 percent stated they had a very high spiritual commitment (see Table 15.2).

Table 15.1   IMPORTANCE OF RELIGION IN ONE'S LIFE BY AGE

Degree of importance	Age group						
	18–24	25–39	40–54	55–64	65–69	70–79	80 and over
Very important	34%	45%	58%	65%	69%	71%	73%
Somewhat important	40%	35%	29%	25%	22%	21%	19%
Hardly important at all	25%	20%	12%	10%	8%	8%	6%
Not sure	1%	—	1%	—	1%	—	2%

Source: Louis Harris and Associates, *The Myth and Reality of Aging in America.* The National Council on the Aging, 1975, p. 181.

Because older people attach more importance to religion than younger adults do, and belief in God is stronger among the elderly than other age groups, many researchers have concluded that religious feelings increase with advancing age. Studies of this relationship have typically been based on cross-sectional data, which compare older and younger people at the same point in time (see Chapter 1, "The Field and Its Methods"). Cross-sectional research makes the assumption that the attitudes and activities of the younger generation accurately represent those of older persons when they were young. But, like political attitudes and behavior discussed in Chapter 14, in order to understand the differences in religious beliefs between the generations we must take into account the time in which older persons were born (cohort effect) and distinguish it from the aging effect. In addition, the period effect must also be considered because of the changing place of religion in our society. As Moberg (1965) observes:

> Whether the differences in religious beliefs between the generations are a result of the aging process [age effect] or of divergent experiences during the formative years of childhood and youth [cohort effect], which are linked with different social and historical circumstances [period effect], is unknown. Longitudinal research might reveal considerably different conclusions from the cross-sectional studies which provide the founda-

Table 15.2   SPIRITUAL COMMITMENT BY AGE

18–24 years	25–29 years	30–49 years	50–64 years	65 years and over
My religious faith is the most important influence in my life.				
59%	54%	67%	76%	82%
I have a very high spiritual commitment.				
3%	10%	11%	12%	23%
I receive a great deal of comfort and support from my religious beliefs.				
71%	66%	77%	85%	87%

Source: Princeton Religion Research Center, *Religion in America, 1982.* Princeton, NJ: The Gallup Poll, 1982.

tion for current generalizations about age variations in the ideological dimension of religion.

One such longitudinal study is reported by Blazer and Palmore (1976) from an analysis of religious activities and attitudes of community residents over an 18-year period. Measures of religious activities included church attendance, listening to church services on the radio, watching religious programs on television, and reading the Bible. Their findings reveal that positive religious attitudes remain fairly stable over time with no significant increase or decrease. In other words, if people were religious or nonreligious when young, chances are they will continue to have the same basic religious orientation when old. This contradicts the common view that people become increasingly religious as they age.

The Ritualistic Dimension

In contrast to what people believe, the ritualistic dimension involves what people do. It includes two types of religious activities—organizational and nonorganizational (Mindel & Vaughan, 1978). Examples of organizational activities include attending church services, prayer meetings, and religious revival meetings, as well as contributing money to religious activities.

Organizational Activities   Going to church is the most prevalent type of organizational activity; about half of all persons age 65 and over attend church in an average week (Princeton Religion Research Center, 1982). A substantial amount of research has been done on the relationship between aging and church attendance. Bahr (1970) has classified the findings of these studies into four major models.

1. *The traditional model.* According to this model there is a steady drop in church attendance from the ages of 18 to 35, the lowest point being between 30 to 35, when parents have young children. After this period, church activity gradually increases until old age before leveling off and then declining.
2. *The stability model.* This model asserts that there is no relationship between aging and church attendance and that the pattern of church attendance remains stable throughout one's lifetime.
3. *The family cycle model.* This model relates church attendance to stages of the family cycle. The peak in church attendance, according to the family cycle model, is when children reach Sunday-school age. As children grow up and leave home, the frequency of church attendance begins to drop.
4. *The disengagement model.* In this model, church attendance begins to decline in the middle years and continues to decline throughout old age.

Each of the foregoing models can claim some research in support of it. However, this may be due to the fact that different methods and measurements were used in these studies (Hunsberger, 1985). Also, because most of the studies were cross-sectional, we cannot reliably distinguish between cohort effects and age effects. The few longitudinal studies available have produced different findings. For example, the longitudinal study done by Wingrove and Alston (1971) found no consistent support for any of the models. Much more work is needed to determine the relationship between

The elderly manifest high rates of religious activities, attitudes, and feelings. (Alex Harris)

age and church attendance. At this time, according to Palmore (1987), "There appears to be little or no aging effect on church attendance in general." Furthermore, a decline in church attendance by those elderly who have physical disabilities may be offset by an increased participation in nonorganizational activities (Ainlay & Smith, 1984; Mindel & Vaughan, 1978).

Nonorganizational Activities   The other aspect of the ritualistic dimension, nonorganizational activities, includes watching religious programs on television, listening to religious programs on the radio, Bible reading, and private prayer.

Religious Television and Radio Programs Often referred to as the electronic church, television has become increasingly important for religious expression in American life. About 13.6 million persons regularly watch religious programs. About half of the audience is age 50 and over and most are women (*U.S. News & World Report*, 1984). A survey by the Good News Broadcasting Association, one of the largest religious radio broadcasting organizations, reports that 68 percent of its listeners are over age 50 and 27 percent are over age 70 (Koenig, Smiley & Gonzales, 1988).

Bible Reading The elderly read the Bible more frequently than do middle-aged and younger age groups. The Gallup poll shows that 27 percent of people age 65 and over read the Bible daily (Princeton Religion Research Center, 1982). In a survey of participants at senior centers, Koenig, Smiley, and Gonzales (1988) found that 38 percent of them reported reading the Bible or other religious literature on a daily basis.

Prayer Nearly 95 percent of older people report that they pray and about 20 percent belong to prayer groups (Princeton Religion Research Center, 1982). According to Koenig, Smiley, and Gonzales (1988), frequency of prayer remains stable with age except for a slight increase in late old age, especially among those who are in poor health. They cite the following case of Mr. Wilaby, a 72-year-old man who has lived alone for the past 10 years since the death of his wife; he suffers from chronic health problems that limit his activity:

> I pray a lot. It settles me down when I get agitated and picks me up when I'm down. I can talk to the Lord about anything. Since my wife passed away, I pray every night and during the day when I can. Since I can't depend on her anymore, I now depend on the Lord.

ADJUSTMENT AND RELIGION

Many investigators have shown positive relationships between religious activities and well-being among older persons, whereas some (Steinitz, 1980; Tellis-Nayak, 1982) have questioned this assumption. An early study by Moberg and Taves (1965) investigated the relationship between church participation and adjustment in old age. They found that church members had higher personal adjustment scores than non-members, and that church leaders (officers and committee members) had higher scores than other church members. The researchers concluded that the evidence overwhelmingly supports the hypothesis that church participation is related to a good personal adjustment in the later years. Blazer and Palmore (1976) found that for the elderly, happiness, a sense of usefulness, and personal adjustment are significantly related to religious activities and attitudes. They suggest that religion becomes increasingly important for the personal adjustment of many elderly. Hunsberger (1985) reports a positive relationship between religiosity and life satisfaction. And more recently, Koenig, Kvale, and Ferrel (1988) find that organizational and nonorgani-

Although some older persons may no longer be able to attend church, they compensate by engaging in religious activities at home such as reading the Bible. Older people read the Bible more frequently than any other age group. (Nick Myers)

zational activities and religious beliefs are correlated with well-being in later life.

The relationship between religious involvement and personal adjustment, however, is still unclear. As Moberg (1965) put it: "Either those who are well-adjusted engage in many religious activities or else engaging in many religious activities contributes to a good adjustment in old age."

FUNCTIONS AND DYSFUNCTIONS OF RELIGION

Religion functions primarily at two levels: the psychological (or individual) level and the social (or group) level. For the individual who in faith accepts the basic teachings of a religion, religion may perform certain psychological functions during the later years. Barron (1961) cites four such functions: (1) to help face impending death; (2) to help find and maintain a sense of meaningfulness and significance in life; (3) to help accept the inevitable losses of old age; and (4) to help discover and utilize the compensatory values that are potential in old age.

At the social level, the church brings together people of all ages and helps reduce isolation of the elderly by affording them the opportunity for social interaction. Twente (1970) observes that for many elderly people, religious pursuits, especially in small communities, help activate and nurture social relationships: "Opportunities to meet friends and exchange news about one another and about mutual acquaintances are important. Sympathy, support, pleasantries, encouragement, and jokes find expression and the older person experiences warmth and reassurance as he feels himself one of the group."

Even when a person can no longer participate in church activities, the importance of continued interaction with church representatives is illustrated by the following example:

> An eighty-one-year-old woman, Mrs. Lang was suffering from a crippling form of arthritis which made her homebound. She had always been a warm, vital, outgoing person who, until three years earlier, was active in her church and contributed her handiwork to the Ladies' Circle. Now, she says, she understands what it means to "cast one's bread upon the waters." She does not know what she would have done were it not for the visits from her minister, who is a source of spiritual comfort, and from the members of the Ladies' Circle. Through these visits she is kept informed as to what is happening in her church, and they make her feel that she still "belongs," that it does not matter that she can no longer help her church—now it is their turn to help her. (Field, 1968)

Visits from a clergyman or the lack of them may also create problems. Many older people who are homebound, hospitalized, or in nursing homes expect to be visited regularly by their clergyman or church representatives. When these expectations are not met, they may feel neglected or offended. Surveying 606 elderly persons in Long Beach, McCann (1969) asked for additional ways in which the church could serve them. They placed home visits at the top of the list. Moberg states that clergy visits to older people when they are ill may have a negative, instead of positive, effect. In some cases when a clergyman calls, ill persons may become afraid that they are about to die.

Many elderly people whose finances are limited feel guilty about attending church because they can afford only a meager contribution or in some instances cannot make one at all. Sometimes older persons may feel that they are being shunned by the church because of this lack of financial support. A case in point is Mrs. Brown: "I was always active in my church and, like my father before me, I always contributed when I was able. Now that I am poor, and cannot make donations, my church seems to have no use for me" (Twente, 1970).

Another problem that many older persons face is the feeling that they no longer have a place in the life of their church. After years of faithful service, many complain that their leadership roles and responsibilities are being taken over by younger persons. In addition, some argue that their advice is no longer sought and their opinions are ignored.

CHURCH PROGRAMS AND ORGANIZATIONS

Churches offer older members a wide range of services and programs. These have been categorized into the following four groups (Tobin, Ellor, & Anderson-Ray, 1986):

1. *Providing religious programs.* This includes not only the regular worship services offered by most churches, but also special worship services designed

Box 15.1 **Religion and Gerontological Theories**

Progressive *disengagement* from social roles is evident in many religious contexts, sometimes as a concomitant of physical deterioration but all too often as a result of ageist policies and practices. Yet, even those who no longer can attend congregational gatherings need not be fully disengaged. They can continue to be socially and spiritually involved, especially if active steps are taken to incorporate them into the spiritual life of the community. Absence from religious meetings need not mean severed relationships.

The ideology of *activity theory* has dominated the orientations of most religious leaders concerned with aging. Much of the denominational literature and educational materials to aid aging ministries has the goal of keeping older members actively involved in congregational and community life. Spiritual ministries of prayer, counsel, encouragement to visitors and friends, and the listening ear are significant contributions that even shut-in elderly can make, and services the young-old can contribute are almost unlimited. Nevertheless, activity theory contributes to . . . ageism when activism is presented as the only suitable way for the aging to function. Insisting that everyone must be active can be a form of tyranny, trying to force all into the same mold instead of allowing them to indulge preferences for "merely" watching television, reading, praying, meditating, or other "passive" behavior. Such policies fail to recognize individual differences, view "nonactive" conduct as a symptom of maladjustment, obstruct some of the ways to nurture spiritual growth (even when opening others), and induce feelings of disappointment and failure. Whenever one judges successful aging only by the retention of activities appropriate to young and middle-aged people, activity theory becomes "little more than a subtle way of glorifying youth at the expense of old age. . . ."

Many older people think in terms of *exchange theory*, feeling that they must compensate tangibly for every service and favor received by equivalent gifts or pay. Usually they fail to recognize important non-material gifts of cheer, counsel, prayer, thankfulness, and simple listening to others. These are spiritual services which older people can provide par excellence, but which usually are ignored in the menus of services suggested for interpersonal and intergenerational exchanges. The life review process of telling one's life story also can greatly benefit listeners or readers as well as the narrators.

Source: David O. Moberg, "Spiritual Maturity and Wholeness in the Later Years." *Journal of Religion & Aging.* [Readers interested in full source citations and footnotes are referred to the original article.]

for older persons as well as religious study groups and prayer groups. Most churches facilitate participation in these activities by providing transportation to them. Many congregations provide ramps, large-print reading materials, and hearing aids for their handicapped and elderly members.

2. *Serving as a host.* Church buildings are often used for a variety of purposes and programs. One of the most popular is the congregate meals program. They also serve as sites for preretirement planning programs, lectures, and conferences.

3. *Providing pastoral care services.* These services are for members of the congregation who may be permanently or temporarily disabled. They include visitation, telephone reassurance, home-delivered meals, and light housekeeping assistance. Another type of service increasingly being offered by churches is peer counseling. The Widow-to-Widow program provides an example of this type of group in which widows are trained as volunteers to help other widows cope with practical and psychological problems resulting from the loss of their spouses.

4. *Providing social services.* Some churches have social service programs to help the needy in the community. Often such a program is developed as a response to a gap in the local community service network.

Churches and religious organizations also sponsor institutional facilities for their elderly. In the past many of these institutions were called "homes for the aged." They were operated for older people who were in relatively good physical and mental health but who needed a place to live because of poverty or social isolation. Today most institutions are now medically oriented, and few of these types of homes remain. However, some institutions still refer to themselves as "homes"; an example is the Jewish Home and Hospital for the Aged in New York City. It was the nation's first teaching nursing home and has long been actively involved in teaching innovative approaches and developing creative programs in the care of the elderly. One of the most advanced nonprofit geriatric centers in the country, as well as the largest, the Jewish Home and Hospital serves 2,500 elderly through a comprehensive range of in-patient and community programs (see Table 15.3).

Table 15.3   CLINICAL AND EDUCATIONAL PROGRAMS
IN GERIATRIC MEDICINE AT THE JEWISH
HOME AND HOSPITAL FOR THE AGED

Rehabilitation unit: return to community
Lifelong care units
Home care: long-term (Nursing Home Without Walls)
Day hospital (for frail elderly and blind elderly)
Special emphasis clinics: interdisciplinary
   Incontinence and urodynamics
   Memory loss
   Impaired vision
   Rehabilitation
   Orthopedics
   Neurology
   Psychiatry
Ambulatory care: senior citizens' apartment house and club
College for patients

Source: Leslie S. Libow, "The Teaching Nursing Home."
Journal of the American Geriatrics Society (32), 1984.

SUMMARY

1. Religion is "a system of beliefs and practices by which a group of people interprets and responds to what they feel is sacred and usually, supernatural as well." The close tie between religion and old age is characteristic not only of primitive but also of modern societies. Though religious movements are often started by younger persons, religious leadership is most likely to be concentrated among the elderly.

2. Religiosity—interest and involvement in religious activities—has many dimensions. Two of these dimensions are the ideological and ritualistic. Older persons tend to have a stronger belief in God and to consider religion more important in their lives than younger persons do. The dissimilarity in the religious orientation between younger and older persons appears to be the result of cohort and period effects rather than of the aging process. Religious attitudes seem to be fairly stable and show no dramatic change in later life.

3. At the present time, there appears to be little or no relationship between aging and church attendance. Church attendance alone is not an adequate measure of religious activity because religious activity also includes listening to religious programs on radio or watching them on television as well as Bible reading and private prayer. Whether religious involvement is positively related to life satisfaction and personal adjustment is unclear.

4. Religion performs many psychological and social functions for older persons. Its psychological functions include helping one to face death and to help find a sense of meaningfulness in life, while at the social level it helps reduce isolation and fosters group interaction. Religion can also be dysfunctional in that homebound elderly often feel neglected when not visited regularly by the clergy. Some older persons also feel that they are being pushed out of their roles in church affairs by younger church members.

5. Churches offer their older members a wide variety of services. These include not only religious services and programs but also the provision of pastoral care and social services.

KEY TERMS

religion	*ritualistic dimension*
sacred	*disengagement*
religiosity	*activity theory*
ideological dimension	*exchange theory*

FOR FURTHER STUDY

Koenig, Harold G., Smiley, Mona, & Gonzales, Jo Ann Ploch. (1988). *Religion, Health, and Aging.* Westport, CT: Greenwood Press.
An interdisciplinary volume that brings together research findings on the relationships among the various aspects of religion and health in later life.

Moberg, David O. (1970). "Spiritual Well-Being in Late Life." In Jaber F. Gubrium (Ed.), *Late Life*. Springfield, IL: Charles C Thomas.

A good overview of the role of religion in the lives of the elderly.

Palmore, Erdman B. (Ed.) (1984). *Handbook of aging in the United States*. Westport, CT: Greenwood Press.

Part II of this volume, "Religious Groups," contains chapters on the elderly in the three major religious groups in the United States: Protestants, Catholics, and Jews.

Thorson, James A. & Cook, Thomas C. (1980). *Spiritual well-being of the elderly*. Springfield, IL: Charles C Thomas.

A collection of essays written from various religious traditions and theoretical perspectives.

Chapter

16

Education

More than 200 years ago the philosopher Immanuel Kant wrote, "Man becomes man through education; he is what education makes him." In this statement Kant emphasizes the primary function of the educational process—socialization. Through socialization people acquire the skills, values, and roles that make it possible for them to become members of society (see Chapter 6, "Socialization"). The school is the agency in our society that has the responsibility of socializing the young in certain skills and values. It gives them much of the knowledge they will need as adults and trains them to do necessary work.

Education is a major social institution in all industrialized societies. The growth of mass education in the United States began about a hundred years ago and coincided with the shift from an agricultural to an industrial economy. Industrialization requires not only that workers be able to read and write but also that they learn new skills and techniques in order to perform specialized roles within the division of labor. Schools were developed to provide such training.

At many university campuses today, one gets the distinct impression of being in a large industrial center, rather than at a center for learning. In fact, when we consider the number of our population involved in formal education in elementary schools, high schools, and colleges either as students, teachers, or suppliers of school goods and services, education is the largest single industry in the United States and the major employer in our society.

BARRIERS TO LEARNING

Kingsley Davis (1949) observes that every society sets up certain barriers to learning through defective instructional techniques and lack of proper motives and incentives: "All told, societies vary enormously in their waste of human learning ability, but they all waste it. Since modern scientists have such difficulty in perfecting teaching techniques, in measuring capacities and talents, and in motivating people to learn, there is little wonder that societies have also bungled the job."

Older people in our society face a formidable barrier to learning because of the many prevailing myths regarding their inability to learn (see Chapter 7, "Changes and Adaptations in Later Life"). Despite evidence that "you are never too old to learn," some educators hold steadfastly to the belief that the elderly cannot benefit from educational activities. More than three decades ago, Tibbitts and Rogers (1955), in noting the lack of interest in adult education for older people, remarked: "Skepticism on the part of adult educators, as well as many aging people themselves, regarding the learning capacity of older men and women seems to be an important factor in retarding a faster growth." As a result, the role of education in old age has been largely neglected in the past.

The myths about the elderly's learning ability not only have affected the attitudes of the general public and the professionals who work with older people but have also served to undermine the confidence of older people in themselves, creating a self-fulfilling prophecy. McClusky (1971) makes the following observation about the elderly's low participation rates in learning activities:

> It is also possible that older people, especially in later years, have gnawing, unacknowledged doubts about their continuing ability to learn. This loss of "educational nerve" may have become so regressive that the elderly are extremely reluctant to expose themselves to the embarrassment, and in their eyes even ridicule, that participation might possibly entail.

EDUCATIONAL LEVELS

Today's older people were born and educated in an era when the opportunity for free mass public education was more limited and less emphasis was placed on education in general. In addition, the large influx of young immigrants who came to this country prior to World War I, and who now make up a substantial proportion of the older population, have lower levels of literacy and educational attainment than the native population. As a result, the educational level of older people, as we have previously noted, is below that of the overall population.

In 1987, as shown in Table 16.1, the median years of school completed for persons 65 and over was 12.0, compared with 12.7 years for those 25 and over. In that same year over 50 percent of the elderly were high school graduates, whereas about 75 percent of the adults in general had received a high school education. Furthermore, only 20 percent of the elderly had completed at least one year of college, as compared with 37 percent of all persons 25 years and over.

The educational gap between the younger and older population has been narrowing in recent years. For example, between 1959 and 1987, the difference in median school years completed between older persons and the overall population has decreased from 2.7 years to 0.7 years.

ADULT EDUCATION

Besides formal schooling, *adult education* opportunities have been increasingly expanded in recent years, especially for older persons. In 1984, of the 23.3 million persons who had taken adult education courses, nearly 900,000 (4 percent) were age 65 and older. Adult education includes credit and noncredit courses, lectures, discussion groups, correspondence courses, education by television, and on-the-job training.

Table 16.1   SELECTED MEASURES OF EDUCATIONAL ATTAINMENT BY AGE GROUP: 1987

Age	Total	Male	Female
Median years of school completed			
25+	12.7	12.7	12.6
65+	12.0	12.0	12.0
65–74	12.2	12.2	12.2
75+	10.3	9.7	10.6
Percent with at least a high school education			
25+	75.6	76.0	75.3
65+	51.2	50.9	51.4
65–74	56.9	56.7	57.1
75+	42.0	39.8	43.3
Percent with one or more years of college			
25+	37.0	40.6	33.6
65+	20.4	23.2	18.4
65–74	21.9	25.2	19.3
75+	18.0	19.5	17.2

Source: U.S. Bureau of the Census, *Current Population Reports,* Series P-20, No. 428, "Educational Attainment in the United States: March 1987 and 1986," August 1988.

These activities are conducted by a variety of institutions and agencies—colleges and universities, public schools, libraries, labor unions, business and industry, churches, and community and senior centers.

Historical Overview

The history of adult education in the United States from colonial times to the present has been a repetitious one, in which specific needs arose and programs were developed to try to meet them. As each need was met or it declined in importance, the focus of adult education shifted to another concern.

In its earliest beginnings, adult education was mainly associated with the task of teaching adults to read so that they could attain salvation through studying the Holy Scriptures. Later, during the Revolutionary and Civil War periods, adult education became closely identified with the need for an enlightened citizenry, a view that was the outgrowth of the ideal that people must be educated to fulfill their responsibilities as citizens of a democracy.

Between the Civil War and World War I, adult education shifted its focus to more specific programs, such as vocational education and public affairs. But the main concern of this period centered on Americanization of the large number of immigrants. In order for them to become assimilated, it was necessary that they learn the common language, attitudes, and values of American society. In 1926 the American

Opportunities for adult education have rapidly expanded in recent years. (Tennessee Commission on Aging)

Association for Adult Education was founded, launching adult education as a distinct field of social practice. Since 1930, adult education has rapidly expanded (Schroeder, 1970).

In the early 1950s Wilma Donahue (1955) conducted a survey of educational programs for older persons. Her findings revealed that although there were many existing programs in which older people might be included, there were few programs specifically designed for them. Her work, along with the 1961 White House Conference on Aging, gave impetus to the development of programs that were specifically designed for the elderly.

The focus of many of these early programs was on the problems and needs of older people. For instance, it was at this time that preretirement planning programs began to emerge to assist older persons in adjusting to retirement and its accompanying role losses. By the time of the 1971 White House Conference on Aging, the emphasis on adult education had begun to shift from a problems approach to a positive approach. McClusky (1971) stressed that education should be an affirmative enterprise in which each person should be allowed to grow and to develop his or her potential, regardless of age. This orientation dominated the field of adult education throughout the 1970s. The theme that emerged from the 1981 White House Conference on Aging and is currently gaining momentum is that of self-help. It emphasizes the development of educational programs whose outcome is to assist persons in increasing their problem-solving skills and abilities (Peterson, 1987a).

Participation in Adult Education

Most studies show that as people advance in age, their level of participation in adult education tends to drop. Johnstone and Rivera (1965) studied the participation rates of people by age categories in lecture series, study groups, and discussion groups sponsored by various organizations and institutions. The researchers found that the highest participation rate, 22 percent, occurs in the 40-to-49 age group, followed by 13 percent of those between the ages of 50 and 59. Only 6 percent participated in the 60-to-69 group, and 2 percent in the over 70 group.

Several reasons account for the lower participation of older people. Many elderly are inhibited from taking part in educational activities because of their fear of failure. Some think that education is for the young and that they would feel childish in such a setting. Another reason is that older people are difficult to reach and recruit for educational programs, as they often are outside the mainstream of the regular channels of communication and community services. Finally, some persons are unable to participate because of their lack of physical mobility or transportation. Transportation becomes even more of a problem for those wishing to attend evening classes because many elderly people find night driving difficult and public transportation generally inadequate.

The lower participation rates of older people in adult education programs are also related to their lower levels of educational attainment. It is generally assumed that education begets education—that is, the more formal education persons have, the more likely they are to participate in educational programs. As Table 16.2, based on the 1981 Harris poll shows, of those 65 and over holding college degrees, 16 percent

Table 16.2 PERCENTAGE THAT TOOK EDUCATIONAL COURSES
IN THE PAST YEAR

Age Group	Total	Some high school or less	High school graduate some college	College graduate
18–54	38	12	38	57
55–64	11	3	14	23
65+	5	2	6	16
Total	29	7	32	49

Source: Louis Harris and Associates, *Aging in the Eighties: America in Transition.* Washington, DC: National Council on the Aging, 1981, p. 34.

were enrolled in educational courses, compared with 2 percent of those with some high school education or less. However, overall, as Table 16.2 demonstrates, comparatively few elderly persons (5 percent) are enrolled in formal education programs. As successive generations of older people continue to have higher levels of educational attainment, we can expect to see a rise in their participation rates.

The Harris poll also revealed that when older persons were asked why they took courses, the majority, 69 percent, said it was to expand their general knowledge about some field or hobby. Thirty-nine percent reported it was to make good use of their time, and 26 percent said it was to be with other people.

SOME FUNCTIONS OF EDUCATION

Education fulfills many important needs in the lives of older people. It serves to maintain contact with others, expands horizons, and helps to create and develop meaningful activities. It also helps older people maintain their physical and mental well-being.

The Theory of Educational Needs

McClusky (1974, 1982) has formulated a hierarchial needs theory to serve as a guide for developing educational programs for older persons. He classifies these needs into the following five categories.

1. *Coping needs.* With aging there is often a decline in income, power, and prestige, as well as in energy. Coping with these reductions becomes the important task at this stage of the life course. Top priority in this category is given to the need to educate for physical and economic well-being in order to meet such survival needs as housing and transportation. In the area of education, primary emphasis is placed on adult basic education (the three Rs), which is the prerequisite for more advanced types of learning.

2. *Expressive needs.* These needs refer to those areas in which people participate for the sake of the activities themselves and not as a means of achieving some goal. Expressive needs can be activated through courses and instruction in such areas as arts and crafts, writing, and drama. Such activities give a person pleasure and enjoyment in their own right and contribute to the enrichment of one's life.

3. *Contributive needs.* This category consists of needs that fulfill the desire to be useful—to find a meaningful role and to be of service to others. These needs often can be realized through participation in various types of community activities and programs. Frequently prior to participating in such programs, new skills must be acquired through training. An example is the Foster Grandparent program. This program provides low-income elderly with the opportunity to make a useful contribution to their community through giving personalized care to children with special needs in both institutional and non-institutional settings. Before starting this service, Foster Grandparents receive 40 hours of pre-service orientation; once in the program, they are given monthly in-service training (see Chapter 12, "The Family").

4. *Influence needs.* Although, in general, older people may have less power, they are not powerless. With the proper kind of education and training they can be more assertive in directing and controlling their own lives as well as in serving their community. The Gray Panthers movement is an example of the influence that older people can have on social policies and national priorities.

5. *The need for transcendence.* Uniquely related to later life, this need involves an elderly person's desire to "rise above and beyond the limitation of declining physical powers and of a diminishing life expectancy." It is at this stage that one looks back on his or her life and attempts to attain a higher level of understanding and find a meaning for one's existence (see life review, Chapter 21, "Death and Dying").

Lifelong Learning

Education is being viewed increasingly as a continuous process of *lifelong learning*, rather than as learning restricted to the early stages of life. Educational opportunities over the life span, especially in the later years, are expected to be in great demand in the future. This demand will be due mainly to the lengthening of life expectancy, the rise in the educational levels of the elderly accompanied by their subsequent interest in education, and the acceleration of change in society.

In describing the role of education throughout adulthood, Houle (1974) divides the adult life span into four periods: young independent adulthood, early middle age, early old age, and later old age. Of particular interest are the last two stages: early old age, beginning at 55 and extending to 75; and later old age, 75 and over.

Education performs several important functions in early old age. First, education can help the individual to plan a strategy to bring about a successful adjustment in the later years. Next, besides diminishing disengagement, it can also assist in reengagement by giving persons the ability to take part in new interests and activities. In addition, education can be one of those activities that help to fill the time for older people.

Learning in later old age is usually related to a sense of personal need, which includes spending time in a satisfying manner and continuing to contribute to society. For many elderly persons, education affords them the opportunity to interact with persons of all age groups and to remain involved in community affairs and activities. Finally, learning in old age, as well as throughout other stages of the life course, contributes to a vitality of both mind and body.

In the past, persons experienced a much slower rate of change in their lifetimes than people do today. This was especially true of those living in farming communities, where the environment remained much the same from one generation to the next. All the necessary skills and knowledge needed for a lifetime were learned in the early years of one's education.

But in today's rapidly changing technological society, education has no cut-off point. The challenges of a changing society demand that education be continuous not only to prevent intellectual obsolescence but also to counterbalance skill obsolescence in the job market. New skills must be learned in order to hold a job or to qualify for reemployment.

For many years it was an accepted fact that obsolescence was an inevitable occurrence among older workers and that not much could be done about it. The older worker is often stereotyped as being inflexible and unwilling or unable to change his or her habits. As a result, employers have been reluctant to offer retraining to retain them. Likewise, older workers themselves are uncomfortable about participating in retraining programs because they feel that they cannot finish the program successfully or compete with younger workers (Sterns, 1986).

Most findings from actual training programs report positive results in the retraining of older workers. Older workers often perform as well as if not better than younger workers (Welford & Birren, 1965; Haberlandt, 1973; Rhodes, 1983). Today lifelong training is a necessity because of the rapid technological changes taking place in our society, which create obsolescence of knowledge among all age groups (Sterns, 1986).

Life-Course Education

Life-course education differs from lifelong learning. Butler (1975) refers to this type of education as that in "which different psychological, personal, familial, occupational and other tasks related to specific processes and stages of life are taught." He emphasizes the need to understand and prepare for the transitions that take place throughout the life course, such as marriage, parenthood, and retirement.

In recent years, one of the most promising areas for life-course education has been retirement planning programs. It has been noted that "The life-course transition from formal education to work takes 12 to 16 years or more, while the transition from work to leisure retirement is expected to be completed over a weekend" (Shrank & Waring, 1989). In order to ease this abrupt transition, retirement planning programs are becoming increasingly available in business and industry.

Currently, most programs are offered three to five years before retirement. For retirement planning to be most beneficial, however, it should begin 20 or 30 years before retirement. Early education for retirement gives one the opportunity to plan for an adequate retirement income, to take preventive measures in health maintenance, and to develop hobbies and interests for the retirement years. In some companies, retirement planning programs are developing into a type of life-course counseling (Shrank & Waring, 1989). Not only retirement preparation but other life-course transitions as well may be taught successfully long before they are experienced.

THE ROLE OF COLLEGES AND UNIVERSITIES

In recent years there has been a dramatic increase in the number of colleges and universities offering courses in gerontology as well as the number of courses per campus. For instance, in 1957, there were 57 campuses offering gerontology instruction; by 1976, the number had increased to 607, and by 1985, there were 1,105 campuses offered gerontology courses. There is every reason to believe that this rate of growth will continue. Existing data reveal that those universities and colleges that do not offer gerontology courses at the present time will have them in the next few years, except for a small number of technical schools (Peterson, 1987b).

Higher education in the field of aging involves two separate but interrelated aspects: education *about* older people and education *for* older people.

Education About Older People

Gerontology education refers to the instruction at the undergraduate and graduate levels of those persons who plan to work in the field of aging, primarily teaching or conducting research. This instruction involves studying the older population and processes of aging.

Box 16.1 **The Graying of the College Classroom**

What are the effects of having people older than 60 years of age participate as peers in the college classroom with college-age students? A study done by Edwin J. Kay and his associates (1983) reports that the young students gained more positive attitudes toward their own aging and toward intergenerational learning. In addition, the amount of activity in the intergenerational class was greater than in a class with only college-age students. The instructor felt that the intergenerational mix made the class livelier and stimulated more discussion. The researchers conclude: "the exchange between generations does more than help older and younger students understand each other; it provides a stimulating atmosphere for learning in which the benefits accrue not only to the older but to the younger students as well."

Source: Edwin J. Kay et al. "The Graying of the College Classroom." *The Gerontologist* (23), 1983, pp. 196–199.

Besides instruction, the university has the responsibility of developing new knowledge through research activities, thus making knowledge available for use in present and future aging programs. University personnel often assist those who work with older people by serving on boards of community organizations, sponsoring seminars and workshops, and speaking to community service groups. Another major service that universities and colleges perform is the dissemination of information about aging through pamphlets, books, and articles. Educational television and radio programs under the auspices of universities have also been especially useful.

Education for Older People

The courses of study offered by colleges and universities that attract older people may be taken for credit or noncredit, often with a reduction in or waiver of tuition. They are typically of two basic types. One type is composed of general courses that lead to self-enrichment and intellectual growth. Such content is often found in the social sciences, arts, history, geography, and the humanities. The other type consists of topics designed to help older persons develop coping skills and competencies for facing the problems of later life, such as estate planning, money management, health care, and retirement preparation (Peterson, 1986).

An example of a short-term program specifically designed for older persons and

Elderhostel offers older persons an opportunity to live on a college or university campus and take courses from regular faculty members. (Nick Myers)

conducted under a separate administration is *Elderhostel.* Its name was inspired by the youth hostels and folk schools of Europe. Elderhostel is a network of colleges and universities that offers one-week academic programs to persons age 60 or older at moderate costs. The participants live on campus and take college-level courses taught by regular faculty members. Most programs are scheduled during the summer months and offer a wide range of liberal arts and sciences courses.

Elderhostel started in 1975 as a summer experiment at the University of New Hampshire and four other New Hampshire colleges with an enrollment of about 200. Since that time, its growth has been dramatic. By 1989, Elderhostel programs were being offered by 1,400 educational institutions in 50 states and in Canada with an enrollment of 148,000 summer and academic-year hostelers. Elderhostel is based on the premise that the later years afford one an opportunity to enjoy new experiences.

Jean Romaniuk and Michael Romaniuk (1982) studied the factors that played a role in the decision of older persons to attend Elderhostel. They found that factors related to learning content and involvement in new experiences were considered to be among the most important motives. Table 16.3 lists the motivational factors for attending Elderhostel in order of their importance.

A national discussion group that provides program units on themes drawn from literature, drama, history, folklore, philosophy, and the visual arts is the Discovery through the Humanities Program. Older persons come together at housing complexes, residential-care centers, senior centers, or churches to discuss distinguished writers, thinkers, and artists. Volunteer leaders facilitate the sharing of ideas and opinions evoked from reading the books supplied by the program. The program is sponsored by the National Council on the Aging, and more than 1,500 groups have participated in the program each year since it began in 1976.

Another type of program designed for older persons is the Institute for Retired Professionals, a special learning community within the New School for Social Research in New York City. Its purpose is to provide an opportunity for persons to share their experience and skills with other retired professionals and executives like themselves. Its 630 members participate in a peer learning program that includes a wide variety of subjects. There is no outside faculty. Each member is both a teacher and a student, helping to select and design the curriculum and then to organize and lead

Table 16.3   FACTORS, IN ORDER OF IMPORTANCE, INFLUENCING THE DECISION TO ATTEND ELDERHOSTEL

1. Catalog course descriptions	6. Time of year
2. Visit new places	7. Special campus features
3. Try something new	8. Visit old familiar places
4. Learn new things	9. Elderhostel reputation
5. Near friends/relatives	

Source: Jean Romaniuk and Michael Romaniuk, "Participation Motives of Older Adults in Higher Education: The Elderhostel Experience." *The Gerontologist* (22), 1982, p. 366.

the groups. In addition, the Institute members also enroll in two regular New School courses each year (see Box 16.2).

Community colleges have been most active in developing innovative credit and noncredit programs for the elderly. Much of their success has been due to their congenial social atmosphere, flexibility in program content, and styles of teaching. In addition, community colleges have employed active recruitment and outreach efforts. Some offer precampus counseling and remedial support. Besides offering courses on campus, many community colleges have developed programs that are offered at various sites in the community, such as in nursing homes, at adult day-care centers, and congregate meal sites.

Box 16.2 # At the New School, Retired Adults Are Educating Each Other

The scene is the weekly session of News and Views, one of about 80 study groups offered at the Institute for Retired Professionals, an adult education program at the New School for Social Research.

In a lecture hall 75 men and women—attorneys, professors, business people—are discussing current events. The talk turns to cocaine abuse, and a social worker tells of her experiences with drug dealers and their motives. Her remarks goad a lawyer formerly with the Department of Labor to defend Government enforcement efforts.

The courses at the institute range from languages to drawing to seminars on Virginia Woolf. But what sets it apart is its peer learning method under which the more than 600 students organize and teach the courses themselves.

After careers that brought responsibility and experience, most of the retirees find peer learning a refreshing alternative to being spoon-fed knowledge in a classroom. The method lets people with high school and college educations immerse themselves in long-buried interests, or interests they never knew they had.

"I came to the I.R.P. trying to stick to my own fields," said Joseph Cresh, a former director of a nursing home, "but now I've become interested in origins, sources, archeology."

Now in its 25th year, the institute owes its peer learning system to its founders, a group of teachers who set out to continue their intellectual activities after retirement. As the method now stands, any group of students can create a course on any topic. The retirees meet to discuss whether there is interest in a new course, then appoint interested students as coordinators to organize the curriculum. Those who plan to take a course offer to prepare papers and conduct individual sessions. A list of courses to be offered is published before each term.

Henry Lipman, director of the institute, said the method encourages interaction among the students, satisfying important social and intellectual needs for retired people.

"One of the biggest problems with retirement is having to replace the social network that went with the job, walking in and being able to say you've just seen a Balanchine ballet, or are in the middle of a book," said Mr. Lipman, a former dean of continuing education at New York University. "When you retire you do not have that kind of contact."

Arno Rosenberger, a retired businessman who runs the News and Views hour, said, "We can stay home and read our newspapers, we can stay home and read our books, but we like to discuss, have an interplay."

Emanuel Klinger, a former high school music teacher, asked: "Where else would you meet people from the Department of Labor, from education, from A.T. & T.? You don't find that variety in college."

Some things are the same as in college, Mr. Cresh interjected, saying that there are "too many single-sex tables" in the cafeteria.

Papers take up to 50 hours to prepare, and are often on a par with graduate-level work, Mr. Lipman said. Using them to teach a class satisfies another important need, he said, the "ego gratification" one gets through employment.

The decibel level after class, he added, could be compared to a "small textiles factory" as class discussions and congratulations spill out into the corridor.

Mildred Fisher, a widow who is a former social worker, said, "The common value system we have here is important, and it's such a pleasure to enrich yourself."

Despite the range of expertise, most of the students do not write papers on fields with which they are familiar. Some are completely new to a subject, while others have approached it from a different angle.

The music component of a recent course on the Bible in the arts was taught by a music teacher who was an expert on Haydn's oratorio "The Creation," but had "never read Genesis before." Mr. Lipman said. Leonard Gelber, a former high school principal and professor of political science at New York University, found a previously undiscovered affinity for women in feudal society, a topic he wrote a paper on last term.

Alfred Plant, a retired vice president of the Block Drug Company, is coordinating a course on stage comedy this year. He said the course started "with the Greeks, with Aristophanes," and is working its way "to Neil Simon, with lots of stops in between." Mr. Plant, who is chairman of the Jewish Repertory Theater, is a former trustee of the National Academy of Arts and Sciences.

The comedy course, he said, brought out surprising interests from other students. "One lady wanted to do a paper on burlesque—a very fine, nice lady," he said with a chuckle. Her lecture is to be given under the rubric "indigenous American comedy."

"Last year," Mr. Plant said, "we did the theater of Great Britain, and the year before that the decade of the 30's—Odets, Irwin Shaw, O'Neill."

Because the institute's re-enrollment rate is about 90 percent, the median age of the students has gone up, from the high 60's at the time of its founding to about 72 today, Mr. Lipman said. He said it has also become the "granddaddy" of about a dozen other peer learning programs for retirees at such places as Harvard, Duke and Brooklyn College.

(continued)

Mr. Lipman said demand for such programs would increase as both the median age and the average level of education of the elderly rises. People now retiring at the age of 65 have an average of three more years of schooling than did their forebears 10 years ago, he said.

"In every school where this has been tried, they have been oversubscribed from day one," Mr. Lipman said, adding that a standard program at City University that offers free courses to the elderly has had few takers. "The problem is not whether the population is there, but whether the universities have the type of insight the New School had, the idea of letting people run their own program."

Mr. Plant said: "The key thing that makes this successful is people studying the things they have always wanted to, but have never had the time. Now I have my chance."

Source: *The New York Times*, December 18, 1986.

SUMMARY

1. The growth of mass education in the United States coincided with the shift from an agricultural to industrial economy. Today, education is the largest single industry in our society. Older people face many barriers to learning because of the many myths regarding their inability to learn.

2. Although the educational level of older persons is below that of the overall population, the gap between the younger and older population has been narrowing and will continue to do so. Adult education opportunities for the elderly have been increasingly expanded in recent years. The lower participation rates of older persons in adult education are related to their lower levels of educational attainment. As successive generations of older people continue to have higher educational levels, we can expect to see a rise in their participation rates.

3. To assist in developing educational programs for the elderly, McClusky has proposed five educational needs of older persons—coping needs, expressive needs, contributive needs, influence needs, and the need for transcendence. Education is being viewed today as a continuous, lifelong process.

4. Gerontology education involves instruction both at the graduate and undergraduate level for those persons who plan to work in the field of aging. A number of educational programs are designed specifically for older persons, such as Elderhostel and the Discovery through the Humanities Program. Community colleges have been very active and successful in providing a variety of programs for the elderly.

KEY TERMS

adult education   *gerontology education*
lifelong learning   *Elderhostel*
life-course education

FOR FURTHER STUDY

Lowy, Louis, & O'Connor, Darlene (1986). *Why education in the later years?* Lexington, MA: Lexington Books.

Provides an overview of the field of educational gerontology, examines knowledge about education in the later years, and analyzes the federal role in education for the elderly.

Peterson, David A. (1983). *Facilitating education for older learners.* San Francisco: Jossey-Bass.

This book was designed to assist teachers and program planners in understanding the educational needs and characteristics of older learners so that they may develop more efficient and rewarding instruction for them.

Peterson, David A., Thorton, James E., & Birren, James E. (Eds.) (1986). *Education and aging.* Englewood Cliffs, NJ: Prentice-Hall.

This volume deals with the role of higher education in an aging society, analyzes some of the resources that facilitate instruction, and suggests some directions for future research and policy.

Sherron, Ronald H., & Lumsden, D. Barry (Eds.) (1985). *Introduction to educational gerontology.* Washington, DC: Hemisphere.

An overview of the factors involved in planning, implementing, and evaluating educational programs for the elderly.

PART
FIVE

Social Problems of the Elderly

Economic Status of the Elderly

All of us are familiar with the plight of elderly people who are struggling to live on a limited income. Should we look on this as a personal or a social problem? What is the distinction between the two? A personal problem is a condition that is linked to individual suffering and does not affect a large number of people; its causes and solutions lie within individuals and their immediate environment. A social problem, on the other hand, is a condition that adversely affects a large number of people, and its causes and solutions lie outside individuals and their immediate environment (Lauer, 1978). For example, if only one or two elderly persons were living in poverty, we might determine that the source of their problem was poor planning, a failure to save for retirement, or laziness. This would constitute a personal problem. But when large numbers of older people are living in poverty, the situation becomes a social problem, and as such it requires that we look beyond individuals and their immediate environment to the economic and political institutions in society for causes and solutions.

Sociologists are primarily interested in social problems, not in personal ones. A *social problem* may be defined as a condition that a significant number of people believe to be undesirable and feel that something should be done to correct. By this definition, the increasing number of older people in our population does not in itself constitute a social problem. Longevity is not considered an undesirable condition, but rather an achievement that has been highly valued and sought after in most societies from the beginning of recorded time (Chapter 2). As for doing something to correct the situation, not many people would advocate employing measures to reduce longevity or the size of the older population. The social problem concerning the elderly lies in the fact that the major social institutions have not kept pace with the rapid increase in the number of older people nor made the necessary adaptations to their needs (Neugarten, 1966). In addition, our society's changing values are beginning to define as no longer tolerable many conditions that have existed among older people. Instead of accepting these conditions as inevitable or taking them for granted as we have done in the past, we are now seeing these conditions as social problems that can be changed through social action.

Throughout this book we have been discussing the problems that the elderly face. Some problems have resulted from physiological changes; others have been associated with societal values and beliefs, role loss, a decline in status, and age discrimination. In this part, we will examine the elderly's problems regarding economic status, health care, transportation, housing, and deviance. Finally, we will discuss death and dying in a social context.

INCOME AND POVERTY

Most people think that the elderly, having met their major economic obligations, need less income than younger persons. In general, except for health expenditures, older people do spend less money, but often it is because they have less money to spend (Chapter 10). For some, poverty is a lifelong condition only worsened in old age. For others, poverty is a new condition, occurring after retirement or widowhood.

Median Income

One way of showing the economic situation of the elderly is by examining their median incomes. In 1987, the median income of families with heads age 65 and over was $20,808. Unrelated individuals (persons who live alone or with nonrelatives) have substantially lower incomes than those who live in family settings. For instance, the median income for older unrelated persons in 1987 was $8,149, or about 40 percent of the income of older families.

Though the median income of older families is still below that of the younger segment of the population, it has been steadily increasing, and the gap in income between the elderly and non-elderly has narrowed (see Figure 17.1). Some factors contributing to the improvement of the economic situation of the elderly have been the increasing coverage of older people by private and public pension plans, the implementation of the Supplemental Security Income (SSI) program, Social Security increases, and improvements in other income maintenance programs.

Income Distribution

Figure 17.2 shows the income distribution of older families and unrelated individuals. In 1987, about 14 percent of the families with a head 65 and over had incomes of less than $10,000 and nearly a third had incomes of less than $15,000. The economic hardships of those elderly living alone or with nonrelatives are reflected in the fact that 60 percent had incomes under $10,000, and about 77 percent had incomes below $15,000.

Though the aged are disproportionately represented in the lower income levels, as we noted in Chapter 10 ("Social Stratification"), they are also disproportionately represented in the higher income levels. In 1987, about 40 percent of those elderly living in families had incomes of $25,000 and over, and 10.5 percent had incomes of $50,000 or more.

Poverty Level

In 1987, 12.2 percent of persons 65 and over, or about 3.6 million people, were living below the officially determined *poverty level*. Calculated for persons age 65 and over, in 1987 this level was $6,872 per year for an older couple and $5,447 per year for an

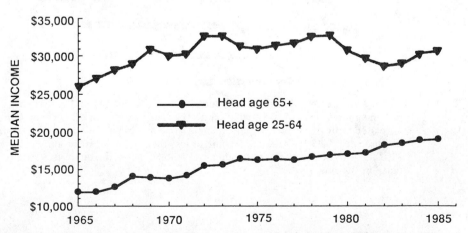

Figure 17.1. Median income of elderly and nonelderly families: 1965–1985. Although the median income of younger families increased during this period, it did not increase as rapidly as the median income of older families.

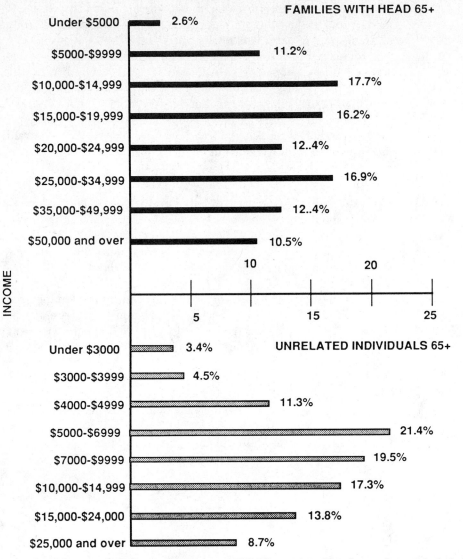

Figure 17.2. Percent distribution by income: 1987. About 14% of families with an elderly head had incomes of less than $10,000, and 40% had incomes of $25,000 or more. In contrast, unrelated individuals (elderly person living alone or with nonrelatives) were more likely to have low incomes: 60% reported an income of less than $10,000, while only 8.7% had incomes of $25,000 or more. (*Note:* Income categories in each half of the chart vary in size and differ from those in the other half.)

older person living alone. About another 2.3 million older persons live on incomes just slightly above the poverty level and are classified as *near poor*.

In addition to these recognized poor, there is a *hidden poor* population among the elderly. Census poverty figures do not include those older persons who, though poor themselves, live with others (mostly relatives) whose incomes are sufficient to raise the older persons out of the poverty level. Also, low-income persons are not counted as poor if they are institutionalized. Thus the number of older persons living in poverty is much higher than the figures show.

Poverty is not evenly distributed throughout the older population but varies by race and sex. In 1987, the percentage of elderly blacks living below the poverty level was 33.9 percent, or over three times that of whites (10.1 percent). Older females living alone or with nonrelatives reflect a higher incidence of poverty than their male counterparts. Minority women living alone have the highest percentage of poverty of all categories. Poverty also varies among the older population by age differences. For instance, the highest incidence of poverty is among the oldest-old (85 and over). In 1987, the poverty rate for the oldest-old was nearly twice the rate for the young-old (65 to 74).

Overall, the proportion of all older persons living below the poverty level has been dropping steadily since the 1960s. Table 17.1 shows the sharp drop in poverty rate over the 1959-to-1987 period. For example, the poverty rate was halved from 28.5 percent in 1966 to 14.6 percent in 1974. Or put another way, in 1959, 35.2 percent of all the elderly were poor, and by 1987 the percentage had dropped by nearly two-thirds to 12.2 percent.

Table 17.1   POVERTY RATES FOR PERSONS
AGE 65 AND OVER: 1959–1987

Year	Poverty rate (percent)	Year	Poverty rate (percent)
1959	35.2	1977	14.1
1966	28.5	1978	14.0
1967	29.5	1979	15.2
1968	25.0	1980	15.7
1969	25.3	1981	15.3
1970	24.5	1982	14.6
1971	21.6	1983	14.1
1972	18.6	1984	12.4
1973	16.3	1985	12.6
1974	14.6	1986	12.4
1975	15.3	1987	12.2
1976	15.0		

Source: U.S. Senate Special Committee on Aging, *Aging America: Trends and Projections.* Washington, DC: U.S. Government Printing Office, 1987–88.

PUBLIC SOURCES OF INCOME

To gain a clearer picture of the financial situation of older people, it is necessary to look at the major sources of their income, both public and private, and to understand some of the programs from which this income is derived.

Social Security

Today about 38 million persons receive monthly Social Security benefits. Although retired workers are the principal beneficiaries of this program (23.3 million), Social Security benefits also go each month to 2.7 million disabled workers, 3 million children, and 3.3 million spouses, as well as other eligible family members. Although Social Security has long been considered the financial bedrock for millions of older Americans, who depend more heavily on income from Social Security than they do

Franklin D. Roosevelt signing the Social Security Act in 1935, the most important single piece of legislation for the elderly in American history. (Social Security Administration)

from any other source, it was originally designed and conceived as a supplement to the income of older people. A recent study of poverty done by the U.S. Bureau of the Census found that Social Security helps more people escape poverty than all federal anti-poverty programs combined. According to the study, in 1986, almost half of the elderly would have been near the poverty level without Social Security (Dolan, 1989).

When the Social Security Act was signed into law in 1935, it made provisions for two federal–state programs: (1) unemployment insurance and (2) assistance to three groups of low-income persons (the aged, the blind, and dependent children). In addition, it established a federal old-age insurance system designed to provide basic retirement income after the age of 65 for workers insured under the system. This old-age insurance became popularly known as Social Security.

Since the passage of the Social Security Act, many changes have been made to improve the protection it gives to wage earners and to extend this protection to their families. Originally, the Act covered only workers when they retired, but in 1939 it was amended to provide benefits to the workers' dependents at retirement, as well as to the workers' survivors at their death. With the addition of these benefits, the program was then called Old-Age and Survivors' Insurance (OASI). In the beginning, the Social Security program covered only those who worked in industry or commerce, but in the 1950s coverage was extended to include household and farm workers, self-employed persons, state and local employees, members of the armed forces, and members of the clergy. To protect workers against the loss of earnings because of total disability, disability insurance was later added to the system (OASDI). In 1965 the Social Security program was expanded once more with the passage of Medicare.

For our present discussion, we will consider the old age and survivors' portion of OASDI. This aspect of the program may be divided into the following categories.

1. *Basic benefits.* These benefits are paid at age 65 and are based on the workers' average yearly earnings under Social Security over a period of years. But, regardless of how much a worker has earned, there is a limit set on the amount of the benefit. For example, the maximum monthly benefit for a worker retiring at age 65 in 1989 was $899, and the maximum benefit payable to a couple was $1,348.50. The normal retirement age for full benefits will gradually be raised to 66 by the year 2009 and then to 67 by the year 2027.

2. *Dependent benefits.* These benefits are equal to half of the worker's basic benefits and may be paid to a spouse and to each child under age 18 (or up to 19 if a full-time high school student). In cases in which a wife has worked and is qualified to receive Social Security, she has the option to draw a pension based either on her work record or on her husband's (reduced by half), depending on which is higher.

   This situation raises the question of whether or not the working wife is being treated fairly. During their working years, a husband and wife are considered separate tax units, and together they pay more into the system than a family in which only the husband works and earns the same amount. Yet, at retirement, the husband and wife are treated as one unit and are thus entitled to only one benefit. Often a working wife may receive no more or even less in retirement benefits than a nonworking wife. The working wife, however, does receive disability protection and has the option to retire at 62 even if her husband continues to work. As the participation rates of women in the labor force continue to increase, the issue of the inequity of their retirement benefits is expected to become highly controversial.

3. *Early-retirement benefits.* Early-retirement benefits may be paid to beneficiaries as early as age 62, but the amount is permanently reduced to 80 percent of full benefits at age 62 to take into account the longer period over which they must be paid. Before 1956, workers could not receive any benefits until they reached the age of 65. The law was changed in 1956 to permit women to receive reduced benefits at 62, and in 1961 the same option was given to men. Early retirement benefits will be reduced to 70 percent of full benefits after the age for full retirement benefits is changed to 67.

4. *Delayed retirement benefits.* Workers who delay retirement receive an increase in retirement benefits for each year that they work beyond age 65, up to age 70. Those persons who are 65 in 1989 will have their benefits increased 3 percent each year. For those who are 65 in 1990 and later, their benefits will gradually be increased until they reach 8 percent in 2009.

5. *Earnings test (retirement test).* According to this test, persons age 65 and up to age 70 are allowed to earn only a certain amount of money and still be eligible to receive their full social security benefits. When this limit was reached ($8,880) in 1989, benefits were reduced one dollar for every two dollars earned. For persons retiring before age 65, their limit was $6,480 in 1989. The earnings test has now been liberalized so that one dollar in benefits is withheld for every three dollars in earnings above the limit.

   The *earnings test* probably has been the target for more criticism than any other aspect of the Social Security program. Opponents argue that it destroys one's incentive to work and penalizes those with low incomes who need to work. They maintain that it is discriminatory because it takes into account only earned income and not income received from nonwork sources such as investments and rents. Many believe that the earnings test should be eliminated completely even though it would be extremely expensive to do so. Estimates are that its removal would cost the federal government an additional $16 billion over a five-year period (U.S. Senate, Special Committee on Aging, 1989). Those who support the earnings limit say that doing away with it would result in a windfall for professionals in the upper-income brackets who have chosen to continue working.

6. *Survivors' benefits.* Survivors' benefits are payable to the widow or widower beginning at age 60 and to young children, if any. In the past, benefits were reduced in most cases by 50 percent if the widow or widower remarried. This reduction resulted in many elderly couples' living together, rather than marrying to avoid a cut in benefits. Since 1979, widows and widowers who remarry after age 60 no longer have their benefits reduced. Also since 1984, a surviving divorced spouse who remarries after age 60 has no reduction in benefits.

Financing Social Security   Social Security is a pay-as-you-go-system that transfers money from the young working population to the elderly retired population. Most of the money is derived from a payroll tax on employees called FICA (Federal Insurance Contribution Act). Employers contribute an equal amount. To support the system, the payroll tax rate and the amount of income taxed has risen over the years. Between 1937 and 1949, the basic Social Security payroll tax rate was 1 percent each from the employee and the employer on the first $3,000 of earned income. By 1989, the tax rate had reached 7.51 percent on the first $48,000 of earned income.

Much criticism of Social Security stems from the larger bite taken out of the worker's paycheck as well as the regressive character of the payroll tax. Unlike the federal income tax, which is progressive—the more you make, the more you pay—the Social Security tax is based on the premise that the more you make, the less you pay. For example, persons earning $48,000 or less in 1989 were taxed at the rate of 7.51 percent on their entire income, whereas those who earned more were not taxed on earnings after the $48,000 mark was reached. Thus, higher-salaried workers pay a lower proportion of their income in Social Security taxes than lower-salaried workers. Put in dollars, a worker earning $96,000 pays the same amount ($3,604.80) into the system as the one earning $48,000, but the amount represents only 3.7 percent of the higher income.

A common argument is that a younger worker could buy retirement coverage such as an *Individual Retirement Account (IRA)* for less than the combined employee–employer tax and get better returns over a lifetime. However, one must bear in mind that Social Security is more than retirement income. It is also insurance against a disabling illness or injury for workers of any age. In addition, it provides life insurance protection for eligible family members in the event that the worker dies before retirement.

With workers retiring earlier and living longer, the ratio between those who pay into the Social Security system and those who collect from it has been changing markedly. This situation, along with a declining birth rate, has caused much concern in the past decade about the depletion of the Social Security trust funds, which act as a cushion against deficits. To help ensure the solvency of Social Security and bring the system into financial balance, in 1983, the year of the "Social Security crisis," Congress passed amendments to the Social Security Act that guaranteed huge reserves. As a result of this legislation, current projections estimate, the program will be sound and solvent for the next 75 years.

The amendments included two major strategies: increase revenues and discourage early retirement. In order to increase revenues, the previous schedule of payroll tax increases was accelerated. Also, the number of persons paying Social Security taxes was expanded to include all new federal employees, who in the past were in a separate federal civil service system. Next, for the first time, Social Security benefits were made taxable. One-half of the Social Security benefits received by persons whose income exceeds $35,000 ($32,000 for a couple) are now subject to federal income tax. The revenue from this tax is then put back into the Social Security trust funds. In order to discourage early retirement, as we have already noted, an increase in the retirement age from 65 to 67 is scheduled to be gradually phased in between 2009 and 2027. And finally, delayed retirement benefits have been increased to encourage persons to remain in the labor force longer.

No matter what changes occur in the financing of Social Security, one thing is certain: To provide adequately for the retirement period in the future, there will be an increasing financial burden on the working population. The question simply comes down to this: whether or not we want to live better during our retirement years at the expense of a lower standard of living during our working years (Schulz, 1988).

Supplemental Security Income

In addition to Social Security, the Social Security Administration operates the *Supplemental Security Income (SSI)* program, which went into operation in 1974. SSI replaced the federal–state assistance program for the low-income aged, blind, and disabled that was originally established under the Social Security Act of 1935. SSI is the first federal program to provide a guaranteed minimum income for the most needy and vulnerable groups in the population. Unlike Social Security, it is financed from income taxes.

Approximately 1.5 million persons aged 65 and over received SSI benefits in 1986. However, more than half of the 4.2 million SSI recipients were disabled and not elderly (U.S. House of Representatives, Committee on Ways and Means, 1987). Persons with no income receive the full amount of SSI. Those who have other sources of income but still fall below the minimum income level receive SSI money to bring them up to this level. In 1989, the minimum level was $368 per month for individuals and $553 for couples.

PRIVATE SOURCES OF INCOME

Figure 17.3 shows the sources of income for the elderly. Although social security is the major source (38 percent), other sources of income such as asset income (26 percent), earnings (17 percent), and pensions (16 percent) make up a large share.

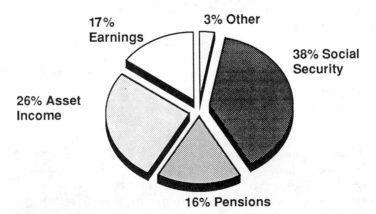

Figure 17.3. Income sources of elderly married couples and individuals: 1986. Income from Social Security is the most important source of income for the elderly, followed by income from assets.

Assets and Earnings

Savings, stocks, bonds, and other asset income have been growing in importance as sources of income in recent years. In 1960 income from assets made up only 16 percent of the total income of the elderly; by 1980 it had increased to 22 percent and by 1986 to 26 percent. However, in 1986 only one-third of the elderly who had asset income received more than $5000 from this source. About 60 percent of the elderly either had no asset income or received less than $500 a year from it.

Earnings from paid employment declined in importance with age. Persons between the ages of 65 and 69 received 30 percent of their income from earnings as compared with those 80 and older, who received only 4 percent.

Older persons depend more heavily on income from Social Security than they do from any other source. (Nick Myers)

Private Pension Plans

In recent years the growth of private pensions throughout industry has been widespread. Today about 40 million workers now have private pension coverage. Private pension plans may be classified into two types: contributory and noncontributory plans. A *contributory pension plan* requires that an employee pay part of the cost, whereas a *noncontributory pension plan,* which is the most common, is financed totally by the employer. Retirement benefits are determined in a variety of ways. Some companies provide the same retirement benefits to all eligible employees. Others base their benefits on the number of years of service, or on the employee's earnings, or on a combination of both (Schulz, 1988).

Two key characteristics of pension plans are vesting and portability. *Vesting* refers to the right of employees to receive the pension benefits they have accumulated if they leave the plan before retirement. *Portability* refers to the transfer of pension rights from one plan to another when the worker changes jobs. Social Security provides a good example of portability in the public sector; credits toward benefits accumulate under the Social Security system for workers no matter how often they change jobs. In the private sector, Teacher's Insurance and Annuity Association–College Retirement Equities Fund (TIAA–CREF) offers portability; university and college professors can transfer their pension benefits from one institution to another as their affiliations change.

Nearly all pension plans contain early-retirement options so that workers can receive their benefits before the customary retirement age. Usually such options require that the worker meet a minimum age requirement, or minimum-years-of-service requirement, or both. The "30 and out" plan of the United Automobile Workers, mentioned in Chapter 12, uses only years of service as qualification for full pension benefits. American Telephone and Telegraph Company combines age with years of service. Employees are given the option to retire at age 55 after 20 years of service on full pension, or they may retire at age 50 after 25 years of service but with reduced benefits.

The flagrant abuse and mismanagement of private pension plans prompted the passage of the *Employment Retirement Income Security Act (ERISA)* in 1974. Prior to this legislation, some companies required 30 years or more of continuous service for an employee to become vested. Many employees often lost their pension rights when they changed jobs, were laid off, or were terminated. When companies went out of business or were purchased by other companies, workers were often unable to collect their pensions, or, at best, only small portions of them. The Studebaker plant closing provides an illustration of this situation.

> In 1963 . . . some four thousand employees of Studebaker Corporation's South Bend, Indiana, plant found that their pensions amounted to little after the factory closed down. There was not enough money in the fund to pay benefits, although Studebaker had honored all its contract obligations. Men who had worked for the company for thirty and forty years got 15 per cent of their promised pensions; many others received nothing. (Butler, 1975)

ERISA has greatly improved the prospects that pension promises will be fulfilled. This legislation regulates and supervises private pension plans and provides basic protection against the loss of retirement benefits. To ensure that there will be enough money to pay the benefits promised, the pension law sets minimum standards for building up the funds that finance pensions. This law regulates both the timing and amount of vesting so that employees may receive a larger part or all of their pension benefits in fewer years. In this way, those who switch jobs will have a better chance to collect a pension when they retire. Also the law provides for a government corporation that will pay pensions up to a certain amount if the company goes out of business or cannot meet its obligations. Finally, the law establishes strict rules to prevent the misuse of pension funds.

INCOME ADEQUACY AND INFLATION

Judging the adequacy of the income of older persons is a difficult task. However, several standards are available in order to measure income adequacy. The most common measure is the poverty index, developed by the Social Security Administration in the early 1960s, and adjusted each year to reflect increases in the consumer price index. Briefly, the key factor in the construction of the index is the amount of money needed to buy food for a minimum but adequate diet that supplies all essential nutrients. The poverty level is then calculated at three times the food budget.

Retired Couple's Budget

Another approach to determining the adequacy of income of the elderly is by the use of budgets prepared by the Bureau of Labor Statistics every year from 1967 to 1982. These budgets were designed for couples in urban areas, with the husband aged 65 or over and both partners retired. It was assumed that the couples were self-supporting and in relatively good health, lived in their own homes, and were able to take care of themselves. The budgets listed the costs of major items required to meet the normal needs of retired couples at three different standards of living: lower, intermediate, and higher. In 1982, the last year for which the budgets were prepared, the Bureau of Labor Statistics set the budgets for retired couples at $7,226 (lower level), $10,226 (intermediate level) and $15,078 (higher level).

Perceptions of Finances

As an alternative to using budgets as an indicator of whether or not income is adequate, Peterson (1972) suggests a perceptual approach for measuring financial adequacy. Through this method, valuable insight into the way older people view their financial situation may be gained.

> This method rests on the assumption that an individual can determine the adequacy of his own finances; in fact, he is probably the only person who is in a position to do so since only he can incorporate consideration of his past level of living, his changing needs, his housing situation, the number of persons he must provide for, his assets, medical expenses, debts, etc. The perceptual method is employed by asking older people how

adequate they think their financial situation is and accepting their judgment as the measure of financial adequacy.

Peterson surveyed older persons in southeastern Michigan to determine how they perceived their financial situation. His findings reveal that 57 percent of the respondents felt their present finances to be inadequate, 35 percent viewed their incomes as adequate, and another 8 percent saw them as partially adequate. He found that females, blacks, and those living alone—the same segments of the population heavily represented among the elderly poor—were more likely to report their finances as inadequate.

Peterson's data also showed that persons in the lower income levels tended to have lower financial expectations than those in the higher levels. Individuals in the lower categories felt that only a small increase was needed in their income to raise them to what they considered to be an adequate level. He concludes that financial adequacy is best seen in relative terms instead of in specific amounts of money: "The average older person regardless of present level of income stated that to reach adequacy, his family income would need to be increased by 33%."

Consumer Patterns

Another way to examine the economic well-being of the elderly is by their consumption patterns. Older persons consume fewer goods and services than their younger counterparts, and their spending is more concentrated into essentials such as housing (including utilities), food, and medical care. These three items account for 60 percent of the elderly's spending, as compared with 49 percent spent by younger households on the same items. Older households spend substantially less on clothing, transportation, and entertainment than do younger households. The one area in which the elderly spend more in actual dollars than any other age group in the population is on health care (U.S. Senate Special Committee on Aging, 1987–1988).

Expenditures differ not only between the elderly and the non-elderly but also between the elderly themselves—the young-old and the old-old. Table 17.2 shows that expenditures for health care for the old-old are greater than for the young-old, whereas the old-old spent less on transportation, pension and life insurance, and entertainment.

Inflation

Many people believe that the elderly live on a fixed income and, as a result, are hit hard by inflation. This simply is not true. According to Robert Clark et al. (1984), most of the sources of income of the elderly rise in value when prices rise. In fact, their findings suggest that the nominal income of older persons rises more rapidly than do prices. For example, Social Security benefits are automatically adjusted to the increase in the consumer price index. Other government programs such as the Supplemental Security Income and food stamp programs also adjust fully for inflation. Thus, the elderly are largely protected from inflation in that the bulk of their income is currently adjusted for inflation with a relatively short lag. The elderly who are most

Table 17.2 AVERAGE ANNUAL EXPENDITURES OF URBAN CONSUMER UNITS BY TYPE OF EXPENDITURE AND AGE OF HOUSEHOLD: 1986

Type of expenditure	Percent distribution	
	65–74	75+
Shelter/furnishings	20.1	23.2
Utilities	9.4	11.5
Food	16.4	16.8
Clothing	4.2	3.5
Health care	9.1	15.0
Transportation	19.1	13.9
Pension and life insurance	5.1	2.2
Entertainment	4.1	2.5
Cash contributions	6.3	5.6
Other	6.2	5.7

Source: Adapted from U.S. Bureau of Labor Statistics, Release 88-175, "Consumer Expenditure Survey Results from 1986," April 14, 1988 (data from interview survey).

vulnerable to inflation are those in the higher-income bracket who suffer a greater loss from inflation in proportion to their incomes because many of their assets come from sources that have fixed dollar amounts such as bonds, private pensions, and personal savings (Schulz, 1988; Clark et al., 1984).

In recent years the overall economic status of the elderly has vastly improved. As we noted earlier, in 1966, 28.5 percent of the population over age 65, or 5.1 million persons, fell below the poverty level. Mainly because of the changes in the income levels of Social Security and private pensions, this percentage has been cut by more than half. Although great gains have been made over the past few decades in improving the elderly's income, still millions of elderly live below the poverty level or just above it—older persons who live alone; women, especially those over age 85; and elderly minority group members. It is to these economically deprived groups that we must now direct our efforts.

SUMMARY

1. Social problems differ from personal problems in that they affect a large number of people and their causes lie outside the individual. A social problem is a condition that a significant number of people believe to be undesirable and feel that something should be done to correct. By this definition, the growing size of the older population does not itself constitute a social

problem. But the fact that needed changes in the major social institutions have not kept pace with the increases in the elderly population has led to social problems.

2. Overall, the economic status of the elderly has been improving. Although the median income of older families is still below that of the younger families, the gap has narrowed in recent years, and the percentage of elderly living below the poverty level has been steadily declining since the 1960s.

3. Older persons depend more heavily on income from social security than they do from any other source. Social Security involves a transfer of money from one generation to the next—the young working population to the elderly retired population. With persons retiring earlier and living longer, the ratio between those who pay into the system and those who receive benefits from it has changed markedly. This situation has placed a heavier burden on the working population.

4. Supplemental Security Income (SSI), which replaced the federal–state assistance program in 1974, was the first federal program to provide a guaranteed minimum income for the most needy groups in the population.

5. Private pension plans have become widespread in recent years. They may be classified into two types: contributory, in which an employee pays part of the cost, and noncontributory, in which the employer pays the entire cost. In 1974, the Employment Retirement Income Security Act (ERISA) was passed to help protect and regulate private pension plans.

6. In order to judge the adequacy of the income of older persons, several standards are used. These include the poverty index, retired couple's budgets, and one's own perception of his or her own financial adequacy.

7. Contrary to popular belief, the elderly who live on a fixed income are not hit as hard by inflation as other segments of the population. The reason for this is that the bulk of their income is currently adjusted for inflation.

KEY TERMS

social problem
poverty level
near poor
hidden poor
earnings test
Individual Retirement Account (IRA)
Supplemental Security Income (SSI)

contributory pension plan
noncontributory pension plan
vesting
portability
Employment Retirement Income
    Security Act (ERISA)

FOR FURTHER STUDY

Berstein, Merton C., & Merton, Joan B. (1988). *Social Security: The system that works.* New York: Basic Books.

Deals with policy issues concerning Social Security and private pensions.

Clark, Robert L. & Spengler, Joseph L. (1980). *The economics of individual and population aging.* Cambridge, England: Cambridge University Press.

See Chapter 4, "Economic Status of the Elderly," for a discussion of the elderly's income and income sources.

Clark, William F., Pelham, Anabel O., & Clark, Marleen (1988). *Old and poor.* Lexington, MA: Lexington Books.

Provides a good description of the poor elderly by using data from the California Senior Survey, a longitudinal study of 2000 elderly persons receiving Medicaid.

Schulz, James H. (1988). *The economics of aging.* Dover, MA: Auburn House.

The standard work in the economics of the elderly that includes the development of public and private pensions, medical insurance, and employment assistance.

Chapter
18

Health

*T*oday we regard epilepsy as an illness, but in some societies in the past the epileptic was glorified. A man subject to such attacks was often the hero of an old Arab epic. He was more likely to receive admiration rather than treatment. Among the Abkhasians, overweight persons are looked on as ill. Though some forms of obesity may require medical attention in American society, nevertheless, we do not believe that all overweight persons are sick.

Health and illness, then, are not only viewed as physical problems but have social aspects as well. What constitutes illness is subject to social definition, a definition in our society that differs greatly from what it was in the past. With advances in modern medicine, the definition has been greatly expanded, and standards of wellness have changed. For example, malaria with its accompanying chills and fever calls for prompt medical attention today. But this was not the case in the mid-1800s when malaria, common among persons in the Mississippi Valley, was referred to as *ague* and accepted as a normal physical condition. People would often remark, "He's not sick, he's just got the ague" (Caudill, 1953). By the same token, it is not uncommon today for physicians and patients alike to define many illnesses as "natural" and dismiss them under the guise of "it's just old age."

Illness affects society in many ways. Persons who are ill are not able to perform the necessary tasks of daily living and their social roles. In turn, they are expected to play a role that Parsons (1951) calls the *sick role*. One of the main characteristics of this role is the shift from independence to dependence. This role is particularly disturbing to most adults in our society because of the high value that we place on independence. Complementary to the sick role are the roles that family, friends, and medical personnel perform to help restore the sick person to a normal functioning state.

Illness and injury exact a high economic cost from our society in lost work days, decreased productivity, and health-care services. Between 1965 and 1987 national health expenditures increased from nearly $42 billion to $500 billion. Even with today's apparent slower rate of increase, health-care expenditures are expected to reach $1.53 trillion by the year 2000. The elderly are the heaviest users of health services. Though persons age 65 and over represent about 12 percent of the total population, they account for about a third of all personal health-care expenditures (U.S. Senate Special Committee on Aging, 1989).

Health looms large as a problem for the elderly. In most opinion polls, older people rank health and health-care costs near the top of their list of concerns. In a 1981 Harris poll, "poor health" was among the most frequently cited "very serious" problems of persons age 65 and older.

HEALTH STATUS OF THE ELDERLY

In order to understand the health-care problems and needs of the elderly, let us begin by discussing their health status. Though health is difficult to measure, a number of indicators are used, including mortality, disease and disability rates, and self-health assessments.

Mortality

Mortality rates are the oldest and a widely accepted indicator of health status. Although two-thirds of deaths in the United States involve older persons, significant declines in death rates have occurred in the older age groups, especially those between 65 and 84 years of age. In addition, declines for older females are greater than for older males, and the declines for older whites are larger than those for older blacks (U.S. Senate Special Committee on Aging, 1987–1988).

Although heart disease has been declining, it remains the major cause of death in the United States. Heart disease, cancer, and stroke are the three leading causes of death among the older population. Seventy-five percent of elderly persons in this country die from these diseases (see Table 18.1 and Figure 18.1).

Box 18.1 **Social Isolation Can Be Hazardous to Health**

Loneliness may be more hazardous to health than smoking, according to a review of scientific data collected over the past 20 years. Statistics have long shown that adults who live alone and have little contact with others are more likely to suffer health problems and die prematurely. Why this is so, however, has never been clear.

A group of researchers at the University of Michigan's Institute for Social Research decided to look into the question by examining the work of other scientists over the past 20 years. The review convinced them, the researchers reported recently, that "social isolation is as significant to mortality rates as smoking, high blood pressure, high cholesterol, obesity, and lack of physical exercise."

All those factors have been demonstrated to put people at higher risk of premature death, although not all the reasons that are risk factors are fully understood. "In fact," said sociologist James House, the lead researcher, "when age is adjusted for, social isolation is as great or greater a mortality risk than smoking."

Source: *Knoxville Journal,* August 8, 1988.

Disease and Disability

The older population has a lower incidence of acute diseases than younger persons have. *Acute conditions* are characterized as having a definite and rapid onset, they usually last only a short time, they have pronounced symptoms, and they generally respond well to the use of drugs or therapy. Colds and influenza are examples of acute illnesses. In contrast, chronic diseases, which constitute the bulk of the health-care problems of the elderly, are characterized as having a gradual onset, they usually persist over a period of time, and there is no medical cure for them. *Chronic conditions* most common among the elderly are arthritis, high blood pressure, heart conditions, and hearing impairments. The likelihood of having a chronic illness not only increases with age but also tends to vary by sex. It is somewhat paradoxical that women have more illnesses than men, yet men die earlier. The reason for this is that although women have higher rates of diseases than men, they have fewer fatal ones. For example, women suffer more than men from arthritis and vision problems, but although these conditions are bothersome, they rarely cause death. In contrast, men have higher rates of life-threatening diseases such as heart disease, stroke, and emphysema.

Although 80 percent of all older persons have at least one chronic condition, for more than half of these persons, these conditions do not interfere with or restrict their activities. On the other hand, for some older persons such conditions may be restrictive and eventually lead to long-term disability.

Long-term disability refers to a reduction in a person's normal activities as a result

Table 18.1   DEATH RATES FOR TEN
             LEADING CAUSES OF DEATH
             AMONG OLDER PEOPLE BY
             AGE: 1986
             (Rates per 100,000 Population in
             Age Group)

Cause of death	Age 65 and over
All causes	5,103
Heart disease	2,122
Cancer	1,057
Stroke	444
Lung disease	215
Pneumonia and influenza	209
Diabetes	93
Accidents	86
Atherosclerosis	74
Kidney disease	61
Blood poisoning	51
All other causes	691

Source: National Center for Health Statistics, "Advance Report of Final Mortality Statistics, 1986," *Monthly Vital Statistics Report,* vol. 37, no. 6, Supplement (2), September 1988.

of a chronic condition. A widely used method of determining disability among older persons is through a personal self-maintenance scale called the *Index of Activities of Daily Living (ADL)*. This scale focuses on the unaided performance of six basic personal-care activities: eating, toileting, dressing, bathing, getting in and out of bed, and maintaining continence (Katz et al., 1963). A second scale, the *Instrumental Activities of Daily Living (IADL)*, refers to the capacity to perform basic activities that focus on home management and independent living. These items include shopping, handling finances, light housekeeping, meal preparation, using the phone, and taking medication (Lawton & Brody, 1969). As one might expect, difficulties with personal care and home management tend to increase with age. In 1984 about one-quarter of the uninstitutionalized population aged 65 and over had difficulty with one or more personal-care activities, and about the same proportion had difficulty with at least one or more of home-management activities (National Center for Health Statistics, 1984).

Another measure of activity limitation is the number of days a person is confined to bed. Table 18.2 reveals that of those in the oldest-old category (age 85 and over), only 3.4 percent were bedridden in 1984, whereas more than 60 percent of the total older population spent no days in bed. Yet, the myth still persists that older people are always ill and spend much of their time in bed.

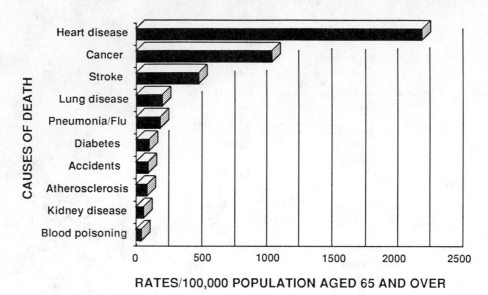

RATES/100,000 POPULATION AGED 65 AND OVER

Figure 18.1. The ten leading causes of death among persons aged 65 and over in the United States, 1984. Three out of four elderly persons die from heart disease, cancer, or stroke in the United States. Heart disease is still the major cause of death, even though its rates have declined since 1968, whereas death rates from cancer continue to rise. Stroke, the third leading cause of death, has declined over the last three decades.

Self-Health Assessment

A third measure of health status is the perception that the individual has of his or her own physical condition. It is interesting to note that the majority of older persons view themselves as being in good health. A 1987 Health Interview Survey reveals that 69 percent of the elderly living in the community report their health to be good or

Table 18.2   PERCENT OF THE 65+ POPULATION IN
THE COMMUNITY CONFINED TO BED:
1984

Number of days per year in bed	Age			
	65–74	75–84	85+	65+
0	63.5	61.3	55.8	62.2
1–6 days	14.5	12.9	12.1	13.8
7–13 days	6.7	7.4	8.7	7.1
14–27 days	6.5	7.0	6.3	6.6
28–365 days	7.8	9.9	13.9	8.9
Always	1.0	1.6	3.4	1.4

Source: National Center for Health Statistics. Unpublished data from the National Health Interview Survey, Supplement on Aging, 1984.

Most older people define their health as good or excellent and only a small minority are unable to carry on normal activities. (Nick Myers)

excellent, whereas 31 percent rate their health as fair or poor (National Center for Health Statistics, 1988). These figures may be a surprise because of the high incidence of chronic illnesses and impairments that afflict the elderly. Good health to most older people, however, does not generally mean the complete absence of disease but only that the condition present does not significantly interfere with physical and social functioning. Maddox and Douglass (1973) found that older persons tend to display a realistic orientation toward evaluating their health status, and that over time their rating tended to coincide with their physician's health assessment.

MAJOR TYPES OF HEALTH CARE

Despite the greater incidence of chronic conditions among persons age 65 and over, they visit a physician only about one-third more times than younger persons. Older persons had, on average, eight visits per year in 1986, compared with five visits by the general population (U.S. Senate Special Committee on Aging, 1987–1988). Since the advent of Medicare, the average number of physician visits have increased substantially, especially for persons with low incomes.

Box 18.2 **Drugs and the Elderly**

As chronic conditions increase with age so does the taking of prescription drugs and over-the-counter medications to manage these conditions. The elderly make up about 12 percent of the population, yet their use of medications accounts for 25 to 30 percent of all drug expenditures. Two of the more common problems associated with medications and the elderly are adverse drug reactions and drug interactions.

1. *Adverse Drug Reactions*. Defined as "any unintended or undesired consequences of drug therapy," adverse drug reactions can be a serious problem in the older person, especially among the institutionalized elderly population (Simonson, 1984). Confusion, forgetfulness, and many other similar symptoms may be mistakenly attributed to a deterioration in the elderly person's condition as result of old age when the true problem may be medication. Drug reactions can also be physically harmful to the patient and may result in such conditions as gastrointestinal irritation, blood loss, and sometimes even death. Adverse drug reactions are more likely to occur among the old-old (those 75 and over), those elderly who are small in stature, and those elderly who take excessive medications.

2. *Drug Interactions*. Drug interaction occurs when two drugs are taken together and one drug modifies the effect of the other. For example, alcohol and barbiturates taken together have a much greater depressing effect than when taken separately. Among the reasons for the high incidence of drug interactions among the elderly is that they take more medications than the general population, so their chances of experiencing drug interactions are greatly increased. Also, the numerous physiological changes that occur with aging affect the absorption and excretion of medications. In an older person, for instance, the kidneys eliminate medications more slowly and increased amounts of both medications may remain in the body for a longer period of time, resulting in a drug interaction. Next, in this age of specialization, it is not uncommon for a person to see several physicians, each of whom may be unaware of the medications prescribed by the others. Finally, elderly persons will sometimes swap or borrow prescription medications from friends or relatives without realizing that these drugs may interact with the medications that they are currently taking.

Source: William Simonson, *Medications and the Elderly,* Rockville, MD: Aspen Systems Corp., 1984.

Physician Services

Although the physician–population ratio has been improving steadily, it still continues to be a problem for older people. Younger physicians are less likely to set up their practice in older central-city neighborhoods, smaller communities, and rural areas— the very places with high proportions of elderly persons. The problem is further aggravated by the lack of mobility among many older people.

Physicians tend to give low priority to the needs of older people for two reasons.

The first reason is the misconception that being sick is a necessary part of being old. But some elderly also believe that symptoms of illness are normal and inevitable results of aging and do not seek help. A study done by the University of Illinois of 900 elderly persons who were homebound revealed that many of them were too ill even to walk to the door (*Time*, 1970). They had gone for months without seeking medical aid and thought that because they were old, they were supposed to be sick. Because older people are expected to be ill, physicians tend to write off as "normal" symptoms in an elderly person. Patients may complain of feeling ill and of being confused and disoriented, and physicians, instead of probing deeper for causes of symptoms, often assure them that such behavior is to be expected with advanced years. Thus, routinely treatable illnesses, such as heart attacks, viral infections, and even appendicitis, may go undiagnosed. Older patients are continually told, "What do you expect for a person of your age?" A story is told of an elderly woman who went to her physician complaining of not feeling well. The doctor said, "You must remember that you're not getting any younger." "I know that, doctor," she replied. "I just want to keep getting older."

The second reason why physicians give low priority to the needs of the elderly relates to their medical training, which focuses primarily on acute illnesses. Physicians often see positive, sometimes dramatic results in the treatment of younger patients with acute illnesses, and they derive reward and satisfaction from curing them. By contrast, older people suffer from chronic illnesses with no known medical cure, a situation particularly frustrating and depressing to many physicians. Unable to heal the older patients, the physician can only help them adapt to their situation.

Hospital Care

The average length of stay in a hospital for the elderly is declining. In 1968 it was 14.2 days per stay, and by 1987 it had dropped to 8.9 days. Men are more likely to be hospitalized than women, but women's average length of stay is longer (U.S. Senate Special Committee on Aging, 1988a).

Many older people who do not have a regular doctor and those whose income is limited rely on the emergency rooms of voluntary, nonprofit, and public hospitals when they become ill. Some strategies used by these hospitals to deal with the elderly include:

1. *The emergency-room hustle.* This is primarily a technique to avoid dealing with the problems of the older person. The doctor gives the patient a cursory examination, decides nothing is wrong, and sends the patient home with instructions to return at another time. Such patients are dubbed "gomers" ("*get out of my emergency room*").
2. *The transfer.* Voluntary hospitals may refuse care to elderly people. They often transfer them to overloaded and underfinanced public hospitals.
3. *The shuttle.* This is a variation of the transfer tactic. Patients are moved from one place to another until a hospital breaks down and admits them. Sometimes patients die in the ambulance (Butler, 1975).

Box 18.3 # The Medicalization of Aging

In recent years the jurisdiction of medicine has extended over areas of life that were considered nonmedical in the past. Problems and behavior become reinterpreted as illness and the medical profession is given a mandate to treat them. Some scholars suggest that a medicalization of society is taking place (Illich, 1976). For example, childbirth has become redefined as a medical procedure. Once considered a natural event that took place without medical supervision, birth today in the United States nearly always occurs in hospitals attended by physicians. Medical intervention through labor-inducing drugs and cesarean section has become commonplace in childbirth. Deviant behaviors such as alcoholism and drug addiction have become medicalized in recent years, and offenders are now being treated instead of punished.

Arluke and Peterson (1981) maintain that aging is increasingly being regarded as a medical problem and that physicians are extending their domain to control the behavior of older people through psychotropic or mind-altering medications. Many of these psychotropic drugs, which constitute a leading source of drug abuse among the elderly, have little to do with their health but rather are used for the care and management of elderly patients. Overprescribing psychotropic drugs is a common way of controlling the behavior of older persons in institutional as well as family settings to make their behavior more socially acceptable and less troublesome. The problem is thus attributed to the elderly individual, not the social institution. With this line of reasoning, older persons are considered to be at fault and so their behavior must be changed through medication. The possibility that their behavior is not an illness but an adaptation to a social situation is ignored, and attention is then diverted away from the family or institution.

According to a recent forum held by the American Psychological Association, large numbers of older persons are being reduced to living in a state of stupor and mental confusion because of overdrugging (AARP News Bulletin, 1989). The overuse and misuse of drugs today among the elderly is creating a serious problem, especially for those living in nursing homes. A contributing factor to the so-called other drug problem is the nursing-home practice of using psychotropic drugs as "chemical straitjackets" to keep older persons quiet and manageable, as well as to induce sleep. About half of all nursing-home residents are given a form of tranquilizer or sedative on a regular basis for extended periods of time. In a study of Tennessee nursing homes, researchers found that antipsychotics were the most common psychotropic drugs prescribed in nursing homes. In one nursing home, out of the 221 residents given antipsychotic drugs, only 36 were actually diagnosed as having a psychosis (Lipton & Lee, 1988).

Sources: Ivan Illich, *Medical Nemesis: The Expropriation of Health*. New York: Pantheon, 1976; Arnold Arluke and John Peterson, "Accidental Medicalization of Old Age." In Christine Fry and Contributors, *Dimensions: Aging, Culture and Health*. New York: Praeger, 1981; Peggy Eastman, " 'America's Other Drug Problem' Overwhelms Thousands, Experts Say," *AARP News Bulletin*, April, 1989; Helene L. Lipton and Philip R. Lee, *Drugs and the Elderly*. Stanford, Calif.: Stanford University Press, 1988. [Readers interested in full source citations are referred to these original sources.]

care facilities (ICFs). A *skilled-nursing facility* was a specially qualified facility with the staff and equipment to provide around-the-clock skilled nursing care or rehabilitation services as well as other related health services. An *intermediate-care facility* was one that provided health-related care and services to those who needed less care than those in a skilled-nursing facility, but more than custodial or residential care. As of 1990 the distinction between the two facilities has been eliminated, and both types of nursing homes must now meet the same requirements for the provision of services, staffing, and other administrative requirements.

Nursing homes may also be classified by whether they are profit or nonprofit. Two types of nonprofit homes are those owned and operated by a government agency, such as the city or county, and those owned by an organization, such as a religious group, labor union, or fraternal association. Another type, a commercial or proprietary home, is operated for profit and owned by an individual or corporation. About 80 percent of all the elderly in nursing homes live in commercial homes.

Some people argue that there is a direct contradiction between society's goal—rehabilitating patients—and the goal of profit-making nursing homes—keeping their beds full to make money. Others contend that in a home run for profit, dollars are the primary goal and patient care is a by-product, whereas in a nonprofit facility, patient care is the sole reason for its existence.

A study sponsored by the AFL-CIO asserted that most of the problems in nursing homes may be traced to the profit motive:

> This is not to state there are no problems in non-profit homes, the most frequent being pressure on relatives to make donations. But the facts are that non-profit nursing homes spend more on patient care and more on staffing than profit-making institutions, and the results are evidenced in better care for nursing home residents. (U.S. Senate Special Committee on Aging, 1978).

Related to the profit motive is the fact that despite the name "nursing home," nurses are scarce in these facilities. The poor image that nursing homes have does not attract registered nurses. Those registered nurses employed in these facilities are often overburdened with paperwork, administrative duties, and awesome responsibilities. Working conditions are often poor, and wages are low. A similar situation

---

Box 18.4 **Nursing Home Services**

A study done by the Health Care Financing Administration (1988) found that more than 4,000 of the nation's 15,000 nursing homes administer drugs without regard to a physician's written orders. Nearly 3,000 nursing homes fail to provide rehabilitative nursing care to prevent conditions ranging from immobility to paralysis. More than 6,500 nursing homes serve food under unsanitary conditions.

Source: Martin Tolchin, *New York Times News Service*, December 2, 1988.

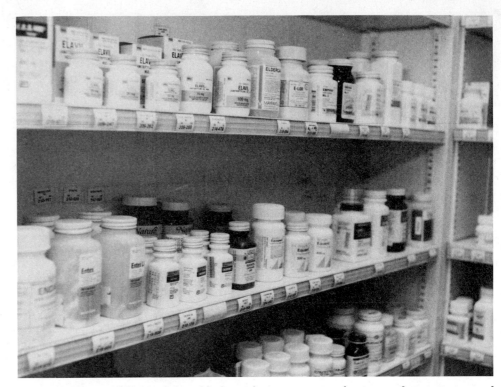

The major drug problem of the elderly is their unintentional misuse of prescription and over-the-counter drugs. (Nick Myers)

Community-Based Care

Many chronically ill elderly persons are able to remain in the community and avoid institutionalization because of the care given them by their informal support system of family, friends, and neighbors. The majority of primary caregivers, those who have the major responsibility for the older person's care, are either wives or adult daughters. Proximity to the elderly person is usually the determining factor in who becomes the *primary caregiver*. Partly because wives tend to outlive their husbands, caregiving differs by sex. The primary caregiver for men is most often the wife, whereas for women the primary caregiver is an adult child. Husbands and especially wives report that being a caregiver makes a major contribution to their sense of self-worth (U.S. Senate Special Committee on Aging, 1988b).

Emotional stress or physical strain is an inevitable accompaniment to caregiving, especially when the one receiving the care is substantially physically or mentally impaired. The difficulties and problems that arise for the caregiver in such a situation are referred to as the *caregiving burden*. Depending on the degree of the older person's impairment, this burden may range from feelings of overload to a dramatic change in the caregiver's lifestyle and daily routine. In recent years a number of intervention programs have focused on ways to reduce the caregiving burden. Such intervention efforts include respite programs to provide time off for caregivers and organizations in which caregivers freely discuss their common problems, offer solutions, and provide support for one another.

Nursing-Home Care

A widely held misconception about older people is that a large percentage of them require institutional care. But only 5 percent of persons 65 and over are in nursing homes at any one time. However, it has been estimated that 20 to 25 percent of the elderly will spend some time in a nursing home at some point in their lives (Kastenbaum & Candy, 1973). Another misconception is that the majority of persons entering a nursing home remain there for the rest of their lives. Seventy-five percent of those entering a nursing home stay less than a year, and about one-third to one-half stay less than three months (U.S. Senate Special Committee on Aging, 1987–1988). The majority of nursing-home patients are over 85 years of age, female, white, and currently unmarried (see Table 18.3).

The greatest impetus to the creation of nursing homes in the United States was the passage of the Social Security Act in 1935. Prior to that time, facilities for the aged were few in number. The majority of the aged who could not provide for themselves and had no family who could help them generally lived in county almshouses, popularly referred to as the "poor farm" or "poor house."

After the advent of Social Security, the number of facilities run for profit to serve the newly monied aged population grew rapidly. Most of these early accommodations were organized as small private boarding homes. At that time, recipients of the federal–state program of Old Age Assistance (OAA) were considered ineligible to collect monthly benefits if they lived in a public institution. Thousands of these residents moved into private boarding homes. With the passage of time, these homes began to hire nurses and to call themselves *nursing homes*. Most states began licensing these facilities by the mid-1950s.

Table 18.3   SELECTED CHARACTERISTICS OF NURSING HOME RESIDENTS 65 YEARS AND OLDER: 1985

	Percent		Percent
Age		*Race*	
65–74	16	White	93
75–84	39	Black	6
85+	45	Other	1
Sex		*Marital status*	
Male	25	Widowed	64
Female	75	Married	16
		Never married	14
		Divorced or separated	6

Note: Total number of residents 65+ : 1,316,000

Source: U.S. Special Committee on Aging, *Aging in America: Trends and Projections,* 1987–88, p. 119.

Organized, systematic pet therapy, which began in the 1960s, brings homeless pets together with persons in health care facilities. Pets often help the patients to feel loved, responsible, and needed. Some studies of pet ownership among elderly persons in the community reveal positive effects on well-being including the reduction of high blood pressure. (Nick Myers)

The passage of the Medicare Bill in 1965 gave nursing homes their biggest boost. The bill provided for federal reimbursement of all reasonable costs incurred by patients who qualified for rehabilitation or skilled-nursing-home services; it also provided, through Medicaid, for nursing-home care for those with limited assets.

This modification in the health-care financing system, together with the increasing demand for beds as the number of elderly persons increased, accounts for most of the current growth in the nursing-home population. Currently, there are 1.5 million persons in nursing homes, and this population is expected to increase to 2 million in another decade.

Nursing Homes

"Nursing home" is a generic term for any residential facility that gives some level of nursing care. Prior to 1990, the Medicare and Medicaid programs classified nursing homes into two major categories: skilled-nursing facilities (SNFs) and intermediate-

applies to the licensed practical nurses who work in these institutions. As a result, much of the care in nursing homes is left in the hands of untrained aides and orderlies, who are paid minimum wages and whose turnover rate is exceedingly high. Most problems of abuse and poor care in nursing homes stem from their almost complete dependence on untrained personnel. Kayser-Jones (1981) classified the most commonly reported incidents of nursing home abuse as:

1. *Infantilization.* Residents are treated like young children. For example, they are scolded, given direct commands, and addressed by such terms as "Honey" or "Baby." In addition, patients may be dressed in childish attire, and women are sometimes given dolls to play with.
2. *Depersonalization.* There is a loss of individuality. Residents are treated with indifference and often ignored as if they had no value or significance.
3. *Dehumanization.* There is a lack of respect for privacy and little regard for patients' dignity as human beings. Cultural norms are often violated, such as having men and women shower or bathe together in the same room or patients having to urinate or defecate in the presence of others.
4. *Victimization.* Besides having their possessions stolen, residents are verbally and sometimes physically abused. They are punished by being tied up or excessively sedated. In one nursing home residents had their mouths taped

These patients in a nursing home are busy arranging flowers in baskets that are to be placed on tables in the dining room. (Nick Myers)

shut with adhesive tape—because they dared to ask for a bedpan at 2 o'clock in the afternoon while aides played cards (Moss & Halamandaris, 1977).

Because of such abuses and the widespread publicity that they have received, the 1975 Amendments to the older Americans Act provided for the creation of an ombudsman program to receive complaints from nursing-home residents. The *ombudsman* acts as an advocate for the institutionalized elderly by assessing and verifying each complaint and then seeking to address it. Today there are about 9000 paid and volunteer ombudsmen in more than 700 state and local programs nationwide (*AARP News Bulletin*, 1988).

Nursing-home reform legislation passed in 1987 spelled out certain rights of nursing-home residents. They include being free from physical and mental abuse, punishment, involuntary seclusion, and any physical or chemical restraints unless absolutely necessary for the resident's safety. In addition, nursing-home residents have the right to choose a personal physician and to have privacy with regard to medical treatments as well as written and telephone communications.

HEALTH-CARE COSTS

Health-care costs in this country are a major problem for all age groups. But the elderly have been most severely affected because of their higher risks of illness and disability, as well as the special services and facilities that they require. In 1965 the *Medicare* program was enacted to help prevent a major illness from depleting the elderly of their savings. All persons over the age of 65 are eligible for Medicare regardless of income. It consists of two parts: Part A (hospital insurance) helps pay for hospital care, some patient care in a skilled nursing facility, home health care, and hospice care. Part B (medical insurance) helps pay for physicians' services, outpatient hospital services, home health care as well as a number of other medical services and supplies that are not covered by the hospital insurance part of Medicare. Part A is supported by the Social Security payroll tax, and Part B is maintained by monthly medical insurance premiums paid by Medicare enrollees and general revenues.

As a companion program to Medicare, *Medicaid* was enacted in 1965 to provide health care for low-income persons of all ages. It is jointly financed by the states and the federal government. Unlike Medicare, it provides for long-term nursing-home care and is the principal public source of financing for nursing-home care.

In the last two decades, the structure and the delivery of health care have resulted in the overutilization of services, inefficiency, and waste. Since the introduction of Medicare in 1965, hospital costs and utilization rates have increased dramatically. In an effort to cut Medicare costs, a reimbursement method was created in 1985 in which a fixed, predetermined amount for a specific diagnosis is paid to a hospital regardless of the type of services given or the length of the stay. Under this prospective payment system (PPS), all Medicare patients are classified into one of about 475 diagnosis-related groups (DRGs), and to cover its costs the hospital receives a fixed payment for each DRG. If a hospital can treat a patient for less than the DRG

Box 18.5 **Is This Any Way to Grow Old?**

My father has Parkinson's disease. My mother and I together could no longer handle him at home. He required physical assistance for every move. We put him in a nursing home, recommended as the top of the line, with one nursing aide for every 15 patients (if everyone shows up for work). My father cannot feed himself nor get to and from the bathroom. One nurse's aide with 15 patients cannot attend to his needs. So my mother spends seven to eight hours a day at the nursing home.

The nursing home costs $45,000 per year. My mother is heartsick. They worked and saved and bought insurance all their lives so that they could grow old in peace. Now she doesn't know how she will live, let alone how to take care of him.

Source: Adapted from Carolyn Kazdin, *New York Times,* June 28, 1988, p. 29.

---

amount, it can keep the savings. If the treatment costs more, the hospital must absorb the loss. Thus, this system discourages overtreatment and overuse of services. Since the introduction of this health care policy, hospitals tend to discharge elderly patients much earlier than they did previously and sometimes it is not in the best interest of the patient. As a result, some critics maintain that hospitals are discharging older patients "quicker and sicker."

Two of the greatest fears that plague the elderly are losing their life's savings if they should have an extended hospital stay or need long-term nursing home care. Such costs can wipe out the resources of all but the very wealthy. To prevent elderly persons from suffering financial disaster due to prolonged hospitalization, Congress passed the Medicare Catastrophic Coverage Act of 1988, the largest expansion of Medicare since its creation in 1965. The new benefits included unlimited hospitalization, improved skilled nursing facility and home health care benefits, and an unlimited number of days of hospice care. These new benefits were financed by a $4 increase in monthly medical insurance premiums and an annual supplemental premium that depended on one's federal income tax liability, the maximum premium being $800 per person and $1600 for a couple.

When signed into law in July 1988, Catastrophic Coverage was hailed as a major breakthrough in health care. But support for it began to decline in the early part of 1989 when angry Medicare beneficiaries claimed that the extra money they had to pay did not justify the benefits they received. Outraged constituents and lobbying groups began demanding that the act be repealed. By November of 1989, lawmakers responded and it was repealed.

The tremendous financial burden for long-term care in a nursing home is the second fear that plagues older people. It continues to threaten the financial security of the majority of the elderly and their families. Contrary to popular belief, Medicare does not cover the cost of long-term care in a nursing home, only short-term acute care. Nursing home residents must deplete all their income and assets in order to qualify for long-term care under Medicare. This situation is known as the "Medicaid spend-down."

Today the cost of staying in a nursing home can range from $12,000 to $50,000 per year, with an average cost of $22,000 per year. Most people who enter a nursing home are not poor, but one out of every three elderly who spend any time in a nursing home end up poor. The future direction of some provision for long-term care insurance in this country remains uncertain at this writing. But it is an issue that undoubtedly will receive increased attention in the near future. (See the Reading on long-term care at the end of this chapter.)

SUMMARY

1. Illness is a social as well as a physical phenomenon. The social definition of illness has varied in different places and at different times. Illness and injury exact a high price from society in terms of lost productivity and the cost of maintaining health-care services.

2. Death rates for the elderly have been steadily declining. Females have had a consistently lower death rate than males, and whites a lower death rate than blacks. The leading causes of death among the older population in the United States are heart disease, cancer, and stroke. Three-quarters of elderly persons die from these diseases.

3. Older people have fewer acute illnesses than younger people do. Acute illnesses generally involve a disability of a short-term nature, whereas chronic diseases persist over time. Unlike acute diseases, they have no known medical cures. About 80 percent of all older persons have one or more chronic conditions.

4. In 1987 nearly 70 percent of uninstitutionalized persons age 65 and over reported that their health was good or excellent. Most older persons are able to realistically evaluate their own health status, and their assessments tend to coincide with those of their physicians.

5. Older people see their physicians about one-third more often than do younger persons. Although the physician–population ratio has improved, the uneven geographical distribution of physicians is still a problem. The needs of the elderly are given low priority by physicians because many physicians write off symptoms of illnesses in older persons as untreatable, and physicians find it more rewarding to treat acute illnesses that can be cured instead of the chronic illnesses that afflict older people.

6. The average length of stay in a hospital for the elderly is declining. Older men are more likely to be hospitalized than older women. Many elderly are able to avoid institutionalization because of the care given them by their family, friends, and neighbors.

7. About 1.5 million elderly are in nursing homes. The development of nursing homes in this country can be traced back to the Social Security Act of 1935. About 80 percent of all nursing homes in this country are profit-making enterprises. Some people argue that the profit motive directly contradicts

the best interests of the nursing-home patient. Accounts in recent years have revealed neglect and abuse of nursing-home patients by the staff. Many of these problems stem from long hours, low pay, and lack of trained personnel. In 1975 the Ombudsman Program was created to receive complaints from nursing-home patients, and in 1987 nursing-home-reform legislation that spelled out nursing-home patients' rights was passed.

8. One of the greatest fears of most elderly is the loss of their savings because of catastrophic illness. Legislation enacted in 1988 helped to alleviate this situation by putting a ceiling on hospital and doctor expenses for the Medicare benefactor. However, paying for long-term care in a nursing home still remains a major problem for the elderly.

KEY TERMS

sick role

acute conditions

chronic conditions

long-term disability

Index of Activities of Daily Living (ADL)

Instrumental Activities of Daily Living (IADL)

adverse drug reactions

drug interactions

medicalization of aging

primary caregiver

caregiving burden

nursing home

skilled nursing facilities

intermediate-care facilities

ombudsman

Medicare

Medicaid

Medicaid spend-down

prospective payment system (PPS)

diagnosis-related groups (DRGs)

FOR FURTHER STUDY

Kart, Cary S., Metress, Eileen K., & Metress, Seamus P. (1988). *Aging, health, and society.* Boston: Jones and Bartlett.

Deals with how the health problems of aging affect both the individual and society.

Wantz, Molly S. & Gay, John E. (1981). *The aging process: A health perspective.* Cambridge, MA: Winthrop.

Provides information on the physical and psychosocial aspects of aging at the various developmental stages.

Ward, Russell A., & Tobin, Sheldon S. (Eds.) (1987). *Health in aging: Sociological issues and policy directions.* New York: Springer.

Focuses on the sociological processes associated with health in later life and the policy implications of those processes.

Reading

Implications of an Aging Population for Long-Term Care

Judith D. Kasper

In this article, Kasper points out that as the number of older people in our society continues to increase, the need for long-term care will also increase.

. . . Elderly people use the bulk of long-term care, both of nursing home care and care provided to those living in the community. One in five Americans will be 65 or older 40 years from now. The sheer increase in numbers of elderly people could mean a substantial increase in the numbers needing long-term care, even if the percentage of people needing assistance remains stable. In addition, the composition of the elderly population is changing in ways that are likely to affect the need for long-term care. By the year 2000, one out of every two elderly people will be 75 or older, indicating a shift within the elderly population toward the older ages. This is the group most vulnerable to the physical and cognitive problems that often require long-term care.

Though the long-term care population represents less than a quarter of the elderly, the specter of frailty and decline leading to admission to a nursing home or dependence on others for help with routine daily tasks haunts older Americans, their children, and their grandchildren. Polls indicate elderly people worry about becoming a burden to their children. In addition, most adult Americans feel the costs of long-term care are beyond their means. In response to these fears, federal legislation to finance long-term care is being proposed for the first time. . . .

WHAT IS LONG-TERM CARE?

Long-term care is usually thought of as assistance provided over an extended period of time because of health problems that limit a person's ability to perform routine,

Source: Judith D. Kasper, "Implications of an Aging Population for Long-Term Care." *The World and I*, December, 1988, pp. 579–589. [Readers interested in full source citations and footnotes are referred to the original article.]

everyday tasks. This type of care goes beyond medical assistance from physicians or nurses to include such services as help with personal hygiene (bathing or dressing, for example) and meal preparation. Some definitions also include transportation services, modifications to housing (to improve mobility, for instance), and psychological care. Two of the difficulties in designing programs or legislation to provide long-term care are the broad range of services that can be included and the gaps in knowledge concerning which services are most appropriate for which people. One recent review of community-based long-term care programs reveals the following range of services across programs: post-hospital skilled nursing care; physical therapy; transportation; home aides to do meal planning, shopping, personal care, and to exercise supervision; and psychosocial counseling.

THE RELATIONSHIP BETWEEN AGING AND LONG-TERM CARE

The notion that age is inevitably linked to decline is gradually being dispelled, with good reason. Nonetheless, the probability of needing long-term care rises with age and is greatest among the very old. . . .

Similarly, the likelihood of experiencing functional impairments that require assistance from others or use of special equipment increases with age. Almost half of those 85 or older living in the community report difficulty in performing one or more routine activities of daily life, ranging from walking to bathing or to using the toilet.

It is important to realize that these difficulties are not the result of the normal aging process. The argument has recently been advanced that many physiological and cognitive declines previously regarded as integral to advancing age do not occur in many individuals, and that when they do, they may even be reversible. At a recent conference on aging, it was pointed out that "People do not become blind, disabled, or demented because of aging."

Many of the problems commonly attributed to aging are the result of chronic illness—conditions that persist over the long term, often require medical management, and usually are not subject to cure. One prominent example is arthritis, which afflicts half of all elderly people, with effects ranging from discomfort to severe limitations in mobility. While aging is not the cause of such diseases, or the functional declines that often accompany them, many are illnesses that are more common in later life. Ironically, success in increasing life expectancy—presently at about 75 years—through the reduction of infant mortality and control of childhood diseases has meant many more people live to an age where the diseases of later life can take their toll.

The relationship between increasing age and the onset of chronic illness that impairs functioning would seem to indicate an inevitable increase in the need for long-term care. If the percentage of elderly needing assistance with some aspects of functioning remains at around 20 percent, about seven million people will need some type of long-term care at the turn of the century, and double that figure by 2050. There are some, however, who question this apparent inevitability.

WILL THE RELATIONSHIP BETWEEN AGING AND THE NEED FOR LONG-TERM CARE CHANGE?

Discovery of a cure or a means of preventing Alzheimer's disease and other severely debilitating chronic illnesses would obviously have a significant impact on the numbers of elderly people needing long-term care. These kinds of medical breakthroughs are difficult to predict. There is evidence, however, that it may be possible to delay the onset of some diseases (if not prevent them altogether), thus reducing the number of years of illness immediately preceding death. This eventuality is referred to as the "compression of morbidity." Those who see it as a likely development point to epidemiological data such as those indicating the average age of first heart attack for men is now four years later than it was two decades ago. In addition, some of the negative physiological changes observed in old age, though previously thought to be irreversible, appear subject to modification through factors such as nutrition and exercise. Osteoporosis, for example, may be preventable through reduction of risk factors for the disease (smoking, heavy drinking, or inadequate calcium intake) and may even be subject to amelioration once it strikes.

Those who are more skeptical about achieving widespread compression of morbidity point to the degree to which projected delays in the onset of disease depend on changes in health habits. Considerable uncertainty remains about how to achieve widespread changes in diet, exercise habits, or reductions in smoking, as well as whether such changes will endure if achieved. An even more pessimistic view of the implications of increased life expectancy is that disease and disability actually will increase, leading to a "pandemic" of mental disorders and chronic diseases.

Whether compression of morbidity can be achieved—thus substantially reducing the need for long-term care among the elderly population—is uncertain. It seems prudent, however, as our society attempts to project future service needs, costs, and availability of care providers, to assume levels of need at least equivalent to those of today's elderly.

WHO NEEDS LONG-TERM CARE?

The parameters of the population in need of long-term care are often treated as synonymous with the number of individuals having limitations in functions of daily living. These limitations are measured by reported difficulty in performing a set of routine activities (ranging from mild difficulties in performance to inability to perform), or by gauging ability to perform these activities without assistance. The most commonly used list includes eating, transferring (from a bed to a chair), dressing, bathing, using the toilet, and walking. These so-called activities of daily living (ADLs) were defined in the 1960s through observation of patients in a rehabilitation facility; their developers believe they reflect primary sociobiological functions. One criticism of this commonly used set of measures is that it focuses on physical functioning and does not adequately capture the problems confronting those with cognitive impairments.

Though the long-term care population may be defined as those people with limitations in performing routine daily tasks, this is by no means a stable estimate. It varies considerably, depending on the set of activities that are selected and whether all levels of impairment performance are included. For example, difficulty in walking is the most commonly mentioned functional limitation among elderly people. The size of the long-term care population (excluding nursing home residents) is close to six million people if one includes those with walking difficulties (in addition to possible problems with bathing, dressing, transferring, getting outside, eating, and using the toilet), but only 4.3 million if those who have trouble walking are excluded. . . .

Similarly, restricting the long-term care population to those elderly people "unable to perform" at least one activity provides a smaller estimate than does using a broader definition to include all those with moderate or mild difficulty. The different ways in which the long-term care population can be estimated—inclusion of both physically and cognitively impaired, restriction by severity of impairment or by numbers or types of impairments—significantly influences the size and nature of the population. . . .

WHAT LONG-TERM CARE SERVICES ARE NEEDED?

There is a tendency to define services as long-term or acute by the setting in which they are provided. Thus, by definition, care provided in nursing homes becomes long-term care and care in hospitals is acute. In fact, according to Rosalie A. Kane and Robert L. Kane, long-term care services can be delivered

> in the client's home, in community foster homes, at central sites within the community such as multipurpose senior centers, day hospitals, and day care centers; in a variety of residential settings, including sheltered housing, board and care homes, retirement hotels, old-age homes, nursing homes, and rehabilitation centers; and in mental hospitals.

The same authors note that "long-term care refers to the range of services needed to compensate for functional problems, not the places where they are offered."

Long-term care encompasses a broad range of both health and social services, which involve in turn a wide spectrum of providers, settings, and needs. It is not specific to a particular set of services or a particular care setting. For this reason the definition of long-term care often hinges on the presence of a functional impairment, the duration of the problem, and whatever services are needed to compensate. (Thus, estimates of the long-term care population rely on numbers of functionally impaired people, as discussed in the previous section, rather than estimates of people using specific types of services or residing in specific settings.)

From existing data it is possible to determine that those with ADL impairments make use of both help from individuals and special equipment. Among people who had difficulty bathing without assistance, for example, about one out of five relied only on special equipment (shower seat, tub stool, or grab bars, for example), while the remaining four relied on other people for help, or a combination of people and equipment. Reliance on people and equipment varies by type of impairment—for example, equipment is more often used to help people "get around inside," while help with eating more often comes from other people. It is also impossible to determine that elderly people with ADL difficulties have more physical visits and hospitalizations than others.

A much better understanding is needed of which services are best suited to particular functional difficulties. Little is known, for example, about the service needs of cognitively impaired versus physically impaired elderly people, or about the needs of people with different numbers or severities of limitations. A variety of options to meet long-term care needs is sometimes available. People may be assisted by special equipment or by other individuals. Assistance may be provided to people in their homes, or they may go to day-care centers for services. Choosing among options requires criteria for choice. At present, these are likely to involve considerations of costs and what services are provided by existing programs. But factors that should also come into play are the quality and appropriateness of the services provided and the preferences of those being helped. Considerations of how help is provided and how best to maximize the autonomy of dependent elderly people are gaining increased attention in discussions of provision of long-term care services.

WHO PROVIDES LONG-TERM CARE TO THE ELDERLY?

Most of the assistance provided to those elderly living in the community is provided by their family or friends. Several surveys have found the majority of functionally disabled elderly people rely solely on their family and friends, and also that this support is crucial in keeping people in the community, thus preventing or postponing nursing home placement. Elderly people in general have considerable contact with their children, which becomes more frequent as they age. Caregivers to disabled elderly people are most often children, though some elderly shoulder this burden as well. Among children, adult middle-aged daughters and daughters-in-law more often take on the care-giving role than do sons or sons-in-law. A number of changes in the size and structure of the family and in female labor-force participation pose potential problems for such extensive reliance on family care giving in the future.

More elderly people will be without children in the future, both because marriage rates have declined and because more couples have not had children. . . .

A second trend that will reduce the availability of family caregivers is the increasing participation of women in the work force. Nearly two-thirds of women in their 30s are in the labor force today. At least four-fifths of women born in the 1960s and 1970s will be in the labor force as their parents turn 65. As one researcher put it in testimony before Congress: "By early in the next century, when people will be longer on life expectancy, they will find themselves shorter on family support where it counts most in old age—at home. Families in the future may still have the emotional will to provide care, but fewer will have a practical way. . . ."

If the ability of the family to provide care declines in the future, there is likely to be greater reliance on professional sources of care such as home health agencies and adult day-care centers. In addition, the need for nursing home beds will increase.

WHO PAYS FOR LONG-TERM CARE?

The aspect of long-term care financing that is most troubling to the public and most often discussed is the cost of nursing home care. . . . The typical nursing home patient either enters as a financially indigent Medicaid patient or becomes one after exhausting his or her assets paying for institutional care.

Medicaid was enacted in 1965 as a program to enable the poor to obtain greater access to medical care. The majority of recipients, then and now, are poor women and children. But after patients, the largest financer of nursing home care for the elderly is Medicaid. About half of nursing home care is paid for by patients, over 40 percent by Medicaid, and the remaining small percentage by Medicare, private insurance, and other sources. Annually, about a third of all Medicaid expenditures now goes for skilled nursing and intermediate care facilities, primarily for the care of the elderly.

Much less is known about the costs of providing long-term care in the community or, more importantly, the potential costs under a publicly financed program providing such care. In part, this is because so much care is now provided by family members, and there is concern about whether this would diminish if care were publicly financed. Estimating the costs of in-home, community-based care is complicated as well by the variety of services provided under the programs that have been studied.

While public awareness of the costs of nursing home care and the lack of coverage provided under Medicare has increased substantially, one recent survey of the elderly indicated 15 percent thought Medicare paid for nursing home care and 23 percent thought their private insurance provided such coverage. Private insurance for institutional care is relatively recent and covers only a few hundred thousand people, most still in the work force. Less than 1 percent of nursing home care is paid for by private insurance today. . . .

CONCLUSIONS

The delivery and cost of long-term care services are issues of importance for many of today's elderly and their families. Finding better ways to finance and provide long-term care has taken on a sense of urgency because of recent demographic changes. It seems certain that as the population ages and more people live into their 80s and 90s, the need for long-term care will grow. The answers to the questions of who needs care, what kind they require, who will provide it, and who will pay are still being formulated, based on present-day evidence and the experience of other countries. For many in our aging population, the quality of life will be profoundly affected by the outcome.

Chapter
19

Housing and Transportation

*B*ecause the elderly spend an increasingly large proportion of their time at home, housing plays an important role in their lives. Their living environment includes not only the housing unit in which they live but also other aspects, such as shopping facilities, medical services, and transportation. In fact, a very important element in the living environment of an older person is the availability of adequate transportation. The value of good transportation may even outweigh the quality of the living unit itself. For an elderly person who does not drive, a home or an apartment may become a virtual prison if transportation is inaccessible.

Both housing and transportation, then, can have a decided impact on the quality of life and the lifestyle of elderly persons. Although there is a growing commitment to provide adequate housing and transportation for the elderly, these items remain major problems for them. In this chapter, after reviewing some of the types of housing in which older people live, we will look at the major federal programs that assist the elderly in their housing needs. Then we will examine the sources of the transportation problem and the government's response to the problem.

TYPES OF HOUSING

Home Ownership

Nearly three-fourths of all persons age 65 and over own their homes, and of these, 80 percent live in homes that are mortgage-free. These homes are generally older and of somewhat lower quality than those owned by younger persons. In 1985 about 45 percent of elderly homeowners lived in housing that was built before 1950. The median value in 1985 of homes built before 1950 and occupied by older homeowners was $45,400, as compared with $70,900 for those built after the early part of 1980 (U.S. Senate Special Committee on Aging, 1989).

Various studies show that many older people are "overhoused" in terms of room and square footage because their children have left home. They often prefer to remain in their own homes amid familiar surroundings, despite the fact that large, older homes are often expensive and difficult to maintain.

Housing costs vary by mortgage status and the age of the homeowner. The percentage of income spent on housing (not including repairs) in 1985 was higher for older households than for younger households. For example, among older homeowners without a mortgage payment, the percentage of income spent on housing was 18 percent, compared with 10 percent for younger homeowners, whereas for those making mortgage payments, it was 28 percent for older households and 21 percent for younger households.

Older persons often spend a disproportionately large percentage of their income on property taxes. As a result, all states have instituted some type of property tax relief programs. One such program, *circuit breaker,* provides complete or partial relief when property taxes exceed a certain percentage of one's income. Another program is homestead exemption, which exempts a dollar amount or percent share from property valuation from their taxes.

Apartments

An alternative to owning a home is renting. About 25 percent of housing units occupied by older persons are rental properties. Older people who rent are often unable to compete with younger persons for the more desirable housing. As a result, many elderly renters live in older apartment buildings located in areas of cities in which rents are low and conveniences are few. Older persons who are more likely to rent than own their homes tend to be 75 years or over, females, and living alone. According to recent data, an elderly woman living alone spends nearly 50 percent of her income on rent (U.S. Senate Special Committee on Aging, 1988).

Mobile Homes

An increasingly popular housing alternative for older people, especially among working-class retirees, is mobile-home living. Older persons make up about 21 percent of the households in mobile homes (Black, 1989). Mobile-home living is most frequently found in states with mild climates like Florida, Arizona, and California. The homogeneity of a mobile-home-park community often provides the elderly with security and companionship in addition to low-cost housing. Many parks have a restriction on the age of a mobile home (usually five years) to be admitted into the park. As a result, owners who want to move to another park with their over-age models often have difficulty finding one that will take them. As Johnson (1971) points out, this problem confronts many older people who buy a mobile home when they retire and later on do not have enough money to replace it.

> Some of these people may spend their 60s in a mobile-home park in a semi-rural, recreation area but find that in their 70s or 80s they want to move back to an urban area in order to be closer to their children or to hospital and shopping facilities. One elderly couple . . . had spent ten years in a mobile-home park near the ocean before they discovered that their mobile home was rusting due to the salt air—a problem they hadn't foreseen and which contributed to their decision to move back to the Bay Area. They spent six months looking for a park that would be willing to take them.

In mobile-home parks in which spaces are rented, the residents are subject to rent increases by park owners. In Florida some mobile home owners have had rents doubled in recent years because the land that their home is situated on has increased in value (Black, 1989). Many older people have no choice but to pay more rent because of the problems involved in moving to another park. Even if they were to find a park that would accept their older mobile home, they often can ill afford the expense of moving. Johnson observes that some older mobile-home parks do cater to the elderly who cannot afford or qualify for the newer mobile-home parks, but "they are often run-down in appearance . . . they are inhabited by retired, working-class individuals, some of them living in ancient and minuscule trailers, who are trying to remain independent on small pension or Social Security payments" (Johnson, 1971).

Single-Room Occupancy

Many elderly persons live in inner-city hotels in which they have *single-room occupancy (SRO)*, usually with shared or community bath and no kitchen unit. Research indicates that the elderly are present in high proportions where SROs are found. SROs are not limited to large cities but are found in smaller communities as well.

The SRO population has been described as the "least visible of an invisible population." The urban renewal efforts of the 1960s first brought the existence of the SRO population to the attention of the public. The demolition of many old hotels sent thousands of older residents into the streets to search for other low-rent accommodations. The commercial areas and centers of the city in which SROs are found have been hardest hit by both public and private development. Ehrlich (1976) notes that about 30 hotels in St. Louis that provided residences for the elderly have been razed since 1960:

> Furthermore, the majority of the hotels in which the aged population now reside were constructed before 1910 and are approaching the point of terminal decay. The elderly manage to stay just one step ahead of the "headache ball" by going from one hotel to another as the structures become dilapidated and slated for redevelopment. . . . The downtown elderly, most with limited incomes, find themselves with fewer and fewer housing and service options.

A situation that aroused much public indignation occurred in San Francisco in 1977. Forty elderly Chinese and Filipino residents were evicted from a hotel located at the edge of Chinatown because it was being torn down for commercial development. More than 330 law-enforcement officers were on the scene as 2000 persons demonstrated against the evictions (U.S. Senate Special Committee on Aging, 1977).

It has been generally accepted that SROs constitute undesirable housing because many units were built for transients and are not suitable for permanent residence. Also, most of these structures are old and deteriorating. Recently, the view has been advanced that SROs help preserve and maintain a distinctive lifestyle that some older persons prefer and find advantageous. Personal security may be enhanced because people are always on the premises, sometimes including a desk clerk or custodian. Also many older persons value the security, cleanliness, and heat that a hotel or rooming house provides more than they do a private bath or kitchen unit. In addition, the downtown location of the SROs allows older people to be within walking distance of nearby stores and restaurants.

Eckert (1980) points out that within these SRO hotels is "a large percentage of persons who have led mobile, single lives in the past and seem to prefer living alone in the present. While they do not romanticize hotel life, they overwhelmingly prefer it to any form of 'institutional' living for older adults." The reading at the end of this chapter ("Loners, Losers, and Lovers") provides some insight into the singular, alienated lifestyle of elderly residents in a slum hotel in Detroit.

Shared Housing

The concept of *shared housing* is not new. It is a modern version of the practice of taking in boarders and lodgers, which was common in this country up until the 1930s. In a shared housing arrangement, a homeowner rents out a room or rooms in exchange for rent or a combination of companionship, housework, yardwork, and/or grocery shopping and rent. Each person has a private bedroom and shares common areas such as the kitchen and living room.

House sharing among the elderly usually involves a frail older person who has a large home with extra room, needs some additional income and help with household tasks, and feels better having someone else in the home. A study done by McConnell and Usher (1980) found that the majority of older persons prefer to share housing with middle-aged persons. However, in a college community, it is not uncommon for an older person to share his or her home with a young person.

To help match people who are seeking housing with those who have extra space in their homes that they would like to share, more than 200 housemate-matching services have been started (Schreter & Turner, 1986). The matching service may range from simple referral to reference checking, counseling, and even structuring an agreement as to what services will be provided in lieu of rent or a rent reduction.

The term *shared housing* is also used to refer to group residences or group-shared housing. The Share-A-Home concept—discussed in Chapter 12, "The Family"—provides an example of this type of living arrangement.

Accessory Apartments and ECHO Housing

Both *accessory apartments* and ECHO housing allow older persons to live close to their families while at the same time maximizing privacy. Accessory apartments involve converting surplus space in an existing single-family home into a separate living unit with its own kitchen, bathroom, and, often, entrance. This type of arrangement is often referred to as a mother-in-law apartment.

ECHO is an acronym for *Elder Cottage Housing Opportunity*. It refers to a small, free-standing, removable housing unit. Such units are typically placed in the side or back yard of a single-family home to provide housing for elderly parents so that they will be near their adult children for mutual aid and support but still maintain their independence. In Australia, where this type of housing originated, such units are called "granny flats" and in Denmark they are referred to as "kangaroo housing." However, the ECHO concept is not new. In many rural and southern areas of the United States, it has long been common to see a mobile home near a single-family unit so that elderly persons can live near their adult children. One of the major drawbacks to this type of housing is that zoning regulations prohibit them in many communities because it is assumed that they will lower property values and overload housing.

FEDERALLY ASSISTED HOUSING PROGRAMS

Federal assistance for low-income housing for the elderly did not begin until the late 1950s. This assistance mainly has been in the form of new construction programs and rent supplements. Although such programs have done much to provide decent housing for many older people, much more needs to be done. Today there is a growing shortage of housing for low-income elderly because since 1980, funds for federally assisted housing have been drastically cut. A recent report of the House Select Committee on Aging estimates that between 25 and 30 percent of all elderly cannot afford adequate housing, and approximately 250,000 persons are on waiting lists for

Box 19.1 ## Community Resistance to Elderly Housing

A study of two suburban communities to determine how residents felt about group housing in their community revealed that all group housing was objectionable to them. However, the least objectionable were one-story apartments, shared housing, and multi-story apartments for the elderly, in that order. The accompanying table shows that housing for the elderly had the lowest mean objection scores (1.7 and 1.8), whereas group housing for male delinquents was the most objectionable (2.8).

RESPONDENTS' OBJECTIONS TO HAVING VARIOUS TYPES OF GROUP HOUSING IN THEIR NEIGHBORHOODS (*N* = 139)

TYPE OF GROUP HOUSING	MEAN OBJECTION[a] SCORE
For male juvenile delinquents	2.8
For female juvenile delinquents	2.7
Public housing	2.6
For former patients of state mental hospitals	2.4
For the mentally retarded	2.3
An ordinary apartment complex	2.2
An apartment complex for students	2.2
For unwed mothers	2.1
A high-rise condominium with units selling for $200,000 and up	2.1
A multi-story apartment building for the elderly	1.8
A large, older home that had been slightly remodeled to house 5 to 10 unrelated older persons	1.7
A cluster of single-story apartments for the elderly	1.7

[a] 3 = *very much*, 2 = *somewhat*, 1 = *not at all.*

Source: Wiley P. Mangum, "Community Resistance to Planned Housing for the Elderly: Ageism or General Antipathy to Group Housing?" *The Gerontologist* (28), 1988, p. 327.

subsidized housing (*The Aging Connection*, 1989). Furthermore, by 1995 the number of households headed by persons age 65 and over will increase from the current 17 million to 21.4 million.

Public housing began with the passage of the Housing Act of 1937, which was designed to assist low-income families. Not until 1956 was the act amended to provide public housing specifically for the elderly, making this the oldest of the federal housing programs for the elderly. In 1987, about 44 percent (537,000 units) of the nation's more than 1.4 million public-housing units were occupied by older persons.

The first housing program specifically designed for older persons was *Section 202* of the 1959 Housing Act. Currently, it is the primary federal means of financing the

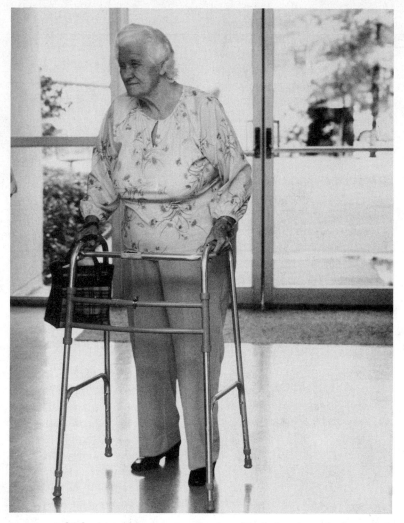

Low-rent, high-rise public housing for the elderly has been built in many towns and cities across the nation. (Nick Myers)

construction of subsidized rental housing for the elderly. Through this program, the government makes low-interest loans to nonprofit sponsors for the construction of housing for the low-income elderly.

The *Section 8* program, created under the 1974 Housing Act, provides subsidized rent to low-income families. Although not designed specifically for the elderly, it has become a major source of assisted housing units for them. Under Section 8, the Department of Housing and Urban Development (HUD) pays the difference between 30 percent of a tenant's income and the fair market rent. This program allows eligible persons to select their own dwellings instead of leaving the selection up to HUD or the local housing authority. They may choose from new construction or

Box 19.2 ## Q's and A's on Housing

Question: Is it better for an older person to live alone or live with others?

Answer: In the end, it depends on the wish of the person. The huge increase in the number of older people who live alone surely reflects their wish for the autonomy afforded by living in one's own place. Many who live alone may not like to, but the psychological cost of moving in with a relative or sharing one's domain with an unrelated person may be worse. In fact, people who live alone are somewhat more likely to visit with friends than are those who live with others, perhaps because the former feel free to make decisions on their own about entertaining.

Question: Is it preferable for older people to live in housing limited to older people or to live with people of all ages?

Answer: Once again, it depends on the person's choice, and data show that only one-third or so of older people who must move would like to live with other elderly. Thus most elderly will continue to remain socially integrated by being with younger people. However, those who do choose age-segregated living also thrive.

Question: What is the effect on older people of moving to planned housing for the elderly?

Answer: Research has been unanimous in concluding that an overall positive effect occurs in such areas as housing satisfaction, morale, activity, and social interaction after an older person moves to planned housing. Of course not all persons respond positively, and we need to know what factors lead to a favorable or unfavorable outcome.

Source: M. Powell Lawton, "Housing." In George L. Maddox (Ed.), *The Encyclopedia of Aging.* New York: Springer, 1987, pp. 335–336.

rehabilitated and existing housing of various types, including apartment hotels, single-family dwellings, and multi-family structures. Section 8 housing assistance payments are also provided for eligible lower-income families who live in projects financed under Section 202. In 1987, Section 8 provided 854,000 units of assisted housing for the elderly.

TRANSPORTATION PROBLEMS

Being without transportation has been compared to having a modern kitchen with all the latest appliances and yet having no electricity. Being denied access to transportation also denies older people access to many services and programs specifically designed for them. The lack of transportation restricts one's lifestyle, limits contacts and activities with others, and makes goods and services difficult, if not impossible, to obtain.

The transportation problems of the elderly originate mainly from these interrelated factors: (1) many older people have low incomes and cannot afford the cost of transportation; (2) physical limitations and design barriers inhibit many elderly from using public transportation as well as from driving; (3) the transportation system in our society is dominated by privately owned and operated automobiles; (4) many older people live in rural and suburban areas in which transportation systems are inadequate or nonexistent (Revis, 1971).

Public Transportation Costs

Transportation costs are sufficiently high to represent one of the largest items in the elderly family's budget. To ease this expense and to encourage the elderly's use of public transportation, by 1974 more than 145 transit systems were offering reduced fares to the elderly (Revis, 1975). Usually this reduction, which runs between 25 and

Being without a car or access to one, a significant number of older people, as well as others in the low-income bracket, are limited to public transportation. (Nick Myers)

50 percent of the regular fare, applies to those persons age 65 and over. In most cases it is offered only at nonpeak hours, when optimum service has substantially tapered off.

Though income is related to automobile ownership at all ages, the relationship is especially pronounced in the case of the elderly with their higher proportion of low incomes. The costs of buying, operating, and maintaining a car have skyrocketed in recent years, with the result that many older people cannot afford to buy a car, and others have been forced to sell theirs.

Transportation Barriers

One reason that older persons do not use public transportation or use it infrequently is that often bus and train schedules are difficult to read and interpret and signs may be confusing and illegible. Also, the information conveyed over a public-address system or by a bus driver is often inaudible or unintelligible even to younger passengers. Another obstacle to the elderly's use of public transportation is that many are afraid to walk from their homes to bus stops or subway stations for fear of street crime. In recent years, older people standing at bus stops have been primary targets for purse snatching and robbery.

Physical barriers to the older person's use of public transportation include high bus steps, rapidly closing doors, poorly placed handrails, narrow seating, and stiff exit

Although the number of licensed drivers decreases with age, the percentage of drivers among the elderly has been increasing in recent years. (Alex Harris)

doors. Equally difficult to cope with are long flights of stairs, turnstiles, and fast-moving escalators in subway stations (see Table 19.1).

Private Automobile Dominance

As Table 19.2 shows, with age the number of licensed drivers begins to decrease. But the percentage of drivers with licenses among the older population has increased. In 1986, approximately 65 percent of persons age 65 and over were licensed drivers. A decade earlier, it was about 42 percent.

Problems often arise with licensing and insurance. Many states require a reexamination of licenses at specified age levels with varying renewal periods and restrictions. Automobile insurance companies frequently discriminate against older drivers by denying them coverage, cancelling their policies, or raising their insurance rates. On the other hand, some insurance companies are now offering reductions in

Table 19.1   TRAVEL BARRIERS CONFRONTING THE ELDERLY AND DISABLED

Physical barriers	Operational barriers
Vehicles	
High step required to enter	Frequency of service
Difficult to get into or out of seats	Driver assistance/attitude
Seats not available/forced to stand	Acceleration/deceleration
Difficult to reach handholds	Information presentation
Cannot see out for landmarks	Schedules maintenance
No place to put packages	Inadequate or inappropriate routes
Cannot see or hear location information	Too many transfers
Nonvisible signs	
Terminals	
Long stairs	Employee assistance/attitude poor
Long walks	Information clarity and dissemination
Poor fare-collection facilities	inadequate
Poor posting of information	Length of stops too short
Poor crowd-flow design	Crowd flow nondirected
Insufficient seating	Little or no interface with other modes
Little interface with other modes	
Transit stops	
Insufficient shelter	Poor location:
Platform incompatible with vehicle	for safety
Inadequate posting of information	for convenience
	Not enough stops
	Information displayed insufficient or confusing

Source: Richard K. Brail, James W. Hughes, and Carol A. Arthur, *Transportation Services for the Disabled and Elderly,* Center for Urban Policy Research, Rutgers University, New Brunswick, NJ, 1976, p. 26

Table 19.2 LICENSED DRIVERS BY AGE OF DRIVER:
1986

Age	Number of licensed drivers (millions)	Percent of total age group
16–24 years	29.0	81.8%
25–34 years	39.9	92.9
35–44 years	30.6	92.4
45–54 years	20.8	91.1
55–64 years	19.3	86.9
65 +	18.8	64.6

Source: U.S. Bureau of the Census, *Statistical Abstract of the United States: 1988,* Washington, DC: U.S. Government Printing Office, 1987. Percentages computed with total population figures from U.S. Bureau of the Census, *Current Population Reports,* Series P-25, No. 1022, "United States Population Estimates, by Age, Sex, and Race: 1980 to 1987," March 1988.

premiums to more and more of the elderly who enroll in special driving-safety courses.

Being without a car or access to one, a significant number of older people are limited to public transportation and walking. As the automobile has become the primary mode of transportation in our society, public-transportation systems have rapidly declined in numbers and scope. With fewer people riding buses, bus fares

---

Box 19.3 **Are Older Drivers Capable?**

A two-year study of older drivers by the National Research Council revealed that age alone is a poor predictor of the ability to drive. As a result, the council concluded that there is no justification to restrict driving based solely on age. There is no particular age at which driving skills begin to falter.

The council found that as a group older drivers are more likely to be involved in automobile accidents. Elderly individuals may have vision problems, a slower reaction time, and difficulties in negotiating heavy traffic and merging onto expressways.

According to the study, although a driver in the over-75 group is twice as likely to be involved in an accident as those in the middle-aged group, many elderly people are capable and safe drivers who are less likely to be involved in accidents than drivers in the under-25 group. Drivers in the 65-to-74 range have a statistical record nearly as good as and sometimes better than drivers in the 25-to-54 range.

Source: "AARP in Action." Washington, DC: *AARP News Bulletin,* December 1988.

have gone up, routes have been cut back or canceled, and hours of service have been reduced. These changes, in turn, result in an even greater decline in ridership. As a consequence, many public-transit systems have experienced financial difficulties or have been forced to discontinue service altogether.

Walking becomes a problem in an automobile-oriented society. The smooth and rapid flow of automobile traffic takes precedence over pedestrian movements. Light signals, traffic and street signs, and the like are geared to the driver, not the pedestrian. Sidewalks, crosswalks, pedestrian routes, and pedestrian control signals are often absent. Often, traffic lights change too rapidly to allow one to walk safely across a street. All these factors contribute to a disproportionately high pedestrian accident rate among persons 65 and over. As Mumford (1970) notes: "To bring the pedestrian back into the picture, one must treat him with the respect and honor we now accord only to the automobile."

In a study of the mobility patterns of 709 retired persons in San Antonio, Texas, Carp (1971) found that walking was not looked on favorably as a means of transportation. Only 3 percent of the respondents said that walking was a satisfactory means of getting places; 53 percent said that it met their needs very poorly, and none felt that it met their needs well. Carp reports that the more the retirees walked, the more negative was their evaluation. The major reasons given for the unsatisfactory evaluation of walking included: (1) most destinations were beyond walking distance, especially if packages or bundles were to be carried on the return trip; (2) fear that walking might result in an injury, such as being hit by a car, falling, or being attacked; and (3) fatigue and chronic health problems.

Place of Residence

Transportation is a particularly acute problem among those elderly who live in suburban and rural areas where transportation is either inadequate or unavailable. Older rural residents who cannot drive or can no longer afford an automobile are in a much worse transportation situation than their urban counterparts. Their isolation is greater, and their incomes are generally less. A report on the transportation problems of the rural elderly found that between 7 and 9 million rural elderly lack adequate transportation and are thus severely restricted in their ability to reach needed services (U.S. Senate Special Committee on Aging, 1984). The needs of the rural elderly have received increased attention in the past few years through a series of hearings conducted by the U.S. Senate and from those who work in the field of aging.

The availability of transportation services for the elderly who live in the suburbs is also problematic. Many of the young families who moved to the suburbs following World War II have "aged in place," thus changing the age composition of suburbia. Since 1980 a greater number of persons age 65 and older live in the suburbs (10.1 million) than in central cities (8.1 million).

> The dispersion of older persons over a suburban landscape poses a challenge for community planners who have specialized in providing services to younger, more mobile dwellers. Transportation to and from service providers is a particularly critical need. . . . Institutions that serve the needs of elderly persons must be designed with supportive

Walking is an important form of transportation for this 93-year old woman. (Nick Myers)

transportation services in mind. . . . Primary transportation systems or mass transit must ensure accessibility from all perimeters of the suburban community to adequately serve the dispersed elderly population. (U.S. Senate Special Committee on Aging, 1988)

FEDERAL LEGISLATION

The federal government did not give major policy attention to the issue of transportation for older people until 1970 with the passage of an amendment to the Urban Mass Transportation Act of 1964. The amendment authorized that a proportion of its funding be directed toward the special transportation needs of the elderly and hand-

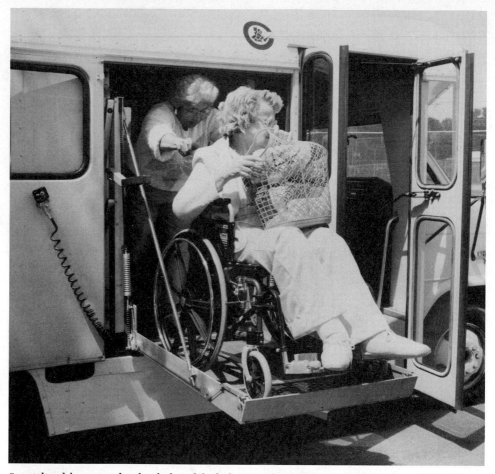

Specialized buses with wheel chair lifts help to make those elderly with physical disabilities more mobile. (Nick Myers)

icapped. It recognized for the first time that the needs of the elderly and handicapped differed from those of other transit users. The amendment stressed that public transportation should be made more available to the elderly and handicapped through the planning and designing of more adequate facilities and services for them. Since 1979, all new public-transit buses purchased with federal assistance have been required to have barrier-free design features that will make them more accessible to the elderly and handicapped.

Another significant development was the passage of the National Mass Transit Act in 1974, which provided for reduced transit fares for the elderly. This Act stipulated that fares paid by the elderly and handicapped during off-peak hours in all projects funded by the Department of Transportation were not to be more than one-half of those paid by general users during peak hours.

Finally, the Surface Transportation Assistance Act of 1978 provided funding at the federal level to support public-transportation costs for non-urban and rural areas that are in need of transportation assistance. This legislation has greatly benefited the elderly and handicapped, as they are the ones who are the most isolated and less mobile in these areas.

SUMMARY

1. Most elderly people live in their own mortgage-free homes. Generally, their homes are older and of lower quality than those of younger persons. Because the elderly often spend a disproportionate share of their income on property taxes, all states now have instituted some type of property tax relief program.

2. About one-fourth of the housing units occupied by the elderly are rental properties. Older renters tend to be 75 years of age and over, female, and living alone. Another housing alternative for the elderly is mobile-home living. Although such an arrangement usually offers security, companionship, and low-cost housing, in some cases the elderly are subjected to unfair rent increases by mobile-home-park owners. Some elderly prefer living in inner-city hotels in which they have single-rooms, share a bath, and have no kitchen unit. This type of housing, referred to as single-room occupancy, or SRO, allows the resident to live in a downtown location and to be within walking distance of stores and eating places.

3. Shared housing usually involves an elderly homeowner who rents out a room or rooms in exchange for companionship and services. Two other types of living arrangements for older persons are accessory apartments and ECHO (Elder Cottage Housing Opportunity). An accessory apartment concerns the conversion of extra space in a home to a separate, independent living unit, whereas the ECHO option involves a free-standing unit usually placed to the back or side of a single-family home so that older persons may live near their adult children.

4. The first public housing specifically designed for the elderly was provided by Section 202 of the 1959 Housing Act. Presently, it provides for the construction of subsidized rental housing. The Section 8 program, which provides subsidized rent to low-income families, has become an important source of assisted-housing units for the elderly.

5. The transportation problems of the elderly stem from low incomes, design barriers, the dominance of the private automobile, and inadequate or non-existent transportation systems in some rural or suburban areas.

6. Attention to the transportation needs of the elderly began with the passage of an amendment in 1970 to the Urban Mass Transportation Act of 1964. Legislation passed in 1974 provided for reduced fares for the elderly, and in 1978 federal funds were allocated to support public transportation for non-urban and rural elderly in need of transportation assistance.

KEY TERMS

circuit breaker
single-room occupancy hotels
(SROs)
shared housing
accessory apartments

Elder Cottage Housing Opportunity
(ECHO)
Section 202
Section 8

FOR FURTHER STUDY

Chillis, Robert D., Seagle, James F., & Seagle, Barbara M. (Eds.) (1982). *Congregate housing for older people.* Lexington, MA: Lexington Books.

A collection of articles dealing with issues related to the nature of congregate housing, its design, and its maintenance.

Powell, M. Lawton (1980). *Environment and aging.* Monterey, CA: Brooks/Cole.

Focuses on how older persons live and cope with the stresses of different environmental features.

Streib, Gordon F., Folts, W. Edward, & Hilker, Mary A. (1984). *Old homes—new families: Shared living for the elderly.* New York: Columbia University Press.

Deals with shared-living households that provide a primary group environment for older persons and offers them services and companionship in a non-institutional setting.

Wachs, Martin (1979). *Transportation for the elderly.* Berkeley, CA: University of California Press.

Contains the results of a two-year study regarding the future transportation needs of the elderly.

Reading

Loners, Losers, and Lovers

Joyce Stephens

The following excerpt is from a participant observation study of elderly tenants in a single-room occupancy slum hotel (SRO), the Guinevere. These tenants are truly loners in that they have broken all ties with families and friends, and make no attempt to form new, long-lasting relationships. Their world is characterized by extreme alienation and isolation. The following paragraphs describe the type of interaction that occurs between the elderly men and women who live in the Guinevere.

The world of the Guinevere aged is a society composed largely of men, and in this way it is typical of SRO hotel populations. Elderly women are considerably less likely to wind up in slum hotels; they tend to live with family members or in their own homes or apartments. The few women who do live in the hotel are in significant ways differentiated from the men.

The dominant values of the SRO society come into conflict with the values supporting sex-role identities in the case of the women. For them, the consequences include a reduced capacity to cope, a greater vulnerability, and an even more extreme isolation and loneliness than the men endure. . . .

The theme of "trying to get something out of them" runs through the relationships established between the men and women. The men are wary and suspicious; the women bitter and resentful. Each assumes that the other is trying to use and exploit him (or her). . . .

The elderly women in the Guinevere Hotel have not always lived in slum hotels; they have not always been alone. They, more than the men, are likely to have been married, to have raised children, and to have been linked to the conventional life presented by the larger society. Roles of a lifetime, especially those that play such a crucial part in buttressing selfhood, do not die easily; thus, the elderly women are prone to attempt to retain these role definitions, behaviors, and associated values regarding self and others, and to act in terms of them. Behaviors so inappropriate to

Joyce Stephens, *Loners, Losers, and Lovers.* Seattle: University of Washington Press, 1976. [Readers interested in full source citations and footnotes are referred to the original source.]

the SRO society are countered by sharp rebuff. The men are wary and determined not to be drawn into relationships which they cannot afford, and to this end they define the women as foolish, boring, and a burden if one is silly enough to give them an opening. The men avoid the women and, in so doing, contribute to a deepening sex-related isolation.

The women appear more vulnerable, less successful at coping, unreconciled to their status. A favorite and familiar story of these women tells of the solicitous care still available to them from their families. All they have to do is pick up the telephone and make a call, and the son, daughter, grandchild, whoever, will come for them, take them home, care for them. There is no viable basis for these daydreams: children are gone or dead, grandchildren are uninvolved or, in some cases, have actively avoided and refused to have anything to do with these women. Nevertheless, it is a favorite story, even if no one believes it.

The women are less in tune with things; they are not aware of current events, political issues. They, more than the men, try to live in the past or in their recon-structions of imagined pasts, in which they are surrounded by loving families, in which they are "somebody." The adjustment of the women to the world of the SRO is more fragile, more tenuous than that of the men. Ironically, their inappropriate need to revive ways of relating that would allow intimacy is looked upon in the society of SRO tenants as a cover-up for an exploitative ruse, another hustle.

The result is that the women become even more isolated and alone than the men, for the men have relinquished the need for intimacy in order to take care of more basic needs, whose satisfaction precludes all forms of intimacy and dependence. The women are shunned, and efforts on their part to initiate contact are viewed with suspicion. Holdover values from another time—family, children, friendship—are inimical to survival in the world of the SRO. The world of the SRO is a tough, hostile place which phases out the need for intimacy and dependency. For the women, this involves giving up roles and attitudes more sharply and profoundly bound up with their sex identity than is true of the men.

One stratagem for dealing with this conflict which comes to assume a major part in the adjustment of these women is a self-imposed isolation. What begins as enforced isolation merges into a kind of self-isolating as they learn (perforce) to live according to the taken-for-granted meanings that define the reality of the SRO society. That they have not learned as well as the men is occasionally revealed in their conversa-tions which center around past status, prestige, and familial relationships, and in their furtive attempts to make contacts with the men and establish quasi-family relation-ships. Such lapses are generally met with derision and hostility, so that, over time, these violations of the norms are so carefully guarded against that the women appear to be more unapproachable, independent, and forbidding than the men. But once we get past their chilly exterior, we find vulnerable and unbelievably lonely people. Their management of social identity represents an enforced adaptation in order to make it in the world of the SRO.

The avoidance that characterizes relationships between the sexes does not mean that there is no inter-sex mingling. The men occasionally seek out female company— typically, the services of a prostitute. Next to sports, the horses, and alcohol, sex is the most popular topic of conversation among the men. The hotel is worked by prostitutes from the area and a few part-timers who live in the hotel itself. When the social security checks arrive on the first of the month, the "prossies" arrive also; all ages, often on narcotics, and attended by the ever watchful eye of their "sponsor" (pimp), they pour into the hotel bar to work the old men. Additionally, there are a few middle-aged and elderly women living in the hotel who "trick" now and then to pay their rent. . . .

Romances between the elderly tenants are rare—sixty-year-old men do not want sixty-year-old women. When romances do develop, they are short-lived and not a subject of bragging. The men will not bring a lady friend into the bar to show her off and are reticent about such relationships. In the words of one seventy-three-year-old woman, "romances here are torrid and end abruptly, usually over trivia." Long-term relationships between these men and women are precluded by the conflicting demands and expectations referred to earlier. The women attempt to use the relationship as a vehicle to establish a quasi-family situation—the man will be asked to do things for her, to accompany her downtown, to have dinner with her. The man views such expectations as exploitative and possessive on her part. At this point, the relationship usually ends. Several of the men reported prior relationships that they had formed with elderly female tenants, only to have to break them off because they became to "possessive," "jealous," and "demanding." Since the men define the women as seeking a relationship that they cannot afford and do not want, they prefer the pay-as-you-go services of the prostitute.

For their part, the elderly women define the men as interested only in sex. (They are correct; the liaison with the prostitute constitutes a casual, sharply delimited transaction in which no ongoing demands are made of the relationship.) Involvement with a man is a source of unrelenting gossip, and any friendship between the sexes is always assumed to be a front for the fact that they are sleeping with each other. The strict proscription against "getting too friendly" applies to male-female interaction particularly. Both men and women are inclined to interpret overtures on the part of the other as attempts at exploitation.

The institutionalization of mutual suspicion and avoidance that characterizes contacts between the elderly men and women has more severe consequences for the women, who must rely on a decreased sociability pool. They do not work and, therefore, do not form work relationships; they do not usually frequent the hotel bar and do not have drinking cronies. And the women, cut off from the company of men, do not relate well to each other either. The attitudes of the women toward each other revolve around the axes of hostility and jealousy. They are in a permanent kind of competition with one another.

Interaction between the women takes the form of one-up-manship, with the goal being to establish that one's family and background are definitely superior to the other. This behavior ought not to be viewed as a feminine counterpart to the "conning" behavior of the hustlers, who are attempting to demonstrate superior abilities over rivals in their occupation. The competition of the hustlers serves as a socially binding force, in that it defines their common interests, skills, and experience. For the women, however, this competitive arena intensifies their bitterness over a life that they cannot leave and cannot live, and drives deep barriers between them.

One informant spoke knowingly of the fragility of relationships between the women:

Friendships between them [women] never last more than a few days. Then they fall out over some paltry matter. Usually, over gossip. Some of the feuds and vendettas are years old. Friendships between the men are more permanent because they are hard-headed and practical. They need each other for their work. Luther [a carny boss], now how could he take care of all that by himself? No, he's got to have someone he will know for sure is going to be there; he's got to have his workers. He makes a lot of contacts and holds on to them. But, the women, they're so out of touch with the mainstream. The men don't have anything to do with them. Well, because they can see that they're just interested in using them. Do this for me; oh, won't you drive me there? And, of course, the women are quite boring; they live in the past. Not like the men, who have to keep up with the times. But to get back to the women, no, I don't know any of them who have stayed friends. Friends? They're too jealous and suspicious of one another, always gossiping and backbiting on each other. And sooner or later, it gets back, and there you are, they're not speaking anymore.

All in all, one cannot help being struck by the poignant appearance of these taciturn and suspicious ladies, with their wigs that don't fit and their veiled hats that, like banners, put forth a brave front. Their loneliness and isolation are tangible. Their adoption of an exaggerated unapproachability underscores what is a poorer mastery of the coping strategies needed to make it in the world of the SRO.

. . . The values of a lifetime, which served to support personal and social identity, are not appropriate in the world of the Guinevere and must be sloughed off. The fracturing of identity that results is the heavy price that these elderly women must pay in order to continue as SRO tenants. They have little choice: they, no less than the men, are locked into their situation by age, poverty, ill health, and their own desire to maintain independence.

Chapter
20

Deviance

*I*f an instructor confided to her Sociology of Aging students that while driving to class she got a ticket for running a stop sign they would probably react with indifference. But if she announced that on the way to class she ran over a student and did not stop her car or even look back, their reaction would probably be one of moral indignation. Although these two acts differ by a matter of degree and content, both are deviant because they violate norms, and both are crimes because the norms violated are formalized by law.

Although all crime is considered deviant, all deviance is not a crime. Crime is but one type of deviant behavior. Mental illness and alcoholism, for example, are considered deviant behavior but are not illegal. *Deviance*, then, is defined as behavior that violates a norm, whereas *crime* is behavior that violates a norm that has been formally enacted into criminal law.

Because any behavior that violates a norm is considered deviant in the sociological sense, all of us are deviant in certain situations and at certain times. But as we mentioned previously, deviance is a matter of degree because norms vary in their importance. In Chapter 3, "Age Norms and Age Status," we discussed how some norms (folkways) are not considered too important, and their violation results in only mild disapproval; however, other norms (mores) are considered extremely important, and their violation results in strong disapproval. Being late to class, for example, violates a folkway and is only mildly deviant, whereas elder abuse, which violates one of society's mores, is considered quite deviant behavior.

DEVIANCE AND RELATIVITY

Because deviance exists only in relation to norms, like norms it varies by culture, social context, and time. Mother-in-law avoidance, for example, is widely practiced in many societies. In some places a man is not permitted to eat with his mother-in-law, look at her, speak to her, or even mention her name. If in such a place a man sees his mother-in-law coming down a path, he will hide behind a tree or dive into some bushes to avoid her. In his culture such behavior is considered appropriate for a son-in-law, whereas Americans would consider a man behaving in this fashion mentally disturbed.

Deviance also varies with the social context in which it occurs. It is perfectly acceptable behavior for two older men to play checkers in the park. But if they moved their checker game inside a church while a service was in progress, then their behavior would be considered unacceptable.

Another way deviance varies is by time. In early America a healthy man who stopped working merely because he reached a certain age would have been considered strange indeed. At that time retirement as we know it today was unheard of. Most men continued to work until they could no longer work (Fischer, 1978). Today a man who continues to work past the customary retirement age of 65 is deviating from the norm. People would wonder why he continues to work and constantly ask such questions as, "Aren't you too old to be working?" or "When are you retiring?"

SUICIDE AND THE ELDERLY

All forms of deviance, with the exception of suicide, tend to decline with age. The suicide rate for older persons is probably much higher than the statistics show. Many older people commit suicide by slow, indirect means, such as self-starvation, not taking medication, or not seeking needed medical help. Such suicides as that described in the following example never make the official statistics.

One elderly man who was confined to a wheelchair became deeply depressed because of his dependent state and the fact that he was a burden to his wife. He lost all will to live, and one day he suddenly stopped eating. Despite the pleadings of his wife and his adult children, he stubbornly refused all food. Within a short time he was dead. (Personal communication)

The suicide rate for the white male is highest of any group; this is true throughout the life course, and the rate steadily increases from age 45 (see Table 20.1). In the United States, suicide rates for white males age 85 and over are about 13 times higher than the rates for white elderly females. The reason why older men are more prone to commit suicide is not clear. Depression is usually given as the main reason, but this state evidently occurs as frequently among older women. Also, women are less successful in their suicide attempts than men, and many women expect or want to be stopped in the act. Men are more violent in their attempts and leave little doubt about their intentions.

Suicide rates vary not only by sex but also by race and marital status. Elderly suicide rates are lower for nonwhites than for whites with the exception of Americans of Japanese, Chinese, and Filipino origin (McIntosh & Santos, 1981). In addition, nonmarried persons are more likely to take their own lives than married persons. Those most at risk for suicide are elderly widowers (Berardo, 1968, 1970).

Emile Durkheim's classic work *Suicide,* first published in 1897, offers an explanation of suicide that has served as a guide for many of the sociological studies on suicide that have followed. In this volume, Durkheim describes four types of suicide, including egoistic and altruistic. He explains both the altruistic and egoistic types in terms of the degree to which people are integrated into society. In the egoistic type of suicide, persons lack the emotional attachments and psychological support that are provided by involvement in group life. Their ties to others are minimal. Elderly

Table 20.1 SUICIDE RATES IN THE UNITED STATES FOR PERSONS 5 YEARS OR OLDER BY AGE, SEX, AND RACE: 1985 (Number of Deaths per 100,000 Population in Specified Group)

Age range	White males	White females	Black males	Black females
5–14	1.3	0.5	0.6	0.2
15–24	22.7	0.7	13.3	2.0
25–34	25.4	6.4	19.6	3.0
35–44	23.5	7.7	14.9	3.6
45–54	25.1	9.0	13.5	3.2
55–64	28.6	8.4	11.5	2.2
65–74	35.3	7.3	15.8	2.0
75–84	57.1	7.0	15.6	4.5
85+	60.3	4.7	7.7	1.4

Source: National Center for Health Statistics, *Health, United States, 1987,* March 1988.

suicide often tends to be of this type in that older people are often socially isolated as a result of the end of their participation in the nuclear family through the death of a spouse and in the occupational structure through retirement. In other words, they are weakly integrated into society. Consequently, in times of emotional crisis an elderly person, especially a widower, has no one or nowhere to turn and, thus, is not constrained against self-destruction.

Whereas *egoistic suicide* results from weak social integration into society, *altruistic suicide,* the second type of suicide delineated by Durkheim, results from individuals' being so strongly integrated into group life that their own self-interests become subordinate to those of the group and they are willing to give their lives for the good of the group. Altruistic suicide was formerly practiced among the aged Eskimos when they became a burden to their families or community and could no longer keep up with the strenuous nomadic life. The story in Chapter 5, "Cultural Diversity," of a Japanese grandmother who wished to die when she thought that she had outlived her usefulness is another illustration of altruistic suicide (Stenback, 1980; Osgood, 1985).

EXPLANATIONS OF DEVIANCE

There are a number of approaches to understanding deviance. Biological and psychological explanations focus on the nature of the deviant person, whereas sociological theories of deviance concentrate on how cultural and social factors shape deviant behavior. Four of the more prominent sociological theories of deviance are now discussed and related to aging.

Durkheim's Anomie Theory

One of the earliest sociological explanations of deviance is contained in Durkheim's study of suicide, mentioned earlier. According to Durkheim, a third type of suicide, *anomic suicide,* results from conditions in which the normal equilibrium of society becomes disturbed, such as during a depression or a period of economic boom. Traditional values and norms become weak or absent, and, therefore, individuals lack guidelines to regulate their behavior. He called this situation "anomie," meaning normlessness or lack of regulation. Some writers contend that a similar condition exists for the elderly in that our society does not specify a definite role for them, and their lives are socially unstructured. In other words, there is a normlessness in the later years in which there are few guidelines for appropriate behavior. As a result, some older persons suffer from feelings of futility, uselessness, and despair and because of these feelings, following Durkheim's thesis, are prone to take their own lives (Rosow, 1973, 1974; Osgood, 1985).

In opposition to anomic, Durkheim called his fourth type of suicide "fatalistic." He considered this type the result of excessive regulation and social oppression. Durkheim gave scant attention to fatalistic suicide, as he felt it was not relevant in our civilized society. According to Kastenbaum (1985), studies suggest that the institutionalized elderly often have serious inclinations to bring their lives to a quick end.

As he so aptly puts it, "visiting a geriatric facility today (or some of our reservations for Native Americans), Durkheim might take his own concept more seriously." (See Figure 20.1.)

Merton's Anomie Theory

Building on Durkheim's concept of anomie, Robert Merton redefined anomie in 1938 to refer to a widespread frustration that occurs when there is an acute gap between cultural goals and socially approved ways to achieve them. Financial success, for example, is a major cultural goal in American society. Persons who retain this goal but find that they are blocked in achieving it through the approved means (hard work and education) may seek success through disapproved means (theft and embezzlement). Merton (1968) called this type of response "innovation."

Ritualism, another source of deviance, involves rejecting the cultural goals but still abiding by the means, sometimes to the point of compulsion. An example of this type of adaptation would be an employee who drops out of the competitive struggle to get ahead by permanently lowering his aspirations and choosing job security over success and routinized activity over trying something new. The employee continues to work diligently at the same job year after year, just marking time until retirement.

Another type of deviance delineated by Merton is *retreatism.* In this mode of adaptation the individual rejects both the cultural goals and the conventional means to achieve them. As Merton points out:

> Retreatism seems to occur in response to acute anomie, involving an abrupt break in the familiar and accepted normative framework and in established social relations, particularly when it appears to individuals subjected to it that the condition will continue indefinitely . . . as, for example, in the case of retirement from the job being imposed upon people without their consent and in the case of widowhood.

Since the widow or widower and the retiree have lost a major role, they experience, to some degree, a feeling of isolation. Retreatism seems to occur more fre-

	WEAK	STRONG
INTEGRATION	Egoistic	Altruistic
REGULATION	Anomic	Fatalistic

Figure 20.1. Durkheim's four types of suicides. Each of these types of suicides suggest a relationship between the individual and society—weakly or strongly integrated into society, or weakly or strongly regulated or constrained by society.

quently among isolated widows. This pattern of response is illustrated by an elderly widow who is reluctant to get involved with others. She dwells on happier times in the past to help ease an unhappy present.

> Sometimes I think, "I just can't stand to be here by myself"; then I say to myself, "You are, so you might as well make the most of it." . . . I'm probably not as dependent on other people as I might be. I've rather got used to being alone. . . . I live in the past, I guess. I have lots of memories of good times, and when I get to feeling lonesome I just try to remember those. (Blau, 1981)

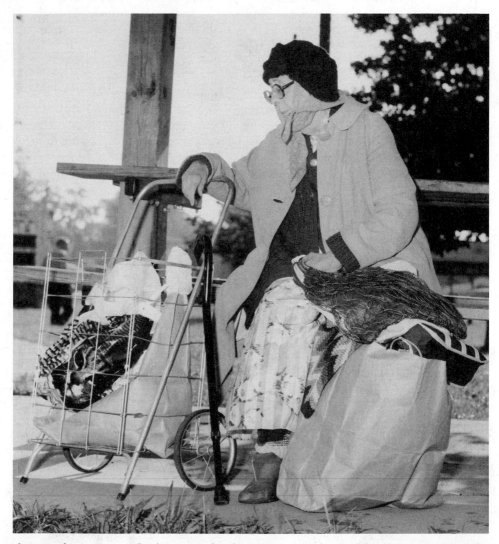

Shopping-bag women who live an isolated existence in urban public places represent the retreatist pattern of deviance. (Nick Myers)

Shopping-bag women also provide an example of this type of deviance with its abrupt break in established social relations and norms. These women live on the streets simply because they have no money to live elsewhere. They must carry all their possessions with them in shopping bags, and because of this they are referred to as "shopping-bag women" or "bag ladies." They have been aptly described as "aging women with swollen ankles and ulcerated feet, toting bags, shuffling slowly across the street, poking into garbage cans, slumped on a park bench, dozing in doorways, sprawling across library steps, huddled among their possessions in dreary waiting rooms of train and bus stations" (Rousseau, 1981).

These homeless women come from a wide variety of social classes and ethnic groups. They are usually old, suffering from the effects of poverty, poor health, and sometimes mental impairment. Some of these women have adapted to life on the streets and prefer living on the outside to living in an institution. As Hand (1983) notes:

> For some women now on the street, their present predicament is the end result of the attenuation of social bonds over many years through deaths, desertion, loss of family, illness, or unemployment until the final catastrophe—loss of a room or a check. . . . Some had lived for years in a situation of narrow social margin. Some had been recently completely dependent on an institution that had met every subsistence need. For others, their present situation of social isolation and physical aloneness was not something they previously had experienced or expected. They had had families, friends, homes and jobs and then, rather rapidly, were bereft of them.

Shopping-bag women tend to be loners, living in their own private worlds. They gravitate toward crowds but manage to keep to themselves; their interaction with others, even other shopping-bag women, is minimal. As Merton notes, retreatists are reluctant to enter into new social relationships with others, the adaptations they make are largely private, and they tend to continue in their apathetic state.

Labeling Theory and the Social Breakdown Syndrome

Another approach to explaining deviance is *labeling theory*. This theory focuses on the process by which some people label other members of society as deviant. According to labeling theorists, it is not a person's acts but rather the way in which he or she is labeled as a deviant that is important.

Edwin Lemert (1951, 1967), who formulated the labeling perspective, distinguished between primary and secondary deviance. Everyone, for example, violates social norms from time to time in ways that are considered deviant. An executive may pad his or her expense account, or an elderly person receiving Social Security may not report some of his or her earnings to avoid a cut in benefits; a person may experiment with drugs or homosexual behavior. The person evading the norm will not think of himself or herself as a deviant. Such behavior is usually short-lived and goes unnoticed by others. This is considered *primary deviance*, whereas *secondary deviance* involves norm violations that are discovered and made public by one's family, friends, employer, or a law-enforcement agency. The individual is then labeled by others as a deviant and typed as a pervert, crook, eccentric, incompetent, or whatever name suits the circumstances. People begin to respond to him or her in terms of this label. As a consequence, the person accepts the label and begins to see himself or herself as a deviant and then behaves in accordance with the label. The following is an example of how the label of mental illness transformed the life of an elderly man.

> Mr. M., an older Japanese gentleman . . . after his wife's death, was admitted to a care home since he had no family to attend to him. He was adjusting quite well, although gradually, to his wife's death by visiting and developing interests in calligraphy, tutoring, and lecturing to students at the local university. However, he did have sporadic depressive events during the holiday season, being alone for the first time without his wife. . . . A graduate student had befriended him and provided support during this period. However, when called upon by the care home to help them deal with his garrulousness, she immediately set up an appointment with a psychiatrist without disclosing the nature of this appointment with Mr. M., even after his many queries as to the kind of doctor to whom she was referring him. [She finally told Mr. M. that he was "manic-depressive."] In this case, the gentleman, who was perfectly capable of handling his own affairs and who had previously not shown signs of maladjustment (other than eccentricity) began to exhibit aberrant behavior. He thus unwillingly accepted the misdiagnosis of "crazy" and began to exhibit those behaviors. The consequence was destructive. The home began fearing his behavior, now labeling him as a psychiatric case and pulling all support which had previously been given him and which he needed even more at this time. (Kobata, Lockery & Moriwaki, 1980)

Labeling has been used by Kuypers and Bengtson (1973) to address the issue of age-related decline. They suggest that the elderly's self-concept as well as their ability to mediate between self and society are related to the kinds of social labeling they experience as they make the transition from middle to old age. Kuypers and Bengtson propose a four-stage cycle that they call the *social breakdown syndrome* (see Figure 20.2).

The first stage is based on the premise that the elderly are highly susceptible to social labeling because they are deprived of positive feedback and support from others in their social world. This susceptibility is due to ambiguous norms, their loss of roles, and their lack of reference groups. Second, because of this lack of positive feedback and support from family, friends, and significant others, the elderly become dependent for self-labeling on the larger society, which often stereotypes and characterizes them as useless, sick, crazy, incompetent, and so on. Third, those older persons who accept such negative labeling learn to act, for example, as if they were incompetent and previous skills of independence are lost. Finally, they accept the external labeling and begin to think of themselves as incompetent, setting the stage for the vicious cycle of increasing incompetence. In other words, the label proves to be a self-fulfilling prophecy.

CRIME

One of the most widespread forms of deviance in our society is crime. Contrary to popular belief, overall the elderly have the lowest victimization rates of any age group in our society. This is true for each of the crime categories with the exception of "personal larceny with contact" (purse snatching and pocket picking). In this cate-

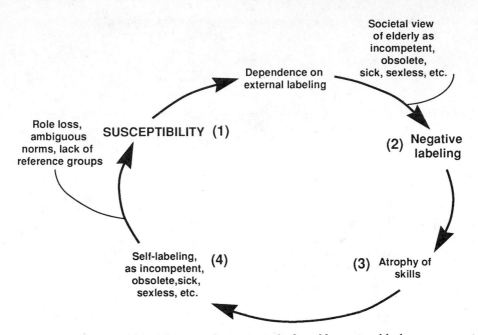

Figure 20.2. The social breakdown syndrome as applied to old age. An elderly person receives negative messages that he or she is incompetent. The older person incorporates this label into his or her self-concept, which in turn produces a cycle of negative feedback.

gory, the rate of crime against the elderly is not very significantly different from that of other age groups (see Table 20.2).

Analyzing data from the National Crime Survey, Whitaker (1987) reports that when crimes are committed against the elderly, in some ways the crimes tend to be more serious than those committed against younger persons. Among the elderly, violent-crime victims age 75 and over were more likely to be injured and to receive medical treatment than victims age 65 to 74. (Box 20.1 presents a summary of the major findings from this survey.)

Fear of Crime

Despite their low victimization rates, fear of crime pervades the lives of many older people. Surveys reveal that the elderly view fear of crime as a major problem. Both the 1975 and 1981 Harris polls found that the elderly ranked fear of crime "a very serious problem," even above health and not having enough money to live on.

The fear of crime greatly diminishes the quality of life for large numbers of older people and restricts their mobility. Much of this fear may come from the fact that older people are acutely aware of their vulnerability to victimization. This condition is probably best summed up in the expression "crib jobs," used by young hoodlums to refer to the crimes they commit against the elderly. In their eyes, robbing an older

Table 20.2   AVERAGE ANNUAL VICTIMIZATION RATES AND NUMBER OF
VICTIMIZATIONS, BY AGE OF VICTIM AND TYPE OF CRIME:
1980–1985

	Age of victim			
	12–24	25–49	50–64	65 +
Crimes of violence	67.5	34.0	11.3	6.0
Robbery	11.4	6.0	3.4	2.7
Assault	54.2	27.1	7.8	3.2
Aggravated	18.4	9.1	2.7	1.0
Simple	35.8	18.0	5.1	2.3
Crimes of theft	126.5	82.4	46.1	22.3
Personal larceny with contact	3.5	2.8	2.8	3.1
Personal larceny without contact	123.0	79.6	43.4	19.2
Household crimes	371.4	242.6	164.4	102.7
Burglary	144.3	86.9	59.4	44.0
Household larceny	196.8	136.5	92.3	53.7
Motor vehicle theft	30.3	19.3	12.7	5.1

*Note: The victimization rate is the annual average of the number of victimizations for 1980–1985
per 1000 persons or households in that age group. Detail may not add to total because of rounding.*

Source: Catherine J. Whitaker, ''Elderly Victims,'' *Bureau of Justice Statistics Special
Report.* Washington, DC: U.S. Government Printing Office, 1987.

person is as easy as taking the proverbial candy from a baby. The special vulnerability
of the elderly to crime results from several factors:

1. Older people have diminished physical strength and are less able to defend
   themselves or to escape from threatening situations. They are also less likely
   to defend themselves for fear of being injured. Diminished hearing and
   vision may also contribute to their victimization.
2. Because of low income, many older people can afford to live only in the
   poorer sections of the city, places where crime rates are the highest. Thus
   they are close to the groups most likely to victimize them—the unemployed,
   the drug addicts, and teenage school dropouts.
3. Many older people live alone, which further increases their chances of
   victimization. Also, the elderly are often unaccompanied on the streets and
   on public transportation.
4. Many older people are without cars and depend on either walking or public
   transportation. This increased exposure makes them an easy target for potential criminals (Goldsmith, 1976).

How does fear of crime among the elderly vary by sex, race, income, and size of
the community? Clemente and Kleiman (1976) explored this relationship in a study
based on national surveys conducted by the National Opinion Research Center in
1973 and 1974. They found that women were more likely to admit fear of crime than

---

Box 20.1 **Elderly Victims of Crime: Some Major Findings from the National Crime Survey**

- Elderly violent-crime victims were more likely than younger victims to face offenders armed with guns (16 percent vs. 12 percent).
- Elderly violent-crime victims were more likely than younger victims to report that the offenders were total strangers (62 percent vs. 47 percent).
- The elderly were more likely than victims under age 65 to be victimized by a violent crime at or near their own homes (45 percent vs. 22 percent). Those 75 and older were the most likely of any age to be victimized in this location (55 percent).
- About 46 percent of elderly victims of violent crimes were attacked, and 29 percent were injured, about the same proportions as victims under 65.
- The elderly were less likely than younger victims to attempt to protect themselves during a crime incident (52 percent vs. 72 percent).
- Among victims who reported financial losses, the elderly reported large losses ($25 or more) about as often as did younger victims.
- Among the elderly, certain groups were more vulnerable to crime than others: Males, blacks, separated or divorced persons, and urban residents generally had the highest victimization rates.

Source: Catherine J. Whitaker, "Elderly Victims," *Bureau of Justice Statistics Special Report.* Washington, DC: U.S. Government Printing Office, 1987.

---

men: About 70 percent of elderly females expressed fear of crime, compared with 34 percent of the elderly males. Aged blacks were more fearful of crime than aged whites; Clemente and Kleiman report that nearly 70 percent of the aged blacks were afraid to walk around in their neighborhood at night alone. Forty-seven percent of the aged whites reported that they were afraid to do so. People at higher income levels reported less fear of crime than those in the lower income brackets. Presumably, those with more income live in better neighborhoods with lower crime rates and thus feel less threatened. Finally, fear of crime decreases as one goes from large cities to rural areas. Three-fourths of the elderly respondents in large cities (where crime rates are highest) expressed fear of crime, compared with one-fourth of those in rural areas.

Fear of crime has profoundly affected the lives of many elderly, especially those who live in the inner cities. There have been reports of older persons' sleeping in the daytime because they were too frightened of break-ins to sleep at night. Many adapt to the threat of crime by making fortresses of their homes and apartments and going outside as little as possible. Social and recreational activities are kept to a minimum. Many refuse to go out after dark, or even after 3 or 4 o'clock in the afternoon when children begin coming home from school; others are afraid to leave their homes or apartments at any time. (See Box 20.2.)

Box 20.2 **Woman Terrorized by Burglars Dies in Sweltering Apartment**

CHICAGO—An elderly woman, described as so terrorized by burglars that she kept all her windows closed and a length of pipe by her bed, died of circulatory disease and heat stroke in her sweltering apartment.

The 79-year-old woman's body was found in the apartment she refused to leave since the purse-snatching 1½ months earlier, says her niece.

"She had all the windows sealed in last week's heat. . . . It must have been 125 degrees in there when we found her," the niece said. "She had barricaded herself in there out of fear of burglars and robbers."

Source: The Associated Press, *The Knoxville Journal*, July 30, 1987.

Crimes of Fraud

In contrast to crimes of force, which more frequently victimize the low-income and minority elderly, confidence games are nonviolent crimes that prey upon the more affluent elderly. In California, the San Francisco and Los Angeles police departments report that 90 percent of the confidence victims are over the age of 65 and are mainly women (Younger, 1976).

Confidence Games   A popular scheme for victimizing older persons is called the *"pigeon drop,"* believed to be the oldest confidence game in existence, having originated in China more than 1000 years ago (St. John, 1977). There are several variations to this scheme, but essentially it works like this: Two girls work together, usually in large shopping malls or department stores. When they spot an elderly, well-dressed woman, one girl approaches the "pigeon" and begins a conversation to try to win her confidence. The second girl then joins them, explaining that she has just found an envelope or a bag. She opens it and finds what appears to be a roll of money with no identification. The girl then offers to go to her lawyer, banker, or employer for advice on what the three of them should do with the money. On her return, she says that her lawyer will keep the money for them for a period of six months, and if no one claims it by then, they will divide the money three ways. But in the meantime, to show "good faith," each of the three must match her share of the find with her own money. The elderly victim then withdraws money from her savings account and gives it to the girl to take to the lawyer for safekeeping. Of course, she never sees the money again. Sometimes these girls get away with up to $25,000 or more in a single incident (see Box 20.3 for a variation of this scheme).

Another favorite confidence game is the "bank examiner" scheme. The swindle works this way: A man calls an elderly woman on the phone, having gotten her name from the telephone book. He identifies himself as a bank examiner. He explains that he is trying to trap a dishonest teller at the bank and asks her to help in apprehending the culprit. Sometimes he offers to pay for her assistance. If she agrees, the "bank examiner" then asks her to go to the bank and withdraw all her money. Later he phones saying that the plan worked, and the culprit has been caught. He offers to send a bank messenger or an FBI agent to pick up her money and redeposit it into her account. The messenger arrives, takes the money, and gives the woman a receipt. She never sees the messenger or her money again.

Another way swindlers exploit older people is by posing as Social Security agents. They extort money from Social Security beneficiaries either by claiming that their victims must pay a set fee to assure continuation of their benefits, or by promising that upon payment of a certain fee, their Social Security benefits will be increased. Another gimmick is to claim that an overpayment has been made and to ask the victim to return the money to the agent.

Consumer Frauds Consumer frauds range from land swindles involving worthless and imaginary property to the use of high-pressure sales techniques that result in elderly people's paying for thousands of dollars' worth of dancing lessons. Though consumer frauds prey on people of all ages, there are some schemes of which the elderly are the favorite targets. The elderly are frequently victimized by unscrupulous insurance agents, who rely upon their fear of illness and disability. For example, an insurance agent told an elderly couple in Ohio that the Medicare program would soon run out of funds and sold them $787 worth of health insurance. In Pennsylvania, six insurance agents teamed up to take the life savings of an 80-year-old woman. Within a three-year period, she paid more than $50,000 to buy 31 different health-insurance policies, all of which were permitted to lapse (Fanning, 1974).

To many older people, their home represents their most prized possession and

---

Box 20.3 Elderly Woman Is Swindled

An elderly woman was swindled out of $7,000 cash and two rings she valued at $13,000 Thursday by two women flim-flam artists who used the "pigeon drop," police said.

The 83-year-old woman was approached in the parking lot of a grocery store by two women who said they had found a bag containing $63,000 in cash by her car.

They offered to split the money with her if she would give them some "good faith" money, police said. Accompanied by one of the women, the elderly lady went to the bank, cashed a check, and gave them the proceeds, plus money from her purse and two rings. This tactic is commonly called the "pigeon drop."

One of the women said she worked at a department store and that her boss would give the older woman her share of the pot.

When the elderly woman arrived at the store, according to the police report, "she found that the boss did not exist and the women were nowhere to be found."

Source: *Knoxville News-Sentinal*, April 2, 1988.

greatest financial asset, so they are particularly susceptible to home-repair schemes. Roving home repairmen offer to do such tasks as installing aluminum siding or painting a house at phony bargains. Their workmanship is shoddy, and their materials are inferior; the aluminum siding soon falls off and the paint washes off in the first rain. Sometimes older people are visited by bogus home inspectors who use scare tactics, saying their homes need repairs. One woman in Pittsburgh had a man come to her house posing as a furnace inspector. He convinced her that her furnace was danger-ously faulty, although in reality it was in good condition. She paid him $14,000 in cash for a new one along with additional equipment (Bennett, 1974).

Real-estate schemes capitalize on the dream of some older people to spend their last days in a warm, sunny climate. Operating through the mail, the brochures promise prospective buyers a retirement paradise in such states as Arizona, New Mexico, and Florida. Particularly appealing to persons on retirement incomes are those advertisements that offer homesites for a low down payment and a low monthly payment. Many advertisements for such lots are deceptive: Persons often find that they have purchased lots in remote areas without access to roads and with no pro-vision for utilities.

Many lonely elderly women fall prey to dance-studio swindles. They are pres-sured and flattered into paying in advance for thousands of hours' worth of dance instructions through a scheme of "lifetime" memberships. A woman may be bilked into buying several such memberships, sometimes costing her her entire life savings or her home. Butler (1975) relates how a lonely 69-year-old woman, in an effort to find companionship, paid $10,000 for dancing lessons. When she became bedridden and tried to get a refund, the studio refused. One elderly widow was conned into eight "lifetime" memberships, which entitled her to 3,100 hours of instruction at a cost of $34,913 (Ducovny, 1969).

Medical Quackery   Older persons are the victims in about seven out of ten cases involving medical fraud coming to the attention of the criminal justice system. The American Medical Association estimates that about a billion dollars a year is wasted on quack schemes. Not only are the elderly victimized financially, but by delaying needed medical attention, they are also endangering their health and sometimes even their lives. The fact that they commonly suffer from chronic illnesses makes them prime targets for "guaranteed cures" and "miracle medicines."

Arthritis, one of the most common chronic conditions of the elderly, is also one of the most profitable for medical frauds. Quack medicines for this condition include alfalfa tea, sea water, and "immune" milk. The devices and methods that have been promoted to cure arthritis almost defy the imagination. One popular article has been uranium ore–lined mittens. Another is a metal disk, which is clipped to the ankle while a person immerses his or her foot in cold water. The Inducto-Scope claimed to cure arthritis through magnetic induction: The arthritic places the rings of the device over the affected areas and inserts the plug into a wall socket, but this only exposes the person to electric shock. Then, there is a device which is supposed to expand all the atoms of the body through its "Z-Rays."

Equally unsound medically as these arthritis "cures" are the thousands of alleged treatments for cancer promoted by quacks. Probably one of the most creative cancer "cures" was an instrument that was called the "Sonus Film-O-Sonic." It "silently" played tape-recorded music and had electrode pads that were attached to the patient.

Appliances such as dentures, eyeglasses, and hearing aids are another lucrative area for quacks. Hoping to save money, many older people fall victim to mail-order dentures at cut-rate prices. They receive ill-fitting dentures that are painful and make eating regular foods impossible. Eyeglasses are also sold through the mails. One mail-order operator claimed to sell lenses ground in accordance with prescriptions; the Federal Trade Commission examined some of the glasses and found 10 out of 15 pairs to be improperly ground. Hearing aids are often sold by unscrupulous door-to-door salesmen. The price is high and the hearing aid is generally useless.

Why are the elderly so vulnerable to confidence games and fraudulent practices? First, being on a fixed income, many elderly are anxious to take advantage of an opportunity that they think will save them money or that promises them additional money. Next, some older people are lonely and frequently taken in by a friendly salesperson or the attentive con artist. Also, many elderly are naïve about the schemes designed to separate them from their money. Impaired hearing may prevent proper understanding of a sales explanation, poor vision may interfere with reading the fine print on a contract. Finally, many older people, facing illness and pain and the possibility of death, are desperate to try almost anything, no matter how outlandish, that promises them a relief or cure.

ELDER ABUSE

Elder abuse, like child abuse and wife battering, is not new, but it is only recently that it has been brought to the public's attention and recognized as a social problem. The abuse and neglect of the elderly in nursing homes came to public notice in the 1970s, and since that time it has been well documented through congressional investigations and state and federal hearings (see Chapter 18, "Health"). Beginning in the late 1970s and early 1980s, attention shifted from the elderly's institutional mistreatment to their mistreatment in family settings.

Estimates reveal that 32 elderly persons per 1000 are the victims of elder abuse (Pillemer & Finkelhor, 1988). Much elder abuse goes unreported because of the fear of reprisal; in the case of elderly parents, they also suffer from the guilt and embarrassment of having raised a child who abuses them. Most studies find that victims of elder abuse are female, white, widowed, and over the age of 75. They tend to be frail and highly dependent. The abuser is often an adult child or relative who lives in the same household (Quinn & Tomita, 1986).

Types of Mistreatment

Elder abuse and *elder neglect* are often used together, and sometimes they are used interchangeably. However, they are not the same. *Elder abuse* refers to the mistreatment of an older person through physical or psychological injury or financial exploitation by a caregiver. *Elder neglect* refers to the failure of a caregiver to fulfill an important need of an older person when resources are available to do so. Abuse, then, is distinguished from neglect on the basis of intent: Abuse involves the committing of an act, whereas neglect involves the omitting of an act (Hudson & Johnson, 1986). Neglect may be classified as either passive or active. *Passive neglect* occurs when a elderly person is left alone for long time periods or isolated, whereas *active neglect* occurs when the caregiver withholds from the older person food, medicine, and other necessities for daily living (Hickey & Douglass, 1981).

Two of the most common types of elder abuse are physical abuse and psychological abuse. Physical abuse involves slapping, beating, or restraining an older person. In one well-publicized case, a daughter chained her 81-year-old father to a toilet for a week and beat him with a hammer every time he dozed off. Psychological abuse involves verbal and emotional abuse as, for example, frightening, threatening, insulting, and humiliating an older person (Hickey & Douglass, 1981). One case was reported in which an elderly woman living with her family was not allowed in the kitchen during mealtimes while the rest of the family ate. She was told to stay in her room and not associate with them because she was not wanted (Robinson, 1985).

Financial exploitation, another type of abuse, occurs when a relative, caregiver,

The lights in this building in Nashville, Tennessee were turned on in such a way as to increase the public's awareness of elder abuse. (Tennessee Commission on Aging)

or some other person improperly or illegally uses or manages an older person's money or property. In some instances elderly persons are forced to give up all their assets.

> An ailing Florida man was swindled out of a 40-acre orange grove by a nephew whom he trusted. The nephew fed him liquor with his medications, then threatened him physically until he signed. The old man had only his social security pension left. "I guess I signed too many papers," he said. (Robinson, 1985)

Abuse may also take the form of a violation of elderly persons' rights, which includes not allowing them to vote or declaring them mentally incompetent and committing them to a mental institution without due process of law.

Reasons for Abuse

Researchers have suggested a number of factors, some of them overlapping, that contribute to the mistreatment of older persons by their families. These factors include:

1. *Environmental conditions.* Some researchers suggest that abuse of the elderly may be due to family conflict and crises that often stem from such factors as crowded living conditions, marital problems, insufficient income, unemployment, and alcoholism. An additional source of stress may result from the caregivers' being caught in the middle between two generations—children and elderly family members (Hickey & Douglass, 1981).
2. *Dependency of the elderly.* It seems that the most abused older persons are those who are impaired physically or mentally or both. Taking care of an elderly person who is frail, incontinent, and/or mentally disordered is a demanding job that may build up resentment and anger in the caregiver. In addition, elderly persons may contribute to this resentment by being demanding or tyrannical.
3. *Early relationship with parents.* Parents who mistreated their children when they were growing up sometimes have children who retaliate by mistreating them in their old age. Also, the motive for revenge tends to be stronger if the child believes that the mistreatment was intentional (Rathbone-McCuan & Hashimi, 1982).
4. *Pathological caregivers.* This category includes caregivers who are psychotic, sadistic, mentally retarded, or drug addicted. One study found that 43 percent of those who abused elders had drug problems, whereas 31 percent had a history of mental illness (Wolf, Strugnell & Godkin, 1982).
5. *Functional impairment of the caregiver.* Sometimes the caregiver is an elderly spouse or relative who is frail, ill, or mentally disordered and may be unaware that he or she is being abusive or neglectful. For example, an elderly caregiver's lack of strength may be the cause of an elderly person's falling, or the caregiver may be suffering from dementia and forget to give food or medication to the dependent elder.

Up to this point, we have been discussing crimes committed against the elderly. We now turn to a discussion of crimes committed by the elderly.

THE OLDER CRIMINAL

When we think of older persons, the picture of decent, honest, law-abiding citizens usually comes to mind. It has been well documented that crime gradually declines with advancing age. Older people in all societies have a lower crime rate than any other adult group. Yet in recent years news magazines, newspapers, and television have devoted much attention to the growing number and seriousness of crimes committed by the elderly. Some scholars (Feinberg, 1984; Malinchak, 1980) have reported an increase in elderly crime, whereas others have challenged this view (Steffensmeier, 1987; Wilbanks, 1984; Sunderland, 1982). Is this so-called "geriatric crime wave" fact or fiction? Is "white-haired crime" becoming a social problem?

Some writers have speculated that the elderly are turning to crime as a response to their declining economic position or the loneliness of growing old in our society. Alston (1987) points out that as the older population continues to increase, so will the number of older offenders. She also suggests that since people are remaining healthier and more active in old age today than ever before, there is a greater potential for them to commit crimes.

Types of Offenses

Older persons commit the same crimes as those of other age groups; there is no one crime or crimes in which older persons are the major offenders. However, the elderly do have different crime patterns from those of younger persons. The most frequent offenses of the elderly regarding arrest tend to be alcohol related, such as driving while under the influence (DUI) and drunkenness, followed by larceny-theft (especially shoplifting). Incidentally, these three offenses also rank high for the younger age groups, though in a different order.

To determine if the elderly's involvement in crime has increased or decreased in recent years, Wilbanks (1984) analyzed data from the FBI *Uniform Crime Reports* (UCR) for 1970 and 1980. He found no increase in total arrests for all offenses for the elderly; in fact, he noted a decline for the decade. In another study of UCR arrest statistics for the years of 1964 and 1984, Steffensmeier (1987) found that elderly crime is about the same now as it was 20 years ago, although there have been fluctuations in arrest rates for some offenses. For example, there have been increases in larceny-theft and driving under the influence (DUI) and decreases for public drunkenness, disorderly conduct, gambling, and vagrancy. If any change has taken place, according to Steffensmeier, it is "a small decline in the relative criminality of the elderly across the majority of the UCR offenses, including 'serious crimes.'"

How, then, do we account for the recent report of an increase in serious crimes by the elderly? Steffensmeier suggests an answer.

> The UCR lists larceny-theft as an Index or serious crime; larceny-theft accounts for virtually all of the increases from 1964 to 1984 in Index crimes by the elderly. But larceny-theft should not be defined as a "serious" crime and lumped together with offenses such as robbery and murder. Most elderly arrests for larceny-theft are for shoplifting or related minor thefts. Neither the general public nor criminal justice

officials regard these minor larcenies as serious crimes. Furthermore, the UCR arrests data on larceny do not distinguish between petty (e.g., under $50) and grand thefts.

There is no evidence of an elderly crime wave at this time. Older people continue to commit fewer crimes and fewer serious crimes than do their younger counterparts (see Table 20.3). According to Wilbanks (1984), the debate should not be about what types of crimes the elderly commit but rather about why they commit so few as compared with other adult age groups.

The Elderly Inmate

Persons 65 years of age and older make up less than 1 percent of the total prison population. The typical older inmate tends to be male, white, unmarried, and usually with less than a high school education (Dickinson & Wheeler, 1980; Alston, 1986). Elderly inmates are described as loners who live quietly without bothering anyone and serve their time with little notoriety (Wiegand & Burger, 1979). Gillespie and Galliher (1972) interviewed inmates in a state penitentiary and found that men in their sixties and seventies claimed that prison had made them age faster than normal. They blamed prison for their physical and mental decline. Aging in prison tends to differ from aging in the community in that prisoners are less aware of chronological age, and productivity, occupation, and retirement are not important issues (Reed & Glamser, 1979).

Long or repeated prison terms may result in institutional dependency. There is some truth in the stories about older men who after serving long prison terms break the law so that they can go back to prison. Many older persons after spending years in prison find it difficult to cope with life on the outside; they miss the security and routine of prison life. As Aday (1984) points out, for those elderly whose ties to family and friends have been broken, whose health is failing, and whose resources and job opportunities are meager, prison may be a refuge.

Table 20.3 MALES ARRESTED BY OFFENSE CHARGED AND
AGE: 1986

| | Percent distribution | | | | |
Serious crimes	18–24	25–44	45–54	55–64	65+
Murder	32.6	49.1	5.6	2.5	1.5
Forcible rape	30.0	47.6	4.5	1.8	0.7
Robbery	39.4	36.2	1.3	0.4	0.2
Aggravated assault	29.6	49.1	5.5	2.3	0.9
Burglary	35.3	27.0	1.2	0.4	0.1

Source: U.S. Bureau of the Census, *Statistical Abstract of the United States: 1988*. Washington, DC: U.S. Government Printing Office, 1987.

SUMMARY

1. *Deviance* is defined as any behavior that violates a norm. But because not all norms are equally important, deviance is a matter of degree. Because deviance exists only in relation to norms, it varies by culture, time, and place. All forms of deviance, except for suicide, tend to decline with age. The elderly white male has the highest suicide rate of any group in our society. Durkheim delineated four types of suicides, including egoistic and altruistic. Egoistic suicide occurs when the individual is not well integrated into the group, whereas altruistic suicide occurs when the individual is over-integrated into the group.

2. Many theories have been proposed to explain deviance. Deviance occurs, according to Durkheim, when there is a lack of guidelines and norms to regulate one's behavior. He called this situation "anomie," meaning normlessness. Some writers claim that such a condition exists for the elderly in our society. Merton redefined Durkheim's concept of anomie to refer to a widespread frustration that occurs when there is a gap between cultural goals and approved ways to achieve them. He delineated several types of deviance that can occur in response to this condition. These include innovation, ritualism, and retreatism. "Shopping-bag women" provide an example of retreatism in which the individual rejects both the cultural goals and the conventional means of achieving them.

3. According to labeling theorists, a violation of a norm that is discovered and made public will label a person as a deviant. People then begin to respond to the person in terms of this label. As a result, the person accepts the label and begins to see himself or herself as a deviant and behaves accordingly. Kuypers and Bengtson use labeling theory to explain age-related decline in the elderly. They propose a four-stage cycle that they call the "social breakdown syndrome."

4. A common form of deviance in our society is crime. Although the elderly have the lowest victimization rates of any age group in our society, the fear of being victimized affects the lives of substantial numbers of older people. The only crime category in which the elderly are victimized at about the same rate as the general population is personal larceny with contact (purse-snatching and pocket picking).

5. Older persons are particularly vulnerable to crimes of fraud. The most common scheme for victimizing the elderly is the "pigeon drop." Consumer frauds that bilk older persons of their money include real-estate frauds and unnecessary health insurance and home repairs. Dance studios often con older women into buying thousands of dollars' worth of dancing lessons that they can never use.

6. Because the elderly commonly suffer from chronic illnesses, they are especially susceptible to medical quackery. Arthritis treatments are one of the lucrative medical frauds. In an effort to save money, older persons lose thousands of dollars a year on ill-fitting dentures, useless hearing aids, and improperly ground eyeglass lenses.

7. Although the terms *elder abuse* and *elder neglect* are often used interchange-

ably, they are not the same. *Elder abuse* refers to mistreating an older person physically, psychologically, or through financial exploitation. *Elder neglect* refers to the failure of a caregiver to fulfill an older person's needs when resources are available to do so.

8. Older persons have lower crime rates and different patterns of crime from their younger counterparts. The most common offenses of the elderly regarding arrest tend to be alcohol related. Persons age 65 and over make up less than 1 percent of the total prison population.

KEY TERMS

deviance	*labeling theory*
crime	*primary deviance*
egoistic suicide	*secondary deviance*
altruistic suicide	*social breakdown syndrome*
anomic suicide	*pigeon drop*
anomie theory	*elder abuse*
ritualism	*elder neglect*
shopping-bag women	*passive neglect*
retreatism	*active neglect*

FOR FURTHER STUDY

Alston, Letitia T. (1986) *Crime and older Americans.* Springfield, IL: Charles C Thomas.
  Discusses victimization of the elderly and its cost as well as older criminals and their treatment.

Carthy, Belinda & Langsworthy, Robert (Eds.) (1988). *Older offenders.* New York: Praeger.
  Deals with criminology and criminal justice as they relate to older offenders.

Ducovny, Amram (1969). *The billion dollar swindle: Frauds against the elderly.* New York: Fleet.
  Deals with the vulnerability of older people to a host of deceptive practices, including medical quackery, investment swindles, and nursing-home frauds.

Kates, Brian (1985). *The murder of a shopping bag lady.* San Diego: Harcourt Brace Jovanovich.
  The true story of a homeless woman that provides valuable insight into a "second America" populated by individuals and families without places to live.

Osgood, Nancy J. (1985). *Suicide in the elderly.* Rockville, MD: Aspen Systems Corporation.
  Examines the problems of elderly suicide in detail and focuses on prevention and intervention strategies.

Quinn, Mary Joy & Tomita, Susan K. (1986). *Elder abuse and neglect.* New York: Springer.
  A comprehensive work that serves both as an introduction to the subject and a guide to effective intervention.

Shover, Neal (1985). *Aging criminals.* Beverly Hills, CA: Sage.
  An excellent study that explores criminal behavior and the aging process.

Chapter
21

Death and Dying

Death is no longer the taboo topic that it once was, but for many of us, it still is difficult to talk about. Some of us are so terrified at the thought of it that we block it out of our minds. We not only avoid the subject, we also avoid the terminally ill. We are uncomfortable when a dying person wants to talk about his or her dying. Displays of grief embarrass us. Many persons are at a loss for words when they meet a bereaved person and try to avoid him or her if at all possible. This avoidance and denial of death contribute toward making death a social problem. It is a social problem at the individual level, because many people do not know how to cope with impending death except possibly to fear it. Next, it is a social problem for the survivors, who often do not know how to handle their feelings or how to prepare and readjust their lives before and after the death of significant others. Finally, it poses a problem for medical personnel, who are oriented toward maintaining and prolonging life (Perry & Perry, 1976).

In many preindustrial societies, the largest number of deaths occurs at the beginning of the life course. For instance, among the Sakai of the Malay Peninsula, about half of the babies die before the age of three. In the Kurnai tribe of Australia, 40 to 50 percent of children die before the age of ten (Blauner, 1966). In contrast, in the United States and other industrialized nations, the majority of deaths are of elderly people. Death thus has become increasingly a phenomenon of the old in our society. Because of this, the problems related to death are those related to aging.

ATTITUDES TOWARD DEATH

Many people assume that because older people have relatively little time left and death is more imminent for them, they are more fearful of death than younger persons are. Research suggests that just the opposite is true. One study found that middle-aged persons (45 to 54) had the greatest fear of death, whereas the older age group (65 to 74) expressed the least amount of fear. There also appears to be no increase in fear of death among older persons, even as the time of death approaches (Bengtson, Cueller, & Ragan, 1977). In fact, the finding that fear of death diminishes with age is one of the most consistent findings in the area of death (e.g., Kalish & Reynolds, 1981; Keller, Sherry, & Piotrowski, 1984).

Fear of Death

Kalish (1976) proposes several reasons why older people are less fearful of death. First, older persons place less value on their lives and recognize that their future is limited. Also, after having lived to old age, most elderly people feel that they have received their fair share of years and that any additional years are a bonus. Third, as people grow older, they frequently have to deal with the deaths of others, which helps to socialize them to accept the appropriateness of their own deaths.

Although the elderly tend to view death with acceptance, not fear, most studies reveal that the elderly think and talk more about death than do those in other age groups. For most older people, death is a frequent and important topic (Riley & Foner, 1968). This preoccupation may be due not only to the imminence of their own deaths but also to their store of death-related experiences, having outlived many friends and relatives.

Fear of death is associated with religious beliefs. Most studies concur that persons who are the most religious are the least fearful of death. Some studies show a curvilinear relationship between religiosity and fear of death. The very religious and irreligious have the least fear of death, whereas the uncommitted or uncertain tend to be the most fearful (Kalish, 1985).

The fact that older people are not usually disturbed by the fear of death may be because, in most respects, they are ready for death. Kastenbaum (1969) observes that although elderly persons face death in a number of ways, two orientations toward death tend to be predominant. The first orientation involves getting ready for death by putting one's house in order, withdrawing from social activities, and then waiting

"Our Mother E. S. Jackson fell asleep. . . ." (Nick Myers)

for the end. The second orientation embodies the "I'll die with my boots on" philosophy; recognizing that death can come at any moment, these individuals remain active to the end. At the same time, they are ready for death. The death of Rosie, a resident of Merrill Court, a small apartment building housing mostly elderly widows, illustrates this second pattern.

> Among the widows, there was a "good" and a "bad" way to die. Rosie's death especially was the community's example of "the right way to die." She was praised as much for remaining active to the end as for "being ready" in both the practical and philosophic sense. Her will and burial were prearranged and she was on good terms with "her people." As they looked around them, some residents were said to be "living on borrowed time" while others had not "lived out their mission." But whatever the case, they were agreed that one should try to face death rather than turn one's back on it, all while living fully to the end. (Hochschild, 1973)

The widows of Merrill Court shared a collective concern for being ready for and facing up to death. They talked freely about death among themselves and accepted it as a fact of life. Marshall (1975) found a similar orientation toward death among residents of Glen Brae, a retirement community located on the eastern seaboard of the United States. About 400 residents lived in Glen Brae; their ages ranged from 64 to 96, the average age being 80.

Socialization for Death

Marshall says that people in communities composed of elderly residents, such as Merrill Court and Glen Brae, socialize one another for impending death. Residents are fairly successful in accepting their approaching deaths as legitimate, that is, appropriate and nonproblematical. They look upon death as part of the natural scheme of things that characterize the social reality shared with others. By legitimating death in this way, they are able to face death—their own and those of others—with equanimity.

Marshall points to three factors that contribute to the process of legitimation of death at Glen Brae: management of grief, talking about death, and role modeling. In

---

Box 21.1 **The Life Review**

The tendency of older persons toward self-reflection and reminiscence used to be thought of as indicating a loss of recent memory and therefore a sign of aging. However, in 1961 Robert N. Butler postulated that reminiscence in the aged was part of a normal *life-review* process brought about by realization of approaching dissolution and death. It is characterized by the progressive return to consciousness of past experiences and particularly the resurgence of unresolved conflicts that can be looked at again and reintegrated. If the reintegration is successful, it can give new significance and meaning to one's life and prepare one for death, by mitigating fear and anxiety.

This is a process that is believed to occur universally in all persons in the final years of their lives. . . . It is spontaneous, unselective, and seen in other age groups as well; but the intensity and emphasis on putting one's life in order are most striking in old age. In late life, people have a particularly vivid imagination and memory for the past and can recall with sudden and remarkable clarity early life events. There is renewed ability to free-associate and bring up material from the unconscious. Individuals realize that their own personal myth of invulnerability and immortality can no longer be maintained. All of this results in a reassesment of life, which brings depression, acceptance, or satisfaction. . . .

As part of the life review, one may experience a sense of regret that is increasingly painful. In severe forms it can yield anxiety, guilt, despair, and depression. . . . The most tragic life review is that in which a person decides life was a total waste.

Some of the positive results of reviewing one's life can be a righting of old wrongs, making up with enemies, coming to acceptance of mortal life, a sense of serenity, pride in accomplishment, and a feeling of having done one's best. . . .

One of the greatest difficulties for younger persons is to listen thoughtfully to the reminiscences of older people. We have been taught that this nostalgia represents living in the past and a preoccupation with self and that it is generally boring, meaningless, and time-consuming. Yet as a natural healing process it represents one of the underlying human capacities on which all psychotherapy depends. The life review as a necessary and healthy process should be recognized in daily life as well as used in the mental health care of older people.

Source: Robert N. Butler and Myrna I. Lewis, *Aging and Mental Health*. St. Louis: C.V. Mosby, 1982.

the first year of its existence, the residents formulated a community policy about the treatment of death that has remained in effect. This point of view is expressed in the following excerpt from the *Glen Call,* the resident newspaper.

> It is forecast that we can expect a death amongst us as frequently as one every two weeks. . . . Our responsibility, therefore, involves a point of view, a determination. Either Glen Brae will turn into a place shrouded in a funeral parlor atmosphere of tears and perpetual sadness, or it will play its intended role—the best place to be when crises occur. It is suggested that . . . we reduce to a minimum the prolongation of sorrow, the discussion of pain, loss, and tragedy. . . . (Marshall, 1975)

In line with this thinking, both the death event and grief are low-keyed at Glen Brae. Deaths are marked only by a discreet notice on the bulletin board and in the *Glen Call.* Funerals are held elsewhere, and the external appearances of grief are minimized. One resident, in discussing the behavior of the survivors, observed: "Most of the time, outside of going to funerals, they pick up and go on in a very remarkable fashion. And they do it purposefully—for the other residents. It's very obvious."

At the same time, death is discussed openly and freely among the residents:

> When people begin to think about their impending deaths, they frequently talk with others about it; this proves beneficial in assisting them to come to terms with it. Glen Brae is, in a sense, organized to provide such assistance by encouraging a high level of social interaction which allows death to be dealt with informally.

Glen Brae also provides the residents with role models that allow them to anticipate their own dying. These models give them a clearer idea of what their own death might be like and assist them in planning for it. Many residents feel that there is an appropriate pattern for dying. For example, one resident stated: "I think the thing that is feared is dying, not death. You see you want to die nobly, and you're afraid you won't be able to." Another said that she would like to die gracefully. "I aim to die without yelling, 'Hey, I'm going.' "

THE PROCESS OF DYING

Dying is viewed by Glaser and Strauss (1968) as a status passage in which the dying person is passing between the status of being alive and the status of being dead. Earlier, we discussed other types of status passages, such as those between adolescence and adulthood or between work and retirement. These passages are regulated by rules designating when the passage should be scheduled, a sequence of prescribed steps, and the actions that must be carried out by various participants in order to accomplish the transition. In contrast to most status passages, "dying is almost always unscheduled; second, the sequence of steps is not institutionally prescribed; and third, the actions of the various participants are only partly regulated."

The Dying Trajectory

To describe the process of going from normal health to the downhill pattern of dying, Glaser and Strauss use the term *trajectory of dying,* which has two major characteristics—duration and shape. *Duration* means that the trajectory of dying takes place over time, and *shape* refers to the fact that it can be charted. Durations of some patterns are slow, whereas others are quite sudden. The shape may be all downhill, or it may go down and then up before going down again. Different patterns include, for example, the familiar lingering pattern, in which the patient is expected to die sooner than he or she does, resulting in a slow downward trend. In the short-reprieve pattern, the patient receives an unexpected postponement of death. Another pattern is the abrupt surprise trajectory: A patient is expected to recover but suddenly dies. Then there is the suspended sentence, in which the patient is sent home from a hospital and may live for several years. Finally, there is the entry–re-entry pattern, in which the patient goes slowly downhill and returns home several times between hospital stays.

Each of these trajectory-of-dying patterns rests on the expectations of medical personnel about how a patient's dying will proceed (duration and shape). In addition, dying trajectories also depend on the nature of the disease or the condition from which the patient suffers. A patient dying from cancer will have a different trajectory from one suffering a fatal heart attack.

A Stage Theory of Dying

From interviews with terminally ill patients, Kübler-Ross (1969) has proposed that persons aware of their impending death pass through five psychological stages in preparation for it: denial, anger, bargaining, depression, and acceptance. In later writings she has said that not every person goes through each stage in sequence, and many individuals may move back and forth between stages.

The first stage, denial ("No, not me"), is characterized by a person's refusing to accept the reality of impending death or feeling that some mistake has been made. Some people frantically go from one doctor or treatment center to another in search of a more positive or satisfactory diagnosis.

In the second stage, denial is replaced by feelings of anger or rate ("Why me?"), which the person directs at family, friends, and medical personnel. Much of this anger is quite justified. Kübler-Ross states that we too would be angry if all our life's activities were suddenly interrupted, "if we had put some hard-earned money aside to enjoy a few years of rest and enjoyment, for travel and pursuing hobbies, only to be confronted with the fact that 'this is not for me.' "

In the third stage, bargaining ("Yes me, but . . ."), the person tries to make a deal with fate to bargain for a postponement of the event. Much of the bargaining is likely to be between God and the patient. Many patients promise "a life dedicated to God" or "a life in the service of the church" and to others in exchange for some additional time.

The next stage is depression ("Woe is me!"), characterized by a sense of great loss. Persons grieve not only for what they have but for what they are in the process of losing. It is a time for saying goodbye to family and friends. This grief helps prepare persons to make the break with those they care about and to separate themselves from this world.

The last stage is acceptance ("It's time for me to go"). The patient now feels neither depression nor anger. There is almost an absence of feelings. This is a time when the dying individual "will contemplate his [or her] coming end with a certain degree of quiet expectation." One patient described it as "the final rest before the long journey." Whitman and Lukes (1975) relate the case of a 70-year-old widow who had reached this stage of acceptance after having undergone surgery and treatment for cancer with no sign of success. In preparation for death, she had made her own funeral arrangements and put her estate in order. She then said goodbye to her family and friends and withdrew into herself to await her fate. But an unusual phenomenon occurred—her condition began miraculously to improve. The hospital personnel were then faced with the task of completely reversing her outlook and attitude from one of dying to one of living.

Although Kübler-Ross's *stage theory of dying* has received considerable recognition and has done much to establish the topic of death and dying as one of general concern and study, at the present time there is little evidence available to support the theory. Some writers have proposed other stages, whereas others maintain that the process of dying is stageless. Kastenbaum (1978) observes that this theory suffers from methodological weaknesses and conceptual flaws. Furthermore, he notes that it does not take into account the type of illness and treatment as well as one's lifestyle and ethnicity.

TWO CONTROVERSIAL ISSUES

Two of the most controversial issues in death and dying are whether or not the dying patient should be told about the medical prognosis, and how long artificial means should be used to keep a hopelessly ill or mentally disabled patient alive.

The Right to Know

The situation involving patients who are terminally ill is defined by hospital personnel, their families, and themselves. Glaser and Strauss (1965) distinguish four types of awareness situations that may develop: closed awareness, suspicion awareness, mutual pretense awareness, and open awareness. The first type, closed awareness, refers to a situation in which patients do not know that they are dying; the information is kept from them by hospital personnel and by family members. In the second situation, suspicion awareness, the patients suspect what their real condition is and attempt to confirm or negate these suspicions. The third situation is mutual pretense awareness, a situation in which patients know they are dying, and the hospital and family members know, but everyone pretends that death is not imminent. Finally, there is the situation of open awareness, in which all concerned are fully aware of what is happening, and thus there is no need to conceal the truth from the patients.

It is often recognized that the closed awareness context is easier in some ways on the dying patient's family, especially if the patient is the kind of person who is not likely to accept death with fortitude. But it can be a very painful and difficult experience for family members to keep the truth from the dying person, especially if the dying trajectory is slow. Closed awareness is generally more comfortable for hospital personnel because an unaware patient is usually easier to handle and less disruptive to hospital routine. On the other hand, the situation may subject nurses to a great deal of strain, as they must constantly be on guard against disclosure.

In an open awareness context, the patient is now openly recognized as having the status of a dying person:

> Once a patient has indicated his awareness of dying, the most important interactional consequence is that he is now responsible for his acts as a *dying* person. He knows now that he is not merely sick but dying. He must face that fact. Sociologically, "facing" an impending death means that the patient will be judged, and will judge himself, according to certain standards of proper conduct. These standards, pertaining to the way a man handles himself during his final hours and to his behavior during the days he spends waiting to die, apply even to physically dazed patients. Similarly, certain standards apply then to the conduct of hospital personnel, who must behave properly as humans and as professionals. (Glaser & Strauss, 1965)

Glaser and Strauss make the point that the problem concerning awareness of dying is more than just a technical one; it is a moral one as well. It raises the question, Has anyone (including the physician) the right "to deny a dying person the opportunity to make peace with his conscience and with his God, to settle his affairs and provide for the future of his family, and to control his style of dying, much as he controlled his style of living?" According to Weisman (1972) "to be informed about a diagnosis, especially a serious one, is to be fortified, not undermined." He notes that many patients realize the diagnosis for themselves long before they are told. Ineffective treatment, persistent symptoms, evasive answers to questions, and cues from relatives and family convey this information indirectly.

In the past most physicians chose not to tell their patients the truth in cases of terminal illness. They were often evasive and ambiguous in discussions with their patients. In a survey of staff members of a Chicago hospital in the mid-70s, Okeon (1977) found that almost 90 percent of the physicians said they preferred to deceive terminal patients by withholding information. Their policy was to tell the patient as little as possible, using the most general terms.

Today there is far more support for informing the patient than in the past, from both physicians and the general public. In fact, the majority of physicians as well as the general public now favor open awareness. Kalish (1985b) points out that "patients are seen as participating more in their own care, and the right to have access to relevant information is also seen as more appropriate."

Although awareness of approaching death gives patients a chance to complete important work, to get their affairs in order, and to make plans for their families, awareness can have certain disadvantages. Other people may not approve of the way the dying persons are managing their death and may try to change their plans. Also, for patients who are unable to face death, an awareness of dying may result in more anguish and less dignity than if they did not know.

Some nurses prefer working with patients who are aware of their impending death. There is no need for pretense, and the nurse can help the patient prepare to confront death. One nurse with considerable experience in dealing with dying patients expresses these feelings about her own death:

> Personally when my time comes, please don't read me scriptures or poetry. Hold my hand and let the light come in. Don't leave me alone because I haven't been through this

experience and it scares me. When my time comes I hope I can accept it. Life is sweet to its bitter end. (Abernathy, 1979)

The Right to Die

As the pain and suffering of a patient with a terminal illness increase, or as the dying patient's life is being prolonged by machines though the patient is comatose, the question arises, How long should life be maintained? Morison (1971) cites three possibilities open to the physician attending the dying patient: (1) use all possible means to keep the patient alive; (2) discontinue artificial means or heroic measures, but continue ordinary procedures; and (3) take some steps to hasten death and the speed of the downhill trajectory of dying.

Although most people admit that there comes a time when it is proper to shift from heroic measures of keeping a patient alive to ordinary medical procedures, there is much less agreement about the decision to accelerate the termination of life. Permitting a patient to die naturally, rather than employing heroic measures to sustain life, is referred to as *passive euthanasia*. When a physician or another person deliberately terminates the life of a patient who is hopelessly ill or nonfunctional, it is called *active euthanasia* (Berdes, 1978). The line between passive and active euthanasia is difficult to draw.

> The more one thinks of actual situations, however, the more one wonders if there is a valid distinction in allowing a person to die and hastening the downward course of life. Sometimes the words "positive" and "negative" are used, with the implication that it is all right to take away from the patient something that would help him to live but wrong to give him something that will help him to die. (Morison, 1971)

In discussing euthanasia, another distinction is the degree of voluntarism involved on the part of the dying patient. In cases when patients are mentally competent and conscious, they may request or consent to passive or active euthanasia—then their death can be termed *voluntary euthanasia*. Imposing passive or active euthanasia upon a patient who is incapable of giving consent, as in the case of a comatose patient, is referred to as *involuntary euthanasia* (Berdes, 1978).

To prevent the prolongation of life when death is inevitable, some persons complete documents referred to as *living wills*. These documents, distributed by the Concern for Dying, an educational council, are intended for future use in the event that persons are unable to participate fully in decisions regarding their treatment during a terminal illness. The living will, prepared while individuals are mentally competent, informs others of their wish not to prolong the inevitability of death by artificial means or heroic measures (see Figure 21.1). In 1976, California became the first state to enact a living-will law. In the past decade, 38 states have followed suit. Although each state's legislation varies, the procedures for executing the living will are generally similar to those of a last will and testament.

Whether or not euthanasia should be regulated or legalized has been the subject of much controversy. Many cases of active euthanasia that have come to the attention of the public involve elderly persons. One of the earliest cases to receive international attention occurred in 1950; it involved Dr. Herman Sanders, who injected air into the

My Living Will
To My Family, My Physician, My Lawyer
and All Others Whom It May Concern

Death is as much a reality as birth, growth, maturity and old age—it is the one certainty of life. If the time comes when I can no longer take part in decisions for my own future, let this statement stand as an expression of my wishes and directions, while I am still of sound mind.

If at such a time the situation should arise in which there is no reasonable expectation of my recovery from extreme physical or mental disability, I direct that I be allowed to die and not be kept alive by medications, artificial means or "heroic measures". I do, however, ask that medication be mercifully administered to me to alleviate suffering even though this may shorten my remaining life.

This statement is made after careful consideration and is in accordance with my strong convictions and beliefs. I want the wishes and directions here expressed carried out to the extent permitted by law. Insofar as they are not legally enforceable, I hope that those to whom this Will is addressed will regard themselves as morally bound by these provisions.

(Optional specific provisions to be made in this space — see other side)

DURABLE POWER OF ATTORNEY (optional)

I hereby designate _____ to serve as my attorney-in-fact for the purpose of making medical treatment decisions. This power of attorney shall remain effective in the event that I become incompetent or otherwise unable to make such decisions for myself.

Optional Notarization:

"Sworn and subscribed to

before me this _____ day

of _____, 19_____."

_____
Notary Public
(seal)

Signed_____

Date _____

Witness _____

_____
Address

Witness _____

_____
Address

Copies of this request have been given to _____

_____   _____

(Optional)   My Living Will is registered with Concern for Dying (No. _____)

Distributed by Concern for Dying, 250 West 57th Street, New York, NY 10107 (212) 246-6962

Figure 21.1. A living will.

veins of an older woman who was suffering from cancer and had only a short time to live. Ninety percent of the residents in his hometown in New Hampshire signed a petition expressing their support of his action. Dr. Sanders was later acquitted of a first-degree murder charge. More recently, a North Carolina judge suspended the sentence of a woman who helped her ailing 80-year-old sister commit suicide by carbon-monoxide poisoning. A grand jury in Florida refused to indict an elderly man who killed his wife, a victim of a serious brain disorder (*U.S. News & World Report,* 1983).

A study by Ward (1980) found that older persons tend to be less accepting of euthanasia than younger persons. However, acceptance of euthanasia is greater among those elderly who tend to be more dissatisfied with their own lives. In general, the public, along with most clinicians, now seems to feel that allowing a person to die is sometimes acceptable, especially in cases of terminal illness. But this is quite different from direct killing, which is difficult to justify (Moody, 1988). Palmore (1977) points out that certain trends in our society are increasing our acceptance of euthanasia:

1. The increasing number of persons who reach very old age when prolonged but terminal illness becomes the typical cause of death.
2. The trend toward more rational allocation of scarce and expensive medical equipment (e.g., kidney machines) and the personnel to those who can benefit most.
3. The growing belief in the right of all persons to do what they want with their own bodies, so long as it does not harm others, as reflected in the growing acceptance of contraceptives, abortion, masturbation, premarital intercourse, and cremation. The right to die under certain circumstances may become another generally accepted civil right.

An innovative approach to dealing with the terminally ill in the last weeks of their lives that perhaps both opponents and proponents of euthanasia can accept is a *hospice.* A hospice may be a separate unit within a hospital, or it may be an independent facility. Originally, the term was used to refer to a way station for travelers, but in modern times a hospice has come to mean a facility devoted specifically to the care of the dying. Because hospices are designed for the dying, their orientation and practice differ from those of a general hospital. They emphasize care, not cure, and schedules are designed to fit the needs of the individual patient and not the institution. The key principle of hospice care is reduction of pain, both physical and psychological, accomplished through administration of pain-killing drugs in doses large enough to keep the patient's pain always below the pain threshold and through humane environment and treatment, psychiatric care, and religious counseling (Berdes, 1978).

Hospices are now found in England, the United States, and Canada. The best known is St. Christopher's Hospice, a facility outside of London. It offers meals on demand and with alcoholic beverages. Private rooms are available for relatives who wish to live with or near the patients. Pets and children are welcome. Patients are permitted to shift back and forth between hospice and home as their strength permits.

> When physicians elsewhere finally give up on treating the disease, St. Christopher's takes over and treats the patient. Noticeably absent are the mechanical respirators, cardiovascular shock equipment, oxygen tents and intravenous feeding apparatus to which such patients are often made an appendage in hospitals. Present is a staff deftly alleviating pain. Here, many of the horrors that make euthanasia seem merciful evaporate in an atmosphere of comfort and safety. (Sage, 1974)

Perhaps the essence of the hospice can best be summed up by the underlying philosophy of the hospice movement, namely that one's last days should be spent in living, not dying.

AFTER THE DEATH

The death of an elderly person in our society is generally perceived as being less disruptive and having less impact on the social structure than the death of a young or middle-aged person. This attitude is explained, in part, by the fact that very old persons are no longer actively engaged in the vital functions of society and therefore leave less of a void. Responsibilities of work have generally been passed on to others, and the tasks of socializing children and of parenthood are over.

On the other hand, when a middle-aged person dies, the social loss felt is much greater. Besides contributing to one's family, occupation, and society, the middle-aged person has time left for further contributions. Cumming and Henry (1961) note that when middle-aged persons die they are torn from the fabric of society, but by the time older people die, they have already unraveled the threads of interaction, with the result that their deaths are not as noticeable. An old person's death, then, is viewed as less of a social loss because it terminates a life that society considers to have reduced value and whose potential has been largely exhausted. Weisman (1972) compares the death of a child whose potential is yet unrealized with that of an elderly person:

> The death of a child is always a tragedy. It is unforgettable and futile, because so much of a child's worth depends upon unrealized potential and its capacity to evoke tenderness. In contrast, the death of the very aged fits into an acceptable order of nature and we find reasons to explain why it is right and proper for an old patient to die when he does. "It is just as well." "He was about ready to die anyway." "I don't think he wanted to live." "He never took care of himself." "He couldn't have lived much longer." The terminally aged may be as helpless as a child, but they seldom arouse tenderness.

Grief and Bereavement

Bereavement is generally composed of three distinct phases. The first phase is a brief period of shock, which lasts for several days. The second is a time of intense grief, characterized by physiological changes, such as the loss of sleep, appetite, and weight, as well as withdrawal from social activities. Finally, there is a period of recovery, in which there is a resumption of social activities and a reawakening of interest in life.

Widows sometimes idealize the memory of their deceased husbands. (Nick Myers)

Older persons often anticipate the death of a spouse or of their peers. As a result, they prepare themselves in advance by rehearsing and experiencing, in part, what life will be like following their anticipated loss. When death does occur, it may be that the task of mourning is eased and reconciliation is accomplished more quickly because a certain amount of the *"grief work"* has preceded the event.

Compared with younger persons, older persons are more likely to suffer from a succession of bereavements by having outlived many friends and relatives. Kastenbaum (1969) suggests that this can cause a "bereavement overload."

> Moreover, bereavement may follow so closely upon bereavement that the elder is never able to complete his "grief work." It is often estimated that normal mourning requires approximately a year to run its course. It is possible that even more time is required when one is an octogenarian who is mourning for the spouse whose life has been shared for thirty, forty, fifty or more years. But other deaths may intervene before the mourning is completed. The elder can reach a point at which he feels he no longer can respond fully to a new death; he is still so closely involved with the old deaths.

Phyllis R. Silverman and Adele Cooperhand (1984) point out that bereavement involves a period of transition in which one learns to accept the fact of loss and make the necessary psychological and social adjustments. One way to facilitate this transition period is through a volunteer, peer-counseling program called *"Widow-to-Widow."* Started in the mid-1960s by Silverman, it is based on the premise that often the most effective person to help a recently widowed person is another widow. This person may be a friend, relative, or someone from a mutual support group. Such help provides the newly widowed with psychological support and an understanding of what feelings are to be expected and are typical in this context. In addition, the volunteer serves as a friend and role model, helping to integrate the widow back into the community.

Funerals

The funeral is an important rite of passage in all societies dating back to prehistoric times. It fulfills many functions, including the affirmation of the fundamental meanings of the society and of group solidarity in the face of the ultimate threat of death. In nearly all societies, these fundamental meanings have been of a religious nature. In a secular society such as ours, however, there has been much difficulty in making these affirmations and in coping with death partly because of the decline in religious beliefs (Berger & Berger, 1975). Death becomes especially difficult to accept when many people no longer believe that there is life after death, or that "all is for the best." There is a tendency to mask the reality of death. Expensive caskets are sold today complete with inner-spring mattresses or "Perfect Posture" beds. There are high-fashion clothes and accessories for the dead, along with special cosmetics for grooming (Mitford, 1963). These cosmetics not only are designed to make the deceased more presentable for viewing but even attempt to make them appear in a state of healthy repose. Foreigners are often amazed by our custom of open-casket viewing. An English woman states:

> I myself have attended only one funeral here—that of an elderly fellow worker of mine. After the service I could not understand why everyone was walking towards the coffin . . . but I thought I had better follow the crowd. It shook me rigid to get there and find the casket open and poor old Oscar lying there in his brown tweed suit, wearing a suntan makeup and just the wrong shade of lipstick. (Mitford, 1963)

In an effort to further disguise and soften the impact of death in our society, a whole new terminology involving death has evolved in the funeral business. For example, the *funeral director* or the *mortician* (not the *undertaker*) sees that *Ms. Jones* (not the *corpse*) is placed in a *casket* (not a *coffin*) in a *slumber room* (not a *laying-out room* or *display room*) before the *service* (not the *funeral*). Later the *coach* or *professional car* (not the *hearse*) will transfer her to a *memorial park* (not a *cemetery* or *graveyard*) where she will be *interred* (not *buried*).

In recent years the funeral industry has been under attack for the high costs of funerals, burials, and related expenses. Americans spend billions of dollars a year on funeral expenses, with average burial costs about $5,000. Mourners are often taken advantage of at a time when they are the most vulnerable and least able to judge what they can afford. Many deplete their savings or go into heavy debt in an effort to "do the right thing for the deceased," or to do what is expected of them by their family and friends.

"Would you mind saying we 'passed away'? I'd feel a lot happier with the euphemism."
(Drawing by Handelsman; © 1985 The New Yorker Magazine, Inc.)

SUMMARY

1. Since the majority of those who die are older people, the problems related to death are also related to aging. The elderly are less fearful of death than younger persons. At the same time, they think about it and discuss it more often than younger persons do. Persons who are the most religious tend to be less afraid of death.

2. Residents of retirement communities like Glen Brae socialize one another for impending death. In such environments, death is legitimized because it is viewed as an appropriate and matter-of-fact aspect of life. This process of legitimation took place in Glen Brae through the management of grief, discussions about death, and role modeling.

3. Dying is viewed as a status passage in which one moves between the statuses

of living and dead. The term *trajectory of dying*, as used by Glaser and Strauss, denotes that dying has both duration and shape. The trajectory may be slow or sudden, and it may reveal a regular or erratic downhill pattern. The pattern of the trajectory depends to a large extent on the nature of the terminal condition. Kübler-Ross has proposed that a person passes through five stages of preparation for death: denial, anger, bargaining, depression, and acceptance. As yet, there is little research that supports the existence of these five stages or that they can be universally applied.

4. Glaser and Strauss distinguish four types of awareness situations as defined by terminally ill patients and those around them: closed awareness, suspicion awareness, mutual pretense awareness, and open awareness. Today most physicians and the general public believe in telling the patient the truth in cases of terminal illness.

5. Most people feel that when a patient is hopelessly ill or disabled, there comes a time when it is proper to withdraw extraordinary measures to sustain life. Permitting a patient to die in this way is called passive euthanasia. When a physician deliberately ends the life of a terminally ill patient, it is referred to as active euthanasia. Euthanasia may also be voluntary or involuntary, depending on whether or not one has the consent of the patient. To prevent the prolongation of life by artificial means when death is inevitable, some persons complete documents called living wills. Palmore observes that certain trends are operating in our society that will increase the acceptance of euthanasia in the future.

6. Hospices are an innovative approach to providing care for the dying. Their goal is to furnish an optimum level of care and comfort for the dying patient. Hospices may be independent facilities or units in hospitals.

7. The death of an older person is likely to have far less impact on the social structure than that of a younger person who is actively engaged in family, work, and community affairs. Older persons often anticipate the death of a spouse or friend and prepare themselves for their expected loss. In comparison with younger persons, older people are much more likely to suffer from a succession of losses, resulting in "bereavement overload."

8. Funerals are important rites of passage in most societies, and they fulfill many valuable functions. Because death is becoming increasingly difficult to accept in secular societies like our own, funerals are designed to mask the reality of death.

KEY TERMS

life review
trajectory of dying
stage theory of dying
passive euthanasia
active euthanasia
voluntary euthanasia

involuntary euthanasia
living wills
hospice
grief work
Widow-to-Widow program

FOR FURTHER STUDY

Aiken, Lewis R. (1985). *Dying, death, and bereavement.* Boston: Allyn and Bacon.
   A comprehensive interdisciplinary survey of death and dying.

Buckingham, Robert W. (1983). *The complete hospice guide.* New York: Harper & Row.
   Focuses on the basic concepts of hospice care.

Kalish, Richard A. (1985). *Death, grief, and caring relationships.* Monterey, CA: Brooks/Cole.
   Deals with relationships, the dying process, and grief as well as philosophical issues and attitudes regarding death.

Marshall, Victor W. (1980). *Last chapters: A sociology of aging and dying.* Monterey, CA: Brooks/Cole.
   A sociological and social psychological analysis of aging and dying both at the individual and societal level.

Reading

Mammaw

Carole F. Byrd

Born August 1, 1890, in Knoxville, Tennessee, Nell Narcissa Badgett was the second of nine children and 54 years later became my maternal grandmother and my friend. I called her Mammaw.

When I was two years old, she would take me by the hand and lead me to the chicken yard, where we would feed the chickens. She taught me the gentleness of the animals—the cows and Bessie, the work mule.

A devout believer in God, she went to the same church from early childhood until her death. At age 12 she began playing the organ every Sunday and did so until she was 79. I remember looking with love down to the organ bench in front of the church where Mammaw sat each Sunday. Her hair—her shining glory—was always neatly in place, and the church light seemed to radiate on her silver waves. In her last

_____

Carole F. Byrd. Personal communication.

years, her hair was tinted a bluish-silver as the result of the weekly rinse to keep it from being "yellow."

In 1955 we moved into Mammaw's home to take care of her after my grandfather died. Mammaw and I shared a bedroom. Many nights we would lie in bed laughing at something when Mom would yell at us to "quieten down" so she could sleep.

I remember one night in particular, not very long after Pappaw died, when she woke me in the middle of the night to tell me my grandfather was standing at the foot of my bed and wanted me to tell him good-bye. I tried to tell her she was having a dream, but she insisted he was there. She believed this until her death. After I humored her by telling him good-bye (even though I did not see anything), she told me he said he would not be back again and for her to find someone else to marry. He told her a man would ask her to marry him but to beware and not say yes to the first man. The second man was the man for her, he said.

Strangely, events happened as she said Pappaw predicted. She turned down the first proposal but accepted the second—the man she lived with until she died.

I began to date about the same time Mammaw began dating. My father imposed strict rules on me. I had to be home at 11 P.M.—on the dot—and I was never allowed to sit in the car in the driveway when I got home. Mammaw had no rules—not even a curfew. I could accept the fact Mammaw had no curfew, but I simply wouldn't let her get by with sitting in the car in the driveway! I would stay awake until I heard her date's car, wait about 10 minutes, and then tiptoe to the living room and start flashing the porch lights. Of course, the rest of my family was asleep. She would eventually get the message and come into the house. I used to tease her by saying I was the only person I knew who had to leave the door unlocked for a grandmother!

When she decided to marry Earl Felix in 1959, Mammaw was 69 years young. He was 59. Being a spunky person, she decided it best to "run off" and get married. She scared us all! When they weren't home from their date at 1 A.M., my mother and I were pacing the floor. We were afraid they had been involved in a wreck. Finally around 2 A.M. they came home. It scared them that all the inside lights were on. This time they didn't stay in the car in the driveway. When they came through the door, my mother demanded they tell her where they had been. When she finished her tirade of how they had managed to ruin everyone's sleep and had nearly caused her to have a heart attack, Mammaw glanced at Mr. Felix and then to Mom. I can still see it clearly today.

"We got married," she said.

We were all stunned, but that ended the reprimand.

Mammaw then moved into Mr. Felix's home nearby, and I missed my room-mate.

In the fall of 1959—the year Mammaw remarried—I started attending high school at Harrison-Chilhowee Academy in Seymour, Tennessee, where I lived in the dormitory during the week and came home only on weekends. I started rolling Mammaw's hair every Saturday so I could have a set time to visit her. We enjoyed those Saturdays. On one of the first Saturdays after she married, we were having our usual chat when I started teasing her about marrying a younger man. I asked her, "Mammaw, is he the man you thought he was?"

And she answered, with a twinkle in her eye, "Yes, honey, but I'm not the woman I thought I was!"

We both laughed so hard our sides hurt!

Some Saturdays I would go to Mammaw's house angry at something or someone, especially when I was in high school, and I'd complain about whatever had annoyed me. She not only was my friend, but she was also my sounding board. She would always have me seeing the situation from a totally different perspective by the time I left her house, and I'd always feel better.

"If you can't say something good about someone," she would say, "then don't say anything at all."

This was her life's motto, and she lived by it. I never heard her say anything bad about anyone in the 42 years I knew her.

Mammaw was 87 years old when she developed cancer of the breast. She had a mastectomy and lived eight years before the cancer returned to take her life. I continued to fix her hair every Saturday until she died.

One of the last things she said in the hospital—just the day before she went into a coma— was "Here comes my hairdresser. Don't you think I need something done?" Three days later she died—May 20, 1986—at the age of 95. She died as she had lived, with all her family around her.

I could not stand the thoughts of someone else going to the funeral home to fix her hair because *I* knew how she liked it. I went to the funeral home and told one of the employees I was going to roll Mammaw's hair. The employee went to get her boss. It was obvious they didn't like the idea, but I was insistent. They finally led me to a room where Mammaw was lying on a cold, steel table. Someone had already washed her hair. The manager asked the lady who was going to fix her hair to leave. For the next 30 minutes, it was just Mammaw and me, again, like it used to be. I gently rolled her hair, talking to her as I had done so many Saturdays in the past. But this time she couldn't talk back to me. As the tears slid silently down my cheeks, I realized my best friend was gone.

Programs and Prospects for the Elderly

Chapter 22

Social Services and Programs for the Elderly

TYPES OF SERVICES AND PROGRAMS

Services and Programs for the Homebound Elderly

Services and Programs for the Well Elderly

Services for the Elderly with Special Problems

SOCIAL SERVICE UTILIZATION

Information and Referral Programs

Outreach Programs

Some of the earliest attempts to intervene in the social conditions of older persons can be traced back to the Byzantines, who honored old age. They established a number of homes for the elderly, which were in existence during the fifth century. These homes, known as *gerocomeia*, were supported by the church, the state, and private persons. Throughout most of history, however, social problems, including those of the elderly, were considered inevitable—nothing could be done to eradicate or ameliorate them.

Today the concept of *social intervention*—which refers to a planned attempt to change, supposedly for the better, the lives of other individuals or groups through the application of skills and knowledge—is a widely accepted attitude and practice in modern societies. Social intervention may take the form of *social services*, which may be defined as "a social mechanism for [the] distribution of resources designed to achieve and maintain a prescribed level of well-being for all members of society" (Shlonsky, 1976). This definition implies that social services are not just for the poor, but that everyone is entitled to a basic level of welfare.

Some groups, such as the elderly, need more social services than others to achieve an acceptable level of well-being. Specialized social services for the elderly did not develop until recent years. This development coincided with the expansion of our knowledge of the biological, psychological, and sociological aspects of aging. Social services for older people generally focus on activities that are supportive; help protect, conserve, and improve physical and social functioning; and provide opportunities for personal fulfillment.

In this chapter we will briefly review some services and programs provided for the elderly in their homes and in community settings (Table 22.1). We will then look at the availability and utilization of social services for older people. Many of these services relate to the problems mentioned in previous chapters.

TYPES OF SERVICES AND PROGRAMS

Most older people prefer to remain in their own homes and retain their independence and autonomy as long as possible. The services listed in the following section are designed to provide some of the necessary resources that the frail, incapacitated elderly need in order to function more independently within their own homes and to prevent or delay the need for institutionalization.

Services and Programs for the Homebound Elderly

Homemaker Services   Homemakers are professionally supervised persons, usually women, who are trained to furnish housekeeping and other help to those elderly who are temporarily incapacitated after hospitalization or who are permanently disabled. The homemaker usually has some training in the home care of the sick, but she is not a substitute for a nurse. She assists her client by shopping for food, preparing the meals, doing light housekeeping, and offering companionship. In addition, she provides personal services, such as helping to bathe and dress the older person. Services may range from a few hours a day several times a week to 24-hour service seven days a week. Some low-income persons are eligible to receive homemaker services without cost through federally subsidized programs such as Medicaid.

Table 22.1   SERVICES AND PROGRAMS FOR THE ELDERLY

For the frail, homebound elderly	For the well elderly	For the elderly with special problems
Homemaker	Transportation and escort	Protective
Home health	Congregate meals	Counseling
Home-delivered meals	Legal services	Adult day-care centers
Friendly visitors	Employment	
Telephone reassurance		
Emergency response systems		

Home-health Services   Home-health aides may provide skilled or paraprofessional nursing care. They may perform such duties as dispensing and supervising medication, changing dressings, giving rehabilitation therapy, and providing personal hygiene services. In some communities, homemaker and home-health aide services are combined so that one person may do both jobs. Both of these services contribute to helping older people remain in their own homes.

In addition, the home-health service shortens or circumvents prolonged hospitalization. Home-health services are covered under Medicare if the patient is homebound and requires skilled-nursing care on an intermittent basis. Under the provisions of the Medicare Catastrophic Coverage Act (1988), annual coverage for home-health services was increased from 15 days to 38 days. Because of the early hospital discharges under the DRG (diagnosis-related groups) system, home-health services have been one of the fastest-growing aspects of the Medicare program.

Home-Delivered Meals   Popularly referred to as meals-on-wheels, this service provides for the delivery of a hot noon meal to elderly persons who are homebound and unable to cook and shop or obtain help to do so. Not only is the older person given a nutritious meal five days a week, but also he or she receives a friendly visit from the volunteer delivering the meal.

> In his garage apartment he was pretty much a prisoner. He didn't dare risk the stairs by himself, now that he was on crutches; and there wasn't another place he could move to on his little pension. His life was bounded by a dirty alley at the back and the tall brick apartment house wall from his living-bedroom. . . . There was just Mr. Wilmont and the impersonal television set. But when Meals-on-Wheels found Mr. Wilmont, Mr. Wilmont found a new way of life. With that nice Mrs. Freedman stopping in every day, he began to get himself cleaned up a little, and the apartment too. He also started listening to the news in order to have something to say to her when she came. Life was different, in a good way. (Smith, 1973)

The hot meal is often delivered along with a cold snack for dinner and cereal and milk for the next day's breakfast. With home-delivered meals, many persons who might othewise require institutional care can remain in their own homes.

Friendly Visitors   Sometimes referred to as "organized neighborliness," this program provides volunteers to visit isolated, homebound persons and institutionalized persons on a regularly scheduled basis. The visitor and older person may do such things as play cards or checkers, watch television together, or just sit and talk. The visitor is usually trained and supervised by a professional person and must have an understanding of the older person's needs and be a good listener. Visitors offer continuing companionship to elderly persons who have no relatives or friends to fill this need. Older persons themselves make especially good visitors.

Many professional workers have observed how this program relieves the loneliness of older people: "Clients look better and take more interest in things outside themselves after receiving friendly visiting. Frequently, there is improvement in actual physical condition, or at least, less absorption in illness" (Administration on Aging, 1972).

In home-delivered meal programs two volunteers are needed—a driver and a visitor. Appropriate equipment is essential so that the food will be kept at the proper temperatures. (Nick Myers)

Telephone Reassurance Services   Many elderly persons who live alone worry that they may become ill or injured without being able to contact anyone for help. The *telephone reassurance service*, just as the name implies, helps allay these concerns by arranging for calls at a certain time each day to persons who live alone. The older person generally informs the telephone reassurance volunteer if he or she does not plan to be home at the time of the regularly scheduled call. If the phone is not answered and the volunteer has not been notified that the client will be away, someone will immediately go to the home to check on the person. Community agencies and churches often provide space and funds for such a service. The callers may range in age from teenagers to older persons. By checking on an elderly person's health and well-being, telephone reassurance provides continuing personal contact and a feeling that someone cares.

Emergency Response Systems There are several types of *emergency response systems* that allow older persons to summon help through an alarm and response system. The subscribers to the Lifeline service wear a button on their neck or wrist. When help is needed the button is pressed; this triggers automatic dialing to the Lifeline center (usually a local hospital). When the call is received, Lifeline workers telephone the elderly person's home. If no one answers, they call a responder (a designated friend or relative) to check out the situation. The responder then calls the center to let them know what further assistance is needed.

Another system, similar to Lifeline, except that it offers voice contact, is called Voice of Help. Still another type of program, Medic-Alert, supplies information about the medical history of an individual in case that person is unconscious or incoherent when help arrives. The elderly person wears a bracelet or necklace that contains his or her medical condition (e.g., diabetic) and identification number along with Medic-Alert's telephone number. In this way, emergency personnel can call and get access to the person's computerized medical records (Crichton, 1987). (See the reading in Chapter 23 for a further discussion of this topic.)

Services and Programs for the Well Elderly

Most communities offer an array of services and programs for those elderly who are relatively well and able to travel to them. The focal point for the delivery of many of these services is the senior center. At such centers, older persons may often avail themselves of a wide range of individual and group services.

Transportation and Escort Services A number of innovative projects for meeting the transportation needs of older people have been developed in many communities across the nation. Some communities provide door-to-door, flexible transportation services (sometimes referred to as dial-a-ride) for the elderly in a variety of vehicles, including station wagons, minibuses, and passenger buses. The older person generally calls a central dispatching office, usually 24 hours in advance, and specifies the trip needed. The scheduling and routing for the next day's transportation requirements are then worked out accordingly. Some senior centers provide a bus that runs between the members' homes and the center. In Menlo Park, California, center members may arrange to be picked up by having a standing reservation or by phoning in advance. The bus is also used for group outings and other occasions.

Another transportation alternative is the use of volunteers driving private cars; this service is especially valuable in rural areas where no accessible public transportation exists. Volunteer drivers pick up older persons at their homes and take them to doctors' offices, clinics, stores, and other essential destinations.

In some communities, escort services are provided for older persons who may need someone to accompany them when walking or traveling either because of their physical impairments or for protection from criminal victimization. In New York City, the police have organized a teenage volunteer escort service. In an inner-city area in Chicago, the police hired a bus and a driver for the day that Social Security checks arrive. The driver picks up the older people from two housing projects and takes them to a bank and a grocery store and then safely home.

Congregate Meals   The federal nutrition program, under provisions of the Older Americans Act, serves more than half a million meals annually to persons age 60 and older. Most *congregate meals* are offered to groups of elderly at midday in central locations, such as senior centers, schools, community centers, and churches. The average site serves about 20 to 60 persons each day (Gelfand, 1988). In addition to a hot, nutritious meal, many of the nation's more than 1300 meal sites offers a variety

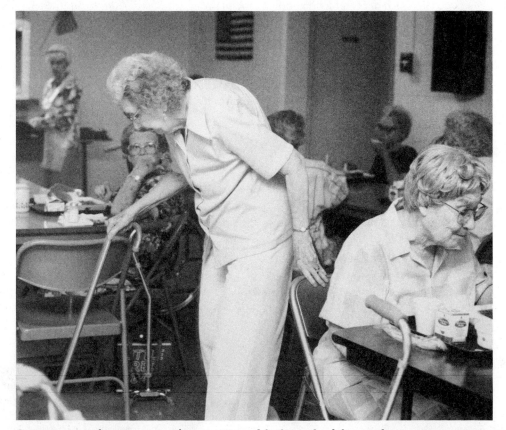

Congregate meals increase social interaction and facilitate the delivery of supportative services as well as improving nutrition. (Nick Myers)

of services and programs, including consumer advice, health and nutrition information, counseling, and arts and crafts. The program also gives the elderly a place where
they can meet, talk, and make friends. In some cases the social aspect is more
important than the meal itself. For example, birthdays and holidays are celebrated at
the meal sites, and in some instances, older men and women who met at the meals
program have decided to marry and have held their weddings at the meal site. (See
Box 22.1.)

Legal Services   It is becoming increasingly apparent that the elderly are in need of
a wide variety of legal services, which range from tenant rights, consumer protection,
and contracts to the preparation of wills. Many older people lack access to the legal
system. Some feel that they cannot afford it, whereas others fear involvement with
lawyers or are unaware of their legal rights.

   To make legal assistance more readily available to the elderly, the Legal Services
Corporation was formed in 1974. This federally funded program provides free legal
services to the elderly poor. The Corporation does not provide legal services directly
but funds local legal-aid projects. Another source of legal assistance for the elderly is
provided through senior center paralegals. These persons, many of whom are aged

---

Box 22.1 The Nutrition Program in Samoa

Cultural relativism warns us that some cultural institutions within one society may not
easily transfer to another. An example of this occurred in American Samoa, where a
nutrition program was attempted. To begin with, Samoa is not a society that understands
volunteerism, a major factor in Meals-on-Wheels and congregate meal success elsewhere. In Samoa, *families*—not neighbors or strangers who volunteer—serve the elderly. Thus, when the government's planning began, Samoans, suggested that food or
money be distributed among families who would then make sure that their elderly got
proper nourishment. American government officials (mostly white contract employees)
objected to this on the grounds that other family members would perhaps get the food
intended for the elderly. After long consideration (with one another but not with the
Samoans), the government officials decided that the food should be cooked in the
kitchens of the 26 consolidated elementary schools, where food was already being
prepared by kitchen personnel for government-subsidized hot meals for the schoolchil-
dren. The elderly could simply go to the school for lunch. This solution led to the demise
of the nutrition program for elders, because it did not take into consideration appropriate
age-status and role behavior, particularly in respect to titled chiefs who maintained that
it was beneath their dignity to go to school and line up like children just for a midday meal.
Also, the usual time for Samoans to eat is not noon but at 10 A.M. and 7 P.M.

Source: Lowell D. Holmes, *Other Cultures, Elder Years*. Minneapolis, Minn.: Burgess, 1983,
p. 7.

themselves, work with the assistance of a lawyer. They are trained to provide legal assistance with problems that confront older people and to serve as advocates for the elderly poor.

Employment Services   A number of nonprofit volunteer employment agencies are specifically designed to help older people secure full-time and part-time jobs. One of the best sources for information about job opportunities is the state employment service offices. Though they offer counseling and job placement to all age groups, these agencies have been expanding their services to older workers. Many have established Older Worker Service Units, while others have personnel who specialize in securing jobs for the older worker.

ACTION, a federal volunteer agency, administers the Foster Grandparent and the Senior Companion programs. These programs provide part-time employment of 20 hours per week at a small hourly stipend and are open to low-income persons who are age 60 and over. Both programs give older persons an opportunity to utilize their skills and experience to meet community needs as well as derive a sense of satisfaction that comes from feeling useful and being of service to others. The Foster Grandparent program offers support and companionship to children with special needs, while the Senior Companion program provides care and assistance to other adults, primarily the homebound elderly with emotional, physical, and mental impairments.

Another federal program is Green Thumb, which operates under grant agreements with the Employment and Training Administration. Green Thumb, like Foster Grandparent and Senior Companion programs, provides part-time employment of 20 hours per week for low-income persons. Eligibility for Green Thumb begins at age 55, but priority is given to those age 60 and over. The Green Thumb program places participants in such areas as education, transportation, recreation, and the like, depending on where their abilities and skills can be used most effectively. The program provides training and work experience for its participants, and each year thousands of them "graduate" and secure employment in the private sector.

Finally, the Job Training Partnership Act of 1983 established a federal program of job training and placement for economically disadvantaged youths and young adults and older persons. However, the impact of the program on older workers appears to be minimal. According to a 1984 Department of Labor study, only 41 percent of those between the ages of 55 and 64 were able to reenter the labor force in any capacity, and only 21 percent of those 65 and over became reemployed.

A unique and innovative employment service is provided by Rent-A-Granny or Grandpa. Sponsored by the Older American Council, this nonfee agency provides employers with older workers that they can use on a temporary, permanent, part-time, or full-time basis. Eighty-year-old Anne Beckman, founder of this service in 1960 in Albuquerque, New Mexico, has an ability for matching talents and jobs. She has secured thousands of jobs for older persons in Albuquerque, from working as domestics and tour directors to being private investigators. In the last few years, the agency has been specializing in home health care.

Beckman finds that most people do not know the wealth that they possess in hidden assets.

Foster Grandparents attend to the physical, mental, and emotional needs of disadvantaged children.

They don't realize that their hobbies, avocations, and special interests often can be recycled and sold as valuable commodities in the job market. For example, one woman came in who casually mentioned that she had won many prizes for garden shows. I had no trouble getting her a job arranging flowers for a nursery. . . . A granny with a flair for whipping up tasty hors d'oeuvres was hired by a party caterer. A learned college professor, exiled into idleness by mandatory retirement policy, was offered a chair in a department store—behind its information booth. (Weisinger, 1976)

Beckman's service is open to persons age 55 and older, but it is not unusual for her to obtain jobs for persons in their seventies and eighties. In one instance she placed a 92-year-old man with a resonant voice as a telephone solicitor (Weisinger, 1976).

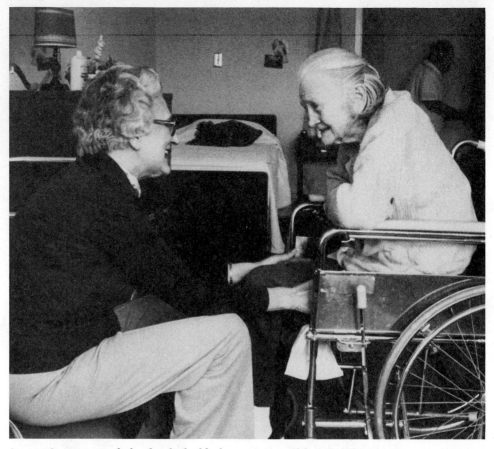

Senior Companions help the frail elderly to gain confidence and a more positive mental attitude.

Services for the Elderly with Special Problems

Protective Services   Usually sponsored by legal-service centers, or voluntary or public agencies, *protective services* are distinguished from other social services in that there is a potential or reason for legal intervention. Protective services provide assistance to older persons who are too mentally or physically incapacitated to manage their own affairs or to act in their own behalf.

One type of protective service is *guardianship*, in which a guardian manages the person and property of another who is found to be legally incompetent. The incompetent, referred to as a "ward," is stripped of all his or her rights such as voting, driving, marrying, or managing an allowance. He or she may not be able to resist admission to a mental hospital or nursing home if the guardian decides to make such arrangements (Cohen, 1985). In certain cases this extreme legal procedure is the most

Box 22.2 <u>**Elderly Volunteers in China**</u>

Volunteer service for retired workers is popular in China. Almost one-third (400,000) of Shanghai's retired workers engage in volunteer activities daily. Certainly a common sight on Nanjing Road, the busiest street in the city, is an old person wearing the red armband of the volunteer while directing the heavy bicycle and pedestrian traffic.

City volunteers also participate in cleaning neighborhood areas; tending city-planted trees and shrubs; running errands, feeding, doing chores, providing physical and social support to the lonely, feeble old people; and chairing or serving on community committees. Their committee service may involve mediation, teaching, and "re-education." Because of their age, they are thought to have the knowledge and tact to intervene and help settle family or neighborhood misunderstandings by counseling the disputing individuals.

Source: Kathleen A. Kalab, "Lives of the Elderly in China." *Journal of Anthropology* (5), 1986, pp. 63–64.

desirable approach, but sometimes guardianship can work against the best interests of the older person (see Box 22.3).

Counseling Services   These services, generally offered by public or voluntary social agencies, provide assistance in many areas, including personal and family problems, retirement adjustment, finances, and living arrangements. Often the request for help comes from the older person's relatives. The referral may also come from other agencies or professionals. The following situation illustrates how uprooting a person from familiar surroundings into an institution, without careful consideration of such a move, can create problems and the need for intervention by a counseling agency:

> Miss R.'s attorney asked the agency to plan with Miss R., a 90-year-old woman who had refused to remain in the institution for the aged where she had been placed by relatives a month previously. . . . It was found that she had a calcium deficiency of the spine which would require her to wear a body-brace and to limit going up and down stairs to once a day. Relatives [had] then arranged for her to enter a sectarian home for the aged by mortgaging her property in order to pay her admission to the home. At the institution Miss R. was placed in the hospital sector where she could not adjust to strangers coming in and out of her room at will. When it came time for Miss R. to sign the permanent contract at the institution, she rebelled and went home. (Leach, 1970).

After Miss R. returned home, a caseworker began visiting her and found that she felt betrayed by her relatives and friends. Her physician confirmed that she was not in need of nursing-home care. In time, Miss R. developed a good relationship with the caseworker and was persuaded to employ a woman on a part-time basis to assist her.

Box 22.3   **Robbed of Her Rights—and $40,000**

Marguerite Van Etten was in her early 60s when she was involved in a near-fatal traffic accident on her way to work at the Florida Department of Health. She suffered severe head trauma and fell into a coma, and it took her two months to recover her faculties, she later told a House subcommittee on health. When she recovered, she found that her daughter had been granted a guardianship petition.

"When I was finally able to return home, it was like a bad dream," she testified. "My furniture was gone—my daughter had it shipped to Maryland even before I was declared incompetent. I had to sleep on a sleeping bag on the bare floor. I lost my job. My driver's license had been revoked. I had trouble drawing on my bank account in my own name."

But Mrs. Van Etten's biggest surprise was when she went to the polls to vote. "I was flabbergasted to learn that I no longer had the right," she said. "I called county officials—there had to be some mistake—and they said they knew me as '83-0449; Van Etten, mentally incompetent.'"

Mrs. Van Etten was ultimately able, a year after the accident, to get the guardianship overturned. "I was restored to competency" as she put it. She testified, however, that her daughter's activities had cost her $40,000 in assets.

Source: William Sherman, "Savage Guardians." *Longevity*, June, 1989, p. 44.

With household help and the support of the caseworker and the agency, Miss R. was able to remain in her own home where she had strong, meaningful ties and felt secure.

Adult Day-Care Centers   Day-care centers are designed to prevent premature institutionalization for those who have mental or physical impairments and are not capable of full-time independent living, but who can manage to stay in the community if professional support is provided. Day-care centers fulfill a variety of needs, including social, psychiatric and rehabilitation services, health maintenance, and recreational activities. These services are usually offered five days a week on an eight-hour basis, along with meals and transportation. The centers are especially valuable for those elderly whose families work and where there is no one at home to care for them during the day. Day-care centers may be located in an independent facility, or they may be part of a senior center, a neighborhood center, or a hospital (Beattie, 1976).

An increasing number of adult day-care centers are offering respite services. This service provides some time off for the primary caregiver (usually a spouse or adult child) from his or her continuing responsibilities in taking care of an older person who cannot be left alone because of physical and mental impairments. This time off may range from three hours a week to a weekend or a vacation period.

Table 22.2   TIMETABLE OF IMPORTANT DEVELOPMENTS IN AGING

1935	Passage of the Social Security Act
1943	First senior center established (New York City)
1945	Gerontological Society of America
1946	Friendly Visitors Program
1947	National Retired Teachers Association (NRTA)
1950	National Council on the Aging (NCOA)
1956	Reduced Social Security benefits for women at age 62
1958	American Association of Retired Persons (AARP)
1961	First White House Conference on Aging (WHCOA)
	Special Committee on Aging, U.S. Senate
	National Council on Senior Citizens (NCSC)
	Reduced Social Security benefits for men at age 62
1964	National Association of State Units on Aging (NASUA)
1965	Older Americans Act (OAA)
	Administration on Aging (AoA)
	Medicare and Medicaid
	Foster Grandparent Program (FGP)
	Service Corps of Retired Executives (SCORE)
	Green Thumb
1967	Age Discrimination in Employment Act (ADEA) covering workers between the ages of 40 and 65
1970	Gray Panthers
1971	Second White House Conference on Aging (WHCOA)
	ACTION agency
	Retired Senior Volunteer Program (RSVP)
1972	National Nutrition Program for the Elderly
	Adult Day-Care Centers
1973	Area Agencies on Aging (AAA)
	Federal Council on Aging
1974	Employee Retirement Income Security Act (ERISA)
	Supplemental Security Income (SSI)
	Association for Gerontology in Higher Education (AGHE)
	National Institute on Aging (NIA)
	Senior Companions Program (SCP)
1975	Age Discrimination Act (ADA)
	Ombudsman program for long-term-care institutions
1976	First hospice in the United States
1978	Amendments to Age Discrimination in Employment Act of 1967 (ADEA), raising upper age limit to 70
1981	Third White House Conference on Aging (WHCOA)
1986	Amendments to Age Discrimination in Employment Act of 1967 (ADEA), removing upper age limit
1988	Medicare Catastrophic Coverage Act (Repealed 1989)

Source: Diana K. Harris, *Dictionary of Gerontology*. Westport, Conn.: Greenwood Press, 1988, pp. xi–xii.

SOCIAL SERVICE UTILIZATION

All these social services and more are needed by the elderly. Yet at present most communities have only some services, and they are not available to all the elderly who need them. Three major concepts involving development and planning of social services are availability, accessibility, and utilization. Social services must not only be available when needed, but they "must be in existence and organized in a comprehensive, coordinated way on a continuous basis, so that older people can utilize them when they are required" (Lowry, 1975). In addition, social services should be geographically accessible to where older people live. Services should be accessible in the sense that they are easily obtainable and not blocked by elaborate procedures and red tape, which discourage their use.

But neither availability nor accessibility will assure that services will be utilized. Often, services are not used by those who need them most. The elderly's sense of dignity and pride often stand in the way of their utilizing services. Many elderly who have been self-sufficient and independent all their lives are too proud to accept free assistance readily. Also, among many ethnic groups, persons will not use a service because they believe that it represents the group's failure to "take care of their own" (Lowry, 1975; Gelfand, 1987).

Probably one of the main reasons for the elderly's not using services is their lack of knowledge about them, especially among the socially isolated elderly. Two programs created in recent years to help alleviate this situation are information and referral programs and outreach programs. Although these programs are often treated as being separate and distinct, there is considerable overlap between them.

Information and Referral Programs

The major purpose of an *information and referral* (I & R) *program* is to link older people with services that have been designed to meet their specific needs. Information and referral agencies maintain continuously updated files of all the services available in their areas. These files are also available to agencies needing service information. People usually call information and referral when they have an immediate problem. The caseworker helps them to formulate their problem in the context of existing services, and then assists them in contacting the appropriate service (Gelfand, 1988). In addition to the initial contact, most information and referral agencies do follow-up work to evaluate whether the client was properly referred and received the needed service. The agency also performs a valuable function by identifying unmet needs in the community and discovering gaps and duplication in available services.

Outreach Programs

While information and referral programs primarily depend on clients to seek them out, *outreach programs* seek out their clients. Outreach workers go into the community to make people aware of available services and how to use them. In addition,

Information and referral programs for the elderly are the same as those for the general population except they focus on the needs of older persons. Each local site generally offers both a telephone and a walk-in service. (Nick Myers)

they attempt to overcome resistance to the elderly's utilization of needed services (Wilson, 1984). For example, when Medicare and SSI programs were first implemented, outreach workers were used to inform many older persons about them. Often outreach workers are older persons themselves. In Operation Medicare Alert, about 14,500 persons—most of them elderly—went into communities across the nation to reach those eligible for the program. Within six months, they had signed up over 4 million elderly for Medicare (Terris, 1977).

Another highly successful and comprehensive outreach program was Project FIND (Friendless, Isolated, Needy or Disabled) conducted by the National Council on the Aging (1967–1968). Older aides ranging in age from 50 to 85 surveyed a dozen communities across the country. The target group was the isolated elderly of low socioeconomic levels. When the aides found elderly persons who needed help, they referred them to services that were available in their community. They found that substantial proportions of older people were unaware of the services they were entitled to. Some did not even know that they were eligible for Social Security (The National Council on the Aging, 1970).

A more recent example of another type of outreach program is Project Rescue. Established in 1985, this program serves the needs of 2000 older men and a small

Homelessness stems from such factors as social service and disability cutbacks, personal crises, and lack of aftercare services for the deinstitutionalized mentally ill. (Black Star)

number of women living in New York City's Bowery, commonly referred to as Skid Row.

> Three days each week, Project Rescue sends outreach workers into the streets, parks, subways, and flophouses on the Bowery to find older homeless men and women. Intervention begins at the lowest level: human contact. Next, food and clothing are offered. Sometimes workers are successful in bringing the homeless to Project Rescue for medical assessment and treatment . . . for alcoholism, for psychiatric services, for housing referral, for assistance with entitlements, for a shower, for a hot meal, or merely to gain respite from the streets. Roughly 110 men and women attend the daily breakfast and lunch programs at Project Rescue. An additional 50 lunches are sent to homebound elderly living in the flophouses. (The Aging Connection, 1989)

In recent years the number of services for the elderly has been greatly expanded, but as the older population continues to grow, so will the demand for services. A challenge for the future appears to be developing and making available a full range of services for the elderly, while at the same time trying to keep pace with the needs of an increasing older population.

SUMMARY

1. Specialized social services and programs for the elderly are of recent origin. Their development has coincided with the expansion of our knowledge about aging. Services for the elderly fall into three major groups: the homebound, the well elderly, and those elderly with special problems.

2. Various services have been designed to help older people remain in their own homes as long as possible. These include homemaker and home-health services, home-delivered meals, friendly visitors, telephone reassurance services, and emergency response systems.

3. For those elderly who are relatively well, most communities offer a wide variety of programs and services, such as transportation, congregate meals, and legal and employment services.

4. Services for the elderly with special problems include protective services, counseling services, and adult day-care centers.

5. Availability, accessibility, and utilization are three major concepts involving the planning and development of social services. Often older persons do not use available services because they lack knowledge of the services that are available. Two programs have been initiated to remedy this situation. Information and referral programs connect older people with needed services, whereas outreach programs send workers out into the community to inform older persons of existing services.

KEY TERMS

gerocomeia
social intervention
social services
telephone reassurance services
emergency response systems
congregate meals

ACTION
protective services
guardianship
information and referral programs
outreach programs

FOR FURTHER STUDY

Dobelstein, Andrew, with Johnson, Ann B. (1985). *Serving older adults: Policy, programs, and professional activities.* Englewood Cliffs, NJ: Prentice-Hall.

An introduction to the problems of older persons and the policies, programs, and methods of helping older persons deal with them.

Gelfand, Donald E. (1988). *The aging network: Programs and services.* New York: Springer.

Discusses existing programs and services for the elderly along with funding and variations in service delivery.

Monk, Abraham (Ed.) (1985). *Handbook of gerontological services.* New York: Van Nostrand Reinhold.

Contains a comprehensive review of social interventions and services available to older persons.

Wilson, Albert J. E. (1984). *Social services for older persons.* Boston: Little, Brown.

Provides an excellent overview of service programs for the elderly.

Chapter
23

Future Trends, Technology, and Aging

O ur society is rapidly changing. Change is reflected in every aspect of our lives, from norms and values to technology. Change has become such a prevalent element that we frequently take it for granted. Throughout this book, we have examined changes that have taken place regarding the elderly. In this final chapter, we shall look at some of the future changes that are likely to occur in the older population, their effect on the general population, and the impact of technological change on the elderly.

Predicting future social changes on the basis of existing trends is called *extrapolation*. Such social forecasting rests on the assumption that any stable society, such as ours, will in the future be much as it is at present, having certain continuities that tend to persist. The possibility of unexpected events or of the intervention of unforeseen factors is largely ignored in extrapolation. Thus, making predictions based on existing trends can be risky. Nevertheless, some attempts at social forecasting are necessary in order to plan more effectively for the future and to develop appropriate solutions for problems that may arise with change.

TWO SOURCES OF SOCIAL CHANGE

Technological change is a major source of social change. Changes in technology usually precede changes in other areas of the culture and, in turn, this situation results in *cultural lag*—a concept introduced by William F. Ogburn (1922). Cultural lag is the time period between the introduction of a change and society's adaptation to it. For example, recent advances in medical technology have made it possible to prolong life or to prolong the dying process through the use of artificial means. But there is a lag in the cultural ideas that regulate how we use this new technology (Kornblum, 1988).

Another source of social change is a change in the demographic structure of the population. The rapid growth of our older population provides an example. The social institutions in our society have not yet adjusted to the change in the size of the older population, thus resulting in cultural lag. As Neugarten (1975) points out:

> Our social institutions were not prepared for the relatively rapid appearance of large numbers of older people since the turn of the century. If our institutions are to be more successful in the next decades, scholarly efforts should now be undertaken to forecast, as best we can, the likely demographic and social developments, to anticipate the problems of aging and the aging society that lie ahead.

DEMOGRAPHIC TRENDS

Our country is in the midst of a demographic transformation that will not have run its course until the middle of the next century. We are in the process of changing from a young nation to an aging nation. This transformation is the result of a declining younger population and a growing older population (Pifer and Bronte, 1986). Contributing to the growth of the older population has been an improvement in life expectancy. But living longer also means a deterioration in health, especially among the oldest-old. Consequently, a large number of people in this age group now require or will require long-term care.

Population

The number and proportion of older people in the population are expected to continue increasing through the first third of the next century. These rises will result from increased life expectancy and the aging of the 76.4 million "baby boomers" born in the 1946-to-1964 period. Table 23.1 shows the projected growth of the older population for the years 2000 to 2050. Notice how in 2010 the population will increase to 39.3 million as the baby boomers begin to reach age 65. This dramatic increase will

Table 23.1   PROJECTED GROWTH OF
THE 65 AND OVER
POPULATION: 2000–
2050
(Numbers in thousands)

Year	Number	Percent
2000	34,882	13.0
2010	39,362	13.9
2020	52,067	17.7
2030	65,604	21.8
2040	68,109	22.6
2050	68,532	22.9

Source: U.S. Bureau of the Census, *Current Population Reports,* Series P-25, No. 1018, "Projections of the Population of the United States, by Age, Sex, and Race: 1988–2080," January 1989. Projection data for 2000–2050 from middle series.

continue until 2030, at which time it will reach 65.6 million (more than twice today's elderly population), and then it will begin to slow down.

Population projections like these can be made with a fair amount of reliability because they are based on death rates, not birth rates, and those who will be 65 in 2050 have already been born. The proportion of older people in the population is more difficult to project than the actual numbers because it depends on birth rates, which are subject to wide fluctuation. Estimates are that the proportion of elderly in the population will reach 13.9 percent in 2010 and 21.8 percent by 2030 (see Table 23.1).

The projected growth of the older population will raise the median age of the U.S. population from 33 today to 36 by the year 2000, and to age 42 by 2050. In 2050, one in five persons will be age 65 and over.

Although the human life span probably has not changed for the last 100,000 years, as we pointed out in Chapter 2, life expectancy has increased by 27 years since 1900. One of the primary reasons for this dramatic increase has been the decline in infant and child death rates because of technological advances in medicine. Through immunization such diseases as smallpox, tuberculosis, diphtheria, typhoid fever, tetanus, and polio have dropped by 99 percent in this century (Fries, 1984).

Most researchers foresee only small improvements in life expectancy from now into the next century. They do not predict any of the spectacular scientific breakthroughs that one so often reads about in the popular press. It is not unusual to read stories about how it will soon be possible to live 200 years or more by taking certain vitamin compounds, anti-aging drugs, or some magic potion. Although such claims have tremendous appeal, they crumble under scientific scrutiny (Fries & Crapo, 1981). Even if heart disease, the number-one cause of death, could be eliminated, only 7 years would be added to life expectancy at age 65, according to Taeuber (1988). The elimination of death fron cancer would add about another 2 to 3 years—certainly a far cry from superlongevity or immortality.

Table 23.2 shows the projected life expectancy at birth by sex from 2000 to 2050. Women will continue to outlive men by about 7 years throughout the first half of the next century.

Health

The future elderly will not only live longer, but they will remain healthier to a later age as compared with today's elderly. In other words, severe diseases will be compressed into the later years. For example, instead of persons having heart attacks in their fifties and sixties, they may be having them in their eighties and nineties. Thus the future elderly will have much the same health needs as the present generation, but at a more advanced age and with larger numbers of older persons, health-care costs will be greater (Neugarten, 1975; Fries and Crapo, 1981). Currently, health-care costs are the largest source of public spending for the elderly.

Caring for older people will continue to be one of the fastest-growing new industries in this country (Henderson, 1988). As the size of the older population increases, so will the nursing-home population. Predictions are that between 1985 and 2000 the nursing home population will increase from 1.4 million to 2 million, and by 2040 it will more than double again, to 4.6 million (Manton & Soldo, 1985). Advances in medical technology will make it possible in the future to replace arteries, nerve cells, and even brain cells. Medical scientists will be able to generate or regenerate body parts such as skin, bones, and vital organs. Other technological advances that are likely to take place in the future, according to Butler (1987), include:

Table 23.2 PROJECTED LIFE EXPECTANCY AT BIRTH BY SEX: 2000–2050

Year	Male	Female	Difference
2000	73.5	80.4	6.9
2010	74.4	81.3	6.9
2020	74.9	81.8	6.9
2030	75.4	82.3	6.9
2040	75.9	82.8	6.9
2050	76.4	83.3	6.9

Source: U.S. Bureau of the Census, *Current Population Reports,* Series P-25, No. 1018, "Projections of the Population of the United States, by Age, Sex, and Race: 1988–2080," January 1989. Projection data from middle series.

1. Medicinal cleansers or lasers that will unclog arteries
2. Antibodies that will treat cancer successfully
3. Artificial hearing
4. Considerable progress toward treating Alzheimer's disease
5. Bionics equipped with microprocessors that will result in "smart" arms and hands (see Box 23.1)

INSTITUTIONAL TRENDS

Technological change touches nearly every aspect of our lives and affects all the social institutions within our society. For example, in the economic institution, the banking industry has been transformed by automated banking procedures. Television has changed the face of politics with presidential debates and election returns, as well as changing our religious practices with the electronic church. Education has been radically altered with the use of computers, television, and videocassette recorders. In fact, the influence of technology is so powerful that it extends from before we are born until after we die—test-tube babies to tubes and machines for prolonging life, and then to cryonics after we die (see Box 23.2).

The Economy

The economic status of the older population will undoubtedly continue to improve. Average incomes will increase while the number of incomes below the poverty level will decrease. Much of this improvement will reflect increased coverage of the elderly under public and private pension programs.

Box 23.1 **Bionic Parts**

Although television promoted the "Six Million Dollar Man" as science fiction, in the very near future continued advances in biomedical research may allow millions of us to replace worn-out or damaged body parts with bionic substitutes.

Originally developed for its possible military applications, the science of bionics weaves together a number of different disciplines—including engineering, computer design, electronics, physics, and medicine—to produce implements for replacing or amplifying the potential of the human body.

According to Vance Packard, in the decades ahead "the production, sale, installation and servicing of human spare parts is likely to become the fastest-growing industry in the modern world. In dollar volumes it will rival the automobile spare-parts industry, conceivably the entire automobile-building industry.

Source: Ken Dychtwald and Joe Flower, *Age Wave.* Los Angeles: Jeremy P. Tarcher, 1989, p. 337.

Box 23.2 **A Prospect for Immortality: Human Cold Storage**

"Freezing is nature's way of saying time out and putting life on hold," according to Paul Segall, a biologist at the University of Southern California at Berkeley who is noted for his experiments with cryonics. *Cryonics* refers to the belief that renewed life is possible after death on this planet by freezing and placing persons in suspension at the time of death until reanimation is possible. Segall is also the director of Trans Time, Inc., where five people have been frozen and stored in liquid-nitrogen-cooled stainless steel tanks.

Although the technology of freezing is still in a primitive stage, according to Segall and other cryobiologists, freezing may hold the promise of biological immortality in that a person with a terminal disease could be frozen and then revived at some future date when a cure for the disease has been found.

With the publication of Robert Ettinger's book in 1964, *The Prospect of Immortality*, the first cryonics group was established in New York City in 1966. The cryonics movement seeks to promote study and interest in life extension, cryonics, and futurism. A typical member of the movement has an average education, comes from a middle to lower socioeconomic background, and is nonreligious. Nearly half of the members indicate no political interest or affiliation and most are married white males in their thirties (Smith, 1983).

Ettinger, regarded as the father of the cryonics movement, says that membership is up in the three American cryonics organizations and that hundreds of people are committed to having their bodies frozen after death. To be a candidate for being frozen, one pays $1,250 down and another $28,000 when death occurs. The money is transferred from the deceased's pre-established trust fund or life insurance policy. The deceased's contract with a cryonics corporation lasts until the time defrosting is considered desirable.

Sources: Carol Kahn, *Health*, March 1987; Joel Shurkin, *Longevity*, April, 1989; George P. Smith, II, *Medical-Legal Aspects of Cryonics: Prospects for Immortality*. Port Washington, NY: Associated Faculty Press, 1983.

In the future, older women will be better off financially than they are now. Some factors contributing to their improved financial status are (1) their higher rates of participation in the labor force; (2) their increased coverage under private pension plans; (3) their greater concentration in higher-paying industries and jobs; and (4) less sex discrimination in wages and salaries (Chen, 1985).

The trend toward early retirement is expected to continue to the turn of the century. At that time, the trend may reverse itself since fewer younger persons will be in the labor force because of the lower birth rates since the mid-1960s. This situation in turn will create a demand for older workers. As a result, business and industry will modify their current employment practices and provide incentives for workers to stay on the job.

What will be the effect of technological change on older workers in the future? There is considerable disagreement concerning this question. One view maintains that because older workers in the future will be better educated and will receive more continuous training, they will not be as disadvantaged as they have been in the past by technological advances. On the other hand, some argue that technological change will result in decline in the overall employment level, underemployment, permanent displacement, and the deskilling of jobs (Coberly & Morrison, 1984). Additional research is needed before the impact of technological advances on the older worker can be fully assessed. (See the reading "Technology and Older Adults" at the end of this chapter for further discussion of this topic.)

Another question to be explored concerns the elderly's attitude toward new

Many older workers, like this pharmacist, now need to use computers and other new technologies in order to perform their jobs. (Nick Myers)

technologies. One of the few studies done in this area reveals that older people have less positive views toward the new products of technology than do younger persons (Brickfield, 1984). As Table 23.3 shows, the higher the age of the person, the less likely that he or she had used such items as electronic calculators, cable TV, computers, video recorders, automatic teller machines, and video games.

The *elderly support ratio*, or dependency ratio (the number of persons age 65 and older to persons of working age, 18 to 64 years) has changed considerably in this century as a result of people living longer and families having fewer children. As Table 23.4 shows, in 1900 there were approximately 7 older persons for every 100 persons of working age; presently the ratio is about 20 per 100 persons. Dramatic changes will occur in this ratio when the baby boomers exit the work force and enter retirement. Predictions are that by 2020, the ratio will climb to 29 elderly per 100 persons of working age, and that by 2030, the ratio will reach 38. It is important to note that this support or dependency ratio is only a rough measure because many persons (65 and older) continue to work, and many younger persons (18 to 64) are not working.

The *total support ratio* (the ratio of the number of persons under 18 and over 65 years of age to the number of persons of working age) has declined dramatically since 1900. As Table 23.4 demonstrates, the total support ratio declines after 1960 until the year 2010. Even though it begins to increase again after that point, it still remains lower than what it was prior to the 1960s.

> This would suggest that fewer economic demands are currently placed on working age Americans for supporting the young and the old. From a public policy standpoint, however, the decline in the total support ratio, caused by a large decline in the number of children, masks the rise in the elderly support ratio. This is an important distinction because it is primarily publicly-funded programs which serve the elderly while mostly private (i.e., family) funds are directed toward the support of the young. Nonetheless, the increasing demands on public programs caused by a burgeoning elderly population are, in large part, offset by declining demands on private funds for supporting children. (U.S. Senate Special Committe on Aging, 1987–1988)

Table 23.3   USE OF TECHNOLOGY BY AGE

Technology	45–54	55–64	65+
Electronic calculator	76%	67%	41%
Cable TV	39	39	37
Computer	40	30	1
Video recorder	12	6	6
Automatic teller machine	19	14	9
Video games	28	13	12

Source: Cyril F. Brickfield. "Attitudes and Perceptions of Older People toward Technology." In P. K. Robinson, J. Livingston, and J. E. Birren (Eds), *Aging and Technological Advances.* New York: Plenum, 1984, p. 32.

Table 23.4   ELDERLY, YOUNG, AND TOTAL
SUPPORT RATIOS: 1900–2050

Year	65 +	Under 18	Total
1900	7.4	76.3	83.7
1920	8.0	67.7	75.7
1940	10.9	51.9	62.8
1960	16.8	65.1	82.0
1980	18.6	45.8	64.4
1990	20.4	41.4	61.7
2000	20.8	39.2	60.0
2010	21.8	34.7	56.5
2020	29.0	35.0	64.1
2030	38.0	36.0	73.9
2040	39.3	34.9	74.2
2050	39.9	34.8	74.8

Source: U.S. Bureau of the Census, *Current Population Reports,* Series P-25, No. 1018, "Projections of the
Population of the United States, by Age, Sex, and
Race: 1988–2080," January 1989. Projection data for
1990–2050 from middle series.

The Political System

As we noted in Chapter 14, despite a rapidly growing elderly population, there
appears to be no evidence of a marked increase in its political power now or in the
foreseeable future. The possibility of "senior power" in the sense of a politics of aging
seems highly unlikely. At present, political attitudes, party affiliations, social class,
ethnicity, and the interests of the elderly are far too diverse to result in a cohesive
aging vote that could determine the outcome of national elections. No great change
is likely in the near future. However, the elderly's participation in politics probably
will be greater as they come to represent a larger proportion of the total population,
and they will have more education than the previous generations of older persons
(Binstock, 1974).

Education

Although the educational attainment of older persons is still well below that of the
younger population, the gap in median school years between older and younger
persons has narrowed over the past three decades and is expected to continue to do
so. In 1987, the median level of education among the elderly had increased to 12
years, as compared with 12.7 years for younger persons. By 2000, the median number
of school years completed for persons age 65 and older is expected to reach 12.4 years,
as compared with 12.8 years for all persons age 25 and older.

Box 23.3 **The Fountain of Age**

Our country has been obsessed with youth for far too many years. Age has deen defined only as a decline from a peak of youth; and male youth at that—a certain kind of strength, prowess, potency, or a male definition of the woman as sex object. Age is denied; a fate worse than death. Negative stereotypes of older people are reinforced daily in the popular media, which contain very few examples of anyone 60 or older doing anything active or dynamic in society.

Meanwhile, we have the reality of people 60 and older who are breaking through this denial of age and defining for themselves a good life that doesn't seek the fountain of youth but instead affirms the fountain of age.

A revolution is implied if we begin to look at the years after 60 as simply another period of human development when *we* start to define the terms.

Research shows us that people in age become more and more themselves; in other words, the diversity of people in age is much greater than it is in youth. Maybe it's because something wonderful happens when we finally get to the point of affirming ourselves. When we free ourselves from conforming to certain imperatives, such as the way we should be as wives or mothers, or as successful men, then we can accept ourselves as we really are. We don't have that win/lose attitude that keeps us from taking risks. And if we take more risks, we can try all sorts of things and we don't have to win. But we do have to free ourselves to be our age and not try to hold on to youth.

Just as the women's movement began in my generation but really exploded in the next, so, I predict, will the age revolution. This is the revolution we will see at the end of the century when we break through the mystique and denial of age and start to define ourselves as persons fulfilling our human potential in unique ways in the new third of life. This revolution will change the music and the values in the same way the Beatles, the civil rights movement and the feminist movement did in the 1960s and 70s.

As we move into our 60s, 70s and 80s, my generation and the generation that follows will show that these can indeed be new, vital years of life satisfying in ways that we, as pioneers, will define.

Source: Betty Friedan, "Not for Women Only," *Modern Maturity*, April–May 1989, pp. 72–73.

Because they will be better educated and have more free time, older persons in the future will become more involved in lifelong learning—in programs of general education and those designed exclusively for the elderly. Prominent among the latter will be preparation-for-retirement programs, which not only will deal with such topics as finances, health, and legal problems but also, according to Pfeiffer (1976), will include "alternative patterns of meaningful participation in community and family life . . . through continued work participation, changed occupational status, second, third, and fourth careers, or through gradual education to leisure." In addition, preretirement programs will also be changed to accommodate the increasing number of women in the labor force. Past programs have primarily concerned the adjustment problems of men as they retired; in the future, such education will also be directed toward meeting the special needs of female retirees (McClusky, 1978).

As the enrollment of older people in educational institutions continues to increase, more offerings will be developed specifically for them. "Educational innovation for an aging society will demand not merely *access* to predetermined programs and materials, but *redesign* of those offerings to meet the needs of learners who bring with them the special strengths of age and experience" (Moody, 1986).

The Family

Families will be smaller in the future. When the baby boomers become parents and grandparents, they will have fewer children and grandchildren as compared with earlier generations. As a result, they will experience a more intense relationship with their adult children, and, with increased life expectancy, their relationship will be of a longer duration (Bengtson & Dannefer, 1987).

Besides being smaller, families will also be more complex in the future. Because of the present divorce and remarriage rate, and with people living longer today,

"Well, the children are grown up, married, divorced, and remarried. I guess our job is done."
(Drawing by Leo Cullum; © 1989 The New Yorker Magazine, Inc.)

generational relationships will be complicated by the development of step-grandparents and step-grandchildren (Brubaker, 1985). In addition, the four- or-five-generation family will be the norm by the next century because of the increasing longevity and shorter gaps between generations. Children will come to know their great-grandparents and even their great-great-grandparents.

Today, persons in their sixties and older have aged parents in their eighties and nineties. This trend should even be more pronounced in the future and may lead to more intergenerational households in which more than one generation is old.

SUMMARY

1. Predicting future trends within a society on the basis of present trends is called extrapolation. Some attempts at social forecasting are necessary in order to plan more effectively for the future and to develop solutions for problems that may arise. Two sources of social change are technology and changes in the demographic structure of the population. The time interval between the introduction of a change and society's adaptation to it is called cultural lag.

2. The older population is expected to continue increasing until the first third of the next century before slowing down. Most researchers do not see any spectacular improvements in life expectancy between now and into the next century. Women will continue to outlive men by about 7 years.

3. Although the future elderly will remain healthier to a later age, they will still have much the same health needs of the present generation of older persons. As the size of the elderly population increases, so will the need for nursing-home care. Many new technological advances in medical science are predicted for the future such as the replacement of nerve and brain cells, and progress toward the treatment of cancer and Alzheimer's disease.

4. The economic status of the elderly will continue to improve as average incomes rise and the number of incomes below the poverty level declines. The early-retirement trend may reverse itself around the beginning of the next century as the demand for older workers increases because of a labor shortage. There appears to be no evidence to justify the possibility of "senior power" in the near future. Presently, the elderly do not constitute a voting bloc, and there is no reason to expect a change.

5. The gap in median years of school between the older and younger population will continue to narrow. In the future, more older persons will be involved in both general education and educational programs that are specifically designed for them. Families in the future will be smaller, and four- or five-generation families will be the norm. Children will not only come to know their great-grandparents but their great-great-grandparents as well.

KEY TERMS

extrapolation   elderly support ratio
cultural lag   total support ratio
cryonics

FOR FURTHER STUDY

Dychtwald, Ken, & Flower, Joe (1989). *Age wave*. Los Angeles: Tarcher.

A highly readable book that discusses the growing older population and its impact on our future society.

Jarvik, Lissy F. (Ed.) (1978). *Aging into the 21st century*. New York: Gardner.

A collection of articles that deals with the future of aging from the perspective of various disciplines.

Kiesler, Sara B., Morgan, James N., & Oppenheimer, Valerie K. (Eds.) (1981). *Aging: Social change*. New York: Academic.

Written by scholars from the social and behavioral sciences, this volume examines the question of social change and its impact on the elderly, especially around the year 2000.

Pampel, Fred C. (1981). *Social change and the aged*. Lexington, MA: Lexington Books.

Examines changes in the position of the elderly in post-industrial society and the effects of these changes at both the individual and societal level of analysis.

Selby, Philip, & Schechter, Mal (1982). *Aging 2000: A challenge for society*. Lancaster, England: MTP Press Limited.

Reports results from a survey conducted in 16 countries to identify the problems of the elderly and the ways for dealing with them in order to guide policy makers in the future.

Reading

Technology and Older Adults

Sara Czaja and Robin Barr

This article shows how technological advances can be adapted to the needs of older people in the workplace, in the home, in medical and health care settings, and on the highways. Older people are viewed as active users of technologies instead of passive recipients.

Rapidly developing technology is changing the nature of work, the form and scope of both mass and interpersonal communications, the goals and settings of education and leisure activities, and most aspects of everyday life. Computer terminals are now commonplace in most public places and are becoming commonplace in home environments. Many routine activities—such as banking, the issuance of airplane tickets, home telephone-answering devices, and automatic monitoring of blood pressure— involve the use of some form of electronic technology or computerization. Technology has also changed the quality and delivery of health services.

How does an aging society adjust to these changes? This question is of interest to scientists, policymakers, manufacturers, and designers as well as older people themselves. The potential importance of technology to the well-being of the elderly clearly requires no proof. However, current cohorts of older people may be especially vulnerable to the negative effects of this technological revolution given that large percentages of them have had limited exposure to technology throughout their life course. This problem is exacerbated by the fact that many system designers assume that older people will have limited interactions with technology and thus they fail to consider them as a potential user group with designing technological systems. In order for the benefits of technology to be realized for this and future generations of older adults, we need to reconceptualize older individuals as active users of technology rather than as passive recipients.

One task of the research and design community is to understand areas where the elderly will interact with technology and to develop ways to facilitate this inter-

Sara J. Czaja and Robin A. Barr. "Technology and the Everyday Life of Older Adults." *The Annals of the American Academy of Political and Social Sciences*, 503, May, 1989. pp. 127–137. [Readers interested in full source citations and footnotes are referred to the original article.]

action. This latter task entails understanding how the processes of aging contribute to changes in physiological and psychological functioning and what the implications of such changes are for the design of technological systems. The critical question is whether technological change will enhance or impede the ability of older adults to live and work with greater independence. There are many potential positive consequences of new technology for older people. They include the reduction of physical demands associated with tasks, facilitation of communication, compensation for infirmities, additional linkage to the outside world, and increased safety. Yet, without attention to the abilities and requirements of older people, these positive consequences may be outweighed by such potential negative consequences as demands for faster-paced work, unnecessarily complex operation sequences, skill obsolescence, displacement of older workers, reduction of face-to-face interactions, and reduced societal ties. The obvious task is to maximize the benefits of technology for older adults while minimizing the potential costs. With careful planning, research, and design, technology can improve the quality of life of older people. . . .

USE OF TECHNOLOGY BY OLDER ADULTS

The following discussion focuses on settings where the older adult will need to interact with technology. Examples are provided to illustrate that technology has become a part of most routine tasks and activities.

At Work

Older adults who are still in the work force are almost certain to interact with new technologies at work. During the past decade, new computer and communication technologies have been, and continue to be, rapidly introduced into most occupational settings. Consequently, most workers now need to interact successfully with technology simply to perform their jobs. One as yet unanswered question is how the influx of this technology into work settings alters the work life of the elderly. Technology obviously changes the nature of work: in some cases, jobs are eliminated and new ones are created, and in other cases, both the context and the demands of the job are altered. How well do older workers cope with these changed contexts and demands? How well-adapted are the new job roles and activities to the aging work force? For example, secretaries and office personnel now need to use word processing, electronic mail, and data-base management packages to perform standard office tasks such as typing and filing. Managers, bank tellers, sales clerks, and cashiers are also using computers on a regular basis to carry out routine tasks and activities, such as sales transactions, inventory management, and decision making. This means that workers now have to learn to operate computers and use software packages to keep abreast of job demands. How well do older workers respond to these challenges? Can the new tasks be better tailored to the capacities of older adults?

Similar observations can be made for blue-collar occupations. Computer-interactive tasks are becoming prevalent within the general manufacturing, chemical, and nuclear power industries. For example, computer-aided manufacturing, now the most important technology within the industry, involves both direct and indirect applications of computers in the manufacturing process. Examples include computer-aided control of machines, process control, process planning, inventory control, and scheduling. In conventional manufacturing operations, machines are operated by humans, and products are scheduled and transported by humans. In automated manufacturing, the process is accomplished by a group of machines that are operated by computer-based controllers. For both blue-collar and white-collar older workers, the resulting challenges include job displacement and changes in job-skill requirements.

To make these challenges easier to overcome, changes both in attitudes toward older workers and in the design of the new technologies are necessary. There is evidence that older workers are less likely to be selected for retraining programs in firms than younger employees. Yet there is little evidence that older workers benefit less from such retraining or stay for a shorter time with the company after retraining than younger workers. As new technologies continue to invade the workplace, especially enterprises experiencing labor shortages, an active policy of selecting older workers for retraining will eventually be instituted. At the same time, new equipment will need to be introduced into the workplace with older workers in mind. Attention to such design aspects as glare from video displays, positioning of keyboard controls, and complexity of operating sequences has the potential to enhance the productivity of all workers and particularly can increase the longevity of employment of older individuals.

Considering future employment opportunities, current projections indicate that jobs in the service sector will increase dramatically over the next few decades. Broadly defined, the service sector includes medical care, business services, and personnel service and nonprofit agencies. Specific types of jobs that will experience growth include clerical workers, cashiers, and office, sales, and banking clerks. Most of these occupations will be highly affected by new technology. Other types of jobs that will increase in upcoming years center around computer programming, servicing, repairs, and operation. Currently, older people tend not to be employed in these occupations, and reasons for their underrepresentation need to be further identified. Their full participation in new and expanding job categories not only will be of benefit to them but will also benefit employers seeking to hire and retain workers in a field where worker shortages will continue to be a problem.

Consequently, the relationship between the new technologies and the employment potential of older adults needs to be considered. This issue must be examined from two perspectives: promoting employment opportunities for unemployed elderly and maintaining currently employed elderly in the labor force. Considering the former, technology may be designed to improve work oppportunities for older people. For example, technological advances are being used to assist people with visual deficits. In addition to traditional optical aids, closed-circuit television is used to magnify flexibly the image of a target object for some low-vision workers. Other aids can be as simple as a piece of cardboard with a slit cut in it; the reader can place the opening over the current line or lines of text to be read, thereby increasing contrast substantially. An equivalent device is easily created for computer screens. Since visual deficits are more likely to occur in older populations, this elementary technology particularly promotes employment opportunities for older adults.

Computer technology also makes paid work at home a more likely option through the use of electronic links between office and home and between coworkers. Older people who find it difficult to leave home because of health or transportation problems can benefit from such arrangements. Also, computer tasks such as data entry are especially amenable to part-time work, and research indicates that such work is a likely and preferred option for many older people.

Depending, however, on the manner in which it is implemented and the employment practices that are adopted, technology may negatively affect the employment status of older people. One obvious problem is that of skill obsolescence and displacement. Unless retraining programs are available, older workers will not have the requisite job skills to compete in the work environment. The manner in which technology changes jobs may also be detrimental to older people. Thoughtless technological innovation can easily replace physically demanding jobs with poorly designed substitutes. Jobs may be created with information-processing demands that unnecessarily restrict the effectiveness of many older adults. For example, many older adults have particular difficulty, relative to younger adults, with complex speeded tasks. Yet well-planned changes in task design can eliminate such age differences and improve the performance of both younger and older people. The technology itself may also create health problems for older people. There are numerous reports in the literature of visual strain and bodily discomfort among people who use computer terminals on a regular basis. It is likely that these complaints will be exacerbated for older people, given age-related problems in vision and physical functioning.

Currently, however, specific knowledge about the impact of technology on an aging work force is limited. As has been suggested, there are a number of issues that need to be addressed by researchers and employers to ensure that technology serves to improve the work life of the older population.

At Home

A broad assortment of devices is now available to assist elderly adults in the activities of home life. Lighted treads on stairs, can openers that can be managed by arthritic hands, grab bars in bathrooms, slip-proof bathtubs, and a host of other low-tech, relatively inexpensive devices all provide substantial assistance. But technology can serve as much more than a prop for elderly adults. In particular, computer technology can substantially enhance the social activities and intellectual challenges that an older adult chooses to engage in. Older people typically have more leisure time than younger people and often spend the majority of their time at home engaged in individual, sedentary activities. Most researchers agree that the elderly need more challenging and enriching leisure and recreational experiences, as these are known to be important to continued health and morale. Computer technology holds the promise of making discretionary time more meaningful to older people and also providing additional links to the outside world.

Older adults often report problems participating in outside activities because of physical restrictions, lack of transportation, inconvenience, and fear of crime. Computers help to alleviate these problems by providing oppportunities for continued education and recreation within home settings. Software is now available for a wide variety of topics, such as nutrition and foreign languages, which make it possible for older people to maintain existing hobbies or to develop new interests. Through computer networks, it is now possible for older people to establish electronic links with universities.

Computers are also being used to facilitate communication between the elderly themselves or with others who share a common interest. Social isolation and loneliness are common problems experienced by older people. Electronic-mail networks are being established that allow people to communicate with one another and to form mutual-support groups. Such electronic networks now make it easier for older people to maintain ties to family and to form new friendships.

Older people are also using computers for retrieval of information, for example, information about transportation, social services, or recreation activities. It is now possible to use computers to carry out routine errands such as shopping, bill payment, and financial management. Computers also offer the potential for augmenting memory functioning by serving as a real-time memory aid. For example, an individual can create a personal data base that contains prompting for important dates, medication schedules, anniversaries, financial due dates, and so forth. All of these computer applications offer the potential for enhancing the functional independence of older adults.

In addition to computers, other forms of technology are also available that can enhance the ability of older people to live at home. For example, electronic emergency alarm systems are available and easily accessible. These systems use a personal transmitter, which, in the case of an emergency such as a fall, sends a signal to a phone that is linked to a hospital emergency room. In addition to emergency response systems, telecommunication devices are being developed that provide home safety and security services. These systems can be linked to a micro-processor to monitor the home's electrical use, heating, ventilation. The system can also be linked to automatic dialers to notify authorities when assistance is needed.

The success of all these applications is dependent on the awareness of their existence and the willingness and ability of the elderly to use the various devices. Research has shown that older people are receptive to technologies such as computers if they perceive them as useful, if they are provided with adequate training, and if the system or device is relatively easy to use. But problems remain to be solved concerning the design of user interfaces that permit easy access and widespread use by a broad spectrum of older adults.

Medical Environments

By now it is common knowledge that medical technologies have had an enormous impact on prolonging life for severely ill patients. Yet the role of technology in the management and prevention of disease has received much less emphasis. One important new challenge for research is to develop ways to enable older people to use technology such as computers to participate directly in disease prevention and management. For example, computers may be used for computer-assisted health instruction. Software programs—some of them adapted from the space program—are being developed concerning health maintenance and disease management. Currently, most of the available health instructional programs are used in hospitals; however, there is a growing awareness of their value for older people at home.

Computers may also be used to assist disease management by giving reminders of medication schedules or instructions on diet or rehabilitation practices. For example, systems are now being developed in which a physician keys in a prescription schedule to a central computer facility. That facility then calls the patient at home at the appropriate times using a computer-activated voice to remind the patient to take the prescription drug. These systems are being further developed to allow patients to key in, through the telephone, any changes in symptoms that can alert the physician to possible side effects or changes in the course of the disease. Also, systems are now available that provide daily appraisals of a patient's vital signs and monitor changes in functioning. In such systems, sensors incorporating microprocessors monitor blood pressure, pulse rate, body temperature, and heart electrical activity. The data are then stored and subsequently compared with later readings to check for changes.

Technology may also be used to aid in long-term care for the elderly. Assistive technologies are available to aid walking, hearing, and vision. In the near future, these technologies will include programmable wheelchairs, voice-activated computer control centers, and robots that aid in the performance of tasks such as meal preparation.

Two obstacles remain before such applications can materially improve the quality of life of a broad range of older people. The first problem is one of design. The applications must be readily available, understandable, and easy to use. The second is one of economics. Not only must software be written and technology be developed that will permit older adults to use the information and to gain from it, but ways must be found to make the cost of such equipment within reach of the intended users. In calculating the costs and benefits of such systems, the obvious task is to show that such systems are effective in maintaining independence—that they do reduce the number and duration of hospitalizations and reduce the probability of entry to extended-care facilities.

On the Highway

Driving is another area where rapid changes in technology can either improve older adults' performance or lead to increased errors and the possibility of serious accident and injury. Violation statistics of older drivers reveal that they are most likely to incur right-of-way and traffic-sign violations. In contrast, they are very much less likely than younger drivers to incur speeding violations. Although more research needs to be done, the available data suggest that older drivers fail to notice some signs rather than deliberately ignore them. Technology can help to reduce the problem in a number of ways. First, new automotive technologies can permit head-up displays on instrument panels. Such displays potentially reduce the amount of time older—or younger—drivers must take their eyes off the road to consult instruments. Second, low-tech strategies can be employed to improve both the design of road signs and their placement. A critical—and often overlooked—variable in this case is ensuring that older drivers are included in any pilot population of drivers who are examined to test the effect on driving of changes in signs.

Current research on serious accidents tells us that individuals over age 65 are substantially more likely to be killed or severely injured than younger people. New technologies can reduce the likelihood of serious injury or death under these circumstances, and some of these technologies are particularly appropriate for older people. For example, relative to younger people, older adults are involved in fewer high-speed frontal collisions and more car-to-car lateral collisions. Technologies under development that protect against the effects of lateral collisions will thus disproportionately improve the survival chances of the population most at risk from such accidents.

The most widely used and effective technology currently available is the seat belt. Evidence indicates, however, that lap-and-shoulder seat belts are less than satisfactory for many older people. Those with arthritic problems have difficulty reaching for and buckling the belts. Neck strains and sprains associated with seat-belt use are particularly likely to occur in older adults. Supplementary air bags do provide a substantial benefit to older adults when used in conjunction with lap-and-shoulder belts; however, the sensors in air bags are not likely to be activated by lateral-impact collisions, which occur disproportionately among older drivers.

Therefore, there is clearly a need for further research in technologies to protect older drivers. Nevertheless, some encouraging trends are evident. For example, power-assisted mounting of the upper section of the lap-and-shoulder seat belt is now becoming available in some models and does diminish discomfort problems for older persons of small stature.

As in other areas, new technology can also exacerbate the problems of older drivers. Unnecessarily cluttered instrument panels, synthesized voices that are difficult for adults with selective hearing impairment to understand, and awkward placement of controls are among the technological errors that will likely disrupt older drivers particularly severely. . . .

SUMMARY

The emergence of a technological revolution at a time when the population of the United States is aging has highlighted the need to design technology that permits older adults to achieve their full potential. . . .

In a society that is growing older, no other incentive to design for older adults seems to be needed. Furthermore, attention to the needs of this population carries with it one likely additional benefit: accommodating the needs of the elderly in the design process typically facilitates the performance of young as well as old.

Glossary

accessory apartments The conversion of surplus space in an existing single-family home into a separate living unit; sometimes referred to as a mother-in-law apartment.

achieved status A position in society earned through competition and individual effort. See also *ascribed status.*

ACTION A federal agency that manages a number of volunteer programs including the Foster Grandparent Program (FGP), Retired Senior Volunteer Program (RSVP), and Senior Companion Program (SCP).

active euthanasia Deliberate termination of the life of a hopelessly ill or nonfunctional patient. See also *passive euthanasia.*

active neglect A condition occurring when a caregiver withholds from an older person food, medicine, and other necessities for daily living. See also *passive neglect.*

activity theory A theory that stresses a continuation of roles and activities as one ages; when roles are lost the individual is expected to find substitutes. See also *disengagement theory.*

acute condition An illness characterized as having a definite and rapid onset, lasting only a short time, having pronounced symptoms, and generally responding well to the use of drugs or therapy.

adult day care centers Facilities designed to prevent premature institutionalization for those who have mental or physical impairments and are not capable of full-time independent living, but who can manage to stay in the community if professional support is provided.

adult education The education of older adults that includes credit and noncredit courses, lectures, discussion groups, correspondence courses, education by television, and on-the-job training.

adverse drug reaction "Any unintended or undesired consequences of drug therapy" (William Simonson)

age consciousness Being aware of one's own aging and the aging of others.

Age Discrimination in Employment Act (ADEA) A law passed in 1967 that banned age discrimination in hiring, promoting, and dismissing employees between the ages of 40 and 65. In 1978 the law was amended to raise the upper limit of protection to age 70. In 1986 the upper limit was removed for nearly all workers. The ADEA now protects virtually all workers age 40 and older.

age effect The impact of maturation on one's behavior or performance. See also *cohort effect; period effect*

age norms Expectations about what is considered appropriate behavior at different ages.

age role The expected behavior of one who holds a certain age status

age–sex structure The number or proportion of males and females in each age group in the population.

age status Differential rights and obligations awarded to individuals on the basis of age.

age stratification Structured social inequality based on age.

age stratification model According to Matilda Riley and her associates, age, much like social class, organizes society into a hierarchy and divides the population into categories on the basis of the amount of social rewards they possess (wealth, power, and prestige) and functions as a means of control over these rewards.

ageism Prejudices and stereotypes applied to older persons based solely on their age. See also *New Ageism.*

aging All the regular changes that occur in biologically mature individuals as they advance in chronological age.

aging subculture According to Arnold Rose, the elderly tend to interact more with one another as they age and less with other age groups because of the common interests that they share and because, to some extent, they are excluded from interacting with other age groups.

altruistic suicide Suicide committed by individuals so strongly integrated into group life that they are willing to give their lives for the good of the group.

Alzheimer's disease An organic disorder characterized by a progressive deterioration of mental functioning.

anomie (1) normlessness or lack of regulation (Emile Durkheim); (2) a widespread frustration that occurs when there is an acute gap between cultural goals and socially approved ways to achieve them (Robert Merton).

anomic suicide Suicide resulting from conditions in which individuals lack guidelines to regulate their behavior because traditional values and norms are weak or absent.

antediluvian theme The idea that people in ancient times lived much longer than they do today. Also referred to as the Methuselah theme.

anticipatory socialization The process of preparing for a new role before assuming it.

ascribed status A person's position in society, which is assigned at birth without regard for individual ability. See also *achieved status.*

baby boom The dramatic increase in births from 1946 to 1964.

bag ladies Impoverished, homeless elderly women who carry all their belongings in shopping bags.

barrio A distinct and relatively closed Mexican-American urban community.

bureaucratization The growth of formal large-scale organizations.

busy ethic The high value that people place on keeping busy in retirement.

caregiver One involved in any phase of health care. See also *primary caregiver.*

caregiving burden The emotional stress and physical strain that accompany the difficulties of caring for a chronically ill person, usually a spouse or elderly parent.

case study A study method that focuses on a single case in considerable depth and detail, usually over a long period of time.

cataract The clouding of the lens inside the eye that leads to reduced vision.

centenarian A person 100 years of age or older.

chronic condition An illness or disease characterized as having a gradual onset and persisting over a period of time for which there is no medical cure.

chronological age The calculation of one's age by the number of years he or she has lived.

circuit breaker A type of property tax relief for low-income elderly homeowners.

class See *social class.*

closed-class system A society in which members' social mobility is severely restricted.

cohabitation Nonmarried members of the opposite sex living together.

cohort Persons born within the same year or same time period.

cohort analysis A technique for examining cross-sectional and longitudinal data at the same time; the comparison of one or more cohorts at two or more points in time.

cohort effect Socialization experiences that are largely shared with other members of the same cohort who grew up during the same time period. See also *age effect*; *period effect*.

community A grouping of people who live in a limited territorial area, where they have a sense of belonging and fulfill most of their daily needs and activities.

congregate meals A federal nutrition program, enacted as part of the Older Americans Act, that serves midday meals to the elderly at central locations, such as senior centers, schools, and churches.

consequential dimension of religion Behavior linked to one's relationship with God.

contributory pension plan A private pension plan in which the employee pays part of the cost.

counterphobia A defense mechanism in which one overcompensates for feared situations.

crime Behavior that violates a norm that has been formally enacted into criminal law.

cross-over phenomenon After a certain age the life expectancies of older blacks and older whites tend to reverse.

cross-sectional study The comparison of two or more groups at one point in time. See also *longitudinal study*.

cryonics The belief that there can be renewed life after death on this planet by freezing and placing persons in suspension at the time of death until reanimation is possible.

cultural lag The time period between the introduction of a change and society's adaptation to it.

cultural relativism An attitude that all patterns of behavior should be analyzed in the cultural context in which they are found and not by the standards of another culture.

cultural universals The general traits or characteristics that exist in all societies.

culture The social heritage of a society that is transmitted to each generation; learned behavior that is shared with others.

demography The scientific study of the size, composition, distribution, and changes in human populations.

denial A defense mechanism in which one refuses to face painful thoughts or feelings.

dependent variable The variable that is assumed to be affected by the independent variable.

deviance Any behavior that violates a norm.

diagnosis-related groups (DRGs) A list of specific medical conditions or combinations of illnesses with preset amounts used by Medicare to reimburse hospitals. See also *prospective payment plan*.

discrimination Unfair or unequal treatment of members of a minority group.

disengagement theory A theory that assumes that it is mutually beneficial for the older individual and society to withdraw from each other.

displacement The shifting of blame from the real cause of difficulty to other persons, objects, or situations.

double jeopardy A term applied to those minority members who are devalued because of old age and are disadvantaged because of their minority status.

double standard of aging A term describing the different forms that aging takes for men and women in our society.

drug interaction When two or more drugs are taken together and one modifies the effect of the other. See also *adverse drug reaction*.

early retirement Retiring before the age of 65.

earnings test (retirement test) A restriction limiting the amount of money persons 65–70 are allowed to earn while remaining eligible for their full Social Security benefits.

economic institution The norms and ideas controlling the production and distribution of scarce foods and services in a society.

egoistic suicide Suicide committed by a person who lacks the emotional attachments and psychological support usually involved in group living.

elder abuse The mistreatment of an older person through physical or psychological injury or by financial exploitation by a caretaker.

elder cottage housing opportunity (ECHO) A small, free-standing, removable housing unit that is typically placed in the side or back yard of a single-family home to provide housing for elderly parents.

elder neglect The failure of a caretaker to fulfill an important need of an older person when resources are available to do so.

Elderhostel A network of colleges and universities that offers one-week academic programs at moderate cost to persons age sixty or older. The participants live on campus and take courses taught by regular faculty members.

elderly support ratio The ratio of the number of persons aged 65 and older to persons of working age (18 to 64 years).

emergency response system A type of communication program that allows older persons to summon help through an alarm-and-response system.

Employment Retirement Income Security Act (ERISA) Legislation that regulates and supervises private pension plans and provides basic protection against the loss of retirement benefits.

ethnic group A group that differs from the larger society in such characteristics as race, religion, nationality, language, or customs.

ethnocentrism The tendency to regard one's own culture as superior to all others.

exchange theory A theory based on the premise that much social interaction can be reduced to rewards and costs.

experiment A research tool in which the investigator controls or manipulates at least one variable being studied.

extended family Several nuclear families who are joined together by extensions of the parent–child relationship.

extrapolation Predicting future social changes on the basis of existing trends.

fatalistic suicide Suicide committed as a result of excessive regulation and social oppression.

filial maturity The developmental process in which the child can be depended upon by the parents and is dependable as far as the parents are concerned.

filial piety An ethic expressed in respect and obedience to one's parents.

folkways Rules that govern the conventions and routines of everyday life, and define what is socially correct.

formal organization A large and impersonal secondary group deliberately designed to achieve specific goals.

Foster Grandparent Program (FGP) A program that provides an opportunity for older persons to work on a one-to-one basis with children who have special needs in a variety of settings.

fountain theme The idea that there is some substance that will bring about rejuvenation. Also referred to as the rejuvenation theme.

Friendly Visitors A program in which older volunteers visit on a regular basis elderly persons that are homebound or institutionalized.

functional disorder A disorder for which no physical cause can be found and the origin of which appears to be emotional.

gay Men or women who engage mainly in homosexual relations.

generation gap Differences in values, norms, and lifestyles in groups or individuals of different ages.

gerocomeia Homes for the elderly in the fifth century, which were supported by the state, the church, and private persons.

gerocomy The belief that an old man may absorb youth from young women.

geronticide The killing of old people.

gerontocracy A society in which old men are the rulers.

gerontology The scientific study of aging.

gerontology education Instruction at both the undergraduate and graduate levels mainly for those persons who plan to teach or conduct research in the field of aging.

Gerovital-H3 A highly questionable drug that is supposed to retard the aging process as well as be effective in treating a number of degenerative diseases.

"golden age" myth The belief that in the past older persons were highly honored and respected in the family and the community.

gradual retirement Giving an employee shorter hours or extended vacations so that retirement may be experienced in small doses.

graying of America A term that denotes the increasing percentage of older persons in the population as well as a rising median age in this country.

grief work A process by which survivors grieve, free themselves from the relationship with the deceased, and then rebuild their lives.

group Two or more people who interact with one another in a standardized pattern and who share a sense of common identity.

guardianship A type of protective service in which a guardian manages the person and property of another who is legally incompetent.

Hayflick limit The finite capacity for cells to divide.

hidden unemployment Older workers who drop out of the labor force after finding their search for employment futile and as a result are no longer classified as unemployed.

hidden poor Older persons who live with others (mostly relatives) whose incomes are sufficient to raise the elderly out of the poverty level. Also low-income persons are not counted as poor if they are institutionalized.

Hispanic Americans of Spanish origin.

homosexual Preferential sexual attraction for persons of the same sex.

hospice A facility devoted specifically to the care of the dying.

hyperborean theme The idea that people in some remote places had extreme longevity; also referred to as Shangri-La theme.

ideological dimension of religion The religious beliefs that one holds.

income The money that people receive in exchange for labor or services or from pensions or investments. See also *wealth*.

independent variable A variable directly manipulated by the investigator so that its effect on the dependent variable may be studied. See also *dependent variable*.

Index of Activities of Daily Living (ADL) A scale that focuses on the unaided performance of six basic personal care activities: eating, toileting, dressing, bathing, getting in and out of bed, and continence.

individual power The ability to control one's life.

Individual Retirement Account (IRA) A custodial retirement account that is tax-free until withdrawal. There is a penalty for withdrawing before the age of 59½ except in cases of disability.

industrialization The shifting of the workplace from the home to the factory, resulting in radical changes in production and economic organization.

information and referral program A program linking older people with services that have been designed to meet their specific needs.

innovation Achieving a desirable goal by undesirable means.

institution An organized cluster of norms—folkways, mores, and laws—that surround an important social need or activity of a society.

Instrumental Activities of Daily Living (IADL) The capacity to perform basic activities that focus on home management and independent living.

interaction The process of acting toward someone who interprets the act and responds to it.

"intergenerational equity" movement Proponents of this movement claim that the progress the elderly has made in recent years in government programs and policies has been achieved at the expense of the young.

intermediate care facility (ICF) A facility that provides less health care than a skilled-nursing facility but more than a custodial or residential care. See also *skilled nursing facility*.

intimacy at a distance The preference of older people to live near, but not with, their children.

involuntary euthanasia A case in which passive or active euthanasia is imposed on a patient who is incapable of giving consent.

Issei First-generation Japanese-Americans (old–old). See also *Nisei*.

kibbutz (pl. kubbutzim) Agricultural settlements organized around the principle of communal living in Israel.

labeling theory A process by which some people label other members of society as deviant.

law A formalized type of control; rules enacted by those who exert political power and that are enforced by the police and other officials who have been given the authority to do so.

lesbian Female homosexual.

life chances The probability that a person will obtain the opportunities that affect health, longevity, and happiness.

life course The sequence of stages that individuals pass through from infancy to old age and the life events that roughly coincide with these stages; often used synonymously with life cycle.

life course education Instruction regarding psychological, personal, familial, occupational and other activities related to specific stages of life.

life expectancy The average number of years remaining at any specified age.

life review A process in which older individuals recall and discuss their past experiences.

life span The average age members of a species can survive free of disease and accident under optimum conditions.

lifelong learning Education and training that continues throughout the life course.

living will A document prepared while individuals are mentally competent to inform others that they do not wish to prolong the inevitability of death by artificial means or heroic measures.

long-term care Services provided over an extended period of time for those persons with chronic physical and mental disabilities.

long-term disability A reduction in a person's normal activities as a result of a chronic condition.

longitudinal study A study method in which repeated measures on the same individuals are made at two or more points in time. See also cross-sectional study.

looking-glass self The concept of self that persons derive from the reactions of others to them.

mandatory retirement Retirement that is forced on a person at a fixed age.

master status A person's occupation, which usually determines his or her general position in society; also known as key status.

maximum life potential The length of life of the longest-lived members of a species.

median age The age that divides the population into two equal segments, one of which is younger than the median and one of which is older than the median.

Medicaid A healthcare program for low-income persons of all ages financed jointly by the states and the federal government.

Medicaid-spend down The requirement that nursing home residents must deplete all their income and assets in order to qualify for long-term care under Medicaid.

medicalization of aging The controlling of the behavior of older people through the use of drugs.

Medicare A federal hospital and medical insurance program for persons age 65 and over.

Medigap insurance Insurance policies that supplement Medicare coverage.

Methuselah theme See *antediluvian theme.*

minority group A group of people who in some ways differ from the dominant group in society and who, because of these differences, are the objects of prejudice and discrimination.

modernization The social changes that occur when a preindustrial society develops economically and the workplace shifts from the home to the factory.

monogamy A form of family organization in which a man can have only one wife.

mores Rules that define what is morally right or wrong in a society and are considered extremely important for the welfare of the group.

multipurpose senior center A designated community facility for older people that offers a wide variety of activities and services.

myth of abandonment The belief that adult children desert their parents in old age.

near poor Persons who live on incomes just slightly above the poverty level.

New Ageism Prejudice against the elderly because they are seen as being responsible for the alleged ills of society. See also *"intergenerational equity" movement.*

Nisei Second-generation Japanese-Americans (young–old). See also *Issei.*

noncontributory pension plan A private pension plan financed totally by the employer.

nonsubsidized retirement community A retirement community in which persons may buy their homes and the land on which the home is built, or the developer may retain ownership.

norms Standards or rules of behavior.

nuclear family The most basic of all family types, composed of a husband, a wife, and their children.

nursing home A generic term for any residential facility that gives some level of nursing care.

Obsute A theme in ancient Japanese literature involving the abandonment of the elderly.

old–old Persons 75 to 84 years of age.

Older American Act (OAA) Legislation to establish programs and allocate funds to improve the life of the elderly.

oldest–old Persons 85 years of age or older.

ombudsman An agency or program that acts as an advocate for the institutionalized elderly by assessing, verifying, and seeking to resolve complaints.

open-class system A society that permits its members to move up or down the social hierarchy, depending on their own accomplishments or failings.

organic disorder A disorder that has a clearly established physical basis.

outreach programs Programs to make people aware of available services in the community as well as attempting to overcome resistance to their use.

participant observation A technique commonly used by sociologists in case studies, in which the investigator takes part in whatever group is being studied.

passive euthanasia Permitting a patient to die naturally, rather than employing heroic measures to sustain life. See also *active euthanasia.*

passive neglect A condition occurring when an older person is left alone for long time periods or isolated. See also *active neglect.*

period effect An historical event that affects the entire population for a limited period of time. See also *age effect; cohort effect.*

pet therapy The use of pets to reduce the elderly's feelings of isolation and loneliness.

Peter Pan syndrome Refusal to face the reality of aging by pretending to stay young.

pigeon drop scheme A confidence game in which older people, especially older women, are duped out of large sums of money.

planned retirement community A retirement community that was originally and deliberately planned as such.

political institution A cluster of norms that serves to maintain social order, to protect against outside enemies, and to plan and coordinate for the general welfare.

politics The process by which people acquire and exercise power over others.

polyandry A form of family organization in which a woman can have more than one husband.

polygyny A form of family organization in which a man can have more than one wife.

population The total collection of individuals or units that the researcher studies.

population pyramid A diagram that graphically depicts the age–sex structure of a population.

portability The transfer of pension rights from one plan to another when the worker changes jobs.

poverty level A specific income used to define the poor.

preindustrial Societies whose economies are based on hunting and gathering.

prejudice A state of mind that entails feelings and attitudes.

presbyopia Farsightedness.

prestige The social recognition and respect that one receives from others.

primary caregiver The person with the major responsibility for an older person's care, usually a wife or adult daughter.

primary deviance A short-lived and mostly unnoticed violation of social norms. See also *secondary deviance.*

primary group A group in which the members have an intimate, direct, and personal relationship with one another. See also *secondary group.*

primary memory The temporary memory system that stores information from a few seconds to a minute or so and has a limited capacity of about seven or eight items.

progeria A rare childhood disease in which its victims resemble very old, small people.

progress Social change of a desirable nature, which implies a value judgement that the change taking place is for the better.

projection Attributing one's undesirable feelings to others, in an effort to relieve one's own anxieties.

prospective payment plan (PPP) A reimbursement method paid by Medicare in which a predetermined amount for a specific diagnosis is paid to hospitals regardless of the type of services or length of stay.

protective services Services that provide assistance to older persons who are too mentally or physically incapacitated to manage their own affairs or act in their own behalf.

Protestant ethic A cluster of values and attitudes surrounding a moral commitment to hard work, frugality, and moderation.

reference group Any group or social category used as a standard of comparison and by which accomplishments and failures are measured.

rehearsal for widowhood Psychological preparations by wives for some of the problems they are likely to encounter when their husbands die.

rejuveration theme See *fountain theme.*

religion "A system of beliefs and practices by which a group of people interpret and respond to what they feel is sacred, and usually, supernatural as well." (Johnstone)

religiosity Interest and involvement in religious activities.

reminiscence The recalling of the past that is part of the normal life review process. See also *life review.*

representative A sample that contains basically the same distribution of pertinent characteristics in the population being studied.

resocialization The replacement of former norms and values with new ones.

retirement "An economically nonproductive role for large numbers of people whose labor is not considered essential to or necessary for the functioning of the economic order." (Orbach)

retirement community A planned, relatively self-sufficient entity, partially separated from the larger community, and whose residents are mainly retired or semi-retired.

retreatism A mode of adaptation in which the individual rejects both the cultural goals and the conventional means to achieve them.

rites-of-passage Ceremonies that mark and publicly announce the transition from one status to the next.

ritualistic dimension of religion Participation in organizational and nonorganizational activities.

ritualism Rejecting the approved cultural goals, while abiding by the approved means, sometimes to the point of obsession.

role The expected behavior of one who holds a certain status.

role ambiguity The result when there are no clearly defined guidelines or expectations concerning requirements of a given role.

role discontinuity The result of a lack of preparation and consistency in training for a role that one will take on at the next consecutive stage.

role model An individual whose behavior in a certain role provides a pattern for another individual to follow in performing the same role.

role rehearsal The process of an individual acting out behavior required in a future role.

role reversal The reversal of the parent–child relationship: as the child takes on the supportive role of the parent, the parent assumes the former dependency role of the child.

role set The entire array of related roles associated with a particular status that an individual occupies.

sacred Elements that are separate from the everyday world and that evoke feelings of respect and awe.

sample The selection of a certain number of units from the entire population being studied.

sample survey A systematic way to gather data about individuals or groups through the use of interviews or mailed questionnaires.

secondary deviance Violations of social norms that are discovered and made public by one's family, friends, employer, or a law enforcement agency. See also *primary deviance*.

secondary memory The memory system that can store limitless amounts of information for long periods of time or even permanently, except in cases of brain injury or disease. See also *primary memory*.

Section 8 A housing program that provides subsidized rent to low-income families and allows eligible persons to select their own dwellings.

Section 202 The primary federal means for financing the construction of subsidized rental housing for the elderly through low-interest government loans.

selective memory The act of remembering only the good.

self-fulfilling prophecy A false belief or prediction that comes true through the behavior that it produces.

senescence The process of growing old; the period of years during which one becomes old.

Senior Companion Program (SCP) A program that provides care and assistance to other adults, primarily the homebound elderly with emotional, physical, and mental impairments.

senior power The political influence of older persons.

sexual preference A term being used more frequently as studies reveal that few persons are exclusively heterosexual or homosexual.

shared housing An arrangement in which a homeowner rents out a room or rooms in exchange for rent or a combination of services and rent; the term also refers to group residences or group-shared housing.

sibling bond A relationship in which there is a reciprocity and sharing among members.

sick role Persons who are no longer able to perform the necessary tasks of daily living and are forced to shift from independence to dependence.

single-room occupancy (SROs) Inner-city hotels and rooming houses, usually with a shared or community bath and no kitchen unit.

skilled nursing home facility (SNF) A facility that provides around-the-clock skilled nursing care or rehabilitation services as well as other related health services. See also *intermediate care facility.*

social breakdown syndrome A stage theory in which older persons are often labeled as incompetent by society, and eventually they in turn label themselves as incompetent.

social category People who have some characteristic in common, such as the same occupation, hobby, or age.

social class A category of individuals and families who share relatively equal amounts of social rewards; one's social class is often determined by occupation, education, and income.

social clocks Age norms that govern the timing of adult behavior.

social gerontology A subfield that focuses mainly on the social aspects of aging while deemphasizing the biological and psychological aspects.

social intervention A planned attempt to change, supposedly for the better, the lives of other individuals or groups through the application of skills and knowledge.

social mobility The vertical movement of persons from one social class to another.

social problem A condition that a significant number of people believe to be undesirable and feel that something should be done to correct it.

social services "A social mechanism for [the] distribution of resources designed to achieve and maintain a prescribed level of well-being for all members of society." (Shlonsky)

socialization The process through which individuals learn their culture and acquire the skills, attitudes, values, and roles that allow them to become members of their society.

societal power The ability to control or influence the lives of others.

sociology The scientific study of human interaction.

sociology of aging The scientific study of the interaction of older persons in society.

status A person's position in society along with the rights and obligations it entails.

status inconsistency A situation in which a person ranks high in one status dimension but low in another.

stereotypes Oversimplified, exaggerated beliefs about a group or category of people.

stratification The ranking of individuals and families into higher and lower social positions according to their share of social rewards.

subsidized retirement community A retirement community that provides public housing.

Sunbelt The southern and southwestern states.

Supplemental Security Income (SSI) The first federal program to provide a guaranteed minimum income for the most needy and vulnerable groups in the population.

synchronized retirement A husband and wife who retire at the same time.

telephone reassurance A program in which calls are made at a certain time each day to older persons who live alone.

theory of shared functions According to this theory, to accomplish most tasks in our society there must be coordination and cooperation between primary groups and formal organizations.

total institution Places of residence where individuals are isolated from the larger society for an extended period of time.

total support ratio The ratio of the number of persons under 18 and over 65 to the number of persons of working age (18 to 64).

trajectory of dying The process of going from normal health to the downhill pattern of dying.

unplanned retirement community A place that was not originally designed as a retirement community, but has become a popular place of retirement migration.

urbanization The social changes that occur as people move from farms into cities where the jobs are.

values Socially learned and shared conceptions of what is desirable, good or right; values serve as criteria for judging ideas, behavior, events, people and things.

variable A concept that can vary from one individual or context to another. See also *dependent variable*; *independent variable*.

vesting The right of employees to receive the pension benefits they have accumulated if they leave the plan before retirement.

voluntary association A type of formal organization that individuals join by choice, is non-profit, and has a specific purpose.

voluntary euthanasia A case in which a mentally competent and conscious patient requests or consents to passive or active euthanasia.

wealth What a person owns, such as property, stocks, and bonds.

Widow-to-Widow program A peer-counseling program in which widows are trained as volunteers to help other widows.

women in the middle Females who have a responsibility to their children in addition to being primary caregivers to their parents.

working retired Those persons who work after officially retiring.

"world we have lost" myth The romantization of the past and the assumption that the elderly in preindustrial societies enjoyed an ideal existence.

References

(1970, August 3) *Time*, p. 5.

(1973, December 10, & 1975, November 5). *The Manchester Evening News.*

(1986, January 13). Ordinary millionaires. *U.S. News & World Report.*

(1986, October 27). The Forbes four-hundred. *Forbes.* pp. 137–232.

Abernathy, A. (1979). Personal communication.

Achenbaum, W. A. (1978). *Old age in the new land.* Baltimore: Johns Hopkins University Press.

Adams, C. F. (1971, November 20). The power of aging in the marketplace. *Business Week.*

Aday, R. H. (1984). Criminals. In E. B. Palmore (Ed.), *Handbook on the aged in the United States* (pp. 295–309). Westport, CT: Greenwood.

Administration on Aging (1972). *Let's end isolation.* Washington, DC: U.S. Government Printing Office.

Ainlay, S. C., & Smith, D. R. (1984). Aging and religious participation. *Journal of Gerontology,* **39,** 357–363.

Albrecht, R. (1973). The family and aging seen cross-culturally. In R. R. Boyd & C. G. Oakes (Eds.), *Foundations of practical gerontology.* (pp. 27–34) Columbia: University of South Carolina Press.

Aldous, J., & Hill, R. (1965). Social cohesion, lineage type, and intergenerational transmission. *Social Forces,* **43,** 471–482.

Alsop, R. (1984, April 24). As early retirement grows in popularity, some have misgivings. *The Wall Street Journal.*

Alston, L. (1986). *Crime and older Americans.* Springfield, IL: Charles C Thomas.

American Association of Retired Persons (1988, July/August). The gentle warriors. *AARP News Bulletin.* pp. 16 and 14.

Arling, G. (1976). The elderly widow and her family, neighbors and friends. *Journal of Marriage and the Family,* **38,** 757–768.

Asimov, I. (1974, June). The pursuit of youth. *Ladies' Home Journal.* pp. 83, 153–154, 160.

Atchley, R. C. (1976). *Sociology of retirement.* Cambridge, MA: Schenkman.

Atchley, R. C. (1976). Selected social and psychological differences between men and women in later life. *Journal of Gerontology,* **31,** 204–211.

Atchley, R. C. (1988). *Social forces and aging.* Belmont, CA: Wadsworth.

Atchley, R. C., & Miller, S. (1983). Types of elderly couples. In T. H. Brubaker (Ed.), *Family relationships in later life.* Beverly Hills, CA: Sage.

Babchuk, N., Peters, G. R., Hoyt, D. R., & Kayser, M. A. (1979). The voluntary associations of the aged. *Journal of Gerontology,* **34,** 579–587.

Bahr, H. M. (1970). Aging and religious disaffiliation. *Social Forces,* **49,** 59–71.

Barfield, R. E., & Morgan, J. N. (1969). *Early retirement: The decision and the experience.* Ann Arbor: University of Michigan, Institute for Social Research.

Barron, M. L. (1961). *The aging American: An introduction to social gerontology and geriatrics.* New York: Thomas Y. Crowell.

Baumhover, L. A., & Jones, J. E. (Eds.). (1977). *Handbook of American aging programs.* Westport, CT: Greenwood.

Beal, E. W. (1979).   Children of divorce: A family systems perspective. *Journal of Social Issues, 35,* 140–154.

Beattie, W. M. (1976).   Aging and the social services. In R. H. Binstock & E. Shanas (Eds.), *Handbook of aging and the social sciences* (pp. 619–642). New York: Van Nostrand Reinhold.

Beauvoir, S. de (1972).   *The coming of age.* New York: G. P. Putnam's.

Bekker, L. deM., & Taylor, C. (1966).   Attitudes toward the aged in a multigenerational sample. *Journal of Gerontology, 21,* 115–118.

Bell, I. P. (1976).   The double standard. *Trans-Action, 8,* 75–80.

Benedict, R. (1938). Continuities and discontinuities in cultural conditioning. *Psychiatry, 1,* 161–167.

Bengtson, V. L. (1970).   The generation gap: A review and typology of social psychological perspectives. *Youth and Society, 2,* 16–25.

Bengtson, V. L. (1975).   Generation and family effects in value socialization. *American Sociological Review, 40,* 358–371.

Bengtson, V. L. (1976). *The social psychology of aging.* Indianapolis: Bobbs-Merrill.

Bengtson, V. L., Cuellar, J. B., & Ragan, P. (1977).   Stratum contrasts and similarities in attitudes toward death. *Journal of Gerontology, 32,* 76–88.

Bengtson, V. L., & Dannefer, D. (1987).   Family, work, and aging: Implications of a disordered cohort flow for the twenty-first century. In R. A. Ward & S. S. Tobin (Eds.), *Health in aging* (pp. 256–289). New York: Springer.

Bengtson, V. L., Kasschau, P. L., & Ragan, P. K. (1977).   The impact of social structure on aging individuals. In J. E. Birren & K. W. Schaie (Eds.), *Handbook of the psychology of aging.* (pp. 327–353). New York: Van Nostrand Reinhold.

Bengtson, V. L., & Manuel, R. C. (1976).   The sociology of aging. In R. H. Davis (Ed.), *Aging: Prospects and issues* (pp. 41–57). Los Angeles: Ethel Percy Andrus Gerontology Center, University of Southern California.

Bengtson, V. L., Manuel, R. C., & Burton, L. M. (1981).   Competence and loss: Perspectives on the sociology of aging. In R. H. Davis (Ed.,), *Aging: Prospects and issues.* (pp. 29–39). Los Angeles: Ethel Percy Andrus University of Southern California Press.

Bengtson, V. L., Olander, E. B., & Haddad, A. A. (1976).   The "generation gap" and aging family members: Toward a conceptual model. In J. F. Gubrium (Ed.), *Time, roles, and self in old age* (pp. 237–263). New York: Human Sciences Press.

Bennett, J. (1974, January).   They're after your money. *Dynamic Maturity.* p. 15.

Berardo, F. M. (1968).   Widowhood status in the U.S.: Perspectives on a neglected aspect of the family life cycle. *Family Coordinator, 17,* 191–203.

Berardo, F. M. (1970).   Survivorship and social isolation: The case of the aged widower. *Family Coordinator, 19,* 11–25.

Berdes, C. (1978).   *Social services for the aged, dying and bereaved in international perspective.* Washington, DC: International Federation on Aging.

Berelson, B., & Steiner, G. A. (1964).   *Human behavior: An inventory of scientific findings.* New York: Harcourt Brace Jovanovich.

Berger, P. L. (1963).   *Invitation to sociology.* Garden City, NY: Anchor Books.

Berger, P. L., & Berger, B. (1975).   *Sociology: A biographical approach.* New York: Basic Books.

Berger, R. M. (1982a).   *Gay and gray.* Urbana: University of Illinois Press.

Berger, R. M. (1982b).   The unseen minority: Older gays and lesbians. *Social Work, 27,* 236–241.

Biesele, M., & Howell, N. (1981).   The old people give you life: Aging among !Kung hunter gatherers. In P. Amoss and S. Harrell (Eds.), *Other Ways of growing old: Anthropological perspectives* (pp. 77–98). Stanford, CA: Stanford University Press.

Binstock, R. H. (1974, September). Aging and the future of American politics. *The Annals of the American Academy of Political and Social Science, 415,* 199–212.

Binstock, R. H. (1988, December).   Aging, politics and public policy. *The World and I* (pp. 533–547).

Birren, J. E. (1964). *The psychology of aging.* Englewood Cliffs, NJ: Prentice-Hall.

Birren, J. E. (1968).   Aging: Psychological aspects. In D. L. Sills (Ed.), *International encyclopedia of the social sciences.* New York: Macmillan.

Birren, J. E. (1976). Aging: The psychologist's perspective. In R. H. Davis (Ed.), *Aging: Prospects and issues*. (pp. 16–28) Los Angeles: Ethel Percy Andrus Gerontology Center, University of Southern California.

Birren, J. E., & Renner, V. J. (1977). Research on the psychology of aging: Principles and experimentation. In J. E. Birren and K. W. Schaie (Eds.), *Handbook of the psychology of aging* (pp. 3–38). New York: Van Nostrand Reinhold.

Black, B. (1989, March). Not so mobile homes. *AARP News Bulletin*.

Blau, P. M. (1964) *Exchange and power in social life*. New York: Wiley.

Blau, Z. S. (1973). *Old age in a changing society*. New York: New Viewpoints.

Blau, Z. S. (1981). *Aging in a changing society*. New York: Watts.

Blauner, R. (1966). Death and social structure. *Psychiatry, 29*, 378–394.

Blazer, D., & Palmore, E. (1976). Religion and aging in a longitudinal panel. *The Gerontologist, 16*, 82–85.

Blenkner, M. (1965). Social work and family relationships in later life, with some thoughts on filial maturity. In E. Shanas & G. Streib (Eds.), *Social structure and the family*. (pp. 46–59) Englewood Cliffs, NJ: Prentice-Hall.

Botwinick, J. (1973). *Aging and behavior*. New York: Springer.

Botwinick, J. (1978). *Aging and behavior*. 2nd ed. New York: Springer.

Botwinick, J. (1984). *Aging and behavior*. 3rd ed. New York: Springer.

Breen, L. Z. (1960). The aging individual. In C. Tibbitts (Ed.), *Handbook of social gerontology* (pp. 145–162). Chicago: University of Chicago Press.

Brickfield, C. F. (1984). *Attitudes and perceptions of older people toward technology*. In P. K. Robinson, J. Livingston, and J. E. Birren (Eds.) *Aging and technological advances* (pp. 31–38). New York: Plenum, 1984.

Brim, O. G., & Wheeler, S. (1966). *Socialization after childhood: Two essays*. New York: Wiley.

Broom, L., & Selznick, P. (1973). *Sociology* (5th ed.). New York: Harper & Row.

Brubaker, T. H. (1985). *Later-life families*. Beverly Hills, CA: Sage.

Bultena, G., & Powers, E. (1976). Effects of age-grade comparisons on adjustment in later life. In J. F. Gubrium (Ed.), *Time, roles, and self in old age* (pp. 165–177). New York: Human Sciences Press.

Bultena, G., & Wood, V. (1969). The American retirement community: Bane or blessing? *Journal of Gerontology, 24*, 209–217.

Burgess, E. W. (Ed.) (1960). *Aging in western societies*. Chicago: University of Chicago Press.

Busse, E. W., & Blazer, D. G. (1980). The theories and processes of aging. In E. W. Busse and D. G. Blazer (Eds.), *Handbook of geriatric psychiatry* (pp. 3–27). New York: Van Nostrand Reinhold.

Busse, E. W., & Pfeiffer, E. (1977). Functional psychiatric disorders in old age. In E. W. Busse & E. Pfeiffer (Eds.), *Behavior and adaptation in late life* (pp. 158–211). Boston: Little, Brown.

Busse, E. W., & Pfeiffer, E. (1977). Introduction. In E. W. Busse & E. Pfeiffer (Eds.), *Behavior and adaptation in late life* (pp. 1–7). Boston: Little, Brown.

Butler, R. N. (1975). *Why survive? Being old in America*. New York: Harper & Row.

Butler, R. N. (1987). Future trends. In G. L. Maddox (Ed.), *Encyclopedia of aging* (pp. 265–267). New York: Springer.

Butler, R. N. (1989). Dispelling ageism: The cross-cutting intervention. *The annals of the American Academy of Political and Social Sciences, 503*, 138–147.

Butler, R. N., & Lewis, M. I. (1977). *Aging and mental health*. St. 2nd ed. Louis: C. V. Mosby.

Butler, R. N. & Lewis, M. I. (1982). *Aging and mental health*. 3rd ed. St. Louis: C. V. Mosby.

Cain, L., Jr. (1968). Age and the character of our times. *The Gerontologist, 8*, 250–258.

Campbell, A. (1971). Politics through the life cycle. *The Gerontologist, 11*, 112–117.

Cantor, M. H. (1979). Neighbors and friends: An overlooked resource in the informal support system. *Research on Aging, 1*, 434–463.

Carp. F. M. (1966). *A future for the aged: Victoria Plaza and its residents*. Austin: University of Texas Press.

Carp. F. M. (1970). Communicating with elderly Mexican-Americans. *The Gerontologist, 10*, 126–133.

Carp. F. M. 1971). Walking as a means of transportation for retired people. *The Gerontologist,* **11,** 104–111.

Carp. F. M., & Kataoka, E. (1976). Health care problems of the elderly of San Francisco's Chinatown. *The Gerontologist,* **16,** 30–38.

Caudill, W. (1953). Applied anthropology in medicine. In A. L. Kroeber (Ed.), *Anthropology today.* Chicago: University of Chicago Press.

Cavan, R. (1949). *Personal adjustment in old age.* Chicago: Science Research Associates.

Chen, Y.-P. (1985). Economic status of the aged. In R. H. Binstock & E. Shanas (Eds.), *Handbook of aging and the social sciences* (pp. 641–665). New York: Van Nostrand Reinhold.

Clark, M., & Anderson, B. (1967). *Culture and aging.* Springfield, IL: Charles C Thomas.

Clark, R. L. et al. (1984). *Inflation and the economic well-being of the elderly.* Baltimore: Johns Hopkins University Press.

Clemente, F., & Kleiman, M. (1976). Fear of crime among the aged. *The Gerontologist,* **16,** 207–210.

Clemente, F., Rexroad, P. A., & Hirsch, C. (1975). The participation of the black aged in voluntary associations. *Journal of Gerontology,* **30,** 469–472.

Coberly, S., & Morrison, M. (1984). Labor force participation. In P. K. Robinson, J. Livingston, and J. E. Birren (Eds.), *Aging and technological advances* (pp. 155–158), New York: Plenum.

Cohen, E. S. (1985). Protective services. In A. Monk (Ed.), *Handbook of gerontological services* (pp. 483–513). New York: Van Nostrand Reinhold.

Cole, W. E., & Harris, D. K. (1977). *The elderly in America.* Boston: Allyn & Bacon.

Coles, R. (1974). *The old ones of New Mexico.* Albuquerque: University of New Mexico Press.

Comfort, A. (1976). *A good age.* New York: Crown.

Commager, H. S. (1970). Quoted in R. Williams, *American society: A sociological interpretation.* New York: Knopf.

Constanelos, D. J. (1968). *Byzantine philanthropy and social welfare.* New Brunswick, NJ: Rutgers University Press.

Cooley, C. H. (1902). *Human nature and the social order.* New York: Scribner's.

Cowgill, D. O. (1974). Aging and modernization: A revision of the theory. In J. F. Gubrium (Ed.), *Late life: Communities and environmental policy* (pp. 123–146). Springfield, IL: Charles C Thomas.

Cowgill, D. O., & Holmes, L. D. (1972). Summary and conclusions: The theory in review. In D. O. Cowgill & L. D. Holmes (Eds.), *Aging and modernization* (pp. 305–323). New York: Appleton-Century-Crofts.

Cox, F. M., & Mberia, N. (1977). *Aging in a changing village society: A Kenyan experience.* Washington, DC: International Federation on Ageing.

Crichton, J. (1987). *Age care sourcebook: Resource guide for the aging and their families.* New York: Simon & Schuster.

Crittenden, J. (1962). Aging and party affiliation. *Public Opinion Quarterly,* **26,** 648–657.

Crouch, B. M. (1972). Age and institutional support: Perceptions of older Mexican-Americans. *Journal of Gerontology,* **27,** 524–529.

Cumming, E., & Henry, W. (1961). *Growing old.* New York: Basic.

Cutler, N. E. (1969). Generation, maturation and party affiliation: A cohort analysis. *Public Opinion Quarterly,* **33,** 583–588.

Cutler, N. E. (1981). Political characteristics of elderly cohorts in the twenty-first century. In S. B. Kiesler, J. N. Morgan, and V. K. Oppenheimer (Eds.), *Aging: Social change* (pp. 127–157). New York: Academic.

Cutler, N. E., & Schmidhauser, J. R. (1975). Age and political behavior. In D. S. Woodruff & J. E. Birren (Eds.), *Aging: Scientific perspectives and social issues* (pp. 397–403). New York: Van Nostrand Reinhold.

Cutler, S. (1973). Voluntary association participation and life satisfaction: A cautionary note. *Journal of Gerontology,* **28,** 96–100.

Cutler, S. (1976). Membership in different types of voluntary associations and psychological well-being. *The Gerontologist,* **16,** 335–339.

Davis, K. (1949). *Human society.* New York: Macmillan.

Davis, R. H., & Davis, J. A. (1985). *TV's image of the elderly: A practical guide for change.* Lexington, MA: Lexington Books.

Dennis, H. (1988). Retirement planning. In H. Dennis (Ed.), *Fourteen steps in managing an* *aging workforce*. Lexington, MA: Lexington Books.

Dennis, W. (1966). Creative productivity between the ages of 20 and 80 years. *Journal of Gerontology, 21*, 1–8.

Dickinson, G. E., & Wheeler, A. L. (1980, July–August). The elderly in prison. *Corrections Today*, p. 10.

Dolan, J. (1989). Fighting poverty. *AARP News Bulletin*, February, p. 7.

Donahue, W., Orbach, H. L., & Pollak, O. (1960). Retirement: The emerging social pattern. In C. Tibbitts (Ed.), *Handbook of social gerontology* (pp.330–406) Chicago: University of Chicago Press.

Donahue, W. (1955). *Education for later maturity*. New York: Whiteside and William Morrow.

Dovenmuehle, R. H., Busse, E. W., & Newman, G. (1970). Physical problems of older people. In E. B. Palmore (Ed.), *Normal aging* (pp. 29–39). Durham, NC: Duke University Press.

Dowd, J. J. (1975). Aging as exchange: A preface to theory. *Journal of Gerontology, 30*, 584–594.

Dowd, J. J. (1980). *Stratification among the aged*. Monterey, CA: Brooks/Cole.

Dowd, J. J., & Bengtson, V. L. (1978). Aging in minority populations: An examination of the double jeopardy hypothesis. *Journal of Gerontology, 33*, 427–436.

Ducovny, A. (1969). *The billion dollar swindle: Frauds against the elderly*. New York: Fleet Press.

Durkheim, E. (1951). *Suicide*. Glencoe, IL: Free Press. (Original work published in 1897.)

Eckert, J. K. (1980). *The unseen elderly*. San Diego, CA: Campanile Press, San Diego State University.

Edsall, T. B. (June 1988). The return of inequality. *Atlantic*, pp. 89–90, 92–94.

Ehrlich, P. (1976). A study: Characteristics and needs of the St. Louis downtown SRO elderly. In *The invisible elderly*. Washington, DC: The National Council on the Aging.

Ekerdt, D. J. (1986). The busy ethic: Moral continuity between work and retirement. *The Gerontologist, 26*, 239–244.

Fanning, P. (1974, November 16). Conning the elderly. *The National Observer*.

Feinberg, G. (1984). White-haired offenders: An emergent social problem. In W. Wilbanks & P. K. H. Kim (Eds.), *Elderly criminals* (pp. 83–105). Lanham, MD: University Press of America.

Fengler, A. P., & Wood, V. (1972). The generation gap: An analysis of attitudes on contemporary issues. *The Gerontologist, 12*, 124–128.

Field, M. (1968). *Aging with honor and dignity*. Springfield, IL: Charles C Thomas.

Fillenbaum, G. (1971). The working retired. *Journal of Gerontology, 29*, 82–89.

Fischer, D. H. (1978). *Growing old in America*. New York: Oxford University Press.

Fleg, J. L. (1987). Heart. In G. L. Maddox (Ed.), *The encyclopedia of aging* (pp. 319–321). New York: Springer.

Flemming, A. S. (1971, November 20). The power of the aging in the marketplace. *Business Week* pp. 52–58.

Flynn, C. B., Longino, C. F., Wiseman, R. F., & Biggar, J. C. (1985). The redistribution of America's older population: Major national migration patterns for three census decades, 1960–1980. *The Gerontologist, 25*, 292–296.

Foner, A. (1986). *Aging and old age: New perspectives*. Englewood Cliffs, NJ: Prentice-Hall.

Foner, A., & Schwab, K. (1981). *Aging and retirement*. Monterey, CA: Brooks/Cole.

Foner, A., & Schwab, K. (1983). Work and retirement in a changing society. In M. W. Riley, B. B. Hess, & K. Bond (Eds.), *Aging in society: Selected review of recent research* (pp. 71–93). Hillsdale, NJ: Erlbaum.

Fox, J. H. (1977). Effects of retirement and former work life on women's adaptation in old age. *Journal of Gerontology, 32*, 196–202.

Fox, N. L. (1980, October). Sex in nursing homes? For Lord's sake, why not? *Registered Nurse* (Annual Review) pp. 95–100.

Friedman, L. A. (1984). *Your time will come: The law of age discrimnation and mandatory retirement*. New York: Russell Sage.

Friedmann, E. A., & Havighurst, R. J. (1954). *The meaning of work and retirement*. Chicago: University of Chicago Press.

Fries, J. F. (1984). The compression of morbidity. In P. K. Robinson, J. Livingston, & J. E. Birren (Eds.), *Aging and technological advances* (pp. 169–187). New York: Plenum.

Fries, J. F., & Crapo, L. M. (1981). *Vitality and aging.* San Francisco: Freeman.

Gallagher, D., & Thompson, L. W. (1983). Cognitive therapy for depression in the elderly: A promising model for treatment and research. In L. Breslau & M. Haug (Eds.), *Depression and aging: Causes, care and consequences* (pp. 168–192). New York: Springer.

Gelfand, D. E. (1987). Ethnicity. In G. L. Maddox (Ed.), *The encyclopedia of aging* (pp. 229–230). New York: Springer.

Gelfand, D. E. (1988). *The aging network: Programs and services.* New York: Springer.

Gerbner, G., Gross, L., Signorielli, N., & Morgan, M. (1980). Aging with television: Images on television drama and conceptions of social reality. *Journal of Communication, 30,* 37–47.

Gilford, R., & Black, D. (1972). *The grandchild–grandparent dyad: Ritual or relationship?* Paper presented at the 25th annual meeting of the Gerontological Society, San Francisco.

Gillespie, M. W., & Galliher, J. F. (1972). Age, anomie, and the inmate's definition of aging in prison: An exploratory study. In D. P. Kent et al. (Eds.), *Research planning and action for the elderly* (pp. 465–483). New York: Behavioral Publications.

Glaser, B. G., & Strauss, A. L. (1965). *Awareness of dying.* Chicago: Aldine.

Glaser, B. G., & Strauss, A. L. (1968). *Time for dying.* Chicago: Aldine.

Glenn, N. (1974, September). Aging and conservatism. *The Annals of the American Academy of Political and Social Science, 415,* 176–186.

Glenn, N., & Grimes, M. (1968). Aging, voting and political interest. *American Sociological Review, 33,* 563–575.

Glenn, N., & Hefner, T. (1972). Further evidence on aging and party identification. *Public Opinion Quarterly, 36,* 31–47.

Glock, C. Y. (1962). On the study of religious commitment. *Religious Education, 57* (July–August), S–98 to S–110.

Goffman, E. (1961). *Asylums.* Chicago: Aldine.

Gold, B. D. (1974, September). The role of the federal government in the provision of social services to older persons. *The Annals of the American Academy of Political and Social Science, 415,* 55–69.

Goldsmith, J. (1976, February). Police and the older victim: Keys to a changing perspective. *Police Chief, 43,* 5–8.

Goode, W. J. (1963). *World revolution and family patterns.* New York: Free Press.

Goody, J. (1976). Aging in nonindustrial societies. In R. H. Binstock & E. Shanas (Eds.), *Handbook of aging and the social sciences* (pp. 117–129). New York: Van Nostrand Reinhold.

Gruman, G. J. (1966). History of ideas about the prolongation of life: The evaluation of prolongevity hypotheses to 1800. *Transactions of the American Philosophical Society, 56*(9), 1–102.

Guemple, L. (1983). Growing old in Inuit society. In J. Sokolovsky (Ed.), *Growing old in different societies* (pp. 24–28). Belmont, CA: Wadsworth.

Haberland, K. F. (1973). Learning, memory and age. *Industrial Gerontology, 19,* 20–37.

Hall, G. S. (1922). *Senescence: The last half of life.* New York: Appleton.

Hand, J. (1983). Shopping-bag women: Aging deviants in the city. In E. W. Markson (Ed.), *Older women: Issues and prospects* (pp. 155–177). Lexington, MA: Lexington Books.

Harris, D. K., & Cole, W. E. (1977). *Study guide and readings for sociology: The study of human interaction.* New York: Knopf.

Harris, L., & Associates (1975). *The myth and reality of aging in America.* Washington, DC: The National Council on the Aging.

Harris, L., & Associates (1979). *1979 Study of American attitudes toward pensions and retirement.* New York: Johnson & Higgins.

Harris, L., & Associates. (1981). *Aging in the eighties: America in transition.* Washington, DC: The National Council on the Aging.

Harris, M. (1985). *Good to eat.* New York: Simon & Schuster.

Havighurst, R. J. (1961). The nature and values of meaningful free-time activities. In R. W. Kleemeier (Ed.), *Aging and leisure* (pp. 309–344). New York: Oxford University Press.

Havighurst, R. J., & Albrecht, R. (1953). *Older people.* New York: Longman's, Green.

Havighurst, R. J., Neugarten, B. L., & Tobin, S. S. (1968). Disengagement and patterns of aging. In B. L. Neugarten (Ed.), *Middle age and aging* (pp. 161–172). Chicago: University of Chicago Press.

Hayflick, L. (1965). The limited in vitro lifetime of human diploid cell strains. *Experimental Cell Research, 37*, 614–636.

Hayflick, L. (1974). The strategy of senescence. *The Gerontologist, 14*, 37–45.

Hayflick, L. (1987). Biological aging theories. In G. L. Maddox (Ed.), *The encyclopedia of aging* (pp. 64–68). New York: Springer.

Heintz, K. M. (1976). *Retirement communities: For adults only.* New Brunswick, NJ: The Center for Urban Policy Research, Rutgers-State University of New Jersey.

Henderson, C. (1988, March/April). Old glory: America comes of age. *The Futurist*, pp. 36–40.

Hess, B. B. (1974). Stereotypes of the aged. *Journal of Communication, 24*, 76–85.

Heyman, D., & Jeffers, F. C. (1968). Wives and retirement: A pilot study. *Journal of Gerontology, 23*, 488–496.

Hickey, T., & Douglass, R. L. (1981). Neglect and abuse of older family members: Professionals' perspectives and case experiences. *The Gerontologist, 21*(2), 171–176.

Hill, C., Thompson, L. W., & Gallagher, D. (1988). The role of anticipatory bereavement in older women's adjustment to widowhood. *The Gerontologist, 28*, 792–799.

Hochschild, A. (1973). *The unexpected community.* Englewood Cliffs, N.J.: Prentice-Hall.

Hochschild, A. (1975). Disengagement theory: A critique and proposal. *American Sociological Review, 40*, 553–569.

Hochschild, A. (1976). Disengagement theory: A logical, empirical, and phenomenological critique. In J. F. Gubrium (Ed.), *Time, roles, and self in old age* (pp. 53–87). New York: Human Sciences Press.

Holmes, T. H., & Rahe, R. H. (1967). The social readjustment rating scale. *Journal of Psychosomatic Research, 11*, 213–218.

Homans, G. C. (1961). *Social behavior: Its elementary forms.* New York: Harcourt Brace Jovanovich.

Houle, C. (1974). The changing goals of education in the perspective of lifelong learning. *International Review of Education, 20*, 430–446.

Howells, W. (1948). *Mankind so far.* Garden City, NY: Doubleday.

Hsu, F. L. K. (1972). American core value and national character. In F. L. K. Hsu (Ed.), *Psychological anthropology.* Cambridge, MA: Schenkman.

Hudson, M. F., & Johnson, T. F. (1986). Elder neglect and abuse: A review of the literature. In C. Eisdorfer (Ed.), *Annual review of gerontology and geriatrics* (pp. 81–134). New York: Springer.

Hudson, R. B., & Binstock, R. H. (1976). Political systems and aging. In R. H. Binstock & E. Shanas (Eds.), *Handbook of aging and the social sciences* (pp. 369–400). New York: Van Nostrand Reinhold.

Hudson, R. B., & Strate, J. (1985). Aging and political system. In R. H. Binstock & E. Shanas (Eds.), *Handbook of aging and the social sciences*, 2nd ed. (pp. 554–585). New York: Van Nostrand Reinhold.

Hughes, E. (1970). Quoted by G. Maddox in Adaptation to retirement. *The Gerontologist, 10*, 14–18.

Hunsberger, B. (1985). Religion, age, life satisfaction and perceived sources of religiousness: A study of older persons. *Journal of Gerontology, 40*, 615–620.

Huyck, M. H. (1974). *Growing older.* Englewood Cliffs, NJ: Prentice-Hall.

Huyck, M. H. (1983). Quoted in Turner, B. F., & Adams, C. The sexuality of older women. In E. W. Markson (Ed.), *Older women* (pp. 55–72). Lexington, MA: Lexington Books.

Inkeles, A. (1969). Social structure and socialization. In D. Goslin (Ed.), *Handbook of socialization theory and research* (pp. 615–632). Chicago: Rand McNally.

Jackson, J. J. (1985). Race, national origin, ethnicity, and aging. In R. H. Binstock & E. Shanas (Eds.), *Handbook of aging and the social sciences* (pp. 264–303). New York: Van Nostrand Reinhold.

Jacobs, J. (1974). *Fun city.* New York: Holt, Rinehart & Winston.

Jacobs, J. (1975). *Older persons and retirement communities.* Springfield, IL: Charles C Thomas.

Johnson, M. T., & Kelly, J. J. (1979). Deviate sex behavior in the aging: Social definitions and the lives of older gay people. In O. J. Kaplan (Ed.), *Psychopathology of aging* (pp. 243–258). New York: Academic Press.

Johnson, S. K. (1971). *Idle Haven: Community*

building among the working-class retired. Berkeley: The University of California Press.

Johnstone, J. W., & Rivera, R. (1965). *Volunteers for learning.* Chicago: Aldine.

Johnstone, R. L. (1988). *Religion and society in interaction.* Englewood Cliffs, NJ: Prentice-Hall.

Jones, R. (1977). *The other generation: The new power of older people.* Englewood Cliffs, NJ: Prentice-Hall.

Kahana, B., & Kahana, E. (1970). Grandparenthood from the perspective of the developing grandchild. *Developmental Psychology, 3,* 98–105.

Kalish, R. A. (1969). The young and old as generation gap allies. *The Gerontologist, 9,* 83–89.

Kalish, R. A. (1975). *Late adulthood: Perspectives on human development.* Monterey, CA: Brooks/Cole.

Kalish, R. A. (1976) Death and dying in a social context. In R. H. Binstock & E. Shanas (Eds.) *Handbook of Aging and the Social Sciences* (pp. 483–507). New York: Van Nostrand Reinhold.

Kalish, R. A. (1985). The social context of death and dying. In R. H. Binstock & E. Shanas (Eds.), *Handbook of aging and the social sciences,* 2nd ed. (pp. 149–170). New York: Van Nostrand Reinhold.

Kalish, R. A., & Johnson, A. I. (1972). Value similarities and differences in three generations of women. *Journal of Marriage and the Family, 34,* 49–54.

Kalish, R. A., & Reynolds, D. K. (1981). *Death and ethnicity: A psychocultural study.* Farmington, NY: Baywood.

Kastenbaum, R. (1978). Death, dying and bereavement in old age. *Aged Care and Services Review, 1,* 1–10.

Kastenbaum, R. (1969). Death and bereavement in later life. In A. Kutscher (Ed.), *Death and bereavement* (pp. 28–54). Springfield, IL: Charles C Thomas.

Kastenbaum, R. (1985). Dying and death: A life-span approach. In J. E. Birren & K. Warner Schaie (Eds.), *Handbook of the psychology of aging* (pp. 619–643). New York: Van Nostrand Reinhold.

Kastenbaum, R., & Candy, S. E. (1973). The four percent fallacy: A methodological and empirical critique of extended care facility population statistics. *International Journal of Aging and Human Development, 4,* 15–21.

Katz, S., et al. (1963). Studies of illness in the aged: The index of ADL—a standardized measure of biological and psychosocial function. *Journal of the American Medical Association, 185,* 914–919.

Kayser-Jones, J. S. (1981). *Old, alone and neglected: Care of the aged in Scotland and the United States.* Berkeley: University of California Press.

Keith, P. M. (1982). Working women versus homemakers: Retirement resources and correlates of well-being. In M. Szinovacz (Ed.), *Women's retirement: Policy implications of recent research* (pp. 77–91). Beverly Hills, CA: Sage.

Keller, J. W., Sherry, D., & Piotrowski, C. (1984). Perspectives on death: A developmental study. *Journal of Psychology, 116,* 137–142.

Kelly, J. (1977). The aging male homosexual: Myth and reality. *The Gerontologist, 17,* 328–332.

Kelly, J. (1980). Homosexuality and aging. In J. Marmor (Ed.), *Multiple roots of homosexual behavior* (pp. 176–193). New York: Basic Books.

Kerckhoff, A. C. (1966). Family patterns and morale in retirement. In I. Simpson (pp. 173–192) & J. McKinney (Eds.), *Social aspects of aging.* Durham, NC: Duke University Press.

Kessel, V. (1970). Polygyny after sixty. In H. A. Otto (Ed.), *The family in search of a future* (pp. 171–181). New York: Appleton-Century-Crofts.

Kimmel, D. C. (1978). Adult development and aging: A gay perspective. *Journal of Social Issues, 34,* 113–130.

Kinsey, A. C., Pomeroy, W. B., & Martin, C. E. (1948). *Sexual behavior in the human male.* Philadelphia: Saunders.

Kinsey, A. C., Pomeroy, W. B., Martin, C. E., & Gebhard, P. H. (1953). *Sexual behavior in the human female.* Philadelphia: Saunders.

Kivett, V. R., & Atkinson, M. P. (1984). Filial expectations, association, and helping as function of number of children among rural-transitional parents. *Journal of Gerontology, 39,* 499–503.

Kluckhohn, C. (1944). *Mirror for man.* Greenwich, CT: Fawcett.

Kobata, F. S., Lockery, S. A., & Moriwaki, S. Y. (1980). Minority issues in mental health and aging. In J. E. Birren & R. B. Sloane (Eds.), *Handbook of mental health and aging.* (pp. 448–467). Englewood Cliffs, NJ: Prentice-Hall.

Koenig, H. Smiley, M., & Gonzales, J. A. P. (1988). *Religion, health, and aging.* Westport, CT: Greenwood Press.

Koenig, H., Kvale, J., & Ferrel, C. (1988). Religion and well-being in later life. *The Gerontologist,* **28,** 18–28.

Kornblum, W. (1988). *Sociology in a changing world.* New York: Holt, Rinehart & Winston.

Kübler-Ross, E. (1969). *On death and dying.* New York: Macmillan.

Kuypers, J., & Bengtson, V. L. (1973). Social breakdown and competence: A model of normal aging. *Human Development,* **16,** 181–201.

Laner, M. R. (1978). Growing older male: Heterosexual and homosexual. *The Gerontologist,* **18,** 496–501.

Laner, M. R. (1979). Growing older female: Heterosexual and homosexual. *Journal of Homosexuality,* **4,** 267–275.

Laslett, P. (1983). *The world we have lost.* New York: Scribners.

Laswell, H. D. (1936). *Politics: Who gets what, when, how?* New York: McGraw-Hill.

Lauer, R. H. (1978). *Social problems and the quality of life.* Dubuque, IA: Wm. C. Brown.

Lawton, M. P., & Brody, E. (1969). Assessment of older people: Self maintaining and instrumental activities of daily living. *The Gerontologist,* **9,** 179–186.

Lead, J. M. (1970). Counseling with older people and their families. *Working with older people: A Guide to Practice* (Vol. 3). Washington, DC: U.S. Government Printing Office.

Lehman, H. C. (1953). *Age and achievement.* Princeton, NJ: Princeton University Press.

Lemert, E. M. (1952). *Social pathology.* New York: McGraw-Hill.

Lemert, E. M. (1967). *Human deviance, social problems and social control.* Englewood Cliffs, NJ: Prentice-Hall.

Lemon, B. W., Bengtson, V. L., & Peterson, J. A. (1972). An exploration of the activity theory of aging, *Journal of gerontology,* **27,** 511–523.

Levin, J., & Levin, W. C. (1980). *Ageism: Prejudice and discrimination against the elderly.* Belmont, CA: Wadsworth.

Levine, M. L. (1988). Age discrimination: The law and its underlying policy. In H. Dennis (Ed.), *Fourteen steps in managing an aging work force* (pp. 25–35). Lexington, MA: Lexington Books.

Light, D., Jr., & Keller, S. (1975). *Sociology.* New York: Knopf.

Linton, R. (1936). *The study of man.* New York: Appleton-Century-Crofts.

Linton, R. (1942). Age and sex categories. *American Sociological Review,* **7,** 589–603.

Litwak, E. (1985). *Helping the elderly: The complementarity of informal networks and formal systems.* New York: Guilford.

Loether, H. J. (1975). *Problems of aging.* Belmont, CA: Dickenson.

Longino, C. F., Jr. (1981). Retirement communities. In F. J. Berghorn, D. Schafer, & Associates (Eds.), *The dynamics of aging* (309–418). Boulder, CO: Westview.

Longino, C. F., Jr. & Kart, C. S. (1982). Explicating activity theory: A formal replication. *Journal of Gerontology,* **37,** 713–722.

Lowenthal, M., & Haven, C. (1968). Interaction and adaptation: Intimacy as a critical variable. *American Sociological Review,* **33,** 20–30.

Lowy, L. (1975). Social welfare and the aging. In M. G. Spencer & C. J. Dorr (Eds.), *Understanding aging.* New York: Appleton-Century-Crofts.

Mace, N. L., & Rabins, P. V. (1981). *The 36-hour day.* Baltimore: Johns Hopkins University Press.

Maddox, G. (1964). Disengagement theory: A critical evaluation. *The Gerontologist,* **4,** 80–82.

Maddox, G., & Douglass, E. (1973). Self-assessment of health: A longitudinal study of elderly subjects. *Journal of Health and Social Behavior,* **14,** 87–93.

Makinodan, T. (1977). Immunity and aging. In C. E. Finch & L. B. Hayflick (Eds.), *Handbook of the biology of aging* (pp. 379–408). New York: Van Nostrand Reinhold.

Makinodan, T., Kawa, K. H., Soto, K., & Hirayama, R. (1985). The aging immune system. In R. J. Morin & R. J. Bing (Eds.), *Frontiers in medicine* (pp. 284–299). New York: Human Sciences Press.

Malinchak, A. (1980). *Crime and gerontology.* Englewood Cliffs, NJ: Prentice-Hall.

Manney, J. D., Jr. (1975). *Aging in American Society.* Ann Arbor: The Institute of Gerontology, University of Michigan–Wayne State University.

Manton, K., & Soldo, B. J. (1985). Dynamics of health changes in the oldest old: New perspectives and evidence. *Milbank Memorial Fund Quarterly, 63,* 206–285.

Marans, R. W., Hunt, M. E., & Vakalo, K. L. (1984). Retirement communities. In I. Altman, M. P. Lawton, & J. F. Wohlwill (Eds.), *Elderly people and their environment* (pp. 57–93). New York: Plenum.

Markides, K. S., & Machalek, R. (1984). Selective survival, aging and society. *Archives of Gerontology and Geriatrics, 24,* 207–222.

Markides, K. S., & Mindel, C. H. (1987). *Aging and ethnicity.* Newbury Park, CA: Sage.

Marshall, V. (1975). Socialization for impending death in a retirement village. *American Journal of Sociology, 80,* 1124–1144.

Masters, W. H., & Johnson, V. E. (1966). *Human sexual response.* Boston: Little, Brown.

Matthews, S. H., & Sprey, J. (1984). The impact of divorce on grandparenthood. *The Gerontologist, 24,* 41–47.

McCann, C. (1969). Quoted in P. E. Hammond, Aging and the minister. In M. Riley, J. Riley, & M. Johnson (Eds.), *Aging and society* (Vol. 2) (292–323). New York: Russell Sage Foundation.

McClusky, H. Y. (1971). *Education.* 1971 White House Conference on aging, background and issues. Washington, DC: U.S. Government Printing Office.

McClusky, H. Y. (1974). Education for aging: The scope of the field and perspectives for the future. In S. M. Grabowski & W. D. Mason (Eds.), *Learning for aging.* Washington, DC: Adult Education Association.

McClusky, H. Y. (1978). Designs for learning. In L. F. Jarvik (Ed.), *Aging into the 21st century* (pp. 169–185). New York: Gardner.

McClusky, H. Y. (1982). Education for older adults. In C. Eisdorfer (Ed.), *Annual review of gerontology and geriatrics* (Vol. 3) (pp. 403–428). New York: Springer.

McConnell, S., & Usher, C. (1980). *Intergenerational house sharing.* Los Angeles: Andrus Gerontology Center, University of Southern California.

McCrae, R. R., & Costa, P. T. (1984). Emerging lives, enduring dispositions. *Personality in Adulthood.* Boston: Little, Brown.

McIntosh, J. L., & Santos, J. F. (1981). Suicide among minority elderly: A preliminary investigation. *Suicide and Life Threatening Behavior, 11,* 151–166.

Mead, M. (1971, November 15). A new style of aging. *Christianity and Crisis.* New York: Christianity and Crisis, Inc.

Medvedev, Z. A. (1974). Caucasus and Altay longevity: A biological or social problem? *The Gerontologist, 14,* 381–387.

Merton, R. K. (1968). *Social theory and social structure.* New York: Free Press.

Metchnikoff, O. (1921). *Life of Elie Metchnikoff.* Boston: Houghton Mifflin.

Miller, S. J. (1965). Social dilemma of the aging leisure participant. In A. M. Rose & W. A. Peterson (Eds.), *Older people and their social world* (pp. 77–92). Philadelphia: Davis.

Milletti, M. A. (1984). *Voices of experience: 1500 retired people talk about retirement.* New York: Educational Research TIAA-CREF.

Mindel, C. H., & Vaughan, C. E. (1978). A multidisciplinary approach to religiosity and disengagement. *Journal of Gerontology, 33,* 103–108.

Minnigerode, F. A. (1976). Age-status labeling in homosexual men. *Journal of Homosexuality, 1,* 273–276.

Mitford, J. (1963). *The American way of death.* New York: Simon & Schuster.

Moberg, D. O. (1965). Religiosity in old age. *The Gerontologist, 5,* 78–87.

Moberg, D. O. (1984). *The church as a social institution.* Grand Rapids, MI: Baker Book House.

Moody, H. R. (1986). Education as a lifelong process. In A. Pifer and L. Bronte (Eds.), *Our aging society* (pp. 199–217). New York: W. W. Norton.

Moody, H. R. (1988). *Abundance of life: Human development policies for an aging society.* New York: Columbia University Press.

Morison, R. S. (1971). Death: Process or event? *Science, 173,* 694–698.

Moss, F. E., & Halamandaris, V. J. (1977). *Too old, too sick, too bad.* Germantown, MD: Aspen Systems Corp.

Mumford, L. (1970). The highway and the city. In G. DeBell (Ed.), *The environmental handbook.* New York: Ballantine.

Murdock, G. P. (1934). *Our primitive contemporaries*. New York: Macmillan.

Murdock, G. P. (1945). The common denominator of culture. In R. Linton (Ed.), *The science of man in the world crisis*. New York: Columbia University Press.

National Center for Health Statistics (1984). [National health interview survey, supplement on aging]. Unpublished data.

National Center for Health Statistics (1988). Current estimates from the National Health Survey, United States, 1987. *Vital and Health Statistics Series, 166* (10). Washington, DC: U.S. Government Printing Office.

National Council on the Aging (1972). *The multipurpose senior center: A model community action program*. Washington, DC: The National Council on the Aging.

National Institute of Senior Centers (1974). *Directory of senior centers and clubs*. Washington, DC: The National Council on the Aging.

Neugarten, B. L. (1966). The aged in American society. In H. S. Becker (Ed.), *Social problems* (pp. 167–196). New York: Wiley.

Neugarten, B. L. (1968). *Middle age and aging*. Chicago: University of Chicago Press.

Neugarten, B. L. (1975). Introduction. *The Gerontologist, 15*, 3.

Neugarten, B. L. (1975). The future and the young–old. *The Gerontologist, 15*, 4–9.

Neugarten, B. L. (1980, April). Acting one's age: New rules for old. *Psychology Today*, pp. 66–80.

Neugarten, B. L., Havighurst, R. J., & Tobin, S. S. (1968). Personality and patterns of aging. In B. L. Neugarten (Ed.), *Middle age and aging* (pp. 173–177). Chicago: University of Chicago Press.

Neugarten, B. L., Moore, J. W., & Lowe, J. C. (1965). Age norms, age constraints, and adult socialization. *American Journal of Sociology, 70*, 710–717.

Neugarten, B. L., & Weinstein, K. K. (1968). The changing American grandparent. In B. L. Neugarten (Ed.), *Middle age and aging* (pp. 280–285). Chicago: University of Chicago Press.

Nie, N., Verba, S., & Petrocik, J. (1976). *The changing American voter*. Cambridge, MA: Harvard University Press.

Ogburn, W. F. (1922). *Social change*. New York: Viking.

Okeon, D. (1977). What to tell cancer patients: A study of medical attitudes. In R. F. Weir (Ed.), *Ethical issues in death and dying*. New York: Columbia University Press.

Orbach, H. L. (1963). Societal values and the institutionalization of retirement. In R. Williams, C. Tibbitts, & W. Donahue (Eds.), *Processes of aging* (Vol. 2) (pp. 389–402). New York: Atherton.

Osako, M. M., & Liu, W. T. (1986). Intergenerational relations and the aged among Japanese-Americans. *Research on Aging, 8*, 129–155.

Osgood, N. J. (1982). *Senior settlers: Social integration in retirement communities*. New York: Praeger.

Osgood, N. J. (1985). *Suicide in the elderly*. Rockville, MD: Aspen Systems Corporation.

Palmore, E. B. (1971). Attitudes toward aging as shown by humor. *The Gerontologist, 12*, 181–186.

Palmore, E. B. (1975). *The honorable elders*. Durham, NC: Duke University Press.

Palmore, E. B. (1977). Sociological aspects of aging. In E. W. Busse & E. Pfeiffer (Eds.), *Behavior and adaptation in late life* (pp. 33–69). Boston: Little, Brown.

Palmore, E. B. (1981). *Social pattern in normal aging: Findings from the Duke longitudinal study*. Durham, NC: Duke University Press.

Palmore, E. B. (1986). Attitudes toward aging as shown by humor: A review. In L. Nahemow, K. A. McCluskey-Fawcett, & P. E. McGhee (Eds.), *Humor and aging* (pp. 101–119). Orlando, FL: Academic.

Palmore, E. B. (1987). Religious organizations. In G. L. Maddox (Ed.), *The encyclopedia of aging* (pp. 561–563). New York: Springer.

Palmore, E. B., et al. (1985). *Retirement: Causes and consequences*. New York: Springer.

Palmore, E. B., & Jeffers, F. C. (1971). *Predictions of life span*. Lexington, MA: Lexington Books.

Palmore, E. B., & Maeda, D. (1985). *The honorable elders revisted*. Durham, NC: Duke University Press.

Palmore, E. B., & Manton, K. (1974). Modernization and the status of the aged: International correlations. *Journal of Gerontology, 29*, 205–210.

Parsons, T. (1951). *The social system.* Glencoe, IL: Free Press.

Passuth, P. M., & Bengtson, V. L. (1988). Sociological theories of aging: Current perspective and future directions. In J. E. Birren & V. L. Bengtson (Eds.), *Emergent theories of aging* (pp. 333–355). New York: Springer.

Pearl, R. (1926). *Alcohol and longevity.* New York: Knopf.

Pearl, R. (1934). *The ancestry of the long-lived.* Baltimore: Johns Hopkins University Press.

Perry, J., & Perry, E. (1976). *Face to face: The individual and social problems.* Boston: Educational Associates.

Peters, G. R., & Kaiser, M. A. (1985). The role of friends and neighbors in providing social support. In W. J. Sauer & R. T. Coward (Eds.), *Social support networks and the care of the elderly.* New York: Springer.

Peterson, D. A. (1972). Financial adequacy in retirement: Perceptions of older Americans. *The Gerontologist,* **12,** 379–383.

Peterson, D. A. (1983). *Facilitating education for older learners.* San Francisco: Jossey-Bass.

Peterson, D. A. (1986). Aging and higher education. In D. A. Peterson, J. E. Thorton, & J. E. Birren (Eds.), *Education and aging* (pp. 30–61). Englewood Cliffs, NJ: Prentice-Hall.

Peterson, D. A. (1987a). Adult education. In G. L. Maddox (Ed.), *The encyclopedia of aging* (pp. 9–10). New York: Springer.

Peterson, D. A. (1987b). *Career paths in the field of aging.* Lexington, MA: Lexington Books.

Pfeiffer, E. (1976). Quoted in R. F. Graber, Aging in 2025: Telling it like it's going to be. *Geriatrics,* **31.**

Pfeiffer, E. (1977). Psychopathology and social pathology. In J. Birren & K. W. Schaie (Eds.), *Handbook of the psychology of aging* (pp. 650–671). New York: Van Nostrand Reinhold.

Pifer, A., & Bronte, L. (1986). Introduction: Squaring the pyramid. In A. Pifer and L. Bronte (Eds.), *Our aging society* (pp. 3–13). New York: W. W. Norton.

Pillemer, K., & Finkelhor, D. (1988). The prevalence of elder abuse: A random sample survey. *The Gerontologist,* **28,** 51–57.

Plath, D. W. (1972). Japan: The after years. In D. O. Cowgill & L. D. Holmes (Eds.) *Aging and Modernization.* (pp. 133–150) New York: Appleton-Century-Crofts.

Pollak, O. (1948). Social adjustment in old age: A research planning report. *Social Science Research Council* (Bulletin 59).

Popenoe, D. (1977). *Sociology.* Englewood Cliffs, NJ: Prentice-Hall.

Princeton Religion Research Center (1966). *Religion in America.* Princeton, NJ: The Gallup Poll.

Princeton Religion Research Center (1976). *Religion in America.* Princeton, NJ: The Gallup Poll.

Princeton Religion Research Center (1982). *Religion in America.* Princeton, NJ: The Gallup Poll.

Quetelet, L. A. J. (1969). *A treatise on man and the development of his faculties* (a facsimile reproduction of the English translation of 1842). Gainesville, FL: Scholars' Facsimiles and Reprints.

Quinn, M. J., and Tomita, S. K. (1986). *Elder abuse and neglect: Causes, diagnosis, and intervention strategies.* New York: Springer.

Rathbone-McCuan, E., & Hashimi, J. (1982). *Isolated elders: Health and social intervention.* Rockville, MD: Aspen Systems Corporation.

Reed, M. B., & Glamser, F. D. (1979). Aging in a total institution: The case of older prisoners. *The Gerontologist,* **19,** 354–360.

Reichard, S., Livson, F., & Petersen, P. G. (1962). *Aging and personality.* New York: Wiley.

Retherford, R. D. (1975). *The changing sex differential in mortality.* Westport, CT: Greenwood.

Revis, J. S. (1971). *Transportation.* 1971 White House conference on aging: Background and issues. Washington, DC: U.S. Government Printing Office.

Revis, J. S. (1975). *Transportation for older Americans: A state of the art report.* Administration on Aging. Washington, DC: U.S. Government Printing Office.

Rhodes, S. R. (1983). Age-related differences in work attitudes and behavior: A review and conceptual analysis. *Psychological Bulletin,* **93,** 328–367.

Riley, M. W., & Foner, A. (1968). *Aging and society, vol 1.: An inventory of research findings.* New York: Russell Sage.

Riley, M. W., Foner, A., Hess, B., & Toby, M. (1969). Socialization for the middle and later years. In D. A. Goslin (Ed.), *Handbook of socialization theory and research* (pp. 951–982). Chicago: Rand McNally.

Robertson, J. (1976). Significance of grandparents: Perceptions of young adult grandchildren. *The Gerontologist,* **16,** 137–140.

Robertson, J. F., Tice, C. H., & Loeb, L. (1985). Grandparenthood: From knowledge to programs and policy. In V. L. Bengtson & J. F. Robertson (Eds.), *Grandparenthood* (pp. 211–224). Beverly Hills, CA: Sage.

Robinson, D. (1985, February 17). How can we protect our elderly? *Parade,* pp. 4–7.

Rockstein, M., & Sussman, M. (1979). *Biology and aging.* Belmont, CA: Wadsworth.

Romaniuk, J., & Romaniuk, M. (1982). Participation motives of older adults in higher education: The elderhostel experience. *The Gerontologist,* **22,** 364–368.

Rose, A. M. (1960). The impact of aging on voluntary associations. In C. Tibbitts (Ed.), *Handbook of social gerontology* (pp. 666–697). Chicago: University of Chicago Press.

Rose, A. M. (1965). The subculture of aging. In A. M. Rose & W. A. Peterson (Eds.), *Older people and their social world* (pp. 3–16). Philadelphia: Davis.

Rose, A. M. (1965). A current theoretical issue in social gerontology. In A. M. Rose & W. A. Peterson (Eds.), *Older people and their social world* (pp. 359–366). Philadelphia: Davis.

Rosenberg, G. S. (1970). Implications of new models of the family for the aging population. In H. A. Otto (Ed.), *The family in search of a future* (pp. 171–181). New York: Appleton-Century-Crofts.

Rosenberg, G. S. (1970). *The worker grows old.* San Francisco: Jossey-Bass.

Rosenman, S. I. (1938). *The public papers and addresses of Franklin D. Roosevelt.* New York: Random House.

Rosenmayr, L. & Kockeis, E. (1963). Propositions for a sociological theory of aging and the family. *International Social Science Journal,* **15,** 410–426.

Rosow, I. (1962). Old age: One moral dilemma of an affluent society. *The Gerontologist,* **2,** 182–191.

Rosow, I. (1967). *Social integration of the aged.* New York: Free Press.

Rosow, I. (1973). The social context of the aging self. *The Gerontologist,* **13,** 82–87.

Rosow, I. (1974). *Socialization to old age.* Berkeley: University of California Press.

Rousseau, A. M. (1981). *Shopping bag ladies: Homeless women speak about their lives.* New York: Pilgrim.

Rubin, I. (1965). *Sexual life after sixty.* New York: Basic Books.

Sage, W. (1974, June). Choosing the good death. *Human Behavior.*

Schaie, K. W. (1983). The Seattle longitudinal study: A 21-year exploration of psychometric intelligence in adulthood. In K. W. Schaie (Ed.), *Longitudinal studies of adult psychological development* (pp. 64–135). New York: Guilford.

Schiffman, S. S., & Covey, E. (1984). Changes in taste and smell with age: Nutritional aspects. In J. M. Ordy, D. Harman, & R. Alfin-Slater (Eds.), *Nutrition in gerontology,* (pp. 43–64). New York: Raven Press.

Schlesinger, J. A. (1966). *Ambition and politics: Political careers in the United States.* Chicago: Rand McNally.

Schrank, H. T., & Waring, J. M. (1989). Older workers: Ambivalence and interventions. *The Annals of the American Academy of Political and Social Science,* **503,** 113–126.

Schreter, C. A., & Turner, L. A. (1986). Sharing and subdividing private market housing. *The Gerontologist,* **26,** 181–186.

Schroeder, W. L. (1970). Adult education defined and described. In R. Smith, G. Aker, & J. R. Kidd (Eds.), *Handbook of adult education.* New York: Macmillan.

Schulz, J. H. (1985). *The Economics of aging.* 3rd ed. Belmont, CA: Wadsworth.

Schulz, J. H. (1988). *The economics of aging.* 4th ed. Dover, MA: Auburn House.

Seigel, J. S., & Passel, J. S. (1976). New estimates of the number of centenarians in the United States. *Journal of the American Statistical Association,* **71,** 559–566.

Shanas, E. (1980). Older people and their families: The new pioneers. *Journal of Marriage and the Family, 42*, 9–15.

Shanas, E., et al. (1968). *Old people in three industrial societies*. New York: Atherton.

Shanas, E., & Sussman, M. B. (Eds.). (1977). *Family, bureaucracy and the elderly*. Durham, NC: Duke University Press.

Sheppard, H. L. (1976). Work and retirement. In R. Binstock & E. Shanas (Eds.), *Handbook of aging and the social sciences* (pp. 286–309). New York: Van Nostrand Reinhold.

Sherman, S. R. (1985). Reported reasons retired workers left their last job: Findings from the new beneficiary survey. *Social Security Bulletin, 48* (11), 22–30.

Shlonsky, H. (1976). Quoted in S. D. Tobin, S. M. Davidson & A. Sack, *Effective services for older Americans*. Ann Arbor: Institute of Gerontology, University of Michigan–Wayne State University.

Shock, N. W. (1977). Biological theories of aging. In J. E. Birren & Schaie, W. K. (Eds.), *Handbook of the psychology of aging* (pp. 103–113). New York: Van Nostrand Reinhold.

Shock, N. W. (1985). The physiological basis of aging. In R. J. Morin & R. J. Bing (Eds.), *Frontiers in medicine* (pp. 300–312), New York: Human Sciences Press.

Silverman, P. (1987). Family life. In P. Silverman (Ed.), *The elderly as pioneers* (pp. 205–223). Bloomington: Indiana University Press.

Silverman, P. R., & Cooperband, A. (1984). Widow to widow: The elderly widow and mutual help. In G. Lesnoff-Caravaglia (Ed.), *The world of the older woman* (pp. 144–161). New York: Human Sciences Press.

Silverstone, B., & Wynter, L. (1975). The effects of introducing a heterosexual living space. *The Gerontologist, 15*, 83–87.

Simmons, L. W. (1945). *The role of the aged in primitive society*. New Haven: Yale University Press.

Simmons, L. W. (1959). Aging in modern society. In *Toward better understanding of the aging*. New York: Council on Social Work Education, pp. 1–8.

Simmons, L. W. (1960). Aging in preindustrial societies. In C. Tibbitts (Ed.), *Handbook of social gerontology* (pp. 65–66). Chicago: University of Chicago Press.

Simonton, D. K. (1984). *Genius, creativity and leadership*. Cambridge, MA: Harvard University Press.

Simpson, I. H. (1973). Problems of the aging in work and retirement. In R. R. Boyd & C. G. Oakes (Eds.), *Foundations of practical gerontology* (pp. 167–170). Columbia: University of South Carolina Press.

Simpson, I. H., Bach, K. W. & McKinney, J. D. (1966). Work and retirement. In I. H. Simpson & J. C. McKinney (Eds.), *Social Aspects of Aging*, pp. 68–74. Durham, NC: Duke University Press.

Smelser, N. J. (1988). *Sociology*. Englewood Cliffs, NJ: Prentice-Hall.

Smith, B. K. (1973). *Aging in America*. Boston: Beacon.

Snyder, J. D., & Engleman, R. M. (1976). Ten social service programs that really work. *Geriatrics, 31*, 118–125.

Sontag, S. (1972, September). The double standard of aging. *Saturday Review*, pp. 29–39.

St. John, D. (1977, May). Beware the flimflam man. *Dynamic Maturity*.

Starr, B. D., & Weiner, M. B. (1981). *The Starr-Weiner report on sex and sexuality in the mature years*. New York: McGraw-Hill.

Stearns, P. N. (1982). *Old age in preindustrial society*. New York: Holmes & Meier.

Stearns, P. N. (1976). *Old age in European society*. New York: Holmes & Meier.

Steffensmeier, D. J. (1987). The invention of the "new" senior citizen criminal; An analysis of crime trends of elderly males and elderly females, 1964–1984. *Research on Aging, 9*(2), 281–311.

Stehouwer, J. (1968). *Old people in three industrial societies*. New York: Atherton.

Steinitz, L. Y. (1980). Religiosity, well-being and weltanschaung among the elderly. *Journal of the Scientific Study of Religion, 19*, 60–67.

Stenback, A. (1980). Depression and suicidal behavior in old age. In J. E. Birren & R. B. Sloane (Eds), *Handbook of mental health and aging*, pp. 616–652. Englewood Cliffs, NJ: Prentice-Hall.

Sterns, H. L. (1986). Training and retraining adults and older adult workers. In J. E. Birren, P. K. Robinson, & J. E. Livingston (Eds.), *Age, health and employment* (pp. 93–113). Englewood Cliffs, NJ: Prentice-Hall.

Stone, R. (1985). *The relationship between retirement and change in functional health among unmarried women.* Paper presented to the annual meeting of the American Public Health Association.

Streib, G. F. (1965). A longitudinal study of retirement. In *Final report to the Social Security Administration.* Washington, DC: U.S. Government Printing Office.

Streib, G. F. (1965). Are the aged a minority group? In A. W. Gouldner & S. M. Miller (Eds.), *Applied sociology* (pp. 311–328). Glencoe, Ill.

Streib, G. F. (1971). *Retirement roles and activities.* 1971 White House Conference on aging, background and issues. Washington, DC: U.S. Government Printing Office.

Streib, G. F. (1972). Old age in Ireland: Demographic and sociological aspects. In D. O. Cowgill & L. D. Holmes (Eds.), *Aging and modernization* (pp. 167–181). New York: Appleton-Century-Crofts.

Streib, G. F. (1985). Social stratification and aging. In R. H. Binstock & E. Shanas (Eds.), *Handbook of aging and the social sciences* (pp. 339–368). New York: Van Nostrand Reinhold.

Streib, G. F., & Schneider, C. J. (1971). *Retirement in American society: Impact and process.* Ithaca, NY: Cornell University Press.

Streib, G. F., & Streib, R. B. (1975). Communes and the aging. *American Behavioral Scientist,* **19,** 176–189.

Sunderland, G. (1982). Geriatric crime wave: The great debate. *Police Chief,* **49,** 40–44.

Sussman, M. B. (1965). Relationships of adult children and their parents in the United States. In E. Shanas & G. Streib (Eds.), *Social structure and the family* (pp. 62–92). Englewood Cliffs, NJ: Prentice-Hall.

Sussman, M. B. (1976). Family life of old people. In R. H. Binstock & E. Shanas (Eds.), *Handbook of aging and the social sciences* (pp. 218–243). New York: Van Nostrand Reinhold.

Sussman, M. B. (1985). Family life of old people. In R. H. Binstock & E. Shanas (Eds.), *Handbook of aging and the social sciences,* 2nd ed. (pp. 415–449). New York: Van Nostrand Reinhold.

Sussman, M. B., & Burchinal, L. (1962). Parental aid to married children: Implications for family functioning. *Marriage and Family Living,* **24,** 320–332.

Szinovacz, M. (1982). Personal problems and adjustment to retirement. In M. Szinovacz (Ed.), *Women's retirement: Policy implications of recent research* (pp. 195–203). Beverly Hills, CA: Sage.

Taeuber, C. (1988, December). Demographic perspectives of an aging society. *The World and I,* pp. 590–603.

Talley, T. & Kaplan, J. (1956). The negro aged. *Newsletter* (December), The Gerontological Society, p. 6.

Talmon, Y. (1971). Aging in Israel: A planned society. *American Journal of Sociology,* **67,** 284–295.

Tellis-Nayak, V. (1982). The transcendant standard: The religious ethos of the rural elderly. *The Gerontologist,* **22,** 359–363.

Terris, B. J. (1977). Legal services for the elderly. In J. R. Berry & C. R. Wingrove (Eds.), *Let's learn about aging.* Cambridge, MA: Schenkman.

The Aging Connection (1989). House committee hits "202" housing cuts. February/March.

The Aging Connection (1989). Project Rescue: Hope for the Bowery's homeless. June/July.

The National Council on the Aging (1970). *The golden years: A tarnished myth.* Washington, DC: The National Council on the Aging.

Thompson, L. W., Breckenridge, J. N., Gallagher, D., & Peterson, J. (1984). Effects of bereavement on self-perceptions of physical health in elderly widows and widowers. *Journal of Gerontology,* **39,** 309–314.

Thompson, W. E. (1958). Pre-retirement anticipation and adjustment in retirement. *Journal of Social Issues,* **14,** 35–45.

Thompson, W. E., Streib, G. F. (1961). Meaningful activity in a family context. In R. W. Kleemeier (Ed.), *Aging and leisure* (pp. 177–211). New York: Oxford University Press.

Tibbitts, C. (1968). Some social aspects of gerontology. *The Gerontologist,* **8,** 131–133.

Tibbitts, C., & Rogers, M. (1955). Aging in the contemporary scene. In W. Donahue (Ed.), *Education for later maturity* (pp. 19–35). New York: Whiteside and William Morrow.

Tobin, S., Ellor, J. W., & Anderson-Ray, S. M. (1986). *Enabling the elderly.* Albany: State University of New York Press.

Tobin, S., & Lieberman, M. A. (1976). *Last home for the aged.* San Francisco: Jossey-Bass.

Torres-Gil, F. (1986). An examination of factors affecting future cohorts of elderly Hispanics. *The Gerontologist, 26,* 140–146.

Trela, J. E. (1976). Status inconsistency and political action. In J. F. Gubrium (Ed.), *Time, roles, and self in old age* (pp. 126–147). New York: Human Sciences Press.

Troll, L. E. (1971). The family of later life: A decade review. *Journal of Marriage and Family, 33,* 263–290.

Troll, L. E. (1982). *Continuations: Adult development and aging.* Monterey, CA: Brooks/Cole.

Troll, L. E., Miller, S. J., & Atchley, R. C. (1979). *Families in later life.* Belmont, CA: Wadsworth.

Turner, B. F., & Adams, C. (1983). The sexuality of older women. In E. W. Markson (Ed.), *Older women* (pp. 55–72). Lexington, MA: Lexington Books.

Turner, G. (1884). *Samoa, a hundred years ago and before.* London: Macmillan.

Twente, E. (1970). *Never too old.* San Francisco: Jossey-Bass.

Tyson, R. (1975, March). Have you discovered the pluses of being over 30? *House and Garden,* pp. 75, 156.

U.S. Bureau of the Census (1986). Household wealth and asset ownership: 1984. *Current population reports.* (Series P-70, No. 7). Washington, DC: U.S. Government Printing Office.

U.S. Department of Health, Education, and Welfare (1976, September–October). Nutrition program aids California's older Native Americans. *Aging.* Washington, DC: U.S. Government Printing Office.

U.S. Department of Health, Education, and Welfare (1976, September–October). Projects in Nevada succeed in helping Indians help themselves. *Aging.* Washington, DC: U.S. Government Printing Office.

U.S. Department of Health and Human Services (1988). *Indian health services, chart services book.* Washington, DC: U.S. Government Printing Office.

U.S. Department of Labor (1971). *Back to work after retirement.* Washington, DC: U.S. Government Printing Office.

U.S. House of Representatives, Committee on Ways and Means (1987). *Background material and data on programs within the jurisdiction of the Committee on Ways and Means.* Washington, DC: U.S. Government Printing Office.

U.S. News & World Report. (1983). December 19, p. 11.

U.S. Senate Special Committee on Aging (1977). *Developments in aging: 1976.* Washington, DC: U.S. Government Printing Office.

U.S. Senate Special Committee on Aging (1978). *Developments in Aging: 1977* (Vol. 1). Washington, DC: U.S. Government Printing Office.

U.S. Senate Special Committee on Aging (1979). *Developments in aging: 1978.* Washington, DC: U.S., Government Printing Office.

U.S. Senate Special Committee on Aging. (1984). *Developments in Aging: 1983.* Washington, DC: U.S. Government Printing Office.

U.S. Senate Special Committee on Aging (1987–1988). *Aging America: Trends and projections.* Washington, DC: U.S. Government Printing Office.

U.S. Senate Special Committee on Aging (1988a). *Developments in aging: 1987* (Vol. 1). Washington, DC: U.S. Government Printing Office.

U.S. Senate Special Committee on Aging (1988b). *Developments in aging: 1987* (Vol. 3). Washington, DC: U.S. Government Printing Office.

U.S. Senate Special Committee on Aging (1989). *Developments in aging: 1988 (Vol. 1).* Washington, DC: U.S. Government Printing Office.

U.S. Senate Special Committee on Aging (1989). *Aging America: Trends and Projections* Washington, DC: U.S. Government Printing Office.

Van Gennep, A. (1960). *Rites of passage* (M. Vizedom & G. Caffee, Trans.). London: Routledge & Kegan Paul.

Vinick, B. H., & Ekerdt, D. J. (1989). Retirement and the family. *Generations, 13,* 53–56.

Waldron, I. (1976). Why do women live longer than men? *Social Science and Medicine, 11,* 349–362.

Walz, T. H., & Blum, N.S. (1987). *Sexual health in later life.* Lexington, MA: Lexington Books.

Ward, R. A. (1980). Age and acceptance of euthanasia. *Journal of Gerontology, 35,* 421–431.

Warner, W. L. (Ed.) (1949). *Democracy in Jonesville.* New York: Harper & Row.

Warner, W. L., & Lunt, P.S. (1941). *The social life of a modern community, Yankee city series* (Vol. 1). New Haven: Yale University Press.

Weber, M. (1922/1968). *Economy and society*. New York: Bedminster.

Wechsler, D. (1958). *The measurement and appraisal of adult intelligence*. Baltimore: Williams & Wilkins.

Weeks, J. R. (1984). *Aging: Concepts and social issues*. Belmont, CA: Wadsworth.

Weinberg, M. S., & Williams, C. J. (1974). *Male homosexuals: Their problems and adaptations*. New York: Oxford University Press.

Weisinger, M. (1976, February 1). How granny power gets jobs for older folks. *Parade*, pp. 14–16.

Weisman, A. D. (1972). *On dying and denying: A psychiatric study of terminality*. New York: Behavioral Publications.

Welford, A. T. (1977). Motor performance. In C. E. Finch & L. B. Hayflick (Eds.), *Handbook of the biology of aging* (pp. 450–496). New York: Van Nostrand Reinhold.

Welford, A. T., & Birren, J. E. (1965). *Behavior, aging, and the nervous system*. Springfield, IL: Charles C Thomas.

Whitaker, C. J. (1987). *Elderly crime victims, Bureau of Justice Statistics Special Report*. Washington, DC: U.S. Government Printing Office.

Whitman, H. H., & Lukes, S. J. (1975). Behavior modification for terminally ill patients. *American Journal of Nursing, 75*, 100–101.

Wiegand, N. D., & Burger, J. C. (1979). The elderly offender and parole. *The Prison Journal, 59* (2), 48–57.

Wilbanks, W. (1984). The elderly offender: Placing the problem in perspective. In W. Wilbanks & P. K. H. Kim (Eds.), *Elderly criminals* (pp. 1–11). Lanham, MD: University Press of America.

Williamson, J. B., Evans, L., & Powell, L. A. (1982). *The politics of aging: Power and policy*. Springfield, IL: Charles C Thomas.

Williams, R. (1970). *American society: A sociological interpretation*. New York: Knopf.

Wilson, A. J. E. (1984). *Social services for older persons*. Boston: Little, Brown.

Wilson, K. B., & DeShane, M. R. (1982). The legal rights of grandparents: A preliminary discussion. *The Gerontologist, 22*, 67–71.

Wingrove, C. R., & Alston, J. P. (1971). Age, aging and church attendance. *The Gerontologist, 11*, 356–358.

Wolf, R., Strugnell, C. P., & Godkin, M. A. (1982). *Elder abuse and neglect: Final report from three model projects*. Worcester: University of Massachusetts Medical Center, Center on Aging.

Wu, F. Y. T. (1975). Mandarin-speaking aged Chinese in the Los Angeles area. *The Gerontologist, 15*, 271–275.

Young, M., & Willmott, P. (1962) *Family and kinship in East London*. Baltimore: Penguin.

Younger, E. J. (1976, February). The California experience: Prevention of criminal victimization of the elderly. *Police Chief, 43*, 13–16.

Index